Middle School 2-2

학교시험 완벽대비

2학기 전과정

적중100plus

영어 기출문제집

중2

시사 | 송미정

*Best Collection*

# 구성과 특징

교과서의 주요 학습 내용을 중심으로 학습 영역별 특성에 맞춰 단계별로 다양한 학습 기회를 제공하여 단원별 학습능력 평가는 물론 중간 및 기말고사 시험 등에 완벽하게 대비할 수 있도록 내용을 구성

## Words & Expressions

**Step1**  Key Words 단원별 핵심 단어 설명 및 풀이
Key Expression 단원별 핵심 숙어 및 관용어 설명
Word Power 반대 또는 비슷한 뜻 단어 배우기
English Dictionary 영어로 배우는 영어 단어

**Step2**  실력평가 단원별 수시평가 대비 주관식, 객관식 문제풀이

**Step3**  서술형 대비 학업성취도 및 수행능력평가 대비 서술형 문제풀이

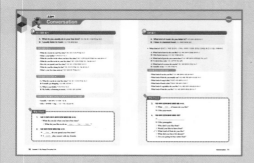

## Conversation

**Step1**  핵심 의사소통 의사소통에 필요한 주요 표현 방법 요약
핵심 Check 기본적인 표현 방법 및 활용능력 확인

**Step2**  대화문 익히기 상황에 따른 대화문 활용 및 연습

**Step3**  기본평가 시험대비 기초 학습 능력 평가

**Step4**  실력평가 단원별 수시평가 대비 주관식, 객관식 문제풀이

**Step5**  서술형 대비 학업성취도 및 수행능력평가 대비 서술형 문제풀이

## Grammar

**Step1**  주요 문법 단원별 주요 문법 사항과 예문을 알기 쉽게 설명

핵심 Check 기본 문법사항에 대한 이해 여부 확인

**Step2**  기본평가 시험대비 기초 학습 능력 평가

**Step3**  실력평가 단원별 수시평가 대비 주관식, 객관식 문제풀이

**Step4**  서술형 대비 학업성취도 및 수행능력평가 대비 서술형 문제풀이

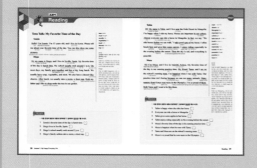

## Reading

**Step1**  구문 분석 단원별로 제시된 문장에 대한 구문별 분석과 내용 설명
확인문제 문장에 대한 기본적인 이해와 인지능력 확인

**Step2**  확인학습A 빈칸 채우기를 통한 문장 완성 능력 확인

**Step3**  확인학습B 제시된 우리말을 영어로 완성하여 작문 능력 키우기

**Step4**  실력평가 단원별 수시평가 대비 주관식, 객관식 문제풀이

**Step5**  서술형 대비 학업성취도 및 수행능력평가 대비 서술형 문제풀이
교과서 구석구석 교과서에 나오는 기타 문장까지 완벽 학습

# Composition

## |영역별 핵심문제|

단어 및 어휘, 대화문, 문법, 독해 등 각 영역별 기출문제의 출제 유형을 분석하여 실전에 대비하고 연습할 수 있도록 문제를 배열

## |서술형 실전 및 창의사고력 문제|

학교 시험에서 점차 늘어나는 서술형 시험에 집중 대비하고 고득점을 취득하는데 만전을 기하기 위한 학습 코너

## |단원별 예상문제|

기출문제를 분석한 후 새로운 시험 출제 경향을 더하여 새롭게 출제될 수 있는 문제를 포함하여 시험에 완벽하게 대비할 수 있도록 준비

## |단원별 모의고사|

영역별, 단계별 학습을 모두 마친 후 실전 연습을 위한 모의고사

## INSIGHT on the textbook.......................................... 교과서 파헤치기

- **단어Test1~2** 영어 단어 우리말 쓰기와 우리말을 영어 단어로 쓰기

- **대화문Test1~2** 대화문 빈칸 완성 및 전체 대화문 쓰기

- **본문Test1~5** 빈칸 완성, 우리말 쓰기, 문장 배열연습, 영어 작문하기 복습 등 단계별 반복 학습을 통해 교과서 지문에 대한 완벽한 습득

- **구석구석지문Test1~2** 지문 빈칸 완성 및 전문 영어로 쓰기

# Lesson 6

# New Places,
# New Experiences

## 🎙 의사소통 기능

- 경험 묻기

  A: Have you ever traveled to another country?

  B: Yes, I have. It was a wonderful experience.

- 만족이나 불만족에 대해 묻기

  A: How do you like this shirt?

  B: It's colorful. I like it.

## 🎙 언어 형식

- 원인과 결과를 나타내는 'so ... that'

  It was **so** delicious **that** I asked for more.

- 목적격 관계대명사

  It was from the *khorkhog* **that** she was cooking for us.

# Words & Expressions

교과서

## Key Words

- □ **abroad**[əbrɔ́ːd] 凰 해외에
- □ **airport**[ɛ́ərpɔrt] 명 공항
- □ **amazing**[əméiziŋ] 형 굉장한, 놀라운
- □ **arrive**[əráiv] 동 도착하다
- □ **asleep**[əslíːp] 형 잠이 든
- □ **barbecue**[báːrbikjùː] 명 바비큐
- □ **beginning**[bigíniŋ] 명 시작, 처음
- □ **bright**[brait] 형 밝은
- □ **camel**[kǽməl] 명 낙타
- □ **capital**[kǽpətl] 명 수도
- □ **chance**[tʃæns] 명 기회
- □ **cheerful**[tʃíərfəl] 형 쾌활한, 유쾌한
- □ **coastline**[kóustlain] 명 해안선
- □ **colorful**[kʌ́lərfəl] 형 화려한, (색이) 다채로운
- □ **cozy**[kóuzi] 형 아늑한
- □ **culture**[kʌ́ltʃər] 명 문화
- □ **during**[djúəriŋ] 전 ~ 동안[내내]
- □ **enough**[inʌ́f] 凰 ~할 만큼 (충분히)
- □ **expect**[ikspékt] 동 기대하다, 예상하다
- □ **flight**[flait] 명 비행
- □ **guest**[gest] 명 손님
- □ **imagine**[imǽdʒin] 동 상상하다

- □ **kid**[kid] 동 농담하다
- □ **lamb**[læm] 명 양고기
- □ **language**[lǽŋgwidʒ] 명 언어
- □ **magical**[mǽdʒikəl] 형 아주 멋진, 마법의, 마술의
- □ **modern**[mádərn] 형 현대의
- □ **moment**[móumənt] 명 순간
- □ **Mongolian**[maŋgóuliən] 형 몽골의 명 몽골 사람
- □ **moved**[muːvd] 형 가슴 뭉클한
- □ **once**[wʌns] 접 ~하자마자
- □ **part**[paːrt] 명 부분, 일부
- □ **rise**[raiz] 동 (해가) 뜨다, 일어나다
- □ **scared**[skɛərd] 형 겁먹은, 무서워하는
- □ **serve**[səːrv] 동 제공하다
- □ **shooting star** 유성
- □ **station**[stéiʃən] 명 역, 정거장
- □ **sweet**[swiːt] 형 달콤한, 단
- □ **tasty**[téisti] 형 맛있는
- □ **traditional**[trədíʃənl] 형 전통적인
- □ **TV station** 텔레비전 방송국
- □ **view**[vjuː] 명 경관, 전망
- □ **wedding**[wédiŋ] 명 결혼(식)
- □ **whole**[houl] 명 전체, 모든

## Key Expressions

- □ **at first** 처음에는
- □ **be cooked with** ~으로 요리되다
- □ **be full of** ~로 가득하다
- □ **be made of** ~로 만들어지다
- □ **be made with** ~로 만들어지다
- □ **can't wait to** 빨리 ~하면 좋겠다
- □ **feel like**+주어+동사 ~인 것처럼 느끼다
- □ **from A to B** A에서 B로
- □ **get used to** ~에 익숙해지다

- □ **Have you been (to)** ~? ~에 가 본 적 있니?
- □ **Have you ever**+과거분사 ~? 너는 ~해 본 적 있니?
- □ **How did you like** ~? ~는 어땠어?
- □ **How do you like** ~? ~는 어떠니?
- □ **How was** ~? ~는 어땠어?
- □ **show A around B** …에게 ~을 둘러보도록 안내하다
- □ **smell**+형용사 ~한 냄새가 나다
- □ **so** 형용사/부사 **that** 주어+동사 매우 ~해서 …하다
- □ **wake up** 잠에서 깨다

## Word Power

※ 동사 – 동사ing – 동사ed

감정을 나타내는 동사에 '-ing'를 붙이면 '~한 감정을 일으키는'의 의미가 되고, '-ed'를 붙이면 '~한 감정을 느끼는'의 의미가 된다.

- □ **amaze**(놀라게 하다) – **amazing**(놀라운) – **amazed**(놀란)
- □ **annoy**(짜증나게 하다) – **annoying**(짜증나게 하는) – **annoyed**(짜증이 난)
- □ **bore**(지루하게 만들다) – **boring**(재미없는, 지루하게 하는) – **bored**(지루해 하는)
- □ **disappoint**(실망시키다) – **disappointing**(실망시키는) – **disappointed**(실망한)
- □ **excite**(신나게 하다) – **exciting**(신나게 하는) – **excited**(신난)
- □ **interest**(흥미를 갖게 하다) – **interesting**(흥미로운) – **interested**(흥미를 느끼는)
- □ **relax**(느긋이 쉬다) – **relaxing**(느긋하게 해 주는) – **relaxed**(느긋함을 느끼는)
- □ **satisfy**(만족시키다) – **satisfying**(만족감을 주는) – **satisfied**(만족하는)
- □ **surprise**(놀라게 하다) – **surprising**(놀라운) – **surprised**(놀란)
- □ **tire**(피곤하게 만들다) – **tiring**(피곤하게 만드는) – **tired**(피곤한)

## English Dictionary

- □ **abroad** 해외에
  → in or to a different country or countries
  다른 나라에서 또는 다른 나라로

- □ **airport** 공항
  → a place where planes take off and land with facilities for passengers
  승객들을 위한 시설을 갖춘 곳으로 비행기가 이륙하고 착륙하는 장소

- □ **asleep** 잠이 든
  → not awake 깨어 있지 않은

- □ **bright** 밝은
  → shining strongly 강하게 빛나는

- □ **chance** 기회
  → an opportunity to do something
  어떤 것을 할 기회

- □ **cheerful** 쾌활한, 유쾌한
  → noticeably happy 현저히 행복한

- □ **expect** 기대하다, 예상하다
  → to believe or think that something will happen
  어떤 것이 발생할 것이라고 믿거나 생각하다

- □ **get used to** ~에 익숙해지다
  → to become familiar with something or someone
  어떤 사람이나 사물과 친숙해지다

- □ **guest** 손님
  → someone who is invited to visit you
  당신을 방문하도록 초대된 사람

- □ **kid** 농담하다
  → to make a joke 농담을 하다

- □ **language** 언어
  → the method of human communication used by the people of a country or region for talking or writing
  한 나라나 지역의 사람들에 의해 말하거나 쓰기 위해서 사용되는 의사소통 방법

- □ **magical** 마법의
  → seems to use special powers
  특별한 힘을 사용하는 것처럼 보이는

- □ **modern** 현대의
  → designed and made using the latest ides or methods
  가장 최신의 생각이나 방법을 사용하여 디자인되고 만들어진

- □ **Mongolian** 몽골의
  → relating to Mongolia or its people
  몽골 혹은 몽골 사람들과 관련된

- □ **part** 부분, 일부
  → one of the pieces, sections, or elements that makes the whole of something
  어떤 것의 전체를 만드는 조각, 부분품 또는 요소들 중의 하나

- □ **rise** (해가) 뜨다
  → appear above the horizon in the sky
  지평선 위로 하늘에 나타나다

- □ **station** 역, 정거장
  → a place where trains or buses stop so that people can get on or off
  사람들이 타거나 내릴 수 있도록 지하철이나 버스가 멈추는 장소

- □ **view** 경관, 전망
  → everything that can be seen from a particular place
  특정한 장소로부터 보여지는 모든 것

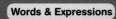
**서답형**

**01** 다음 괄호 안의 단어를 문맥에 맞게 빈칸에 써 넣으시오.

(1) The soccer game last night was really _____ . (excite)

(2) He was _____ with the test results. (disappoint)

**02** 〈보기〉에 주어진 단어를 이용해 빈칸을 채울 때 들어갈 말이 다른 하나를 고르시오.

┌─── 보기 ───┐
interest
└─────────┘

① Math is the most _____ subject to me.

② The subject in which I'm _____ is computer technology.

③ This is the most _____ part in this movie.

④ Is there any _____ news in the paper?

⑤ I watched a very _____ show last weekend.

**중요**

**03** 밑줄 친 부분과 의미가 가장 가까운 것을 고르시오.

As soon as he went to bed, he fell asleep.

① Since          ② Until

③ Once          ④ In case

⑤ After

**04** 빈칸에 알맞은 단어를 고르시오.

I was surprised because I didn't _____ to see him there.

① expect          ② arrive

③ allow          ④ encourage

⑤ decide

**중요**

**05** 다음 밑줄 친 부분의 의미로 알맞지 않은 것은?

① The coach called the whole team over. (전체)

② Do you mean I don't practice enough? (충분히)

③ Many people were moved by his songs and his beautiful voice. (움직였다)

④ I've waited a long time for a moment like this. (순간)

⑤ Cars have become an important part of our modern lifestyle. (현대의)

**서답형**

**06** 다음 주어진 우리말에 맞게 빈칸을 채우시오. (철자가 주어진 것도 있음)

(1) 나는 곧 그 일에 익숙해질 거라고 생각한다.

➡ I think I will soon g_____ the work.

(2) 우리 삼촌은 내게 그 도시 곳곳을 안내하기로 약속했다.

➡ My uncle promised to _____ me _____ the city.

**01** 다음 괄호 안의 단어를 문맥에 맞게 고쳐 쓰시오.

(1) The movie was so _____ that I fell asleep while watching it. (bore)

(2) We were all _____ at his speed of working. (amaze)

**02** 두 문장이 같은 의미가 되도록 빈칸을 채우시오.

> I think that you are familiar with my accent now.
> = I think that you _____ my accent now.

**03** 다음 우리말에 맞도록 빈칸에 알맞은 말을 쓰시오. (철자가 주어진 경우 주어진 철자로 시작할 것)

(1) 유성은 사실 전혀 별이 아니다.
➡ A _____ is not actually a star at all.

(2) 그는 너무 무서워서 결국 남은 하루를 차 속에서 머무르는 것으로 끝냈다.
➡ He was _____ s_____ _____ he ended up staying in the car for the rest of the day.

(3) 네가 만약 쉽게 잠들 수 없다면, 지루한 것을 해라.
➡ If you can't fall _____ easily, do something b_____.

(4) 캔버라는 호주의 수도이다.
➡ Canberra is the _____ city of Australia.

**04** 다음 빈칸에 공통으로 들어갈 말을 쓰시오.

> • Do you know what dish is made _____ red beans, milk and ice?
> • Usually, spaghetti is cooked _____ tomato sauce.

**05** 다음 빈칸에 들어갈 말을 〈보기〉에서 찾아 쓰시오.

> ┤ 보기 ├
> at    for    like    up

(1) She set a clock but she didn't wake _____.

(2) _____ first, I thought I understood what you said

(3) He can't wait _____ the party.

(4) I feel _____ I am much taller.

**06** 다음 우리말에 맞게 주어진 단어를 바르게 배열하시오.

(1) 올해에 기쁨이 가득하길 바란다.
(be, joy, hope, I, of, will, this, full, year)
➡ _____

(2) 이 장소는 아주 멋져서 나는 여기서 살고 싶다.
(this, magical, here, is, want, I, so, live, place, that, to)
➡ _____

# Conservation

교과서

## ① 경험 묻기

> **A** Have you ever traveled to another country? 다른 나라로 여행 가 본 적 있니?
> **B** Yes, I have. It was a wonderful experience. 응. 있어. 그것은 멋진 경험이었어.

- 'Have you ever+과거분사 ~?'는 '너는 ~해 본 적 있니?'의 뜻으로, 상대방에게 경험을 묻는 표현으로 ever 다음에는 동사의 과거분사형을 써야 한다. 보통 before나 ever 등의 부사가 자주 함께 사용된다. 상대방에게 경험을 묻는 질문을 되물을 때는 Have you?만 써서 물을 수 있다.

- 'Have you ever+과거분사 ~?'로 물었을 때 'Yes, I have.'로 응답하는 경우 구체적인 설명을 덧붙이면 좋다. 해 본 적이 없으면 'No, I haven't.'로 답한다.

### 경험을 물어보는 표현들

- Have you (ever) 과거분사 ~? 너는 ~해 본 적 있니?
- Do you have any experience of 동명사 ~? 너는 ~해 본 경험이 있니?

### 경험을 묻는 말에 답하는 표현

- I have 과거분사 ~. 나는 ~해 본 적이 있어요.
- I have never 과거분사 ~. 나는 ~해 본 적이 없어요.
- I have a lot of experience. 나는 경험이 풍부해요.
- I don't have any experience of ~. 나는 ~해 본 경험이 전혀 없어요.

### 핵심 Check

**1.** 다음 우리말과 일치하도록 빈칸에 알맞은 말을 쓰시오.

 (1) **A:** _____ a marathon? (너는 마라톤을 뛰어 본 적 있니?)

  **B:** Yes, I have. (응. 있어.)

 (2) **A:** Do you have any experience of meeting a famous actor?

   (너는 유명한 배우를 만나 본 경험이 있니?)

  **B:** No, _____. (아니. 난 전에 유명한 배우를 만나 본 적이 전혀 없어.)

**2.** 대화의 순서를 바르게 배열하시오.

 (A) I hope you have a chance to do that some time.

 (B) No, I haven't.

 (C) Have you been to Africa before?

 ➡ _____

## ② 만족이나 불만족에 대해 묻기

**A** How do you like this shirt? 이 셔츠가 마음에 드니?

**B** It's colorful. I like it. 그것은 색이 화려하구나. 마음에 들어.

■ 'How do you like ~?'는 어떤 것에 대한 만족이나 불만족에 대해 물을 때 사용하며 '~는 어떠니?'라는 의미이다. 유사한 표현으로 'What do you think of[about] ~?', 'What is your opinion of[on] ~?' 등의 표현을 사용한다.

■ 'What do you think of[about] ~?'의 경우 우리말로 '어떻게'라는 말이 들어간다고 What 대신 How를 쓰지 않도록 유의한다.

■ 과거의 경험에 대한 의견을 물을 때는 'How did you like ~?'라고 한다. 묻는 사람이 상대방의 경험에 대해 알고자 할 때 쓰는 표현으로 '~가 어땠니?'라는 의미이다. 'How was ~?'로 바꾸어 쓸 수 있다.

### 만족이나 불만족에 대해 묻기

• How do you like ~? ~는 어떠니?

• How is ~? ~는 어떠니?

■ 'How do you like ~?'의 대답으로 긍정의 경우에는 'Great!'이나 'Terrific!' 등으로, 부정의 대답은 'It was terrible.'이나 'It was not so good.' 등으로 할 수 있다.

### 핵심 Check

**3.** 다음 우리말과 일치하도록 빈칸에 알맞은 말을 쓰시오.

(1) **A:** _____ as your present? (너의 선물로 이 책 어떠니?)

   **B:** It is wonderful. (훌륭해.)

(2) **A:** _____ (영화 어땠어?)

   **B:** It was great. I love the scene with the festival. (매우 좋았어. 나는 축제 장면이 정말 좋았어.)

**4.** 다음 대화에서 <u>어색한</u> 부분을 찾아 바르게 고치시오.

   **A:** What did you like the dance festival?

   **B:** It was really nice.

   ➡ _____

### A. Listen & Speak 1 B-1

G: ❶You look excited, Inho. ❷What's up?

B: I'm going to Jejudo with my family this weekend. ❸Have you ever been there?

G: Yes, ❹many times. I love the coastline. How about you?

B: It'll be my first visit to Jejudo. ❺I can't wait for this weekend!

G: 인호야. 너 신나 보인다. 무슨 일이니?

B: 이번 주말에 가족들과 함께 제주도에 가거든. 넌 가 본 적 있니?

G: 응. 여러 번 가 봤어. 나는 그 해안선을 좋아해. 너는 어떠니?

B: 난 이번이 제주도 첫 방문이야. 이번 주말이 빨리 왔으면 좋겠다!

❶ look+형용사: ~하게 보이다 excited: 신난
❷ 상대방이 신난 이유를 'What's up?'으로 물어보고 있다.
❸ 'Have you ever+과거분사 ~?'는 '너는 ~ 해 본 적 있니?'의 뜻으로, 상대방에게 경험을 묻는 표현이다.
❹ many times 앞에 I have been there가 생략되어 있다.
❺ 'I can't wait for ~.'는 원하던 일이 다가오고 있어 빨리하고 싶은 기대감을 나타내는 표현이며, '~하는 것을 기다릴 수 없다' 또는 '당장 ~하고 싶다, 빨리 ~했으면 좋겠다' 정도로 해석한다.

**Check(√) True or False**

(1) The girl has never been to Jejudo.　　　　T ☐ F ☐

(2) The boy will go to Jejudo this weekend.　　T ☐ F ☐

### B. Listen & Speak 2 B-1

G: ❶How was your vacation?

B: Great. I went to Dokdo with my family.

G: ❷How did you like it?

B: It was ❸amazing. I want to visit ❹there again.

G: 방학 잘 보냈니?

B: 좋았어. 가족과 함께 독도에 다녀왔어.

G: 어땠어?

B: 굉장했어. 다시 한 번 가 보고 싶어.

❶ 'How was ~?'는 묻는 사람이 상대방의 의견에 대해 알고자 할 때 쓰는 표현으로 '~가 어땠니?'라는 의미이다. 'How did you like ~?'로 바꾸어 쓸 수 있다.
❷ 'How do you like ~?'는 어떤 것에 대해 만족하는지를 물을 때 사용하며 '~는 어떠니?'라는 의미이다. 유사한 표현으로 'What do you think of[about] ~?', 'What is your opinion of[on] ~?' 등의 표현을 사용한다.
❸ amazing: 굉장한, 놀라운
❹ there는 장소 부사로 여기서는 Dokdo를 나타낸다.

**Check(√) True or False**

(3) The boy went to Dokdo with his family.　　T ☐ F ☐

(4) The boy wants to visit Dokdo again.　　　T ☐ F ☐

### Listen & Speak 1 A

B: ❶Have you ever tried Spanish food?

G: ❷Yes, I have. It's really ❸tasty.

❶ Have you ever+과거분사 ~?: 너는 ~해 본 적 있니?

❷ 'Yes, I have tried Spanish food.'가 원래의 문장으로, 경험을 묻는 질문에 긍정으로 답할 때는 보통 질문과 중복되는 부분은 생략하고 'Yes, I have.'로 답한다.

❸ tasty: 맛있는

### Listen & Speak 1 B-2

B: ❶Have you ever watched the sun rise over the ocean?

G: ❷No. ❸How about you?

B: ❹I watched the sun rise in Gangneung on New Year's Day. It was great.

G: I ❺tried several times, but I just couldn't ❻ wake up early ❼enough.

❶ Have you ever+과거분사 ~?: 너는 ~해 본 적 있니?

❷ 'No, I haven't watched the sun rise over the ocean.'이 원래의 문장으로 질문과 중복되는 부분은 생략되었다.

❸ 경험을 묻는 질문을 되물을 때 사용하는 'Have you?'를 'How about you?' 대신에 사용해도 된다.

❹ 'on New Year's Day'가 과거의 시점이므로 'watched'라고 동사의 과거형을 사용하였다. New Year's Day는 날짜 관련 표현이므로 날짜 앞에 쓰는 전치사 on을 사용한다.

❺ try: 시도하다

❻ wake up: 잠에서 깨다

❼ enough: ~할 만큼 (충분히)

### Listen & Speak 2 A

G: ❶How do you like your new house?

B: ❷It's great. I have a bigger room now.

❶ 'How do you like ~?'는 어떤 것에 대한 만족이나 불만족에 대해 물을 때 사용하며 '~는 어떠니?'라는 의미이다.

❷ It은 앞에서 나온 'my new house'를 가리킨다.

### Listen & Speak 2 B-2

B: ❶Have you been to the new Chinese restaurant?

G: ❷Yes. ❸I had dinner there last Saturday.

B: ❹How did you like it?

G: The ❺service was bad. I ❻won't go back there again.

❶ 어떤 장소에 다녀온 적이 있는지 경험을 물어볼 때는, 'Have you gone ~?'이 아닌 'Have you been (to) ~?'의 표현을 사용하는 것에 유의해야 한다.

❷ 경험을 묻는 질문에 긍정으로 답할 때 'Yes, I have.'로 대답할 수 있다. 'I have'가 생략되어 있다.

❸ 'last Saturday(지난주 토요일)'가 과거를 나타내는 부사구로, 과거동사 'had'를 사용하였다.

❹ 여기서 it은 앞에 나온 the new Chinese restaurant을 의미하고, 'How did you like it?'은 새로 생긴 중국 음식점에 대해 어떻게 생각하는지를 묻는 표현이다.

❺ service: 서비스

❻ won't = will not

### Real-Life Zone

B: ❶Have you ever traveled abroad, Sujin?

G: Yes, I went to Cambodia last summer.

B: Wow. ❷How did you like it?

G: It was really hot, but I enjoyed the trip.

B: Tell me some ❸interesting experiences you had during the trip.

G: Hmm... ❹let me think. I ate fried spiders!

B: What? ❺You're kidding. ❻How did you like them?

G: They were really big, so I was a little ❼scared at first. But the taste was okay.

B: Really? I cannot ❽imagine eating spiders.

❶ Have you ever+과거분사 ~?: 너는 ~해 본 적 있니? abroad: 해외에

❷ 과거의 일에 대해 만족하는지를 물을 때 'How did you like ~?'로 표현한다.

❸ interesting은 동사 'interest(흥미를 갖게 하다)'에서 파생된 현재분사형 형용사로 '흥미로운'의 뜻이다.

❹ 대화 중에 질문을 받았을 때, 생각할 시간이 필요하면 'Let me think'나 'Let me see'를 말할 수 있다.

❺ 'You're kidding.'은 '설마, 농담이지.'라는 뜻으로, 상대방이 방금 한 말이 믿기지 않아서 놀람을 나타낼 때 쓰는 표현이다.

❻ How did you like ~?: ~는 어땠어?

❼ scared 겁먹은, 무서워하는 at first: 처음에는

❽ imagine: 상상하다

● 다음 우리말과 일치하도록 빈칸에 알맞은 말을 쓰시오.

**Listen & Speak 1 A**

B: _____ _____ _____ tried Spanish food?

G: Yes, I _____. It's really _____.

**Listen & Speak 1 B**

1. G: You _____ excited, Inho. What's up?

   B: I'm _____ to Jejudo _____ my family this weekend. _____ you ever _____ there?

   G: Yes, many times. I love the _____. How about you?

   B: It'll be my first visit to Jejudo. I _____ wait _____ this weekend!

2. B: _____ you _____ watched the sun _____ over the ocean?

   G: No. How about you?

   B: I _____ the sun rise in Gangneung _____ New Year's Day. It was great.

   G: I _____ several times, but I just couldn't _____ up _____ enough.

1. G: 인호야, 너 신나 보인다. 무슨 일이니?
   B: 이번 주말에 가족들과 함께 제주도에 가거든. 넌 가 본 적 있니?
   G: 응. 여러 번 가 봤어. 나는 그 해안선을 좋아해. 너는 어떠니?
   B: 난 이번이 제주도 첫 방문이야. 이번 주말이 빨리 왔으면 좋겠다!

2. B: 바다 위로 해가 뜨는 것을 본 적 있니?
   G: 아니. 너는?
   B: 나는 새해 첫날에 강릉에서 해돋이를 봤어. 멋지더라.
   G: 나는 몇 번 시도해 봤는데 일찍 일어나지 못했어.

**Listen & Speak 1 C**

1. A: _____ _____ _____ traveled to another country?

   B: Yes, I have. It was a wonderful _____.

2. A: Have _____ _____ _____ a horse?

   B: Yes, I have. It was a wonderful _____.

1. A: 다른 나라로 여행 가 본 적 있니?
   B: 응, 있어. 그것은 멋진 경험이었어.

2. A: 말을 타 본 적 있니?
   B: 응, 있어. 그것은 멋진 경험이었어.

**Listen & Speak 2 A**

G: _____ _____ _____ like your new house?

B: It's great. I have a _____ room now.

G: 새 집은 어때?
B: 좋아. 나는 이제 더 큰 방을 가졌어.

### Listen & Speak 2 B

1. **G:** _____ was your _____?

   **B:** Great. I _____ to Dokdo with my family.

   **G:** _____ _____ you like it?

   **B:** It was _____. I want to visit there again.

2. **B:** _____ _____ _____ _____ the new Chinese restaurant?

   **G:** Yes. I _____ dinner there last Saturday.

   **B:** _____ _____ _____ like it?

   **G:** The service was bad. I _____ go back there again.

### Listen & Speak 2 C

1. **A:** _____ do you like this shirt?

   **B:** It's _____. I like it.

2. **A:** How _____ _____ _____ your ice cream?

   **B:** It's _____. I like it.

### Real-Life Zone A

**B:** _____ _____ _____ _____ _____, Sujin?

**G:** Yes, I _____ to Cambodia last summer.

**B:** Wow. _____ did you like it?

**G:** It was really hot, but I _____ the trip.

**B:** Tell me some _____ experiences you _____ during the trip.

**G:** Hmm... _____ me think. I ate _____ spiders!

**B:** What? You're kidding. _____ did you _____ _____?

**G:** They were really big, _____ I was a little _____ _____
_____. But the taste was okay.

**B:** Really? I cannot _____ eating spiders.

### Communication Task

**A:** _____ _____ _____ _____ tacos?

**B:** Yes, I have. They were _____.

   / No, I _____. I want to _____ some someday.

---

해석

1. G: 방학 잘 보냈니?
   B: 좋았어. 가족과 함께 독도에 다녀
      왔어.
   G: 어땠어?
   B: 굉장했어. 다시 한 번 가 보고 싶
      어.

2. B: 새로 생긴 중국 음식점에 가 봤
      니?
   G: 응. 지난주 토요일에 거기서 저녁
      을 먹었어.
   B: 어땠어?
   G: 서비스가 형편없었어. 그곳에 다
      시는 가지 않을 거야.

1. A: 이 셔츠가 마음에 드니?
   B: 그것은 색이 화려하구나. 마음에
      들어.

2. A: 너의 아이스크림은 어떠니?
   B: 그것은 달콤해. 마음에 들어.

B: 수진아 해외여행 가 본 적 있니?
G: 응, 지난여름에 캄보디아에 다녀왔
   어.
B: 와. 여행은 어땠니?
G: 날씨가 너무 더웠지만 여행은 즐거
   웠어.
B: 여행하면서 재미있었던 경험 좀 이야
   기해 줘.
G: 음… 생각 좀 해 볼게. 거미 튀김을
   먹었어!
B: 뭐라고? 진짜로? 거미 튀김은 어땠
   는데?
G: 너무 커서 처음엔 조금 무서웠는데.
   맛은 괜찮았어.
B: 정말? 난 내가 거미를 먹는 걸 상상
   할 수가 없어.

A: 타코를 먹어본 적 있니?
B: 응, 먹어 봤어. 맛있었어.
   / 아니, 안 먹어 봤어. 언젠간 한 번
   먹어 보고 싶어.

[01~02] 다음 대화의 빈칸에 알맞은 것을 고르시오.

**01**

> B: _____
>
> G: Yes, I have. It's really tasty.

① Did you have tacos?

② How is the new Chinese restaurant?

③ Have you ever traveled to another country?

④ Have you ever tried Spanish food?

⑤ Have you ever seen the picture before?

**02**

> A: How do you like this song?
>
> B: _____

① I listened to it on my cell phone.　② It's cheerful. I like it.

③ I like pop songs.　④ It was played at the concert.

⑤ Yes, it does. It sounds like a song.

**03** 대화 순서를 바르게 배열하시오

> (A) Yes, many times. I love the coastline. How about you?
>
> (B) I'm going to Jejudo with my family this weekend. Have you ever been there?
>
> (C) You look excited, Inho. What's up?
>
> (D) It'll be my first visit to Jejudo. I can't wait for this weekend!

➡ _____

**04** 다음 대화의 밑줄 친 부분과 바꾸어 쓸 수 있는 것을 고르시오.

> G: How did you like it?
>
> B: It was amazing. I want to visit there again.

① What did you do?

② What did you think of it?

③ What was an amazing experience?

④ What do you like?

⑤ What is your view about it?

[01~02] 다음 대화를 읽고 물음에 답하시오.

> B: _____
>
> G: No. How about you?
>
> B: I watched the sun rise in Gangneung on New Year's Day. It was great.
>
> G: I tried several times, but I just couldn't wake up early enough.

**01** 빈칸 (A)에 알맞은 말을 고르시오.

① Have you ever been to Jejudo?

② Have you ever watched the sun rise over the ocean?

③ Have you ever had *tteokguk* on New Year's Day?

④ Have you ever woken up early in the morning?

⑤ Have you ever traveled to another country?

**02** 위의 대화를 읽고 답할 수 <u>없는</u> 질문은?

① Has the girl watched the sun rise?

② Has the boy watched the sun rise?

③ When did the boy watch the sun rise?

④ How many times has the boy watched the sun rise?

⑤ Where did the boy watch the sun rise?

**03** 다음 중 짝지어진 대화가 <u>어색한</u> 것은?

① A: How did you like the new movie?

　B: It was okay. The story was good, but the acting was bad.

② A: How was the English test today?

　B: I didn't do well. I was sleepy during the test.

③ A: Have you ever made a pizza?

　B: Yes, I have. I have only eaten it many times.

④ A: Have you ever been to the Mexican food restaurant?

　B: Yes, I have. The food was delicious and the service was good.

⑤ A: How do you like this restaurant?

　B: The food is okay, but the service is terrible.

**04** 대화의 순서를 바르게 배열한 것을 고르시오.

> (A) It was amazing. I want to visit there again.
>
> (B) How did you like it?
>
> (C) How was your vacation?
>
> (D) Great. I went to Dokdo with my family.

① (B) – (A) – (C) – (D)

② (B) – (C) – (A) – (D)

③ (C) – (A) – (B) – (D)

④ (C) – (B) – (A) – (D)

⑤ (C) – (D) – (B) – (A)

[05~06] 다음 대화를 읽고 물음에 답하시오.

> B: Have you ___(A)___ to the new Chinese restaurant?
>
> G: Yes. I had dinner there last Saturday.
>
> B: ___(B)___ did you like it?
>
> G: The service was bad. I won't go back there again.

**05** 빈칸 (A)에 알맞은 말을 고르시오.

① watched    ② had    ③ went

④ gone    ⑤ been

**06** 빈칸 (B)에 알맞은 것을 고르시오.

① How    ② Who    ③ When

④ What    ⑤ Where

**07** 다음 대화의 빈칸에 들어갈 말을 〈보기〉에서 골라 순서대로 옳게 배열한 것은?

> B: Have you ever traveled abroad, Sujin?
> G: _____
> B: _____
> G: _____
> B: _____
> G: _____
> B: What? You're kidding. How did you like them?
> G: They were really big, so I was a little scared at first. But the taste was okay.
> B: Really? I cannot imagine eating spiders.

┤ 보기 ├

(A) Hmm... let me think. I ate fried spiders!

(B) Wow. How did you like it?

(C) Yes, I went to Cambodia last summer.

(D) It was really hot, but I enjoyed the trip.

(E) Tell me some interesting experiences you had during the trip.

① (B) – (A) – (E) – (D) – (C)

② (B) – (E) – (D) – (A) – (C)

③ (C) – (A) – (B) – (E) – (D)

④ (C) – (B) – (D) – (E) – (A)

⑤ (C) – (D) – (A) – (E) – (B)

**[08~09] 다음 대화를 읽고 물음에 답하시오.**

> G: ___(A)___ was your weekend, Tony?
> B: It was great. I went to the International Food Festival with my parents.
> G: ___(B)___ food did you try?
> B: I had a traditional Chinese dessert, *tangyuan*.
> G: ___(C)___ did you like it?
> B: I enjoyed it. It's made with sweet rice balls. Chinese people usually serve it to guests at a wedding.

**08** 빈칸 (A)~(C)에 알맞은 말로 짝지어진 것을 고르시오.

   (A)   (B)   (C)

① How – How – How

② How – What – How

③ How – What – What

④ What – How – What

⑤ What – What – How

**09** 대화의 내용과 일치하지 않는 것을 고르시오.

① Tony는 주말에 탕위안을 먹었다.

② 중국 사람들은 보통 결혼식에서 손님들에게 탕위안을 대접한다.

③ 탕위안은 중국의 전통 후식이다.

④ Tony는 국제 음식 축제에 친구들과 다녀왔다.

⑤ 탕위안은 달콤한 맛이 난다.

[01~03] 다음 대화를 읽고 물음에 답하시오.

G: You look ___(A)___ (excite), Inho. What's up?

B: I'm going to Jejudo with my family this weekend. ⓐ넌 거기 가 본 적 있니?

G: Yes, many times. I love the coastline. How about you?

B: It'll be my first visit to Jejudo. I can't wait ___(B)___ this weekend!

**01** 빈칸 (A)를 괄호 안의 주어진 단어를 이용하여 채우시오.

➡ _____

**02** 밑줄 친 ⓐ의 우리말을 주어진 단어를 이용해 영작하시오.

➡ _____
(there, ever)

**03** 빈칸 (B)에 알맞은 전치사를 쓰시오.

➡ _____

**04** 괄호 안에 주어진 단어를 알맞게 배열하시오.

G: _____ (new, like, how, do, your, you, house)

B: It's great. I have a bigger room now.

➡ _____

[05~06] 다음 대화를 읽고 물음에 답하시오.

A: I have ___(A)___ (ride) a water slide.

B: _____(B)

A: It was really exciting. It was faster than I expected.

**05** 빈칸 (A)를 괄호 안의 주어진 단어를 이용해 채우시오.

➡ _____

**06** 빈칸 (B)에 적절한 말을 주어진 단어를 이용하여 채우시오.

➡ _____ (like)

[07~08] 다음 대화를 읽고 물음에 답하시오.

B: (A)해외여행 가 본 적 있니(traveled, have, abroad, you, ever), Sujin?

G: Yes, ⓐI have been to Cambodia last summer.

B: Wow. ⓑHow did you like it?

G: It was really hot, but I enjoyed the trip.

B: ⓒTell me some interesting experiences you had during the trip.

G: Hmm... let me think. ⓓI ate fried spiders!

B: What? You're kidding. How did you like them?

G: They were really big, ⓔso I was a little scared at first. But the taste was okay.

B: Really? I cannot imagine eating spiders.

**07** 괄호 안의 주어진 단어를 알맞게 배열하여 밑줄 친 (A)의 우리말을 영작하시오.

➡ _____

**08** ⓐ~ⓔ 중 어법상 어색한 것을 바르게 고치시오.

_____ ➡ _____

교과서
# Grammar

### ① 원인과 결과를 나타내는 'so ... that'

> • It was **so** delicious **that** I asked for more. 그것은 너무 맛있어서 나는 더 달라고 했다.

- **형태:** so+형용사/부사+that+주어+동사

  **의미:** 매우 …해서 (주어가) ~하다

- 'that' 앞의 내용은 원인을 나타내고, 'that' 이하는 결과를 나타내며 'so+형용사/부사+that+주어+동사'의 어순이 된다.

- (원인) Julie is so kind / (결과) that everybody likes her. (Julie는 매우 친절해서 모든 사람이 그녀를 좋아한다.)

- 'so+형용사/부사+that+주어+can+동사원형'은 '형용사/부사+enough+to부정사'로 바꿔 쓸 수 있다.

  • He is **so** rich **that** he **can** buy the building. 그는 매우 부자여서 그 건물을 살 수 있다.

  = He is rich **enough to** buy the building.

- 'so+형용사/부사+that+주어+cannot[can't]+동사원형'은 'too+형용사/부사+to부정사'로 바꿔 쓸 수 있다.

  • She is **so** poor **that** she **can't** buy the house. 그녀는 너무 가난해서 그 집을 살 수 없다.

  = She is **too** poor **to** buy the house.

- 'so that 주어+동사'는 '~하기 위해서'라는 의미로 목적을 나타낸다.

  • She ran fast **so that** she could catch the thief. 그녀는 그 도둑을 잡기 위해서 빨리 뛰었다.

### 핵심 Check

1. 다음 우리말에 맞게 빈칸에 알맞은 말을 고르시오.

   (1) 바람이 매우 강해서 나는 문을 열 수 없었다.

   ➡ The wind was (too / so) strong that I couldn't open the door.

   (2) 그 반지는 매우 커서 그녀는 그 반지를 낄 수 없었다.

   ➡ The ring was so big (because / that) she couldn't wear it.

## 2 목적격 관계대명사

> • It was from the *khorkhog* **that** she was cooking for us.
> 그것은 그녀가 우리를 위해 요리하고 있던 호르호그에서 나는 냄새였다.

- **형태**: 사람 who(m)/that 주어+동사
  사물, 동물 which/that 주어+동사

  **의미**: '~하는, ~하고 있는'

- 목적격 관계대명사는 관계사절에서 선행사가 목적어 역할을 할 때 사용하며 관계사절은 선행사를 '~하는, ~하고 있는'으로 뒤에서 꾸며준다.

  - She is the doctor **who(m)[that]** I respect. 그녀는 내가 존경하는 의사이다.
    선행사　　목적격 관계대명사

  - The cake **which[that]** he made was delicious. 그가 만든 케이크는 맛있었다.
    선행사　목적격 관계대명사

- 목적격 관계대명사는 흔히 생략할 수 있다.

  - She is the girl (**whom**) I told you about. 그녀는 내가 너에게 말했던 소녀야.

  - This is the book (**which**) I borrowed yesterday. 이것은 내가 어제 빌렸던 책이야.

- 관계대명사가 전치사의 목적어인 경우 전치사를 빠뜨리지 않는다.

  - The lady is very considerate. + I always talk about her.

  → The lady **who** I always talk **about** is very considerate. 내가 항상 이야기하는 그 여성분은 매우 사려 깊다.

- 목적격 관계대명사는 흔히 생략할 수 있지만 그것이 전치사의 목적어이고 그 전치사가 관계대명사 앞에 위치하는 경우는 생략할 수 없고 선행사가 사람은 'whom', 사물은 'which'를 쓴다.

  - The girl **with whom** he is talking is Sue. 그가 함께 이야기를 하고 있는 소녀는 Sue이다.

  - The tent **in which** they lived was very big. 그들이 살고 있는 텐트는 매우 컸다.

### 핵심 Check

**2.** 다음 우리말에 맞게 빈칸을 알맞게 채우시오.

(1) 우리가 만난 남자는 배우였다.

➡ The man _____ we met was an actor.

(2) 이것은 할머니가 나를 위해 만들어 주신 케이크이다.

➡ This is the cake _____ Grandma made for me.

## 01 다음 빈칸에 들어갈 말로 알맞지 <u>않은</u> 것은? (2개)

> • This is the author _____ I wanted to meet.

① who       ② what       ③ that
④ whom      ⑤ whose

## 02 다음 문장에서 어법상 <u>어색한</u> 부분을 바르게 고쳐 쓰시오.

(1) The music is so loud which I cannot sleep.

_____ ➡ _____

(2) The question is very difficult that nobody can answer it.

_____ ➡ _____

(3) The mirror who you broke is my sister's.

_____ ➡ _____

(4) Did you see the book which I left it on the desk?

_____ ➡ _____

## 03 다음 우리말에 맞게 괄호 안에 주어진 어휘에 한 단어를 추가하여 바르게 배열하시오. (필요하면 어형을 바꿀 것)

(1) 그가 너무 빨리 말해서 나는 그의 말을 이해할 수 없었다. (he, fast, I, him, could not, spoke, that, understand)

➡ _____

(2) Eric이 사고 싶은 자전거는 매우 비싸다. (the bike, wants, expensive, is, to buy, Eric, very)

➡ _____

## 04 빈칸에 공통으로 들어갈 말로 알맞은 것은?

> • The village _____ I was born in was very small.
> • Julie is so kind _____ everybody likes her.

① which       ② who       ③ that
④ what       ⑤ whom

**01** 다음 빈칸에 들어갈 수 있는 말이 <u>다른</u> 하나는?

① The man _____ is playing with the dogs is my husband.

② This is the teacher _____ everyone respects.

③ We want to see the movie _____ you chose.

④ I want to eat fruit _____ I grew in my garden.

⑤ I'm looking for the car _____ color is purple.

**02** 다음 중 어법상 바르지 <u>않은</u> 것은?

① The boy who the teacher is waiting for is my classmate.

② The car which Ms. Kim wants to buy is expensive.

③ This is the dog that I found in the park.

④ He is so strong that he can lift the box.

⑤ He was so young that he can't drive.

**03** 다음 밑줄 친 부분의 쓰임이 나머지 넷과 <u>다른</u> 하나는?

① The students <u>that</u> she invited couldn't come to the class.

② The vase <u>that</u> you broke is my mom's.

③ The old lady <u>that</u> Jimin helped is my grandmother.

④ This is the cap <u>that</u> I bought last month.

⑤ The computer <u>that</u> makes a lot of noise is Tom's.

**04** 다음 밑줄 친 that의 성격이 나머지 넷과 다른 것은?

① It is surprising <u>that</u> he knows the answer.

② I asked my mom to buy me a dress <u>that</u> I wanted to wear.

③ This is the pig <u>that</u> my grandfather raises.

④ It is the question <u>that</u> nobody solved.

⑤ This is the movie <u>that</u> we produced.

**05** 주어진 어휘를 이용하여 다음 우리말을 영어로 쓰시오.

그 의자는 매우 편안해서 그녀는 잠이 들었다.
(comfortable, fell, asleep)

➡ _____

**06** 다음 괄호 안에서 알맞은 말을 고르시오.

(1) I will join the camp (which / who) I have been interested in.

(2) Penguins are birds (who / which) cannot fly.

(3) Look at the boy and his dog (that / which) are running.

(4) The boxes which you placed on the table (is / are) very heavy.

(5) She spoke so (clear / clearly) that I could understand her.

(6) She is (so / enough) tall that she can reach the ceiling.

**서답형**

**07** 다음 중 생략할 수 있는 것을 찾아 쓰시오.

(1) He teaches me the things that I never knew before.

➡ _____

(2) I have seen the boy who is wearing a blue jacket.

➡ _____

**08** 다음 중 어법상 어색한 문장을 고르시오.

① Diana was too young to be a driver.
② The car is too expensive for us to buy.
③ This book is enough easy for your kids to understand.
④ She's so wise that she doesn't make any trouble.
⑤ This juice is so cold that I can't drink it.

**09** 다음 중 어법상 올바른 문장을 고르시오.

① Is he enough strong to lift it?
② The dinner yesterday was too awful to eat it.
③ This watch is so expensive that I can't buy.
④ The box is so heavy that we can't carry it.
⑤ I got up too late that I couldn't have breakfast this morning.

**서답형**

**10** 밑줄 친 부분을 생략할 수 있으면 O표, 그렇지 않으면 X표를 하시오.

(1) This is all that I can give you. (    )
(2) Do you know the girl who is singing loudly? (    )

(3) I lost the watch of which my father was fond. (    )
(4) Jin is a student who everyone likes. (    )
(5) I want smartphone apps that translate English sentences into Korean. (    )

**중요**

**11** 다음 두 문장을 한 문장으로 바르게 바꾸면?

> • The woman is a famous writer.
> • You met her at Dan's party.

① The woman is a famous writer who you met her at Dan's party.
② The woman who you met at Dan's party is a famous writer.
③ The woman who you met her at Dan's party is a famous writer.
④ The woman is a famous writer that you met her at Dan's party.
⑤ The woman whose you met at Dan's party is a famous writer.

**서답형**

**12** 다음 괄호 안에 주어진 어구들을 바르게 배열하여 문장을 완성하시오.

> • She is wearing (which, the wedding dress, left, her mother) her.

➡ _____

_____

**서답형**

**13** 우리말에 맞게 괄호 안의 어휘를 바르게 배열하시오.

> 그는 매우 일찍 일어나서 아침 내내 졸렸다. (he, early, that, he, sleepy, got up, so, was, all morning)

➡ _____

**14** 다음 그림을 보고 괄호 안에 주어진 어휘를 이용하여 빈칸을 알맞게 채우시오.

➡ The _____ _____ so heavy _____ the man _____ carry _____. (bag)

**15** 다음 두 문장이 같은 뜻이 되도록 빈칸에 알맞은 말을 쓰시오.

(1) They are too strong for us to defeat.
→ They are so strong that _____ _____ defeat _____.

(2) She was so slow that she couldn't win the race.
→ She was _____ _____ _____ _____ the race.

(3) Sean was so cute that I could fall in love with him.
→ Sean was _____ _____ for me _____ fall in love with.

**16** 주어진 문장의 밑줄 친 부분과 동일한 역할을 하는 것을 고르시오.

• Every doctor that I've ever seen is kind.

① That is my house.
② That book is mine.
③ I think that she can take care of you.
④ This is the movie that I am interested in.
⑤ That she went out with James is not true.

**17** 다음 중 주어진 문장의 밑줄 친 that과 쓰임이 같은 것은?

• The advice that he gave me was useful.

① Do you know the girl that is dancing on the stage?
② That is not similar with me.
③ I knew that she was there yesterday.
④ That you're doing very well is true.
⑤ The book that I bought is not the best seller.

**18** 빈칸에 들어갈 말을 순서대로 바르게 연결한 것은?

• My house is _____ small for all of us to live in together.
• My house is _____ small that all of us can't live in together.

① too – enough
② so – enough
③ too – so
④ enough – so
⑤ so – too

**19** 관계대명사를 이용하여 만든 다음 문장을 원래의 두 문장으로 쓰시오.

(1) The boy band that I like most is BTS.
➡ _____

(2) This is the picture which I took three days ago.
➡ _____

(3) I know some people who work for Google.
➡ _____

**01** 다음 두 문장을 관계대명사를 이용하여 한 문장으로 연결하시오. (that을 사용하지 말 것)

(1) • The story was surprising.
   • She told me the story.
   ➡ _____

(2) • This is the money.
   • I really need it.
   ➡ _____

(3) • I have a friend.
   • She lives in Canada.
   ➡ _____

(4) • This is the movie.
   • It has a sad ending.
   ➡ _____

(5) • I met a person.
   • Her hobby is mountain climbing.
   ➡ _____

**02** 다음 문장에서 관계대명사가 생략된 곳에 써넣으시오. (필요하면 be동사도 추가할 것)

(1) This is the apartment she lives in.
   ➡ _____

(2) I like the jacket my wife bought for me.
   ➡ _____

(3) Aladdin is the movie I like best.
   ➡ _____

(4) Look at the cloud floating in the sky.
   ➡ _____

**03** 다음 두 문장의 뜻이 같도록 빈칸에 알맞은 말을 쓰시오.

(1) I am too young to take care of myself.
   → I am _____ young _____
   _____ _____ take care of myself.

(2) The book that I bought yesterday is hard to read.
   → The book _____ I bought yesterday is hard to read.

**04** 잘못된 부분을 바르게 고쳐 문장을 다시 쓰시오.

(1) The boy has no toys with that he can play.
   ➡ _____
   _____

(2) He is the mechanic which I want to introduce to you.
   ➡ _____
   _____

(3) The girls who I took care of was my nieces.
   ➡ _____
   _____

(4) The pen that I'm writing is Mike's.
   ➡ _____
   _____

(5) Everything what I told you was true.
   ➡ _____
   _____

**05** 다음 그림을 보고 주어진 어휘를 이용하여 문장의 빈칸에 알맞은 말을 쓰시오.

(1) (cook, well)

• My mother _____ _____ _____ _____ everybody loves her food.

(2) (run, fast)

• Kelly _____ _____ _____ _____ no one can win her in a race.

(3) (smart, get)

• He is _____ _____ _____ always _____ A in math.

**06** 다음은 "Can You Guess What It Is?" 퀴즈 문제이다. 빈칸에 적절한 말을 써 넣어 퀴즈 문제를 완성하시오.

(1)
1. It is something _____ _____ _____. (3 points)

2. Its color is white. (2 points)
3. It comes from cows. (1 point)
→ Answer: milk
(2)
1. It is _____ _____ _____ _____ _____. (3 points)
2. It is usually written in European countries. (2 points)
3. Mozart and Bach are the most well-known composers of it. (1 point)
→ Answer: classical music

**07** 다음 우리말을 주어진 어휘를 이용하여 영어로 옮기시오.

(1) 나는 매우 피곤해서 더 이상 일을 할 수 없었다. (tired, that, work, any more)

➡ _____

(2) 그 고양이는 너무 조용히 움직여서 아무도 그 것을 눈치채지 못했다. (move, quietly, no one, notice)

➡ _____

(3) 그 계단은 매우 높고 가팔라서 나는 어지러움을 느꼈다. (stairs, high and steep, feel, dizzy)

➡ _____

**08** 다음 중 어법상 어색한 것을 바르게 고쳐 다시 쓰시오.

(1) This game console is so small that you can take anywhere.

➡ _____
_____

(2) The bags are too heavy for you to carry them to the airport.

➡ _____
_____

## A Trip to Mongolia

This year, I had a special summer because I visited Mongolia for the
　　　　　　　　　　　　　　　　= as
first time. My friend Altan is from Mongolia. His grandmother invited
　　　　　　　　　　　　= comes from
me to Ulaanbaatar, the capital of Mongolia.
　　　　　　　└ 동격 ┘

After a four-hour flight from Seoul, Altan and I arrived at Chinggis
'숫자+단위 명사'가 하나의 낱말로 형용사처럼 쓰일 경우에 하이픈으로 연결
Khaan International Airport in Ulaanbaatar. It took thirty minutes
by taxi from the airport to Altan's grandmother's house.
교통, 통신 수단을 나타낼 때: by+무관사 명사

Her house is a *ger*, a traditional Mongolian house. It is a big tent,
　　　　　　　└ 동격 ┘
but it is cozy inside. When we entered, something smelled wonderful.
　　　　　　　　　　　　　　　　　　　S　　　　V　　　C
It was from the *khorkhog* that she was cooking for us. *Khorkhog* is a
　　　　　　　　　　목적격 관계대명사
Mongolian barbecue. It is made of lamb and cooked with hot stones.
　　　　　　　　수동태(be동사+pp): ~로 만들어지다
I was moved when Altan said Mongolians serve *khorkhog* to special
　　　= touched
guests. It was so delicious that I asked for more. After dinner, Altan
　　　　　　└ 매우 …해서 ~하다 ┘
and I went outside to see the night sky. The sky was full of bright stars.
　　　　　　to부정사의 부사적 용법(목적)　　　　　　　~로 가득했다
I felt like I was in a magical place.
└ ~인 것처럼 느꼈다

capital: 수도
flight: 비행
arrive: 도착하다
airport: 공항
Mongolian: 몽골의; 몽골 사람
barbecue: 바비큐
lamb: 양고기
moved: 감동한
guest: 손님
magical: 마법의, 신비한

📎 확인문제

● 다음 문장이 본문의 내용과 일치하면 T, 일치하지 <u>않으면</u> F를 쓰시오.

1　Altan comes from Mongolia. ☐

2　Altan's parents invited the writer to Ulaanbaatar, the capital of Mongolia. ☐

3　It took four hours by plane from Seoul to Chinggis Khaan International Airport in
　　Ulaanbaatar. ☐

4　A ger is a modern Mongolian house. ☐

5　*Khorkhog* is a Mongolian barbecue. ☐

6　*Khorkhog* is made of beef and cooked with hot stones. ☐

During the next three days, Altan showed me around and helped me
during+특정 기간을 나타내는 명사                      (목적어)가 ~하도록 돕다

experience Mongolian culture. Every moment was fun and exciting,

but I had the most fun when I rode a camel in the Gobi Desert. At first,
       형용사(much)의 최상급                                   처음에

I was scared because the camel was taller than I expected. But once
                         형용사의 비교급+than             ~하자마자(접속사)

I sat on its back, I soon got used to its movement. From the camel's
               get used to: ~에 익숙해지다

back, the view of the desert was truly amazing.
                             감정을 나타내는 동사는 감정을 유발할 때 현재분사를 쓰는 것이 적절하다.

My visit to Mongolia was a special experience in many ways. It gave

me a great chance to get to know my friend's country and culture. I
                  to부정사의 형용사적 용법

want to visit Mongolia again someday!
   to부정사의 명사적 용법

experience: 경험
culture: 문화
moment: 순간
fun: 재미있는; 재미
scared: 겁먹은
have fun: 재미있게 놀다
ride: 타다
camel: 낙타
expect: 기대하다, 예상하다
once: ~하자마자
special: 특별한
chance: 기회
get to 원형동사: ~하게 되다

---

### 확인문제

● 다음 문장이 본문의 내용과 일치하면 T, 일치하지 않으면 F를 쓰시오.

1  During the next three days, Altan showed the writer around. ☐

2  The writer didn't like to ride a camel in the Gobi Desert. ☐

3  The writer was scared because the camel was taller than the writer expected. ☐

4  The writer couldn't get used to the camel's movement. ☐

5  From the camel's back, the view of the desert was truly amazing. ☐

6  The writer's visit to Mongolia was a terrible experience in many ways. ☐

● 우리말을 참고하여 빈칸에 알맞은 말을 쓰시오.

**1** A _____ to Mongolia

**2** This year, I had a special summer because I visited Mongolia _____ _____ _____ _____.

**3** My friend Altan _____ _____ Mongolia.

**4** His grandmother _____ me _____ Ulaanbaatar, the capital of Mongolia.

**5** After _____ _____ _____ from Seoul, Altan and I _____ _____ Chinggis Khaan International Airport in Ulaanbaatar.

**6** _____ _____ thirty minutes _____ _____ from the airport to Altan's grandmother's house.

**7** Her house is a *ger*, a _____ Mongolian house.

**8** It is a big tent, but it is _____ _____.

**9** When we entered, something _____ _____.

**10** It was _____ the *khorkhog* that she was _____ _____ us.

**11** *Khorkhog* is a _____ _____.

**12** It _____ _____ _____ lamb and cooked _____ hot stones.

**13** I _____ _____ when Altan said Mongolians _____ *khorkhog* _____ special guests.

---

**1** 몽골 여행

**2** 나는 올해 몽골을 처음으로 방문해서 특별한 여름을 보냈다.

**3** 내 친구 알탕은 몽골 출신이다.

**4** 그의 할머니께서는 몽골의 수도인 울란바토르에 나를 초대하셨다.

**5** 서울에서 네 시간 비행 후 알탕과 나는 울란바토르의 칭기즈 칸 국제공항에 도착했다.

**6** 공항에서 알탕의 할머니 댁까지 택시로 30분이 걸렸다.

**7** 할머니의 집은 몽골 전통 가옥인 게르이다.

**8** 큰 텐트이지만 내부는 아늑하다.

**9** 우리가 들어갔을 때. 뭔가 좋은 냄새가 났다.

**10** 그녀가 우리를 위해 요리하고 있던 호르호그에서 나는 냄새였다.

**11** 호르호그는 몽골식 바비큐이다.

**12** 그것은 양고기로 만들어졌으며 뜨거운 돌로 요리되었다.

**13** 나는 알탕이 몽골인들은 특별한 손님에게 호르호그를 대접한다고 말했을 때 감동을 받았다.

**14** It was _____ delicious _____ I asked for more.

**15** After dinner, Altan and I _____ _____ to see the night sky.

**16** The sky _____ _____ _____ bright stars.

**17** I _____ _____ I was in a magical place.

**18** _____ the next three days, Altan _____ _____ _____ and helped me experience Mongolian culture.

**19** Every moment was fun and exciting, but I _____ _____ _____ _____ when I rode a camel in the Gobi Desert.

**20** _____ _____, I was scared because the camel was _____ _____ I expected.

**21** But _____ I sat on its back, I soon _____ _____ _____ its movement.

**22** From the camel's back, _____ _____ _____ _____ _____ was truly amazing.

**23** My visit to Mongolia was a special experience _____ _____ _____.

**24** It gave me a great chance _____ _____ _____ _____ my friend's country and culture.

**25** I want to visit Mongolia _____ _____!

**14** 그것은 너무 맛있어서 나는 더 달라고 했다.

**15** 저녁 식사 후, 알탕과 나는 밤하늘을 보기 위해 밖으로 나갔다.

**16** 하늘은 밝은 별들로 가득했다.

**17** 나는 신비한 장소에 있는 것처럼 느꼈다.

**18** 그 후 3일 동안, 알탕은 나를 구경시켜 주었고 몽골 문화를 경험할 수 있게 도와주었다.

**19** 매 순간이 재미있고 흥미진진했지만, 고비 사막에서 낙타를 탈 때가 가장 재미있었다.

**20** 처음에는 내가 예상했던 것보다 낙타의 키가 커서 무서웠다.

**21** 그러나 낙타 등에 앉자 곧 움직임에 익숙해졌다.

**22** 낙타의 등에서 보는 사막의 경치는 정말로 놀라웠다.

**23** 내가 몽골을 방문한 것은 여러 면에서 특별한 경험이었다.

**24** 내 친구의 나라와 문화를 알 수 있는 좋은 기회가 되었다.

**25** 나는 언젠가 몽골을 다시 방문하고 싶다!

● 우리말을 참고하여 본문을 영작하시오.

**1** 몽골 여행

➡ _____

**2** 나는 올해 몽골을 처음으로 방문해서 특별한 여름을 보냈다.

➡ _____

**3** 내 친구 알탕은 몽골 출신이다.

➡ _____

**4** 그의 할머니께서는 몽골의 수도인 울란바토르에 나를 초대하셨다.

➡ _____

**5** 서울에서 네 시간 비행 후 알탕과 나는 울란바토르의 칭기즈 칸 국제공항에 도착했다.

➡ _____

**6** 공항에서 알탕의 할머니 댁까지 택시로 30분이 걸렸다.

➡ _____

**7** 할머니의 집은 몽골 전통 가옥인 게르이다.

➡ _____

**8** 큰 텐트이지만 내부는 아늑하다.

➡ _____

**9** 우리가 들어갔을 때, 뭔가 좋은 냄새가 났다.

➡ _____

**10** 그녀가 우리를 위해 요리하고 있던 호르호그에서 나는 냄새였다.

➡ _____

**11** 호르호그는 몽골식 바비큐이다.

➡ _____

**12** 그것은 양고기로 만들어졌으며 뜨거운 돌로 요리되었다.

➡ _____

**13** 나는 알탕이 몽골인들은 특별한 손님에게 호르호그를 대접한다고 말했을 때 감동을 받았다.

➡ _____

**14** 그것은 너무 맛있어서 나는 더 달라고 했다.

➡ _____

**15** 저녁 식사 후, 알탕과 나는 밤하늘을 보기 위해 밖으로 나갔다.

➡ _____

**16** 하늘은 밝은 별들로 가득했다.

➡ _____

**17** 나는 신비한 장소에 있는 것처럼 느꼈다.

➡ _____

**18** 그 후 3일 동안, 알탕은 나를 구경시켜 주었고 몽골 문화를 경험할 수 있게 도와주었다.

➡ _____

**19** 매 순간이 재미있고 흥미진진했지만, 고비 사막에서 낙타를 탈 때가 가장 재미있었다.

➡ _____

**20** 처음에는 내가 예상했던 것보다 낙타의 키가 커서 무서웠다.

➡ _____

**21** 그러나 낙타 등에 앉자 곧 움직임에 익숙해졌다.

➡ _____

**22** 낙타의 등에서 보는 사막의 경치는 정말로 놀라웠다.

➡ _____

**23** 내가 몽골을 방문한 것은 여러 면에서 특별한 경험이었다.

➡ _____

**24** 내 친구의 나라와 문화를 알 수 있는 좋은 기회가 되었다.

➡ _____

**25** 나는 언젠가 몽골을 다시 방문하고 싶다!

➡ _____

[01~04] 다음 글을 읽고 물음에 답하시오.

This year, I had a special summer because I visited Mongolia for the first time. My friend Altan is ⓐ Mongolia. His grandmother invited me ⓑ Ulaanbaatar, the capital of Mongolia.

ⓒ서울에서 네 시간 비행 후, Altan and I arrived at Chinggis Khaan International Airport in Ulaanbaatar. ⓓIt took thirty minutes by a taxi from the airport to Altan's grandmother's house.

**01** 위 글의 빈칸 ⓐ와 ⓑ에 들어갈 전치사가 바르게 짝지어진 것은?

① from – for
② in – for
③ in – at
④ from – to
⑤ for – to

**서답형**

**02** 위 글의 밑줄 친 ⓒ의 우리말에 맞게 주어진 어휘를 이용하여 6 단어로 영작하시오.

> flight, from

➡ _____

**서답형**

**03** 위 글의 밑줄 친 ⓓ에서 어법상 틀린 부분을 찾아 고치시오.

_____ ➡ _____

**중요**

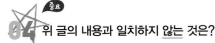 위 글의 내용과 일치하지 않는 것은?

① This year, the writer visited Mongolia for the first time.
② Altan's mother invited the writer to Ulaanbaatar.
③ Ulaanbaatar is the capital of Mongolia.

④ It took four hours by plane from Seoul to Chinggis Khaan International Airport.
⑤ After a thirty-minute taxi ride from the airport, Altan and the writer arrived at Altan's grandmother's house.

[05~07] 다음 글을 읽고 물음에 답하시오.

Her house is a *ger*, a traditional Mongolian house. ⓐIt is a big tent, but it is cozy inside. When we entered, something smelled wonderful. ⓑ그녀가 우리를 위해 요리하고 있던 호르호그에서 나는 냄새였다. *Khorkhog* is a Mongolian barbecue. It is made of lamb and cooked with hot stones. I was moved when Altan said Mongolians serve *khorkhog* to special guests. ⓒIt was so delicious that I asked for more. After dinner, Altan and I went outside to see the night sky. ⓓThe sky was full of bright stars. I felt like I was in a magical place.

**서답형**

**05** 위 글의 밑줄 친 ⓐIt과 ⓒIt이 가리키는 것을 본문에서 각각 찾아 쓰시오.

➡ ⓐ _____  ⓒ _____

**서답형**

**06** 위 글의 밑줄 친 ⓑ의 우리말에 맞게 한 단어를 보충하여, 주어진 어휘를 알맞게 배열하시오.

> the *khorkhog* / for us / it / was cooking / was / she / that

➡ _____

**서답형**

**07** 위 글의 밑줄 친 ⓓ를 다음과 같이 바꿔 쓸 때 빈칸에 들어갈 알맞은 말을 쓰시오.

➡ The sky was _____ _____ bright stars.

**[08~10] 다음 글을 읽고 물음에 답하시오.**

During the next three days, Altan showed me around and helped me experience Mongolian culture. Every moment was fun and exciting, but I had the most fun when I rode a camel in the Gobi Desert. At first, I was scared because the camel was taller than I expected. But @once I sat on its back, I soon got used to its movement. From the camel's back, the view of the desert was truly amazing.

My visit to Mongolia was a special experience in many ways. It gave me a great chance to ___(A)___ know my friend's country and culture. I want to visit Mongolia again someday!

**08** 위 글의 빈칸 (A)에 들어갈 알맞은 말을 모두 고르시오.

① get to      ② arrive at      ③ reach
④ come to      ⑤ go to

**09** 위 글의 밑줄 친 @once와 같은 의미로 쓰인 것을 고르시오.

① I've only been there once.
② There was once a giant.
③ The water is fine once you're in!
④ He cleans his car once a week.
⑤ He once lived in Zambia.

**10** 위 글의 주제로 알맞은 것을 고르시오.

① how to enjoy every exciting moment
② the scary experience of riding a camel
③ the view of the desert from the camel's back
④ the mystery of the Gobi Desert
⑤ a special experience in Mongolia

**[11~12] 다음 글을 읽고 물음에 답하시오.**

**A Trip to Suncheon**

My family took a trip to Suncheon last summer. We visited the National Garden. It was so large that we could not see the whole garden. After three hours' walking, we were really hungry. For dinner, we had Gukbap @that my parents like. Suncheon is famous for Gukbap and we enjoyed it.

This trip was so good that I would never forget it for a long time.

**11** 아래 〈보기〉에서 위 글의 밑줄 친 @that과 문법적 쓰임이 같은 것의 개수를 고르시오.

> ┤ 보기 ├
> ① Are you mad that you should do such a thing?
> ② It is natural that he should say so.
> ③ There's a man that you want to meet.
> ④ It's true that we were a little late.
> ⑤ This is the pen that I bought yesterday.

① 1개      ② 2개      ③ 3개      ④ 4개      ⑤ 5개

**12** 위 글의 내용과 일치하지 않는 것은?

① 글쓴이의 가족은 작년 여름에 순천으로 여행을 갔다.
② 글쓴이의 가족은 순천 국가 정원을 방문했다.
③ 세 시간에 걸쳐 글쓴이의 가족은 국가 정원 전체를 다 볼 수 있었다.
④ 저녁 식사로 글쓴이의 가족은 국밥을 먹었다.
⑤ 순천은 국밥으로 유명하다.

[13~15] 다음 글을 읽고 물음에 답하시오.

(①) This year, I had a special summer because I visited Mongolia for the first time. (②) His grandmother invited me to Ulaanbaatar, the capital of Mongolia. (③) After a four-hour ⓐ_____ from Seoul, Altan and I arrived at Chinggis Khaan International Airport in Ulaanbaatar. (④) It took thirty minutes by taxi from the airport to Altan's grandmother's house. (⑤)

**서답형**

**13** 위 글의 빈칸 ⓐ에 fly를 알맞은 형태로 쓰시오.

➡ _____

**14** 위 글의 흐름으로 보아 주어진 문장이 들어가기에 가장 적절한 곳은?

My friend Altan is from Mongolia.

①       ②       ③       ④       ⑤

**중요**

**15** 위 글의 제목으로 가장 알맞은 것을 고르시오.

① How to Spend a Summer Vacation
② A Special Summer I Spent in Mongolia
③ Altan, My friend, Is from Mongolia.
④ Let Me Introduce Chinggis Khaan International Airport!
⑤ Altan's Grandmother's House Is Only a Thirty-Minute Taxi Ride Away.

[16~18] 다음 글을 읽고 물음에 답하시오.

Her house is a *ger*, a traditional Mongolian house. It is a big tent, but it is cozy inside. When we entered, something smelled wonderful. It was from the *khorkhog* that she was cooking for us. *Khorkhog* is a Mongolian barbecue. It is made of lamb and cooked with hot stones. I was moved when Altan said Mongolians serve *khorkhog* to special guests. It was ⓐ_____ delicious ⓑ_____ I asked for more. After dinner, Altan and I went outside ⓒto see the night sky. The sky was full of bright stars. I felt like I was in a magical place.          *she: Altan's grandmother

**서답형**

**16** 위 글의 빈칸 ⓐ와 ⓑ에 들어갈 알맞은 말을 쓰시오.

➡ ⓐ _____   ⓑ _____

**17** 위 글의 밑줄 친 ⓒto see와 to부정사의 용법이 같은 것을 모두 고르시오. (3개)

① Ann has no one to love her.
② She studied hard to pass the exam.
③ How stupid she was to marry such a man!
④ He promised me to be here at ten o'clock.
⑤ He got up early to catch the first train.

**중요**

**18** 위 글을 읽고 대답할 수 없는 질문은?

① What is a *ger*?
② Who was cooking *khorkhog*?
③ What is *khorkhog* made of?
④ Why is *khorkhog* cooked with hot stones?
⑤ To whom do Mongolians serve *khorkhog*?

[19~22] 다음 글을 읽고 물음에 답하시오.

During the next three days, Altan showed me around and helped me experience Mongolian culture. Every moment was fun and exciting, but I had the most fun when I rode a camel in the Gobi Desert. At first,

I was scared because the camel was taller than I expected. But once I sat on its back, I soon got used to its movement. From the camel's back, the view of the desert was truly amazing.

My visit ____@____ Mongolia was a special experience ____ⓑ____ many ways. It gave me a great chance to get to know my friend's country and culture. I want to visit Mongolia again someday!

**19** 위 글의 빈칸 @와 ⓑ에 들어갈 전치사가 바르게 짝지어진 것은?

① to – in      ② in – by
③ in – for     ④ for – in
⑤ to – for

**20** At first, when the writer rode a camel in the Gobi Desert, why was the writer scared? Fill in the blank with a suitable word.

➡ It was because the camel was _____ than the writer expected.

**21** 다음 문장에서 위 글의 내용과 다른 부분을 찾아서 고치시오.

> After sitting on the camel's back, the writer couldn't get used to the camel's movement.

_____ ➡ _____

**22** 위 글의 마지막 부분에서 알 수 있는 'I'의 심경으로 가장 알맞은 것을 고르시오.

① bored           ② disappointed
③ satisfied        ④ self-confident
⑤ upset

[23~24] 다음 글을 읽고 물음에 답하시오.

**A Trip to Ulleungdo**
Last summer, my parents and I went to Ulleungdo. Ulleungdo is an island ____@____ I always wanted to visit. We walked along the road around the island. ⓑThis trip was so great that I would never forget for a long time.

**23** 위 글의 빈칸 @에 들어갈 알맞은 말을 모두 고르시오.

① which      ② where      ③ when
④ that       ⑤ what

**24** 위 글의 밑줄 친 ⓑ에서 어법상 어색한 것을 고치시오.

_____ ➡ _____

[25~26] 다음 글을 읽고 물음에 답하시오.

This is your captain speaking. We @have just arrived at the airport. Welcome to Mongolia, a country full of the beauty of nature and culture. The time in Ulaanbaatar is now ⓑ4:30 p.m. and there is a chance of rain. We hope you had a nice flight. Thank you for flying with us. We hope to see you again.

**25** 위 글의 밑줄 친 @have just arrived와 현재완료의 용법이 같은 것을 모두 고르시오.

① She hasn't washed the dishes yet.
② Have you ever been to Japan?
③ I have never seen a koala before.
④ We have known her for a long time.
⑤ I have already seen it.

**26** 위 글의 ⓑ의 읽는 법을 영어로 쓰시오.

➡ _____

[01~03] 다음 글을 읽고 물음에 답하시오.

This year, I had a (A)[general / special] summer because I visited Mongolia for the first time. My friend Altan is from Mongolia. His grandmother (B)[invited / visited] me to Ulaanbaatar, the capital of Mongolia.

After a (C)[four-hour / four-hours] flight from Seoul, Altan and I arrived at Chinggis Khaan International Airport in Ulaanbaatar. It took thirty minutes by taxi from the airport to Altan's grandmother's house.

**01** 위 글의 괄호 (A)~(C)에서 문맥이나 어법상 알맞은 낱말을 골라 쓰시오.

➡ (A) _____ (B) _____ (C) _____

**02** How long did it take from Seoul to Chinggis Khaan International Airport in Ulaanbaatar by airplane? Answer in English in a full sentence. (4 words)

➡ _____

**03** 본문의 내용과 일치하도록 다음 빈칸 (A)와 (B)에 알맞은 단어를 쓰시오.

This summer, the writer visited (A)_____ for the first time. Altan and the writer went to Altan's (B)_____ house.

[04~06] 다음 글을 읽고 물음에 답하시오.

Her house is a *ger*, a traditional Mongolian house. It is a big tent, but it is cozy inside. When we entered, something smelled wonderful. ⓐIt was from the *khorkhog* that she was cooking for us. *Khorkhog* is a Mongolian barbecue. It is made of lamb and cooked with hot stones. I was moved when Altan said Mongolians serve *khorkhog* to special guests. It was so delicious that I asked for more. After dinner, Altan and I went outside to see the night sky. The sky was full of bright stars. I felt like I was in a magical place.           *she: Altan's grandmother

**04** 위 글에서 주어진 영영풀이에 해당하는 단어를 찾아 쓰시오.

| comfortable and warm |
|---|

➡ _____

**05** 위 글의 밑줄 친 ⓐIt이 가리키는 내용을 우리말로 쓰시오.

➡ _____

**06** 본문의 내용과 일치하도록 다음 빈칸 (A)와 (B)에 알맞은 단어를 쓰시오.

Altan's grandmother cooked delicious (A)_____ for Altan and the writer. After eating it, Altan and the writer went outside to see the (B)_____ _____ which was full of bright stars.

**[07~09]** 다음 글을 읽고 물음에 답하시오.

During the next three days, ⓐAltan showed me around and helped me experience Mongolian culture. Every moment was fun and exciting, but I had the most fun when I rode a camel in the Gobi Desert. At first, ⓑ내가 예상했던 것보다 낙타의 키가 커서 무서웠다. But once I sat on its back, I soon got used to its movement. From the camel's back, the view of the desert was truly amazing.

My visit to Mongolia was a special experience in many ways. ⓒIt gave me a great chance to get to know my friend's country and culture. I want to visit Mongolia again someday!

**07** 위 글의 밑줄 친 ⓐ를 다음과 같이 바꿔 쓸 때 빈칸에 들어갈 알맞은 말을 쓰시오.

➡ Altan showed me around and helped me _____ _____ Mongolian culture.

**08** 위 글의 밑줄 친 ⓑ의 우리말에 맞게 한 단어를 보충하여, 주어진 어휘를 알맞게 배열하시오. (I로 시작할 것)

expected / the camel / scared / was / I / because / was / taller / I

➡ _____

_____

**09** 위 글의 밑줄 친 ⓒIt이 가리키는 것을 본문에서 찾아 쓰시오.

➡ _____

**[10~12]** 다음 글을 읽고 물음에 답하시오.

Her house is a *ger*, a traditional Mongolian house. It is a big tent, but it is cozy inside. When we entered, something smelled wonderful. It was from the *khorkhog* that she was cooking for us. *Khorkhog* is a Mongolian barbecue. It is made of lamb and cooked with hot stones. I ____ⓐ____ when Altan said Mongolians serve *khorkhog* to special guests. It was so delicious that I asked for more. After dinner, Altan and I went outside ⓑto see the night sky. The sky was full of bright stars. I felt like I was in a magical place.

**10** 위 글의 빈칸 ⓐ에 move를 알맞은 형태로 쓰시오.

➡ _____

**11** 위 글의 밑줄 친 ⓑ를 다음과 같이 바꿔 쓸 때 빈칸에 들어갈 알맞은 말을 쓰시오.

➡ in order that _____ see the night sky

= _____ we could[might] see the night sky

**12** 다음 빈칸 (A)와 (B)에 알맞은 단어를 넣어 *ger*에 대한 소개를 완성하시오.

It is a (A)_____ _____ house. Though it is a big tent, it is (B)_____ inside.

## Writing Workshop - Step 2

**A Trip to Suncheon**

My family took a trip to Suncheon last summer. We visited the National
　　　　　　 ~으로 여행을 갔다

Garden. It was so large that we could not see the whole garden. After three
The National Garden　　so ~ that+주어+can't … = too ~ to …: 너무 ~해서 …할 수 없다

hours' walking, we were really hungry. For dinner, we had Gukbap that my
　　　　　　　　　　　　　　　　　　　　　　　　　　　　　= which(목적격 관계대명사)

parents like. Suncheon is famous for Gukbap and we enjoyed it.
　　　　　　　　　　　　　　　　　　　　　　　　　= Gukbap

This trip was so good that I would never forget it for a long time.
　　　　　　　　　　　　　　　　　　　 = This trip

구문해설　• take a trip: 여행하다　• whole: 전체[전부]의　• be famous for: ~으로 유명하다
　　　　　• for a long time: 오랫동안

## Wrap Up 1-2

G: How was your weekend, Tony?
　　'~가 어땠니?'라는 의미이다. 'How did you like ~?'로 바꾸어 쓸 수 있다.

B: It was great. I went to the International Food Festival with my parents.
　　=My weekend

G: What food did you try?
의문 형용사: 어떤, 무슨

B: I had a traditional Chinese dessert, *tangyuan*.
　　= eat

G: How did you like it?
　How did you like ~?: ~는 어땠어?

B: I enjoyed it. It's made with sweet rice balls. Chinese people usually serve it
　　= *tangyuan*　be made with: ~로 만들어지다

to guests at a wedding.

구문해설　• traditional: 전통적인　• serve: 제공하다, 대접하다

## Wrap Up 7

How was the restaurant that just opened around the corner?
　　　　　　　　　　　 주격 관계대명사

⌐ The restaurant was so crowded that I had to wait for an hour to get in.
　　　　　　　　　 so+형용사(원인)　that+주어+동사(결과)　　　　　 부사적 용법(목적)

⌐ The cheese cake tasted so good that I ate all of it.
　　　　　　　　　　　　　　　　　　　 =the cheese cake

⌐ The restaurant was so noisy that I couldn't talk with my friends.

구문해설　• crowed: 붐비는　• get in: ~에 들어가다

해석

**순천으로의 여행**

나의 가족은 작년 여름에 순천으로 여행을 갔다. 우리는 순천 국가 정원을 방문했다. 그곳은 너무 넓어서 우리는 정원 전체를 다 볼 수 없었다. 세 시간 동안 걸은 후, 우리는 정말 배가 고팠다. 저녁 식사로 우리는 부모님들이 좋아하시는 국밥을 먹었다. 순천은 국밥으로 유명하고, 우리는 그것을 즐겼다.

이번 여행은 너무 좋아서 나는 오랫동안 그것을 결코 잊지 않을 것이다.

G: 토니야, 주말 잘 보냈니?

B: 좋았어. 부모님과 함께 국제 음식 축제에 다녀왔어.

G: 무슨 음식 먹어 봤니?

B: 중국 전통 후식인 탕위안을 먹었어.

G: 어땠어?

B: 맛있었어. 그건 달콤하고 동그란 떡으로 만들었어. 중국 사람들은 보통 결혼식에서 손님들에게 이것을 대접해.

모퉁이에 막 오픈한 그 식당은 어땠나요?

⌐ 그 식당은 매우 붐벼서 나는 안에 들어가기 위해 한 시간 동안 기다려야 했어요.

⌐ 그 치즈 케이크는 매우 맛있어서 나는 전부 먹어 치웠어요.

⌐ 그 식당은 매우 시끄러워서 나는 친구와 이야기할 수 없었어요.

## 영역별 핵심문제

**01** 다음 대화의 빈칸 (A)와 (B)에 들어갈 말로 알맞은 것끼리 짝지어진 것을 고르시오.

> **A:** Wow! It's a new movie. When did you watch it?
> **B:** I watched it last Monday.
> **A:** It looks really interesting. Are you _____(A)_____ with it?
> **B:** No, I am not. It's __(B)__.

|   | (A) | (B) |
|---|-----|-----|
| ① | satisfied | interesting |
| ② | satisfied | bored |
| ③ | satisfied | boring |
| ④ | satisfying | interesting |
| ⑤ | satisfying | bored |

**02** 다음 우리말에 맞도록 빈칸에 알맞은 말을 쓰시오.

(1) 이 탁자는 나무로 만들어졌다.
➡ This table _____ of wood.

(2) 박물관 가이드는 우리에게 둘러보도록 안내해 줄 것이다.
➡ The guide at the museum will _____ us _____.

(3) 내 방은 현대식 스타일로 꾸며져 있다.
➡ My room is decorated in a _____ style.

**03** 빈칸에 알맞은 말을 고르시오.

> Take a look at this picture _____ right to left.

① from  ② for  ③ with
④ in  ⑤ by

**04** 다음 영영풀이가 나타내는 말을 고르시오.

> an opportunity to do something

① chance  ② experience
③ effort  ④ effect
⑤ purpose

**05** 다음 대화의 빈칸에 들어갈 말을 고르시오.

> **A:** Have you _____ won a prize?
> **B:** Yes, I have.

① always  ② still  ③ yet
④ just  ⑤ ever

**[06~08]** 다음 대화를 읽고 물음에 답하시오.

> **G:** How was your weekend, Tony?
> **B:** It was great. I went to the International Food Festival with my parents.
> **G:** What food did you try?
> **B:** I had a traditional Chinese dessert, *tangyuan*.
> **G:** How did you like it?
> **B:** I enjoyed it. It's made _____ sweet rice balls. Chinese people usually serve it to guests at a wedding.

**06** 빈칸에 들어갈 말을 고르시오.

① by  ② about  ③ as
④ for  ⑤ with

**07** 대화에서 다음 영영풀이에 해당하는 단어를 찾아 쓰시오.

> someone who is invited to visit you

➡ _____

## 08 위의 대화를 읽고 답할 수 있는 질문을 〈보기〉에서 모두 고르시오.

┌─ 보기 ┐
ⓐ Has the girl ever eaten *tangyuan*?
ⓑ Who did Tony go to the International Food Festival with?
ⓒ What is *tangyuan*?
ⓓ Where did Tony go on weekend?
ⓔ What did Tony have at the International Food Festival?

➡ _____

## 09 대화의 흐름상 어색한 것을 고르시오.

B: ⓐHave you been to the new Chinese restaurant?
G: ⓑNo. I had dinner there last Saturday.
B: ⓒHow did you like it?
G: ⓓThe service was bad. ⓔI won't go back there again.

① ⓐ    ② ⓑ    ③ ⓒ    ④ ⓓ    ⑤ ⓔ

**[10~12]** 다음 대화를 읽고 물음에 답하시오.

B: Have you ever traveled abroad, Sujin?
G: Yes, I went to Cambodia last summer. (①)
B: Wow. How did you like it?
G: It was really hot, but I enjoyed the trip. (②)
B: Tell me some interesting experiences you had during the trip.
G: Hmm... let me think. (③)

B: What? You're kidding. (④)_____
G: They were really big, so I was a little scared at first. But the taste was okay. (⑤)
B: Really? I cannot imagine eating spiders.

## 10 ①~⑤ 중 주어진 문장이 들어갈 곳은?

┌──────────────────────┐
│ I ate fried spiders! │
└──────────────────────┘

①    ②    ③    ④    ⑤

## 11 위 대화의 표현을 이용해 흐름에 맞게 빈칸을 채우시오.

➡ _____

## 12 대화의 내용과 일치하지 않는 것을 고르시오.

① 수진이가 캄보디아 여행을 갔을 때 날씨가 너무 더웠다.
② 수진이는 해외여행을 간 경험이 있다.
③ 남자아이는 수진이가 거미를 먹는 걸 상상할 수 없었다.
④ 수진이는 지난여름에 캄보디아에 다녀왔다.
⑤ 수진이는 거미 튀김이 맛이 없다고 생각했다.

### Grammar

## 13 다음 괄호 안에서 알맞은 말을 고르시오.

(1) Is it (warm enough / enough warm) to go swimming?
(2) This black tea is (too / so) hot that you can't drink it.
(3) The shoes are too big (to / for) me to wear.

**14** 주어진 문장의 밑줄 친 <u>that</u>과 용법이 <u>다른</u> 하나는?

> • The cheese cake tasted so good <u>that</u> I ate all of it.

① He studied hard so <u>that</u> he could pass the test.
② The tea is so hot <u>that</u> I can't drink it.
③ She was so beautiful <u>that</u> I couldn't take my eyes off her.
④ This book was so interesting <u>that</u> I read it all day.
⑤ I was so tired <u>that</u> I slept all day.

**15** 다음 중 어법상 어색한 문장을 고르시오.

① This is the game I really want to play.
② The doctor you visited is my aunt.
③ The song the cellist is playing is Verdi's.
④ The road which he was driving was not safe.
⑤ The woman who is shaking hands with my teacher is my mom.

**16** 다음 우리말을 주어진 어휘를 이용하여 영어로 옮기시오.

(1) 내가 초대한 소녀들이 나의 생일 파티에 오지 않았다. (girls, invite)
➡ _____

(2) 내가 보고 싶었던 TV 프로그램이 있었다. (there, a TV program, watch)
➡ _____

(3) 네가 먹을 수 있는 쿠키가 좀 있어. (there, some cookies)
➡ _____

(4) 그 가방은 매우 튼튼해서 나는 많은 책을 넣고 다닐 수 있어. (bag, strong, that, a lot of, carry, in)
➡ _____

(5) 나는 매우 바빠서 쇼핑을 갈 수 없었다. (busy, shopping)
➡ _____

(6) 그건 매우 쉬워서 누구든지 그것을 할 수 있어. (anyone, it, can)
➡ _____

**17** 다음 빈칸에 공통으로 알맞은 말을 쓰시오.

> • The skirt _____ you are wearing is mine. Take it off right now!
> • I can't decide _____ to buy. All the skirts you showed me are awesome.

➡ _____

**18** 관계대명사를 이용하여 만든 다음 문장을 원래의 두 문장으로 쓰시오.

(1) The radio which I bought isn't working.
➡ _____

(2) That's the coach who I saw at the soccer match.
➡ _____

**19** 다음 중 두 문장을 한 문장으로 만들 때 의미가 <u>다른</u> 하나는?

① The traffic was very heavy. + We were late.
　→ The traffic was so heavy that we were late.

② I missed you very much. + I could do anything to see you.
　→ I missed you so much that I could do anything to see you.

③ It was raining very hard. + We had to stop playing soccer.
　→ It was raining too hard for us to play soccer.

④ I worked very hard. + I was promoted to director.
　→ I worked hard enough to be promoted to director.

⑤ I got up late. + I couldn't catch the bus.
　→ I got up too late to miss the bus.

**Reading**

[20~21] 다음 글을 읽고 물음에 답하시오.

This year, I had a special summer because I visited Mongolia for the first time. ⓐ My friend Altan is from Mongolia. His grandmother invited me to Ulaanbaatar, the capital of Mongolia.

After a four-hour flight from Seoul, Altan and I arrived at Chinggis Khaan International Airport in Ulaanbaatar. ⓑIt took thirty minutes by taxi from the airport to Altan's grandmother's house.

**20** 위 글의 밑줄 친 ⓐ를 다음과 같이 바꿔 쓸 때 빈칸에 들어갈 알맞은 말을 쓰시오.

➡ My friend Altan _____ from Mongolia.

**21** 위 글의 밑줄 친 문장 ⓑ에서 생략할 수 있는 한 단어를 생략하여 문장을 다시 쓰시오.

➡ _____
_____

[22~24] 다음 글을 읽고 물음에 답하시오.

Her house is a *ger*, a traditional Mongolian house. (①) It is a big tent, but it is cozy inside. (②) When we entered, something smelled wonderful. (③) *Khorkhog* is a Mongolian barbecue. (④) It is made of lamb and cooked with hot stones. (⑤) I was moved when Altan said Mongolians serve *khorkhog* to special guests. ⓐ그것은 너무 맛있어서 나는 더 달라고 했다. After dinner, Altan and I went outside to see the night sky. The sky was full of bright stars. I felt like I was in a magical place.

**22** 위 글의 흐름으로 보아, 주어진 문장이 들어가기에 가장 적절한 곳은?

It was from the *khorkhog* that she was cooking for us.

①　　②　　③　　④　　⑤

**23** 다음 문장에서 위 글의 내용과 다른 부분을 찾아서 고치시오.

A *ger* is a big tent, so it isn't cozy inside.

_____ ➡ _____

**24** 위 글의 밑줄 친 ⓐ의 우리말에 맞게 주어진 어휘를 이용하여 9단어로 영작하시오.

so, that, for, more

➡ _____

**[25~27]** 다음 글을 읽고 물음에 답하시오.

During the next three days, Altan showed me around and helped me experience Mongolian culture. Every moment was fun and exciting, but I had the most fun when I rode a camel in the Gobi Desert. At first, I was scared because the camel was taller than I expected. But once I sat on its back, I soon got used to its movement. From the camel's back, the view of the desert was truly amazing.

My visit to Mongolia was a special experience in many ways. ⓐ그것은 내 친구의 나라와 문화를 알 수 있는 좋은 기회가 되었다. I want to visit Mongolia again someday!

**25** 위 글의 밑줄 친 ⓐ의 우리말에 맞게 주어진 어휘를 알맞게 배열하시오.

> my friend's country and culture / me / to know / it / a great chance / gave / to get

➡ _____

_____

**26** 위 글의 제목으로 가장 알맞은 것을 고르시오.

① My Visit to Mongolia, a Special Experience
② A Special Mongolian Culture
③ Enjoy Riding a Camel!
④ Let Me Introduce Mongolia to You!
⑤ When Can I Visit Mongolia Again?

**27** 위 글을 읽고 대답할 수 <u>없는</u> 질문은?

① How long did Altan show the writer around?
② What did the writer experience with Altan?
③ When was the most fun moment to the writer during the trip?
④ How long did the writer ride a camel in the Gobi Desert?
⑤ What gave the writer a great chance to get to know Mongolia and its culture?

**[28~30]** 다음 글을 읽고 물음에 답하시오.

(A)[I am / This is] your captain speaking. We have just arrived at the airport. <u>자연과 문화의 아름다움으로 가득 찬 나라 몽골에 오신 것을 환영합니다.</u> The time in Ulaanbaatar is now 4:30 p.m. and there is a chance of rain. We hope you (B) [had / will have] a nice flight. Thank you for flying with us. We hope (C)[seeing / to see] you again.

**28** 위 글의 괄호 (A)~(C)에서 문맥이나 어법상 알맞은 낱말을 골라 쓰시오.

➡ (A) _____ (B) _____ (C) _____

**29** 위 글의 종류로 알맞은 것을 고르시오.

① live broadcast       ② boarding call
③ travel essay         ④ traffic report
⑤ in-flight announcement

**30** 위 글의 밑줄 친 우리말을 주어진 어휘를 알맞게 배열하여 영작하시오.

> Mongolia, the beauty, a country, nature and culture, welcome, full of, of, to

➡ _____

_____

**01** 출제율 85%

제시된 영영풀이의 단어로 대화의 빈칸을 채우시오. (주어진 철자로 시작할 것)

> c_____ : noticeably happy

> A: How do you like this song?
> B: It's c_____. I like it.

**02** 출제율 95%

다음 빈칸에 공통으로 들어갈 말을 쓰시오.

> • It was full _____ animals waiting for their new owner.
> • This pink dress is made _____ silk.

**03** 출제율 100%

다음 중 〈보기〉에 있는 단어를 사용하여 자연스러운 문장을 만들 수 없는 것은?

> ┤ 보기 ├
> abroad    bright    modern    whole

① The moon was very _____ last night.
② You must see many small dots in order to see the _____ painting.
③ From ancient buildings to _____ works of art, you can find them.
④ I'm planning to travel _____.
⑤ After a busy day, he falls _____.

**04** 출제율 95%

다음 영영풀이에 해당하는 단어를 고르시오.

> to believe or think that something will happen

① wait        ② require        ③ decide
④ expect        ⑤ explain

**[05~07]** 다음 대화를 읽고 물음에 답하시오.

> B: 바다 위로 해가 뜨는 것을 본 적 있니?
> G: ⓐNo. ⓑHow about you?
> B: ⓒI watched the sun rise in Gangneung on New Year's Day. It was great.
> G: ⓓI tried several times, ⓔso I just couldn't wake up early enough.

**05** 출제율 95%

밑줄 친 우리말과 일치하도록 주어진 단어를 이용해 문장을 만드시오.

> ➡ _____
>   _____ (over, ever, watch, rise)

**06** 출제율 90%

위 대화에서 다음 영영풀이에 해당하는 단어를 찾아 쓰시오.

> to appear above the horizon in the sky

> ➡ _____

**07** 출제율 100%

위 대화의 문맥상 어색한 것을 고르시오.

① ⓐ        ② ⓑ        ③ ⓒ        ④ ⓓ        ⑤ ⓔ

**08** 출제율 95%

다음 대화의 빈칸에 알맞은 말을 고르시오.

> A: Have you ever gone camping?
> B: _____ It was a wonderful experience.

① Yes, I have.
② No, I haven't.
③ Of course, I did.
④ No, I didn't.
⑤ I have never had it.

**09** 빈칸 (A)와 (B)에 어울리는 의문사를 각각 쓰시오.

> G: (A)_____ was your vacation?
> B: Great. I went to Dokdo with my family.
> G: (B)_____ did you like it?
> B: It was amazing. I want to visit there again.

**[10~12]** 다음 대화를 읽고 물음에 답하시오.

> B: Have you ever traveled abroad, Sujin?
> G: (A)[No, I haven't. / Yes, I have.] I went to Cambodia last summer.
> B: Wow. How did you like it?
> G: It was really hot, but I enjoyed the trip.
> B: Tell me some ___ⓐ___ (interest) experiences you had (B)[during / while] the trip.
> G: Hmm... let me think. I ate fried spiders!
> B: What? You're kidding. How did you like them?
> G: They were really big, so I was a little ___ⓑ___ (scare) at first. ___(C)___ the taste was okay.
> B: Really? I cannot imagine eating spiders.

**10** 위 대화의 괄호 (A), (B)에서 적절한 것을 고르시오.

➡ (A) _____ (B) _____

**11** 괄호 안에 주어진 단어를 이용해 빈칸 ⓐ와 ⓑ를 채우시오.

➡ ⓐ _____ ⓑ _____

**12** 빈칸 (C)에 알맞은 말을 고르시오.

① Because  ② When  ③ But
④ Therefore  ⑤ Since

**13** 잘못된 부분을 바르게 고치시오.

(1) He teaches me new things that I have never tried them before.
➡ _____

(2) Jack is the boy who she is in love.
➡ _____

(3) My sister likes the cake who I baked.
➡ _____

(4) I know the boys which she is talking to.
➡ _____

(5) This is the tablet PC that I really want to buy it.
➡ _____

(6) I was too tired that I couldn't work out.
➡ _____

(7) The girl is enough fast that she can catch the bus.
➡ _____

(8) The man is very smart that he solves any problem.
➡ _____

**14** 다음 중 어법상 어색한 문장을 고르시오.

① The house in which we lived was beautiful.
② This is the issue that everyone is talking about.
③ The city I visited is called the windy city.
④ The women I talked with just a minute ago are my aunts.
⑤ That is the cousin whom played with me when I was young.

**15** 빈칸에 공통으로 알맞은 말을 쓰시오. *출제율 90%*

> • It was raining, _____ we didn't go to the park.
> • It was _____ cold that we couldn't go outside.

**16** 다음 중 어법상 올바른 문장을 고르시오. *출제율 100%*

① This is the video camera who he lent me.
② I'm listening to the music who you recommended.
③ I know a boy which speaks English very well.
④ This is the book I read last year.
⑤ I don't like people whom tells a lie.

**17** 다음 문장을 어법에 맞게 고쳐 쓰시오. *출제율 95%*

(1) This report was so difficult that you can't read it.

➡ _____
_____

(2) I was so tired to finish my task.

➡ _____
_____

(3) I was stupid enough for believe what you said.

➡ _____
_____

(4) The rings that she was wearing was fantastic.

➡ _____
_____

(5) I've found the dog whom you lost.

➡ _____
_____

---

[18~20] 다음 글을 읽고 물음에 답하시오.

> ⓐThis year, I had a special summer though I (A)[invited / visited] Mongolia for the first time. My friend Altan is from Mongolia. His grandmother invited me to Ulaanbaatar, the (B)[capital / capitol] of Mongolia.
>
> After a four-hour flight from Seoul, Altan and I arrived at Chinggis Khaan International Airport in Ulaanbaatar. It (C)[spent / took] thirty minutes by taxi from the airport to Altan's grandmother's house.

**18** 위 글의 괄호 (A)~(C)에서 문맥이나 어법상 알맞은 낱말을 골라 쓰시오. *출제율 95%*

➡ (A) _____ (B) _____ (C) _____

**19** 위 글의 밑줄 친 ⓐ에서 흐름상 어색한 부분을 찾아 고치시오. *출제율 90%*

_____ ➡ _____

**20** 위 글을 읽고 대답할 수 없는 질문은? *출제율 100%*

① When did the writer take a trip to Mongolia?
② Has the writer ever been to Mongolia before?
③ Who invited the writer to Ulaanbaatar?
④ Why was the writer invited to Ulaanbaatar?
⑤ How long did it take from the airport to Altan's grandmother's house by taxi?

**[21~23]** 다음 글을 읽고 물음에 답하시오.

Her house is a *ger*, a traditional Mongolian house. It is a big tent, but it is cozy inside. When we entered, something smelled wonderful. It was ①from the *khorkhog* that she was cooking ②for us. *Khorkhog* is a Mongolian barbecue. It is made ③of lamb and cooked ④with hot stones. I was moved when Altan said Mongolians serve *khorkhog* to special guests. It was so delicious that I asked ⑤of more. After dinner, Altan and I went outside to see the night sky. The sky was full of bright stars. I felt like I was in a magical place.

출제율 90%

**21** 밑줄 친 전치사 ①~⑤ 중에서 그 쓰임이 알맞지 <u>않은</u> 것을 고르시오.

①     ②     ③     ④     ⑤

출제율 100%

**22** 위 글의 제목으로 알맞은 것을 고르시오.

① What Is a *Ger*?
② Have you Ever Eaten *Khorkhog*?
③ I Enjoyed a *Ger* and *Khorkhog*
④ Serve *Khorkhog* to Special Guests
⑤ The Night Sky Full of Bright Stars

출제율 95%

**23** 위 글의 내용과 일치하지 <u>않는</u> 것은?

① 게르는 큰 텐트이지만 내부는 아늑하다.
② 호르호그는 몽골식 바비큐이다.
③ 호르호그는 양고기로 만들어졌다.
④ 몽골인들은 저녁식사로 주로 호르호그를 먹는다.
⑤ 글쓴이는 호르호그가 너무 맛있어서 더 달라고 했다.

**[24~26]** 다음 글을 읽고 물음에 답하시오.

During the next three days, Altan showed me around and helped me experience ⓐ \_\_\_\_\_ culture. (①) Every moment was fun and exciting, but I had the most fun when I rode a camel in the Gobi Desert. (②) At first, I was scared because the camel was taller than I expected. (③) From the camel's back, the view of the desert was truly amazing. (④)
My visit to Mongolia was a special experience in many ways. (⑤) It gave me a great chance ⓑto get to know my friend's country and culture. I want to visit Mongolia again someday!

출제율 95%

**24** 본문의 한 단어를 변형하여 위 글의 빈칸 ⓐ에 들어갈 알맞은 말을 쓰시오.

➡ _____

출제율 100%

**25** 위 글의 흐름으로 보아, 주어진 문장이 들어가기에 가장 적절한 곳은?

> But once I sat on its back, I soon got used to its movement.

①     ②     ③     ④     ⑤

출제율 90%

**26** 위 글의 밑줄 친 ⓑto get과 to부정사의 용법이 <u>다른</u> 것을 <u>모두</u> 고르시오.

① The house to spend the night in was cozy.
② You will find it difficult to read the novel.
③ He is the man to blame for the mistake.
④ Literature is not something to study.
⑤ He is rich enough to buy a plane of his own.

**01** 대화의 흐름상 또는 어법상 어색한 것을 하나 찾아서 고치시오.

> B: Have you been to the new Chinese restaurant?
> G: Yes. I had dinner there last Saturday.
> B: How did you like it?
> G: The service was good. I won't go back there again.
> B: Really? I wanted to go there, but I won't go, either.

_____ ➡ _____

**02** 밑줄 친 부분 앞에 생략된 부분을 대화에서 찾아 완전한 문장으로 쓰시오.

> G: You look excited, Inho. What's up?
> B: I'm going to Jejudo with my family this weekend. Have you ever been there?
> G: Yes, many times. I love the coastline. How about you?
> B: It'll be my first visit to Jejudo. I can't wait for this weekend!

➡ _____
_____

**03** 대화의 밑줄 친 부분과 같은 뜻이 되도록 주어진 단어를 이용해 문장을 완성하시오.

> A: How do you like your ice cream?
> B: It's sweet. I like it.

➡ (1) _____
(think)
(2) _____
(opinion)

**04** 다음 두 문장을 'so ... that' 구문을 이용하여 한 문장으로 연결하여 쓰시오.

(1) • Jack was very sleepy.
• Jack couldn't work any more.

➡ _____

(2) • Mason is very short.
• Mason can't ride a roller coaster.

➡ _____
_____

(3) • The man is very busy.
• He can't play with his daughter.

➡ _____
_____

(4) • It was too hot.
• Children couldn't play outside.

➡ _____
_____

**05** 다음 두 문장을 관계대명사를 이용하여 한 문장으로 연결하여 쓰시오.

(1) • I want a robot.
• I can control the robot.

➡ _____
_____

(2) • Look at the picture.
• My classmate drew the picture.

➡ _____
_____

(3) • Daniel is the boy.
• I met the boy at the concert.

➡ _____
_____

(4) • The cathedral was beautiful.
• We visited the cathedral last year.

➡ _____
_____

**06** 우리말과 일치하도록 주어진 단어를 바르게 배열하시오.

(1) 그는 매우 정직해서 거짓말을 못한다.
→ He is (so, he, honest, that, tell, can't) a lie.

➡ _____

(2) 그는 나이가 들어 대학교에 입학할 수 있다.
→ He is (that, old, enter, he, can, so) a university.

➡ _____

**[07~09]** 다음 글을 읽고 물음에 답하시오.

Her house is a *ger*, a traditional Mongolian house. It is a big tent, but it is cozy inside. When we entered, something smelled (A) [wonderful / wonderfully]. It was from the *khorkhog* that she was cooking for us. *Khorkhog* is a Mongolian barbecue. It is made of lamb and (B)[cooking / cooked] with hot stones. I was moved when Altan said Mongolians serve *khorkhog* to special guests. It was (C)[so / such] delicious that I asked for more. After dinner, Altan and I went outside to see the night sky. The sky was full of bright stars. I felt ___ⓐ___ I was in a magical place.

**07** 위 글의 빈칸 ⓐ에 들어갈 알맞은 한 단어를 쓰시오.

➡ _____

**08** 위 글의 괄호 (A)~(C)에서 어법상 알맞은 낱말을 골라 쓰시오.

➡ (A) _____ (B) _____ (C) _____

**09** 다음 빈칸 (A)와 (B)에 알맞은 단어를 넣어 *khorkhog*에 대한 소개를 완성하시오.

*Khorkhog* is a (A)_____ _____ which is made of lamb and cooked with hot stones. Mongolians serve it to (B)_____ _____.

**[10~12]** 다음 글을 읽고 물음에 답하시오.

During the next three days, Altan showed me around and helped me experience Mongolian culture. Every moment was fun and exciting, but I had the most fun when I rode a camel in the Gobi Desert. At first, I was scared because the camel was taller than I expected. But once I sat on its back, I soon ⓐ익숙해졌다 its movement. From the camel's back, the view of the desert was truly amazing.

My visit to Mongolia was a special experience in many ways. ⓑIt gave me a great chance to get to know my friend's country and culture. I want to visit Mongolia again someday!

**10** 위 글의 밑줄 친 ⓐ의 우리말을 got을 사용하여 세 단어로 쓰시오.

➡ _____

**11** 위 글의 밑줄 친 ⓑ를 3형식 문장으로 고치시오.

➡ _____

_____

**12** 본문의 내용과 일치하도록 다음 빈칸 (A)와 (B)에 알맞은 단어를 쓰시오.

Altan helped the writer experience (A)_____ _____, and the visit to Mongolia was a (B)_____ _____ in many ways.

# 창의사고력 서술형 문제

**01** 그림과 관련된 경험을 해 본 적이 있는지 묻고 대답하는 대화를 완성하시오.

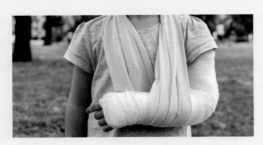

┌─── 조건 ────────────────────────┐
│ • break를 이용할 것 │
└─────────────────────────────────┘

┌─────────────────────────────────┐
│ A: _____ │
│ B: _____ │
└─────────────────────────────────┘

**02** 과거의 자신의 모습을 생각하며 할 수 있었던 것과 할 수 없었던 것을 'so … that ~' 구문을 이용하여 〈보기〉와 같이 쓰시오.

┌─── 보기 ────────────────────────┐
│ I was so young that I couldn't ride a bike. │
└─────────────────────────────────┘

(1) I _____ I couldn't _____ .

(2) I _____ I couldn't _____ .

(3) I _____ I could _____ .

(4) I _____ I could _____ .

**03** 다음 내용을 바탕으로 기행문을 쓰시오.

┌─────────────────────────────────────────────────┐
│ **My trip** │
│ Where: Ulleungdo │
│ When: Last summer │
│ Who With: My parents │
│ What I Did: │
│ - walked along the road around the island │
└─────────────────────────────────────────────────┘

┌─────────────────────────────────────────────────┐
│ **A Trip to Ulleungdo** │
│ (A)_____, my parents and I went to (B)_____. Ulleungdo is an island that │
│ I always wanted to visit. We (C)_____ along the road around (D)_____. │
│ This trip was so great that I would never forget it for a long time. │
└─────────────────────────────────────────────────┘

**단원별 모의고사**

**01** 빈칸에 알맞은 말을 〈보기〉에서 골라 쓰시오. (2번 사용 가능)

┌─ 보기 ─┐
at   for   to   about   in   of

(1) The room was full _____ smoke. So I opened the windows.

(2) _____ first, his accent was difficult to understand. But soon, we got used _____ it.

(3) *Feijoada* is a Brazilian national dish. It is made _____ black beans and meat.

**02** 우리말과 일치하도록 주어진 단어를 알맞게 배열하시오.

(1) 내 친구는 지금 유학 중입니다.

➡ _____

(now, friend, studying, abroad, my, is)

(2) 우리는 서로 다시 만날 것을 기대했다.

➡ _____

(expected, again, see. we, other, to, each)

**03** 다음 빈칸에 공통으로 들어갈 말을 쓰시오.

┌─────────────────────────┐
│ • Let's talk more about snowboarding _____ the break. │
│ • I have traveled _____ the winter vacation. │
└─────────────────────────┘

**04** 단어와 영영풀이의 연결이 잘못된 것을 고르시오.

① get used to: to become familiar with something or someone

② kid: to make a joke

③ station: a place where trains or buses stop so that people can get on or off

④ part: one of the pieces, sections, or elements that makes the whole of something

⑤ modern: designed and made using the oldest ides or methods

**05** 다음 대화의 문맥상 어색한 것을 고르시오.

┌─────────────────────────┐
│ B: ⓐHave you ever watched the sun rise over the ocean? │
│ G: No. ⓑHow about you? │
│ B: ⓒI watched the sun rise in Gangneung on New Year's Day. It was great. │
│ G: ⓓI tried several times, ⓔbut I just couldn't wake up late enough. │
└─────────────────────────┘

① ⓐ   ② ⓑ   ③ ⓒ   ④ ⓓ   ⑤ ⓔ

**[06~07]** 다음 대화를 읽고 물음에 답하시오.

┌─────────────────────────┐
│ G: 방학은 어땠니? │
│ B: Great. I went to Dokdo with my family. │
│ G: How did you like it? │
│ B: It was   (A)   (amaze). I want to visit there again. │
└─────────────────────────┘

**06** 밑줄 친 우리말을 how를 사용해 두 가지로 영작하시오.

➡ (1) _____
   (2) _____

**07** 빈칸 (A)에 알맞은 말을 주어진 단어를 이용해 쓰시오.

➡ _____

## 08 다음 대화의 빈칸에 들어갈 말을 〈보기〉에서 골라 순서대로 바르게 배열한 것은?

> G: How was your weekend, Tony?
> B: _____
> G: _____
> B: _____
> G: _____
> B: I enjoyed it. It's made with sweet rice balls. Chinese people usually serve it to guests at a wedding.

보기

> (A) What food did you try?
> (B) I had a traditional Chinese dessert, *tangyuan*.
> (C) It was great. I went to the International Food Festival with my parents.
> (D) How did you like it?

① (B) – (A) – (C) – (D)
② (B) – (C) – (D) – (A)
③ (C) – (A) – (B) – (D)
④ (C) – (B) – (A) – (D)
⑤ (C) – (D) – (B) – (A)

## [09~10] 다음 대화를 읽고 물음에 답하시오.

> B: 새로 생긴 중국 음식점에 가 봤니?
> G: Yes. I had dinner there last Saturday.
> B: _____(A)_____
> G: The service was bad. I won't go back there again.

## 09 빈칸 (A)에 알맞은 말을 고르시오.

① Why did you go there?
② How did you like it?
③ What did you like?
④ What didn't you like about it?
⑤ Why do you think so?

## 10 밑줄 친 우리말을 영작하시오.

➡ _____

## [11~12] 다음 대화를 읽고 물음에 답하시오.

> B: Have you ever traveled abroad, Sujin?
> G: Yes, I went to Cambodia last summer. (①)
> B: Wow. (②)
> G: It was really hot, but I enjoyed the trip.
> B: Tell me some interesting experiences you had during the trip. (③)
> G: Hmm... let me think. I ate fried spiders! (④)
> B: What? You're kidding. How did you like them?
> G: They were really big, so I was a little scared at first. But the taste was okay. (⑤)
> B: Really? I cannot imagine eating spiders.

## 11 ①~⑤ 중 주어진 문장이 들어갈 곳은?

> How did you like it?

①          ②          ③          ④          ⑤

## 12 위 대화를 읽고 대답할 수 없는 질문을 고르시오.

① How was the weather when Sujin went to Cambodia?
② Where did Sujin travel last summer?
③ Who did Sujun travel to Cambodia with?
④ Has Sujin ever been abroad before?
⑤ What did Sujin eat in Cambodia?

**13** 다음 중 어법상 <u>어색한</u> 것은?

① Give me a pen I can write with.
② There are many products which are made in China.
③ The boy who playing the violin is my son.
④ The movie I watched yesterday was fantastic.
⑤ I haven't heard the language which is spoken in that country.

**14** 빈칸에 공통으로 들어갈 알맞은 것은?

- It is the notebook _____ you lent me.
- Look at the boys and their bikes _____ are under the tree.

① who      ② which      ③ that
④ what      ⑤ whose

**15** 두 문장을 관계대명사를 사용하여 한 문장으로 쓰시오.

(1) There is a shop in front of my office.
　　+ It sells good coffee.

➡ _____

_____

(2) I like the game.
　　+ The boys are downloading the game now.

➡ _____

_____

**16** 다음 문장에서 생략된 말이 있는 곳은?

The man ① I sat ② next to ③ on the train ④ slept ⑤ all the way.

**17** 다음 우리말에 맞게 괄호 안에 주어진 어휘를 바르게 배열하시오.

(1) 네가 가장 존경하는 사람에 대해 얘기해 봐라. (most, tell, about, me, the man, you, whom, admire)

➡ _____

(2) 그녀는 옆집에 사는 여자이다. (she, next door, is, the woman, lives, who)

➡ _____

(3) Mandy는 매우 빠르게 수영해서 금메달을 딸 수 있었다. (swam, that, won, so, Mandy, fast, the gold medal, she)

➡ _____

**[18~19]** 다음 글을 읽고 물음에 답하시오.

This year, I had a special summer because I visited Mongolia for the first time. My friend Altan is from Mongolia. His grandmother invited me to Ulaanbaatar, the capital of Mongolia.

After a four-hour flight from Seoul, Altan and I arrived at Chinggis Khaan International Airport in Ulaanbaatar. ⓐ공항에서 알탕의 할머니 댁까지 택시로 30분이 걸렸다.

**18** What's the capital of Mongolia? Answer in English in a full sentence. (2 words)

➡ _____

**19** 위 글의 밑줄 친 ⓐ의 우리말에 맞게 한 단어를 보충하여, 주어진 어휘를 알맞게 배열하시오.

to Altan's grandmother's house / took / taxi / from the airport / it / thirty minutes

➡ _____

_____

**[20~22] 다음 글을 읽고 물음에 답하시오.**

Her house is a *ger*, a traditional Mongolian house. It is a big tent, but it is cozy inside. When we entered, something smelled wonderful. It was from the *khorkhog* _____ⓐ_____ she was cooking for us. *Khorkhog* is a Mongolian barbecue. It is made of lamb and cooked with hot stones. I was ⓑmoved when Altan said Mongolians serve *khorkhog* to special guests. It was so delicious that I asked for more. After dinner, Altan and I went outside to see the night sky. The sky was full of bright stars. I felt like I was in a magical place.

**20** 위 글의 빈칸 ⓐ에 들어갈 알맞은 말을 <u>모두</u> 고르시오.

① who          ② that          ③ whom
④ what          ⑤ which

**21** 위 글의 밑줄 친 ⓑmoved와 바꿔 쓸 수 있는 단어를 쓰시오.

➡ _____

**22** 위 글의 주제로 알맞은 것을 고르시오.

① a special Mongolian house
② the Mongolians who like lamb
③ a traditional Mongolian house and food
④ a special recipe using hot stones
⑤ the Mongolian night sky full of bright stars

**[23~25] 다음 글을 읽고 물음에 답하시오.**

During the next three days, Altan showed me around and helped me (A)[experience / experiencing] Mongolian culture. Every moment was fun and exciting, but I had the most fun when I rode a camel in the Gobi Desert. At first, I was (B)[scared / scary] because the camel was taller than I expected. But once I sat on its back, I soon got used to its movement. From the camel's back, the view of the desert was truly (C)[amazing / amazed].

My visit to Mongolia was a special experience in many ways. It gave me a great chance to get to know my friend's country and culture. I want ⓓto visit Mongolia again someday!

**23** 위 글의 괄호 (A)~(C)에서 어법상 알맞은 낱말을 골라 쓰시오.

➡ (A) _____    (B) _____    (C) _____

**24** 〈보기〉에서 위 글의 밑줄 친 ⓓto visit와 문법적 쓰임이 같은 것의 개수를 고르시오.

┤ 보기 ├
① It was impossible to solve the problem.
② He is the last man to tell a lie.
③ To hear him talk, you would take him for a fool.
④ My goal is to become a great doctor.
⑤ She tried not to weep at the sad news.

① 1개    ② 2개    ③ 3개    ④ 4개    ⑤ 5개

**25** 위 글의 내용과 일치하지 <u>않는</u> 것은?

① 알탄은 3일 동안 글쓴이를 구경시켜 주었다.
② 글쓴이는 고비 사막에서 낙타를 탈 때가 가장 재미있었다.
③ 처음에 글쓴이는 예상했던 것보다 낙타의 키가 커서 무서웠다.
④ 낙타의 등에서 보는 사막의 경치는 정말로 무서웠다.
⑤ 글쓴이는 언젠가 몽골을 다시 방문하고 싶다.

# Lesson 7

# Living in the AI World

## 🎙 의사소통 기능

- 의견 표현하기
  A: I'm going to fly a drone.
  B: That sounds like fun.

- 가능 여부 표현하기
  A: Is it possible for you to text with your eyes closed?
  B: Sure. I can do that.

## 🎙 언어 형식

- 지각동사
  I **see** a cat **crossing** the street.

- 가주어 'it'
  **It** is hard **to believe** that you can understand us.

# Words & Expressions
교과서

## Key Words

- **AI** 인공지능(artificial intelligence)
- **amusement**[əmjúːzmənt] 명 즐거움, 오락
- **animated**[ǽnəmèitid] 형 동영상의, 생기 있는
- **beat**[biːt] 동 이기다
- **beatbox**[bíːtbɑks] 동 비트박스를 하다
- **bedroom**[bédrùːm] 명 침실
- **burn**[bəːrn] 동 불타다
- **chance**[tʃæns] 명 기회
- **check**[tʃek] 동 확인하다, 점검하다
- **closet**[klɑ́zit] 명 옷장
- **cloudy**[kláudi] 형 구름의, 흐린
- **cross**[krɔːs] 동 건너다
- **danger**[déindʒər] 명 위험
- **dictionary**[díkʃənèri] 명 사전
- **easily**[íːzili] 부 쉽게
- **else**[els] 부 그 밖의
- **exciting**[iksáitiŋ] 형 흥미진진한, 신나는
- **freeze**[friːz] 동 얼리다, 얼다
- **impossible**[impásəbl] 형 불가능한
- **intelligent**[intélədʒənt] 형 똑똑한
- **interesting**[íntərəstiŋ] 형 재미있는, 흥미로운
- **like**[laik] 전 ~ 같이, ~처럼
- **lucky**[lʌ́ki] 형 행운의

- **machine**[məʃíːn] 명 기계
- **mean**[miːn] 동 의미하다
- **off**[ɔːf] 부 할인되어
- **perfect**[pə́ːrfikt] 형 완벽한
- **point**[pɔint] 동 돌리다, 향하게 하다
- **possible**[pásəbl] 형 가능한
- **predict**[pridíkt] 동 예측하다
- **project**[prádʒekt] 명 과제
- **replace**[ripléis] 동 대체하다
- **select**[silékt] 동 선택하다
- **sense**[sens] 동 감지하다
- **situation**[sìtʃuéiʃən] 명 상황
- **space**[speis] 명 공간, 우주
- **strange**[streindʒ] 형 이상한
- **take**[teik] 동 선택하다, 사다
- **teleport**[téləpɔ̀ːrt] 동 순간 이동하다
- **text**[tekst] 동 (휴대전화로) 문자를 보내다
- **theater**[θíːətər] 명 극장
- **through**[θruː] 부 ~을 통해, ~ 사이로
- **translate**[trænsléit] 동 번역하다
- **translator**[trænsléitər] 명 번역가
- **unbelievable**[ənbilívəbəl] 형 믿기 어려운, 놀랄만한
- **without**[wiðáut] 전 ~ 없이

## Key Expressions

- **based on** ~에 근거하여
- **be able to 동사원형** ~할 수 있다
- **because of** ~ 때문에
- **by the way** 그런데, 그건 그렇고
- **by 동사ing** ~함으로써
- **don't have to** ~할 필요가 없다(need not)
- **face to face** (~와) 서로 얼굴을 맞대고
- **free from** ~의 염려가 없는
- **get in** ~에 타다
- **get off** ~에서 내리다, ~에서 떨어지다
- **get to** ~에 도착하다
- **get 비교급** 점점 더 ~해지다
- **go with** 같이 가다, 어울리다
- **in danger** 위험에 처한, 위험에 빠진
- **Is it possible (for 목적격) to 동사원형 ~?**
  (…가) ~하는 것이 가능할까?

- **keep 동사ing** 계속 ~하다
- **look for** ~을 찾다
- **look ~ up** (사전·참고 자료·컴퓨터 등에서 정보를) 찾아보다
- **look 형용사** ~하게 보이다
- **move on** ~로 이동하다
- **not just** 단지 ~뿐이 아니다
- **no longer** 더 이상 ~하지 않다
- **out of** (원천·출처) ~에서, ~으로부터
- **over there** 저쪽에
- **see if 주어 동사** ~인지 아닌지 확인하다
- **slow down** 속도를 늦추다
- **sound like 명사** ~처럼 들리다
- **sound 형용사** ~하게 들리다
- **try to 동사원형** 노력하다
- **watch out** 조심하다

## Word Power

※ 명사 + 접미사 -y → 형용사

- □ **dust**(먼지) – **dusty**(먼지가 많은)
- □ **ease**(쉬움) – **easy**(쉬운)
- □ **fun**(재미) – **funny**(재미있는)
- □ **greed**(욕심) – **greedy**(욕심 많은)

- □ **health**(건강) – **healthy**(건강한)
- □ **luck**(행운) – **lucky**(운이 좋은)
- □ **noise**(소음) – **noisy**(시끄러운)
- □ **sleep**(잠) – **sleepy**(졸린)

※ 날씨 관련 명사에 **y**가 붙어 형용사가 되는 경우

- □ **cloud**(구름) – **cloudy**(흐린)
- □ **rain**(비) – **rainy**(비가 오는)
- □ **snow**(눈) – **snowy**(눈이 내리는)

- □ **sun**(태양) – **sunny**(맑은)
- □ **wind**(바람) – **windy**(바람이 부는)
- □ **fog**(안개) – **foggy**(안개가 낀)

※ 음식 관련 명사에 **y**가 붙어 형용사가 되는 경우

- □ **oil**(기름) – **oily**(기름기가 있는)
- □ **salt**(소금) – **salty**(짠)

- □ **taste**(맛) – **tasty**(맛있는)

## English Dictionary

- □ **amusement** 즐거움, 오락
  → the enjoyment that you get from being entertained
  즐겁게 되는 것에서 얻는 기쁨

- □ **beat** 이기다
  → to defeat someone in a game
  경기에서 누군가를 패배시키다

- □ **beatbox** 비트박스를 하다
  → to create the sounds of powerful rhythm with the voice and the hands
  목소리와 손으로 강력한 리듬의 소리를 만들다

- □ **burn** 불타다
  → to be destroyed by fire 불에 의해서 파괴되다

- □ **closet** 옷장
  → a large piece of furniture with a door used for storing clothes 의복을 저장하기 위해 만들어진 문이 있는 큰 가구

- □ **cloudy** 구름의, 흐린
  → when the sky is covered with a lot of clouds
  하늘이 많은 구름으로 덮인

- □ **cross** 건너다
  → to go from one side to the other side of an area
  한 지역의 한쪽에서 다른 쪽으로 가다

- □ **dictionary** 사전
  → a book that contains a list of words and phrases alphabetically with their meanings or their translations in another language
  알파벳순으로 그것의 의미 또는 다른 언어로의 번역이 있는 일련의 단어와 구를 포함하는 책

- □ **lucky** 행운의
  → having desirable things unexpectedly happen to you
  바람직한 상황이 예기치 않게 일어난

- □ **perfect** 완벽한
  → the best possible 가능한 최고의

- □ **possible** 가능한
  → able to happen or be done
  일어나거나 발생할 수 있는

- □ **predict** 예측하다
  → to say that an event will happen in the future
  미래에 어떤 일이 발생할 것이라고 말하다

- □ **replace** 대체하다
  → to take the place of …에 대신하다, …을 대리하다

- □ **select** 선택하다
  → to choose something from a number of things
  많은 것들 중에서 어떤 것을 고르다

- □ **sense** 감지하다
  → to perceive or realize something
  어떤 것을 인지하거나 깨닫다

- □ **situation** 상황
  → what is happening at a particular time and place
  특정한 시간과 장소에서 발생하는 것

- □ **translate** 번역하다
  → to change words in another language
  말들을 다른 언어로 바꾸다

**01** 다음 중 밑줄 친 부분의 뜻풀이가 바르지 <u>않은</u> 것은?

① Some animals have the ability to <u>predict</u> earthquakes. (예측하다)
② I hope my water pipes in the house don't <u>freeze</u>. (얼다)
③ I can <u>teleport</u> through time and space. (전화하다)
④ Please <u>check</u> the password and try again. (확인하다)
⑤ I <u>selected</u> a toy for a child. (선택했다)

**서답형**

**02** 주어진 단어를 이용해 빈칸을 완성하시오.

> Your story is so _____ that I can't stop laughing. (fun)

**[03~04]** 다음 빈칸에 알맞은 것을 고르시오.

**03**
> Do you know anyone who can _____ French into English?

① translate   ② transform   ③ prevent
④ select   ⑤ mean

**04**
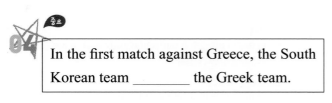
> In the first match against Greece, the South Korean team _____ the Greek team.

① fell   ② hit   ③ beat
④ broke   ⑤ predicted

**05** 다음 밑줄 친 단어의 성격이 <u>다른</u> 하나를 고르시오.

① Doesn't it sound <u>like</u> fun to learn in a forest?
② You look <u>like</u> a totally new person in that suit.
③ Why do you <u>like</u> it so much?
④ Doesn't it seem <u>like</u> a chess game of some sort?
⑤ They are sad for a long time <u>like</u> humans.

**06** 다음 밑줄 친 부분과 의미가 가장 가까운 것은?

> After the test, the people were asked if they saw anything <u>strange</u>.

① natural      ② unusual
③ expected     ④ familiar
⑤ necessary

**서답형**

**07** 다음 주어진 우리말에 맞게 빈칸을 채우시오. (철자가 주어진 것도 있음)

(1) 우리는 Oliver가 이 마을에 더 이상 살지 않기 때문에 그를 자주 볼 수 없다.
   ➡ We cannot see Oliver very often because he _____ _____ lives in this town.
(2) 더 이상 저를 걱정할 필요 없어요. 전 괜찮아요.
   ➡ You _____ h_____ to worry about me. I'm fine.

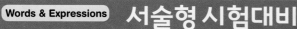
**01** 다음 〈보기〉의 단어를 골라 문맥에 맞게 고쳐 쓰시오.

> ┤ 보기 ├
> cloud   fun   greed   luck   sun

(1) Scrooge was a _____ old man.

(2) I like this book because the story is _____.

(3) It was _____ today, but it will be _____ tomorrow. You will have to bring your umbrella.

(4) I met my favorite movie star by chance. It's my _____ day!

**02** 두 문장이 같은 의미가 되도록 빈칸을 채우시오. (주어진 철자로 시작할 것)

> The new cells take the place of the old cells.
> = The new cells r_____ the old cells.

**03** 다음 빈칸에 공통으로 들어갈 말을 쓰시오.

> • _____ the way, are you still working at the public library?
> • You can learn time management skills _____ doing it.

**04** 다음 우리말에 맞도록 빈칸에 알맞은 말을 쓰시오. (철자가 주어진 경우 주어진 철자로 시작할 것)

(1) 영어를 한국어로 번역할 수 있나요?
➡ Can you _____ English into Korean?

(2) 마감 시간 전에 숙제를 끝내는 것이 가능한가요?
➡ Is it p_____ to _____ your homework before deadline?

(3) 그 밖에 또 필요한 것이 있나요?
➡ Do you need anything e_____?

(4) 그것은 완벽할 필요는 없다.
➡ It doesn't h_____ to be _____.

**05** 다음 빈칸에 들어갈 말을 〈보기〉에서 찾아 쓰시오.

> ┤ 보기 ├
> in   off   to

(1) Get _____ the car right now, or you'll be late.

(2) When I got _____ the top of the mountain, it was very dark.

(3) We will see him soon. Passengers are getting _____ the plane now.

**06** 다음 우리말에 맞게 주어진 단어를 바르게 배열하시오.

(1) 나는 그가 길을 건너는 것을 봤다.
(saw, the, crossing, I, him, street)
➡ _____

(2) 그는 국내 총 생산량이 오를 것이라고 예측했다.
(he, up, go, that, would, the, predicted, GDP)
➡ _____

# Conksation 교과서

## Conversation

### ❶ 의견 표현하기

> **A** I'm going to fly a drone. 난 드론을 날릴 거야.
>
> **B** That sounds like fun. 그거 재미있겠다.

- 의견을 물어 보는 질문에 대한 답으로 동사 'sound(~하게 들리다)'를 사용해 의견을 표현할 수 있다. 'sound+형용사'를 사용하거나, 'sound+like+명사'를 이용하여 말할 수 있다.
  - It sounds interesting. 그거 재미있겠다.
  - It sounds like fun. 그거 재미있겠다.

- 'It'이나 'That'을 생략해서 'Sounds interesting/good/terrible.'로도 말할 수 있다.

- 의견을 나타내는 다른 표현들로는 'I think ~.', 'It seems that ~.', 'In my opinion, ~.' 등이 있다.

- 자신의 의견을 나타낸 뒤, 자신의 생각을 뒷받침하는 이유나 근거를 함께 언급하기도 한다. 또는 'How about you?(너는 어때?)'를 사용해 상대방의 의견을 다시 물어볼 수도 있다.

#### 의견 표현하기

- (That) Sounds (very) interesting.
- How interesting!
- I think (that) it's interesting.
- In my opinion, it's interesting.

### 핵심 Check

**1.** 다음 우리말과 일치하도록 빈칸에 알맞은 말을 쓰시오.

A: I will go swimming with my friends. (내 친구들과 수영하러 갈 거야.)

B: _____ like fun. (재미있겠다.)

**2.** 다음 우리말과 일치하도록 주어진 단어를 바르게 배열하시오.

A: Why don't we make a movie together? (함께 영화를 만드는 것은 어때?)

B: _____ _____ _____. (good, that, sounds) How about you? (좋아. 너는 어때?)

C: _____ _____ _____ _____. (exciting, it's, I, think)
(나는 그것이 재미있다고 생각해.)

**2** **가능 여부 표현하기**

> **A** Is it possible for you to text with your eyes closed?
> 눈 감고 문자 메시지 보내는 것이 가능하니?
>
> **B** Sure. I can do that. 물론이지. 할 수 있어.

■ 'Is it possible for 목적격 to 동사원형 ~?'은 상대방에게 어떤 것을 하는 것이 가능한지 물어볼 때 쓰는 표현이다. 여기서 it은 가주어이며 to 동사원형이 to부정사로 진주어이며 for 목적격은 to부정사의 의미상 주어이다. to부정사 대신에 that절을 사용해서 말할 수도 있다.

- • Is it possible for you to text with your eyes closed?
  = Is it possible that you text with your eyes closed?

■ possible 대신에 likely(~할 것 같은)나 probable((현실로) 있음직한, 가망이 있는)을 사용할 수도 있다.

■ 조동사 'can(~할 수 있다)'을 사용해서 'Can+주어+동사원형 ~?(~을 할 수 있니?)'으로 질문할 수 있다.

**가능 여부 표현하기**

- • Is it possible[probable/likely] that 주어 동사 ~?
- • Is it possible[probable/likely] for 목적격 to 동사원형 ~?
- • Can 주어 동사원형 ~?

**핵심 Check**

**3.** 다음 우리말과 일치하도록 빈칸에 알맞은 말을 쓰시오.

A: _____ _____ _____ _____ I can carry that box?
(제가 저 상자를 운반할 수 있을까요?)

B: I think it's possible with some help. I'll help you.
(전 약간의 도움으로 가능하다고 생각해요. 제가 도와드릴게요.)

A: Thanks. (고마워요.)

**4.** 다음 대화에서 밑줄 친 부분과 같은 의미가 되도록 주어진 단어를 이용해 문장을 만드시오.

A: Is it possible that he can finish this marathon?
B: Yes, it's possible.

➡ _____ (possible, to)
➡ _____ (can)

**5.** 다음 우리말과 일치하도록 주어진 어구를 빈칸에 알맞게 배열하시오.

A: _____ (a cake, it, you, to, is, possible, for, make)
(케이크를 만들 수 있니?)

B: Yes, it is. (응. 할 수 있어.)

🔖 **Listen & Speak 1 B-1**

B: Do you have any ideas for our group project?

G: No. What about you?

B: ❶I'm thinking we should talk about future jobs. ❷What do you think?

G: ❸That sounds perfect for our project. ❹Let's look for some information on the Internet.

| |
|---|
| B: 우리 조별 프로젝트에 대한 좋은 생각이 있니? |
| G: 아니. 너는 어때? |
| B: 나는 미래 직업에 대해 이야기 하면 좋겠다고 생각하고 있어. 너는 어떻게 생각해? |
| G: 우리 프로젝트에 완벽한 것 같아. 인터넷에서 정보를 찾아 보자. |

❶ 'we should talk about future jobs'는 think의 목적어이며 앞에 접속사 that이 생략되어 있다. talk about: ~에 대해서 이야기하다

❷ 'What do you think?'는 자신의 의견을 말한 뒤, 상대방의 의견을 물어볼 때 쓰며 '너는 어떻게 생각하니?'의 의미이다. 바꿔서 쓸 수 있는 표현으로 'How about you?', 'What about you?' 등이 있다.

❸ sound 형용사: ~하게 들리다 perfect: 완벽한

❹ 'Let's 동사원형'은 '~하자'라는 의미로 어떤 것을 제안하고자 할 때 사용한다. 'Why don't we ~?'로 바꿔 쓸 수 있다.

**Check(√) True or False**

(1) They are going to look for some information for their group project in the book.　　T ☐ F ☐

(2) They will look for some information about future jobs.　　T ☐ F ☐

🔖 **Listen & Speak 2 B-1**

G: This computer ❶looks nice. ❷How much is it?

M: ❸It's 500 dollars. It's ❹the newest one.

G: ❺Is it possible to use this coupon?

M: Let me ❻check. Yes, you can. So, you'll get 30 dollars ❼off.

G: Perfect. I'll ❽take it.

| |
|---|
| G: 이 컴퓨터가 좋아 보이네요. 얼마예요? |
| M: 500달러예요. 가장 최신 컴퓨터예요. |
| G: 이 쿠폰을 사용하는 것이 가능한가요? |
| M: 확인해 볼게요. 네, 사용할 수 있어요. 그러면, 30달러 할인 돼요. |
| G: 좋아요. 이걸로 살게요. |

❶ look 형용사: ~하게 보이다

❷ 가격을 묻고자 할 때 'How much ~?(~은 얼마인가요?)' 표현을 사용한다.

❸ 'How much ~?'의 질문에 'It's+가격.'으로 대답한다.

❹ the newest는 형용사 new의 최상급으로 '가장 최신의'의 의미이다. one = computer

❺ 'Is it possible to+동사원형 ~?'은 '~하는 것이 가능한가요?'라는 의미로 가능 여부를 물을 때 사용하는 표현이다. 이때 it은 가주어이고 to부정사구가 진주어이다.

❻ check: 확인하다, 점검하다

❼ off: 할인되어

❽ take: 선택하다, 사다

**Check(√) True or False**

(3) The girl has a coupon which cannot be used.　　T ☐ F ☐

(4) The girl will buy the newest computer.　　T ☐ F ☐

### Listen & Speak 1 A

B: ❶Why don't we try a new VR game?

G: ❷That sounds interesting.

❶ '～을 하자'라는 제안을 하고자 할 때 'Why don't we ～?' 외에도 'Let's ～'의 표현을 쓸 수 있다.

❷ 'That sounds interesting.' 상대방이 한 말에 대하여 '재미있겠다'라는 표현으로 'How interesting!'이나 'Sounds interesting!'으로 바꾸어 사용할 수 있다.

### Listen & Speak 1 B-2

G: The Robot Expo begins next week. ❶Why don't you go with me?

B: ❷Yes, I'd love to. ❸That sounds exciting.

G: We'll have ❹a chance to meet robotics engineers.

B: ❺That'll be great.

❶ Why don't you ～?: ～하는 게 어때? (= What about ～? = How about ～?) go with: 같이 가다, 어울리다

❷ 상대방의 제안에 응할 때는 'Yes, I'd love to.', 그렇지 않을 때는 'Sorry, but I can't.'로 대답할 수 있다.

❸ sound 형용사: ～하게 들리다 exciting: 흥미진진한

❹ to meet이 a chance(기회)를 수식하는 형용사적 용법으로 사용되고 있다. robotics: 로봇 공학 engineer: 기술자

❺ That'll be great.: 그러면 아주 좋겠다.

### Listen & Speak 2 A

G: ❶Is it possible for you to live without your smartphone?

B: No, it's ❷not possible.

❶ Is it possible (for 목적격) to 동사원형 ～?: (…가) ～하는 것이 가능할까? without: ～ 없이

❷ 'not possible'을 'impossible(불가능한)'로 바꿔 쓸 수 있다.

### Listen & Speak 2 B-2

B: ❶We took lots of pictures during our trip.

G: We sure ❷did. We have more than 500 pictures.

B: ❸Is it possible to make an animated photo album out of them?

G: Yes, it's ❹possible. I have an app for that.

❶ take a picture: 사진을 찍다 lots of: 많은 during: ～ 동안

❷ did는 'took lots of pictures'를 의미한다.

❸ Is it possible (for 목적격) to 동사원형 ～?: (…가) ～하는 것이 가능할까? 'it'은 가주어, 'to make an animated photo album out of them'은 진주어이다. out of: (원천 · 출처) ～에서, ～으로부터

❹ possible: 가능한

### Listen & Speak 2 C-1

A: ❶Is it possible for you to text ❷with your eyes closed?

B: Sure. I can ❸do that.

❶ Is it possible (for 목적격) to 동사원형 ～?: (…가) ～하는 것이 가능할까? text: (휴대전화로) 문자를 보내다

❷ with+명사구(your eyes)+과거분사(closed): 너의 눈을 감은 채로 / 명사구가 과거분사된 채로(부대상황)

❸ do = text with my eyes closed

### Real-Life Zone

G: Look at those words on the board.

B: ❶What do they mean? Let's ❷look them up in the dictionary.

G: ❸What about using the AI translator?

B: How do I use ❹it?

G: ❺You point your smartphone camera at the words and ask AI to translate. You will get an answer.

B: ❻Is it possible for AI to read those words?

Speaker: Sure. I can read any language and translate it.

B: ❼Wow, that sounds unbelievable. So, AI, what do those words mean?

Speaker: ❽They mean "Dreams come true!"

B: ❾That's amazing.

❶ 'What do they mean?'은 '그 말들은 무슨 뜻이지?'란 의미로 의미를 묻는 말이다.

❷ look ～ up: (사전 · 참고 자료 · 컴퓨터 등에서 정보를) 찾아보다

❸ What about 동명사 ～?: ～하는 게 어때? translator: 번역가

❹ it은 앞에 나온 'the AI translator'를 가리킨다.

❺ point: 돌리다, 향하게 하다 point와 ask는 접속사 and로 연결된 병렬 관계이다. translate: 번역하다

❻ Is it possible (for 목적격) to 동사원형 ～?: (…가) ～하는 것이 가능할까?

❼ sound 형용사: ～하게 들리다 unbelievable: 믿기 어려운, 놀랄만한

❽ 'What does[do] it[they] mean?'으로 의미를 물었을 때 'mean(의미하다)'을 이용해 'It/They mean(s) ～.(～라는 뜻이에요.)'로 대답할 수 있다.

❾ 놀람을 표현할 때는 'That's surprising.', 'That's amazing.', 'I can't believe it.' 등으로 말할 수 있다.

● 다음 우리말과 일치하도록 빈칸에 알맞은 말을 쓰시오.

**Listen & Speak 1 A**

B: Why _____ we try a new VR game?

G: That _____ interesting.

B: 우리 새로운 VR 게임을 해 보는 게 어때?

G: 그거 재미있겠다.

**Listen & Speak 1 B**

1. B: Do you _____ _____ ideas _____ our group _____?

   G: No. _____ _____ you?

   B: I'm thinking we should _____ _____ _____ jobs. _____ do you _____?

   G: That _____ _____ for our project. Let's _____ _____ some information on the Internet.

2. G: The Robot Expo _____ next week. _____ don't you go _____ me?

   B: Yes, I'd love _____. That _____ exciting.

   G: We'll have a _____ _____ _____ _____ engineers.

   B: That'll be _____.

1. B: 우리 조별 프로젝트에 대한 좋은 생각이 있니?

   G: 아니. 너는 어때?

   B: 나는 미래 직업에 대해 이야기하면 좋겠다고 생각하고 있어. 너는 어떻게 생각해?

   G: 우리 프로젝트에 완벽한 것 같아. 인터넷에서 정보를 찾아보자.

2. G: 로봇 박람회가 다음 주에 시작돼. 나와 함께 가는 게 어때?

   B: 응, 가고 싶어. 그거 재미있겠는데.

   G: 우리는 로봇 공학자를 만날 기회가 있을 거야.

   B: 그거 아주 좋겠다.

**Listen & Speak 1 C**

1. A: I'm _____ to fly a _____.

   B: That sounds _____ _____.

2. A: I'm _____ to _____ a model car.

   B: That sounds _____ _____.

1. A: 난 드론을 날릴 거야.

   B: 그거 재미있겠다.

2. A: 난 모형 자동차를 조립할 거야.

   B: 그거 재미있겠다.

**Listen & Speak 2 A**

G: It is _____ for you _____ _____ your smartphone?

B: No, it's not _____.

G: 네가 스마트폰 없이 사는 것이 가능할까?

B: 아니, 그건 불가능해.

### Listen & Speak 2 B

1. **G:** This computer _____ nice. _____ _____ is it?

   **M:** It's 500 dollars. It's the _____ one.

   **G:** _____ _____ _____ _____ _____ this coupon?

   **M:** Let me _____. Yes, you can. So, you'll get 30 dollars _____.

   **G:** _____. I'll take it.

2. **B:** We _____ lots of _____ _____ our trip.

   **G:** We sure _____. We have more _____ 500 pictures.

   **B:** Is _____ _____ _____ _____ an animated photo album _____ _____ them?

   **G:** Yes, it's possible. I _____ an app for that.

### Listen & Speak 2 C

1. **A:** _____ _____ _____ for you _____ _____ _____ your eyes _____?

   **B:** Sure. I can do that.

2. **A:** Is it _____ _____ _____ to travel around Gangwondo _____ bicycle?

   **B:** Sure. I can do that.

### Real-Life Zone A

**G:** Look _____ those words on the board.

**B:** _____ do _____ _____? Let's _____ _____ _____ in the _____.

**G:** What _____ _____ the AI translator?

**B:** _____ do I use it?

**G:** You _____ your smartphone camera at the words and ask AI to _____. You will _____ an answer.

**B:** Is it _____ _____ _____ _____ _____ those words?

**Speaker:** Sure. I can _____ any language and _____ it.

**B:** Wow, that sounds _____. So, AI, what do those words _____?

**Speaker:** They mean "Dreams come true!"

**B:** That's _____.

해석

1. G: 이 컴퓨터가 좋아 보이네요. 얼마예요?
   M: 500달러예요. 가장 최신 컴퓨터예요.
   G: 이 쿠폰을 사용하는 것이 가능한가요?
   M: 확인해 볼게요. 네, 사용할 수 있어요. 그러면, 30달러 할인돼요.
   G: 좋아요. 이걸로 살게요.

2. B: 우리는 여행 동안 사진을 많이 찍었어.
   G: 진짜 그랬어. 500장 넘게 있어.
   B: 그 사진들로 동영상 앨범을 만드는 것이 가능하니?
   G: 응, 가능해. 나는 그것을 위한 앱이 있어.

1. A: 눈 감고 문자 메시지 보내는 것이 가능하니?
   B: 물론이지. 할 수 있어.

2. A: 자전거로 강원도를 여행하는 것이 가능하니?
   B: 물론이지. 할 수 있어.

G: 저기 칠판에 있는 글자 좀 봐.
B: 무슨 뜻이지? 사전에서 찾아보자.
G: AI 번역기를 사용하는 게 어때?
B: 어떻게 사용하는 거니?
G: 스마트폰 카메라를 글자 위에 댄 후에 AI에게 번역해 달라고 해 봐. 아마 답을 해 줄 거야.
B: AI가 저런 글자를 읽는 것이 가능해?
Speaker: 물론이에요. 저는 어떤 언어도 읽을 수 있고 번역할 수 있어요.
B: 오, 정말 놀라워. 그럼 AI, 이 글자는 뜻이 뭐니?
Speaker: "꿈은 이루어진다."라는 뜻이에요.
B: 정말 대단하구나.

**Conversation** 시험대비 기본평가

**01** 다음 대화의 밑줄 친 부분과 바꿔 쓸 수 있는 것을 고르시오.

> A: <u>Is it possible for you to read 50 novels during summer vacation?</u>
> B: Sure. I can do that.

① Should you read 50 novels during summer vacation?
② Are you going to read 50 novels during summer vacation?
③ Is it possible that you read 50 novels during summer vacation?
④ Is it unlikely for you to read 50 novels during summer vacation?
⑤ Are you thinking of reading 50 novels during summer vacation?

**02** 다음 대화의 빈칸에 알맞은 것을 고르시오.

> B: Do you have any ideas for our group project?
> G: No. What about you?
> B: I'm thinking we should talk about future jobs. What do you think?
> G: _____ Let's look for some information on the Internet.

① That sounds perfect for our project.
② I have a different idea about our project.
③ I think it's too small for us.
④ In my opinion, that's not true.
⑤ I agree with you. That sounds bad.

**03** 주어진 문장 뒤에 올 대화의 순서가 바르게 배열된 것을 고르시오.

> The Robot Expo begins next week. Why don't you go with me?

> (A) We'll have a chance to meet robotics engineers.
> (B) Yes, I'd love to. That sounds exciting.
> (C) That'll be great.

① (A) – (C) – (B)        ② (B) – (A) – (C)
③ (B) – (C) – (A)        ④ (C) – (A) – (B)
⑤ (C) – (B) – (A)

**[01~02]** 다음 대화를 읽고 물음에 답하시오.

> G: The Robot Expo begins next week. Why don't you go with me?
> B: Yes, I'd love to. _____(A)_____
> G: We'll have a chance to meet robotics engineers.
> B: That'll be great.

**01** 위 대화의 빈칸 (A)에 알맞은 말을 고르시오.

① I think it's very boring.
② That sounds exciting.
③ In my opinion, it will be crowded.
④ It doesn't sound like fun.
⑤ I'm not interested in robots.

**02** 위 대화를 읽고 답할 수 <u>없는</u> 질문은?

① What does the boy think about the Robot Expo?
② Who can they meet at the Robot Expo?
③ Where does the girl want to go with the boy?
④ Where will they meet to go to the Robot Expo?
⑤ When does the Robot Expo begin?

**[03~04]** 다음 대화를 읽고 물음에 답하시오.

> G: Look at those words on the board.
> B: What do they mean? Let's look them up in the dictionary. (①)
> G: What about using the AI translator?
> B: How do I use it? (②)
> G: You point your smartphone camera at words and ask AI to translate. (③) You will get an answer. (④)
> B: Is it possible for AI to read those words?
> Speaker: Sure. I can read any language and translate it.
> B: Wow, that sounds unbelievable. So, AI! (⑤)
> Speaker: They mean "Dreams come true!"
> B: That's amazing.

**03** 위 대화의 ①~⑤ 중 주어진 문장이 들어갈 곳은?

> What do those words mean?

①　　②　　③　　④　　⑤

**04** 위 대화의 내용과 일치하지 <u>않는</u> 것을 고르시오.

① AI 번역기는 모든 언어를 읽을 수 있고 번역할 수 있다.
② 여자아이는 AI 번역기를 사용하는 방법을 알고 있다.
③ 칠판에 있는 글자는 "꿈은 이루어진다."라는 뜻을 가지고 있다.
④ 여자아이와 남자아이는 칠판 위의 모르는 글자를 사전에서 찾아봤다.
⑤ AI 번역기를 사용하기 위해서 먼저 스마트폰 카메라를 글자 위에 대야 한다.

**[05~07]** 다음 대화를 읽고 물음에 답하시오.

> G: Minseok, there is a smart food-ordering machine over there. (①) Why don't we try it?
> B: _____(A)_____ We'll be able to order easily and fast by using it.
> G: I hope so. (②) By the way, do you think maybe it will be possible for robots to replace humans someday?
> B: I'm not sure. (③) But we will be free from danger because of robots.
> G: What do you mean?
> B: (④) Robots can do the dangerous work so humans don't have to.
> G: You're right. We should always try to look on the bright side. (⑤)

**05** 위 대화의 ①~⑤ 중 주어진 문장이 들어갈 곳은?

> Robots can help people in danger.

①     ②     ③     ④     ⑤

**06** 위 대화의 빈칸 (A)에 알맞은 말을 고르시오.

① I think that it is delicious.
② In my opinion, robots are necessary in our lives.
③ I don't want to try it.
④ We don't have to use it.
⑤ That sounds interesting.

**07** 위 대화의 내용과 일치하지 <u>않는</u> 것을 고르시오.

① 민석이는 로봇 덕분에 사람들이 위험한 일을 하지 않을 것이라고 생각한다.
② 민석이는 로봇이 인간을 대체할 수 있을 거라고 생각한다.
③ 민석이는 스마트 음식 주문 자판기가 주문을 쉽고 빠르게 해 줄 것이라고 생각한다.
④ 여자아이는 항상 좋은 면을 봐야 한다고 말하고 있다.
⑤ 그들은 스마트 음식 주문 자판기를 사용할 것이다.

**[08~09]** 다음 중 짝지어진 대화가 <u>어색한</u> 것은?

**08** ① A: I go to the farm with my family on weekends.
     B: That sounds interesting.
② A: Is it possible that I finish my homework by tomorrow?
     B: Sure. You can.
③ A: Is it possible that I keep a pet?
     B: Yes, I can.
④ A: Do you know that ice cream is from China?
     B: No. That sounds interesting.
⑤ A: Is it possible that you go abroad alone?
     B: Of course. I can.

**09** ① A: Is it possible to drink juice in space?
     B: Sure, it's possible.
② A: What do you think about this place?
     B: I like it. I think it's very comfortable.
③ A: Why don't we join the Mozart Club?
     B: That sounds like fun. I love music.
④ A: Why don't we watch a movie tonight?
     B: I don't think so. It sounds like fun.
⑤ A: Is it possible that a dog solves a math problem?
     B: No. That sounds impossible.

**01** 다음 대화의 밑줄 친 문장과 의미가 같도록 빈칸에 알맞은 말을 쓰시오.

> G: Is it possible for you to live without your smartphone?
> B: No, it's not possible.

> _____ _____ live without your smartphone?

[02~03] 다음 대화를 읽고 물음에 답하시오.

> G: This computer looks nice. How much is it?
> M: It's 500 dollars. It's the newest one.
> G: 이 쿠폰을 사용하는 것이 가능한가요?
> M: Let me check. Yes, you can. So, you'll get 30 dollars off.
> G: Perfect. I'll take it.

**02** 다음 밑줄 친 우리말을 주어진 단어를 이용해 영작하시오.

> (possible, use)

➡ _____

**03** 다음 질문에 주어진 단어를 이용해 완전한 문장으로 대답하시오.

> How much will the girl pay for the computer?

➡ _____ (will)

[04~05] 다음 대화를 읽고 물음에 답하시오.

> G: Look at those words on the board.
> B: What do they mean? Let's look them __(A)__ in the dictionary.
> G: What __(B)__ using the AI translator?
> B: How do I use it?
> G: You point your smartphone camera at the words and ask AI to translate. You will get an answer.
> B: Is it possible for AI to read those words?
> Speaker: Sure. I can read any language and translate it.
> B: Wow, that sounds (C)believe. So, AI, what do those words mean?
> Speaker: They mean "Dreams come true!"

**04** 위 대화의 빈칸 (A)와 (B)에 알맞은 것을 쓰시오.

(A) _____ (B) _____

**05** 위 대화의 밑줄 친 believe를 알맞은 형으로 고치시오.

➡ _____

**06** 다음 괄호 안에 주어진 단어를 알맞게 배열하시오.

> G: _____
> (Gangwondo, travel, is, bicycle, for, to, possible, you, it, by, around)
> B: Sure. I can do that.

➡ _____
_____

## 교과서 Grammar

**1** 지각동사

> • I **see** a cat **crossing** the street. 고양이가 길을 건너고 있는 게 보여.
> • I **heard** him **sing**. 나는 그가 노래하는 소리를 들었다.

■ 지각동사는 감각 기관을 통하여 인지하는 것을 나타내는 동사로, '보다, 듣다, 느끼다' 등의 의미를 갖는 see, look at, watch, hear, listen to, feel 등의 동사를 말한다. 'see/hear/feel+목적어+원형부정사/현재분사'의 형태로 '목적어가 ~하는 것을[~하는 중인 것을] 보다/듣다/느끼다'라는 의미를 갖는다. 목적격보어 자리에 원형부정사와 현재분사를 모두 사용할 수 있으나 의미상 그 동작이 진행 중인 것을 나타낼 때에는 주로 현재분사를 사용한다.

  • They **saw** him **read** a book. 그들은 그가 책을 읽는 것을 보았다.

  • Did you **hear** the baby **crying**? 너는 그 아기가 울고 있는 소리를 들었니?

  ■ '지각동사+목적어+원형부정사[현재분사]'로 쓰이는 경우, 목적어와 목적격보어는 능동 관계가 된다. '지각동사+목적어+과거분사'로 쓰이는 경우 목적어와 목적격보어의 관계는 수동 관계이다.

  • She **felt** him **touch** her hand. 그녀는 그가 손을 만지는 것을 느꼈다.

  • I **heard** my name **called**. 나는 내 이름이 불리는 소리를 들었다.

■ 사역동사 make, have, let과 혼동하지 않도록 한다. 사역동사도 5형식 동사로 목적어와 목적격보어를 취하지만, 사역동사의 목적격보어로는 동사원형이 나온다. have나 make는 목적격보어로 과거분사를 취할 때도 있다.

  • The teacher **made** me **do** my homework. 선생님은 나에게 숙제를 하도록 시키셨다.

  • I **had** my computer **fixed** yesterday. 나는 어제 내 컴퓨터가 수리되도록 했다.

### 핵심 Check

**1.** 다음 괄호 안에서 알맞은 말을 고르시오.

　(1) She saw him (to do / doing) his homework.

　➡ ＿＿＿＿＿＿＿

　(2) I heard my sister (sing / sang) in her room.

　➡ ＿＿＿＿＿＿＿

　(3) He had his car (washing / washed).

　➡ ＿＿＿＿＿＿＿

## ② 가주어 'it'

- **It** is hard **to believe** that you can understand us.
  네가 우리를 이해할 수 있다는 것을 믿기 힘들어.

- **It** is interesting **to play** soccer. 축구하는 것은 재미있다.

■ 비교적 긴 to부정사 부분이 문장의 주어로 쓰일 때 그 to부정사 부분을 보통의 주어 자리인 문장의 맨 앞에 두지 않고 문장 뒤에 두고, 대신 그 주어 자리에 it을 넣어주는데 그것이 가주어 it이며 뒤로 간 to부정사 부분은 진주어라고 한다. 이때 쓰인 가주어 'it'은 해석하지 않는다.

- **It** is not easy **to study** hard every day. 매일 열심히 공부하는 것은 쉽지 않다.
  = **To study** hard every day is not easy.

- **It** is a lot fun **to draw** cartoons. 만화를 그리는 것은 아주 재미있다.
  = **To draw** cartoons is a lot fun.

■ to부정사의 의미상 주어

'to부정사'가 행하는 동작의 주체를 to부정사의 의미상 주어라고 한다. to부정사의 의미상 주어를 나타낼 때는 to부정사 바로 앞에 'for+목적격'의 형태로 쓴다. 문장에 쓰인 형용사가 kind, foolish, rude, careless, wise 등과 같이 사람의 성질을 나타내는 말일 때는 'of+목적격'을 쓴다. 또한 to부정사의 부정은 to부정사 앞에 not[never]을 써서 'not[never]+to V'로 나타낸다.

- **It** is necessary **for you to be** careful all the time. 너는 항상 조심할 필요가 있다.
- **It** is kind **of you to show** me the way. 길을 가르쳐 주셔서 감사합니다.
- **It** was difficult **for him not to smoke**. 그가 담배를 피우지 않는 것은 힘들었다.

■ 주어로 쓰인 'that'절의 경우에도 보통 가주어 'it'을 쓰고 'that'절을 문장 뒤로 보낸다.

- **That** he should attend the meeting every day is important. 그가 매일 회의에 참석하는 것이 중요하다.
  = **It** is important **that** he should attend the meeting every day.

### 핵심 Check

2. 다음 괄호 안에서 알맞은 말을 고르시오.

(1) It is fun (play / to play) basketball.

  ➡ _____

(2) It was hard for him (solve / to solve) the problem.

  ➡ _____

(3) (It / That) is necessary for you to exercise.

  ➡ _____

**01** 다음 문장에서 어법상 <u>어색한</u> 부분을 바르게 고쳐 쓰시오.

(1) The girl heard the birds sang.

_____ ➡ _____

(2) He saw a drone to fly.

_____ ➡ _____

(3) It is important choose good friends.

_____ ➡ _____

(4) That is necessary to learn a new language.

_____ ➡ _____

**02** 주어진 단어를 어법에 맞게 빈칸에 쓰시오.

(1) I heard her _____ in the room. (cry)
(2) They saw the room _____. (clean)
(3) People came to watch them _____ the game. (play)
(4) Helen felt the water _____ with her hands. (flow)

**03** 다음 우리말을 영어로 바르게 옮긴 것은?

> 그 여행 가방들을 들고 다니는 것은 불가능하다.

① That is impossible to carry the suitcases.
② That is impossible carrying the suitcases.
③ It is impossible carry the suitcases.
④ It is impossible to carry the suitcases.
⑤ It is impossible carries the suitcases.

**04** 주어진 어구를 바르게 배열하여 다음 우리말을 영어로 쓰시오. 필요하다면 단어를 추가하거나 변형하시오.

> 당신은 쉬는 것이 필요하다.
> (a rest, you, it, take, is, necessary, to)

➡ _____

**중요**

**01** 다음 빈칸에 알맞은 말이 순서대로 바르게 짝지어진 것은?

- I saw a cat _____ the street.
- It is a lot of fun _____ cartoons.

① cross – drawing
② crossed – draw
③ crossed – to draw
④ crossing – draw
⑤ crossing – to draw

**02** 다음 빈칸에 들어갈 말로 가장 적절한 것은?

David felt the dog _____ his clothes.

① pulls      ② pulled
③ pulling      ④ to pull
⑤ to pulling

**03** 다음 빈칸에 알맞은 말로 바르게 짝지어진 것을 고르시오.

_____ is very exciting _____ the soccer game in the stadium.

① It – to watch
② It – watch
③ That – watching
④ That – watch
⑤ That – to watch

**서답형**

**04** 주어진 단어를 이용하여 다음 우리말을 영어로 쓰시오. (10단어)

주말에 재미로 자전거를 타는 것은 좋다. (it, for fun, good, ride bicycles)

➡ _____

**중요**

**05** 다음 중 어법상 바르지 <u>않은</u> 것은?

① I saw a boy helping an old lady cross the road.
② They listened to Michelle singing on the stage.
③ Jekyll heard someone coming up the stairs.
④ At times, Nora felt him to stare at her.
⑤ She watched her father come toward her.

**서답형**

**06** 다음 괄호 안에서 알맞은 말을 고르시오.

(1) Did you see many people (to wait / waiting) in a line?
(2) I heard Jack (played / playing) the guitar.
(3) I watched the game (played / playing) from beginning to end.
(4) Why are you making him (listening / listen) to Wayne?
(5) (That / It) is not easy to speak in front of many people.
(6) It is dangerous (swims / to swim) in the sea.
(7) It's so kind (for / of) you to show me the way to the station.

**07** 다음 중 어법상 바르지 **않은** 것은?

> Max ①sat ②in front of the oven and ③ watched her ④to bake ⑤the cookies.

①　　　　②　　　　③　　　　④　　　　⑤

**08** 다음 문장에서 어법상 **틀린** 부분을 찾아 바르게 고쳐 쓰시오.

> This isn't true that Ella likes to speak in front of people.

_____ ➡ _____

[09~10] 다음 우리말을 영어로 바르게 옮긴 것을 **모두** 고르시오.

**09**
> 나는 누군가 내 어깨를 만지는 것을 느꼈다.

① I felt someone touches my shoulder.
② I felt someone touched my shoulder.
③ I felt someone touch my shoulder.
④ I felt someone touching my shoulder.
⑤ I felt someone to touch my shoulder.

**10**
> 여름에 선글라스를 쓰는 것은 도움이 된다.

① It is helpful wears sunglasses in summer.
② It is helpful wore sunglasses in summer.
③ It is helpful wear sunglasses in summer.
④ It is helpful to wear sunglasses in summer.
⑤ It is helpful to wearing sunglasses in summer.

서답형
**11** 다음 대화의 빈칸에 알맞은 말을 4단어로 쓰시오.

> **A:** It is cold here. Who turned off the stove?
> **B:** Bill did. I saw _____.

➡ _____

**12** 다음 중 어법상 올바른 문장을 **모두** 고르시오.

① Jane heard the dog barking at a stranger.
② I saw a boy to solve math problems.
③ By the way, do you think it will be possible of robots to replace humans someday?
④ Is it possible to flying through a rainbow?
⑤ It is not dangerous to do bungee jumping.

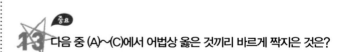
**13** 다음 중 (A)~(C)에서 어법상 옳은 것끼리 바르게 짝지은 것은?

> • I heard the boy (A)(shouting / to shout).
> • We can see the sky (B)(turn / turned) yellow with dust.
> • He was almost asleep when he heard his name (C)(calling / called).

① to shout – turn – calling
② to shout – turned – called
③ shouting – turn – called
④ shouting – turn – calling
⑤ shouting – turned – calling

**14** 다음 중 밑줄 친 부분의 쓰임이 <u>다른</u> 하나는?

① Is <u>it</u> possible for AI to read those words?

② Look! <u>It</u> is going up that tree.

③ <u>It</u> is hard to believe that you can understand us.

④ <u>It</u> is difficult to remember all my friends' birthdays.

⑤ Of course <u>it</u> was not easy to break my old habit.

**15** 다음 주어진 문장의 밑줄 친 부분과 쓰임이 같은 것은?

> Jekyll's friend saw Jekyll <u>drinking</u> strange water.

① <u>Watching</u> the movie, we had some popcorn.

② The smell was from the soup that she was <u>cooking</u> for us.

③ We all heard a baby <u>crying</u> loudly.

④ <u>Driving</u> a smart car was not so difficult.

⑤ When I was standing in front of the screen on the smart closet door, my clothes kept <u>changing</u>.

서답형

**16** 다음 문장을 it을 이용하여 바꿔 쓰시오.

(1) To make her laugh is not easy.

➡ _____

(2) To read 10 books during winter vacation is my plan.

➡ _____

_____

서답형

**17** 다음 문장에서 어법상 <u>어색한</u> 부분을 바르게 고치시오.

(1) Stephanie watched her husband to paint the wall.

_____ ➡ _____

(2) It is safer wears a helmet when riding a bike.

_____ ➡ _____.

(3) Is it possible of you to live without your smartphone?

_____ ➡ _____.

서답형

**18** 다음 괄호 안에 주어진 단어를 이용하여 우리말을 영어로 옮기시오.

(1) 민수는 그 집을 지나갈 때마다 개가 짖는 소리를 듣는다. ( Minsu로 시작할 것)
(a dog, bark, hear, pass by, whenever)

➡ _____

_____

(2) 나는 새가 하늘 높이 나는 것을 봤다.
(see, a bird, fly, high)

➡ _____

(3) 내가 친구들과 함께 야구 경기를 관람하는 것은 재미있다.
(my friends, exciting, watch, baseball games, it) (12 단어)

➡ _____

_____

(4) 종이를 불 근처에 두는 것은 위험하다.
(dangerous, near the fire, put, it) (9 단어)

➡ _____

**01** 다음 문장에서 어법상 어색한 부분을 찾아 바르게 고쳐 다시 쓰시오.

(1) I saw them to play soccer in the playground.

➡ _____

(2) Barbara felt her heart beaten faster.

➡ _____

(3) Aaron looked at Sylvia came with Alex hand in hand.

➡ _____

_____

(4) A farmer bought 43 sheep at the market and saw them steal 24 hours later.

➡ _____

_____

(5) It is hard take care of a baby.

➡ _____

(6) That is a lot of fun to go on a picnic.

➡ _____

(7) It is difficult of me to learn a new language.

➡ _____

**02** 〈보기〉와 같이 다음 두 문장을 하나의 문장으로 쓰시오.

┤ 보기 ├
• I saw a boy. • He was reading a book.
➡ I saw a boy reading a book.

• I heard Sam.
• Sam was baking some cookies.

➡ _____

**03** 다음 문장을 It으로 시작하여 다시 쓰시오.

(1) To answer the math questions was very difficult.

➡ _____

(2) To swim in the blue sea was a great experience.

➡ _____

(3) To exercise regularly is good for your health.

➡ _____

(4) To learn English is not easy for me.

➡ _____

(5) That a friend in need is a friend indeed is true.

➡ _____

**04** 〈보기〉에서 의미상 적절한 단어를 골라 빈칸에 알맞은 형태로 쓰시오.

┤ 보기 ├
pull / stay / take / sing

(1) The doctor told me _____ _____ in bed for one more day.

(2) He saw the building _____ down by the workers.

(3) Can you hear my sister _____ upstairs?

(4) She made him _____ off his shirt.

**05** 다음 빈칸에 적절한 말을 쓰시오.

Is it possible for you _____ _____ _____ _____ during summer vacation? (50 novels)

**07** 다음 빈칸에 적절한 말을 쓰시오.

I saw Jane _____ a website.

**08** 다음 두 문장을 〈보기〉와 같이 한 문장으로 고쳐 쓰시오.

┤ 보기 ├
I saw him. + He was running with his dog.
= I saw him running with his dog.

(1) He heard them.
   + They were playing the drums.
   ➡ _____

(2) Suhan looked at AI Speaker.
   + AI Speaker was playing a movie.
   ➡ _____

**06** 두 문장이 같은 뜻이 되도록 (1)~(3)은 to부정사를 이용하여, (4)는 that절을 이용하여 빈칸을 완성하시오.

(1) I have difficulty in passing the driver's test.
   ➡ It is difficult _____.

(2) Watching the view as we went higher and higher was so exciting.
   ➡ It was so exciting _____ _____.

(3) You are kind to help that old woman.
   ➡ It is kind _____.

(4) In fact, Annabelle didn't tell him a lie.
   ➡ It is true _____.

**09** to부정사를 진주어로 하여 주어진 문장과 같은 의미가 되도록 쓰시오.

(1) She is very smart to solve that problem.
   ➡ _____

(2) This river is not safe to swim in as it is very deep.
   ➡ _____
   _____

## A Day at the AI Expo

Jina and Suhan are at the World AI Expo. They are entering the AI home.
현재진행형(be+~ing): ~하고 있다

Suhan: Look at this! It's a house of the future.

Jina: Let's go into the bedroom first. Look, there's a smart closet.
~으로 들어가다

Suhan: I'm standing in front of this screen on the closet door and my
~ 앞에
clothes keep changing.
keep -ing: 계속 ~하다

Jina: The screen suggests clothes that suit the weather.
주격 관계대명사

Suhan: That's amazing! We no longer have to worry about dressing for
더 이상 ~하지 않다          ~에 대해 걱정하다
the weather.

Jina: Right. Let's move on to the living room.
~로 이동하다

Suhan: Oh, I like this music speaker.

AI Speaker: I'm not just a music speaker. I can do more than you can
단지 ~이 아닌                    ~ 이상
imagine.

Jina: It's hard to believe that you can understand us. What can you do?
가주어      진주어

AI Speaker: How about watching a movie? I'll play one for you.
제안, 권유: ~하는 것이 어때?                              = a movie

Suhan: Look, those smart windows are getting darker. I feel like I'm in
get+비교급: 점점 ~해지다        ~인 것 같다
a movie theater.

AI 인공 지능

Expo 박람회

enter 들어가다

future 미래

bedroom 침실

closet 옷장

suggest 제안하다

dress 옷을 입다; 옷, 드레스

imagine 상상하다

window 창문

theater 극장

dark 어두운

📎 확인문제

● 다음 문장이 본문의 내용과 일치하면 T, 일치하지 <u>않으면</u> F를 쓰시오.

1  Jina and Suhan are at the World AI Expo. ☐

2  Suhan actually keeps changing his clothes. ☐

3  AI Speaker can do more than people can imagine. ☐

4  Jina and Suhan are in a movie theater now. ☐

**Jina:** What else can you do?
그 밖의

**AI Speaker:** I can beatbox, too. Here comes, "cats and boots and cats and boots."

**Suhan:** You're funny. Good job!
잘했어!

**Jina:** Hurry! There's a smart car station outside! Let's go and ride in that red car.

**Suhan:** This car is so cool. Let's get in.
타다

**AI Car:** Welcome. Are you ready to go?
be ready to: ~할 준비가 되다

**Jina:** Yes, what should we do now? It's my first time to ride in a smart car.
to부정사의 형용사적 용법

**AI Car:** You don't need to do anything. I will drive and take you to the
~할 필요가 없다    아무것도    데리고 가다
next station.

**Suhan:** Watch out! I see a cat crossing the street.
조심해!    지각동사+목적어+목적격보어(원형부정사/현재분사)

**AI Car:** Don't worry. I have just sensed it. When I sense dangerous
have+pp: 현재완료의 완료 용법(막 ~했다)
situations, I slow down or stop.
속도를 늦추다

**Jina:** How can you do that?
= slow down or stop

**AI Car:** I'm a very intelligent robotic car. I know all about driving. I can predict danger based on knowledge and experience.
~에 근거하여

**Suhan:** How smart! You think and act like a person. You are really like
감탄문 How+형용사(+주어+동사)!    ~처럼    ~와 같은
a human.

---

else 그 밖의

beatbox 비트박스를 하다

boot 부츠, 목이 긴 신발

funny 재미있는

station 정류장

outside 밖에

cross 건너다

sense 감지하다

dangerous 위험한

situation 상황

intelligent 지능적인, 똑똑한

predict 예측하다

person 사람, 개인

human 인간, 인간의

---

### 확인문제

● 다음 문장이 본문의 내용과 일치하면 T, 일치하지 <u>않으면</u> F를 쓰시오.

1  AI Speaker can beatbox, too. ☐

2  Jina has ridden in a smart car before. ☐

3  When AI Car senses dangerous situations, it slows down or stops. ☐

4  AI Car can't drive as well as humans. ☐

● 우리말을 참고하여 빈칸에 알맞은 말을 쓰시오.

**1** A Day _____ the AI Expo

**2** Jina and Suhan are _____ _____ _____ _____ .

**3** They are _____ the AI home.

**4** Suhan: Look at this! It's a house _____ _____ _____ .

**5** Jina: Let's _____ _____ the bedroom first. Look, there's a smart closet.

**6** Suhan: I'm standing in front of this screen _____ _____ _____ _____ and my clothes _____ _____ .

**7** Jina: The screen suggests clothes _____ _____ _____ _____ .

**8** Suhan: That's amazing! We _____ _____ have to worry about _____ _____ _____ _____ .

**9** Jina: Right. Let's _____ _____ _____ the living room.

**10** Suhan: Oh, I like _____ _____ _____ .

**11** AI Speaker: _____ _____ _____ a music speaker.

**12** I can do _____ _____ you can imagine.

**13** Jina: _____ _____ _____ _____ that you can understand us. What can you do?

**14** AI Speaker: _____ _____ watching a movie?

**15** I'll _____ _____ for you.

**16** Suhan: Look, those smart windows are _____ _____ .

**17** I _____ _____ I'm in a movie theater.

**1** 인공 지능 박람회에서의 하루

**2** 진아와 수한이가 세계 인공 지능 박람회에 있다.

**3** 그들은 인공 지능 집으로 들어가고 있다.

**4** 수한: 이것 봐! 미래의 집이야.

**5** 진아: 침실 먼저 들어가 보자. 이거 봐, 스마트 옷장이 있어.

**6** 수한: 옷장 문에 있는 스크린 앞에 서 있으니까 내 옷이 계속해서 바뀌어.

**7** 진아: 스크린이 날씨에 적합한 옷을 제안하는 거야.

**8** 수한: 놀라워! 우린 더 이상 날씨 때문에 무슨 옷을 입을지 걱정할 필요가 없겠다.

**9** 진아: 맞아. 이제 거실로 가 보자.

**10** 수한: 오, 이 음악 스피커 마음에 들어.

**11** 인공 지능 스피커: 저는 그냥 음악 스피커가 아니에요.

**12** 저는 당신이 상상하는 것 이상의 것을 할 수 있어요.

**13** 진아: 네가 우리를 이해한다니 믿기 어려운 걸! 넌 뭘 할 수 있어?

**14** 인공 지능 스피커: 영화 보는 건 어때요?

**15** 하나 틀어 줄게요.

**16** 수한: 이것 봐, 스마트 창문이 점점 어두워지고 있어.

**17** 마치 내가 영화관 안에 있는 것 같아.

**18** Jina: _____ _____ can you do?

**19** AI Speaker: I can beatbox, too. _____ _____, "cats and boots and cats and boots."

**20** Suhan: You're funny. _____ _____!

**21** Jina: _____! There's a smart car station outside!

**22** Let's go and _____ _____ that red car.

**23** Suhan: This car is _____ _____. Let's _____ _____.

**24** AI Car: Welcome. Are you _____ _____ _____?

**25** Jina: Yes, _____ _____ we do now?

**26** It's _____ _____ _____ to ride in a smart car.

**27** AI Car: You _____ _____ _____ do anything.

**28** I will drive and _____ _____ _____ the next station.

**29** Suhan: Watch out! I see a cat _____ the street.

**30** AI Car: Don't worry. I _____ _____ _____ it.

**31** When I _____ _____ _____, I slow down or stop.

**32** Jina: _____ can you do that?

**33** AI Car: I'm a very _____ _____ car.

**34** I know _____ _____ _____.

**35** I can predict danger _____ _____ knowledge and experience.

**36** Suhan: _____ smart! You think and act _____ a person.

**37** You are really _____ a human.

**18** 진아: 또 뭘 할 수 있어?

**19** 인공 지능 스피커: 비트박스도 할 수 있어요. "북치기 박치기 북치기 박치기."

**20** 수한: 넌 정말 재미있구나. 잘했어!

**21** 진아: 서둘러! 밖에 스마트 자동차 정류장이 있어.

**22** 가서 저 빨간 차를 타 보자.

**23** 수한: 이 차 정말 멋지다. 차에 타자.

**24** 인공 지능 자동차: 어서 오세요. 갈 준비 됐나요?

**25** 진아: 응. 우린 이제 뭘 해야 하지?

**26** 스마트 자동차에 타는 건 처음이야.

**27** 인공 지능 자동차: 아무 것도 하지 않아도 돼요.

**28** 제가 운전해서 다음 정류장까지 데려다줄 거니까요.

**29** 수한: 조심해! 고양이가 길을 건너고 있는 게 보여.

**30** 인공 지능 자동차: 걱정 말아요. 이미 감지했어요.

**31** 저는 어떤 위험 상황을 감지하면 속도를 늦추거나 멈춰요.

**32** 진아: 어떻게 그렇게 할 수 있어?

**33** 인공 지능 자동차: 전 아주 지능적인 로봇 차예요.

**34** 저는 운전에 대한 모든 걸 알고 있어요.

**35** 저는 제 지식과 경험을 바탕으로 위험을 예측할 수 있어요.

**36** 수한: 정말 똑똑하구나! 사람처럼 생각하고 행동하는구나.

**37** 정말 인간 같아.

● 우리말을 참고하여 본문을 영작하시오.

**1** 인공 지능 박람회에서의 하루

➡ _____

**2** 진아와 수한이가 세계 인공 지능 박람회에 있다.

➡ _____

**3** 그들은 인공 지능 집으로 들어가고 있다.

➡ _____

**4** 수한: 이것 봐! 미래의 집이야.

➡ _____

**5** 진아: 침실 먼저 들어가 보자. 이거 봐, 스마트 옷장이 있어.

➡ _____

**6** 수한: 옷장 문에 있는 스크린 앞에 서 있으니까 내 옷이 계속해서 바뀌어.

➡ _____

**7** 진아: 스크린이 날씨에 적합한 옷을 제안하는 거야.

➡ _____

**8** 수한: 놀라워! 우린 더 이상 날씨 때문에 무슨 옷을 입을지 걱정할 필요가 없겠다.

➡ _____

**9** 진아: 맞아. 이제 거실로 가 보자.

➡ _____

**10** 수한: 오, 이 음악 스피커 마음에 들어.

➡ _____

**11** 인공 지능 스피커: 저는 그냥 음악 스피커가 아니에요.

➡ _____

**12** 저는 당신이 상상하는 것 이상의 것을 할 수 있어요.

➡ _____

**13** 진아: 네가 우리를 이해한다니 믿기 어려운 걸! 넌 뭘 할 수 있어?

➡ _____

**14** 인공 지능 스피커: 영화 보는 건 어때요?

➡ _____

**15** 하나 틀어 줄게요.

➡ _____

**16** 수한: 이것 봐, 스마트 창문이 점점 어두워지고 있어.

➡ _____

**17** 마치 내가 영화관 안에 있는 것 같아.

➡ _____

**18** 진아: 또 뭘 할 수 있어?

➡ _____

**19** 인공 지능 스피커: 비트박스도 할 수 있어요. "북치기 박치기 북치기 박치기."

➡ _____

**20** 수한: 넌 정말 재미있구나. 잘했어!

➡ _____

**21** 진아: 서둘러! 밖에 스마트 자동차 정류장이 있어.

➡ _____

**22** 가서 저 빨간 차를 타 보자.

➡ _____

**23** 수한: 이 차 정말 멋지다. 차에 타자.

➡ _____

**24** 인공 지능 자동차: 어서 오세요. 갈 준비 됐나요?

➡ _____

**25** 진아: 응, 우린 이제 뭘 해야 하지?

➡ _____

**26** 스마트 자동차에 타는 건 처음이야.

➡ _____

**27** 인공 지능 자동차: 아무 것도 하지 않아도 돼요.

➡ _____

**28** 제가 운전해서 다음 정류장까지 데려다줄 거니까요.

➡ _____

**29** 수한: 조심해! 고양이가 길을 건너고 있는 게 보여.

➡ _____

**30** 인공 지능 자동차: 걱정 말아요. 이미 감지했어요.

➡ _____

**31** 저는 어떤 위험 상황을 감지하면 속도를 늦추거나 멈춰요.

➡ _____

**32** 진아: 어떻게 그렇게 할 수 있어?

➡ _____

**33** 인공 지능 자동차: 전 아주 지능적인 로봇 차예요.

➡ _____

**34** 저는 운전에 대한 모든 걸 알고 있어요.

➡ _____

**35** 저는 제 지식과 경험을 바탕으로 위험을 예측할 수 있어요.

➡ _____

**36** 수한: 정말 똑똑하구나! 사람처럼 생각하고 행동하는구나.

➡ _____

**37** 정말 인간 같아.

➡ _____

[01~03] 다음 글을 읽고 물음에 답하시오.

Jina and Suhan are at the World AI Expo. ⓐThey are entering the AI home.

Suhan: Look at this! It's a house of the future.

Jina: Let's go into the bedroom first. Look, there's a smart closet.

Suhan: I'm ⓑstanding in front of this screen on the closet door and my clothes keep changing.

Jina: The screen suggests clothes that suit the weather.

Suhan: That's amazing! We no longer have to worry about dressing for the weather.

Jina: Right. Let's move on to the living room.

서답형

**01** 위 글의 밑줄 친 ⓐThey가 가리키는 것을 본문에서 찾아 쓰시오.

➡ _____

**02** 위 글의 밑줄 친 ⓑstanding과 문법적 쓰임이 같은 것을 고르시오. (3개)

① You must stop smoking for your health.
② I smelled something burning.
③ My plan is going to Paris.
④ Kids are playing on the sand.
⑤ I saw him playing tennis.

중요

**03** 위 글의 내용과 일치하지 않는 것은?

① 진아와 수한이는 세계 인공 지능 박람회에 있다.
② 수한이는 침실에 먼저 들어가 보자고 말한다.
③ 옷장 문에 있는 스크린 앞에 서 있으면 옷이 계속해서 바뀐다.
④ 옷장 문에 있는 스크린이 날씨에 적합한 옷을 제안해 준다.
⑤ 수한이는 더 이상 날씨 때문에 무슨 옷을 입을지 걱정할 필요가 없겠다고 말한다.

[04~06] 다음 글을 읽고 물음에 답하시오.

Suhan: Oh, I like this music speaker. (①)

AI Speaker: (②) I'm not just a music speaker. (③) I can do more than you can imagine. (④)

Jina: (⑤) What can you do?

AI Speaker: How about watching a movie? I'll play (A)[it / one] for you.

Suhan: Look, those smart windows are getting darker. ⓐ마치 내가 영화관 안에 있는 것 같아.

Jina: (B)[What / What else] can you do?

AI Speaker: I can beatbox, too. Here (C)[come / comes], "cats and boots and cats and boots."

Suhan: You're funny. Good job!

**04** 위 글의 흐름으로 보아, 주어진 문장이 들어가기에 가장 적절한 곳은?

It's hard to believe that you can understand us.

①        ②        ③        ④        ⑤

서답형

**05** 위 글의 괄호 (A)~(C)에서 문맥이나 어법상 알맞은 낱말을 골라 쓰시오.

(A) _____ (B) _____ (C) _____

서답형

**06** 위 글의 밑줄 친 ⓐ의 우리말에 맞게 주어진 어휘를 이용하여 8단어로 영작하시오.

feel like

➡ _____

[07~09] 다음 글을 읽고 물음에 답하시오.

Jina: Hurry! There's a smart car station outside! Let's go and ride in that red car.

Suhan: This car is so ⓐcool. Let's get in.

AI Car: Welcome. Are you ready to go?

Jina: Yes, what should we do now? It's my first time to ride in a smart car.

AI Car: You don't need to do anything. I will drive and take you to the next station.

Suhan: Watch out! I see a cat ___(A)___ the street.

AI Car: Don't worry. I have just sensed it. When I sense dangerous situations, I slow down or stop.

Jina: How can you do that?

AI Car: I'm a very intelligent robotic car. I know all about driving. I can predict danger based on knowledge and experience.

Suhan: How smart! You think and act like a person. You are really like a human.

**07** 위 글의 빈칸 (A)에 들어갈 알맞은 말을 고르시오. (2개)

① cross
② to cross
③ crosses
④ crossing
⑤ crossed

**08** 위 글의 밑줄 친 ⓐcool과 같은 의미로 쓰인 것을 모두 고르시오.

① I like a cool breeze in autumn.
② You look pretty cool with that new haircut.
③ How did you keep cool in the moment of danger?
④ Store lemons in a cool dry place.
⑤ How cool my new smart phone is!

**09** 위 글의 제목으로 가장 알맞은 것을 고르시오.

① Let's Go and Ride in a Smart Car
② My First Time to Ride in a Smart Car
③ Don't Worry! I Know All about Driving
④ Watch Out! A Cat Is Crossing the Street
⑤ I've Already Sensed a Dangerous Situation!

[10~12] 다음 글을 읽고 물음에 답하시오.

Jina and Suhan are at the World AI Expo. They are entering the AI home.

Suhan: Look at this! It's a house of the future.

Jina: Let's go into the bedroom first. Look, there's a smart closet.

Suhan: I'm standing in front of this screen on the closet door and my clothes keep ___ⓐ___.

Jina: The screen suggests clothes that suit the weather.

Suhan: That's amazing! We no longer have to ⓑworry about dressing for the weather.

Jina: Right. Let's move on to the living room.

**10** 위 글의 빈칸 ⓐ에 change를 알맞은 형태로 쓰시오.

➡ _____

**11** 위 글의 밑줄 친 ⓑworry about과 바꿔 쓸 수 없는 것을 모두 고르시오.

① be concerned about
② be anxious for
③ be worried about
④ be anxious about
⑤ be concerned with

**12** 위 글을 읽고 대답할 수 없는 질문은?

① Where are Jina and Suhan entering?
② Where do Jina and Suhan enter first at the AI home?
③ Where is Suhan standing?
④ How does Suhan's clothes keep changing?
⑤ What does the screen on the closet door suggest?

[13~16] 다음 글을 읽고 물음에 답하시오.

Suhan: Oh, I like this music speaker.
AI Speaker: I'm not just a music speaker. ①I can do more than you can imagine.
Jina: It's hard to believe that you can understand us. What can ②you do?
AI Speaker: How about watching a movie? I'll play one for ③you.
Suhan: Look, those smart windows are getting darker. I feel ⓐlike I'm in a movie theater.
Jina: What else can you do?
AI Speaker: ④I can beatbox, too. Here comes, "cats and boots and cats and boots."
Suhan: ⑤You're funny. Good job!

**13** 다음 밑줄 친 ①~⑤ 중에서 가리키는 대상이 나머지 넷과 다른 것은?

①        ②        ③        ④        ⑤

**14** 위 글의 밑줄 친 ⓐlike와 문법적 쓰임이 같은 것을 고르시오. (2개)

① No one sings the blues like she did.
② I like my coffee strong.
③ Cut the cabbage like this.
④ It looks like her bed wasn't slept in.
⑤ She responded in like manner.

**15** 위 글의 주제로 알맞은 것을 고르시오.

① the speaker that Suhan likes most at the World AI Expo
② the reason why Jina can't believe that the speaker can understand them
③ how to watch a movie using AI Speaker
④ AI Speaker that can beatbox
⑤ what AI Speaker can do besides playing its original role

서답형

**16** 본문의 내용과 일치하도록 다음 빈칸 (A)와 (B)에 알맞은 단어를 쓰시오.

> AI Speaker not only is a (A)_____ _____ but also can play a movie and (B)_____.

[17~19] 다음 글을 읽고 물음에 답하시오.

Jina: Hurry! There's a smart car station outside! Let's go and ride in that red car.
Suhan: This car is so cool. Let's get in.
AI Car: Welcome. Are you ready ⓐto go?
Jina: Yes, what should we do now? It's my first time to ride in a smart car.
AI Car: You don't need to do anything. I will drive and take you ___(A)___ the next station.
Suhan: Watch out! I see a cat crossing the street.
AI Car: Don't worry. I have just sensed it. When I sense dangerous situations, I slow down or stop.

Jina: How can you do that?

AI Car: I'm a very intelligent robotic car. I know all about driving. I can ___(B)___ based ___(C)___ knowledge and experience.

Suhan: How smart! You think and act like a person. You are really like a human.

## 17 위 글의 빈칸 (A)와 (C)에 들어갈 전치사가 바르게 짝지어진 것은?

① to – on
② in – by
③ in – from
④ to – by
⑤ for – on

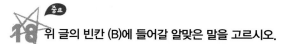

**18** 위 글의 빈칸 (B)에 들어갈 알맞은 말을 고르시오.

① predict safety
② protect cats
③ decide routes
④ predict danger
⑤ generate danger

**19** 위 글의 밑줄 친 ⓐto go와 to부정사의 용법이 다른 것을 고르시오. (2개)

① I have nothing particular to do today.
② He must be a liar to say such a thing.
③ He is rich enough to buy large house.
④ I told him to clean the room.
⑤ I am sorry to have to leave so early.

[20~23] 다음 글을 읽고 물음에 답하시오.

### DAILY NEWS

**AI Beats Human!**

An AI program has ___(A)___ a human in a baduk match. The AI had a match with Lee Sedol, ⓐ그는 가장 위대한 바둑기사들 중의 한 명이다. Baduk is a board game, and the rules are difficult to understand. Many people believed ___(B)___ would be impossible for an AI to beat a human player. However, the AI was able to predict Lee's play, and it finally won the game. People are shocked that an AI can be more intelligent than a human.

**서답형**

**20** 본문의 한 단어를 변형하여 위 글의 빈칸 (A)에 들어갈 알맞은 말을 쓰시오.

➡ _____

**서답형**

**21** 위 글의 빈칸 (B)에 들어갈 알맞은 말을 쓰시오.

➡ _____

**서답형**

**22** 위 글의 밑줄 친 ⓐ의 우리말에 맞게 주어진 어휘를 이용하여 8단어로 영작하시오.

| who, baduk players |
|---|

➡ _____

**23** 위 글의 내용과 일치하지 <u>않는</u> 것은?

① 바둑 대국에서 AI 프로그램이 인간을 이겼다.
② 바둑은 보드 게임이고, 그 규칙은 이해하기 어렵다.
③ 많은 사람들은 AI가 인간 기사를 이기는 것은 불가능할 것이라고 믿었다.
④ 이세돌은 경기를 예측할 수 있었고, 그리고 마침내 AI와의 경기에서 이겼다.
⑤ 사람들은 AI가 인간보다 더 똑똑할 수 있다는 것에 충격을 받았다.

**[01~03]** 다음 글을 읽고 물음에 답하시오.

Jina and Suhan are at the World AI Expo. ⓐ They are entering into the AI home.

Suhan: Look at this! It's a house of the future.

Jina: Let's go into the bedroom first. Look, there's a smart closet.

Suhan: I'm standing in front of this screen on the closet door and my clothes keep changing.

Jina: (A)The screen suggests clothes that suit the weather.

Suhan: That's amazing! ⓑ우린 더 이상 날씨 때문에 무슨 옷을 입을지 걱정할 필요가 없겠다.

Jina: Right. Let's move on to the living room.

**01** 위 글의 밑줄 친 ⓐ에서 어법상 틀린 부분을 찾아 고치시오.

_____ ➡ _____

**02** 위 글의 밑줄 친 ⓑ의 우리말에 맞게, 주어진 어휘를 알맞게 배열하시오.

> the weather / dressing / have to / we / about / no longer / for / worry

➡ _____

_____

**03** 다음 빈칸 (a)와 (b)에 알맞은 단어를 넣어 위 글의 밑줄 친 (A)The screen에 대한 소개를 완성하시오.

> It is the screen on the smart (a)_____
> _____ and suggests clothes that suit
> (b)_____ _____ to the person who
> is standing in front of it.

**[04~07]** 다음 글을 읽고 물음에 답하시오.

Suhan: Oh, I like this music speaker.

AI Speaker: I'm not just a music speaker. I can do more ⓐ you can imagine.

Jina: It's hard to believe that you can understand us. What can you do?

AI Speaker: ⓑHow about watching a movie? I'll play one for you.

Suhan: Look, those smart windows are ⓒ getting darker. I feel like I'm in a movie theater.

Jina: What else can you do?

AI Speaker: I can beatbox, too. Here comes, "cats and boots and cats and boots."

Suhan: You're funny. Good job!

**04** 위 글의 빈칸 ⓐ에 들어갈 알맞은 말을 쓰시오.

➡ _____

**05** 위 글의 밑줄 친 ⓑ를 다음과 같이 바꿔 쓸 때 빈칸에 들어갈 알맞은 말을 쓰시오.

> _____ _____ watching a movie?
> = _____ _____ _____ watch a movie?

**06** 위 글의 밑줄 친 ⓒgetting과 바꿔 쓸 수 있는 단어를 쓰시오.

➡ _____

**07** 위 글을 읽고 '음악 스피커의 역할' 외에 AI Speaker가 할 수 있는 일 두 가지를 우리말로 쓰시오.

(1) _____

(2) _____

**[08~11]** 다음 글을 읽고 물음에 답하시오.

Jina: Hurry! There's a smart car station outside! Let's go and ride in that red car.

Suhan: This car is so cool. Let's get in.

ⓐAI Car: Welcome. Are you ready to go?

Jina: Yes, what should we do now? It's my first time to ride in a smart car.

AI Car: ⓑYou don't need to do anything. I will drive and take you to the next station.

Suhan: Watch out! I see a cat crossing the street.

AI Car: ⓒDon't worry. I have just sensed ⓓit. When I sense dangerous situations, I slow down or stop.

Jina: How can you do that?

AI Car: I'm a very intelligent robotic car. I know all about driving. I can predict danger based on knowledge and experience.

Suhan: How smart! You think and act like a person. You are really like a human.

**08** 다음 빈칸에 본문의 한 단어를 알맞은 형태로 바꿔 넣어, 위 글의 밑줄 친 ⓐAI의 줄이지 않은 형태를 완성하시오.

> Artificial _____

**09** 위 글의 밑줄 친 ⓑ를 다음과 같이 바꿔 쓸 때 빈칸에 들어갈 알맞은 말을 쓰시오.

(1) You _____ _____ _____ do anything.

(2) You _____ _____ do anything.

**10** 위 글에서 AI Car가 밑줄 친 ⓒ처럼 말한 이유를 우리말로 쓰시오.

➡ _____

_____

_____

**11** 위 글의 밑줄 친 ⓓit이 가리키는 것을 본문에서 찾아 쓰시오.

➡ _____

**[12~14]** 다음 글을 읽고 물음에 답하시오.

Jina and Suhan are at the World AI Expo. They are entering the AI home.

Suhan: Look at this! It's a house of the future.

Jina: Let's go into the bedroom first. Look, there's a smart closet.

Suhan: I'm standing in front of this screen on the closet door and my clothes keep changing.

Jina: The screen suggests clothes that suit the weather.

Suhan: ⓐThat's amazed! We no longer have to worry about dressing for the weather.

Jina: Right. Let's move on to the living room.

**12** 위 글의 본문의 내용과 일치하도록 다음 빈칸 (A)와 (B)에 알맞은 단어를 쓰시오.

> (A)_____ doesn't actually keep changing his clothes. He is only standing in front of the screen on the closet door and (B)_____ _____ keep changing.

**13** 위 글의 밑줄 친 ⓐ에서 어법상 틀린 부분을 찾아 고치시오.

_____ ➡ _____

**14** Why does Suhan say that they no longer have to worry about dressing for the weather? Fill in the blanks with suitable words.

> Because the screen on the closet door _____ _____ that suit the weather.

## Before You Read

DAILY NEWS

AI Beats Human!

An AI program has beaten a human in a baduk match. The AI had a match
beat-beat-beaten
with Lee Sedol, who is one of the greatest baduk players.
one+of+the+복수명사: ~ 중의 하나
Baduk is a board game, and the rules are difficult to understand. Many people
to부정사의 부사적 용법(형용사 수식)
believed it would be impossible for an AI to beat a human player. However,
가주어          의미상 주어   진주어
the AI was able to predict Lee's play, and it finally won the game.
= AI       win the game: 시합에 이기다
People are shocked that an AI can be more intelligent than a human.
감정을 나타내는 동사는 수식받는 명사가 감정을 느끼게 되는 경우에 과거분사를 쓴다.

구문해설  • **beat**: 이기다  • **match**: 경기, 시합  • **board game**: 보드 게임(판을 놓고 그 위에서 말을 이
동시켜 가며 하는 모든 게임)  • **intelligent**: 총명한, 똑똑한  • **shocked**: 충격을 받은

## Focus on Expressions

In 2099, people get in a flying car to get to the moon. Kids love to go to the
날아다니는                                목적어로 쓰인 부정사(= going)
moon because the greatest amusement park is there. Above all, horse-riding is
최상급                      = in the moon          동명사(주어)
their favorite activity. They don't want to get off the horses.
목적어로 쓰인 부정사

구문해설  • **get in**: ~에 들어가다, ~에 타다  • **get to**: ~에 도착하다  • **above all**: 다른 무엇보다도 특
히, 우선 첫째로  • **get off**: ~에서 내리다, ~에서 떨어지다

## Wrap Up 1-2

**G:** Minseok, there is a smart food-ordering machine over there. Why don't we
there is 단수명사: ~가 있다                    Why don't we+동사 ~?: 함께 ~하자, ~하지 않을래?
try it?

**B:** That sounds interesting. We'll be able to order easily and fast by using it.
sound 형용사: ~하게 들리다        order(동사)를 수식하고 있으므로 부사를 사용    by 동사ing: ~함으로써
**G:** I hope so. By the way, do you think maybe it will be possible for robots to

replace humans someday?

**B:** I'm not sure. But we will be free from danger because of robots.

**G:** What do you mean?
'무슨 뜻이야?'(의미를 물을 때 사용)
**B:** Robots can help people in danger. Robots can do the dangerous work so
위험에 처한, 위험에 빠진                              그래서
humans don't have to.
~할 필요가 없다(= need not). 뒤에 do the dangerous work가 생략되었음
**G:** You're right. We should always try to look on the bright side.

구문해설  • **machine**: 기계  • **over there**: 저쪽에  • **be able to**: ~할 수 있다(= can)  • **by the
way**: 그런데, 그건 그렇고 (대화에서 화제를 바꿀 때 씀)  • **possible**: 가능한  • **replace**: 대체
하다  • **free from**: ~이 없는  • **danger**: 위험  • **because of**: ~ 때문에

해석

데일리 뉴스
AI가 인간을 이기다!
바둑 대국에서 AI 프로그램이
인간을 이겼다. AI가 이세돌과
대국을 벌였는데, 그는 가장
위대한 바둑기사들 중의 한 명
이다.
바둑은 보드 게임이고, 그 규
칙은 이해하기 어렵다. 많은
사람들은 AI가 인간 기사를 이
기는 것은 불가능할 것이라고
믿었다. 그러나, AI는 이세돌의
경기를 예측할 수 있었고, 그
리고 마침내 경기에서 이겼다.
사람들은 AI가 인간보다 더 똑
똑할 수 있다는 것에 충격을
받았다.

2099년에 사람들은 달에 가
기 위해 날아다니는 차를 탑
니다. 아이들은 가장 멋진 놀
이공원이 그곳에 있기 때문에
달에 가는 것을 좋아합니다.
다른 무엇보다도, 말타기는
그들이 가장 좋아하는 활동입
니다. 그들은 말에서 내리기
를 원하지 않습니다.

**G:** 민석아, 저쪽에 스마트 음
식 주문 자판기가 있어.
가서 해 보지 않을래?
**B:** 재미있겠다. 저걸 사용하
면 우린 쉽고 빠르게 주문
할 수 있을 거야.
**G:** 그러길 바라. 그건 그렇
고, 너는 로봇이 언젠가
인간을 대체할 수 있을 거
라고 생각하니?
**B:** 잘 모르겠어. 하지만 우리
는 로봇 덕분에 위험이 없
어질 거야.
**G:** 무슨 뜻이야?
**B:** 로봇은 위험에 처한 사람
들을 도울 수 있어. 로봇
이 위험한 일을 할 수 있
어서 사람들이 그 일을 하
지 않아도 되지.
**G:** 네 말이 맞아. 우리는 항상
좋은 면을 보도록 해야 해.

**01** 다음 빈칸에 공통으로 들어갈 말을 쓰시오.

> • He will give you enough time to
> _____ them up on the Internet.
> • These whales _____ for their food as
> a team.

**02** 다음 빈칸에 알맞은 말을 고르시오.

> She is never free _____ worry.

① from    ② for    ③ at
④ in    ⑤ on

**03** 다음 문장의 빈칸에 알맞은 것을 〈보기〉에서 찾아 쓰시오.

> ┤ 보기 ├
> if  just  longer  on

(1) The movie is based _____ a famous
novel.
(2) It's not _____ about the money.
(3) She is no _____ a child.
(4) Go and see _____ the door is locked.

**04** 다음 우리말에 맞도록 빈칸에 알맞은 말을 쓰시오. (주어진
철자로 시작할 것.)

(1) 이 경기에선 우리 팀이 너희 팀을 이길 것이다.
  ➡ Our team will b_____ your team in
  this match.
(2) Dave는 잘생겼을 뿐만 아니라 똑똑하기까지
하다.
  ➡ Dave is not only handsome but also
  i_____.
(3) 너는 쉽게 전구를 교체할 수 있다.
  ➡ You can easily r_____ the bulb.

**[05~06]** 다음 대화를 읽고 물음에 답하시오.

> B: We took lots of pictures during our trip.
> G: We sure ___(A)___ . We have more than 500
> pictures.
> B: Is it possible ___(B)___ an animated photo
> album out of them?
> G: _____(C)_____ I have an app for that.

**05** 빈칸 (A)와 (B)에 들어갈 말이 순서대로 바르게 짝지어진 것은?

① do – making    ② do – to make
③ did – make    ④ did – to make
⑤ can – making

**06** 빈칸 (C)에 알맞은 말을 고르시오.

① No, I think it's impossible.
② Yes, I am able to take many pictures.
③ Yes, it's possible.
④ Yes, it sounds interesting.
⑤ That sounds perfect.

**07** 다음 대화의 빈칸 (A)와 (B)에 들어갈 말이 순서대로 바르게 짝지어진 것은?

> B: ___(A)___ don't we try a new VR game?
> G: That ___(B)___ interesting.

① What – sounds
② What – was
③ Why – thinks
④ Why – was
⑤ Why – sounds

**[08~10]** 다음 대화를 읽고 물음에 답하시오.

> B: Do you have any ideas for our group project? (①)
> G: No. (②) What about you?
> B: I'm thinking we should talk about future jobs. (③)
> G: That sounds perfect ___(A)___ our project. (④) Let's look ___(B)___ some information on the Internet. (⑤)

**08** ①~⑤ 중 주어진 문장이 들어갈 알맞은 곳은?

> What do you think?

①          ②          ③          ④          ⑤

**09** 다음 빈칸 (A)와 (B)에 공통으로 들어갈 말을 쓰시오.

➡ _____

**10** 위 대화의 내용과 일치하지 않는 것을 고르시오.

① The girl doesn't have any ideas about the group project.
② Their group project will be about future jobs.
③ The girl disagrees with the boy's idea about the group project.
④ They are talking about their group project.
⑤ They will use the Internet to find some information.

**11** 다음 대화의 빈칸에 들어갈 말을 고르시오.

> G: The Robot Expo begins next week. Why don't you go with me?
> B: _____ That sounds exciting.
> G: We'll have a chance to meet robotics engineers.
> B: That'll be great.

① Yes, I'd love to.
② Really? Me, too.
③ That's too bad.
④ I think it's not perfect.
⑤ I don't want to go with you.

**12** 다음 대화의 빈칸에 들어갈 말을 고르시오.

> A: Is it possible (A)[for / of] you to read 50 novels during summer vacation?
> B: (B)[Sure not / Sure]. I can (C)[do / be] that.

(A) _____  (B) _____  (C) _____

**[13~14]** 다음 빈칸에 알맞은 말이 순서대로 짝지어진 것은?

**13**

> • I can smell the bread _____.
> • I watched the people _____ in the river.

① bake – to swim
② bakes – swimming
③ baked – swam
④ to bake – swims
⑤ baking – swim

**14**

> _____ is good for both body and mind _____ every day.

① This – exercising
② That – exercise
③ That – to exercise
④ It – exercise
⑤ It – to exercise

**15** 다음 그림을 보고 괄호 안에 주어진 어휘를 이용하여 빈칸에 알맞은 말을 쓰시오.

(1) I saw a person _____ badminton. (play)
(2) I saw a person _____ in the pool. (swim)
(3) I saw a person _____ a horse. (ride)

**16** 다음 중 어법상 올바르지 <u>않은</u> 것은?

① It is impossible to finish the work in time.
② It was interesting that compare their situation and ours.
③ It is hard to believe that he knows all the answers to the problems.
④ It is true that nature itself is a teacher and a school.
⑤ Is it possible to make energy from waste?

**17** 다음 중 어법상 올바르지 <u>않은</u> 것은?

① She had him throw away the trash yesterday.
② I often watch her talking on the phone.
③ It is important to wash your hands before doing an experiment.
④ Now it is not hard to see AI robots to serve dishes in the school cafeteria.
⑤ Is it possible to drink while standing on your head?

**18** 괄호 안에 주어진 어휘를 이용하여 다음을 영작하시오.

(1) 나는 그가 공원에서 자전거를 타고 있는 것을 보았다. (ride, see, a bike)
➡ _____

(2) 나는 부엌에서 무언가가 타고 있는 냄새를 맡았다. (smell, something, burn)
➡ _____

(3) 달에서 말하는 것은 가능하지 않다. (not, talk, the moon, it)
➡ _____

(4) 친구들과 농구하는 것은 흥미롭다. (it, exciting, with friends)
➡ _____

**19** 다음 문장에서 어법상 어색한 부분을 바르게 고치시오.

(1) We saw him danced on the street.

_____ ➡ _____

(2) Hyde smells something burns in the room.

_____ ➡ _____

(3) I felt my heart tearing to pieces by regret.

_____ ➡ _____

(4) It is dangerous of you to swim in the sea.

_____ ➡ _____

(5) Many people believed it would be impossible for an AI beating a human player.

_____ ➡ _____

(6) Is it possible make an animated photo album out of them?

_____ ➡ _____

**Reading**

**[20~22]** 다음 글을 읽고 물음에 답하시오.

Jina and Suhan are at the World AI Expo. They are entering the AI home.

Suhan: Look at this! It's a house of the future.

Jina: Let's go into the bedroom first. Look, there's a smart closet.

Suhan: I'm standing in front of this screen on the closet door and my clothes keep changing.

Jina: The screen suggests clothes ⓐ suit the weather.

Suhan: That's amazing! We no longer have to worry about dressing for the weather.

Jina: Right. Let's move on to the living room.

**20** 위 글의 빈칸 ⓐ에 들어갈 알맞은 말을 모두 고르시오.

① that
② who
③ what
④ whom
⑤ which

**21** 위 글의 제목으로 가장 알맞은 것을 고르시오.

① The World AI Expo
② The House of the Future
③ There's a Screen on the Closet Door!
④ The Screen Which Suggests Clothes
⑤ How to Wear Clothes Suitable for the Weather

**22** 주어진 영영풀이에 해당하는 단어를 위 글에서 찾아 쓰시오.

| a small room or cabinet used for storage space |
|---|

➡ _____

**[23~24]** 다음 글을 읽고 물음에 답하시오.

Suhan: Oh, I like this music speaker.

AI Speaker: I'm not just a music speaker. ⓐ저는 당신이 상상하는 것 이상의 것을 할 수 있어요.

Jina: ⓑIt's hard to believe that you can understand us. What can you do?

AI Speaker: How about watching a movie? I'll play one for you.

Suhan: Look, those smart windows are getting darker. I feel like I'm in a movie theater.

Jina: What else can you do?

AI Speaker: I can beatbox, too. Here comes, "cats and boots and cats and boots."

Suhan: You're funny. Good job!

**23** 위 글의 밑줄 친 ⓐ의 우리말에 맞게 주어진 어휘를 알맞게 배열하시오.

> more / can / you / do / than / imagine / can / I

➡ _____

**24** 위 글의 밑줄 친 ⓑIt과 문법적 쓰임이 같은 것을 고르시오.

① It was raining this morning.
② It's impossible to get there in time.
③ I find it strange that she doesn't want to go.
④ It's two miles from here to the beach.
⑤ Look! It's going up that tree.

**[25~27]** 다음 글을 읽고 물음에 답하시오.

Jina: Hurry! There's a smart car station outside! Let's go and ride in that red car.
Suhan: This car is so cool. Let's get in.
AI Car: Welcome. Are you ready to go?
Jina: Yes, what should we do now? It's my first time to ride in a smart car.
AI Car: You don't need to do anything. I will drive and take you to the next station.
Suhan: ⓐWatch out! I see a cat crossing the street.
AI Car: Don't worry. I ⓑhave just sensed it. When I sense dangerous situations, I slow down or stop.
Jina: How can you ⓒdo that?
AI Car: I'm a very intelligent robotic car. I know all about driving. I can predict danger based on knowledge and experience.
Suhan: How smart! You think and act like a person. You are really like a human.

**25** 위 글의 밑줄 친 ⓐWatch out!과 바꿔 쓸 수 있는 말을 쓰시오.

➡ _____

**26** 아래 〈보기〉에서 위 글의 밑줄 친 ⓑhave just sensed와 현재완료의 용법이 다른 것의 개수를 고르시오.

> ① We have already done it.
> ② I have never read the book.
> ③ They have lived in Seoul for ten years.
> ④ He has gone to Busan.
> ⑤ She has waited for you since last night.

① 1개   ② 2개   ③ 3개   ④ 4개   ⑤ 5개

**27** 위 글의 밑줄 친 ⓒdo that이 가리키는 것을 본문에서 찾아 영어로 쓰시오.

➡ _____

_____

**[28~29]** 다음 글을 읽고 물음에 답하시오.

> Messi Is Playing at Our School!
> Scientists have developed a soccer robot ___ⓐ___ "Alpha-Foot." Alpha-Foot is almost human looking and is programmed as Messi. Next week, Alpha-Foot will play in his first soccer match with our soccer team. We are all excited to see the AI robot play for our school.

**28** 위 글의 빈칸 ⓐ에 call을 알맞은 형태로 쓰시오.

➡ _____

**29** 위 글의 종류로 알맞은 것을 고르시오.

① review          ② book report
③ essay           ④ diary
⑤ a school paper article

**01** 제시된 영영풀이의 단어로 빈칸을 채우시오. (주어진 철자로 시작할 것)

*출제율 90%*

| b_____ : to be destroyed by fire |
| --- |

| Lower the heat, or it'll _____. |
| --- |

**02** 다음 밑줄 친 부분을 알맞은 형태로 고치시오.

*출제율 95%*

| The next night was dark and <u>cloud</u>. |
| --- |

➡ _____

**03** 다음 중 〈보기〉에 있는 단어를 사용하여 자연스러운 문장을 만들 수 없는 것은?

*출제율 100%*

┌─── 보기 ───┐
point   take   text   freeze
└───────────┘

① It takes all day just to _____ a tray of ice cubes.
② It is widely used to _____ down aging.
③ Do you like _____ or talking to your friends online?
④ It's not polite to _____ at strangers in public.
⑤ I'll _____ two adult tickets, please.

**04** 주어진 우리말에 맞게 빈칸을 채우시오.

*출제율 95%*

(1) 얼마나 많은 공장 노동자들이 일자리를 잃을 위험에 처해 있는가?
➡ How many factory workers are _____ _____ of losing their jobs?

(2) 너의 성적은 네 개의 과제물과 기말 고사를 기준으로 매겨질 것이다.
➡ Your grade will be _____ _____ four papers and a final exam.

[05~08] 다음 대화를 읽고 물음에 답하시오.

G: Look at those words on the board.
B: What do they mean? Let's look them up in the dictionary.
G: What about using the AI ___(A)___?
B: _____(B)_____
G: You point your smartphone camera at the words and ask AI to translate. You will get an answer.
B: AI가 저 글자들을 읽는 것이 가능해?
Speaker: Sure. I can read any language and translate it.
B: Wow, that sounds unbelievable. So, AI, what do those words mean?
Speaker: They mean "Dreams come true!"
B: That's amazing.

**05** 위의 대화에 나온 단어를 이용해 빈칸 (A)에 알맞은 말을 쓰시오. (주어진 철자로 시작할 것)

*출제율 90%*

➡ t_____

**06** 위 대화의 빈칸 (B)에 알맞은 말을 고르시오.

*출제율 95%*

① What do you think?
② Why don't you use those words?
③ What about you?
④ Do you have any ideas for those words?
⑤ How do I use it?

출제율 90%

**07** 밑줄 친 우리말과 일치하도록 주어진 단어를 이용해 문장을 만드시오.

> (AI, possible, those)

➡ _____

출제율 85%

**08** 위 대화에서 다음 영영풀이에 해당하는 단어를 찾아 쓰시오.

> a book that contains a list of words and phrases alphabetically with their meanings or their translations in another language

➡ _____

**[09~10]** 문장을 대화의 흐름에 맞게 배열하시오.

출제율 95%

**09**
> (A) That sounds perfect for our project. Let's look for some information on the Internet.
> (B) I'm thinking we should talk about future jobs. What do you think?
> (C) Do you have any ideas for our group project?
> (D) No. What about you?

➡ _____

출제율 100%

**10**
> (A) We sure did. We have more than 500 pictures.
> (B) Yes, it's possible. I have an app for that.
> (C) Is it possible to make an animated photo album out of them?
> (D) We took lots of pictures during our trip.

➡ _____

**[11~12]** 다음 대화를 읽고 물음에 답하시오.

> A: Let's see (A)[which / if / what] we can answer these science questions.
> B: That sounds like fun.
> A: 불을 얼리는 것이 가능할까?
> B: Yes, I think it's possible.

출제율 85%

**11** 위 대화의 괄호 (A)에서 적절한 것을 고르시오.

➡ _____

출제율 85%

**12** 밑줄 친 우리말과 일치하도록 주어진 단어를 이용하여 영작하시오. (6단어)

> (possible)

➡ _____

출제율 90%

**13** 다음 빈칸에 들어갈 말이 바르게 짝지어진 것은?

> _____ is possible _____ a robot _____ me how to play the piano.

① It – of – teach
② It – for – to teach
③ That – of – teach
④ That – for – to teach
⑤ This – of – to teach

✏️ 출제율 95%

**14** 다음 빈칸에 들어갈 말이 바르게 짝지어진 것은?

> • I noticed the man _____ slowly toward me.
> • It is fun _____ together with Ella and Jaden every day.

① coming – get  ② coming – to get

③ to come – get  ④ to come – to get

⑤ come – get

**[15~16]** 다음 중 어법상 올바른 문장을 <u>모두</u> 고르시오.

✏️ 출제율 100%

**15** ① Alice saw him running toward her.

② I heard my name calling repeatedly.

③ Jenny felt somebody pulling her hair.

④ Mick watched them fought each other.

⑤ He was looking at the dog to eat the bones.

✏️ 출제율 95%

**16** ① That is necessary to come early in the morning.

② It is good to go for a walk on holidays.

③ It is helpful read many kinds of books.

④ It was really boring of me to memorize English words.

⑤ It is important that you follow the rules.

**[17~19]** 다음 글을 읽고 물음에 답하시오.

> Jina and Suhan are at the World AI Expo. They are entering the AI home.
> Suhan: Look at this! It's a house of the future.
> Jina: Let's go into the bedroom first. Look, there's a smart closet.
> Suhan: I'm standing in front of this screen on the closet door and my clothes keep changing.

Jina: ⓐThe screen suggests clothes that suits the weather.

Suhan: That's amazing! We no longer have to worry __(A)__ dressing __(B)__ the weather.

Jina: Right. Let's move on to the ⓑliving room.

✏️ 출제율 90%

**17** 위 글의 빈칸 (A)와 (B)에 들어갈 전치사가 바르게 짝지어진 것은?

① for – from  ② about – for

③ at – for  ④ for – to

⑤ about – to

✏️ 출제율 85%

**18** 위 글의 밑줄 친 ⓐ에서 어법상 <u>틀린</u> 부분을 찾아 고치시오.

_____ ➡ _____

✏️ 출제율 95%

**19** 위 글의 밑줄 친 ⓑliving과 문법적 쓰임이 <u>다른</u> 것을 <u>모두</u> 고르시오.

① a <u>sleeping</u> car  ② a <u>waiting</u> lady

③ a <u>walking</u> stick  ④ a <u>waiting</u> room

⑤ a <u>walking</u> dictionary

**[20~22]** 다음 글을 읽고 물음에 답하시오.

> Suhan: Oh, I like this music speaker.
> AI Speaker: I'm not just a music speaker. I can do more than ⓐyou can imagine.
> Jina: It's hard (A)to believe that ⓑyou can understand ⓒus. What can you do?
> AI Speaker: How about watching a movie? ⓓI'll play one for you.

Suhan: Look, those smart windows are getting darker. I feel like I'm in a movie theater.
Jina: What else can ⓔyou do?
AI Speaker: How
Suhan: You're funny. Good job!

**20** 위 글의 밑줄 친 ⓐ~ⓔ 중 가리키는 대상이 같은 것끼리 짝지어진 것은?

① ⓐ - ⓑ　② ⓐ - ⓓ　③ ⓑ - ⓒ
④ ⓑ - ⓓ　⑤ ⓒ - ⓔ

**21** 아래 보기에서 위 글의 밑줄 친 (A)to believe와 to부정사의 용법이 다른 것의 개수를 고르시오.

① This plan leaves nothing to be desired.
② To read these books is important.
③ He was too foolish to solve it.
④ Would you like to leave a message?
⑤ To read is to feed the mind.

① 1개　② 2개　③ 3개　④ 4개　⑤ 5개

**22** 위 글의 내용과 일치하지 않는 것은?

① 수한이는 음악 스피커가 마음에 든다.
② 인공 지능 스피커는 사람들이 상상하는 것 이상의 것을 할 수 있다고 말한다.
③ 화면이 점점 어두워지고 있다.
④ 수한이는 마치 영화관 안에 있는 것 같이 느낀다.
⑤ 인공 지능 스피커는 비트박스도 할 수 있다.

[23~25] 다음 글을 읽고 물음에 답하시오.

Jina: Hurry! There's a smart car station outside! Let's go and ride in that red car.
Suhan: This car is so cool. Let's get in.
AI Car: Welcome. Are you ready to go?
Jina: Yes, what should we do now? It's my first time to ride in a smart car.

AI Car: You don't need to do anything. I will drive and take you to the next station.
Suhan: Watch out! I see a cat crossing the street.
AI Car: Don't worry. (①) I have just sensed it. (②)
Jina: How can you do that? (③)
AI Car: I'm a very intelligent robotic car. (④) I know all about driving. (⑤) I can predict danger based on knowledge and experience.
Suhan: How smart! You think and act like a person. You are really like a human.

**23** 위 글의 흐름으로 보아, 주어진 문장이 들어가기에 가장 적절한 곳은?

When I sense dangerous situations, I slow down or stop.

①　②　③　④　⑤

**24** 위 글의 주제로 알맞은 것을 고르시오.

① People want to ride in a cool smart car.
② People share the experience to ride in a smart car.
③ What should we do to ride in a smart car?
④ The AI car knows all about driving.
⑤ How does a smart car sense dangerous situations?

**25** 다음 빈칸 (A)와 (B)에 알맞은 단어를 넣어 '인공 지능 자동차'에 대한 소개를 완성하시오.

It's a very intelligent (A)_____ which knows all about driving. People don't need to (B)_____ _____ while they are riding in this smart car.

# 서술형 실전문제

**01** 대화의 흐름상 또는 어법상 어색한 것을 하나 찾아서 고치시오.

> A: Do you have any questions?
> B: Yes. Is that possible to communicate face to face with other people without speaking?
> A: Not now. But maybe someday.

_____ ➡ _____

**02** 대화의 밑줄 친 부분과 같은 뜻이 되도록 주어진 단어를 이용하여 문장을 완성하시오.

> B: Do you have any ideas for our group project?
> G: No. What about you?
> B: I'm thinking we should talk about future jobs. What do you think?
> G: That sounds perfect for our project. Let's look for some information on the Internet.

➡ _____ (think)

**03** 밑줄 친 우리말과 일치하도록 주어진 단어를 이용하여 문장을 만드시오.

> A: 눈 감고 문자 메시지 보내는 것이 가능하니?
> B: Sure. I can do that.

(it. for, close, with)

➡ _____

**04** 주어진 어휘를 이용하여 다음 우리말을 (1) to부정사 주어를 써서, (2) 가주어를 써서 영작하시오.

> 우리 일상생활에서 에너지를 절약하는 것이 중요하다. (save, our daily lives)

(1) _____
(2) _____

> 퇴근 후 피곤함을 느끼는 것은 당연하다. (natural, tired, after work)

(1) _____
(2) _____

**05** 다음 그림을 보고 괄호 안에 주어진 어휘를 이용하여 빈칸을 알맞게 채우시오.

I watched Jane _____ _____ _____.
(ride)

Jina and Suhan are at the World AI Expo. They are entering the AI home.

Suhan: Look at this! It's a house of the future.

Jina: Let's ⓐgo into the bedroom first. Look, there's a smart closet.

Suhan: I'm standing in front of this screen on the closet door and my clothes keep changing.

Jina: ⓑ스크린이 날씨에 적합한 옷을 제안하는 거야.

Suhan: That's amazing! ⓒWe no longer have to worry about dressing for the weather.

Jina: Right. Let's move on to the living room.

**06** 위 글의 밑줄 친 ⓐgo into와 바꿔 쓸 수 있는 한 단어를 본문에서 찾아 알맞은 형태로 쓰시오.

➡ _____

**07** 위 글의 밑줄 친 ⓑ의 우리말에 맞게 주어진 어휘를 이용하여 8단어로 영작하시오.

| suggests, suit, weather |
|---|

➡ _____

_____

**08** 위 글의 밑줄 친 ⓒ를 다음과 같이 바꿔 쓸 때 빈칸에 들어갈 알맞은 말을 쓰시오.

We don't have to worry about dressing for the weather _____ _____.

Jina: Hurry! There's a smart car station outside! Let's go and ride in that red car.

Suhan: This car is so cool. Let's get in.

AI Car: Welcome. Are you ready to go?

Jina: Yes, (A)[how / what] should we do now? It's my first time to ride in a smart car.

AI Car: You don't need to do anything. I will drive and take you to the next station.

Suhan: Watch out! I see a cat crossing the street.

AI Car: Don't worry. I have just sensed it. ⓐ When I sense dangerous situations, I speed up or stop.

Jina: (B)[How / What] can you do that?

AI Car: I'm a very intelligent robotic car. I know all about driving. I can predict danger (C)[basing / based] on knowledge and experience.

Suhan: ⓑHow smart! You think and act like a person. You are really like a human.

**09** 위 글의 괄호 (A)~(C)에서 어법상 알맞은 낱말을 골라 쓰시오.

(A) _____ (B) _____ (C) _____

**10** 위 글의 밑줄 친 ⓐ에서 흐름상 어색한 부분을 찾아 고치시오.

_____ ➡ _____

**11** 위 글의 밑줄 친 ⓑHow smart!를 What을 사용하여 고치시오.

➡ _____

# 창의사고력 서술형 문제

**01** 가능 여부를 묻고 대답하는 다음 대화를 완성하시오.

조건
- 더운 날 길 위에서 계란을 부치는 것이 가능한지에 대해 이야기할 것.
- possible을 이용할 것.

A: _____

B: _____

**02** 지각동사 see를 이용하여 다음 그림을 묘사하는 문장을 완성하시오. (괄호 안에 주어진 어휘를 이용할 것.)

(1) I can see a man and a woman _____ a song together. (sing)

(2) I can see _____ an ice corn with her left arm raised. (girl, eat)

(3) I can see _____ the shirts in the store. (boy, look)

**03** 다음 내용을 바탕으로 기획한 제품을 쇼핑 호스트가 되어 홍보하는 대본을 쓰시오.

AI Cook
- It selects vegetables and meat from the refrigerator.
- It cooks a delicious meal with these vegetables and meat.

Today, I'll tell you about the "(A)_____." It can select (B)_____ from the refrigerator for you. It can cook (C)_____ with these (D)_____. When the meal is ready, it'll let you know. Now, please call 800-1234-8282 if you'd like to buy one of these AI Cooks.

## 단원별 모의고사

**01** 다음 문장에 공통으로 들어갈 말을 고르시오.

• The story is _____ more and more interesting.

• He is _____ in the front seat of the taxi.

**02** 다음 빈칸에 알맞은 말을 〈보기〉에서 골라 쓰시오.

┌─ 보기 ─
of  on  to
└─

(1) They are sitting face _____ face and looking at each other.

(2) Now, let's move _____ to the next story.

(3) They make plastics out _____ plant materials such as corn and soybeans.

**03** 다음 빈칸에 알맞은 말을 고르시오.

We are offering 25% _____ all furniture purchased on the day of our grand opening.

① on       ② in       ③ off
④ from     ⑤ to

**[04~05]** 다음 대화를 읽고 물음에 답하시오.

G: 네가 스마트폰 없이 사는 것이 가능할까?
B: No, it's (A)not possible.

**04** 밑줄 친 우리말과 일치하도록 주어진 단어를 이용하여 영작하시오.

(possible)

➡ _____

**05** 위 대화의 밑줄 친 (A)를 한 단어로 바꾸시오.

➡ _____

**[06~08]** 다음 대화를 읽고 물음에 답하시오.

G: This computer looks nice. How much is ⓐit?
M: ⓑIt's 500 dollars. ⓒIt's the newest one.
G: Is ⓓit possible to use this coupon?
M: Let me check. Yes, you can. __(A)__, you'll get 30 dollars off.
G: Perfect. I'll take ⓔit.

**06** 위 대화의 ⓐ~ⓔ 중 대상이 다른 하나를 고르시오.

① ⓐ    ② ⓑ    ③ ⓒ    ④ ⓓ    ⑤ ⓔ

**07** 위 대화의 빈칸 (A)에 알맞은 말을 고르시오.

① So                  ② However
③ Unfortunately      ④ Also
⑤ In addition

**08** 위 대화를 읽고 대답할 수 없는 질문을 고르시오.

① Is the coupon which the girl has available to use?
② Will the girl pay in cash or credit card?
③ Where are they?
④ How much discount does the girl get?
⑤ What does the girl want to buy?

**[09~12]** 다음 대화를 읽고 물음에 답하시오.

G: Minseok, there is a smart food-ordering machine over there. ⓐWhy don't we try it?

B: That sounds ___(A)___ (interest). ⓑWe'll be able to order easily and fast by using it.

G: ⓒI hope so. By the way, do you think maybe it will be possible for robots ___(B)___ (replace) humans someday?

B: I'm not sure. But we will be free ___(C)___ danger because ___(D)___ robots.

G: ⓓWhat do you mean?

B: Robots can help people in danger. Robots can do the dangerous work so humans don't have to.

G: You're right. ⓔWe should always try to look on the dark side.

**09** 위 대화의 괄호 안에 주어진 단어를 이용하여 빈칸 (A)와 (B)를 채우시오.

(A) _____ (B) _____

**10** 위 대화의 빈칸 (C), (D)에 알맞은 전치사를 쓰시오.

(C) _____ (D) _____

**11** 위 대화의 문맥상 어색한 것을 고르시오.

① ⓐ  ② ⓑ  ③ ⓒ  ④ ⓓ  ⑤ ⓔ

**12** 위 대화에서 다음 영영풀이에 해당하는 단어를 찾아 쓰시오.

| able to happen or be done |
| --- |

➡ _____

**13** 다음 문장을 it을 주어로 하여 다시 쓰시오.

(1) To eat a lot of vegetables is good for your health.

➡ _____

(2) That people may not want to talk to each other anymore is possible.

➡ _____
_____

**14** 다음 중 어법상 어색한 것은?

① Mike heard his phone ringing.
② It is my plan to read 10 books during the winter vacation.
③ It was exciting to watch them singing and dancing to the music.
④ She watched him to cut the paper.
⑤ Is it possible for you to text with your eyes closed?

**15** 다음 중 어법상 어색한 것은?

① She heard someone crying.
② I saw the boy singing in the classroom.
③ She watched him helping the lady get into the bus.
④ Is it possible to freeze fire?
⑤ It is very kind for you to help us.

## 16 주어진 단어를 이용하여 다음 우리말을 영어로 쓰시오.

(1) 민아는 양파가 튀겨지는 냄새를 맡았다.
(smell, fry)

➡ _____

(2) 우리는 그들이 서로에게 속삭이고 있는 것을 들었다. (whisper, each other)

➡ _____

(3) 새로운 것들을 찾아서 만드는 것은 흥미롭다.
(new things, interesting, find and create, it)

➡ _____

(4) 당신이 이메일을 보내는 것은 쉽다.
(it, send e-mails)

➡ _____

## 17 다음 어법상 틀린 문장의 개수는?

ⓐ I saw my brother singing a song.
ⓑ We heard Yena played the violin.
ⓒ She noticed him shaking his head.
ⓓ Jeniffer felt him came closer.
ⓔ It is good to volunteer at the community center.
ⓕ I think it's possible that a spacecraft can be controlled by a computer program.
ⓖ Is it safe swim in this river?

① 1개　② 2개　③ 3개　④ 4개　⑤ 5개

## [18~20] 다음 글을 읽고 물음에 답하시오.

Jina and Suhan are at the World AI Expo. They are entering the AI home.

Suhan: Look at this! It's a house of the future.
Jina: Let's go into the bedroom first. Look, there's a smart closet.
Suhan: I'm standing in front of this screen on the closet door and my clothes keep changing.
Jina: The screen suggests clothes ⓐthat suit the weather.
Suhan: ⓑThat's amazing! We no longer have to worry about dressing for the weather.
Jina: ⓒRight. Let's move on to the living room.

## 18 아래 보기에서 위 글의 밑줄 친 ⓐthat과 문법적 쓰임이 다른 것의 개수를 고르시오.

① I believe that you'll pass the exam.
② He is the only man that I love.
③ I'm glad that you like it.
④ I was so busy that I could not help him.
⑤ This is the pen that he bought yesterday.

① 1개　② 2개　③ 3개　④ 4개　⑤ 5개

## 19 위 글의 밑줄 친 ⓑThat이 가리키는 것을 본문에서 찾아 쓰시오.

➡ _____

## 20 위 글의 밑줄 친 ⓒRight과 바꿔 쓸 수 없는 말을 고르시오.

① You got it.
② You can say that again.
③ I agree with you.
④ That's all right.
⑤ You said it.

[21~22] 다음 글을 읽고 물음에 답하시오.

Suhan: Oh, I ___(A)___ this music speaker.

AI Speaker: I'm not just a music speaker. I can do more than you can imagine.

Jina: It's hard to believe that you can understand us. What can you do?

AI Speaker: How about watching a movie? I'll play one for you.

Suhan: Look, ⓐthat smart windows are getting darker. I feel ___(B)___ I'm in a movie theater.

Jina: What else can you do?

AI Speaker: I can beatbox, too. Here comes, "cats and boots and cats and boots."

Suhan: You're funny. Good job!

**21** 위 글의 빈칸 (A)와 (B)에 공통으로 들어갈 알맞은 말을 쓰시오.

➡ _____

**22** 위 글의 밑줄 친 ⓐ에서 어법상 틀린 부분을 찾아 고치시오.

_____ ➡ _____

[23~25] 다음 글을 읽고 물음에 답하시오.

Jina: Hurry! There's a smart car station outside! Let's go and ride in that red car.

Suhan: This car is so cool. Let's get in.

AI Car: Welcome. Are you ready to go?

Jina: Yes, what should we do now? It's my first time ⓐto ride in a smart car.

AI Car: You don't need to do anything. I will drive and take you to the next station.

Suhan: Watch out! I see a cat crossing the street.

AI Car: Don't worry. I have just sensed it. When I sense dangerous situations, I slow down or stop.

Jina: How can you do that?

AI Car: I'm a very intelligent robotic car. I know all about driving. ⓑ저는 제 지식과 경험을 바탕으로 위험을 예측할 수 있어요.

Suhan: How smart! You think and act like a person. You are really like a human.

**23** 위 글의 밑줄 친 ⓐto ride와 to부정사의 용법이 같은 것을 모두 고르시오.

① I don't know when to begin the work.
② Does she have a house to live in?
③ I had an opportunity to see him last year.
④ It is best not to make him angry.
⑤ You must work hard to succeed in the examination.

**24** 위 글의 밑줄 친 ⓑ의 우리말에 맞게 한 단어를 보충하여, 주어진 어휘를 알맞게 배열하시오.

> and / predict / experience / can / based / I / knowledge / danger

➡ _____
_____

**25** 위 글의 내용과 일치하지 않는 것은?

① 진아는 스마트 자동차 정류장에 가서 빨간 차를 타 보기를 원한다.
② 진아는 스마트 자동차에 처음 타 본다.
③ 인공 지능 자동차는 고양이가 길을 건너고 있는 것을 감지했다.
④ 인공 지능 자동차는 어떤 위험 상황을 감지하면 속도를 늦추거나 멈춘다.
⑤ 인공 지능 자동차는 자신의 학습 능력을 바탕으로 위험을 예측할 수 있다.

# Lesson 8

# The Unknown Hero

## 의사소통 기능

- 알고 있는지 묻기
  A: Do you know anything about King Sejong?
  B: No, I don't.

- 설명 요청하기
  A: Could you explain the rules of *bisachigi*?
  B: Each player throws a stone at another stone.

## 언어 형식

- 동사+목적어+to부정사
  Japanese officials **pressed** him **to build** Japanese houses.

- 과거분사
  Through his efforts, we now have Bukchon **filled** with its beautiful hanoks.

# Words & Expressions

## Key Words

- **affair** [əféər] 몡 사건, 일
- **alive** [əláiv] 혭 살아 있는
- **another** [ənʌ́ðər] 혭 또 다른, 다른 하나의
- **architecture** [á:rkrtèktʃər] 몡 건축
- **businessman** [bíznəsmæn] 몡 사업가
- **collect** [kəlékt] 동 모으다, 수집하다
- **community** [kəmjú:nəti] 몡 지역사회, 주민
- **dynasty** [dáinəsti] 몡 왕조, 시대
- **explain** [ikspléin] 동 설명하다
- **fan** [fæn] 몡 부채, 선풍기
- **fit** [fit] 동 적합하다
- **found** [faund] 동 설립하다
- **hometown** [hóumtaun] 몡 고향
- **independence** [ìndipéndəns] 몡 독립
- **interest** [íntərəst] 몡 관심, 흥미
- **land** [lænd] 몡 땅, 토지
- **meaning** [mí:niŋ] 몡 의미
- **modern** [mádərn] 혭 현대의
- **movement** [mú:vmənt] 몡 운동
- **nature** [néitʃər] 몡 자연
- **novel** [návəl] 몡 소설
- **official** [əfíʃəl] 몡 공무원, 당국

- **part** [pɑ:rt] 몡 부분, 일부
- **poem** [póuəm] 몡 시
- **pottery** [pátəri] 몡 도자기
- **press** [pres] 동 압박하다
- **property** [prápərti] 몡 재산
- **royal** [rɔ́iəl] 혭 왕의, 왕실의
- **rule** [ru:l] 동 통치하다 몡 규칙, 원칙
- **society** [səsáiəti] 몡 사회, 단체
- **Spanish** [spǽniʃ] 혭 스페인의
- **stone** [stoun] 몡 돌
- **store** [stɔ:r] 동 저장하다, 보관하다
- **suffer** [sʌ́fər] 동 고통 받다, 시달리다
- **support** [səpɔ́:rt] 동 지원하다
- **taste** [teist] 몡 맛, 취향
- **through** [θru:] 전 ~을 통하여
- **tourist** [túərist] 몡 여행객
- **tradition** [trədíʃən] 몡 전통
- **unknown** [ənnóun] 혭 알려지지 않은
- **village** [vílidʒ] 몡 마을
- **waste** [weist] 동 낭비하다
- **Western** [wéstərn] 혭 서양의

## Key Expressions

- **a lot** 많이
- **be famous for** ~으로 유명하다
- **be filled with** ~으로 가득하다
- **be in harmony with** ~와 조화를 이루다
- **be interested in** ~에 흥미를 가지다
- **be known as** ~으로 알려지다
- **care for** ~을 돌보다
- **fall off** (사업, 세력 등이) 쇠퇴하다

- **hundreds of** 수백의, 수많은
- **in danger** 위험에 빠진
- **in need** 어려움에 처한
- **in part** 부분적으로는
- **rise up** 일어서다
- **set foot** 발을 들여놓다
- **take care of** ~을 돌보다
- **thanks to** ~ 덕분에

## Word Power

※ 국가와 관련된 여러 가지 어휘

☐ **Korea**(한국) – **Korean**(한국어; 한국의)

☐ **China**(중국) – **Chinese**(중국어; 중국의)

☐ **Japan**(일본) – **Japanese**(일본어; 일본의)

☐ **Vietnam**(베트남) – **Vietnamese**(베트남어; 베트남의)

☐ **England**(영국) – **English**(영어; 영국의)

☐ **France**(프랑스) – **French**(프랑스어; 프랑스의)

☐ **Spain**(스페인) – **Spanish**(스페인어; 스페인의)

☐ **Germany**(독일) – **German**(독일어; 독일의)

## English Dictionary

☐ **alive** 살아 있는
→ not dead
죽지 않은

☐ **architecture** 건축, 건축학
→ the art of planning, designing and constructing buildings
건물을 계획하고, 설계하고 짓는 기술

☐ **businessman** 사업가, 실업가
→ a man who works in business
사업에 종사하는 사람

☐ **explain** 설명하다
→ to give details about something or describe it so that it can be understood
어떤 것이 이해될 수 있도록 그것에 관해 상세히 기술하거나 묘사하다

☐ **found** 설립하다
→ to get an institution, company, or organization started, often by providing the necessary money
종종 필요한 돈을 제공해서, 어떤 단체, 회사, 조직이 시작되게 하다

☐ **hometown** 고향
→ the place where someone lives or the town that they come from 어떤 사람이 살거나 그들이 출생한 장소

☐ **land** 토지, 땅
→ an area of ground, especially one that is used for a particular purpose such as farming or building
특히 농사나 건축과 같은 특별한 목적을 위해 사용되는 지역

☐ **nature** 자연
→ all the animals, plants, and other things in the world that are not made by people, and all the events and processes that are not caused by people
사람들에 의해 만들어지지 않은 모든 동물, 식물, 그리고 자연의 사물들과 사람들에 의해 일어나지 않은 모든 사건과 과정

☐ **novel** 소설
→ a long written story about imaginary people and events
상상의 사람들이나 사건들에 관해 쓰인 긴 이야기

☐ **property** 재산
→ all the things that belong to someone or something that belongs to them
어떤 사람에게 속해 있는 모든 것들 또는 그들에게 속해 있는 어떤 것

☐ **stone** 돌, 석조
→ a hard solid substance found in the ground and often used for building houses 땅에서 발견되며 종종 집들을 짓는 데 사용되는 딱딱한 고체의 물질

☐ **store** 저장하다
→ to put things in a container or other places and leave them there until they are needed
물건들을 용기나 다른 장소에 넣고 나중에 필요할 때까지 그곳에 두다

**서답형**

**01** 다음 〈보기〉와 같은 관계가 되도록 빈칸에 알맞은 말을 써 넣으시오.

┌─ 보기 ┤
> Korea – <u>Korean</u>

(1) China – _____
(2) Spain – _____

**중요**

**04** 다음 빈칸에 알맞은 단어를 고르시오.

> We _____ goods in a warehouse.

① save      ② waste
③ allow      ④ store
⑤ decide

**중요**

**02** 다음 중 밑줄 친 부분의 의미로 알맞지 않은 것은?

① My hobby is to <u>collect</u> stamps. (수집하다)
② Do you mean I didn't practice <u>enough</u>? (충분히)
③ Why <u>waste</u> money on clothes you don't need? (저축하다)
④ The colour and style is a matter of personal <u>taste</u>. (취향)
⑤ Be careful not to damage other people's <u>property</u>. (재산)

**05** 다음 중 밑줄 친 부분이 어색한 것을 고르시오.

① We don't know whether he's <u>alive</u> or dead.
② There is no <u>loyal</u> road to learning.
③ I need <u>another</u> computer.
④ The burglar got in <u>through</u> the window.
⑤ The company will <u>support</u> customers in Europe.

**서답형**

**06** 다음 주어진 우리말에 맞게 빈칸을 채우시오.

(1) 우리는 다른 사람들과 조화를 이루며 살 수 있기를 원한다.
➡ We want to be able to live in _____ with other people.

(2) 그녀의 발명 덕분에 많은 사람들이 더 나은 생활을 하고 있다.
➡ _____ to her invention, many people live better lives.

**03** 다음 빈칸에 알맞은 전치사로 짝지어진 것은?

> The place is famous _____ its beauty.
> I will take care _____ the patient.

① for – of      ② of – with
③ to – with      ④ in – of
⑤ at – from

**01** 다음 괄호 안의 단어를 문맥에 맞게 고쳐 쓰시오.

(1) Jackson is so _____ in fine arts.
(interest)

(2) We were all _____ at the news.
(amaze)

**02** 다음 두 문장이 같은 의미가 되도록 빈칸을 채우시오.

She moved back home to _____ for her elderly parents.
= She moved back home to _____ care of her elderly parents.

**03** 다음 우리말에 맞도록 빈칸에 알맞은 말을 쓰시오.

(1) 허리케인 시즌만 되면 수백 명의 사람들이 목숨을 잃습니다.
➡ _____ of people lose their lives every hurricane season.

(2) 네가 싫다. 그러니까 내 땅에 발을 들여놓지 마라.
➡ I hate you. So don't _____ foot on my property.

(3) 나는 새해가 행복으로 가득 차기를 바란다.
➡ I hope the New Year will be _____ with happiness!

**04** 다음 빈칸에 공통으로 들어갈 말을 쓰시오.

• Mr. Smith will _____ a company next year.
• Mike _____ something to eat in the room.

**05** 다음 빈칸에 들어갈 말을 〈보기〉에서 찾아 쓰시오.

보기
as    at    for    in

(1) _____ last we won the game.
(2) The children are _____ danger now.
(3) He can't wait _____ the party.
(4) Ann's father is known _____ a great scientist.

**06** 다음 우리말에 맞게 주어진 단어를 바르게 배열하시오.

(1) 올해에 기쁨이 가득하길 바란다.
(be, joy, hope, I, of, will, this, full, year)
➡ _____

(2) 나는 그 드레스를 입어 보았지만 맞지가 않았다.
(I, it, the, on, fit, tried, didn't, dress, but)
➡ _____

# Conversation

**①** 알고 있는지 묻기

> A: Do you know anything about King Sejong? (너는 세종대왕에 대해 아는 것이 있니?)
> B: No, I don't. (아니, 없어.)

■ 어떤 것에 관해 알고 있는지 물을 때는 'Do you know ~?'를 이용해 표현한다.

### 알고 있는지 묻기

- Do you know anything about that singer? (너는 저 가수에 대해 아는 것이 있니?)
- Do you know who Jane Goodall is? (Jane Goodall이 누구인지 알고 있니?)
- Do you know that Ann's father is an actor? (너는 Ann의 아버지가 배우라는 것을 알고 있니?)
- What do you know about BTS? (너는 BTS에 대해 무엇을 알고 있니?)
- Can you guess what it is? (이게 무엇인지 추측할 수 있겠니?)

### 알고 있는지 답하기

- No, I don't. (아니, 몰라.)
- Yes, I do. (응, 알아.)
- Yes, a little. (응, 조금 알아.)
- Sure, I do. They're famous singers. (물론, 알지. 그들은 유명한 가수야.)

A: Do you know anything about Changdeoggung? (너는 창덕궁에 대해 아는 것이 있니?)
B: Yes, a little. It's famous for its beautiful garden. (응, 조금. 그것은 아름다운 정원으로 유명해.)

### 핵심 Check

1. 다음 우리말과 일치하도록 빈칸에 알맞은 말을 쓰시오.

   A: _____ the musical *Cats*? (너는 뮤지컬 Cats에 대해 아는 것이 있니?)

   B: Yes. It's famous for the song "Memory". (응. 그것은 Memory라는 노래로 유명해.)

   A: _____ giraffes sleep only about 2 hours a day? (너는 기린이 하루에 겨우 2시간만 자는 것을 아니?)

   B: No, I don't. That's surprising! (아니, 몰라. 그거 참 놀랍구나!)

## ② 설명 요청하기

A: Could you explain the rules of *bisachigi*? (너 비사치기의 규칙에 대해 설명해 줄 수 있니?)
B: Each player throws a stone at another stone. (각 경기자가 돌을 던져 다른 돌에 맞히는 거야.)

■ 'Can[Could] you explain ~?'은 '너는 ~을 설명해 줄 수 있니?'라는 뜻으로, 상대방에게 설명을 요청할 때 쓰는 표현이다. 공손하게 표현할 때는 can 대신 could를 쓰며 explain 대신 tell을 쓸 수 있다.

### 설명 요청하기

• Can you explain this painting? (이 그림을 설명해 줄 수 있니?)

• Could you explain what this meaning is? (이 의미가 무엇인지 설명해 주실 수 있나요?)

• I don't get it. Can you explain why? (이해가 안 가요. 이유를 설명해 줄 수 있나요?)

• Can you tell me how to use the buttons? (버튼 사용법을 말해 줄 수 있니?)

• Can you show me how to use this machine? (어떻게 이 기계를 사용하는지 알려줄 수 있나요?)

### 핵심 Check

2. 다음 우리말과 일치하도록 빈칸에 알맞은 말을 쓰시오.

A: Can you _____ this poem? (이 시를 설명해 줄 수 있니?)

B: Sure. (물론이지.)

A: _____ you _____ this painting? (이 그림에 대해 설명을 해 주시겠습니까?)

B: Sure. It's *the Two Sisters* by Renoir. (물론이죠. 이 그림은 르누아르의 "두 자매"예요.)

3. 다음 우리말과 일치하도록 주어진 단어를 배열하여 문장을 만드시오.

A: _____ (you, your, to, plan, save, money, could, explain) (돈을 절약할 너의 계획에 대해 설명해 줄 수 있니?)

B: I won't waste my money on snacks. (간식에 돈을 낭비하지 않을 거야.)

### Listen & Speak 1 B-1

B: ❶Do you know anything about Korean history?

G: ❷I don't know much about it but I'm interested in it.

B: ❸Can you help me with my history homework?

G: Sure. ❹No problem.

B: 너는 한국 역사에 대해 아는 것이 있니?

G: 그것에 대해 많이 알지는 못하지만, 관심은 있어.

B: 내 역사 숙제를 도와 줄 수 있니?

G: 물론이지. 문제없어.

❶ Do you know anything about ∼?은 어떤 것에 대해 알고 있는지 묻는 표현이다.

❷ it=Korean history / be interested in: ∼에 관심이 있다

❸ help A with ∼: A가 ∼하는 것을 돕다

❹ No problem.: 문제없어. (상대방의 제안에 승낙하는 표현)

**Check(√) True or False**

(1) The boy knows much about Korean history.   T ☐ F ☐

(2) The girl will help the boy with his history homework.   T ☐ F ☐

### Wrap Up

B: Do you know anything about a *dol* party?

G: Yes. ❶It's the birthday party for a one-year-old baby.

B: ❷Could you tell me more about it?

G: ❸Well, the family members get together for the party, and the birthday baby wears a *hanbok*.

B: ❹That sounds interesting.

G: ❺The family members share food and wish for a long life for the baby. It's a Korean tradition.

B: 넌 돌잔치에 대해 아는 것이 있니?

G: 응. 그건 한 살 먹은 아기를 위한 생일잔치야.

B: 그것에 대해 더 말해 줄 수 있니?

G: 음. 그 잔치를 위해 가족들이 함께 모이고 생일을 맞은 아기는 한복을 입어.

B: 그거 재미있구나.

G: 가족들은 음식을 함께 나누어 먹고 아기가 오래 살기를 바라. 그건 한국의 전통이야.

❶ a one-year-old baby: 한 살 먹은 아기

❷ Could you tell me more about it?: 그것에 대해 더 말해 줄 수 있니? (상대방에게 설명을 요청하는 표현이다.)

❸ get together: 함께 모이다

❹ That은 지시대명사로 앞 문장의 내용을 가리킨다.

❺ share food: 음식을 나누어 먹다 wish for: ∼을 바라다

**Check(√) True or False**

(3) The *dol* party is the birthday party for a one-year-old baby.   T ☐ F ☐

(4) The boy has attended the *dol* party before.   T ☐ F ☐

### Listen & Speak 1 B-3

B: Do you know anything about this writer?

G: Yes. ❶I've read some of his novels. Why?

B: ❷How were they? ❸I'm thinking of buying his books.

G: ❹You shouldn't. ❺I didn't enjoy his books that much.

❶ I've read=I have read 'have+p.p.'의 현재완료 구문이다.

❷ they=his novels

❸ think of ~ing: ~할 생각이다

❹ shouldn't=should not: 금지를 나타낸다.

❺ that much: 그렇게 많이 that은 지시부사로 쓰여 '그렇게, 그만큼'의 뜻을 나타낸다.

### Listen & Speak 2 B-1

G: ❶Can you explain this poem?

B: Sure. ❷It was written by Yun Dongju.

G: What's it about?

B: It's about him missing his hometown.

❶ Can you explain ~?은 어떤 것에 대해 설명을 요청하는 표현이다. Can 대신에 Could를 쓰면 더 정중한 요청이 된다.

❷ It=this poem / was written은 과거형 수동태이다.

### Listen & Speak 2 B-2

B: ❶Could you explain what Helping Hands is?

G: ❷It's a volunteer group in our community.

B: Could you tell me more about it?

G: ❸Well, they take care of children in need.

❶ what Helping Hands is는 간접의문문으로 explain의 목적어이다.

❷ community: 지역 사회

❸ take care of: ~을 돌보다 in need: 어려움에 처한

### Listen & Speak 2 C

A: ❶Could you explain your plan to save money?

B: ❷I won't waste my money on snacks.

❶ to save money는 plan을 수식하는 형용사적 용법이다.

❷ waste one's money on: ~에 돈을 낭비하다

### Real-Life Zone

G: What are *hanoks*? Do you know anything about them?

M: *Hanoks* are traditional Korean houses. ❶They are designed to be in harmony with nature.

G: ❷Could you explain a little more about them?

M: *Hanoks* are cool in the summer and warm in the winter.

W: ❸That sounds interesting. Where can I see these traditional houses?

M: There's a *hanok* village near here.

G: ❹How about going there and seeing the *hanoks*?

W: Good idea! ❺How can we get there?

M: ❻You can take Bus Number 5 over there at the bus stop.

❶ be designed to ~: ~하도록 설계되다 be in harmony with: ~와 조화를 이루다

❷ a little more: 좀 더 많이

❸ That은 지시대명사로 앞 문장의 내용을 가리킨다.

❹ How about ~ing?: ~하는 게 어때?

❺ get there=get to the *hanok* village

❻ over there at the bus stop: 저기 버스 정류장에서

● 다음 우리말과 일치하도록 빈칸에 알맞은 말을 쓰시오.

### Listen & Speak 1 B-2

G: _____ you know _____ about Changdeokgung?

B: Yes, a _____ . It's _____ _____ its beautiful garden.

G: I'm _____ _____ go there _____ my Chinese friend.

B: I _____ you'll _____ it.

### Listen & Speak 2 A

B: Could you _____ this _____?

W: Sure. It's the *Two Sisters* by Renoir. He _____ it in 1881.

### Listen & Speak 2 B-1

1. G: Can you _____ this poem?

   B: Sure. It _____ _____ by Yun Dongju.

   G: What's it _____?

   B: It's _____ him _____ his hometown.

2. B: Could you _____ what Helping Hands is?

   G: It's a _____ _____ in our community.

   B: Could you _____ me _____ about it?

   G: Well, they _____ _____ of children in need.

### Listen & Speak 2 C

A: _____ you _____ your plan to save money?

B: I won't _____ my money _____ snacks.

### Real-Life Zone A

G: _____ are *hanoks*? Do you know _____ _____ them?

M: *Hanoks* are traditional _____ _____. They _____ _____ to be _____ _____ with nature.

G: Could you explain _____ _____ more about them?

M: *Hanoks* are _____ in the summer and _____ in the winter.

해석

G: 너는 창덕궁에 대해 아는 것이 있니?
B: 응, 조금. 그것은 아름다운 정원으로 유명해.
G: 난 내 중국인 친구와 함께 그곳에 갈 거야.
B: 그곳이 마음에 들 거야.

B: 이 그림에 대해 설명을 해 주시겠습니까?
W: 물론이죠. 이 그림은 르누아루의 "두 자매"예요. 그는 1881년에 이 그림을 그렸어요.

1. G: 이 시를 설명해 줄 수 있니?
   B: 그럼. 그것은 윤동주에 의해 씌어졌어.
   G: 그것은 무엇에 관한 거니?
   B: 그것은 고향을 그리워하는 작가에 관한 거야.
2. B: '도움의 손길'이 무엇인지 설명해 줄 수 있니?
   G: 그것은 우리 지역 사회에 있는 자원봉사 단체야.
   B: 그것에 관해 더 말해 줄 수 있니?
   G: 음, 그들은 어려움에 처한 어린이들을 돌봐.

A: 돈을 절약할 너의 계획에 대해 설명해 줄 수 있니?
B: 간식에 돈을 낭비하지 않을 거야.

G: 한옥은 무엇이에요? 한옥에 대해 아는 것이 있으세요?
M: 한옥은 전통적인 한국 가옥이에요. 그것들은 자연과 조화를 이루도록 설계되었어요.
G: 그것들에 대해 좀 더 설명하실 수 있어요?
M: 한옥은 여름에는 시원하고 겨울에는 따뜻해요.

W: That _____ interesting. _____ can I _____ these traditional houses?

M: There's a *hanok* village _____ _____.

G: How _____ _____ there and _____ the *hanoks*?

W: Good _____! _____ can we _____ there?

M: You can _____ Bus Number 5 _____ _____ at the bus stop.

### Real-Life Zone B

1. A: Do you _____ _____ about the Great Wall of China?

   B: Yes. It is one of the _____ _____ in the world.

   A: Can you explain _____ it is _____?

   B: It's _____ it is the _____ _____ in the world.

2. A: Do you know anything _____ the _____ *The Old Man and the Sea*?

   B: Yes. It is a _____ _____ written by Ernest Hemingway.

   A: Can you _____ _____ it is famous?

   B: It's because Hemingway _____ the Pulitzer Prize in 1953 _____ this novel.

### Real-Life Zone B e.g.

A: Do you _____ _____ about the Eiffel Tower?

B: Yes. It _____ _____ in 1889 by Gustave Eiffel.

A: Can you _____ _____ it is famous?

B: _____ _____ it was the _____ _____ in the world at that time.

### Wrap Up

B: Do you _____ _____ about a *dol* party?

G: Yes. It's the _____ party for a one-year-old baby.

B: Could you _____ me _____ about it?

G: Well, the family members _____ _____ for the party, and the birthday baby _____ a *hanbok*.

B: That sounds _____.

G: The family members _____ _____ and _____ _____ a long life for the baby. It's a _____ _____.

W: 그거 재미있네요. 이 전통 가옥을 어디에서 볼 수 있어요?

M: 이 근처에 한옥 마을이 있어요.

G: 거기 가서 한옥들을 보는 게 어때요?

W: 좋은 생각이구나! 그곳에 어떻게 갈 수 있죠?

M: 저기 버스 정류장에서 5번 버스를 타시면 돼요.

1. A: 중국의 만리장성에 대해 아는 것이 있나요?

   B: 네. 그것은 세계에서 멋진 광경들 중의 하나예요.

   A: 그것이 왜 유명한지 설명해 줄 수 있나요?

   B: 세계에서 가장 긴 성벽이기 때문이죠.

2. A: '노인과 바다'라는 소설에 대해 아는 것이 있나요?

   B: 네. 그것은 어니스트 헤밍웨이가 쓴 소설이에요.

   A: 그것이 왜 유명한지 설명해 줄 수 있나요?

   B: 헤밍웨이가 이 책으로 1953년 풀리쳐상을 받았기 때문이죠.

A: 너는 에펠탑에 대해 아는 것이 있니?

B: 응. 그것은 1889년에 Gustave Eiffel에 의해 세워졌어.

A: 그것이 왜 유명한지 설명할 수 있니?

B: 그것은 그 당시 그 탑이 세계에서 가장 높은 탑이었기 때문이야.

B: 넌 돌잔치에 대해 아는 것이 있니?

G: 응. 그건 한 살 먹은 아기를 위한 생일잔치야.

B: 그것에 대해 더 말해 줄 수 있니?

G: 음, 그 잔치를 위해 가족들이 함께 모이고 생일을 맞은 아기는 한복을 입어.

B: 그거 재미있구나.

G: 가족들은 음식을 함께 나누어 먹고 아기가 오래 살기를 바라. 그건 한국의 전통이야.

**01** 다음 대화의 빈칸에 알맞은 것을 고르시오.

> B: _____
>
> G: I don't know much about it but I'm interested in it.
>
> B: Can you help me with my history homework?
>
> G: Sure. No problem.

① Are you interested in Korean history?

② What do you know about Korean history?

③ Have you ever studied Korean history?

④ Do you know anything about Korean history?

⑤ May I help you with your history homework?

**02** 다음 대화의 순서를 바르게 배열하시오.

> (A) I'm going to go there with my Chinese friend.
>
> (B) Yes, a little. It's famous for its beautiful garden.
>
> (C) Do you know anything about Changdeokgung?
>
> (D) I think you'll like it.

➡ _____

**03** 다음 대화의 밑줄 친 부분의 의도로 알맞은 것을 고르시오.

> B: <u>Could you explain what Helping Hands is?</u>
>
> G: It's a volunteer group in our community.
>
> B: Could you tell me more about it?
>
> G: Well, they take care of children in need.

① 안부 묻기      ② 설명 요청하기

③ 충고 구하기      ④ 직업 묻기

⑤ 취미 말하기

[01~03] 다음 대화를 읽고 물음에 답하시오.

> G: (A) _____
> B: Sure. It (B) (wrote / was written) by Yun Dongju.
> G: What's it about?
> B: It's about him missing his hometown.

**01** 위 대화의 빈칸 (A)에 알맞은 말을 고르시오.

① Who wrote this poem?
② Can you explain this poem?
③ Why do you like this poem?
④ Do you like poems?
⑤ Do you know that Yun Donju wrote many poems?

**02** 위 대화의 괄호 (B)에 알맞은 것을 고르시오.

➡ _____

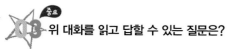

위 대화를 읽고 답할 수 있는 질문은?

① Does the girl like poems?
② What is the title of this poem?
③ Does the boy like Yun Dongju?
④ What is this poem about?
⑤ Why is the girl interested in this poem?

**04** 다음 중 짝지어진 대화가 어색한 것은?

① A: Could you explain the rules of *bisachigi*?
　 B: Sure. Each player throws a stone at another stone.
② A: How was the English test today?
　 B: I didn't do well. I was sleepy during the test.
③ A: Do you know anything about your sister's interest?
　 B: Yes. She's into making pottery.
④ A: Do you know anything about King Sejong?
　 B: No, I don't. He is the king who invented Hangeul.
⑤ A: How do you like this restaurant?
　 B: The food is okay, but the service is terrible.

 다음 대화의 순서를 바르게 배열한 것을 고르시오.

> (A) It's because it was the tallest tower in the world at that time.
> (B) Can you explain why it is famous?
> (C) Do you know anything about the Eiffel Tower?
> (D) Yes. It was built in 1889 by Gustave Eiffel.

① (B) - (A) - (C) - (D)
② (B) - (C) - (A) - (D)
③ (C) - (A) - (B) - (D)
④ (C) - (B) - (A) - (D)
⑤ (C) - (D) - (B) - (A)

[06~09] 다음 대화를 읽고 물음에 답하시오.

B: Do you know anything about a *dol* party?
G: Yes. It's the birthday party for a one-year-old baby.
B: (A) _____
G: Well, the family members get together for the party, and the birthday baby wears a *hanbok*.
B: (B)That sounds interesting.
G: The family members (C)_____ food and wish for a long life for the baby. It's a Korean tradition.

**06** 위 대화의 빈칸 (A)에 알맞은 것은?

① Could you tell me more about it?
② Why do they have a *dol* party?
③ Do your family members get together often?
④ Shall I tell you about the *dol* party?
⑤ When do your family members get together?

서답형
**07** 위 대화의 밑줄 친 (B)가 가리키는 것을 우리말로 쓰시오.

➡ _____

서답형
**08** 위 대화의 빈칸 (C)에 다음 정의에 해당하는 단어를 써 넣으시오.

to have something, use it, or occupy it with another person

➡ _____

중요
**09** 위 대화의 내용으로 보아 알 수 없는 것은?

① The boy knows about a *dol* party.
② A *dol* party is the birthday party for a one-year-old baby.
③ The birthday baby wears a hanbok at a *dol* party.
④ The boy wants to attend a *dol* party.
⑤ A *dol* party is a Korean tradition.

[10~12] 다음 대화를 읽고 물음에 답하시오.

A: Do you know anything about the novel *The Old Man and the Sea*?
B: Yes. It is a short novel (A)write by Ernest Hemingway.
A: Can you (B)_____ why it is famous?
B: It's because Hemingway won the Pulitzer Prize in 1953 for this novel.

서답형
**10** 위 대화의 밑줄 친 (A)를 알맞은 형으로 고치시오.

➡ _____

중요
**11** 위 대화의 빈칸 (B)에 알맞은 것은?

① know          ② explain
③ think          ④ imagine
⑤ suggest

서답형
**12** What did Hemingway win in 1953? Answer in English.

➡ _____

[01~05] 다음 대화를 읽고 물음에 답하시오.

> G: What are *hanoks*? Do you know anything about them?
>
> M: *Hanoks* are traditional Korean houses. They are designed to be (A)_____ harmony with nature.
>
> G: Could you explain a little more about them?
>
> M: *Hanoks* are (B)_____ in the summer and warm in the winter.
>
> G: That sounds (C)_____ (interest). Where can I see these traditional houses?
>
> M: There's a *hanok* village near here.
>
> G: (D)How about going there and seeing the *hanoks*?
>
> W: Good idea! (E)How can we get there?
>
> M: You can take Bus Number 5 over there at the bus stop.

**01** 위 대화의 빈칸 (A)에 알맞은 전치사를 쓰시오.

➡ _____

**02** 위 대화의 빈칸 (B)에 흐름상 알맞은 말을 쓰시오.

➡ _____

**03** 빈칸 (C)를 괄호 안에 주어진 단어를 이용하여 채우시오.

➡ _____

**04** 위 대화의 밑줄 친 (D)와 같은 뜻이 되도록 다음 문장의 빈칸에 알맞은 말을 쓰시오.

➡ _____ we go there and see the *hanoks*?

**05** 위 대화의 밑줄 친 (E)와 같은 뜻이 되도록 다음 문장의 빈칸에 알맞은 말을 쓰시오.

➡ Do you know _____ _____ get there?

[06~07] 다음 대화를 읽고 물음에 답하시오.

> A: Do you know anything about the Great Wall of China?
>
> B: Yes. (A)It is one of the greatest sight in the world.
>
> A: Can you explain (B)_____ it is famous?
>
> B: It's (C)_____ it is the longest wall in the world.

**06** 위 대화의 밑줄 친 (A)에서 어법상 어색한 것을 고치시오.

_____ ➡ _____

**07** 위 대화의 빈칸 (B)와 (C)에 각각 알맞은 말을 쓰시오.

(B) _____ (C) _____

# Grammar

## ① 목적격보어로 to부정사를 취하는 동사

> • Japanese officials **pressed** him to **build** Japanese houses.
> 일본인 관리들은 그에게 일본식 가옥을 지으라고 압박했다.
> • The woman **asked** me **to wait** for her at the hall.
> 그 여인은 내게 홀에서 자기를 기다리라고 요청했다.

- 형태: want/ask/tell/advise/order 등 + 목적어 + to부정사
- 의미: ~가 …하기를 바라다, ~에게 …하기를 요청하다, ~에게 …하라고 말하다, ~에게 …하라고 충고하다, ~에게 …하라고 명령하다

  • I **want** you **to finish** your homework first. 나는 네가 숙제를 먼저 끝내길 원해.

  • Mom **told** me **to put** out the trash. 엄마는 나에게 쓰레기를 내놓으라고 말씀하셨다.

- to부정사를 목적격보어로 취하는 동사에는 want, ask, tell 외에도 advise, allow, beg, cause, enable, encourage, expect, force, get, order, persuade, press 등이 있다.

  • They **advised** him **to leave** the place as soon as possible.
  그들은 그에게 가능한 한 빨리 그곳을 떠나라고 조언했다.

- to부정사의 부정형은 'not[never]+to 동사원형'이다.

  • She **asked** me **not to say** anything. 그녀는 나에게 아무 말도 하지 말라고 요청했다.

  • The doctor **ordered** me **not to drink** alcohol. 의사는 나에게 술을 마시지 말라고 명령했다.

### 핵심 Check

**1.** 다음 괄호 안에서 알맞은 것을 고르시오.

(1) She wanted me (to buy / buy) her a bag.

(2) I expected him (to be / being) a soccer player.

(3) He asked them (be / to be) quiet.

**2.** 다음 우리말과 일치하도록 빈칸에 알맞은 말을 쓰시오. (철자가 주어진 것도 있음.)

(1) 우리는 그녀가 늦을 것이라고 예상했다.

➡ We _____ her _____ _____ late.

(2) 갑작스런 굉음 때문에 나는 펄쩍 뛰었다.

➡ A sudden noise c_____ me _____ j_____.

(3) 그들은 그에게 서류에 서명하도록 강요했다.

➡ They f_____ him _____ _____ the paper.

## ② 명사를 수식하는 현재분사와 과거분사

- Jeong Segwon wanted to help the **suffering** people.
  정세권은 고통 받는 사람들을 돕기를 원했다.
- Through his efforts, we now have Buckchon **filled** with its beautiful *hanoks*.
  그의 노력으로 우리에게는 지금 아름다운 한옥으로 가득 차 있는 북촌이 있다.

■ 분사는 Ving 형태를 취하는 **현재분사**와, p.p. 형태를 취하는 **과거분사**로 나뉘며, 모두 명사를 수식하거나 설명하는 형용사 역할을 한다. **현재분사**는 '~하는'이라는 의미로 **능동**이나 **진행**의 의미를 나타내고, **과거분사**는 '~된'이라는 의미로 **수동**이나 **완료**의 의미를 나타낸다.

- I saw a **crying** baby. 나는 우는 아기를 봤어.
- Look at the water **polluted** by the waste. 쓰레기로 오염된 물을 보세요.

■ 분사가 단독으로 명사를 수식할 때에는 일반적으로 명사 앞에서 수식하지만, 다른 어구와 함께 명사를 수식할 때에는 명사 뒤에서 수식한다.

- Look at the **laughing** children. 웃고 있는 아이들을 보아라.
- People **living** in the village felt happy. 그 마을에 사는 사람들은 행복했다.
- I found a **broken** vase. 나는 깨진 꽃병을 발견했다.
- Kevin found a letter **written** on his notebook. Kevin은 자신의 공책 위에 쓰여진 편지를 발견했다.

■ **have[get]+목적어+과거분사**', '**지각동사+목적어+과거분사**'는 목적어와 목적격보어의 관계가 수동인 경우 쓰인다.

- Jason **had** the man **repair** his car. Jason은 그 남자가 자신의 차를 수리하게 했다.
  = Jason **had** his car **repaired** by the man. Jason은 그의 차가 그 남자에 의해 수리되게 했다.

■ 'Ving'로 형태가 같은 현재분사와 동명사의 차이를 구별하자. 현재분사는 '~하는', '~하는 중인'이라고 해석되고, 동명사는 '~하는 것'이라고 해석되거나 'V를 용도로 하는 명사'로 해석된다.

- There is a **sleeping** baby. [현재분사] 잠자는 아기가 있다.
- Did you find your **sleeping** bag? [동명사] 너의 침낭을 찾았니? (잠자는 데 쓰이는 가방 – 침낭)

### 핵심 Check

**3.** 다음 주어진 동사를 어법에 맞게 빈칸에 쓰시오.

(1) 너는 그 노래 부르는 소녀를 보았니?

➡ Did you see the _____ girl? (sing)

(2) 나는 John에 의해 쓰여진 책을 읽었어.

➡ I read the book _____ by John. (write)

(3) 너는 무언가를 쓰고 있는 그 소녀를 아니?

➡ Do you know the girl _____ something? (write)

**01** 다음 빈칸에 알맞은 것은?

> I asked him _____ off the TV.

① turn      ② turns      ③ turned

④ turning      ⑤ to turn

**02** 다음 괄호 안에서 알맞은 것을 고르시오.

(1) The girl (eating / eaten) cookies is Susan.

(2) We want to find the treasure (hiding / hidden) in the ocean.

(3) The two boys (talking / talked) to each other are Tom and Sam.

(4) All the people (inviting / invited) to the party are enjoying themselves.

**03** 다음 문장에서 어법상 <u>어색한</u> 것을 찾아 바르게 고쳐 다시 쓰시오.

(1) I want you clean the windows.

➡ _____

(2) Timothy got an email sending by a stranger this morning.

➡ _____

(3) Who are the boys played soccer on the ground?

➡ _____

(4) Tell her buying a comfortable pair of shoes!

➡ _____

**04** 다음 우리말에 맞게 주어진 어구를 바르게 배열하시오.

(1) Jack은 그의 아내에게 진주로 만든 목걸이를 주었다.
(Jack, pearls, his wife, made, gave, a, necklace, of)

➡ _____

(2) 칼로 소고기 샌드위치를 자르고 있는 남자는 누구니? (the beef sandwiches, knife, the man, a, who, cutting, is, with)

➡ _____

(3) Mike는 그녀에게 일찍 잠자리에 들라고 충고했다. (Mike, go, her, advised, early, to, to, bed)

➡ _____

**01** 다음 중 빈칸에 들어갈 말로 가장 적절한 것은?

My dad had his shoes _____.

① to shine
② shining
③ shined
④ to shining
⑤ shine

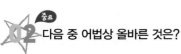

**02** 다음 중 어법상 올바른 것은?

① Do you want me clean your house for you?
② He told Perry putting on a yellow shirt.
③ She didn't allow us to play the piano.
④ The doctor advised Ted stopped smoking.
⑤ Ms. Green asked him carried the boxes.

**03** 다음 밑줄 친 부분의 쓰임이 나머지 넷과 다른 하나는?

① The girl walking in the park is my sister.
② Do you know the woman talking to Tom?
③ The alarm clock ringing noisily is Jason's.
④ The boy singing on the stage is my best friend.
⑤ I started taking the chess class on weekends.

**04** 다음 빈칸에 알맞은 말이 바르게 짝지어진 것은?

• Who is the girl _____ beside the piano?
• Frank expected Jane _____ him.

① singing – helped
② singing – to help
③ sang – helped
④ sang – to help
⑤ sings – helping

**05** 다음 빈칸에 공통으로 들어갈 수 있는 것을 고르시오.

• Kirk _____ Jenny to take part in the party.
• Harold _____ to know what was in the box.

① asked
② wanted
③ invited
④ told
⑤ advised

**06** 다음 괄호 안에서 알맞은 말을 고르시오.

(1) Who is the girl (carries / carrying) a basket?
(2) I got an e-mail (written / writing) in Chinese.
(3) Look at the (cat sleeping / sleeping cat).

**07** 다음 빈칸에 들어갈 말로 알맞게 짝지어진 것은?

> • Kate warned her son _____ fast food.
> • Jerome asked me _____ the TV volume.

① not to eat – to turn down
② not eating – to turn down
③ to not eat – turning down
④ not eating – turning down
⑤ not eat – turn down

 다음 밑줄 친 부분이 어법상 어색한 것을 고르시오.

① The boy played soccer on the ground is my brother.
② The man driving the red car almost hit my sister.
③ He bought a cell phone made in Korea.
④ Who is the boy drinking milk at the table?
⑤ This is the picture painted by Gogh.

**서답형**
**09** 주어진 동사를 어법에 맞게 빈칸에 쓰시오.

(1) My best friend Bill often asks me _____ him. (help)
(2) My dad doesn't allow me _____ out at night. (go)
(3) Marianne ordered him _____ with her. (stay)
(4) The manager warned him _____ any pictures here. (take, not)

**서답형**
**10** 다음 문장에서 어법상 어색한 부분을 바르게 고쳐 쓰시오.

(1) I know the boy kick a ball there.
　_____ ➡ _____
(2) Who is the playing badminton man?
　_____ ➡ _____
(3) The baby crying is Kate's son.
　_____ ➡ _____

 다음 빈칸에 들어갈 괄호 안에 주어진 동사의 형태가 다른 하나는?

① I want you _____ the dishes. (wash)
② Mom made me _____ playing the computer games. (stop)
③ They got him _____ a new contract. (sign)
④ She asked him _____ to the movies together. (go)
⑤ He didn't allow me _____ camping. (go)

**12** 다음 밑줄 친 부분의 쓰임이 어색한 것은?

① I'm reading a play written by Shakespeare.
② You can see many people dancing to the music.
③ Who is the man playing the piano?
④ I found a cat lie in the sun.
⑤ Do you know the boy sitting next to David?

**중요**
다음 중 어법상 어색한 부분을 찾아 바르게 고친 것은?

> Mom wants Tom come home by 5:30.

① wants → want　② Tom → Tom's
③ come → to come　④ home → to home
⑤ by → to

**14** 다음 빈칸에 들어갈 말이 바르게 짝지어진 것은?

> • The man _____ the phone is my uncle.
> • The boys _____ to dinner were two hours late.

① answering – inviting
② answers – invited
③ answering – invited
④ answers – inviting
⑤ answering – to invite

**15** 다음 중 어법상 올바르지 <u>않은</u> 것은?

① They asked me to stay there.
② Susan, do you want me to dance?
③ I made her clean her room.
④ Tell her to come to my office.
⑤ Dad didn't allow me going to the dance party.

**서답형**
**16** 동사 write를 어법에 맞게 빈칸에 쓰시오.

> • My cousin is the boy _____ something on his notebook.
> • Did you see the letter _____ in Korean?

➡ _____, _____

**17** 다음 문장의 빈칸에 알맞지 <u>않은</u> 것은?

> Yuna _____ him to follow her advice.

① made           ② wanted
③ asked          ④ expected
⑤ advised

**18** 다음 우리말에 맞게 영작한 것을 고르시오.

> 너는 태권도를 배우고 있는 저 여자아이를 아니?

① Do you know that girl learn *taekwondo*?
② Do you know that girl learns *taekwondo*?
③ Do you know that girl to learn *taekwondo*?
④ Do you know that girl learning *taekwondo*?
⑤ Do you know that girl to learning *taekwondo*?

**서답형**
**19** 주어진 어구를 활용하여 다음 우리말을 영어로 쓰시오.

(1) 나의 부모님은 항상 내게 학교에서 최선을 다하라고 말씀하신다. (always, do, best, in school)
➡ _____

(2) 건강했기 때문에 그는 그 계획을 수행할 수 있었다. (good health, carry out, enable)
➡ _____

**20** 다음 밑줄 친 부분의 쓰임이 나머지와 <u>다른</u> 것은?

① Look at the woman <u>walking</u> down the road.
② Do you know the boy <u>wearing</u> a mask?
③ Jenny loves <u>going</u> hiking.
④ My brother is <u>washing</u> the dishes.
⑤ The girls <u>dancing</u> to the music are my friends.

**01** 다음 문장에서 어법상 <u>어색한</u> 부분을 바르게 고쳐 쓰시오.

(1) She asked her brother helping her with her homework.

＿＿＿＿＿＿＿＿＿ ➡ ＿＿＿＿＿＿＿＿＿

(2) Jim wanted her go shopping with him.

＿＿＿＿＿＿＿＿＿ ➡ ＿＿＿＿＿＿＿＿＿

(3) They advised him left the place as soon as possible.

＿＿＿＿＿＿＿＿＿ ➡ ＿＿＿＿＿＿＿＿＿

(4) I watched the excited bowling game on TV.

＿＿＿＿＿＿＿＿＿ ➡ ＿＿＿＿＿＿＿＿＿

(5) Who is the boy throws a ball?

＿＿＿＿＿＿＿＿＿ ➡ ＿＿＿＿＿＿＿＿＿

(6) Nancy had his husband to repair their car.

＿＿＿＿＿＿＿＿＿ ➡ ＿＿＿＿＿＿＿＿＿

**02** 주어진 어휘를 어법에 맞게 빈칸에 쓰시오.

(1) The name of a fruit ＿＿＿＿＿＿ with "m" is melon. (begin)

(2) It looks like a person ＿＿＿＿＿＿ with open arms. (dance)

(3) The woman ＿＿＿＿＿＿ at the news started to cry. (frighten)

(4) They are the photos ＿＿＿＿＿＿ there. (take)

**03** 다음 괄호 안에서 알맞은 것을 고르시오.

(1) He told me (came / to come) home before 9 o'clock.

(2) Harry wanted me (doing / to do) it at once.

(3) My mom (expects / hopes) me to be a teacher.

(4) She allowed her daughter (go / to go) to the K-pop concert.

**04** 주어진 어휘를 이용하여 다음 우리말을 영작하시오.

(1) 선생님은 내게 문을 닫아달라고 부탁하셨다. (the teacher, ask, the door)

➡ ＿＿＿＿＿＿＿＿＿＿＿＿＿＿＿＿

(2) 엄마는 내게 그 개를 산책시키라고 말씀하셨다. (mom, walk the dog)

➡ ＿＿＿＿＿＿＿＿＿＿＿＿＿＿＿＿

(3) Kate는 눈으로 덮인 산을 올라갔다. (climb, cover)

➡ ＿＿＿＿＿＿＿＿＿＿＿＿＿＿＿＿

(4) 언제 깨진 창문을 고칠 거예요? (going, fix, break)

➡ ＿＿＿＿＿＿＿＿＿＿＿＿＿＿＿＿

(5) Mariko는 공원에서 그녀의 딸이 놀고 있는 것을 바라보았다. (look, play)

➡ ＿＿＿＿＿＿＿＿＿＿＿＿＿＿＿＿

**05** 다음 두 문장을 같은 뜻을 갖는 한 문장으로 바꿔 쓰시오.

(1) • The business woman is Sophie.
 • She is running a big company.

➡ _____

_____

(2) • There is a bridge in our village.
 • It was built long time ago.

➡ _____

**06** 다음 상황에 알맞은 말을 어법에 맞게 빈칸에 쓰시오.

(1) The driver drove the car very fast. He said to his driver, "Don't drive so fast."

➡ He ordered his driver _____

_____ _____ _____ _____ .

(2) Paul is good at playing the guitar. So Bella said to him, "Will you play the piano for us?"

➡ Bella asked Paul _____ _____

_____ _____ _____ _____ .

**07** 다음 주어진 단어를 어법에 맞게 빈칸에 쓰시오.

| hit / excite / play / amaze / repair |

(1) The girl _____ badminton is my sister.

(2) I have an _____ story to tell you.

(3) We had the car _____ by Potter and Parker.

(4) Jina is an _____ basketball player.

(5) Did you see the building _____ by a dump truck?

**08** 다음 괄호 안에 주어진 단어를 사용해 다음을 영작하시오.

(1) 그 여자는 그 남자에게 자기의 가방을 들어달라고 요청했다. (ask, carry)

➡ _____

(2) Emma는 나에게 내일까지 기다리라고 충고했다. (advise, till)

➡ _____

(3) Peter는 Sylvia에게 자기와 함께 춤을 추자고 말했다. (tell, dance)

➡ _____

(4) 그들은 그가 축제에 참가할 것으로 기대했다. (expect, participate, the festival)

➡ _____

(5) 좋은 건강이 그가 그 계획을 마칠 수 있도록 했다. (good, enable, finish)

➡ _____

**09** 다음 우리말의 의미에 맞게 빈칸에 알맞은 말을 쓰시오.

(1) 그 어린 주자들은 응원하는 군중 옆을 지나갔다.

➡ The young runners passed by the _____ crowd.

(2) 그 요리사는 얇게 잘린 양파를 차가운 물에 넣었다.

➡ The chef put the _____ onions in cold water.

**10** 다음 밑줄 친 부분이 동명사인지 현재분사인지 구별하고, 그 이유를 서술하시오.

| (1) They are <u>waiting</u> for you. |
| (2) The <u>waiting</u> room is full of people. |

(1) _____ ➡ 이유: _____

(2) _____ ➡ 이유: _____

_____

_____

## The King of Architecture in Gyeongseong

Have you been to Bukchon? There is a beautiful *hanok* village in
<u>have been to</u>: ~에 가 본 적이 있다(경험을 나타내는 현재완료)
Bukchon. It is popular with tourists <u>who</u> <u>want to see</u> Korea's past.
=The beautiful *hanok* village    주격 관계대명사    want의 목적어

However, not many people know <u>that</u> Bukchon <u>was created</u> <u>through</u>
명사절을 이끄는 접속사    과거형 수동태    ~을 통해
one man's efforts. That man was Jeong Segwon, <u>known as</u> the King of
~으로 알려진(과거분사)
Architecture in Gyeongseong.

Jeong Segwon was a businessman who <u>founded</u> Geonyangsa in
found(설립하다)의 과거형
1920. <u>At the time</u>, Korea <u>was ruled by</u> Japan, and the Japanese <u>were</u>
그때, 그 당시에    ~에 의해 통치되었다(과거형 수동태)
<u>changing</u> Gyeongseong <u>to fit</u> their taste. Many Japanese <u>moving</u>
과거진행형    부사적 용법(목적)    Japanese를 수식하는 현재분사
<u>into</u> Gyeongseong <u>were building</u> Japanese or Western houses. Jeong
과거진행형
Segwon wanted to protect the *hanok* and <u>help</u> the <u>suffering</u> people.
protect와 함께 wanted to에 연결됨    고통 받는(people을 수식하는 현재분사
He said, "People are power. We <u>Joseon people</u> <u>should</u> keep Jongno
We와 동격 관계    ~해야 한다
and <u>not</u> let the Japanese <u>set foot</u> here." He bought the land <u>between</u>
keep과 함께 should에 연결됨    let의 목적격보어로 쓰이는 원형부사
<u>Gyeongbokgung and Changdeokgung</u>.
between A and B: A와 B 사이에 (있는)
<u>There</u> he built small, modern *hanoks* for the people. Through his
= At the land
efforts, we now have Bukchon <u>filled</u> with its beautiful *hanoks*.
Bukchon을 수식하는 과거분사

architecture: 건축
popular: 인기 있는
tourist: 여행객
past: 과거
create: 만들다
effort: 노력
businessman: 사업가
rule: 지배하다, 통치하다
fit: ~에 맞추다
taste: 맛, 취향
move into: ~으로 이사 오다
set foot: 발을 들여놓다
modern: 현대적인

📎 **확인문제**

● 다음 문장이 본문의 내용과 일치하면 T, 일치하지 <u>않으면</u> F를 쓰시오.

**1** Tourists who want to see Korea's past go to Bukchon. ☐

**2** Bukchon was created through many people's efforts. ☐

**3** Japanese people who moved into Gyeongseong built Japanese or Western houses. ☐

**4** Jeong Segwon built ancient *hanoks* to protect the *hanok*. ☐

Jeong Segwon helped the independence movement in many ways.
여러 방법으로

For example, he built the office building for the Joseon Language
예를 들면                                    ~을 위한

Society and supported its efforts to keep the Joseon language alive.
                        efforts를 수식하는 형용사적 용법          목적격보어

When the Joseon Language Affair happened, he was caught by the
                                    was happend (x)   과거형 수동태

police and suffered a lot. Japanese officials pressed him to build
                      많이                      press A to ~: ~하도록 A에게 압박을 가하다

Japanese houses. He said, "I don't know how to build Japanese
                                          ~하는 방법(know의 목적어)

houses." An official said, "You know how to build *hanoks*, so you can
                                =how you should build          그래서

build Japanese houses, too." But he did not do what the Japanese told
                                              명사절로 do의 목적어

him to do. The cost was high. His business fell off, and he lost his
                                                      lose(잃다)의 과거형

property. However, in part, thanks to Jeong Segwon, the traditions of
            그러나

Korea still live with us today.

---

independence: 독립
movement: 운동
office: 사무실
language: 언어
society: 사회, 학회
support: 지원하다
affair: 사건, 사태
happen: 일어나다, 발생하다
police: 경찰
suffer: 고통을 겪다
official: 관리
press: 압박을 가하다
cost: 비용, 대가
business: 사업
fall off: 쇠퇴하다
property: 재산
in part: 부분적으로는
thanks to: ~ 덕분에
tradition: 전통
still: 아직도, 여전히

---

 확인문제

● 다음 문장이 본문의 내용과 일치하면 T, 일치하지 <u>않으면</u> F를 쓰시오.

1  Jeong Segwon didn't participate in the independence movement. ☐

2  Jeong Segwon made an effort to keep the Joseon language alive. ☐

3  Jeong Segwon was caught by the police after the Joseon Language Affair. ☐

4  A Japanese official told Jeong Segwon to build Korean houses. ☐

5  Jeong Segwon lost his property because he didn't follow the Japanese official's order. ☐

● 우리말을 참고하여 빈칸에 알맞은 말을 쓰시오.

**1** The King of _____ in Gyeongseong

**2** _____ you _____ to Bukchon?

**3** _____ _____ a beautiful *hanok* village in Bukchon.

**4** It is _____ with tourists _____ want to see Korea's _____.

**5** However, not many people _____ that Bukchon _____ _____ through one man's _____.

**6** That man was Jeong Segwon, _____ _____ the King of Architecture in Gyeongseong.

**7** Jeong Segwon was a businessman _____ _____ Geonyangsa in 1920.

**8** At the _____, Korea _____ _____ by Japan, and the Japanese were changing Gyeongseong to _____ their _____.

**9** Many Japanese _____ _____ Gyeongseong were building _____ or _____ houses.

**10** Jeong Segwon _____ to _____ the *hanok* and help the _____ people.

**11** He said, "People are _____. We Joseon people should _____ Jongno and not _____ the Japanese _____ _____ here."

**12** He bought the land _____ Gyeongbokgung _____ Changdeokgung.

**13** There he built small, _____ *hanoks* for the _____.

**14** Through his _____, we now have Bukchon _____ _____ its beautiful *hanoks*.

| | |
|---|---|
| **1** | 경성의 건축왕 |
| **2** | 당신은 북촌에 다녀온 적이 있는가? |
| **3** | 북촌에는 아름다운 한옥 마을이 있다. |
| **4** | 그곳은 한국의 과거를 보고 싶어 하는 관광객들에게 인기가 있다. |
| **5** | 그러나 북촌이 한 사람의 노력으로 만들어졌다는 것을 아는 사람은 많지 않다. |
| **6** | 그 사람은 경성의 건축왕으로 알려진 정세권이었다. |
| **7** | 정세권은 **1920**년에 건양사를 설립한 사업가였다. |
| **8** | 그 당시 한국은 일본의 지배를 받았고, 일본인들은 경성을 그들의 취향에 맞게 바꾸고 있었다. |
| **9** | 경성으로 이주하는 많은 일본인들은 일본식이나 서양식 집들을 짓고 있었다. |
| **10** | 정세권은 한옥을 지키고 고통받는 사람들을 돕기를 원했다. |
| **11** | 그는 말했다. "사람이 힘이다. 우리 조선 사람들은 종로를 지켜야 하며, 일본인들이 이곳에 발을 붙이지 못하게 해야 한다." |
| **12** | 그는 경복궁과 창덕궁 사이의 땅을 샀다. |
| **13** | 거기에 그는 사람들을 위해 작은 현대식 한옥들을 지었다. |
| **14** | 그의 노력으로 북촌은 현재 아름다운 한옥으로 가득 차 있다. |

**15** Jeong Segwon helped the _____ _____ in many _____.

**16** For _____, he built the office building for the Joseon Language Society and _____ its efforts to _____ the Joseon language _____.

**17** When the Joseon Language Affair _____, he was _____ by the police and _____ a lot.

**18** Japanese officials _____ him to _____ Japanese houses.

**19** He said, "I don't know _____ _____ build Japanese houses."

**20** An _____ said, "You _____ how to build *hanoks*, _____ you can _____ Japanese houses, too."

**21** But he did not do _____ the Japanese _____ him to do.

**22** The _____ was _____.

**23** His business _____ off, and he lost his _____.

**24** However, in _____, thanks _____ Jeong Segwon, the _____ of Korea _____ live with us today.

● 우리말을 참고하여 본문을 영작하시오.

**1** 경성의 건축왕
➡ _____

**2** 당신은 북촌에 다녀온 적이 있는가?
➡ _____

**3** 북촌에는 아름다운 한옥 마을이 있다.
➡ _____

**4** 그곳은 한국의 과거를 보고 싶어 하는 관광객들에게 인기가 있다.
➡ _____

**5** 그러나 북촌이 한 사람의 노력으로 만들어졌다는 것을 아는 사람은 많지 않다.
➡ _____

**6** 그 사람은 경성의 건축왕으로 알려진 정세권이었다.
➡ _____

**7** 정세권은 1920년에 건양사를 설립한 사업가였다.
➡ _____

**8** 그 당시 한국은 일본의 지배를 받았고, 일본인들은 경성을 그들의 취향에 맞게 바꾸고 있었다.
➡ _____

**9** 경성으로 이주하는 많은 일본인들은 일본식이나 서양식 집들을 짓고 있었다.
➡ _____

**10** 정세권은 한옥을 지키고 고통받는 사람들을 돕기를 원했다.
➡ _____

**11** 그는 말했다. "사람이 힘이다. 우리 조선 사람들은 종로를 지켜야 하며, 일본인들이 이곳에 발을 붙이지 못하게 해야 한다."
➡ _____
_____

**12** 그는 경복궁과 창덕궁 사이의 땅을 샀다.
➡ _____

**13** 거기에 그는 사람들을 위해 작은 현대식 한옥들을 지었다.
➡ _____

**14** 그의 노력으로 북촌은 현재 아름다운 한옥으로 가득 차 있다.
➡ _____

**15** ▶ 정세권은 여러 방법으로 독립운동을 도왔다.

➡ _____

**16** ▶ 예를 들면, 그는 조선어 학회를 위한 회관을 지었고 조선어를 지키려는 그들의 노력을 지원했다.

➡ _____

_____

**17** ▶ 조선어 학회 사건이 발생했을 때 그는 경찰에 잡혀 많은 고통을 겪었다.

➡ _____

**18** ▶ 일본인 관리들은 그에게 일본식 가옥을 지으라고 압박했다.

➡ _____

**19** ▶ 그는 말했다. "나는 일본식 가옥을 지울 줄 모르오."

➡ _____

**20** ▶ 한 관리가 말했다. "당신은 한옥을 지을 줄 아오. 그러니 일본식 가옥도 지을 수 있소."

➡ _____

**21** ▶ 그러나 그는 그 일본인이 그에게 요구한 것을 하지 않았다.

➡ _____

**22** ▶ 그 대가는 컸다.

➡ _____

**23** ▶ 그의 사업은 쇠퇴했고, 그는 재산을 잃었다.

➡ _____

**24** ▶ 그러나 부분적으로나마, 정세권 덕분에 한국의 전통이 오늘날 여전히 우리와 함께 살아 있다.

➡ _____

[01~05] 다음 글을 읽고 물음에 답하시오.

Jeong Segwon was a businessman ⓐ_____ founded Geonyangsa in 1920. At the time, Korea was ruled by Japan, and the Japanese were changing Gyeongseong to fit their taste. ⓑMany Japanese moved into Gyeongseong were building Japanese or Western houses. Jeong Segwon wanted to _____ⓒ_____ the hanok and help the suffering people. He said, "People are power. ⓓWe Joseon people should keep Jongno and not let the Japanese set foot here."

**서답형**

**01** 위 글의 빈칸 ⓐ에 알맞은 말을 쓰시오.

➡ _____

**서답형**

**02** 위 글의 밑줄 친 ⓑ의 문장에서 어법상 어색한 것을 고치시오.

➡ _____

**중요**

**03** 위 글의 빈칸 ⓒ에 알맞은 것은?

① found     ② protect
③ invent    ④ exchange
⑤ destroy

**서답형**

**04** 위 글의 밑줄 친 ⓓ를 우리말로 옮기시오.

➡ _____

**중요**

**05** 위 글의 내용과 일치하지 <u>않는</u> 것은?

① 정세권은 1920년에 건양사를 설립했다.
② 그 당시 일본인들은 경성을 그들의 취향에 맞게 바꾸고 있었다.
③ 많은 일본인들이 경성으로 이주해 왔다.
④ 일본인들은 일본식 가옥과 서양식 가옥을 짓고 있었다.
⑤ 정세권은 일본인들이 종로에 발을 들여놓는 것에 신경 쓰지 않았다.

[06~08] 다음 글을 읽고 물음에 답하시오.

Have you been ⓐ_____ Bukchon? There is a beautiful hanok village in Bukchon. ⓑ그곳은 한국의 과거를 보기를 원하는 사람들에게 인기가 있다. However, not many people know that Bukchon was created _____ⓒ_____ one man's efforts. That man was Jeong Segwon, ⓓknow as the King of Architecture in Gyeongseong.

**중요**

**06** 위 글의 빈칸 ⓐ와 ⓒ에 들어갈 전치사가 바르게 짝지어진 것은?

① from – by      ② in – by
③ for – from     ④ to – through
⑤ for – through

**서답형**

**07** 위 글의 밑줄 친 ⓑ의 우리말에 맞게 주어진 어휘를 이용하여 11단어로 영작하시오.

┌─────────────────────────────┐
│      with, tourists, who     │
└─────────────────────────────┘

➡ _____

**서답형**

**08** 위 글의 밑줄 친 ⓓ를 알맞은 어형으로 고치시오.

➡ _____

[09~12] 다음 글을 읽고 물음에 답하시오.

Jeong Segwon helped the independence movement ⓐ many ways. For example, he built the office building for the Joseon Language Society and supported its efforts ⓑto keep the Joseon language alive. When the Joseon Language Affair happened, he was caught by the police and suffered a lot. Japanese officials pressed him ⓒ Japanese houses. He said, "I don't know how to build Japanese houses."

**09** 위 글의 빈칸 ⓐ에 알맞은 전치사는?

① in
② to
③ at
④ from
⑤ with

**10** 위 글의 밑줄 친 ⓑto keep과 같은 용법으로 쓰인 것을 고르시오.

① I want to learn Chinese culture.
② Is there anything to eat in the fridge?
③ Were you glad to hear the news?
④ Love is to trust each other.
⑤ Her daughter grew up to be an actress.

**11** 위 글의 빈칸 ⓒ에 알맞은 것은?

① build
② built
③ to build
④ building
⑤ to building

**12** 위 글의 내용으로 보아 대답할 수 없는 것은?

① Why did Jeong Segwon help the independence movement?
② Who built the office building for the Joseon Language Society?
③ Did Jeong Segwon make an effort to keep the Joseon language alive?
④ When was Jeong Segwon caught by the police?
⑤ Did Jeong Segwon build Japanese houses?

[13~14] 다음 글을 읽고 물음에 답하시오.

An official said, "You know how to build *hanoks*, so you can build Japanese houses, too." But he did not do ⓐwhat the Japanese told him to do. The cost was high. His business fell ⓑ , and he lost his property. However, in part, thanks ⓒ Jeong Segwon, the traditions of Korea still live with us today.

**13** 아래 보기에서 위 글의 밑줄 친 ⓐwhat과 문법적 쓰임이 같은 것의 개수를 고르시오.

> ┌──── 보기 ────
> ① Guess what is in this box.
> ② He spent what he had earned.
> ③ What you must do is very important.
> ④ I gave her what she needed.
> ⑤ Ask her what she wants.
> └────

① 1개　② 2개　③ 3개　④ 4개　⑤ 5개

**14** 위 글의 빈칸 ⓑ와 ⓒ에 알맞은 것으로 짝지어진 것은?

① of – to
② from – in
③ with – of
④ from – of
⑤ off – to

[15~18] 다음 글을 읽고 물음에 답하시오.

① Jeong Segwon said, "People are power. ② We Joseon people should keep Jongno and not ⓐ the Japanese set foot here." ③ He bought the land between Gyeongbokgung and Changdeokgung. ④ ⓑThrough his efforts, we now have Bukchon filled ⓒ its beautiful *hanoks*. ⑤

**15** 위 글의 흐름으로 보아, 주어진 문장이 들어가기에 가장 적절한 곳은?

There he built small, modern *hanoks* for the people.

①     ②     ③     ④     ⑤

**16** 위 글의 빈칸 ⓐ에 알맞은 것은?

① get
② make
③ let
④ take
⑤ allow

**17** 위 글의 밑줄 친 ⓑ와 같은 뜻으로 쓰인 것은?

① The doctor pushed his way <u>through</u> the crowd.
② The Charles River flows <u>through</u> Boston.
③ The children are too young to sit <u>through</u> a concert.
④ I couldn't hear their conversation <u>through</u> the wall.
⑤ You can only achieve success <u>through</u> hard work.

**18** 위 글의 빈칸 ⓒ에 알맞은 것은?

① of
② with
③ for
④ from
⑤ along

[19~21] 다음 글을 읽고 물음에 답하시오.

Have you been to Bukchon? There is a beautiful *hanok* village in Bukchon. ⓐIt is popular with tourists who want to see Korea's ⓑ . However, not many people know that Bukchon was created through one man's efforts. That man was Jeong Segwon, known ⓒas the King of Architecture in Gyeongseong.

**서답형**

**19** 위 글의 밑줄 친 ⓐIt이 가리키는 것을 영어로 쓰시오.

➡ _____

**서답형**

**20** 위 글의 빈칸 ⓑ에 다음 정의에 해당하는 단어를 쓰시오.

the time before the present, and the things that have happened

➡ _____

**21** 위 글의 밑줄 친 ⓒas와 같은 뜻으로 쓰인 것은?

① My mother often sings <u>as</u> she works.
② I wish to work <u>as</u> an interpreter.
③ <u>As</u> it rained too much, we couln't go hiking.
④ Can you run as fast <u>as</u> Mike?
⑤ <u>As</u> we go higher, the air gets colder.

[22~25] 다음 글을 읽고 물음에 답하시오.

ⓐJeong Segwon was a businessman. He founded Geonyangsa in 1920. At the time, Korea was ruled by Japan, and the Japanese were changing Gyeongseong ⓑto fit their taste. Many Japanese moving into Gyeongseong were building Japanese or Western houses. Jeong Segwon wanted to protect the *hanok* and help the suffering people. He said, "People are power. We Joseon people should keep Jongno and not let the Japanese set foot here."

**서답형**

**22** 위 글의 밑줄 친 ⓐ를 관계대명사를 써서 한 문장으로 만드시오.

➡ _____

_____

**23** 위 글의 밑줄 친 ⓑ와 용법이 같은 것은?

① My hope is to work as a doctor in Africa.
② It's time to go to bed now.
③ My job is to report the news.
④ The boys hoped to find the hidden treasure.
⑤ Kate went to a shopping mall to buy clothes.

**중요**

**24** 위 글의 내용으로 보아 정세권에 대한 묘사로 가장 알맞은 것을 고르시오.

① creative
② negative
③ patriotic
④ friendly
⑤ passionate

**서답형**

**25** What houses were many Japanese building? Answer in English. (7 words)

➡ _____

[26~28] 다음 글을 읽고 물음에 답하시오.

Jeong Segwon helped the independence movement in many ways. ⓐ example, he built the office building for the Joseon Language Society and supported its efforts to keep the Joseon language ⓑlive. ⓒWhen the Joseon Language Affair was happened, he was caught by the police and suffered a lot. Japanese officials pressed him to build Japanese houses.

**26** 위 글의 빈칸 ⓐ에 들어갈 알맞은 것은?

① For
② In
③ At
④ With
⑤ From

**서답형**

**27** 위 글의 밑줄 친 ⓑ를 알맞은 어형으로 고치시오.

➡ _____

**서답형**

**28** 위 글의 밑줄 친 ⓒ에서 어법상 어색한 것을 고치시오.

_____ ➡ _____

**[01~04]** 다음 글을 읽고 물음에 답하시오.

Japanese officials pressed Jeong Segwon to build Japanese houses. ⓐHe said, "I don't know how to build Japanese houses." An official said, "You know how to build *hanoks*, ⓑ[so / for] you can build Japanese houses, too." But he did not do ⓒ[that / what] the Japanese told him to do. The cost was high. His business fell off, and he lost his property. However, in part, thanks ⓓ[to / of] Jeong Segwon, the traditions of Korea still live with us today.

**01** 위 글의 밑줄 친 ⓐ를 간접화법의 문장으로 바꿔 쓰시오.

➡ _____

_____

**02** 위 글의 괄호 ⓑ~ⓒ에서 문맥이나 어법상 알맞은 낱말을 골라 쓰시오.

➡ ⓑ _____ ⓑ _____ ⓒ _____

**03** 위 글의 내용과 일치하도록 다음 빈칸 (A)와 (B)에 알맞은 단어를 쓰시오.

Despite a Japanese official's pressure, Jeong Segwon didn't (A)_____ Japanese houses. As the result, he lost his (B)_____ .

**04** What houses did Japanese officials press Jeong Segwon to build? Answer in English. (7 words)

➡ _____

**[05~07]** 다음 글을 읽고 물음에 답하시오.

Jeong Segwon said, "People are power. We Joseon people should keep Jongno and not ⓐ let the Japanese set foot here." He bought the ⓑ_____ between Gyeongbokgung (A)[or / and] Changdeokgung. There he built small, modern *hanoks* for the people. (B)[Until / Through] his efforts, we now have Bukchon filled (C)[with / of] its beautiful *hanoks*.

**05** 위 글의 밑줄 친 ⓐ와 같은 뜻이 되도록 다음 문장의 빈칸에 알맞은 말을 쓰시오.

allow the Japanese _____ _____ foot here

**06** 위 글의 빈칸 ⓑ에 다음 정의에 해당하는 말을 쓰시오.

an area of ground, especially one that is used for a particular purpose such as farming or building

➡ _____

**07** 위 글의 괄호 (A)~(C)에서 어법상 알맞은 낱말을 골라 쓰시오.

➡ (A) _____ (B) _____ (C) _____

[08~12] 다음 글을 읽고 물음에 답하시오.

Jeong Segwon helped the ⓐdepend movement in many ways. ⓑ_____ example, he built the office building for the Joseon Language Society and supported its efforts to keep the Joseon language alive. ⓒ조선어 학회 사건이 일어났을 때, 그는 경찰에 잡혀 많은 고통을 겪었다. Japanese officials pressed him (A)[building / to build] Japanese houses. He said, "I don't know (B) [how / what] to build Japanese houses."

**08** 위 글의 밑줄 친 ⓐ를 문맥상 알맞은 말로 어형을 바꾸시오.

➡ _____

**09** 위 글의 빈칸 ⓑ에 알맞은 말을 쓰시오.

➡ _____

**10** 위 글의 밑줄 친 ⓒ의 우리말에 맞게 한 단어를 보충하여, 주어진 어구를 알맞게 배열하시오. (when으로 시작할 것.)

was / the police / happened / he / when / and / suffered / caught / a lot / the Choseon Language Affair

➡ _____
_____

**11** 위 글의 괄호 (A)~(B)에서 어법상 알맞은 낱말을 골라 쓰시오.

➡ (A) _____ (B) _____

**12** What did the Joseon Language Society make an effort to do? Answer in English.

➡ _____

[13~15] 다음 글을 읽고 물음에 답하시오.

Have you been (A)[for / to] Bukchon? ⓐThere is a beautiful *hanok* village in Bukchon. It is popular (B)[with / from] tourists who want to see Korea's past. However, not many people know that Bukchon was created (B)[among / through] one man's efforts. That man was Jeong Segwon, ⓑknow as the King of Architecture in Gyeongseong.

**13** 위 글의 괄호 (A)~(C)에서 어법상 알맞은 낱말을 골라 쓰시오.

➡ (A) _____ (B) _____ (C) _____

**14** 위 글의 밑줄 친 ⓐ와 같은 뜻이 되도록 다음 문장의 빈칸에 알맞은 말을 쓰시오.

➡ Bukchon _____ a beautiful *hanok* village.

**15** 위 글의 밑줄 친 ⓑ를 알맞은 어형으로 고치시오.

➡ _____

해석

## Before You Read

Japanese officials pressed the Joseon people to use the Japanese language.
목적격보어

The Joseon people tried to keep the Joseon language alive.
명사적 용법(tried의 목적어)                          살아 있는

The Joseon people wanted to protect the country. Soon, the independence

movement rose up.
rise의 과거형

구문해설 · alive: 살아 있는 · protect: 지키다 · rise up: 일어나다, 봉기하다

일본 관리들은 조선 사람들에게 일본어를 쓰도록 압박했다. 조선 사람들은 조선어를 살아 있게 지키려고 노력했다.

조선 사람들은 나라를 지키기를 원했다. 이윽고, 독립운동이 일어났다.

## Language in Use

A woman moved into the building next to Joe's store. She opened up a new
building을 수식하는 형용사구

store. Many people started to go to the woman's new store instead of Joe's
~하기 시작했다.                                          ~ 대신에

store. Few people set foot in Joe's store. His food business fell off.
~에 발을 들여 놓았다

구문해설 · next to: ~ 옆에 open up: 열다, 개점하다 · few: 거의 ~ 않는 · fall off: 쇠퇴하다

한 여인이 Joe의 가게 옆에 있는 건물로 이사 왔다. 그녀는 새로운 가게를 열었다. 많은 사람들이 Joe의 가게 대신에 그 여인의 새 가게로 가기 시작했다. Joe의 가게에 들어오는 사람들은 거의 없었다. 그의 음식 장사는 쇠퇴했다.

## Writing Workshop

Who is An Yongbok?

He lived during the Joseon Dynasty, and his job was catching fish. When he
~ 중에, ~ 동안(during+특정한 기간)

was fishing, he saw the Japanese people fishing near Ulleungdo. He visited
지각동사                    목적격보어(현재분사)

Japan twice and said that Ulleungdo and Dokdo were part of Korea. In 1696,
be part of: ~의 일부이다

the Japanese ruler officially told the Japanese people not to fish near Ulleugdo
물고기를 잡지 말라고(to부정사의 부정)

and Dokdo. He did his best to protect Ulleungdo and Dokdo.

구문해설 · dynasty: 왕조 · twice: 두 번 · officially: 공식적으로 · do one's best: 최선을 다하다

안용복은 누구인가?
그는 조선왕조 시대에 살았으며, 그의 직업은 물고기를 잡는 것이었다. 그가 물고기를 잡고 있었을 때 그는 일본 사람들이 울릉도 근처에서 물고기를 잡는 것을 보았다. 그는 일본을 두 번 방문해서 울릉도와 독도는 한국에 속해 있다고 말했다. 1696년에 일본인 통치자는 일본인들에게 울릉도와 독도 근처에서 물고기를 잡지 말라고 공식적으로 말했다. 그는 울릉도와 독도를 지키기 위해 최선을 다했다.

**01** 다음 짝지어진 단어의 관계가 같도록 빈칸에 알맞은 말을 쓰시오.

(1) China – Chinese : France : _____
(2) poem – poet : architecture : _____

**02** 다음 우리말에 맞도록 빈칸에 알맞은 말을 쓰시오

(1) 그녀는 실내에서 할 수 있는 일에 관심이 있다.
  ➡ She is _____ in working indoors.
(2) 우리가 그 일의 힘든 부분은 다 했다.
  ➡ We've done the difficult _____ of the job.
(3) 내 방은 현대식 스타일로 꾸며져 있다.
  ➡ My room is decorated in a _____ style.

**03** 다음 빈칸에 알맞은 말을 고르시오.

The city is famous _____ its scenery.

① from          ② for
③ with          ④ in
⑤ by

**04** 다음 영영풀이가 나타내는 말을 고르시오.

a long written story about imaginary people and events

① novel          ② article
③ report          ④ essay
⑤ diary

**05** 다음 대화의 빈칸에 들어갈 말을 고르시오.

B: Could you _____ this painting?
W: Sure. It's *the Two Sisters* by Renoir. He painted it in 1881.

① view          ② tell
③ show          ④ excuse
⑤ explain

**06** 다음 대화가 자연스럽게 이어지도록 순서대로 배열하시오.

(A) It's a volunteer group in our community.
(B) Well, they take care of children in need.
(C) Could you tell me more about it?
(D) Could you explain what Helping Hands is?

➡ _____

**07** 다음 대화의 흐름상 어색한 것을 고르시오.

B: ⓐDo you know anything about this writer?
G: Yes. ⓑI've read some of his novels. Why?
B: ⓒHow were they? I'm thinking of buying his books.
G: ⓓYou should. ⓔI didn't enjoy his books that much.

① ⓐ     ② ⓑ     ③ ⓒ     ④ ⓓ     ⑤ ⓔ

**[08~11]** 다음 대화를 읽고 물음에 답하시오.

G: What are *hanoks*? ①

M: Hanoks are traditional Korean houses. ② ⓐ <u>They design to be in harmony with nature.</u>

G: Could you explain a little more about them? ③

M: *Hanoks* are cool in the summer and warm in the winter. ④

G: That sounds interesting. ⑤ Where can I see these traditional houses?

M: There's a *hanok* village near here.

G: How about going there and seeing the hanoks?

W: Good idea!     ⓑ     can we get there?

M: You can take Bus Number 5 over there at the bus stop.

**08** ①~⑤ 중 주어진 문장이 들어갈 곳은?

> Do you know anything about them?

①     ②     ③     ④     ⑤

**09** 위 대화의 밑줄 친 ⓐ에서 어법상 어색한 것을 고쳐 다시 쓰시오.

➡ _____

**10** 위 대화의 빈칸 ⓑ에 알맞은 것은?

① What          ② When
③ How           ④ Why
⑤ Where

**11** 위 대화의 내용과 일치하지 <u>않는</u> 것을 고르시오.

① 소녀는 한옥이 무엇인지 모른다.
② 한옥은 자연과 조화를 이루도록 설계되었다.
③ 소녀는 한국의 전통 마을을 방문하기를 원한다.
④ 전통 마을은 대화자들이 이야기하는 장소에서 멀리 있다.
⑤ 소녀와 여인은 버스를 타고 전통 마을에 갈 것이다.

**Grammar**

**12** 다음 중 주어진 문장의 밑줄 친 부분과 쓰임이 <u>다른</u> 하나는?

> Did you see the <u>swimming</u> pool?

① Kevin was not interested in <u>fishing</u>.
② My hobby is <u>taking</u> pictures.
③ The boys are <u>riding</u> bikes together.
④ They enjoyed <u>cooking</u> with her.
⑤ Tanya focused on <u>studying</u> English.

**13** 다음 문장에서 어법상 잘못된 것을 고치시오.

(1) They asked him give a speech.
_____ ➡ _____

(2) Clara made him to wait for her for an hour outside.
_____ ➡ _____

(3) I will have Mike to repair my cellphone.
_____ ➡ _____

(4) I saw the boys played soccer at the park.
_____ ➡ _____

(5) He was reading a letter writing in English.
_____ ➡ _____

**14** 다음 우리말을 올바르게 영작한 것은?

> 그는 Christine에게 집에 조금 일찍 도착하라고 요청했다.

① He asked Christine arrive home a little early.

② He asked Christine arrives home a little early.

③ He asked Christine arrived home a little early.

④ He asked Christine to arrive home a little early.

⑤ He asked Christine arriving home a little early.

**15** 다음 중 어법상 어색한 문장은?

① I liked the pictures painted by Mike.

② He knows the girl dancing on the stage.

③ I saw the dog sleeping on the sofa.

④ The baby smiled at me is very cute.

⑤ They watched the birds singing on the tree.

**16** 다음 중 빈칸에 들어갈 말이 바르게 짝지어진 것은?

> • Did you find your (A)[breaking / broken] camera?
>
> • I saw an (B)[exciting / excited] movie yesterday.
>
> • I can't open the (C)[locking / locked] door.

|  | (A) | (B) | (C) |
|---|---|---|---|
| ① | breaking | – exciting | – locked |
| ② | breaking | – excited | – locked |
| ③ | breaking | – excited | – locking |
| ④ | broken | – exciting | – locking |
| ⑤ | broken | – exciting | – locked |

**17** 다음 중 어법상 어색한 부분을 찾아 바르게 고쳐 다시 쓰시오.

(1) Lucy's dad wants her being a police officer.

➡ _____

(2) My mother asked me buy some milk on my way home.

➡ _____

(3) The teacher told the students bringing some water.

➡ _____

(4) She got her two sons divided a cake exactly in half.

➡ _____

**18** 주어진 단어를 활용하여 다음 우리말을 영어로 쓰시오.

(1) 우리는 낙엽 위를 걷는 것을 좋아합니다. (like / on / fall / leaves)

➡ _____

(2) 그는 그 날아오는 공을 쳤다. (hit / fly)

➡ _____

**19** 다음 두 문장의 해석을 쓰고 밑줄 친 부분의 어법상 차이를 설명하시오.

> (1) Jane likes sliced cheese.
> (2) Jane likes slicing cheese.

(1) 해석: _____

(2) 해석: _____

(3) 어법상 차이: _____

_____

**Reading**

**[20~23]** 다음 글을 읽고 물음에 답하시오.

(①) An Yongbok lived during the Joseon Dynasty, and his job was ⓐcatching fish. (②) When he was fishing, he saw the Japanese people fishing near Ulleungdo. (③) In 1696, the Japanese ___ⓑ___ officially told the Japanese people not to fish near Ulleugdo and Dokdo. (④) He did his best to protect Ulleungdo and Dokdo. (⑤)

**20** 위 글의 흐름으로 보아, 주어진 문장이 들어가기에 가장 적절한 곳은?

He visited Japan twice and said that Ulleungdo and Dokdo were part of Korea.

①        ②        ③        ④        ⑤

**21** 위 글의 밑줄 친 ⓐ와 같은 용법으로 쓰인 것은?

① Barking dogs seldom bite.
② Working in the field was very interesting.
③ The girl reading a book is Mary.
④ We saw Mike climbing the mountain alone.
⑤ Turning to the left, you will find a hotel.

**22** 위 글의 빈칸 ⓑ에 다음 정의에 해당하는 단어를 쓰시오.

the person who rules a country

➡ _____

**23** 위 글을 읽고 대답할 수 없는 질문은?

① Did An Yongbok live during the Joseon Dynasty?
② What did he do for a living?
③ Was he good at catching fish?
④ How many times did he visit Japan?
⑤ Could the Japanese people fish near Dokdo after 1696?

**[24~26]** 다음 글을 읽고 물음에 답하시오.

ⓐHave you ever seen this kind of pot? It is an onggi. People in the old times used it for storing rice for a long time.
We have designed a modern onggi with flowers ⓑpaint on it, and it even has handles.

**24** 위 글의 밑줄 친 ⓐ를 우리말로 옮기시오.

➡ _____

**25** 위 글의 밑줄 친 ⓑpaint를 알맞은 형으로 고치시오.

➡ _____

**26** Why did people in the old times use this kind of pot? Answer in English. (6 words)

➡ _____

**[27~30]** 다음 글을 읽고 물음에 답하시오.

ⓐHow about learning *taegwondo* at the Buckon *Hanok* Village? People can experience the Korean ⓑnation sport. They will learn that *taegwondo* is a sport ⓒthat trains both the spirit and the ___ⓓ___.

**27** 위 글의 밑줄 친 ⓐ를 다음과 같이 바꿔 쓸 때 빈칸에 들어갈 알맞은 말을 쓰시오.

➡ _____ don't you learn *taegwondo* at the Buckon *Hanok* Village?

**28** 위 글의 밑줄 친 ⓑnation을 알맞은 형으로 고치시오.

➡ _____

**29** 위 글의 밑줄 친 ⓒthat와 용법이 같은 것은? (2개)

① It is strange that she doesn't come.
② I know that you don't like cats.
③ Look at the trees that stand on the hill.
④ It was here that she first met Mike.
⑤ This is the doll that my mother made for me.

**30** 위 글의 빈칸 ⓓ에 다음 정의에 해당하는 단어를 쓰시오.

all your physical parts, including your head, arms, and legs

➡ _____

**[31~33]** 다음 글을 읽고 물음에 답하시오.

Jeong Segwon was a businessman who founded Geonyangsa in 1920. At the time, Korea was ruled by Japan, and the Japanese were changing Gyeongseong to fit their taste. Many Japanese moving into Gyeongseong were building Japanese or ⓐWest houses. Jeong Segwon wanted to protect the *hanok* and help the suffering people. He said, "People are power. We Joseon people should keep Jongno and not let the Japanese ___ⓑ___ foot here."

**31** 위 글의 밑줄 친 ⓐWest를 알맞은 형으로 고치시오.

➡ _____

**32** 위 글의 빈칸 ⓑ에 알맞은 것은?

① get          ② set
③ fix          ④ put
⑤ take

**33** 위 글을 읽고 대답할 수 <u>없는</u> 질문은?

① What did Jeong Segwon do for a living?
② When did Jeong Segwon found Geonyangsa?
③ Why were the Japanese changing Gyeongseong?
④ What did Jeong Segwon want to do?
⑤ How did Jeong Segwon keep Jongno?

**01** 다음 두 문장이 같은 뜻이 되도록 빈칸에 알맞은 것은?

> Who's taking care of the children while you're away?
> = Who's caring _____ the children while you're away?

① of     ② to     ③ at
④ for     ⑤ with

**02** 다음 빈칸에 공통으로 들어갈 말을 쓰시오.

> • He sensed that his life was _____ danger.
> • Jake is interested _____ chess.

**03** 다음 중 〈보기〉에 있는 단어를 사용하여 자연스러운 문장을 만들 수 없는 것은?

> ── 보기 ──
> abroad   known   explain   meaning   waste

① What's the _____ of this word?
② First, I'll _____ the rules of the game.
③ Why did you _____ money on clothes you didn't need?
④ I'm planning to travel _____.
⑤ The boy was trying, for some _____ reason, to count the stars.

**04** 다음 영영풀이에 해당하는 단어를 고르시오.

> to feel pain in your body or in your mind

① store     ② require
③ suffer     ④ expect
⑤ endure

**[05~08]** 다음 대화를 읽고 물음에 답하시오.

B: Do you know anything about a *dol* party?
G: Yes. ⓐIt's the birthday party for a one-year-old baby.
B: Could you tell me more about it?
G: Well, the family members get together for the party, and the birthday baby wears a *hanbok*.
B: That sounds interesting.
G: The family members share food and wish ____ⓑ____ a long life for the baby. It's a Korean ____ⓒ____.

**05** 위 대화의 밑줄 친 It이 가리키는 것을 우리말로 쓰시오.

➡ _____

**06** 위 대화의 빈칸 ⓑ에 알맞은 것은?

① to     ② for
③ of     ④ with
⑤ from

**07** 위 대화의 빈칸 ⓒ에 다음 영영풀이에 해당하는 단어를 쓰시오.

> a custom or belief that has existed for a long time

➡ _____

출제율 100%

**08** 위 대화를 읽고 대답할 수 <u>없는</u> 질문은?

① Does the boy know much about a *dol* party?
② What is a *dol* party?
③ Can the girl tell the boy about a *dol* party?
④ How many family members get together for the party?
⑤ What do family members do at the *dol* party?

**[09~12]** 다음 대화를 읽고 물음에 답하시오.

Reporter: You founded Geonyangsa. What does Geonyangsa do?
Jeong: We build houses. We build *hanoks* on the land between Gyeongbokgung and Changdeokgung.
Reporter: Why did you build *hanoks* ⓐthere?
Jeong: Many Japanese are moving into Gyeongseong and changing ⓑit to fit their taste. So I want to protect the *hanok*.
Reporter: You are also helping the independence ⓒ_____(move) in many ways. How have you helped?
Jeong: I know a lot about architecture, so I have built the office building for the Joseon Language Society.

출제율 90%

**09** 위 대화의 밑줄 친 ⓐthere가 가리키는 것을 영어로 쓰시오.

➡ _____
_____

출제율 85%

**10** 위 대화의 밑줄 친 ⓑ가 가리키는 것을 영어로 쓰시오.

➡ _____

출제율 90%

**11** 괄호 안에 주어진 단어를 이용해 빈칸 ⓒ를 채우시오.

➡ _____

출제율 100%

**12** 위 대화의 내용으로 보아 알 수 <u>없는</u> 것은?

① A reporter is interviewing Jeong.
② Jeong founded Geonyangsa.
③ There are a lot of *hanoks* between Gyeongbokgung and Changdeokgung.
④ Many Japanese are changing Gyeongseong to fit their taste.
⑤ Jeong wants to protect the *hanok*.

출제율 90%

**13** 다음 빈칸에 들어갈 말이 바르게 짝지어진 것은?

> • The girl _____ a book is my sister.
> • There was a _____ window.

① read – breaking
② read – broken
③ reading – broken
④ read – break
⑤ reading – break

**14** 다음 우리말에 맞도록 빈칸에 알맞은 말을 차례대로 쓰시오. *출제율 95%*

(1) 그가 돌아오면 저를 도와주라고 부탁해 주시겠어요?
= Will you ask him _____ me when he _____ back?

(2) 그녀는 자기 딸에게 고양이에게 밥을 주라고 말했다.
= She told her daughter _____ the cat.

**15** 다음 중 어법상 어색한 것을 고르시오. *출제율 100%*

① Is snow falling?
② I met a girl naming Kate in the park.
③ There was a fence painted green.
④ Who is the man cooking *bibimbap*?
⑤ A spectator is someone watching a game or a play.

**16** 다음 중 밑줄 친 부분의 쓰임이 바르지 못한 것은? *출제율 95%*

① Jack wants Jane to water the plants.
② He asked her teach math to his son.
③ He made her do her work right now.
④ We saw him singing in the rain.
⑤ He advised me not to smoke.

**17** 다음 문장의 빈칸에 알맞은 것은? *출제율 90%*

> She told me _____ careful when I crossed the road.

① be
② was
③ is
④ being
⑤ to be

**[18~20]** 다음 글을 읽고 물음에 답하시오.

When the Joseon Language Affair (A)[happened / was happened], Jeong Segwon was caught by the police and suffered a lot. Japanese officials pressed him (B)[building / to build] Japanese houses. He said, "I don't know how to build Japanese houses." An official said, "You know how to build hanoks, so you can build Japanese houses, too." But he did not do (C)[what / that] the Japanese told him to do. (D)대가는 컸다. His business fell off, and he lost his property.

**18** 위 글의 괄호 (A)~(C)에서 문맥이나 어법상 알맞은 낱말을 골라 쓰시오. *출제율 100%*

➡ (A)_____ (B)_____ (C)_____

**19** 위 글의 밑줄 친 (D)를 영어로 옮길 때 빈칸에 알맞은 것은? *출제율 90%*

> The cost was _____.

① much
② many
③ high
④ large
⑤ expensive

**20** 위 글의 내용과 일치하지 않는 것은? *출제율 95%*

① 조선어 학회 사건이 발생했을 때 정세권은 경찰에 체포되었다.
② 일본인 관리들은 정세권에게 일본식 집을 짓도록 강요했다.
③ 정세권은 일본식 집을 짓기로 마음먹었다.
④ 정세권은 일본식 집을 짓지 않았다.
⑤ 정세권은 일본인 관리의 말을 듣지 않은 결과 재산을 잃게 되었다.

[21~23] 다음 글을 읽고 물음에 답하시오.

The woman ⓐwear a pink dress opens the window. The sun is shining in the sky. Johnsy looks at a leaf (A)[painted / painting] on the wall. Johnsy looks happy. The man (B)[held / holding] a brush sees the happy face.

✎ 출제율 90%
**21** 위 글의 밑줄 친 ⓐwear를 알맞은 형으로 고치시오.

➡ _____

✎ 출제율 95%
**22** 위 글의 괄호 (A), (B)에서 어법상 알맞은 낱말을 골라 쓰시오.

➡ (A) _____ (B) _____

✎ 출제율 100%
**23** 위 글의 분위기로 가장 알맞은 것은?
① exciting ② sad
③ scary ④ hopeful
⑤ lonely

[24~26] 다음 글을 읽고 물음에 답하시오.

Have you been to Bukchon? ⓐThere is a beautiful *hanok* village in Bukchon. It is ⓑ_____ with tourists who want to see Korea's past. ⓒHowever, not many people know that Bukchon created through one man's efforts. That man was Jeong Segwon, known as the King of Architecture in Gyeongseong.

✎ 출제율 90%
**24** 위 글의 밑줄 친 ⓐ와 같은 뜻이 되도록 다음 문장의 빈칸에 알맞은 말을 쓰시오.

➡ Bukchon _____ a beautiful *hanok* village.

✎ 출제율 100%
**25** 위 글의 빈칸 ⓑ에 알맞은 것은?
① known ② well
③ popular ④ familiar
⑤ unknown

✎ 출제율 85%
**26** 위 글의 밑줄 친 ⓒ에서 어법상 어색한 것을 고치시오.

_____ ➡ _____

[27~28] 다음 글을 읽고 물음에 답하시오.

(①) A woman moved into the building next to Joe's store. (②) She opened up a new store. (③) Many people started to go to the woman's new store instead of Joe's store. (④) ___ⓐ___ people set foot in Joe's store. (⑤)

✎ 출제율 100%
**27** 위 글의 ①~⑤ 중 주어진 문장이 들어갈 곳은?

His food business fell off.

① ② ③ ④ ⑤

✎ 출제율 90%
**28** 위 글의 빈칸 ⓐ에 알맞은 것은?
① Few ② A few
③ Many ④ Much
⑤ A little

**01** 다음 대화의 흐름상 <u>어색한</u> 것을 하나 찾아서 고치시오.

> B: Do you know anything about Korean history?
> G: I don't know much about it and I'm interested in it.
> B: Can you help me with my history homework?
> B: Sure. No problem.

➡ _____

_____

[02~03] 다음 대화를 읽고 물음에 답하시오.

> G: Do you know anything about Changdeokgung?
> B: ⓐYes, a little. It's famous for its beautiful garden.
> G: I'm going to go ⓑthere with my Chinese friend.
> B: I think you'll like it.

**02** 위 대화의 밑줄 친 ⓐ를 생략되지 않은 문장으로 쓰시오.

➡ _____

**03** 위 대화의 밑줄 친 ⓑ가 가리키는 것을 영어로 쓰시오.

➡ _____

**04** 다음 대화의 빈칸에 알맞은 단어를 쓰시오.

> A: Could you _____ your plan to save money?
> B: I won't waste my money on snacks.

➡ _____

**05** 괄호 안의 동사를 어법에 맞게 고쳐 쓰시오.

(1) The policeman asked her (tell) him the truth.

➡ _____

(2) Her parents encouraged her (study) hard.

➡ _____

(3) Please help me (push) the boat.

➡ _____

**06** 주어진 단어를 어법에 맞게 빈칸에 쓰시오.

(1) A girl _____ Jiho called you an hour ago. (name)

(2) The _____ robot is really expensive. (talk)

**07** 다음 상황에 알맞은 말을 어법에 맞게 빈칸에 쓰시오.

(1) This morning he was late for school. The teacher said to him, "Don't be late."
➡ The teacher told him _____ late for school.

(2) Mr. White said to me, "Don't give up."
➡ Mr. White encouraged me _____ up.

**08** 다음 우리말에 맞게 주어진 어구를 배열하시오.

(1) 이것은 그에 의해서 쓰인 유일한 책이다.
   (the / him / only / by / book / written / this / is)

➡ _____

(2) 이 집에 사는 소년은 Andy이다.
   (house / living / the / in / is / Andy / this / boy)

➡ _____

(3) 선생님은 우리에게 체육관에 모이라고 말씀하셨다. (the teacher / the gym / us / gather / told / at / to)

➡ _____

(4) 지호는 도훈이에게 창문을 닦아 달라고 부탁했다. (Jiho / Dohun / the window / clean / asked / to)

➡ _____

[09~11] 다음 글을 읽고 물음에 답하시오.

Who is An Yongbok?

He lived ___@___ the Joseon Dynasty, and his job was catching fish. When he was fishing, he saw the Japanese people fishing near Ulleungdo. He visited Japan twice and said that Ulleungdo and Dokdo were part of Korea. ⓑIn 1696, the Japanese ruler officially told the Japanese people to not fish near Ulleugdo and Dokdo. He did his best to protect Ulleungdo and Dokdo.

**09** 위 글의 빈칸 @에 알맞은 전치사를 쓰시오.

➡ _____

**10** 위 글의 밑줄 친 ⓑ에서 어법상 어색한 것을 고치시오.

_____ ➡ _____

**11** What did An Yongbok do for a living? Answer in English. (4 words)

➡ _____

[12~13] 다음 글을 읽고 물음에 답하시오.

Have you ever seen this kind of pot? It is an onggi. People in the old times used it for @ store rice for a long time.

We have designed a modern onggi with flowers painted on ⓑit, and it even has handles.

**12** 위 글의 밑줄 친 @를 알맞은 형으로 고치시오.

➡ _____

**13** 위 글의 밑줄 친 ⓑ가 가리키는 것을 우리말로 쓰시오.

➡ _____

**01** 다음 주어진 동사와 to부정사를 이용하여 보기와 같이 여러 가지 문장을 쓰시오.

order  want  ask  tell  allow  advise  force  persuade

┤ 보기 ├

My boss ordered me to go to London.

(1) _____

(2) _____

(3) _____

(4) _____

(5) _____

(6) _____

(7) _____

**02** 다음 대화를 읽고 대화의 내용을 요약한 문장을 완성하시오.

**Reporter:** You founded Geonyangsa. What does Geonyangsa do?

**Jeong:** We build houses. We build *hanoks* on the land between Gyeongbokgung and Changdeokgung.

**Reporter:** Why did you build *hanoks* there?

**Jeong:** Many Japanese are moving into Gyeongseong and changing it to fit their taste. So I want to protect the *hanok*.

**Reporter:** You are also helping the independence movement in many ways. How have you helped?

**Jeong:** I know a lot about architecture, so I have built the office building for the Joseon Language Society.

This is a dialogue (A)_____ Jeong Segwon and a reporter. His job is (B)_____ houses. Many Japanese (C)_____ into Gyeongseong are changing it to fit their (D)_____. So he wants to (E)_____ the *hanok*. He is also helping the (F)_____ movement in many ways. For (G)_____, he has built the office (H)_____ for the Joseon Language Society.

## 단원별 모의고사

**01** 다음 문장의 빈칸에 알맞은 것으로 짝지어진 것은?

> • Hundreds _____ people lose their lives every hurricane season.
> • Thanks _____ her invention, many people live better lives.

① of - for
② of - to
③ at - for
④ from - to
⑤ with - from

**02** 다음 우리말을 영어로 옮길 때 빈칸에 알맞은 것으로 짝지어진 것은?

> • 그 물고기는 아직 살아 있니?
> ➡ Is the fish still _____?
> • 커피 한 잔 더 드시겠어요?
> ➡ Won't you have _____ cup of coffee?

① live - other
② living - other
③ living - another
④ alive - other
⑤ alive - another

**03** 다음 밑줄 친 단어의 뜻이 잘못된 것을 고르시오.

① Don't <u>waste</u> your time and money. (낭비하다)
② He got the job <u>through</u> a friend of his. (~을 통하여)
③ Mike read a historical <u>novel</u>. (소설)
④ The house is made of <u>stone</u>. (흙)
⑤ Ants <u>store up</u> food for winter. (저장하다)

**[04~06]** 다음 대화를 읽고 물음에 답하시오.

> B: Do you know anything about a *dol* party?
> G: Yes. It's the birthday party for a one-year-old baby.
> B: Could you tell me more about ⓐit?
> G: Well, the family members get together for the party, and the birthday baby _____ⓑ_____ a *hanbok*.
> B: That sounds interesting.
> G: The family members share food and wish for a long life for the baby. It's a Korean tradition.

**04** 위 대화의 밑줄 친 ⓐit이 가리키는 것을 우리말로 쓰시오.

➡ _____

**05** 위 대화의 빈칸 ⓑ에 다음 정의에 해당하는 단어를 쓰시오.

> to have something such as clothes, shoes, or gloves on your body or on part of your body

➡ _____

**06** 위 대화의 내용으로 보아 대답할 수 <u>없는</u> 질문은?

① Does the boy know a lot about a *dol* party?
② What is a *dol* party?
③ Do the family members get together for the party?
④ What food the family members eat at the *dol* party?
⑤ Do the family members wish for a long life for the baby?

**07** 다음 대화를 순서대로 바르게 배열한 것은?

> (A) Yes. It is one of the greatest sights in the world.
> (B) Can you explain why it is famous?
> (C) Do you know anything about the Great Wall of China?
> (D) It's because it is the longest wall in the world.

① (B) – (A) – (C) – (D)　② (B) – (C) – (D) – (A)

③ (C) – (A) – (B) – (D)　④ (C) – (B) – (A) – (D)

⑤ (C) – (D) – (B) – (A)

**[08~11]** 다음 대화를 읽고 물음에 답하시오.

> Reporter: You founded Geonyangsa. What does Geonyangsa do?
> Jeong: We build houses. (①) We build *hanoks* on the land between Gyeongbokgung and Changdeokgung. (②)
> Reporter: Why did you build hanoks ⓐthere?
> Jeong: (③) Many Japanese are moving into Gyeongseong and changing it to fit their taste. (④)
> Reporter: ⓑ당신은 또한 여러 방법으로 독립 운동을 도와주고 있습니다. How have you helped?
> Jeong: I know a lot about architecture, so I have built the office building for the Joseon Language Society. (⑤)

**08** ①~⑤ 중 주어진 문장이 들어갈 곳은?

> So I want to protect the *hanok*.

①　　②　　③　　④　　⑤

**09** 밑줄 친 ⓐthere가 가리키는 것을 우리말로 쓰시오.

➡ _____

**10** 밑줄 친 ⓑ를 괄호 안에 주어진 단어를 이용하여 영작하시오. (also, way)

➡ _____

_____

**11** 위 대화의 내용으로 보아 알 수 없는 것을 고르시오.

① Jeong founded Geonyangsa.

② Jeong builds *hanoks*.

③ Jeong doesn't know how to build Japanese houses.

④ Many Japanese are changing Gyeongseong to fit their taste.

⑤ Jeong has built the office building for the Joseon Language Society.

**12** 다음 빈칸에 들어갈 동사 do의 형태가 다른 하나는?

① Jim wanted me _____ the dishes.

② She advised him _____ some exercise regularly.

③ Our teacher told us _____ our homework.

④ Did you expect him _____ his best?

⑤ My mom made us _____ it.

**13** 다음 중 빈칸에 들어갈 단어 use의 형태가 <u>다른</u> 하나는?

① I found her _____ my pen.
② The boy _____ your computer is my son.
③ David is _____ the copy machine.
④ They bought a _____ car.
⑤ Ann is _____ a special knife to cut meat.

**14** 다음 중 어법상 올바른 것을 고르시오.

① The typhoon caused the old bridge to fall.
② They expect her participating in the ceremony.
③ Judy asked him make sandwiches.
④ Do you want me waking you up tomorrow morning?
⑤ The math teacher told us solved 10 problems every day.

**15** 다음 두 문장을 관계대명사를 사용하지 않고 하나의 문장으로 바꿔 쓰시오.

• She bought a smartphone.
• The smartphone was made in Korea.

➡ _____

**16** 다음 빈칸에 알맞은 말을 쓰시오.

그는 충격을 받은 것처럼 보인다.
He looks _____.

**17** 다음 빈칸에 적절하지 <u>않은</u> 것은?

I _____ her to take part in the party.

① watched          ② wanted
③ told             ④ persuaded
⑤ expected

[18~19] 다음 글을 읽고 물음에 답하시오.

ⓐHave you been to Bukchon? There is a beautiful hanok village in Bukchon. It is popular with tourists who want to see Korea's past. However, not many people know that Bukchon was created through one man's efforts. That man was Jeong Segwon, known ⓑas the King of Architecture in Gyeongseong.

**18** 위 글의 밑줄 친 ⓐ와 용법이 같은 것은?

① I have been in this country since last month.
② Yumi has seen this movie many times.
③ Mike has just cleaned his room.
④ Lisa has had this cat for ten years.
⑤ She has gone out and this room is cold.

**19** 위 글의 밑줄 친 ⓑas와 의미가 같은 것은?

① He came up as I was speaking.
② When in Rome, do as the Romans do.
③ He is famous as an artist.
④ As it rained, they stopped the game.
⑤ As we go higher, the air gets colder.

**[20~22]** 다음 글을 읽고 물음에 답하시오.

When the Joseon Language Affair happened, ⓐ Jeong Segwon caught by the police and suffered a lot. Japanese officials pressed him to build Japanese houses. He said, "I don't know how to build Japanese houses." An official said, "You know how to build *hanoks*, ___ⓑ___ you can build Japanese houses, too." But he did not do what the Japanese told him to do. The cost was high. His business fell off, and he lost his property. ___ⓑ___, in part, thanks to Jeong Segwon, the traditions of Korea still live with us today.

**20** 위 글의 밑줄 친 ⓐ에서 어법상 어색한 것을 고치시오.

_____  ➡ _____

**21** 위 글의 빈칸 ⓑ에 알맞은 것은?

① so
② or
③ for
④ but
⑤ though

**22** 위 글의 빈칸 ⓑ에 알맞은 것은?

① Though
② However
③ Besides
④ Furthermore
⑤ Therefore

**[23~25]** 다음 글을 읽고 물음에 답하시오.

An Yongbok lived during the Joseon Dynasty, and his ___ⓐ___ was catching fish. When he was fishing, he saw the Japanese people fishing near Ulleungdo. He visited Japan twice and said that Ulleungdo and Dokdo were part of Korea. In 1696, the Japanese ruler ⓑofficial told the Japanese people not to fish near Ulleugdo and Dokdo. He did his best to protect Ulleungdo and Dokdo.

**23** 위 글의 빈칸 ⓐ에 다음 정의에 해당하는 단어를 쓰시오.

the work that someone does to earn money

➡ _____

**24** 위 글의 밑줄 친 ⓑ를 알맞은 형으로 고치시오.

➡ _____

**25** 위 글의 내용과 일치하지 <u>않는</u> 것은?

① 안용복은 조선 왕조 시대에 살았다.
② 안용복의 직업은 어부였다.
③ 안용복은 일본인들이 울릉도 부근에서 고기를 잡는 것을 보았다.
④ 안용복은 일본을 한 번 방문했다.
⑤ 안용복은 울릉도와 독도를 지키려고 노력했다.

# Manners Make the Man

 의사소통 기능

- 약속 정하기
  A: How about going to the hot spring on Thursday at 2:00? Can you make it?

  B: Yes. That would be great.

- 상기시키기
  A: Don't forget to turn off your cellphone in the theater.
  B: Okay, I won't.

 언어 형식

- 관계부사
  Today's quiet concerts began in the 19th century **when** many big concert halls were built.

- 간접의문문
  We do not know **what concerts will look like in the future**.

# Words & Expressions

## Key Words

- **actually** [ǽktʃuəli] 부 사실은
- **appear** [əpíər] 동 나타나다
- **audience** [ɔ́:diəns] 명 관객
- **between** [bitwí:n] 전 (위치가) ~ 사이[중간]에
- **blame** [bleim] 동 비난하다
- **book fair** 도서 박람회
- **bright** [brait] 형 밝은
- **century** [séntʃəri] 명 세기, 100년
- **clap** [klæp] 동 박수치다
- **classical** [klǽsikəl] 형 고전의, 클래식 음악의
- **concerto** [kəntʃéərtou] 명 협주곡
- **correct** [kərékt] 형 올바른, 정확한
- **dependent** [dipéndənt] 형 의존적인, 의존하는
- **disturb** [distə́:rb] 동 방해하다
- **enjoyable** [indʒɔ́iəbl] 형 즐거운, 즐길 수 있는
- **event** [ivént] 명 행사
- **familiar** [fəmíljər] 형 익숙한
- **forget** [fərgét] 동 잊다
- **freely** [frí:li] 부 자유롭게
- **healthy** [hélθi] 형 건강한
- **imagine** [imǽdʒin] 동 상상하다
- **increased** [inkrní:st] 형 증가된
- **inside** [ìnsáid] 전 ~ 안에
- **manners** [mǽnərz] 명 예절
- **memorable** [mémərəbl] 형 기억에 남을, 기억할 만한
- **mostly** [móustli] 부 주로
- **movement** [mú:vmənt] 명 움직임, (큰 교향곡 따위의) 악장[부분]
- **nobleman** [nóublmən] 명 귀족
- **noise** [nɔiz] 명 소음, 잡음
- **orchestra** [ɔ́:rkəstrə] 명 오케스트라
- **pause** [pɔ:z] 명 정지, 멈춤 동 정지하다
- **performance** [pərfɔ́:rməns] 명 공연
- **place** [pleis] 명 장소
- **quiet** [kwáiət] 형 조용한
- **remember** [rimémbər] 동 기억하다
- **result** [rizʌ́lt] 명 결과
- **return** [ritə́:rn] 동 돌려주다, 반납하다
- **scene** [si:n] 명 장면
- **secret** [sí:krit] 명 비밀
- **serious** [síəriəs] 형 심각한, 진지한
- **silent** [sáilənt] 형 조용한
- **social** [sóuʃəl] 형 사회적인, 사교적인
- **surprisingly** [sərpráiziŋli] 부 놀랍게도
- **trash can** 쓰레기통
- **volunteer work** 자원봉사
- **whistle** [hwísl] 동 휘파람을 불다
- **work** [wə:rk] 명 작품

## Key Expressions

- **after some time** 얼마 후
- **as a result** 그 결과(=**consequently**)
- **at any time** 아무 때나
- **dependent on** ~에 의존하는
- **be on time** 제시간에 오다, 시간을 맞추다
- **blame A for B** B 때문에 A를 비난하다
- **by the way** 그건 그렇고
- **for example** 예를 들면(=**for instance**)
- **for now** 우선은, 현재로는, 지금은
- **go back in time** 과거로 거슬러 올라가다
- **no longer** 더 이상 ~하지 않는
- **part of** ~의 부분
- **take a look at** ~을 보다
- **take care of** ~을 돌보다
- **with time** 시간이 지남에 따라

## Word Power

※ '~하는 사람'의 뜻을 갖는 '-ist'

□ **art** (예술) → **artist** (예술가)

□ **tour** (관광) → **tourist** (관광객)

□ **journal** (저널, 신문[잡지]) → **journalist** (기자)

□ **piano** (피아노) → **pianist** (피아노 연주자)

□ **novel** (소설) → **novelist** (소설가)

□ **science** (과학) → **scientist** (과학자)

□ **medal** (메달) → **medalist** (메달 딴 선수)

□ **violin** (바이올린) → **violinist** (바이올린 연주자)

※ 서로 반대되는 뜻을 가진 어휘

□ **dark** (어두운) ↔ **bright** (밝은)

□ **familiar** (익숙한) ↔ **unfamiliar** (익숙하지 않은)

□ **increase** (증가하다) ↔ **decrease** (감소하다)

□ **appear** (나타나다) ↔ **disappear** (사라지다)

□ **dependent** (의존적인) ↔ **independent** (독립적인)

□ **blame** (비난하다) ↔ **praise** (칭찬하다)

## English Dictionary

□ **appear**: 나타나다
→ to start to be seen
보이기 시작하다

□ **blame**: 비난하다
→ to think or say that someone or something is responsible for something bad
누군가 또는 무언가가 나쁜 일에 책임이 있다고 생각하거나 말하다

□ **clap**: 박수치다
→ to hit your open hands together
두 손뼉을 마주 치다

□ **concerto**: 협주곡
→ a piece of music for one or more solo instruments playing with an orchestra
오케스트라와 연주하는 하나 이상의 독주 악기를 위한 음악

□ **disturb**: 방해하다
→ to interrupt someone when they are trying to work, sleep, etc.
일을 하거나 잠을 자려고 할 때 누군가를 방해하다

□ **nobleman**: 귀족
→ a man from a family of high social rank; a female member of the nobility 신분이 높은 집안의 남자; 귀족 출신의 여자

□ **noise**: 소음, 잡음
→ a loud or unpleasant sound
크거나 불쾌한 소리

□ **orchestra**: 오케스트라
→ a group of musicians who play usually classical music together and who are led by a conductor
대개 고전 음악을 함께 연주하며 지휘자가 이끄는 음악가 모임

□ **pause**: 정지하다, 멈추다
→ to stop talking or doing something for a short time before continuing
계속하기 전에 잠시 말하거나 무언가를 하는 것을 멈추다

□ **performance**: 공연
→ the act of performing a play, concert, or some other form of entertainment
연극, 콘서트 또는 다른 형태의 오락물을 공연하는 행위

□ **result**: 결과
→ something that is caused by something else that happened or was done before 이전에 발생하거나 행해진 다른 것에 의해 유발된 것

□ **return**: 돌려주다, 반납하다
→ to bring something to the place that it came from or the place where it should go
어떤 것을 원래 있던 곳이나 가야 할 곳으로 가져가다

□ **secret**: 비밀
→ a fact or piece of information that is kept hidden from other people
남들에게 숨겨진 사실이나 정보

□ **whistle**: 휘파람을 불다
→ to make a high sound by blowing air through your lips or teeth
입술이나 치아 사이로 공기를 내보내어 고음을 내다

□ **work**: 작품
→ something such as a book, song, or painting that is produced by a writer, musician, artist, etc.
작가, 음악가, 화가 등이 만든 책, 노래, 그림 같은 것

**01** 다음 짝지어진 단어의 관계가 같도록 빈칸에 알맞은 말을 쓰시오.

library : librarian = tour : _____

**02** 다음 중 밑줄 친 단어의 우리말 뜻이 **잘못된** 것은?

① He has good manners. 예절
② They look serious nowadays. 심각한
③ Let's clap along to the music. 박수치다
④ The number of students increased last year. 감소했다.
⑤ They blamed each other for the failure. 비난했다.

**03** 다음 중 밑줄 친 단어와 의미가 같은 것은?

Don't disturb Jane. She's studying for her exam.

① pause
② appear
③ whistle
④ interrupt
⑤ depend

**04** 다음 영영풀이에 해당하는 단어는?

to think or say that someone or something is responsible for something bad

① connect
② worry
③ blame
④ cause
⑤ predict

**05** 다음 중 〈보기〉의 밑줄 친 단어와 같은 의미로 쓰인 것은?

┤ 보기 ├
Their dancing was a work of art.

① He's still looking for work.
② She goes to work at 8 o'clock.
③ Taking care of a baby is hard work.
④ When do you leave for work?
⑤ She put her works on display in the art gallery.

**06** 다음 빈칸에 들어갈 말이 바르게 짝지어진 것은?

• You must be _____ time.
• Take a look _____ her old picture.

① in - to
② on - at
③ at - in
④ of - by
⑤ in - with

**07** 다음 우리말에 맞게 빈칸에 알맞은 말을 쓰시오.

(1) 그녀는 밝은 색을 좋아한다.
  ➡ She likes _____ colors.
(2) 그 새는 하늘에서 자유롭게 날고 있다.
  ➡ The bird is flying _____ in the sky.
(3) 이것은 유명한 피아노 협주곡이다.
  ➡ This is a famous piano _____.

**01** 다음 빈칸에 들어갈 말을 〈보기〉에서 골라 알맞은 형태로 쓰시오.

┤ 보기 ├
novel   tour   science   art

(1) A figure skater is an _____ on the ice.
(2) Sumi wants to be a _____ who studies the stars.
(3) Emily Bronte is an English female _____.
(4) Please tell me the way to the _____ information center.

**02** 다음 영영풀이에 해당하는 말을 한 단어로 쓰시오.

to hit your open hands together

➡ _____

**03** 다음 문장의 빈칸에 들어갈 말을 〈보기〉에서 골라 쓰시오.

┤ 보기 ├
mostly   serious   blame   audience

(1) Don't _____ him. He did his best.
(2) The _____ was moved by the play.
(3) The consequences were _____.
(4) The readers are _____ women and children.

**04** 다음 밑줄 친 부분과 의미가 같은 단어를 주어진 철자로 시작하여 쓰시오.

As a <u>result</u>, my team lost.

➡ C_____

**05** 다음 우리말과 같도록 빈칸에 알맞은 말을 써 넣으시오.

(1) 나는 더 이상 오래 머물 수 없다.
➡ I can stay _____ _____.
(2) 아이는 부모에 의존한다.
➡ A child is _____ _____ his parents.
(3) 그들은 아무 때나 휘파람을 불고 박수를 친다.
➡ They whistle and clap _____ _____ _____.

**06** 다음 우리말에 맞게 주어진 단어를 바르게 배열하시오.

(1) 나는 작은 쓰레기통이 필요하다. (need / can / a / I / trash / small)
➡ _____
(2) 소음은 단지 콘서트의 일부였다.
(just / noise / concert / of / was / the / part)
➡ _____
(3) 모차르트 시대의 콘서트는 주로 사교적 행사였다.
(time / mostly / in / events / concerts / social / Mozart's / were )
➡ _____

**①** **약속 정하기**

> A: How about going to the hot spring on Thursday at 2:00? Can you make it?
> (목요일 2시에 온천에 가는 게 어때? 갈 수 있니?)
>
> B: Yes. That would be great. (응. 그거 좋겠다.)

■ 'Can you make it?'은 '갈 수 있니?'라는 뜻으로 약속을 정할 때 쓰는 표현이다. 'make it'은 '해내다, 성공하다'라는 의미를 갖고 있지만, 시간이나 장소의 표현과 함께 쓰여 '시간에 맞춰 가다' 또는 '도착하다'라는 의미를 갖는다.

### 약속 정하기 표현

- Can you make it at six? 6시에 올 수 있니?
- Why don't we meet at the park? 공원에서 만나는 게 어떠니?
- How[What] about meeting at six? 6시에 만나는 게 어떠니?
- Shall we meet after school? 방과 후에 만날까?
- Let's meet at ten on Saturday. 토요일 10시에 만나자.

### 약속 정하기에 답하는 표현

〈승낙하기〉

That would be great. / That's fine with me. / No problem. / Why not? / Sure, I'd love to. / That's a good idea. / (That) Sounds great.

〈거절하기〉

I'm sorry, I can't. / I'm afraid not. / I'd love to, but I can't. / Not this time, thanks. / Maybe next time.

### 핵심 Check

1. 다음 우리말과 일치하도록 빈칸에 알맞은 말을 쓰시오.

(1) A: Can you _____ _____ at five? (5시에 올 수 있니?)

　　 B: That's _____ with me. (난 괜찮아.)

(2) A: How _____ _____ to the movie theater tomorrow?

　　 (우리 내일 영화관에 가는 게 어때?)

　　 B: No _____. (문제없어.)

## ② 상기시키기

A: Don't forget to turn off your cellphone in the theater. (너의 휴대 전화를 극장에서 끄는 것을 잊지 마.)

B: Okay, I won't. (알았어. 잊지 않을게.)

■ 'Don't forget to ~'는 상대방에게 어떤 일을 해야 한다고 알려 주거나 해야 할 일을 상기시켜 주기 위해 사용하는 표현으로 'Remember to+동사원형 ~' 또는 'Make sure that 주어+동사 ~' 또는 'Make sure to+동사원형 ~'으로 바꾸어 쓸 수 있다.

### 어떤 일을 해야 한다고 알려 주기

- Don't forget to bring your lunch box. 도시락을 가져오는 것을 잊지 마라.
- Remember to bring your lunch box. 도시락을 가져와야 한다는 것을 기억해라.
- Make sure that you should bring your lunch box. 도시락을 가져와야 함을 명심해라.
- Make sure to bring your lunch box. 도시락을 가져와야 함을 명심해라.
- Keep in mind that you should bring your lunch box. 도시락을 가져와야 한다는 것을 명심해라.

■ forget이나 remember 뒤에 -ing를 쓰면 '(과거에) ~했던 것을 잊다[기억하다]'라는 의미가 되고, 'to+동사원형'을 쓰면 '(미래에) ~해야 할 것을 잊다[기억하다]'라는 의미를 나타낸다.

- forget + -ing: (과거에) ~한 것을 잊다
- remember + -ing: (과거에) ~한 것을 기억하다
- forget + to 동사원형: (미래에) ~해야 할 것을 잊다
- remember + to 동사원형: (미래에) ~해야 할 것을 기억하다

### 핵심 Check

2. 다음 우리말과 일치하도록 빈칸에 알맞은 말을 쓰시오.

(1) A: _____ _____ _____ bring your umbrella. (너의 우산을 가져올 것을 잊지 마라.)

B: Okay, I see. (네. 알겠어요.)

(2) A: It looks like it's going to rain soon. _____ _____ close the windows.
(창문을 닫아야 한다는 것을 기억해라.)

B: Okay, I will. (네. 그럴게요.)

(3) A: I'm going skating tomorrow. (나는 내일 스케이트를 타러 갈 거야.)

B: _____ _____ _____ put your gloves on. (장갑 끼는 것을 명심해라.)

(4) A: Don't forget to turn off the light before you leave. (떠나기 전에 불을 끌 것을 잊지 마라.)

B: Okay, I _____. (알았어, 잊지 않을게.)

### Listen & Speak 1 B-1

B: ❶Are you interested in going to an opera? I have two tickets.

G: Yes, I love opera. When is ❷it?

B: It's this Saturday at 5:00. ❸Can you make it?

G: Yes, ❹thanks so much for asking me.

B: 너 오페라에 가는 것에 관심이 있니? 내게 표가 두 장 있어.

G: 응. 나 오페라 아주 좋아해. 언제야?

B: 이번 주 토요일 5시야. 갈 수 있니?

G: 응. 나한테 물어봐 줘서 정말 고마워.

❶ be interested in: ～에 관심이 있다
❷ it=the opera
❸ Can you make it?: 갈 수 있니?
❹ thanks so much=thank you so much

**Check(√) True or False**

(1) The boy isn't interested in going to an opera.　　T ☐ F ☐

(2) The girl will go to the opera with the boy.　　T ☐ F ☐

### Wrap Up

G: Yunho! ❶Have you heard about the Christmas concert at the city hall?

B: Yes. ❷I heard that a famous opera singer will be on the stage.

G: Oh, ❸then why don't we go on Christmas Day? Can you make it?

B: Sure. ❹Do you know what time the concert starts?

G: It starts at 5:30. Let's meet at the bus stop at 4:00.

B: Good. ❺Don't forget to dress up.

G: Okay. I won't.

G: 윤호야! 너 시청에서 하는 크리스마스 콘서트에 대해 들어 봤어?

B: 응. 유명한 오페라 가수가 무대에 오를 것이라고 들었어.

G: 오, 그러면 크리스마스 날에 가는 게 어때? 갈 수 있니?

B: 물론이지. 너는 콘서트가 언제 시작하는지 아니?

G: 5시 30분에 시작해. 버스 정류장에서 4시에 만나자.

B: 좋아. 옷을 차려 입는 것 잊지 마.

G: 알았어. 잊지 않을게.

❶ Have you heard about ～?: ～에 대해 들어 봤니? (경험을 나타내는 현재완료이다.)
❷ that은 접속사로 heard의 목적어가 되는 명사절을 이끈다. be on the stage: 무대에 오르다
❸ why don't we ～?: 우리 ～하는 게 어때? (제안을 나타내는 표현이다.)
❹ what time the concert starts는 간접의문문으로 know의 목적어이다.
❺ Don't forget to ～.: ～하는 것을 잊지 마. (상기시키는 표현이다.) dress up: 옷을 갖춰[격식을 차려] 입다

**Check(√) True or False**

(3) The Christmas concert will be held at the city hall.　　T ☐ F ☐

(4) The girl won't dress up when she goes to the oprea.　　T ☐ F ☐

### Listen & Speak 1 B-2

B: ❶Why don't we go to the new shoe shop this weekend?

G: Okay. ❷What about at 2:00 on Saturday?

B: ❸Can you make it at 1:00? ❹I have to take care of my sister at 3:00.

G: Sure. ❺See you then.

❶ Why don't we go ～?=Shall we go ～?
❷ What about ～?: ～은 어때?
❸ Can you make it at 1:00?: 1시에 올 수 있니?
❹ take care of: ～을 돌보다
❺ See you then.: 그때 보자.

### Listen & Speak 2 B-1

B: ❶We're going to Hangang this weekend. Do you remember?

G: Of course. ❷Don't forget to bring your camera.

B: Okay. ❸I won't. I'll bring some snacks, too.

G: ❹Sounds great.

❶ We're going to Hangang=We're going to go to Hangang
❷ Don't forget to ～: ～할 것을 잊지 마. (상기시키는 표현이다.)
❸ I won't.=I won't forget to bring my camera.
❹ Sounds great.: 그거 좋은데.

### Listen & Speak 2 B-2

G: You look healthy. What's your secret?

B: Thanks. ❶Well, I go swimming every day. You should go with me sometime.

G: ❷That sounds like fun. ❸Any other things I should do?

B: ❹Don't forget to eat many kinds of fruits and vegetables, too.

❶ go swimming: 수영하러 가다
❷ That sounds like fun.: 그거 재미있는 것 같구나. fun이 명사이므로 앞에 like를 붙인다.
❸ Any other things I should do?=Are there any other things (which) I should do?
❹ many kinds of fruits: 많은 종류의 과일 (fruit은 보통 단수형으로 쓰이지만, 과일의 종류를 나타낼 때는 복수형을 취한다.)

### Real-Life Zone A

G: What are you listening to?

B: Classical music. ❶I'm going to a concert tomorrow and I'd like to know about the music before I go.

G: ❷I guess it's more enjoyable if you know the music.

B: ❸Actually, I don't want to clap at the wrong time.

G: Don't you just clap when the music stops?

B: No. ❹In classical music, one piece of music may have several pauses. ❺You should wait and clap at the very end.

G: I see. ❻Make sure you don't forget to clap at the real ending. ❼By the way, can you make it to our soccer practice tomorrow at 4:00?

B: Sure. ❽I'll come to the practice after the concert finishes.

G: Okay. See you then.

❶ I'm going to a concert tomorrow=I'm going to go to a concert tomorrow / I'd like to: ～하고 싶다
❷ I guess=I think
❸ at the wrong time: 잘못된 때에
❹ may: ～일지도 모른다 (추측을 나타내는 조동사)
❺ at the very end: 맨 마지막에
❻ Make sure (that) you don't forget to ～: ～할 것을 잊지 말도록 해라.
❼ by the way: 그런데 / can you make it to ～: ～에 올 수 있니?
❽ after the concert finishes: 콘서트가 끝난 후에 (때를 나타내는 부사절은 현재형으로 미래의 일을 나타낸다.)

다음 우리말과 일치하도록 빈칸에 알맞은 말을 쓰시오.

### Listen & Speak 1 B

1. B: Are you _____ _____ going to an opera? I have two _____.

   G: Yes, I love opera. _____ is it?

   B: It's _____ Saturday _____ 5:00. Can you _____ _____?

   G: Yes, _____ so much for _____ me.

2. B: _____ _____ we go to the new shoe shop _____ weekend?

   G: Okay. _____ _____ at 2:00 on Saturday?

   B: Can you _____ _____ at 1:00? I _____ _____ take care of my sister at 3:00.

   G: Sure. _____ you then.

해석

1. B: 너 오페라에 가는 것에 관심이 있니? 내게 표가 두 장 있어.
   G: 응, 나 오페라 아주 좋아해. 언제야?
   B: 이번 주 토요일 5시야. 갈 수 있니?
   G: 응. 나한테 물어봐 줘서 정말 고마워.

2. B: 우리 이번 주말에 새로 생긴 신발 가게에 가는 거 어때?
   G: 좋아. 토요일 2시 어때?
   B: 1시에 가능하니? 난 3시에 여동생을 돌봐야 해.
   G: 당연하지. 그때 보자.

### Listen & Speak 2 B

1. B: We're _____ _____ Hangang this weekend. Do you _____?

   G: Of course. _____ _____ to bring your camera.

   B: Okay. I _____. I'll bring some snacks, too.

   G: _____ great.

2. G: You _____ healthy. What's your _____?

   B: Thanks. Well, I _____ _____ every day. You should go with me _____.

   G: That _____ _____ fun. _____ _____ things I should do?

   B: Don't _____ _____ eat _____ _____ of fruits and vegetables, too.

1. B: 우리 이번 주말에 한강 가잖아. 기억하니?
   G: 물론이지. 카메라 가져 오는 것 잊지 마.
   B: 알았어. 잊지 않을게. 나는 약간의 간식도 가져올게.
   G: 아주 좋아.

2. G: 너 건강해 보여. 비결이 뭐니?
   B: 고마워. 음, 나는 매일 수영하러 가. 너도 언젠가 나와 함께 가는 게 좋겠어.
   G: 재밌을 것 같은데. 내가 또 해야 하는 다른 것들이 있니?
   B: 다양한 종류의 과일과 채소를 먹는 것도 잊지 마.

### Real-Life Zone A

**G:** What are you _____ _____?

**B:** Classical music. I'm _____ _____ a concert tomorrow and I'd _____ _____ know about the music _____ I go.

**G:** I _____ it's _____ enjoyable _____ you know the music.

**B:** Actually, I don't want to _____ at the _____ time.

**G:** Don't you just clap _____ the music _____?

**B:** No. In classical music, one piece of music _____ have several _____. You should _____ and clap at the _____ _____.

**G:** I _____. _____ _____ you don't _____ _____ clap at the _____ _____. By the _____, can you _____ _____ to our soccer _____ tomorrow at 4:00?

**B:** Sure. I'll come to the practice _____ the concert _____.

**G:** Okay. _____ you then.

### Real-Life Zone B

**A:** _____ _____ we go to the library on Monday _____ school? Can you _____ it?

**B:** Sorry, but I _____. How _____ on Tuesday?

**A:** Okay. _____ _____ to bring your library card.

**B:** All _____. I _____.

### Wrap Up

**G:** Yunho! _____ you _____ about the Christmas concert at the city hall?

**B:** Yes. I heard _____ a famous opera singer _____ _____ on the stage.

**G:** Oh, then _____ _____ we go on Christmas Day? Can you _____ _____?

**B:** Sure. Do you know _____ _____ the concert starts?

**G:** It starts _____ 5:30. _____ _____ at the bus stop at 4:00.

**B:** Good. Don't _____ _____ dress up.

**G:** Okay. I _____.

**01** 다음 대화의 빈칸에 알맞은 것을 고르시오.

> B: Are you interested in going to an opera? I have two tickets.
> G: Yes, I love opera. When is it?
> B: It's this Saturday at 5:00. _____
> G: Yes, thanks so much for asking me.

① Do you like operas?
② What opera are you interested in?
③ Let's go to an opera.
④ Can you make it?
⑤ How can you go there?

**02** 다음 대화의 순서를 바르게 배열하시오.

> (A) Sure. See you then.
> (B) Okay. What about at 2:00 on Saturday?
> (C) Why don't we go to the new shoe shop this weekend?
> (D) Can you make it at 1:00? I have to take care of my sister at 3:00.

➡ _____

**03** 다음 대화의 밑줄 친 부분의 의도로 알맞은 것을 고르시오.

> B: We're going to Hangang this weekend. Do you remember?
> G: Of course. <u>Don't forget to bring your camera.</u>
> B: Okay. I won't. I'll bring some snacks, too.
> G: Sounds great.

① 계획 묻기　　　　　② 상기시키기
③ 충고 구하기　　　　④ 문제점 제안하기
⑤ 약속 정하기

**[01~03]** 다음 대화를 읽고 물음에 답하시오.

> G: You look ⓐhealth. What's your secret?
> B: Thanks. Well, I go swimming every day. You should go with me sometime.
> G: That sounds like fun. ⓑAny other things I should do?
> B: Don't forget to eat many kinds of fruits and vegetables, too.

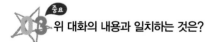
**01** 위 대화의 밑줄 친 ⓐ를 알맞은 형으로 고치시오.

➡ _____

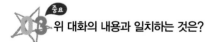
**02** 위 대화의 밑줄 친 ⓑ를 괄호 안에 주어진 단어를 보충하여 다시 쓰시오. (are, that)

➡ _____

**03** 위 대화의 내용과 일치하는 것은?

① 소녀는 소년이 건강해 보이는 비결을 알고 있다.
② 소년은 매일 수영을 한다.
③ 소년은 소녀가 언젠가 함께 수영하러 가기를 원한다.
④ 소녀는 소년과 함께 수영하러 가는 것을 재미있게 생각한다.
⑤ 소년은 소녀에게 많은 과일과 채소를 먹으라고 충고한다.

**04** 다음 대화의 밑줄 친 부분과 의미가 같도록 한 단어로 바꾸어 쓰시오.

> A: Don't forget to look to the right before you cross the street in London.
> B: Okay, I see.

➡ _____

**05** 다음 대화의 순서를 바르게 배열한 것을 고르시오.

> (A) Okay. Don't forget to bring your library card.
> (B) All right. I won't.
> (C) Why don't we go to the library on Monday after school? Can you make it?
> (D) Sorry, but I can't. How about on Tuesday?

① (B) - (A) - (C) - (D)
② (B) - (C) - (A) - (D)
③ (C) - (A) - (B) - (D)
④ (C) - (B) - (A) - (D)
⑤ (C) - (D) - (A) - (B)

**06** 다음 밑줄 친 말과 바꾸어 쓸 수 있는 것을 고르시오. (2개)

> A: What time should we meet tomorrow?
> B: Can you make it at five?

① I need to meet you at five.
② Let's meet tomorrow.
③ Let's meet at five.
④ How about meeting at five?
⑤ I can't make it at five.

Conversation **173**

[07~12] 다음 대화를 읽고 물음에 답하시오.

G: What are you listening ⓐ ?

B: Classical music. I'm going to a concert tomorrow and I'd like to know about the music (A) I go.

G: I guess it's more enjoyable (B) you know the music.

B: Actually, I don't want to clap at the wrong time.

G: Don't you just clap when the music stops?

B: No. In classical music, one piece of music ⓑmay have several pauses. You should wait and clap at the very end.

G: I see. Make sure you don't forget to clap at the real ending. By the way, can you ⓒ it to our soccer practice tomorrow at 4:00?

B: Sure. ⓓI'll come to the practice after the concert will finish.

G: Okay. See you then.

**07** 위 대화의 빈칸 ⓐ에 알맞은 것은?

① at  ② to
③ of  ④ for
⑤ with

위 대화의 빈칸 (A)와 (B)에 알맞은 것은?

|  | (A) | (B) |
|---|---|---|
| ① | before | if |
| ② | after | if |
| ③ | after | when |
| ④ | before | until |
| ⑤ | before | after |

**09** 위 대화의 밑줄 친 ⓑ와 용법이 같은 것은?

① You may come in if you wish.
② May she rest in peace!
③ The rumor may be false.
④ May I take a picture here?
⑤ You may stay at this hotel for a week.

**10** 위 대화의 빈칸 ⓒ에 알맞은 것은?

① do  ② let
③ get  ④ make
⑤ find

**11** [서답형] 위 대화의 밑줄 친 ⓓ에서 어법상 어색한 것을 고쳐 다시 쓰시오.

➡ _____

**12** 위 대화의 내용으로 보아 알 수 없는 것은?

① The boy is listening to classical music.
② The boy often claps at the wrong time.
③ The girl advises the boy to clap at the real ending.
④ The girl knows that there is their soccer practice tomorrow at 4:00.
⑤ The boy will come to the soccer practice tomorrow.

[01~05] 다음 대화를 읽고 물음에 답하시오.

> G: Yunho! Have you heard about the Christmas concert at the city hall?
> B: Yes. I heard ____ⓐ____ a famous opera singer will be on the stage.
> G: ⓑOh, then why don't we go on Christmas Day? Can you make it?
> B: Sure. ____(A)____
> G: It starts at 5:30. Let's meet at the bus stop at 4:00.
> B: Good. (B) 옷을 차려 입는 것을 잊지 마.
> G: Okay. I won't.

**01** 위 대화의 빈칸 ⓐ에 알맞은 말을 쓰시오.

➡ _____

**02** 위 대화의 밑줄 친 ⓑ와 같은 뜻이 되도록 다음 문장의 빈칸에 알맞은 말을 쓰시오.

➡ Oh, then _____ go on Christmas Day.

**03** 위 대화의 빈칸 (A)에 다음 두 문장을 한 문장으로 바꿔 채우시오.

> Do you know?+What time does the concert start?

➡ _____

**04** 위 대화의 밑줄 친 우리말 (B)를 주어진 단어를 이용하여 옮기시오. (5 words)

> forget / up

➡ _____

**05** When and where will the girl and the boy meet?

➡ _____

[06~07] 다음 대화를 읽고 물음에 답하시오.

> A: (A)How don't we go to the library on Monday after school? Can you make it?
> B: Sorry, but I can't. (B)How about on Tuesday?
> A: Okay. Don't forget to bring your library card.
> B: All right. I won't.

**06** 위 대화의 밑줄 친 (A)에서 어법상 어색한 것을 고치시오.

_____ ➡ _____

**07** 위 대화의 밑줄 친 (B)와 같은 뜻이 되도록 빈칸에 알맞은 말을 쓰시오.

➡ _____ _____ go to the library on Tuesday?

# Grammar

교과서

## ① 관계부사

- Today's quiet concerts began in the 19th century **when** many big concert halls were built.
  오늘날의 조용한 콘서트는 많은 대형 콘서트홀이 지어진 19세기에 시작되었다.
- Leipzig is the city **where** Wagner was born in 1813.
  라이프치히는 와그너가 1813년에 태어난 도시이다.

■ 관계부사는 접속사와 부사의 역할을 동시에 하며, 관계대명사처럼 선행사를 수식하는 형용사절을 이끈다. 선행사가 '때'를 나타낼 때는 when, '장소'는 where를 쓴다. 관계부사는 '전치사(at, in, on)+관계대명사(which)'로 바꿔 쓸 수 있다.

| | 선행사 | 종류 | 전치사+관계대명사 |
|---|---|---|---|
| 장소 | the place, the city, the house 등 | where | in[at/on] + which |
| 때 | the time, the day 등 | when | in[at/on] + which |
| 이유 | the reason | why | for + which |
| 방법 | the way | how | in + which |

- I remember the day. She left for Busan on the day.
  = I remember the day **on which** she left for Busan. 난 그녀가 부산으로 떠난 날을 기억한다.
  = I remember the day **when** she left for Busan.

- A desert is an amazing place **where** a variety of animals survive in their own way.
  사막은 다양한 동물들이 그들만의 방식대로 살아가는 놀라운 장소이다.

- Do you know the reason **why**(= **for which**) Dan didn't come? 넌 Dan이 오지 않는 이유를 알고 있니?

■ 선행사가 방법을 나타내는 the way일 경우에는 the way와 how를 함께 쓸 수 없다.

- This is **the way** the man opened the door. 이것이 그 남자가 문을 연 방법이다.
- This is **how** the man opened the door.
- This is the way how the man opened the door. (×)

### 핵심 Check

1. 다음 문장의 괄호 안에서 알맞은 것을 고르시오.

   (1) Sam knows the exact time (when / where) Kate will come.

   (2) I'd like to visit the city (why / where) I was born.

   (3) Tell me the reason (why / which) you were late for school.

   (4) This is (the way how / how / the way) he killed the big bear.

## ② 간접의문문

> • We do not know **what concerts will look like in the future.**
> 우리는 콘서트가 미래에 어떤 모습일지 알지 못한다.
>
> • I remember **when I went to a concert for the first time.**
> 나는 내가 처음으로 콘서트에 갔던 때를 기억한다.

■ 간접의문문은 의문문이 '의문사+주어+동사' 형태로 문장 안에서 목적어의 역할을 하는 것을 말한다.

　• I don't know **why he was absent.** 〈목적어 역할〉 나는 그가 왜 결석했는지 모른다.

■ 의문사가 주어인 경우에는 의문사가 주어 역할을 동시에 하므로 직접의문문처럼 '의문사+동사'의 어순임에 유의한다.

　• Do you know **who wrote this book**? 너는 누가 이 책을 썼는지 아니?

■ 간접의문문으로 바꾸어 쓸 때에는 조동사 do를 삭제한다. 이때, 조동사 do의 시제를 간접의문문의 동사에 반영해야 한다는 점에 유의해야 한다.

　• Please tell me. + What did you do last night?
　→ Please tell me **what you did last night.** 너는 어젯밤 무엇을 했는지 내게 말해 줘.

■ 의문사가 없는 경우에는 의문사 대신에 if나 whether를 쓴다.

　• Will you tell me? + Are you hungry?
　→ Will you tell me **if[whether] you are hungry**? 배가 고픈지 내게 말해 줄래?

■ believe, imagine, suppose, consider, expect, think, guess 등과 같은 동사가 주절에 있을 경우 간접의문문의 의문사를 문장 맨 앞으로 배치한다.

　• Do you think? + Who is he?
　→ **Who** do you think **he is**? 너는 그가 누구라고 생각하니?
　→ Do you think who he is? (×)

### 핵심 Check

**2.** 다음 우리말과 일치하도록 빈칸에 알맞은 말을 쓰시오.

(1) 네가 무엇을 샀는지 말해 줄 수 있니?

➡ Can you tell me ＿＿＿＿ ＿＿＿＿ ＿＿＿＿?

(2) 나는 네가 그것을 좋아하는지 궁금해.

➡ I wonder ＿＿＿＿ ＿＿＿＿ ＿＿＿＿ it.

(3) 너는 누가 그 경기에서 이길 거라고 생각하니?

➡ ＿＿＿＿ ＿＿＿＿ ＿＿＿＿ ＿＿＿＿ ＿＿＿＿ win the game?

**01** 다음 두 문장을 한 문장으로 연결할 때 올바른 것은?

> • Do you know?
> • What is it famous for?

① Do you know what is it famous for?
② Do you know what it is famous for?
③ Do you know it is famous for what?
④ What do you know it is famous for?
⑤ What do you know is it famous for?

**02** 다음 괄호 안에서 알맞은 것을 고르시오.

(1) November is the month (when / where) I was born.

(2) This is the restaurant (when / where) I first met him.

(3) I can't forget the day (when / where) I arrived in Canada.

(4) That is the reason (which / why) I came back so soon.

**03** 우리말과 의미가 같도록 빈칸에 들어갈 말로 알맞은 것을 고르시오.

> • 나는 그가 내일 집으로 돌아올지 알 필요가 있어.
> ➡ I need to know _____ back home tomorrow.

① if he will come
② he will come
③ will he come
④ whether will he come
⑤ that he will come

**04** 다음 빈칸에 알맞은 말을 〈보기〉에서 골라 쓰시오.

> why   how   when   where

(1) This is the park _____ I often take a walk.

(2) I'll never forget the day _____ I met my favorite soccer player.

(3) I know the reason _____ Jack loves you.

(4) This is _____ Miss White could marry Johnson.

**01** 다음 빈칸에 알맞은 것을 고르시오.

> A: Do you know _____?
> B: It's on the desk.

① where does the book
② where the books are
③ where are the books
④ where is the book
⑤ where the book is

**02** 다음 문장의 빈칸에 알맞은 것은?

> I remember the day on _____ we started the work.

① which      ② when
③ that       ④ where
⑤ how

**03** 다음 우리말을 영어로 바르게 옮긴 것은?

> 너는 그의 생일이 언제인지 기억하니?

① When do you remember his birthday is?
② When do you remember is his birthday?
③ Do you remember when is his birthday?
④ Do you remember his birthday is when?
⑤ Do you remember when his birthday is?

**서답형**
**04** 다음 문장의 괄호 안에서 알맞은 것을 고르시오.

(1) I know the hotel (which / where) he is staying.
(2) This is (the way / the way how) she opened the door.
(3) Do you know the reason (which / for which) he didn't go to the meeting?

**서답형**
**05** 다음을 간접의문문을 이용하여 한 문장으로 쓰시오.

(1) Do you know? Who is that tall guy over there?
➡ _____

(2) Tell me. Who made this chocolate cake?
➡ _____

(3) I wonder. Did Marianne get married?
➡ _____

(4) Do you think? Where is Snow White?
➡ _____

**06** 다음 중 밑줄 친 부분의 쓰임이 나머지와 다른 하나는?

① Do you know <u>when</u> to stop?
② He forgot the day <u>when</u> he had first met her.
③ <u>When</u> does he go to the library?
④ I wonder <u>when</u> he will arrive at home.
⑤ <u>When</u> did you last see your friend Mike?

**07** 다음 중 어법상 바르지 않은 것은?

① Do you know where the first train station in Korea is?

② Tell me whether he is at home.

③ She wants to know who the winner is.

④ The woman is asking me where the library is.

⑤ I'm not sure if or not this answer is right.

**08** 다음 빈칸에 들어갈 말로 알맞게 짝지어진 것은?

> • Tell me the reason _____ he came here.
> • I will explain _____ the detective cleared up the mystery.

① why – how
② that – what
③ which – how
④ why – which
⑤ that – which

**09** 다음 두 문장을 간접의문문을 이용하여 한 문장으로 쓰시오.

(1) I know. + Who won the race?

➡ _____

(2) Do you know? + When will the bus come?

➡ _____

(3) The man is asking her. + How long does it take to get to TIG Market?

➡ _____
_____

(4) Do you think? + Who will win the game?

➡ _____

(5) Do you guess? + What does she want to buy?

➡ _____

**10** 다음 빈칸에 들어갈 말이 나머지와 다른 하나는?

① Today is the day _____ I have a test.

② This is the place _____ we held a party.

③ This is the room _____ I sleep every day.

④ This is the library _____ I read the book.

⑤ The town _____ I was born had a large river.

**11** 다음 중 어법상 어색한 것을 찾아 바르게 고치시오.

(1) Tell me when does the show start.

_____ ➡ _____

(2) Please let me know that does the bag have some pockets.

_____ ➡ _____

(3) Do you think who runs fastest?

_____ ➡ _____

**12** 다음 두 문장을 한 문장으로 바르게 연결한 것은? (2개)

> • This is a famous restaurant.
> • Many people go there in France.

① This is a famous restaurant many people go there in France.

② This is a famous restaurant to which many people go in France.

③ This is a famous restaurant which many people go in France.

④ This is a famous restaurant where many people go in France.

⑤ This is a famous restaurant where many people go there in France.

**13** 다음 두 문장을 간접의문문으로 바르게 바꾼 것은?

> • Do you know?
> • Who is Leonardo da Vinci?

① Who is Leonardo da Vinci do you know?
② Who do you know is Leonardo da Vinci?
③ Who do you know Leonardo da Vinci is?
④ Do you know who is Leonardo da Vinci?
⑤ Do you know who Leonardo da Vinci is?

**서답형**
**14** 다음 괄호 안의 말을 이용하여 우리말을 영작하시오.

(1) 나는 그녀가 그 문제를 푼 방법을 안다. (how, solve)

➡ _____

(2) 나는 Jerry가 화가 났던 이유를 안다. (why, angry)

➡ _____

(3) 이곳은 내가 집에 가는 길에 종종 들르는 도서관이다. (where, stop by, on)

➡ _____

**15** 다음 문장의 밑줄 친 when과 쓰임이 같은 것은?

> Tell me the day <u>when</u> he will come.

① <u>When</u> you go out, take your umbrella.
② I didn't have a bike <u>when</u> I was a kid.
③ I was sleeping <u>when</u> the phone rang.
④ I remember the day <u>when</u> I started the work.
⑤ She waved her hand at Tom <u>when</u> she saw him.

**16** 다음 괄호 안의 단어를 바르게 배열할 때 다섯 번째로 오는 단어는?

> (is / house / this / live / with / I / parents / the / where / my)

① is          ② I
③ house       ④ where
⑤ live

**17** 다음 우리말을 영어로 바르게 옮긴 것은? (2개)

> 나는 프랑스를 방문했던 그 여름을 잊지 못한다.

① I can't forget the summer what I visited France.
② I can't forget the summer which I visited France.
③ I can't forget the summer when I visited France.
④ I can't forget the summer where I visited France.
⑤ I can't forget the summer in which I visited France.

**서답형**
**18** 다음 두 문장을 한 문장으로 만들었을 때, 나머지 한 문장을 쓰시오.

(1) • He is asking her.
  + • _____
  ➡ He is asking her how long it takes to reach the top.

(2) • The woman was not sure.
  + • _____
  ➡ The woman was not sure if the thief was a man or a woman.

(3) • Do you believe?
  + • _____
  ➡ What do you believe the secret of his success is?

**01** 다음 두 문장을 하나의 문장으로 바꿔 쓰시오.

(1) Tell me. + What do you want for Christmas?

➡ _____

(2) She asks me. + How much sugar is there in the bottle?

➡ _____

(3) Do you know? + Where is Greece on the map?

➡ _____

(4) I wonder. + Is he a singer?

➡ _____

(5) I have no idea. + Will he join us soon?

➡ _____

(6) Do you think? + Where does your soul go after you die?

➡ _____

**02** 다음 두 문장을 한 문장으로 바르게 연결하시오.

(1) This is the house. I was born in this house.

➡ _____

(2) December 25th is the day. Christmas is celebrated on that day.

➡ _____

_____

(3) There is a small bed. I always sleep on it.

➡ _____

(4) This is the way. I solved the problem in the way.

➡ _____

**03** 다음 괄호 안에서 알맞은 말을 고르시오.

(1) Mike asked me what (did I eat / I ate) for breakfast.

(2) We have no idea when (she left / did she leave).

(3) She knows who (is he / he is).

(4) I don't know (that / if) he will come here.

**04** 다음 문장의 밑줄 친 부분을 바르게 고쳐 쓰시오.

(1) I don't know the reason which my mom was angry.

➡ _____

(2) Write the name of the city where you live in.

➡ _____

(3) This is the way how we found the answers.

➡ _____

(4) He was born in the year which the war ended.

➡ _____

**05** 다음 문장을 어법에 맞게 고쳐 쓰시오.

(1) The doctor will ask you what did you eat for breakfast.

➡ _____

(2) Please let us know are you able to attend the meeting.

➡ _____

_____

(3) Do you suppose what they are thinking?

➡ _____

**06** 다음 우리말을 참고하여 빈칸에 알맞은 말을 쓰시오.

(1) 나는 그가 편지를 감춘 곳을 알고 있다.

➡ I know the place _____ he hid the letter.

(2) 너는 그가 너에게 돈을 준 이유를 아니?

➡ Do you know the reason _____ he gave you money?

(3) 너는 자동차가 없던 시절을 상상할 수 있니?

➡ Can you imagine the days _____ there were no cars?

**07** 괄호 안에 주어진 어휘를 이용하여 다음 우리말을 영작하시오.

(1) Daniel은 그가 어떻게 가수가 되었는지 우리에게 말해 주었다. (become, a singer)

➡ _____

(2) 그가 올지 안 올지 의심스럽다. (it, doubtful, whether, come, or)

➡ _____

**08** 다음 우리말과 같도록 주어진 단어를 배열하여 문장을 완성하시오.

(1) 너는 네 여동생을 처음 본 날을 기억하니?

(sister / you / little / first / you / remember / your / do / the / day / when / saw)?

➡ _____

_____

(2) 공원은 사람들이 산책을 하는 곳이다.

(where / park / walk / take / people / a / place / a / is / a)

➡ _____

(3) Mariel은 자기가 아사코를 만나게 될지 어떨지 알고 싶어 한다.

(Mariel / to / to / is / know / wants / meet / he / whether / Asako / going)

➡ _____

**09** 다음 문장을 두 문장으로 나누어 쓰시오.

(1) Nobody knows why Lauren left the office early.

➡ _____

(2) It is difficult to understand what the teacher says.

➡ _____

(3) Steve didn't tell me when the movie began.

➡ _____

(4) What do you think the most typical Korean dish is?

➡ _____

(5) They wonder if they can borrow some books today.

➡ _____

# Reading

## The History of Classical Concert Manners

Imagine yourself at a classical music concert. The orchestra starts
재귀대명사(재귀 용법)                                                  ~하기 시작하다
to play one of Mozart's piano concertos. The concert hall is dark and
silent. Nobody makes a sound. Everybody looks serious.
        누구도 ~하지 않는                    단수 취급

The audiences only clap after the concerto finishes. This is a familiar
            부사절 after 이하를 수식
scene at concerts today.

Let's go back in time and take a look at one of Mozart's concerts in
                            go와 병렬 구조
the 18th century. You are in a bright hall inside a nobleman's house.
Mozart is playing the piano. Surprisingly, however, the audiences are
        눈앞에 벌어지는 일을 나타내는 현재진행형        문장 전체를 수식하는 부사
eating, drinking, and talking freely. They whistle and clap at any time.
You are shocked by their bad manners, but Mozart himself would be
주어가 충격을 받는 입장을 나타내는 수동태                        강조 용법의 재귀대명사(생략 가능)
surprised by today's quiet audiences.

Concerts in Mozart's time were mostly social events. They were
good places to meet people. Noise was just part of the concert.
        places를 수식하는 형용사적 용법의 부정사

---

imagine 상상하다
classical 고전적인
concerto 협주곡, 콘체르토
silent 조용한
look ~해 보이다
serious 진지한, 심각한
audience 청중, 관객
clap 박수를 치다
finish 끝나다
familiar 친숙한
scene 장면
nobleman 상류층, 귀족
surprisingly 놀랍게도
whistle 휘파람을 불다
mostly 주로
social 사교적인, 사회적인

---

### 확인문제

● 다음 문장이 본문의 내용과 일치하면 T, 일치하지 않으면 F를 쓰시오.

1 The concert hall is dark and silent. ☐

2 The audiences only clap after the concerto finishes. ☐

3 Mozart's concert hall in the 18th century was bright. ☐

4 Mozart wouldn't be surprised by today's quiet audiences. ☐

5 Concerts in Mozart's time weren't mostly social events. ☐

Today's quiet concerts began in the 19th century when many big
concert halls were built. More people, not just noblemen, went to
concerts. Artists were no longer dependent on noblemen for money.
The artists had more power over their works and started to use their
increased power. For example, Wagner blamed the audience for
making noise. After some time, a no-clapping-between-movements
rule appeared.

As a result, here we are today, very quiet and serious. We do not
know what concerts will look like in the future because manners
change with time. For now, however, if you want to enjoy classical
music concerts, just remember this: Enjoy the music, but do not
disturb those around you.

not just 단지 ~ 뿐만 아니라
no longer 더 이상 ~ 아닌
dependent 의존하는
increase 증가시키다
for example 예를 들면
blame 비난하다
movement 악장, 움직임
appear 나타나다
as a result 결과적으로
look like ~처럼 보이다
in the future 미래에
manners 예의범절
for now 지금은
disturb 방해하다

 확인문제

● 다음 문장이 본문의 내용과 일치하면 T, 일치하지 않으면 F를 쓰시오.

1  Today's quiet concerts began in the 19th century. ☐

2  Many big concert halls were built in the 18th century. ☐

3  Just noblemen, not most people, went to concerts in the 19th century. ☐

4  Artists were dependent on noblemen for money in the 19th century. ☐

5  The artists had less power over their works in the 19th century. ☐

6  We know what concerts will look like in the future because manners don't change

   with time. ☐

● 우리말을 참고하여 빈칸에 알맞은 말을 쓰시오.

**1** **The History of _____ Concert _____**

**2** _____ _____ at a _____ music concert.

**3** The _____ starts to _____ _____ of Mozart's _____ concertos.

**4** The concert _____ is _____ and _____ .

**5** _____ makes a _____ .

**6** _____ looks _____ .

**7** The _____ only _____ after the concerto _____ .

**8** This is a _____ _____ _____ concerts today.

**9** Let's _____ _____ in _____ and _____ a _____ at one of Mozart's concerts in the 18th century.

**10** You are in a _____ hall _____ a _____ house.

**11** Mozart is _____ the _____ .

**12** _____ , however, the _____ are eating, drinking, and _____ _____ .

**13** They _____ and _____ at any time.

**14** You are _____ by their _____ manners, but Mozart _____ would be _____ by today's _____ audiences.

**15** Concerts in Mozart's time _____ _____ _____ events.

**16** They were _____ _____ _____ _____ people.

**17** Noise was _____ _____ of the concert.

| | |
|---|---|
| **1** | 클래식 콘서트 관람 예절의 역사 |
| **2** | 당신이 클래식 공연장에 있다고 상상해 보아라. |
| **3** | 오케스트라가 모차르트의 피아노 협주곡들 중 한 곡을 연주하기 시작한다. |
| **4** | 콘서트장은 어둡고 조용하다. |
| **5** | 아무도 소리를 내지 않는다. |
| **6** | 모두가 진지하게 보인다. |
| **7** | 청중은 오직 협주곡이 끝난 후에만 손뼉을 친다. |
| **8** | 이것이 오늘날 콘서트에서 익숙한 장면이다. |
| **9** | 과거로 거슬러 올라가서 18세기 모차르트의 콘서트들 중 하나를 살펴보자. |
| **10** | 당신은 한 귀족의 집안 밝은 홀에 있다. |
| **11** | 모차르트는 피아노를 치고 있다. |
| **12** | 하지만 놀랍게도, 청중들은 먹고 마시며 자유롭게 대화하고 있다. |
| **13** | 그들은 아무 때나 휘파람을 불고 박수를 친다. |
| **14** | 당신은 그들의 나쁜 매너에 충격을 받지만, 모차르트 자신은 오늘날의 조용한 청중에게 놀랄지도 모른다. |
| **15** | 모차르트 시대의 콘서트는 주로 사교적인 행사였다. |
| **16** | 콘서트는 사람을 만나기에 좋은 장소였다. |
| **17** | 소음은 그저 콘서트의 일부였다. |

**18** Today's _____ concerts began in the 19th _____ _____ many big concert halls _____ _____.

**19** More people, _____ _____ _____, went to concerts.

**20** Artists were _____ _____ _____ on noblemen for money.

**21** The artists had _____ _____ over their works and started to _____ their _____ power.

**22** _____ _____, Wagner _____ the audience _____ making noise.

**23** _____ some time, a no-clapping-between-movements _____ _____.

**24** _____ _____ _____, here we are today, very _____ and serious.

**25** We do not know _____ _____ will _____ _____ in the future _____ manners _____ with time.

**26** For now, _____, if you want to _____ _____ music concerts, _____ _____ this:

**27** _____ the music, but do not _____ _____ around you.

**18** 오늘날의 조용한 콘서트는 많은 대형 공연장이 생긴 19세기에 시작됐다.

**19** 귀족뿐만 아니라 더 많은 사람들이 콘서트에 갔다.

**20** 예술가들은 더 이상 돈을 벌기 위해 귀족들에게 의존하지 않았다.

**21** 예술가들은 자신의 작품에 더 많은 권한이 생겼고 그 힘을 사용하기 시작했다.

**22** 예를 들어, 바그너는 소음을 낸다는 것 때문에 관객들을 비난했다.

**23** 얼마 후에 '악장 사이 박수 금지 규칙'이 생겼다.

**24** 그 결과, 오늘날 우리는, 매우 조용하고 진지하다.

**25** 예절은 시대에 따라 변하기 때문에 우리는 콘서트가 미래에는 어떤 모습일지 모른다.

**26** 하지만 지금은 당신이 클래식 음악 공연을 즐기고 싶다면 이것만은 기억해라:

**27** 음악은 즐기되 당신 주변의 다른 사람들을 방해하지 마라.

● 우리말을 참고하여 본문을 영작하시오.

**1** **클래식 콘서트 관람 예절의 역사**
➡ _____

**2** 당신이 클래식 공연장에 있다고 상상해 보아라.
➡ _____

**3** 오케스트라가 모차르트의 피아노 협주곡들 중 한 곡을 연주하기 시작한다.
➡ _____

**4** 콘서트장은 어둡고 조용하다.
➡ _____

**5** 아무도 소리를 내지 않는다.
➡ _____

**6** 모두가 진지하게 보인다.
➡ _____

**7** 청중은 오직 협주곡이 끝난 후에만 손뼉을 친다.
➡ _____

**8** 이것이 오늘날 콘서트에서 익숙한 장면이다.
➡ _____

**9** 과거로 거슬러 올라가서 18세기 모차르트의 콘서트들 중 하나를 살펴보자.
➡ _____

**10** 당신은 한 귀족의 집안 밝은 홀에 있다.
➡ _____

**11** 모차르트는 피아노를 치고 있다.
➡ _____

**12** 하지만 놀랍게도, 청중들은 먹고 마시며 자유롭게 대화하고 있다.
➡ _____

**13** 그들은 아무 때나 휘파람을 불고 박수를 친다.
➡ _____

**14** 당신은 그들의 나쁜 매너에 충격을 받지만, 모차르트 자신은 오늘날의 조용한 청중에게 놀랄지도 모른다.
➡ _____

**15** 모차르트 시대의 콘서트는 주로 사교적인 행사였다.
➡ _____

**16** 콘서트는 사람을 만나기에 좋은 장소였다.
➡ _____

**17** 소음은 그저 콘서트의 일부였다.
➡ _____

**18** 오늘날의 조용한 콘서트는 많은 대형 공연장이 생긴 19세기에 시작됐다.

➡ _____

**19** 귀족뿐만 아니라 더 많은 사람들이 콘서트에 갔다.

➡ _____

**20** 예술가들은 더 이상 돈을 벌기 위해 귀족들에게 의존하지 않았다.

➡ _____

**21** 예술가들은 자신의 작품에 더 많은 권한이 생겼고 그 힘을 사용하기 시작했다.

➡ _____

**22** 예를 들어, 바그너는 소음을 낸다는 것 때문에 관객들을 비난했다.

➡ _____

**23** 얼마 후에 '악장 사이 박수 금지 규칙'이 생겼다.

➡ _____

**24** 그 결과, 오늘날 우리는, 매우 조용하고 진지하다.

➡ _____

**25** 예절은 시대에 따라 변하기 때문에 우리는 콘서트가 미래에는 어떤 모습일지 모른다.

➡ _____

**26** 하지만 지금은 당신이 클래식 음악 공연을 즐기고 싶다면 이것만은 기억해라.

➡ _____

**27** 음악은 즐기되 당신 주변의 다른 사람들을 방해하지 마라.

➡ _____

**[01~03]** 다음 글을 읽고 물음에 답하시오.

Imagine yourself at a classical music concert. The orchestra starts ⓐto play one of Mozart's piano concertos. The concert hall is dark and silent. Nobody makes a sound. Everybody looks serious. The audiences only clap after the concerto finishes. ⓑThis is a familiar scene at concerts today.

**01** 위 글의 밑줄 친 ⓐto play와 문법적 쓰임이 같은 것을 모두 고르시오.

① He wants to see the game this weekend.
② The old lady came here to meet you yesterday.
③ For the work, I need a pen to write with.
④ My sister hopes to be a doctor in the future.
⑤ We decided to finish the work.

**서답형**

**02** 위 글의 밑줄 친 ⓑThis가 가리키는 것을 본문에서 찾아 영어로 쓰시오.

➡ _____

_____

**중요**

**03** 위 글의 내용과 일치하지 <u>않는</u> 것은?

① 오늘날의 콘서트홀은 밝다.
② 오늘날의 콘서트홀은 조용하다.
③ 연주회에서는 소음을 내지 않는다.
④ 관객의 표정은 진지하다.
⑤ 관객들은 연주 중간에 박수를 치지 않는다.

**[04~06]** 다음 글을 읽고 물음에 답하시오.

Let's go back in time and take a look ⓐ____ one of Mozart's concerts in the 18th century. You are in a bright hall inside a nobleman's house. Mozart is playing the piano. Surprisingly, however, the audiences are eating, drinking, and ⓑtalking freely. They whistle and clap at any time. You are shocked by their bad manners, but Mozart himself would be surprised ⓒ____ today's quiet audiences. Concerts in Mozart's time were mostly social events. They were good places to meet people. Noise was just part of the concert.

**중요**

**04** 위 글의 빈칸 ⓐ와 ⓒ에 들어갈 전치사가 바르게 짝지어진 것은?

① for - about     ② in - by
③ at - by         ④ at - about
⑤ by - on

**서답형**

**05** By what would Mozart be surprised? Fill in the blanks with the suitable words.

➡ He would be surprised by _____

_____.

**06** 위 글의 밑줄 친 ⓑtalking과 문법적 쓰임이 <u>다른</u> 것을 모두 고르시오.

① He was talking with his friends.
② You must be proud of being a member of the team.
③ She will be listening to music.
④ They were playing basketball after the class.
⑤ He enjoyed watching the movie.

[07~09] 다음 글을 읽고 물음에 답하시오.

Today's quiet concerts began in the 19th century when many big concert halls were built. More people, not just noblemen, went to concerts. Artists were no longer dependent on noblemen for money. The artists had more power over their works and started to use their increased power. For example, Wagner blamed the audience for making noise. After some time, a no-clapping-between-movements rule appeared.

**서답형**

**07** 위 글의 밑줄 친 when과 바꿔 쓸 수 있는 두 단어를 쓰시오.

➡ _____

**08** 위 글의 제목으로 알맞은 것을 고르시오.

① Today's Quiet Concerts
② How Today's Quiet Concerts Began
③ What Made Artists Dependent on Noblemen?
④ Why Wagner Blamed the Audience
⑤ How Did Artists Have More Power over Their Works?

**09** 위 글을 읽고 19세기의 Artists에 대해 알 수 있는 것을 모두 고르시오.

① They could use many big concerts halls.
② They made more money than before.
③ Their works were better than ever.
④ Wagner didn't like the audience making noise.
⑤ They made a no-clapping-between-movements rule.

[10~12] 다음 글을 읽고 물음에 답하시오.

As a result, here we are today, very quiet and serious. We do not know (A)[how / what] concerts will look like in the future because (B)[manners / manner] change with time. For now, ⓐ_____, if you want to enjoy classical music concerts, just remember this: Enjoy the music, but do not disturb (C)[that / those] ⓑ_____ you.

**10** 위 글의 괄호 (A)~(C)에서 문맥이나 어법상 알맞은 낱말을 골라 쓰시오.

➡ (A)_____ (B)_____ (C)_____

**11** 위 글의 밑줄 친 빈칸 ⓐ에 들어가기에 자연스러운 것은?

① however
② therefore
③ as a result
④ at last
⑤ for instance

**12** 위 글의 빈칸 ⓑ에 들어가기에 적절한 전치사는?

① with     ② around     ③ in
④ for     ⑤ over

[13~15] 다음 글을 읽고 물음에 답하시오.

Imagine ⓐyourself at a classical music concert. ⓑThe orchestra starts to play one of Mozart's piano concerto. The concert hall is dark and silent. Nobody makes a sound. Everybody looks serious. The audiences only clap after the concerto finishes. This is a familiar scene at concerts today.

**13** 위 글의 밑줄 친 문장 ⓐ에 나오는 yourself와 용법이 다른 것을 모두 고르시오.

① He himself drove the car in the rain yesterday.
② She prepared this food herself for her family.
③ He expresses himself in good clear English.
④ She watched herself in the mirror for a long time.
⑤ He will do the work himself after he comes home.

**14** 위 글의 밑줄 친 ⓑ에서 어법이 어색한 것을 찾아 올바른 형태로 바꾸어 쓰시오.

➡ _____

**15** 위 글을 읽고 대답할 수 없는 질문은?
① Does everybody look serious at the concert?
② How is the concert hall?
③ What is a familiar scene at concerts today?
④ When do the audiences clap?
⑤ Why did the orchestra play Mozart's piano concerto?

[16~18] 다음 글을 읽고 물음에 답하시오.

Let's go back in time and take a look at one of Mozart's concerts in the 18th century. You are in a bright hall inside a nobleman's house. Mozart is playing the piano. Surprisingly, however, the audiences are eating, drinking, and talking freely. They whistle and clap at any time. You are shocked by their bad manners, but Mozart himself would be surprised by today's quiet audiences. Concerts in Mozart's time were mostly social events. They were good places ⓐto meet people. Noise was just part of the concert.

**16** What is the passage mainly talking about?
① What did Mozart play at the concert in the 18th century?
② When did the audiences clap at the concert?
③ By what was Mozart shocked at the concert?
④ What was the concert like in Mozart's time?
⑤ Why did the audiences make noise at the concert?

**17** 위 글의 밑줄 친 ⓐto meet과 to부정사의 용법이 다른 것을 모두 고르시오.

① The kind woman wants to meet you.
② She needs some friends to help her with the work.
③ His brother gave me some interesting books to read.
④ I am sorry to hear that.
⑤ He has some work to finish now.

**18** 위 글의 내용과 일치하지 <u>않는</u> 것은?

① In the 18th century, concerts were held in  bright halls.

② A concert hall was inside a nobleman's house at the time.

③ The audiences were talking freely during the concert.

④ The audiences didn't whistle and clap at any time.

⑤ Concerts were good places to meet people.

**[19~21]** 다음 글을 읽고 물음에 답하시오.

@<u>Today's quiet concerts began in the 19th century when many big concert halls built.</u> More people, not just noblemen, went ①_____ concerts. Artists were no longer dependent ②_____ noblemen for money. The artists had more power ③_____ their works and started to use their increased power. For example, Wagner blamed the audience ④_____ making noise. ⑤_____ some time, a no-clapping-between-movements rule appeared.

**19** 위 글의 빈칸 ①~⑤에 들어갈 단어 중 적절하지 <u>않은</u> 것은?

① to      ② on      ③ over

④ by      ⑤ After

서답형
**20** 위 글의 밑줄 친 @에서 어법상 <u>틀린</u> 부분을 찾아 고치시오.

_____ ➡ _____

**21** 위 글의 내용과 일치하지 <u>않는</u> 것은?

① 오늘날의 조용한 콘서트는 18세기에 시작되었다.

② 19세기에는 많은 사람들이 콘서트에 갔다.

③ 예술가들이 귀족의 후원에서 벗어날 수 있었다.

④ 바그너는 소음을 내는 것을 싫어했다.

⑤ 악장 사이에 박수 치지 않는 규칙이 생겼다.

**[22~23]** 다음 글을 읽고 물음에 답하시오.

As a result, here we are today, very (A)[quiet / noisy] and serious. We do not know what concerts will look @_____ in the future (B)[because of / because] manners change with time. For now, however, if you want to enjoy classical music concerts, just remember this: Enjoy the music, but do not (C)[watch / disturb] those around you.

**22** 위 글의 빈칸 @에 들어가기에 알맞은 말을 고르시오.

① after      ② into

③ at      ④ like

⑤ out

중요
**23** 위 글의 괄호 (A)~(C)에서 문맥이나 어법상 알맞은 것은?

| | (A) | (B) | (C) |
|---|---|---|---|
| ① | quiet | because | watch |
| ② | quiet | because | disturb |
| ③ | quiet | because of | watch |
| ④ | noisy | because of | disturb |
| ⑤ | noisy | because | disturb |

Reading **193**

**[01~03]** 다음 글을 읽고 물음에 답하시오.

①Imagine yourself at a classical music concert. ②The orchestra starts to play one of Mozart's piano concertos. ③The concert hall is dark and silent. ④Nobody makes a sound. ⑤Everybody look serious. The audiences only clap after the concerto finishes. @This is a familiar scene at concerts today.

**01** 위 글의 밑줄 친 ①~⑤ 중에서 어법상 틀린 것을 찾아 번호를 쓰고, 고치시오.

➡ 번호: _____ 틀린 것: _____

올바른 형태: _____

**02** 위 글에서 다음 설명에 해당하는 단어를 찾아 쓰시오.

> a group of people who come to watch and listen to someone speaking or performing in public

➡ _____

**03** 밑줄 친 @가 가리키는 것을 우리말로 쓰시오.

➡ _____

_____

_____

**[04~06]** 다음 글을 읽고 물음에 답하시오.

Let's go back in time and (A)[take] a look at one of Mozart's concerts in the 18th century. You are in a bright hall inside a nobleman's house. Mozart is playing the piano. Surprisingly, however, the audiences are eating, drinking, and talking (B)[free]. They whistle and clap at any time. You are shocked by their bad manners, but Mozart himself would be surprised by today's quiet audiences. Concerts in Mozart's time were mostly social events. They were good places to meet people. Noise was just part of the concert.

**04** 위 글 (A)에 주어진 단어의 적절한 형태를 쓰시오.

➡ (A) _____

**05** 위 글에서 다음 영영사전의 뜻을 나타내는 단어를 찾아 쓰시오.

> a man who is a member of the highest social class and has a title such as 'Duke'

➡ _____

**06** 위 글 (B)에 주어진 단어의 적절한 형태를 쓰시오.

➡ (B) _____

**[07~09]** 다음 글을 읽고 물음에 답하시오.

Today's quiet concerts began in the 19th century when many big concert halls were built. More people, not just noblemen, went to concerts. @Artists were no longer dependent on noblemen for money. The artists had more power over their works and started to use their increased power. For example, Wagner blamed the audience for making noise. After some time, a no-clapping-between-movements rule appeared.

**07** Why did Wagner blame the audience? Fill in the blanks with suitable words.

➡ Wagner blamed the audience because they made _____.

**08** 다음 문장에 적절한 말을 채워, 위 글 ⓐ와 같은 뜻의 문장을 완성하시오.

> Artists _____ dependent on noblemen for money any longer.

**09** 위 글에 어울리도록 아래 주어진 문장의 빈칸에 적절한 말을 쓰시오.

> Many big concerts hall began to (A)_____ _____ in the 19th century and artists had more (B)_____ over their works.

**[10~12]** 다음 글을 읽고 물음에 답하시오.

As a result, here we are today, very quiet and serious. We do not know (A)_____ concerts will look like in the future ⓐ[because / because of] manners change with time. For now, however, if you want to enjoy classical music concerts, just remember (B)this: Enjoy the music, but do not disturb ⓑ[ones / those] around you.

**10** 위 글의 빈칸 (A)에 들어가기에 적절한 단어를 쓰시오.

➡ _____

**11** 위 글 ⓐ와 ⓑ에 어법상 적절한 것을 고르시오.

➡ ⓐ _____ ⓑ _____

**12** 위 글의 밑줄 친 (B)의 this가 가리키는 것을 찾아 우리말로 쓰시오.

➡ _____

**[13~15]** 다음 글을 읽고 물음에 답하시오.

Imagine yourself at a classical music concert. The orchestra starts to play one of Mozart's piano concertos. The concert hall is dark and silent. ⓐ_____ makes a sound. ⓑ모두가 진지해 보인다. The audiences only clap after the concerto finishes. This is a familiar scene at concerts today.

**13** 위 글의 빈칸 ⓐ에 들어갈 알맞은 말을 쓰시오.

➡ _____

**14** 위 글의 밑줄 친 ⓑ의 우리말을 세 단어로 쓰시오.

➡ _____

**15** 다음 빈칸 (A)와 (B)에 알맞은 단어를 넣어 오늘날의 연주회장을 설명하시오.

> Today the concert hall is (A)_____ and (B)_____ and the audiences (C)_____ only after the concerto is over.

### Before You Read B

**A Guide to Good Concert Manners**

Watching a classical music concert can be a memorable experience if you keep these tips in mind.
keep ~ in mind: ~을 명심하다

Before You Go In:
• Plan to arrive 20-30 minutes before concert time.
• Find out what music will be played.
~을 알아내다         미래 수동태: 조동사+be+과거분사(p.p.)

When Music Is Playing:
• Turn off your cellphone!
~을 끄다
• Stay quiet. No talking, whistling, singing along to the music.
No -ing: ~하지 마라(=Don't+동사원형 ~)
• Don't clap until the whole piece is over. It is safe to clap when the audience starts clapping.
It 가주어 ~ to 동사원형 구문
=starts to clap

구문해설  • classical: 고전의, 클래식 음악의  • memorable: 기억에 남을 만한, 기억할 만한
• experience: 경험하다  • whistle: 휘파람을 불다  • clap: 박수치다  • audience: 관객

### Writing Workshop

**Music Concert Review**

On February 2, I went to a concert hall at the Seoul Arts Center where Jo
on+특정한 날                                              선행사              관계부사
Seongu's piano concert was held. It was a great opportunity to listen to him
수동태: be+p.p.                              지각동사+목적어+목적격보어(동사원형 또는 현재분사)
play live. He played Chopin's Piano Concerto No. 1. I did not know how
beautiful the classical music was. I liked his live performance. I will not forget
간접의문문: 의문사+주어+동사
this experience.

구문해설  • review: 논평, 비평  • hold: 열다, 개최하다  • opportunity: 기회  • live: (공연이) 라이브의;
라이브로  • performance: 공연  • forget: 잊다  • experience: 경험

### Wrap Up 7

Reporter: When is your new album coming out?
come out: 나오다
Justin Otter: It's coming out next month.
=my new album
Reporter: What are your plans for the new album?
Justin Otter: I'm planning to have a concert at the Super Stadium. My hero
be planning to: ~할 계획이다
Michael Johnson held one of his concerts during his world tour at the place.
one of+복수명사: ~ 중 하나

구문해설  • plan: 계획  • hero: 영웅  • tour: 순회공연  • place: 장소

해석

**콘서트 예절에 대한 안내**
당신이 이와 같은 조언들을 명심한다면 클래식 콘서트를 보는 것은 기억에 남는 경험이 될 것이다.

들어가기 전:
• 콘서트 시간 20-30분 전에 도착하기를 계획하라.
• 어떤 음악이 연주될지 알아보아라.

음악이 연주될 때:
• 휴대 전화를 꺼라.
• 조용히 있어라. 말하거나 휘파람을 불거나 음악에 따라 노래하지 말아라.
• 전체의 곡이 끝날 때까지 박수치지 말아라. 관객들이 박수 치기 시작할 때 박수를 치는 것이 안전하다.

**음악 콘서트 리뷰**
2월 2일에 나는 조성우의 피아노 콘서트가 열린 서울 아트 센터의 콘서트홀에 갔다. 그가 라이브로 연주하는 것을 듣는 것은 훌륭한 기회였다. 그는 쇼팽의 피아노 협주곡 1번을 연주했다. 나는 클래식 공연이 얼마나 아름다운지 몰랐다. 나는 그의 라이브 공연이 아주 마음에 들었다. 나는 이 경험을 잊지 않을 것이다.

기자: 당신의 새 앨범은 언제 나오나요?
저스틴 오터: 다음 달에 나옵니다.
기자: 새 앨범에 대한 계획은 무엇인가요?
저스틴 오터: 저는 수퍼 스타디움에서 콘서트를 가질 계획입니다. 저의 영웅인 마이클 존슨이 세계 공연 동안 콘서트들 중 하나를 그 장소에서 열었거든요.

# 영역별 핵심문제

**01** 다음 짝지어진 단어의 관계가 같도록 빈칸에 알맞은 말을 쓰시오.

> appear : disappear = familiar : _____

**02** 다음 영영풀이에 해당하는 단어는?

> to bring something to the place that it came from or the place where it should go

① free      ② accept      ③ gather
④ receive      ⑤ return

**03** 다음 중 밑줄 친 단어의 뜻풀이가 바르지 <u>않은</u> 것은?

① Press <u>pause</u> to stop the tape. 멈춤
② That is not a <u>correct</u> answer. 정확한
③ This is a <u>serious</u> problem. 심각한
④ I am <u>dependent</u> on others. 독립적인
⑤ I don't want to <u>disturb</u> you. 방해하다

**04** 주어진 단어를 이용해서 다음 우리말에 맞게 빈칸에 알맞은 말을 쓰시오.

(1) 너는 아무 때나 도움을 요청해도 좋다.
➡ You can ask me for help _____
_____ _____ . (time)

(2) 지금은 그가 혼자 있고 싶어 한다.
➡ He wants to be left alone _____
_____ . (now)

(3) 그 결과 그녀는 무대 위에서 굉장히 잘했다.
➡ _____ _____ _____ ,
she did a great job on stage. (result)

**05** 다음 대화의 빈칸에 들어갈 말을 고르시오.

> A: How _____ going to the music festival on Friday at 5:00? Can you make it?
> B: Yes. That would be great.

① to      ② of
③ from      ④ with
⑤ about

**06** 다음 대화가 자연스럽게 이어지도록 순서대로 배열하시오.

> (A) Yes, I love opera. When is it?
> (B) Yes, thanks so much for asking me.
> (C) It's this Saturday at 5:00. Can you make it?
> (D) Are you interested in going to an opera? I have two tickets.

➡ _____

**07** 다음 대화에서 어법이나 흐름상 어색한 것을 고르시오.

> B: We're going to Hangang ⓐ<u>this</u> weekend. Do you remember?
> G: Of course. Don't forget ⓑ<u>bringing</u> your camera.
> B: Okay. I ⓒ<u>won't</u>. I'll bring some snacks, ⓓ<u>too</u>.
> G: Sounds ⓔ<u>great</u>.

① ⓐ    ② ⓑ    ③ ⓒ    ④ ⓓ    ⑤ ⓔ

**[08~11]** 다음 대화를 읽고 물음에 답하시오.

> G: What are you listening to?
> B: Classical music. I'm going to a concert tomorrow and I'd like to know about the music before I go.
> G: I guess it's more enjoyable ___ⓐ___ you know the music.
> B: ⓑActual, I don't want to clap at the wrong time.
> G: Don't you just clap when the music stops?
> B: No. In classical music, one piece of music may have several pauses. You should wait and clap at the very end.
> G: I see. ⓒMake sure you don't forget to clap at the real ending. By the way, can you make it to our soccer practice tomorrow at 4:00?
> B: Sure. I'll come to the practice after the concert finishes.
> G: Okay. See you then.

**08** 위 대화의 빈칸 ⓐ에 알맞은 것은?

① if      ② as
③ since      ④ before
⑤ though

**09** 위 대화의 밑줄 친 ⓑ를 알맞은 어형으로 바꿔 쓰시오.

➡ _____

**10** 위 대화의 밑줄 친 ⓒ와 같은 뜻이 되도록 다음 문장의 빈칸에 알맞은 말을 쓰시오.

➡ Make sure you _____ to clap at the real ending.

**11** 위 대화의 내용과 일치하지 <u>않는</u> 것을 고르시오.

① 소년은 클래식 음악을 듣고 있다.
② 소년은 콘서트에 가기 전에 그 음악에 대해 알고 싶어 한다.
③ 소녀는 콘서트에서 연주하는 음악을 알면 더 재미있을 것이라고 생각한다.
④ 콘서트에서는 음악 연주가 완전히 끝난 후에 박수를 쳐야 한다.
⑤ 소년은 콘서트 때문에 내일 축구 연습에 갈 수 없다.

**Grammar**

**12** 다음 빈칸에 들어갈 말로 가장 적절한 것은?

> Do you know _____?

① Hammington is from where
② where is Hammington from
③ where Hammington is from
④ is where Hammington from
⑤ from Hammington is where

**13** 다음 문장의 괄호 안에서 알맞은 말을 고르시오.

(1) This is the reason (why / how) he came here.
(2) Tell me the date on (which / when) you will travel.
(3) Tokyo is a city (where / which) you can easily get lost.
(4) Do you remember the day (when / which) we spent at the beach?
(5) This is (the way how / how) Jake caught the monkey.

**14** 다음 중 어법상 어색한 것은?

① Do you know when World War II ended?
② Who do you think killed the old woman?
③ I wondered if she would come to the party or not.
④ Tell me if or not you like Jenny.
⑤ I'm not sure whether she is fond of music or not.

**15** 다음 주어진 단어를 바르게 배열하여 문장을 완성하시오.

(crying, is, know, I, Jane, the, why, reason)

➡ _____

**16** 다음 중 어법상 바르지 <u>않은</u> 문장의 개수는?

ⓐ I don't know why did he come here.
ⓑ Do you know how dogs swim?
ⓒ I wonder will he come today.
ⓓ Can you tell me which flower he likes better?
ⓔ Do you think where Ann spent her spring vacation?

① 1개  ② 2개  ③ 3개  ④ 4개  ⑤ 5개

**17** 다음 문장에서 어법상 어색한 부분을 바르게 고쳐 쓰시오.

This is the house which Shakespeare was born.

➡ _____
_____

**18** 다음 그림을 참고하여 주어진 대화의 빈칸을 완성하시오.

A: Look at this picture. Do you know (1)_____ ?
B: Yeah, it's Moai.
A: Could you tell me (2)_____ ?
B: It is in Easter island in Chile.

**19** 다음 두 문장의 해석을 쓰고 밑줄 친 부분의 어법상 차이를 설명하시오.

(1) This is the park <u>which</u> I used to visit while young.
(2) This is the park <u>where</u> I used to go while young.

(1) 해석: _____
(2) 해석: _____
(3) 어법상 차이: _____
_____

**Reading**

**[20~22] 다음 글을 읽고 물음에 답하시오.**

Imagine (A)[you / yourself] at a classical music concert. The orchestra starts ⓐto play one of Mozart's piano (B)[concertos / concerto]. The concert hall is dark and silent. Nobody makes a sound. Everybody looks serious. The audiences only clap after the concerto (C)[will finish / finishes]. This is a familiar scene at concerts today.

**20** 위 글의 괄호 (A)~(C)에서 문맥이나 어법상 알맞은 낱말을 골라 쓰시오.

➡ (A)_____  (B)_____  (C)_____

**21** 위 글의 밑줄 친 ⓐto play와 같은 용법으로 쓰인 것을 고르시오.

① She is happy to see you again.
② He must be tired to walk such a long distance.
③ She called you to ask about your plan.
④ They want to take a break after the class.
⑤ We will go to the beach to swim.

**22** 위 글을 읽고 대답할 수 없는 질문은?

① How is the concert hall?
② Is there anyone that makes a sound?
③ Why do the audiences clap?
④ How does everybody look?
⑤ When do the audiences clap?

**[23~25] 다음 글을 읽고 물음에 답하시오.**

Let's go back (A)_____ time and take a look at one of Mozart's concerts in the 18th century. You are in a bright hall inside a nobleman's house. Mozart is playing the piano. Surprisingly, however, the audiences are eating, ⓐdrinking, and talking freely. They whistle and clap at any time. You are shocked (B)_____ their bad manners, but Mozart ⓑhimself would be surprised by today's quiet audiences. Concerts in Mozart's time were mostly social events. They were good places to meet people. Noise was just part of the concert.

**23** 위 글의 빈칸 (A)와 (B)에 들어갈 전치사가 바르게 짝지어진 것은?

① on - to        ② by - in
③ in - from      ④ in - by
⑤ on - by

**24** 위 글의 밑줄 친 ⓐdrinking과 문법적 쓰임이 같은 것을 고르시오.

① His job was driving a taxi.
② She is taking a walk in the park.
③ How about playing outside?
④ My plan is going to America.
⑤ The car was making a loud noise.

➡ ⓐ와 같은 것:_____

## 25 위 글의 내용과 일치하지 <u>않는</u> 것은?

① 모차르트 시대의 관객들은 연주회장에서 음식을 먹었다.

② 18세기에 관객들은 연주회장에서 술을 마셨다.

③ 모차르트 시대의 관객들은 연주가 끝난 후 박수를 쳤다.

④ 모차르트는 오늘날 연주회장의 관행에 놀랄 것이다.

⑤ 18세기에 소음은 연주회의 한 부분으로 여겨졌다.

## 27 위 글의 주제로 알맞은 것을 고르시오.

① the area where many big concert halls were built

② the people who went to the concert in the 19th century

③ the reason artists blamed the audience

④ how today's quiet concerts began

⑤ the rule people liked in the 19th century

**[28~29]** 다음 글을 읽고 물음에 답하시오.

As a result, here we are today, very quiet and serious. We do not know (A)[how / what] concerts will look like in the future (B)[though / because] manners change with time. For now, however, if you want to enjoy classical music concerts, just (C)[forget / remember] this: Enjoy the music, but do not disturb those around you.

## 28 위 글의 내용과 일치하지 <u>않는</u> 것은?

① 오늘날의 연주회는 조용하다.

② 오늘날의 연주회는 진지하다.

③ 미래의 연주회는 오늘날과 같을 것이다.

④ 예의범절은 시간과 함께 변한다.

⑤ 음악을 즐길 때는 주변 사람들에게 방해가 되지 않아야 한다.

**[26~27]** 다음 글을 읽고 물음에 답하시오.

Today's quiet concerts began in the 19th century ⓐ<u>when</u> many big concert halls were built. More people, not just noblemen, went to concerts. Artists were no longer dependent on noblemen for money. The artists had more power over their works and started to use their increased power. For example, Wagner blamed the audience for making noise. After some time, a no-clapping-between-movements rule appeared.

## 26 위 글의 밑줄 친 ⓐ<u>when</u>을 대신하여 쓸 수 있는 것은?

① about which ② in which
③ with which ④ to what
⑤ during what

## 29 위 글의 괄호 (A)~(C)에서 문맥이나 어법상 알맞은 낱말을 골라 쓰시오.

➡ (A)_____ (B)_____ (C)_____

**[01~02]** 다음 빈칸에 알맞은 단어를 고르시오.

출제율 90%

**01**

Don't _____ me. I have done nothing wrong to you.

① clap      ② blame
③ appear      ④ increase
⑤ disturb

출제율 100%

**02**

Let me _____ a look at the map.

① let      ② hold
③ allow      ④ take
⑤ make

출제율 90%

**03** 다음 영영풀이에 해당하는 단어를 쓰시오.

a piece of music for one or more solo instruments playing with an orchestra

➡ _____

출제율 90%

**04** 다음 빈칸에 들어갈 말이 바르게 짝지어진 것은?

• The photo will lose color _____ time.
• _____ the way, are you free for dinner tomorrow evening?

① at - With      ② on - In
③ with - By      ④ from - At
⑤ out - On

출제율 95%

**05** 다음 중 〈보기〉에 있는 단어를 사용하여 자연스러운 문장을 만들 수 없는 것은?

┌─ 보기 ┐
volunteer   century   classical   social

① We are living in the 21th ____.
② He is slow in ____.
③ She went to a ____ music concert.
④ They ____ at children's center.
⑤ Join a ____ club to make new friends.

**[06~09]** 다음 대화를 읽고 물음에 답하시오.

G: Yunho! Have you heard about the Christmas concert at the city hall?
B: Yes. I heard that a famous opera singer will be ____ⓐ____ the stage.
G: Oh, then why don't we go on Christmas Day? Can you ____ⓑ____ it?
B: Sure. Do you know what time the concert starts?
G: It starts at 5:30. ⓒLet's meet at the bus stop at 4:00.
B: Good. Don't forget to dress up.
G: Okay. I won't.

출제율 85%

**06** 위 대화의 빈칸 ⓐ에 알맞은 말을 쓰시오.

➡ _____

**07** 위 대화의 빈칸 ⓑ에 알맞은 것은?

① get      ② do
③ arrive      ④ make
⑤ finish

**08** 위 대화의 밑줄 친 ⓒ와 같은 뜻이 되도록 다음 문장의 빈칸에 알맞은 말을 쓰시오.

> How _____ _____ at the bus stop at 4:00?

**09** 위 대화의 내용과 일치하지 <u>않는</u> 것은?

① 소년은 크리스마스 콘서트에 대해 알고 있다.
② 콘서트에는 유명한 오페라 가수가 출연한다.
③ 소녀는 콘서트에 가지 않을 것이다.
④ 콘서트는 5시 30분에 열린다.
⑤ 소년은 콘서트에 정장을 차려 입고 갈 것이다.

[10~13] 다음 대화를 읽고 물음에 답하시오.

G: What are you listening to?
B: Classical music. I'm going to a concert tomorrow and I'd like to know about the music ⓐ I go. ( ① )
G: I guess it's more enjoyable if you know the music. ( ② )
B: Actually, I don't want to clap at the wrong time. ( ③ )
G: Don't you just clap when the music stops? ( ④ )
B: No. In classical music, one piece of music may have several pauses. ( ⑤ )
G: I see. Make sure you don't forget to clap at the real ending. ⓑ , can you make it to our soccer practice tomorrow at 4:00?
B: Sure. I'll come to the practice after the concert finishes.
G: Okay. See you then.

**10** 위 대화의 ①~⑤ 중 다음 주어진 문장이 들어갈 알맞은 곳은?

> You should wait and clap at the very end.

①     ②     ③     ④     ⑤

**11** 위 대화의 빈칸 ⓐ에 알맞은 것은?

① when       ② though
③ before       ④ until
⑤ after

**12** 위 대화의 빈칸 ⓐ에 알맞은 것은?

① However       ② Therefore
③ Consequently       ④ In the end
⑤ By the way

**13** 위 대화의 내용으로 보아 대답할 수 <u>없는</u> 것은?

① What is the boy listening to?
② Where is the boy going to tomorrow?
③ Does the boy often go to a concert?
④ When is their soccer practice?
⑤ Will the boy come to the soccer practice tomorrow?

**14** 다음 빈칸에 들어갈 말로 알맞은 것은?

> I'd like to ask you _____ you're free tonight.

① because       ② that
③ as       ④ if
⑤ what

**15** 다음 두 문장을 한 문장으로 바르게 연결한 것은? 출제율 90%

> • This is the town.
> • I was born here.

① This is the town which I was born.
② This is the town in that I was born.
③ This is the town where I was born.
④ This is the town where I was born here.
⑤ This is where the town I was born.

**16** 다음 밑줄 친 부분의 쓰임이 어색한 것은? 출제율 95%

① Do you know why leaves turn red in autumn?
② Luke's mother knew where he kept the comic books.
③ I wonder that there's an easy way to improve my grade.
④ Do you know how many books your brother has?
⑤ I asked her when she had left her home country.

**17** 다음 밑줄 친 부분의 쓰임이 나머지 넷과 다른 것은? 출제율 95%

① I wonder if my child expresses himself well in English.
② Is it okay if I use your phone to call my mom?
③ Let's wait and see if the weather will be nice.
④ Please tell me if there's anything I can do to help you.
⑤ Alex asked me if I wanted a massage.

**[18~20]** 다음 글을 읽고 물음에 답하시오.

Let's go back in time and take a look at one of Mozart's concerts in the 18th century. You are in a bright hall inside a nobleman's house. Mozart is playing the piano. Surprisingly, however, the audiences are eating, drinking, and talking freely. They whistle and clap at any time. You are (A)[shock] by their bad manners, but Mozart himself would be surprised by today's quiet audiences. Concerts in Mozart's time were mostly (B)_____ events. They were good places to meet people. Noise was just part of the concert.

**18** 위 글의 (A)에 주어진 단어의 알맞은 형태를 쓰시오. 출제율 90%

➡ _____

**19** 위 글의 내용을 참고하여 빈칸 (B)에 알맞은 한 단어를 쓰시오 출제율 90%

➡ _____

**20** 위 글에 어울리도록 다음 빈칸 (A)~(C)에 알맞은 단어를 쓰시오. 출제율 100%

> Concert halls in Mozart's time were (A)_____ and noisy and the audiences (B)_____ and (C)_____ at any time.

**[21~23]** 다음 글을 읽고 물음에 답하시오.

Today's (A)[quiet / bright] concerts began in the 19th century ⓐwhen many big concert halls were built. More people, not (B)[because / just] noblemen, went to concerts. Artists were no longer dependent on noblemen for money. The artists had more power over their works and started to use their (C)[increased / increasing] power. For example, Wagner blamed the audience for making noise. After some time, a no-clapping-between-movements rule appeared.

출제율 100%

**21** 위 글의 괄호 (A)~(C)에서 문맥이나 어법상 알맞은 낱말을 골라 쓰시오.

➡ (A)_____ (B)_____ (C)_____

출제율 90%

**22** 위 글의 밑줄 친 ⓐwhen과 같은 용법으로 쓰인 것을 고르시오.

① She was busy when I arrived home.
② When it rains, you should drive carefully.
③ Do you know when she will come here?
④ He doesn't tell me the time when she will arrive.
⑤ She asked me when they would call her.

출제율 95%

**23** 위 글을 읽고 대답할 수 없는 질문은?

① When did the quiet concerts begin?
② Did noblemen go to concerts in the 19th century?
③ How many artists were dependent on noblemen?
④ Who blamed the audience for making noise?
⑤ What kind of rule appeared in the 19th century?

---

**[24~27]** 다음 글을 읽고 물음에 답하시오.

As a result, here we are today, very quiet and serious. ⓐWe do not know what will concerts look like in the future because manners change with time. For now, ⓑ_____, if you want (A)[enjoy] classical music concerts, just remember this: (B)Enjoy the music, but do not disturb those around you.

출제율 95%

**24** 위 글의 밑줄 친 ⓐ의 문장에서 어법이 어색한 것을 바로잡아 문장을 다시 쓰시오.

➡ _____
_____

출제율 85%

**25** 위 글의 빈칸 ⓑ에 들어가기에 적절한 한 단어를 쓰시오.

➡ _____

출제율 90%

**26** 위 글의 (A)에 주어진 단어를 어법상 적절한 형태로 쓰시오.

➡ _____

출제율 95%

**27** 위 글의 밑줄 친 (B)를 우리말로 옮기시오.

➡ _____
_____

**01** 다음 대화의 흐름상 어색한 것을 하나 찾아서 고치시오.

> A: Why don't we go to the library on Monday after school? Can you make it?
>
> B: Sure, I can. How about on Tuesday?
>
> A: Okay. Don't forget to bring your library card.
>
> B: All right. I won't.

➡ _____

**[02~04]** 다음 대화를 읽고 물음에 답하시오.

> G: You look healthy. What's your secret?
>
> B: Thanks. Well, I go ⓐswim every day. You should go with me sometime.
>
> G: That sound's like fun. ⓑ내가 해야 할 다른 어떤 일이 있니? (any, should)
>
> B: Don't forget ⓒ(eating, to eat) many kinds of fruits and vegetables, too.

**02** 위 대화의 밑줄 친 ⓐ를 알맞은 형으로 고치시오.

➡ _____

**03** 위 대화의 밑줄 친 ⓑ를 주어진 단어를 이용하여 영작하시오. (6 words)

➡ _____

**04** 위 대화의 ⓒ의 괄호 안에 알맞은 것을 고르시오.

➡ _____

**05** 다음을 간접의문문을 이용하여 한 문장으로 쓰시오.

(1) • I'll tell you.
 • Where has he been since last Monday?

➡ _____

(2) • I'd like to know.
 • Did you meet her?

➡ _____

(3) • Do you think?
 • Where can I find some fruit?

➡ _____

**06** 다음 우리말과 일치하도록 빈칸에 알맞은 말을 쓰시오.

> 나는 우리가 수영하러 갔던 그 날을 기억한다.

➡ I remember the day _____ we went swimming.

**07** 괄호 안에 주어진 어휘를 이용하여 다음 우리말을 영작하시오.

> 다음 기차가 언제 오는지 말해 줄 수 있습니까?
> (could, the next train) (9 words)

➡ _____

**08** 다음 우리말을 참고하여 빈칸에 알맞은 단어를 쓰시오.

> 이곳은 내가 종종 공부하는 도서관이다.

➡ This is the library _____ I often study.

**09** 주어진 두 문장을 한 문장으로 연결하시오.

(1) Do you know? + Does Anna love me?

&#10142; _____

(2) I don't know. + Why was Kate so surprised?

&#10142; _____

(3) Cathy will tell me. + Who broke the window yesterday?

&#10142; _____

(4) Can you imagine? + Which book did Jennifer buy?

&#10142; _____

**[10~12]** 다음 글을 읽고 물음에 답하시오.

Imagine (A)_____ at a classical music concert. ①The orchestra starts to play one of Mozart's piano concertos. ② The concert hall is dark and silent. ③ Nobody makes a sound. ④Everybody looks serious. ⑤The audiences only clap after the concerto will finish. This is a familiar scene at concerts today.

**10** 다음과 같은 뜻의 문장이 되도록 위 글의 빈칸 (A)에 알맞은 단어를 쓰시오.

> • Imagine that you are in a concert hall and the orchestra plays a famous piece of classical music.

&#10142; _____

**11** 위 글의 ①~⑤ 중 어법이 어색한 문장을 찾아 쓰고, 올바른 형태로 바로 잡으시오.
&#10142; 번호: _____

_____

**12** What do the audiences do after the concerto is over?

&#10142; They _____.

**[13~15]** 다음 글을 읽고 물음에 답하시오.

(A)Let's go back in time and take a look at one of Mozart's concerts in the 18th century. You are in a bright hall inside a nobleman's house. Mozart is playing the piano. Surprisingly, however, the audiences are eating, drinking, and talking freely. They whistle and clap at any time. You are shocked by their (B) _____ manners, but Mozart himself would be surprised by today's quiet audiences. Concerts in Mozart's time were mostly social events. (C) Mozart 시대의 콘서트는 사람을 만나기 좋은 장소이었다. Noise was just part of the concert.

**13** 밑줄 친 (A)와 같은 뜻의 문장이 되도록 아래 빈칸에 알맞은 한 단어를 쓰시오.

> • Let's go back in time _____ take a look at one of Mozart's concerts in the 18th century.

**14** 위 글의 내용으로 보아 빈칸 (B)에 들어가기에 적절한 한 단어를 쓰시오.

&#10142; _____

**15** 위 글의 밑줄 친 (C)에 해당하는 문장을 영어로 완성하시오. (주어진 단어 활용)

> (concerts in Mozart's time, places, meet)

&#10142; _____

_____

## 창의사고력 서술형 문제

**01** 주어진 어구를 활용하여 〈보기〉와 같이 문장을 쓰시오.

> Tell me … / Did you ask …? / Do you know …? / I wonder … / I don't know … / Can you tell me …? / do you think …?

┌─ 보기 ─┐
Did you ask him what he wanted?

(1) _____

(2) _____

(3) _____

(4) _____

(5) _____

(6) _____

(7) _____

**02** 다음 대화를 읽고 대화의 내용을 요약한 문장을 완성하시오.

> G: Yunho! Have you heard about the Christmas concert at the city hall?
> B: Yes. I heard that a famous opera singer will be on the stage.
> G: Oh, then why don't we go on Christmas Day? Can you make it?
> B: Sure. Do you know what time the concert starts?
> G: It starts at 5:30. Let's meet at the bus stop at 4:00.
> B: Good. Don't forget to dress up.
> G: Okay. I won't.

The girl asks Yunho (A)_____ he has heard about the Christmas concert at the city hall. He says (B)_____ he heard that a famous opera singer will be on the stage. The girl suggests (C)_____ to the concert with her on Christmas Day. Yunho agrees and asks her what time the concerts starts. The girl says that the concert starts at 5:30. So they will (D)_____ at the bus stop at 4:00. Yunho tells her (E)_____ to forget (F)_____ dress up. The girl says that she won't.

## 단원별 모의고사

**01** 다음 짝지어진 단어의 관계가 같도록 빈칸에 알맞은 말을 쓰시오.

> dark : bright : dependent : _____

**02** 다음 빈칸에 공통으로 알맞은 것은?

> • He has a lot of stress at _____ .
> • This picture is a _____ of great artistic value.

① result      ② office
③ work      ④ shape
⑤ business

**03** 다음 영영풀이에 해당하는 것은?

> to disturb someone when they are trying to work, sleep, etc.

① blame      ② appear
③ support      ④ whistle
⑤ interrupt

**04** 다음 우리말에 맞게 빈칸에 알맞은 말을 쓰시오.

(1) 그건 그렇고 나는 내 열쇠를 찾을 수 없어.
➡ _____ _____ _____, I can't find my key.

(2) 방을 좀 볼 수 있을까요?
➡ Can I take _____ _____ _____ your room?

(3) 예술가들은 더 이상 돈 때문에 귀족에게 의존하지 않았다.
➡ Artists were no longer _____ _____ noblemen for money.

**[05~08]** 다음 대화를 읽고 물음에 답하시오.

> G: Yunho! Have you heard about the Christmas concert at the city hall? ( ① )
> B: Yes. I heard that a famous opera singer will be on the stage. ( ② )
> G: Oh, then _____ⓐ don't we go on Christmas Day? ( ③ )
> B: Sure. Do you know what time the concert starts? ( ④ )
> G: It starts at 5:30. Let's meet at the bus stop at 4:00. ( ⑤ )
> B: Good. Don't forget to dress ____ⓑ____ .
> G: Okay. I won't.

**05** 위 대화의 ①~⑤ 중 다음 주어진 문장이 들어갈 알맞은 곳은?

> Can you make it?

①      ②      ③      ④      ⑤

**06** 위 대화의 빈칸 ⓐ에 알맞은 것은?

① How      ② Why
③ When      ④ What
⑤ Where

**07** 위 대화의 빈칸 ⓑ에 알맞은 것은?

① up      ② on
③ off      ④ from
⑤ with

**08** 위 대화의 내용으로 보아 대답할 수 없는 것은?

① When did the girl hear about the concert?

② Where will the concert be held?

③ Who will be on the stage?

④ What time does the concert start?

⑤ Where and when will the boy and girl meet?

**[09~11]** 다음 대화를 읽고 물음에 답하시오.

G: You look healthy. ( ① )

B: Thanks. Well, I go swimming every day. ( ② ) You should go with me sometime. ( ③ )

G: ⓐ그거 재미있을 것 같구나. Any other things I should do? ( ④ )

B: Don't forget ____ⓑ____ many kinds of fruits and vegetables, too. ( ⑤ )

**09** 위 대화의 ①~⑤ 중 다음 주어진 문장이 들어갈 알맞은 곳은?

What's your secret?

①        ②        ③        ④        ⑤

**10** 위 대화의 밑줄 친 ⓐ의 우리말을 주어진 단어를 이용하여 영어로 옮기시오. (that, fun) (4 words)

➡ _____

**11** 위 대화의 빈칸 ⓑ에 알맞은 것은?

① eat         ② eating        ③ ate

④ to eat      ⑤ to eating

**12** 다음 대화의 빈칸에 알맞은 것을 고르시오.

A: Let's go see a movie tomorrow.

B: Good idea!

A: _____

B: Okay. Let's meet at 5 o'clock.

① Where can we meet?

② When can you come?

③ How would you like it?

④ Can you make it at 5?

⑤ What time shall we meet?

**13** 다음 빈칸에 알맞은 말이 바르게 짝지어진 것은?

• This is the place _____ I lost my bag.

• Kate remembers the day _____ we first met.

① where – which       ② where – when

③ how – what          ④ when – where

⑤ what – how

**14** 다음 문장에서 어법상 어색한 것을 바르게 고쳐 다시 쓰시오.

(1) The girl is asking where is the nearest bus stop.

➡ _____

(2) Do you know will the leaves turn yellow in autumn?

➡ _____

(3) Will you tell me when did you meet her?

➡ _____

**15** 다음 밑줄 친 부분의 쓰임이 나머지와 다른 하나는?

① I remember the day when Jerry left Paris.

② 2001 was the year when I visited my cousin in the USA.

③ She was washing the dishes when I came home.

④ Do you know the time when the accident happened?

⑤ Christmas season is a time when people feel happy.

**16** 주어진 어휘를 이용하여 다음 우리말을 영작하시오. (간접의문문을 이용하여 쓸 것.)

(1) 나는 그 소녀가 어디에 살았는지 기억한다.
(remember, live)

➡ _____

(2) Anna는 내게 Angelina를 사랑하는지 물었다.
(ask, love)

➡ _____

**17** 다음 두 문장이 같은 뜻이 되도록 빈칸에 알맞은 말을 쓰시오.

> This is how we caught the thief.
> = This is the way _____ _____ we caught the thief.

**[18~20]** 다음 글을 읽고 물음에 답하시오.

Today's quiet concerts began in the 19th century ①which many big concert halls were built. More people, ②not just noblemen, went to concerts. Artists were ③no longer dependent on noblemen for money. The artists had more power over their works and started ④to use their increased power. For example, Wagner ⑤blamed the audience for making noise. After some time, a no-clapping-between-movements rule appeared.

**18** 위 글에 어울리도록 다음 빈칸 (A)와 (B)에 알맞은 단어를 쓰시오.

> Artists became (A)_____ of the noblemen and a no-clapping-between-movements rule (B)_____ in the 19th century.

**19** Why were artists no longer dependent on noblemen for money?

➡ Because many big concerts _____ _____ and more people _____ to concerts in the 19th century.

**20** 위 글의 밑줄 친 ①~⑤ 중에서 어법상 틀린 것을 찾아 번호를 쓰고, 고치시오.

➡ 번호: _____ 틀린 것: _____
올바른 형태: _____

**[21~23]** 다음 글을 읽고 물음에 답하시오.

As a result, here we are today, very quiet and serious. We do not know ⓐwhat concerts will look like in the future because manners change (A)_____ time. For now, however, ⓑif you want to enjoy classical music concerts, just remember this: Enjoy the music, but do not disturb those (B)_____ you.

**21** 위 글의 밑줄 친 ⓐ와 같은 용법으로 쓰인 것을 고르시오.

① She showed me the book which he had bought.

② I know the boy who called you.

③ Do you know the time when she will come?

④ She asked us who could move her desk.

⑤ The air was cool when I opened the door.

**[24~26]** 다음 글을 읽고 물음에 답하시오.

Let's go back in time and take a look at one of Mozart's concerts in the 18th century. You are in a bright hall inside a nobleman's house. Mozart is playing the piano. (A)[Surprise / Surprisingly], however, the audiences are eating, drinking, and talking freely. They whistle and clap at any time. You are shocked by their bad manners, but Mozart (B)[him / himself] would be surprised by today's quiet audiences. Concerts in Mozart's time were (C)[mostly / most] social events. They were good places (D)to meet people. Noise was just part of the concert.

**24** 위 글의 괄호 (A)~(C)에서 문맥이나 어법상 알맞은 낱말을 골라 쓰시오.

➡ (A)_____ (B)_____ (C)_____

**22** 위 글의 빈칸 (A)와 (B)에 들어갈 전치사가 바르게 짝지어진 것은?

① without – by

② about – around

③ in – from

④ with – around

⑤ with – despite

**25** 위 글의 밑줄 친 (D)to meet와 같은 용법으로 쓰인 것을 고르시오.

① They want to watch the movie.

② He will turn on the TV to see the news.

③ She was happy to receive so many messages.

④ I need a book to read during the night.

⑤ She began to study math.

**23** 위 글의 밑줄 친 ⓑif와 문법적 쓰임이 같은 것을 고르시오. (2개)

① Do you know if he is ready?

② If you are busy, I will wait.

③ She asked me if I had any questions.

④ I will see if he has enough time.

⑤ He will call you if he needs help.

➡ ⓑ와 같은 것: _____

**26** 위 글을 읽고 대답할 수 없는 질문은?

① How were the concert halls in the 18th century?

② Where was the concert hall in the 18th century?

③ How many concert halls did they built?

④ What were the audiences doing during the concert?

⑤ What were concerts in Mozart's time?

# Special

# Charlotte's Web

# Words & Expressions

## Key Words

- **above** [əbʌv] 전 ~보다 위에
- **ad** [æd] 명 광고
- **as** [əz] 접 ~하다시피, ~할 때
- **attention** [əténʃən] 명 관심
- **barn** [bɑːrn] 명 헛간
- **crowd** [kraud] 명 군중, 무리
- **dead** [ded] 형 죽은
- **die** [dai] 동 죽다
- **dump** [dʌmp] 명 쓰레기 폐기장
- **enter** [éntər] 동 ~에 들어가다, (~을) 출전시키다
- **excitement** [iksáitmənt] 명 흥분, 신남
- **fair** [fɛər] 명 박람회
- **farm** [fɑːrm] 명 농장
- **feed** [fiːd] 동 먹이를 주다
- **human** [hjúːmən] 형 인간의
- **last** [læst] 동 지속되다

- **miracle** [mírəkl] 명 기적
- **must** [məst] 조 ~해야 하다
- **narrator** [nǽreitər] 명 서술자, 내레이터
- **nobody** [nóubàdi] 대 아무도 ~ 않다
- **pen** [pen] 명 (가축의) 우리
- **pig** [pig] 명 돼지
- **rat** [ræt] 명 쥐
- **save** [seiv] 동 구하다
- **sheep** [ʃiːp] 명 양
- **shining** [ʃáiniŋ] 형 반짝이는, 빛나는
- **spider** [spáidər] 명 거미
- **terrific** [tərífik] 형 훌륭한
- **weave** [wiːv] 동 (실을) 엮다
- **web** [web] 명 거미줄
- **without** [wiðáut] 전 ~ 없이, ~하지 않고

## Key Expressions

- **between A and B** A와 B 사이에
- **care for** ~을 돌보다
- **fatten up** 살찌우다
- **get[win] a prize** 상을 받다
- **look+형용사** ~하게 보이다
- **out of** (재료) ~으로

- **right away** 즉시, 곧바로
- **run out of** ~이 다 떨어지다
- **share A with B** A를 B와 나누다
- **too 형용사 to 동사원형** 너무 ~해서 …할 수 없다
- **Why don't you ~?** ~하는 게 어때?

## Word Power

※ 접속사 **as**의 여러 뜻

□ ～이기 때문에

**As she has a phobia of water, she doesn't swim.** (그녀는 물 공포증이 있기 때문에, 수영을 하지 않는다.)

□ ～하면서

**You can enjoy the scenery as you run or exercise.** (당신은 뛰거나 운동을 하면서 경치를 즐길 수 있다.)

□ ～하다시피, ～이듯이

**As you know, David has been with us for 14 years.** (여러분들이 아시다시피, David는 저희와 14년간이나 근무해 왔습니다.)

※ 감정과 관련된 명사

□ **boredom** 지루함

□ **calmness** 평온

□ **depression** 우울

□ **enthusiasm** 열광, 열정

□ **excitement** 흥분, 신남

□ **happiness** 기쁨

□ **relief** 안심

□ **sadness** 슬픔

## English Dictionary

□ **above** ～보다 위에
→ higher than something else
다른 어떤 것보다 더 높이

□ **crowd** 군중, 무리
→ a large group of people who have gathered together in one place in a disorganized way
무질서한 방식으로 한 장소에 모여 있는 큰 무리의 사람들

□ **dump** 쓰레기 폐기장
→ a place for depositing rubbish
쓰레기를 두는 장소

□ **enter** (～을) 출전시키다
→ to officially state that someone will participate in a competition, race, or examination
어떤 사람이 대회, 경주 또는 시험에 참여할 것이라고 공식적으로 언급하다

□ **excitement** 흥분, 신남
→ a feeling of enthusiasm and interest
열정과 흥미의 느낌

□ **human** 인간의
→ relating to people
사람과 관련된

□ **last** 지속되다
→ to continue to exist or happen for a specified period of time
특정한 기간 동안 계속 발생하거나 존재하다

□ **miracle** 기적
→ a good event that is very surprising or difficult to believe
매우 놀랍거나 믿기 어려운 좋은 일

□ **narrator** 서술자, 내레이터
→ a person who tells a story in a book, movie, or play or gives an account of something
책, 영화 또는 연극에서 이야기를 말해 주거나 어떤 것을 설명해 주는 사람

□ **pen** (가축의) 우리
→ a small area with a fence round it where farm animals are kept
농장 동물을 가두어 두는 주위에 울타리가 있는 작은 지역

□ **rat** 쥐
→ an animal that has a long tail and looks like a large mouse
큰 생쥐같이 생긴 긴 꼬리를 가진 동물

□ **sheep** 양
→ a farm animal whose skin is covered with thick curly hair called wool
피부가 양모라고 불리는 두꺼운 곱슬거리는 털로 덮인 농장 동물

□ **shining** 반짝이는, 빛나는
→ making or reflecting bright light
밝은 빛을 만들어 내거나 반사하는

□ **spider** 거미
→ a creature with eight legs that catches insects for food
먹이로 곤충을 잡는 8개의 다리를 가진 생물

□ **weave** (실을) 엮다
→ to form cloth by crossing threads over and under each other by hand or by using a machine
손이나 기계를 이용해 위아래로 서로 실을 교차함으로써 천을 만들다

□ **web** 거미줄
→ a thin net made by a spider to catch insects
곤충을 잡기 위해서 거미가 만든 얇은 그물망

## Charlotte's Web

Setting: The pen of Wilbur the pig on Mr. and Mrs. Allen's farm

Roles: Narrator 1, 2, 3, Wilbur: A pig, Charlotte: A spider, Mr. and Mrs. Allen: Farm owners, Old Sheep, Duck, Rat

**Scene 1**

Narrator 1: *Charlotte's Web* is a story of friendship between Wilbur the pig and Charlotte the spider.
between A and B: A와 B 사이의

Narrator 2: They lived on Mr. and Mrs. Allen's farm with Old Sheep, Duck, and Rat.

Narrator 3: One day, Mr. and Mrs. Allen were talking outside the barn.
앨런 부부

Mrs. Allen: Wilbur looks very good.
~해 보인다

Mr. Allen: He'll make good bacon for Christmas.
~이 되다

Old Sheep: They are fattening Wilbur up for Christmas!
fatten up: 체중을 늘리다

Duck: For bacon!

Wilbur: No! I'm too young to die!   too+형용사/부사+to부정사: 너무 …해서 ~할 수 없다

Charlotte: You won't, Wilbur. I'll save you.

Wilbur: How?

Charlotte: I don't know yet, but remember? You saved me when Mr. Allen tried to clean my web off. Now it's my turn to save you.
부정문에서 '아직'   to부정사의 형용사적 용법

**Scene 2**

Charlotte: How can I save Wilbur? Hmm....  Oh, I have an idea!

Narrator 1: That night, Charlotte started to weave something above Wilbur's pen. She worked hard all night without sleeping.
to부정사의 명사적 용법   ~ 없이, ~하지 않고

Narrator 2: The next morning, Mr. and Mrs. Allen came to feed Wilbur.
to부정사의 부사적 용법 (~하기 위해서)

Mrs. Allen: Look! There are words in the web. "Some Pig"!
'대단한 돼지'

Mr. Allen: A miracle!

Narrator 3: Soon, a large crowd came to see Wilbur.
to부정사의 부사적 용법 (~하기 위해서)

---

web 거미줄
pen 우리
pig 돼지
narrator 서술자, 내레이터
sheep 양
rat 쥐
die 죽다
fatten up 살찌우다
weave (실을) 엮다
above ~보다 위에
miracle 기적
crowd 군중, 무리

---

 확인문제

● 다음 문장이 본문의 내용과 일치하면 T, 일치하지 않으면 F를 쓰시오.

1  Mr. Allen says Wilbur looks very good. ☐

2  Mr. Allen says Wilbur will make good bacon for Christmas. ☐

3  Wilbur saved Charlotte when Mr. Allen tried to clean her web off. ☐

4  Soon, a large crowd came to see Charlotte. ☐

**Scene 3**

Narrator 1: As time passed, only a few people came. Charlotte called a meeting.

Charlotte: As we saw, human attention does not last long. If nobody
cares for Wilbur, he will be dead before Christmas. We must
write another word soon.

Duck: I have an idea! How about "Terrific"?

Old Sheep: I like it!

**Scene 4**

Narrator 2: Again, Charlotte worked hard all night. Two days later, a
bigger crowd came.

Charlotte: This also will be forgotten soon. We have to prepare the next
word right away.

Duck: Uh, oh. I have run out of ideas.

Rat: What's all the excitement?

Old Sheep: Why don't you help us? Will you bring some ads from the dump?

Duck: We're trying to find new words.

Charlotte: We're trying to save Wilbur's life.

Rat: Okay, if Wilbur shares his meal with me.

**Scene 5**

Narrator 3: With Rat's help, they finally chose "Shining." The biggest
ever crowd came.

Mr. Allen: You know what? I won't make bacon out of Wilbur. I'll
enter him in the fair!

Mrs. Allen: Great idea! Our famous Wilbur will get a prize!

Wilbur: Did you hear that? I'm going to the fair! Thank you, Charlotte!
You saved me. Thank you all!

human 인간의
last 지속되다
terrific 훌륭한
excitement 흥분, 신남
ad 광고
dump 쓰레기 폐기장
run out of ~을 다 써버리다
shining 빛나는, 반짝이는
enter (~을) 출전시키다

---

**확인문제**

• 다음 문장이 본문의 내용과 일치하면 T, 일치하지 않으면 F를 쓰시오.

1 As time passed, more people came to the farm. ☐

2 If nobody cares for Wilbur, he will be dead before Christmas. ☐

3 Charlotte has already prepared the next word. ☐

4 If Wilbur shares his meal with Rat, Rat will bring some ads from the dump. ☐

5 With Rat's help, they finally chose "Shining." ☐

6 Mr. Allen will make bacon out of Wilbur. ☐

● 우리말을 참고하여 빈칸에 알맞은 말을 쓰시오.

**1** Charlotte's _____

**2** _____: The _____ of Wilbur the pig on Mr. and Mrs. Allen's farm

**3** _____: Narrator 1, 2, 3, Wilbur: A pig, Charlotte: A spider, Mr. and Mrs. Allen: Farm owners, Old Sheep, Duck, Rat

**Scene 1**

**4** Narrator 1: *Charlotte's Web* is a story of _____ _____ Wilbur the pig _____ Charlotte the spider.

**5** Narrator 2: They _____ _____ Mr. and Mrs. Allen's farm with Old Sheep, Duck, and Rat.

**6** Narrator 3: One day, Mr. and Mrs. Allen were talking _____ _____ _____.

**7** Mrs. Allen: Wilbur _____ very _____.

**8** Mr. Allen: He'll _____ _____ _____ for Christmas.

**9** Old Sheep: They _____ _____ Wilbur _____ for Christmas!

**10** Duck: _____ bacon!

**11** Wilbur: No! I'm _____ young _____ die!

**12** Charlotte: You _____, Wilbur. I'll _____ you.

**13** Wilbur: _____?

**14** Charlotte: I don't know _____, but remember?

**15** You saved me when Mr. Allen tried to _____ my web _____!

**16** Now it's _____ _____ to save you.

**Scene 2**

**17** Charlotte: _____ can I save Wilbur?

**18** Hmm.... Oh, I _____ an idea!

**19** Narrator 1: That night, Charlotte started _____ _____ something _____ Wilbur's pen.

**20** She worked _____ all night _____ _____.

**21** Narrator 2: The next morning, Mr. and Mrs. Allen came _____ _____ Wilbur.

**22** Mrs. Allen: Look! There are _____ in the web. "_____ _____"!

**23** Mr. Allen: A _____!

**24** Narrator 3: Soon, a _____ _____ came to see Wilbur.

---

**1** 샬럿의 거미줄

**2** 배경: 앨런 부부 농장의 돼지 윌버의 우리

**3** 배역: 서술자 1, 2, 3, 돼지 윌버, 거미 샬럿, 농장 주인 앨런 부부, 늙은 양, 오리, 쥐
**장면 1**

**4** 서술자 1: "샬럿의 거미줄"은 돼지 윌버와 거미 샬럿 사이의 우정 이야기다.

**5** 서술자 2: 그들은 늙은 양, 오리, 쥐와 함께 앨런 부부의 농장에서 살았다.

**6** 서술자 3: 어느 날, 앨런 부부는 헛간 밖에서 이야기하고 있었다.

**7** 앨런 부인: 윌버가 아주 좋아 보여요.

**8** 앨런 씨: 그는 크리스마스에 좋은 베이컨이 될 거예요.

**9** 늙은 양: 그들은 크리스마스를 위해 윌버를 살찌우고 있어.

**10** 오리: 베이컨을 위해!

**11** 윌버: 안 돼! 나는 죽기에 너무 어려.

**12** 샬럿: 죽지 않을 거야, 윌버. 내가 널 구할게.

**13** 윌버: 어떻게?

**14** 샬럿: 아직 잘 모르겠어. 그런데 기억나?

**15** 앨런 씨가 거미줄을 없애려고 했을 때 네가 나를 구했잖아.

**16** 이제 내가 너를 구할 차례야.
**장면 2**

**17** 샬럿: 내가 어떻게 윌버를 구할 수 있을까?

**18** 음… 오, 좋은 생각이 났어!

**19** 서술자 1: 그날 밤, 샬럿은 윌버의 우리 위에 무언가를 짜기 시작했다.

**20** 그녀는 밤새도록 자지 않고 열심히 일했다.

**21** 서술자 2: 다음 날 아침, 앨런 부부는 윌버에게 먹이를 주러 왔다.

**22** 앨런 부인: 보세요! 거미줄에 단어들이 있어요. '대단한 돼지'!

**23** 앨런 씨: 기적이야!

**24** 서술자 3: 곧 많은 군중들이 윌버를 보러 왔다.

---

**Scene 3**

**25** Narrator 1: _____ time passed, _____ _____ _____ people came.

**26** Charlotte _____ _____ _____.

**27** Charlotte: _____ we saw, _____ _____ does not _____ long.

**28** If nobody _____ for Wilbur, he _____ _____ _____ before Christmas.

**29** We must write _____ _____ soon.

**30** Duck: I have an idea! _____ _____ "Terrific"?

**31** Old Sheep: I like _____!

**Scene 4**

**32** Narrator 2: Again, Charlotte worked hard _____ _____.

**33** Two days _____, a bigger crowd came.

**34** Charlotte: This also _____ _____ _____ soon.

**35** We have to prepare the next word _____ _____.

**36** Duck: Uh, oh. I have _____ _____ _____ ideas.

**37** Rat: What's all the _____?

**38** Old Sheep: _____ _____ _____ help us?

**39** Will you _____ some ads _____ the dump?

**40** Duck: We're _____ _____ find new words.

**41** Charlotte: We're trying _____ _____ Wilbur's life.

**42** Rat: Okay, if Wilbur _____ his meal _____ me.

**Scene 5**

**43** Narrator 3: _____ Rat's help, they _____ chose "Shining."

**44** The _____ _____ crowd came.

**45** Mr. Allen: You know _____? I won't _____ bacon _____ Wilbur.

**46** I'll _____ _____ in the fair!

**47** Mrs. Allen: Great idea! Our famous Wilbur will _____ _____ _____!

**48** Wilbur: Did you hear that? I'm going to _____ _____!

**49** Thank you, Charlotte! You _____ me. Thank you all!

---

**장면 3**

**25** 서술자 1: 시간이 지날수록 극소수의 사람들만이 왔다.

**26** 샬럿은 회의를 소집했다.

**27** 샬럿: 보았다시피 인간의 관심은 오래 지속되지 않아.

**28** 아무도 윌버를 돌보지 않는다면, 그는 크리스마스 전에 죽을 거야.

**29** 우리는 곧 다른 단어를 써야 해.

**30** 오리: 내게 생각이 있어. '훌륭한'은 어때?

**31** 늙은 양: 좋아!

**장면 4**

**32** 서술자 2: 다시 샬럿은 밤새도록 열심히 일했다.

**33** 이틀 후, 더 많은 군중이 왔다.

**34** 샬럿: 이것 또한 곧 잊힐 거야.

**35** 우리는 곧바로 다음 단어를 준비해야 해.

**36** 오리: 오. 나는 아이디어가 바닥이 나 버렸어.

**37** 쥐: 모두들 뭐가 그렇게 신나니?

**38** 늙은 양: 우릴 도와주는 게 어때?

**39** 쓰레기 더미에서 광고 몇 개를 가져다줄래?

**40** 오리: 우리는 새로운 단어를 찾으려고 노력하고 있어.

**41** 샬럿: 우리는 윌버의 생명을 구하려고 노력하고 있어.

**42** 쥐: 알았어. 윌버가 음식을 나와 나눈다면.

**장면 5**

**43** 서술자 3: 쥐의 도움으로, 그들은 마침내 '빛나는'을 선택했다.

**44** 이제껏 가장 많은 군중이 왔다.

**45** 앨런 씨: 그거 알아요? 나는 윌버로 베이컨을 만들지 않을 거예요.

**46** 나는 그를 박람회에 출전시킬 거예요.

**47** 앨런 부인: 좋은 생각이에요! 우리 유명한 윌버가 상을 받을 거예요!

**48** 윌버: 들었어? 내가 박람회에 나갈 거야!

**49** 고마워, 샬럿! 네가 나를 구했어. 모두들 고마워!

● 우리말을 참고하여 본문을 영작하시오.

**1** 샬럿의 거미줄
➡ _____

**2** 배경: 앨런 부부 농장의 돼지 윌버의 우리
➡ _____

**3** 배역: 서술자 1, 2, 3, 돼지 윌버, 거미 샬럿, 농장 주인 앨런 부부, 늙은 양, 오리, 쥐
➡ _____

**Scene 1**
**4** 서술자 1: "샬럿의 거미줄"은 돼지 윌버와 거미 샬럿 사이의 우정 이야기다.
➡ _____

**5** 서술자 2: 그들은 늙은 양, 오리, 쥐와 함께 앨런 부부의 농장에서 살았다.
➡ _____

**6** 서술자 3: 어느 날, 앨런 부부는 헛간 밖에서 이야기하고 있었다.
➡ _____

**7** 앨런 부인: 윌버가 아주 좋아 보여요.
➡ _____

**8** 앨런 씨: 그는 크리스마스에 좋은 베이컨이 될 거예요.
➡ _____

**9** 늙은 양: 그들은 크리스마스를 위해 윌버를 살찌우고 있어.
➡ _____

**10** 오리: 베이컨을 위해!
➡ _____

**11** 윌버: 안 돼! 나는 죽기에 너무 어려.
➡ _____

**12** 샬럿: 죽지 않을 거야, 윌버. 내가 널 구할게.
➡ _____

**13** 윌버: 어떻게?
➡ _____

**14** 샬럿: 아직 잘 모르겠어. 그런데 기억나?
➡ _____

**15** 앨런 씨가 거미줄을 없애려고 했을 때 네가 나를 구했잖아.
➡ _____

**16** 이제 내가 너를 구할 차례야.
➡ _____

**Scene 2**
**17** 샬럿: 내가 어떻게 윌버를 구할 수 있을까?
➡ _____

**18** 음… 오, 좋은 생각이 났어!
➡ _____

**19** 서술자 1: 그날 밤, 샬럿은 윌버의 우리 위에 무언가를 짜기 시작했다.
➡ _____

**20** 그녀는 밤새도록 자지 않고 열심히 일했다.
➡ _____

**21** 서술자 2: 다음 날 아침, 앨런 부부는 윌버에게 먹이를 주러 왔다.
➡ _____

**22** 앨런 부인: 보세요! 거미줄에 단어들이 있어요. '대단한 돼지'!
➡ _____

**23** 앨런 씨: 기적이야!
➡ _____

**24** 서술자 3: 곧 많은 군중들이 윌버를 보러 왔다.
➡ _____

**Scene 3**

**25** 서술자 1: 시간이 지날수록 극소수의 사람들만이 왔다.
➡ _____

**26** 샬럿은 회의를 소집했다.
➡ _____

**27** 샬럿: 보았다시피 인간의 관심은 오래 지속되지 않아.
➡ _____

**28** 아무도 윌버를 돌보지 않는다면, 그는 크리스마스 전에 죽을 거야.
➡ _____

**29** 우리는 곧 다른 단어를 써야 해.
➡ _____

**30** 오리: 내게 생각이 있어. '훌륭한'은 어때?
➡ _____

**31** 늙은 양: 좋아!
➡ _____

**Scene 4**

**32** 서술자 2: 다시 샬럿은 밤새도록 열심히 일했다.
➡ _____

**33** 이틀 후, 더 많은 군중이 왔다.
➡ _____

**34** 샬럿: 이것 또한 곧 잊힐 거야.
➡ _____

**35** 우리는 곧바로 다음 단어를 준비해야 해.
➡ _____

**36** 오리: 오. 나는 아이디어가 바닥이 나 버렸어.
➡ _____

**37** 쥐: 모두들 뭐가 그렇게 신나니?
➡ _____

**38** 늙은 양: 우릴 도와주는 게 어때?
➡ _____

**39** 쓰레기 더미에서 광고 몇 개를 가져다줄래?
➡ _____

**40** 오리: 우리는 새로운 단어를 찾으려고 노력하고 있어.
➡ _____

**41** 샬럿: 우리는 윌버의 생명을 구하려고 노력하고 있어.
➡ _____

**42** 쥐: 알았어, 윌버가 음식을 나와 나눈다면.
➡ _____

**Scene 5**

**43** 서술자 3: 쥐의 도움으로, 그들은 마침내 '빛나는'을 선택했다.
➡ _____

**44** 이제껏 가장 많은 군중이 왔다.
➡ _____

**45** 앨런 씨: 그거 알아요? 나는 윌버로 베이컨을 만들지 않을 거예요.
➡ _____

**46** 나는 그를 박람회에 출전시킬 거예요.
➡ _____

**47** 앨런 부인: 좋은 생각이에요! 우리 유명한 윌버가 상을 받을 거예요!
➡ _____

**48** 윌버: 들었어? 내가 박람회에 나갈 거야!
➡ _____

**49** 고마워, 샬럿! 네가 나를 구했어. 모두들 고마워!
➡ _____

**중요**
**01** 다음 빈칸에 공통으로 들어갈 단어를 쓰시오.

> (1) _____ you can see, I still have a long way to go.
> (2) It's hard to reject _____ they offer me a nice bit of money.
> (3) They cried _____ they said goodbye to each other.

**02** 다음 주어진 단어를 이용해 우리말에 맞게 빈칸을 완성하시오.

> 나는 여기에서 엄청난 흥분을 느낄 수 있다.
> ➡ I can feel lots of _____ here.
> (excite)

**03** 다음 밑줄 친 부분과 의미가 가장 가까운 단어를 주어진 철자로 시작하여 쓰시오.

> It seems that our work will be continued without end.

> ➡ l_____

**중요**
**04**  다음 빈칸에 알맞은 단어를 〈보기〉에서 골라 쓰시오.

> ─┤ 보기 ├─
> at / for / in / of / to / with

(1) Can you stop by the store for some milk? We've run out _____ it.
(2) I am happy to share that information _____ you.
(3) I had to care _____ my nephew yesterday.
(4) They are made out _____ trees and bamboo plants.

**중요**
**05** 다음 주어진 우리말에 맞게 빈칸을 채우시오. (철자가 주어진 경우 주어진 철자로 시작할 것)

(1) 그 훈련사는 말 몇 마리를 경주에 출전시킬 것이다.
  ➡ The trainer will e_____ several horses in the race.
(2) 우리는 30분 후에 떠나야 한다.
  ➡ We m_____ leave in thirty minutes.
(3) 동물들이 우리에 갇혀 있다.
  ➡ The animals are kept in the _____.
(4) 매년 이 시기에, 곰들은 겨울을 위해 살을 찌워야 한다.
  ➡ At this time of the year, bears should be _____ _____ for the winter.
(5) 맛이 훌륭해!
  ➡ It tastes t_____.

**06** 다음 영영풀이에 해당하는 단어를 〈보기〉에서 찾아 쓰시오.

> ─┤ 보기 ├─
> dump / enter / narrator / weave

(1) _____: to form cloth by crossing threads over and under each other by hand or by using a machine
(2) _____: to officially state that someone will participate in a competition, race, or examination
(3) _____: a place for depositing rubbish
(4) _____: a person who tells a story in a book, movie, or play or gives an account of something

**07** 다음 문장에서 어법상 <u>어색한</u> 부분을 바르게 고쳐 다시 쓰시오.

(1) I have ran out of ideas.

➡ _____

(2) Bring some ads from the dump, do you?

➡ _____

(3) If Wilbur will share his meal with me, I'll bring some ads from the dump.

➡ _____

_____

(4) A prize will get our famous Wilbur.

➡ _____

_____

(5) John needed someone talking about his troubles.

➡ _____

(6) Though we saw, human attention does not last long.

➡ _____

**08** 다음 빈칸에 알맞은 말을 〈보기〉에서 골라 쓰시오. (한 단어는 한 번만 쓸 것)

┌─ 보기 ─────────────────────┐
as / that / if / when
└──────────────────────────┘

(1) _____ time passed, only a few people came.

(2) _____ nobody cares for Wilbur, he will be dead before Christmas.

(3) You saved me _____ Mr. Allen tried to clean my web off.

[09~11] 다음 글을 읽고, 물음에 답하시오.

(A)[Scene / Scenery] 1

Narrator 1: *Charlotte's Web* is a story of friendship between Wilbur the pig and Charlotte the spider.

Narrator 2: ⓐThey lived on Mr. and Mrs. Allen's farm with Old Sheep, Duck, and Rat.

Narrator 3: One day, Mr. and Mrs. Allen were talking outside the barn.

Mrs. Allen: Wilbur looks very good.

Mr. Allen: He'll make good bacon for Christmas.

Old Sheep: ⓑThey are fattening Wilbur up for Christmas!

Duck: For bacon!

Wilbur: No! ⓒI'm too young to die!

Charlotte: You won't, Wilbur. I'll save you.

Wilbur: (B)[How / Why]?

Charlotte: I don't know (C)[already / yet], but remember? You saved me when Mr. Allen tried to clean my web off. Now it's my turn to save you.

**09** 위 글의 괄호 (A)~(C)에서 문맥이나 어법상 알맞은 낱말을 골라 쓰시오.

(A) _____ (B) _____ (C) _____

**10** 위 글의 밑줄 친 ⓐ와 ⓑ의 They가 가리키는 것을 본문에서 찾아 각각 쓰시오.

ⓐ _____

ⓑ _____

**11** 위 글의 밑줄 친 ⓒI'm too young to die!를 복문으로 고치시오.

➡ _____

**01** 출제율 95%

다음 빈칸에 알맞은 단어를 고르시오.

> Ella cares only about herself. _____ wants to be her friends.

① Somebody ② Nobody
③ Something ④ Nothing
⑤ Everyone

**02** 출제율 90%

다음 빈칸에 알맞은 단어를 모두 고르시오.

> Congratulations! I heard that you _____ first prize.

① took ② won ③ did
④ got ⑤ lost

**03** 출제율 95%

다음 중 밑줄 친 부분의 뜻풀이가 바르지 않은 것은?

① How many times a day should I feed the cat? (먹이를 주다)
② The battery can last for a few days. (지속되다)
③ It was a miracle that he survived. (기적)
④ He's the person who can save you. (돕다)
⑤ Look at the stars shining in the sky. (반짝이는)

**04** 출제율 95%

다음 빈칸에 알맞은 말이 순서대로 바르게 배열된 것은?

> • Leave right _____, and you will get to the airport by three.
> • Is it too late _____ change a small detail on the design?

① on – on ② on – to
③ away – on ④ away – to
⑤ away – for

**05** 출제율 100%

다음 주어진 우리말에 맞게 빈칸을 채우시오.

(1) 한 무리의 사람들이 현장에 몰려갔다.
➡ A _____ of people rushed to the scene.

(2) 경찰이 거기에 도착했을 때, 그는 이미 죽어 있었다.
➡ When the police got there, he was _____ already.

(3) 쓰레기 폐기장에서 악취가 난다.
➡ The _____ smells bad.

(4) 아이들이 신나서 펄쩍펄쩍 뛰고 있다.
➡ The children are jumping up and down with _____.

**06** 출제율 85%

다음 우리말에 맞게 주어진 단어를 바르게 배열하시오.

(1) 해가 구름 위에 있다.
(the, above, the, clouds, is, sun)
➡ _____

(2) 그녀의 부모님은 그녀를 살찌우려고 노력했다.
(tried, up, her, to, parents, fatten, her)
➡ _____

(3) 나는 돈이 다 떨어졌다.
(money, I, of, ran, out)
➡ _____

(4) 나는 당장 가야 한다.
(to, away, have, I, go, right)
➡ _____

(5) 그녀는 부모님을 보살피기 위해 다시 집으로 이사를 했다. (she, parents, care, her, moved back, home, to, for)
➡ _____

**07** 출제율 85%

다음 밑줄 친 make와 같은 문장 형식으로 쓰인 것은?

He'll make good bacon for Christmas.

① I made him a new suit.
② Flowers make our rooms cheerful.
③ He made a model plane for his son.
④ I'll make him go there whether he wants to or not.
⑤ Mary will make a wise mother and good wife for him.

**08** 출제율 100%

다음 밑줄 친 to save와 같은 용법으로 쓰인 것을 고르시오.

Now it's my turn to save you.

① Old Sheep asked Rat to bring some ads from the dump.
② It's time for you to go to bed.
③ Mr. Allen tried to clean my web off.
④ The next morning, Mr. and Mrs. Allen came to feed Wilbur.
⑤ Charlotte wove something to save Wilbur.

**09** 출제율 90%

다음 주어진 문장과 같은 의미의 문장을 so를 이용하여 쓰시오.

I'm too sleepy to drive.

➡ _____

**10** 출제율 90%

다음 문장을 수동태로 바꿔 쓰시오.

(1) Eddie gave Ruth a nice present. (두 가지로 쓸 것.)

➡ _____
_____

(2) Alex bought Stephanie a pretty dress.

➡ _____

(3) Wilbur asked Charlotte an interesting question.

➡ _____
_____

**11** 출제율 90%

다음 문장을 수동태로 바르게 바꾼 것은?

We have to prepare the next word right away.

① The next word has to prepare us right away.
② The next word has to prepare right away by us.
③ The next word has to prepared by us right away.
④ The next word has to be prepared us right away.
⑤ The next word has to be prepared right away by us.

**12** 출제율 100%

다음 중 어법상 옳은 것은?

① I need someone to depend upon very honest.
② Charlotte started weaving something above Wilbur's pen.
③ Dan looks very honestly.
④ "Shining" was finally chosen them.
⑤ If nobody will care for Wilbur, he will be dead before Christmas.

**[13~16]** 다음 글을 읽고, 물음에 답하시오.

**Scene 1**

Narrator 1: *Charlotte's Web* is a story of friendship between Wilbur the pig and Charlotte the spider.

Narrator 2: They lived on Mr. and Mrs. Allen's farm with Old Sheep, Duck, and Rat.

Narrator 3: One day, Mr. and Mrs. Allen were talking outside the barn.

Mrs. Allen: Wilbur looks very good.

Mr. Allen: ①He'll make good bacon for Christmas.

Old Sheep: They are fattening Wilbur up for Christmas!

Duck: For bacon!

Wilbur: No! ②I'm too young to die!

Charlotte: ③You won't, Wilbur. I'll ⓐsave you.

Wilbur: How?

Charlotte: I don't know yet, but remember? You saved ④me when Mr. Allen tried to clean my web off. Now it's my turn to save ⑤you.

✏ 출제율 90%

**13** 위 글의 종류로 알맞은 것을 고르시오.

① review ② play scenario
③ book report ④ essay
⑤ article

✏ 출제율 90%

**14** 위 글의 밑줄 친 ①~⑤ 중에서 가리키는 대상이 나머지 넷과 다른 것은?

①　　②　　③　　④　　⑤

✏ 출제율 95%

**15** 위 글의 밑줄 친 ⓐsave와 같은 의미로 쓰인 것을 고르시오.

① You should save a little each week.
② Save some food for me.
③ We'll take a taxi to save time.
④ Don't forget to save data after word processing.
⑤ Doctors were unable to save her.

✏ 출제율 100%

**16** 위 글의 내용과 일치하지 않는 것은?

① "샬럿의 거미줄"은 돼지 월버와 거미 샬럿 사이의 우정 이야기다.
② 월버와 샬럿은 늙은 양, 오리, 쥐와 함께 앨런 부부의 농장에서 살았다.
③ 앨런 부인은 월버가 크리스마스에 좋은 베이컨이 될 것이라고 말한다.
④ 늙은 양은 앨런 부부가 크리스마스를 위해 월버를 살찌우고 있다고 말한다.
⑤ 월버는 자신이 죽기에는 너무 어리다고 말한다.

**[17~19]** 다음 글을 읽고, 물음에 답하시오.

**Scene 2**

Charlotte: How can I save Wilbur? Hmm.... Oh, I have an idea!

Narrator 1: That night, Charlotte started to ＿＿ⓐ＿＿ something above Wilbur's pen. She worked hard all night without sleeping.

Narrator 2: The next morning, Mr. and Mrs. Allen came ⓑto feed Wilbur.

Mrs. Allen: Look! There are words in the web. "Some Pig"!

Mr. Allen: A miracle!

Narrator 3: Soon, a large crowd came to see Wilbur.

**17** 다음 주어진 영영풀이를 참고하여 빈칸 ⓐ에 철자 w로 시작하는 단어를 쓰시오.

> to make cloth or a carpet by crossing threads over and under each other using a frame or machine

➡ _____

**18** 위 글의 밑줄 친 ⓑto feed와 to부정사의 용법이 다른 것을 모두 고르시오.

① She grew up to be the president.
② I want someone to talk to me.
③ It is interesting to learn a foreign language.
④ I use the computer to do my homework.
⑤ My dream is to be an English teacher.

**19** 본문의 내용과 일치하도록 다음 빈칸 (A)와 (B)에 알맞은 단어를 쓰시오.

> Charlotte ___(A)___ the words "Some Pig" into the web above Wilbur's ___(B)___.

(A) _____ (B) _____

[20~22] 다음 글을 읽고 물음에 답하시오.

> **Scene 3**
> Narrator 1: As time passed, only (A)[a few / a little] people came. Charlotte (B)[called / cancelled] a meeting.
> Charlotte: As we saw, human attention does not last long. ⓐIf nobody will care for Wilbur, he will be dead before Christmas. We must write another word soon.
> Duck: I have an idea! How about "(C)[Terrible / Terrific]"?
> Old Sheep: I like it!

**20** 위 글의 괄호 (A)~(C)에서 문맥이나 어법상 알맞은 낱말을 골라 쓰시오.

(A) _____ (B) _____ (C) _____

**21** 위 글의 밑줄 친 ⓐ에서 어법상 틀린 부분을 찾아 고치시오.

_____ ➡ _____

**22** 위 글을 읽고 대답할 수 없는 질문은?

① As time passed, did many people come constantly?
② Who held a meeting?
③ Does human attention last long?
④ Why do they have to write another word soon?
⑤ What was the first word Charlotte wove in the web?

**[23~24]** 다음 글을 읽고 빈칸에 알맞은 답을 쓰시오.

**Scene 4**

Narrator 2: Again, Charlotte worked hard all night. Two days later, a bigger crowd came.

Charlotte: This also will be forgotten soon. We have to prepare the next word right away.

Duck: Uh, oh. I have run out of ideas.

Rat: What's all the excitement?

Old Sheep: Why don't you help us? Will you bring some ads from the dump?

Duck: We're trying to find new words.

Charlotte: We're trying to save Wilbur's life.

Rat: Okay, if Wilbur shares his meal with me.

출제율 90%

**23** 위 글의 내용과 어울리는 속담을 고르시오.

① Do to others as you would be done by.

② Many hands make light work.

③ A stitch in time saves nine.

④ Too many cooks spoil the broth.

⑤ As you sow, so shall you reap.

출제율 95%

**24** 위 글의 내용과 일치하지 <u>않는</u> 것은?

① 샬럿은 다시 밤새도록 열심히 일했다.

② 샬럿은 곧바로 다음 단어를 준비해야 한다고 말했다.

③ 늙은 양은 아이디어가 바닥이 나 버렸다.

④ 늙은 양은 쥐에게 쓰레기 더미에서 광고 몇 개를 가져다 달라고 부탁했다.

⑤ 쥐는 윌버가 음식을 자신과 나눈다면 도와주겠다고 했다.

**[25~28]** 다음 글을 읽고, 물음에 답하시오.

**Scene 5**

Narrator 3: With Rat's help, they ⓐfinally chose "Shining." ⓑ이제껏 가장 많은 군중이 왔다.

Mr. Allen: You know what? I won't make bacon out of Wilbur. I'll enter ⓒhim in the fair!

Mrs. Allen: Great idea! Our famous Wilbur will get a prize!

Wilbur: Did you hear that? I'm going to the fair! Thank you, Charlotte! You saved me. Thank you all!

출제율 100%

**25** 위 글의 제목으로 가장 알맞은 것을 고르시오.

① Rat's Practical Help

② Wow, We Chose "Shining"

③ Lots of Crowd Came!

④ How to Make Bacon out of Wilbur

⑤ Thank You All! I'm Going to the Fair!

출제율 90%

**26** 위 글의 밑줄 친 ⓐfinally와 바꿔 쓸 수 <u>없는</u> 말을 <u>모두</u> 고르시오.

① at last          ② in the long run

③ completely      ④ in the end

⑤ immediately

출제율 95%

**27** 위 글의 밑줄 친 ⓑ의 우리말에 맞게 한 단어를 보충하여, 주어진 어휘를 알맞게 배열하시오.

crowd / biggest / came / ever

➡ _____

출제율 85%

**28** 위 글의 밑줄 친 ⓒhim이 가리키는 것을 본문에서 찾아 쓰시오.

➡ _____

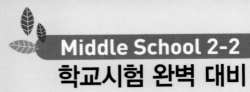

Middle School 2-2
학교시험 완벽 대비

2학기 전과정
적중 100 plus
영어 기출문제집

영어 중 2
시사 | 송미정

*Best Collection*

내용문의 중등영어발전소 적중100 편집부  TEL 070-4416-3636

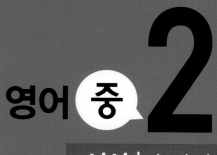

# INSIGHT
## on the textbook
교과서 파헤치기

※ 다음 영어를 우리말로 쓰시오.

| 01 | abroad | _____ |
| 02 | camel | _____ |
| 03 | cheerful | _____ |
| 04 | beginning | _____ |
| 05 | colorful | _____ |
| 06 | bright | _____ |
| 07 | sweet | _____ |
| 08 | enough | _____ |
| 09 | view | _____ |
| 10 | flight | _____ |
| 11 | capital | _____ |
| 12 | guest | _____ |
| 13 | modern | _____ |
| 14 | lamb | _____ |
| 15 | coastline | _____ |
| 16 | scared | _____ |
| 17 | language | _____ |
| 18 | magical | _____ |
| 19 | asleep | _____ |
| 20 | expect | _____ |
| 21 | whole | _____ |

| 22 | moment | _____ |
| 23 | amazing | _____ |
| 24 | culture | _____ |
| 25 | moved | _____ |
| 26 | tasty | _____ |
| 27 | once | _____ |
| 28 | wedding | _____ |
| 29 | rise | _____ |
| 30 | cozy | _____ |
| 31 | serve | _____ |
| 32 | imagine | _____ |
| 33 | chance | _____ |
| 34 | traditional | _____ |
| 35 | be full of | _____ |
| 36 | get used to | _____ |
| 37 | be made of | _____ |
| 38 | show A around B | _____ |
| 39 | be cooked with | _____ |
| 40 | Have you been (to) ~? | _____ |
| 41 | can't wait to | _____ |
| 42 | feel like+주어+동사 | _____ |
| 43 | wake up | _____ |

※ 다음 우리말을 영어로 쓰시오.

| | | |
|---|---|---|
| 01 | 기회 | |
| 02 | 화려한, (색이) 다채로운 | |
| 03 | 순간 | |
| 04 | 아늑한 | |
| 05 | 잠이 든 | |
| 06 | ~할 만큼 (충분히) | |
| 07 | 낙타 | |
| 08 | 비행 | |
| 09 | 손님 | |
| 10 | 상상하다 | |
| 11 | 시작, 처음 | |
| 12 | 제공하다 | |
| 13 | 농담하다 | |
| 14 | 해외에 | |
| 15 | 경관, 전망 | |
| 16 | 양고기 | |
| 17 | 맛있는 | |
| 18 | 밝은 | |
| 19 | 아주 멋진, 마법의 | |
| 20 | 쾌활한, 유쾌한 | |
| 21 | 결혼(식) | |

| | | |
|---|---|---|
| 22 | 현대의 | |
| 23 | 굉장한, 놀라운 | |
| 24 | 수도 | |
| 25 | ~하자마자 | |
| 26 | 문화 | |
| 27 | 부분, 일부 | |
| 28 | 해안선 | |
| 29 | (해가) 뜨다 | |
| 30 | 겁먹은, 무서워하는 | |
| 31 | 가슴 뭉클한 | |
| 32 | 전통적인 | |
| 33 | 기대하다, 예상하다 | |
| 34 | 전체, 모든 | |
| 35 | 잠에서 깨다 | |
| 36 | A에서 B로 | |
| 37 | ~인 것처럼 느끼다 | |
| 38 | ~에 익숙해지다 | |
| 39 | 빨리 ~하면 좋겠다 | |
| 40 | 처음에는 | |
| 41 | ~로 가득하다 | |
| 42 | ~로 만들어지다(재료) | |
| 43 | ~에 가 본 적 있니? | |

※ 다음 영영풀이에 알맞은 단어를 <보기>에서 골라 쓴 후, 우리말 뜻을 쓰시오.

1 _____ : shining strongly:: _____

2 _____ : not awake: _____

3 _____ : to make a joke: _____

4 _____ : noticeably happy: _____

5 _____ : appear above the horizon in the sky: _____

6 _____ : an opportunity to do something: _____

7 _____ : in or to a different country or countries: _____

8 _____ : seems to use special powers: _____

9 _____ : someone who is invited to visit you: _____

10 _____ : designed and made using the latest ideas or methods: _____

11 _____ : relating to Mongolia or its people: _____

12 _____ : believe or think that something will happen: _____

13 _____ : everything that can be seen from a particular place: _____

14 _____ : a place where planes take off and land with facilities for passengers: _____

15 _____ : one of the pieces, sections, or elements that makes the whole of something: _____

16 _____ : a place where trains or buses stop so that people can get on or off: _____

| 보기 | | | |
|---|---|---|---|
| part | station | magical | view |
| asleep | kid | bright | guest |
| Mongolian | expect | airport | rise |
| chance | abroad | modern | cheerful |

**Step1**

※ 다음 우리말과 일치하도록 빈칸에 알맞은 말을 쓰시오.

**Listen & Speak 1 A**

**B:** _____ _____ _____ _____ Spanish food?

**G:** Yes, I _____ . It's really _____ .

B: 스페인 음식을 먹어 본 적 있니?
G: 응, 먹어 봤어. 매우 맛있어.

**Listen & Speak 1 B**

1. **G:** You _____ _____ , Inho. What's _____ ?

   **B:** I'm _____ _____ Jejudo _____ my family this weekend. _____ you _____ _____ there?

   **G:** Yes, many times. I love the _____ . _____ _____ you?

   **B:** It'll be my first visit to Jejudo. I _____ _____ _____ this weekend!

2. **B:** _____ you _____ watched the sun _____ _____ the ocean?

   **G:** No. _____ _____ you?

   **B:** I _____ the sun _____ in Gangneung _____ New Year's Day. It was great.

   **G:** I _____ _____ _____ , but I just couldn't _____ _____ _____ enough.

1. G: 인호야, 너 신나 보인다. 무슨 일이니?
   B: 이번 주말에 가족들과 함께 제주도에 가거든. 넌 가 본 적 있니?
   G: 응. 여러 번 가 봤어. 나는 그 해안선을 좋아해. 너는 어떠니?
   B: 난 이번이 제주도 첫 방문이야. 이번 주말이 빨리 왔으면 좋겠다!

2. B: 바다 위로 해가 뜨는 것을 본 적 있니?
   G: 아니. 너는?
   B: 나는 새해 첫날에 강릉에서 해돋이를 봤어. 멋지더라.
   G: 나는 몇 번 시도해 봤는데 일찍 일어나지 못했어.

**Listen & Speak 1 C**

1. **A:** _____ _____ _____ traveled to _____ _____ ?

   **B:** Yes, I _____ . It was a wonderful _____ .

2. **A:** _____ _____ _____ _____ a horse?

   **B:** Yes, I have. It was a _____ _____ .

1. A: 다른 나라로 여행 가 본 적 있니?
   B: 응, 있어. 그것은 멋진 경험이었어.

2. A: 말을 타 본 적 있니?
   B: 응, 있어. 그것은 멋진 경험이었어.

**Listen & Speak 2 A**

**G:** _____ _____ _____ _____ your new house?

**B:** It's great. I have a _____ _____ now.

G: 새 집은 어때?
B: 좋아. 나는 이제 더 큰 방을 가졌어.

### Listen & Speak 2 B

1. **G:** _____ was your _____?

   **B:** Great. I _____ _____ Dokdo _____ my family.

   **G:** _____ _____ you _____ it?

   **B:** It was _____. I want _____ _____ there again.

2. **B:** _____ _____ _____ _____ the new Chinese restaurant?

   **G:** Yes. I _____ _____ there last Saturday.

   **B:** _____ _____ _____ _____ it?

   **G:** The service was bad. I _____ _____ _____ there again.

<br>

1. G: 방학 잘 보냈니?
   B: 좋았어. 가족과 함께 독도에 다녀
   왔어.
   G: 어땠어?
   B: 굉장했어. 다시 한 번 가 보고 싶어.

2. B: 새로 생긴 중국 음식점에 가 봤니?
   G: 응. 지난주 토요일에 거기서 저녁
   을 먹었어.
   B: 어땠어?
   G: 서비스가 형편없었어. 그곳에 다
   시는 가지 않을 거야.

### Listen & Speak 2 C

1. **A:** _____ do you _____ this shirt?

   **B:** It's _____. I like it.

2. **A:** _____ _____ _____ _____ your ice cream?

   **B:** It's _____. I like it.

<br>

1. A: 이 셔츠가 마음에 드니?
   B: 그것은 색이 화려하구나. 마음에
   들어.
2. A: 너의 아이스크림은 어떠니?
   B: 그것은 달콤해. 마음에 들어.

### Real-Life Zone A

**B:** _____ _____ _____ _____ _____ _____, Sujin?

**G:** Yes, I _____ to Cambodia _____ _____.

**B:** Wow. _____ _____ you _____ it?

**G:** It was really _____, but I _____ the trip.

**B:** Tell me some _____ _____ you _____ _____ the trip.

**G:** Hmm... _____ me _____. I ate _____ spiders!

**B:** What? You're kidding. _____ did you _____ _____?

**G:** They were really big, _____ I was a little _____ _____ _____. But the taste was okay.

**B:** Really? I cannot _____ _____ _____.

<br>

B: 수진아 해외여행 가 본 적 있니?
G: 응, 지난여름에 캄보디아에 다녀왔어.
B: 와. 여행은 어땠니?
G: 날씨가 너무 더웠지만 여행은 즐거
웠어.
B: 여행하면서 재미있었던 경험 좀 이야
기해 줘.
G: 음… 생각 좀 해 볼게. 거미 튀김을
먹었어!
B: 뭐라고? 진짜로? 거미 튀김은 어땠
는데?
G: 너무 커서 처음엔 조금 무서웠는데.
맛은 괜찮았어.
B: 정말? 난 내가 거미를 먹는 걸 상상
할 수가 없어.

### Communication Task

**A:** _____ _____ _____ _____ tacos?

**B:** Yes, I have. They were _____.

/ No, I _____. I want to _____ some _____.

<br>

A: 타코를 먹어본 적 있니?
B: 응, 먹어 봤어. 맛있었어.
/ 아니, 안 먹어 봤어. 언젠간 한 번
먹어 보고 싶어.

※ 다음 우리말에 맞도록 대화를 영어로 쓰시오.

### Listen & Speak 1 A

**B:** _____

**G:** _____

해석

B: 스페인 음식을 먹어 본 적 있니?
G: 응, 먹어 봤어. 매우 맛있어.

### Listen & Speak 1 B

1. **G:** _____
   **B:** _____
   **G:** _____
   **B:** _____

2. **B:** _____
   **G:** _____
   **B:** _____
   **G:** _____

1. G: 인호야, 너 신나 보인다. 무슨 일이니?
   B: 이번 주말에 가족들과 함께 제주도에 가거든. 넌 가 본 적 있니?
   G: 응. 여러 번 가 봤어. 나는 그 해안선을 좋아해. 너는 어떠니?
   B: 난 이번이 제주도 첫 방문이야. 이번 주말이 빨리 왔으면 좋겠다!

2. B: 바다 위로 해가 뜨는 것을 본 적 있니?
   G: 아니. 너는?
   B: 나는 새해 첫날에 강릉에서 해돋이를 봤어. 멋지더라.
   G: 나는 몇 번 시도해 봤는데 일찍 일어나지 못했어.

### Listen & Speak 1 C

1. **A:** _____
   **B:** _____

2. **A:** _____
   **B:** _____

1. A: 다른 나라로 여행 가 본 적 있니?
   B: 응, 있어. 그것은 멋진 경험이었어.

2. A: 말을 타 본 적 있니?
   B: 응, 있어. 그것은 멋진 경험이었어.

### Listen & Speak 2 A

**G:** _____

**B:** _____

G: 새 집은 어때?
B: 좋아. 나는 이제 더 큰 방을 가졌어.

## Listen & Speak 2 B

1. G: _____
   B: _____
   G: _____
   B: _____

2. B: _____
   G: _____
   B: _____
   G: _____

## Listen & Speak 2 C

1. A: _____
   B: _____

2. A: _____
   B: _____

## Real-Life Zone A

B: _____
G: _____
B: _____
G: _____
B: _____
G: _____
B: _____
G: _____
B: _____

## Communication Task

A: _____
B: _____

---

1. G: 방학 잘 보냈니?
   B: 좋았어. 가족과 함께 독도에 다녀
      왔어.
   G: 어땠어?
   B: 굉장했어. 다시 한 번 가 보고 싶어.

2. B: 새로 생긴 중국 음식점에 가 봤니?
   G: 응. 지난주 토요일에 거기서 저녁
      을 먹었어.
   B: 어땠어?
   G: 서비스가 형편없었어. 그곳에 다
      시는 가지 않을 거야.

1. A: 이 셔츠가 마음에 드니?
   B: 그것은 색이 화려하구나. 마음에
      들어.
2. A: 너의 아이스크림은 어떠니?
   B: 그것은 달콤해. 마음에 들어.

B: 수진아 해외여행 가 본 적 있니?
G: 응, 지난여름에 캄보디아에 다녀왔어.
B: 와. 여행은 어땠니?
G: 날씨가 너무 더웠지만 여행은 즐거
   웠어.
B: 여행하면서 재미있었던 경험 좀 이야
   기해 줘.
G: 음… 생각 좀 해 볼게. 거미 튀김을
   먹었어!
B: 뭐라고? 진짜로? 거미 튀김은 어땠
   는데?
G: 너무 커서 처음엔 조금 무서웠는데.
   맛은 괜찮았어.
B: 정말? 난 내가 거미를 먹는 걸 상상
   할 수가 없어.

A: 타코를 먹어본 적 있니?
B: 응, 먹어 봤어. 맛있었어.
   / 아니, 안 먹어 봤어. 언젠간 한 번
   먹어 보고 싶어.

※ 다음 우리말과 일치하도록 빈칸에 알맞은 것을 골라 쓰시오.

**1** A _____ to _____

    A. Mongolia        B. Trip

**2** This year, I had a _____ summer _____ I visited Mongolia _____ the first _____.

    A. because        B. for        C. special        D. time

**3** _____ friend Altan _____ _____ Mongolia.

    A. from        B. is        C. my

**4** His grandmother _____ me _____ Ulaanbaatar, the _____ of Mongolia.

    A. to        B. capital        C. invited

**5** _____ a four-hour _____ from Seoul, Altan and I _____ Chinggis Khaan International Airport in Ulaanbaatar.

    A. at        B. arrived        C. flight        D. after

**6** It _____ thirty minutes _____ taxi _____ the airport _____ Altan's grandmother's house.

    A. by        B. took        C. to        D. from

**7** _____ house is a *ger*, a _____ _____ house.

    A. traditional        B. her        C. Mongolian

**8** It is a big _____, but it is _____ _____.

    A. tent        B. inside        C. cozy

**9** When we _____, something _____ _____.

    A. wonderful        B. entered        C. smelled

**10** It was _____ the *khorkhog* _____ she was _____ _____ us.

    A. from        B. cooking        C. that        D. for

**11** *Khorkhog* is a _____ _____.

    A. barbecue        B. Mongolian

**12** It is _____ _____ lamb and _____ _____ hot stones.

    A. of        B. with        C. made        D. cooked

**13** I was _____ when Altan said Mongolians _____ *khorkhog* _____ special _____.

    A. serve        B. moved        C. to        D. guests

**1** 몽골 여행

**2** 나는 올해 몽골을 처음으로 방문해서 특별한 여름을 보냈다.

**3** 내 친구 알탕은 몽골 출신이다.

**4** 그의 할머니께서는 몽골의 수도인 울란바토르에 나를 초대하셨다.

**5** 서울에서 네 시간 비행 후 알탕과 나는 울란바토르의 칭기즈 칸 국제공항에 도착했다.

**6** 공항에서 알탕의 할머니 댁까지 택시로 30분이 걸렸다.

**7** 할머니의 집은 몽골 전통 가옥인 게르이다.

**8** 큰 텐트이지만 내부는 아늑하다.

**9** 우리가 들어갔을 때, 뭔가 좋은 냄새가 났다.

**10** 그녀가 우리를 위해 요리하고 있던 호르호그에서 나는 냄새였다.

**11** 호르호그는 몽골식 바비큐이다.

**12** 그것은 양고기로 만들어졌으며 뜨거운 돌로 요리되었다.

**13** 나는 알탕이 몽골인들은 특별한 손님에게 호르호그를 대접한다고 말했을 때 감동을 받았다.

**14** It was _____ delicious _____ I asked _____ more.
    A. for             B. so             C. that

**15** _____ dinner, Altan and I _____ _____ to see the night sky.
    A. went             B. after             C. outside

**16** The sky _____ _____ _____ bright stars.
    A. full             B. of             C. was

**17** I _____ _____ I was in a _____ place.
    A. like             B. magical             C. felt

**18** _____ the next three days, Altan _____ me _____ and helped me _____ Mongolian culture.
    A. showed             B. during             C. around             D. experience

**19** Every _____ was fun and _____, but I had the _____ fun when I _____ a camel in the Gobi Desert.
    A. exciting             B. moment             C. rode             D. most

**20** _____ first, I was _____ because the camel was taller _____ I _____.
    A. expected             B. scared             C. than             D. at

**21** But _____ I sat on its _____, I soon got _____ _____ its movement.
    A. back             B. used             C. once             D. to

**22** _____ the camel's _____, the _____ of the desert was truly _____.
    A. view             B. amazing             C. from             D. back

**23** My _____ to Mongolia was a _____ experience _____ many _____.
    A. ways             B. visit             C. in             D. special

**24** It _____ me a great _____ to _____ to know my friend's country and _____.
    A. chance             B. get             C. culture             D. gave

**25** I want to _____ Mongolia _____ _____ !
    A. again             B. visit             C. someday

---

**14** 그것은 너무 맛있어서 나는 더 달라고 했다.

**15** 저녁 식사 후, 알탕과 나는 밤하늘을 보기 위해 밖으로 나갔다.

**16** 하늘은 밝은 별들로 가득했다.

**17** 나는 신비한 장소에 있는 것처럼 느꼈다.

**18** 그 후 3일 동안, 알탕은 나를 구경시켜 주었고 몽골 문화를 경험할 수 있게 도와주었다.

**19** 매 순간이 재미있고 흥미진진했지만, 고비 사막에서 낙타를 탈 때가 가장 재미있었다.

**20** 처음에는 내가 예상했던 것보다 낙타의 키가 커서 무서웠다.

**21** 그러나 낙타 등에 앉자 곧 움직임에 익숙해졌다.

**22** 낙타의 등에서 보는 사막의 경치는 정말로 놀라웠다.

**23** 내가 몽골을 방문한 것은 여러 면에서 특별한 경험이었다.

**24** 내 친구의 나라와 문화를 알 수 있는 좋은 기회가 되었다.

**25** 나는 언젠가 몽골을 다시 방문하고 싶다!

※ 다음 우리말과 일치하도록 빈칸에 알맞은 말을 쓰시오.

**1** A _____ _____ _____

**2** _____ _____, I had a _____ _____ because I visited Mongolia _____ _____ _____ _____.

**3** My friend Altan _____ _____ _____.

**4** His grandmother _____ me _____ Ulaanbaatar, _____ _____ of Mongolia.

**5** _____ _____ _____ _____ from Seoul, Altan and I _____ _____ Chinggis Khaan International Airport in Ulaanbaatar.

**6** _____ _____ thirty minutes _____ _____ _____ the airport _____ Altan's grandmother's house.

**7** Her house is a *ger*, a _____ _____ _____.

**8** It is a _____ _____, but it is _____ _____.

**9** _____ we _____, something _____ _____.

**10** It was _____ the *khorkhog* that she was _____ _____ us.

**11** *Khorkhog* is a _____ _____.

**12** It _____ _____ _____ lamb and _____ _____ hot stones.

**13** I _____ _____ when Altan said Mongolians _____ *khorkhog* _____ _____ _____.

**1** 몽골 여행

**2** 나는 올해 몽골을 처음으로 방문해서 특별한 여름을 보냈다.

**3** 내 친구 알탕은 몽골 출신이다.

**4** 그의 할머니께서는 몽골의 수도인 울란바토르에 나를 초대하셨다.

**5** 서울에서 네 시간 비행 후 알탕과 나는 울란바토르의 칭기즈 칸 국제공항에 도착했다.

**6** 공항에서 알탕의 할머니 댁까지 택시로 30분이 걸렸다.

**7** 할머니의 집은 몽골 전통 가옥인 게르이다.

**8** 큰 텐트이지만 내부는 아늑하다.

**9** 우리가 들어갔을 때, 뭔가 좋은 냄새가 났다.

**10** 그녀가 우리를 위해 요리하고 있던 호르호그에서 나는 냄새였다.

**11** 호르호그는 몽골식 바비큐이다.

**12** 그것은 양고기로 만들어졌으며 뜨거운 돌로 요리되었다.

**13** 나는 알탕이 몽골인들은 특별한 손님에게 호르호그를 대접한다고 말했을 때 감동을 받았다.

**14** It was _____ delicious _____ I _____ _____ more.

**15** After dinner, Altan and I _____ _____ _____ _____ the night sky.

**16** The sky _____ _____ _____ _____ stars.

**17** I _____ _____ I was in a _____ _____.

**18** _____ the next three days, Altan _____ _____ _____ and _____ _____ _____ Mongolian culture.

**19** _____ _____ was fun and exciting, but I _____ _____ _____ _____ when I _____ a camel in the Gobi Desert.

**20** _____ _____, I was _____ because the camel was _____ _____ I _____.

**21** But _____ I _____ _____ its back, I soon _____ _____ _____ its movement.

**22** From the camel's back, _____ _____ _____ _____ _____ was _____ _____.

**23** My visit to Mongolia was a special experience _____ _____ _____.

**24** It gave me a great chance _____ _____ _____ _____ my friend's _____ and _____.

**25** I want to _____ Mongolia _____ _____!

14 그것은 너무 맛있어서 나는 더 달라고 했다.

15 저녁 식사 후, 알탕과 나는 밤하늘을 보기 위해 밖으로 나갔다.

16 하늘은 밝은 별들로 가득했다.

17 나는 신비한 장소에 있는 것처럼 느꼈다.

18 그 후 3일 동안, 알탕은 나를 구경시켜 주었고 몽골 문화를 경험할 수 있게 도와주었다.

19 매 순간이 재미있고 흥미진진했지만, 고비 사막에서 낙타를 탈 때가 가장 재미있었다.

20 처음에는 내가 예상했던 것보다 낙타의 키가 커서 무서웠다.

21 그러나 낙타 등에 앉자 곧 움직임에 익숙해졌다.

22 낙타의 등에서 보는 사막의 경치는 정말로 놀라웠다.

23 내가 몽골을 방문한 것은 여러 면에서 특별한 경험이었다.

24 내 친구의 나라와 문화를 알 수 있는 좋은 기회가 되었다.

25 나는 언젠가 몽골을 다시 방문하고 싶다!

※ 다음 문장을 우리말로 쓰시오.

**1** A Trip to Mongolia

➡ _____

**2** This year, I had a special summer because I visited Mongolia for the first time.

➡ _____

**3** My friend Altan is from Mongolia.

➡ _____

**4** His grandmother invited me to Ulaanbaatar, the capital of Mongolia.

➡ _____

**5** After a four-hour flight from Seoul, Altan and I arrived at Chinggis Khaan International Airport in Ulaanbaatar.

➡ _____

**6** It took thirty minutes by taxi from the airport to Altan's grandmother's house.

➡ _____

**7** Her house is a *ger*, a traditional Mongolian house.

➡ _____

**8** It is a big tent, but it is cozy inside.

➡ _____

**9** When we entered, something smelled wonderful.

➡ _____

**10** It was from the *khorkhog* that she was cooking for us.

➡ _____

**11** *Khorkhog* is a Mongolian barbecue.

➡ _____

**12** It is made of lamb and cooked with hot stones.

➡ _____

**13** I was moved when Altan said Mongolians serve *khorkhog* to special guests.

➡ _____

**14** It was so delicious that I asked for more.

➡ _____

**15** After dinner, Altan and I went outside to see the night sky.

➡ _____

**16** The sky was full of bright stars.

➡ _____

**17** I felt like I was in a magical place.

➡ _____

**18** During the next three days, Altan showed me around and helped me experience Mongolian culture.

➡ _____

**19** Every moment was fun and exciting, but I had the most fun when I rode a camel in the Gobi Desert.

➡ _____

**20** At first, I was scared because the camel was taller than I expected.

➡ _____

**21** But once I sat on its back, I soon got used to its movement.

➡ _____

**22** From the camel's back, the view of the desert was truly amazing.

➡ _____

**23** My visit to Mongolia was a special experience in many ways.

➡ _____

**24** It gave me a great chance to get to know my friend's country and culture.

➡ _____

**25** I want to visit Mongolia again someday!

➡ _____

※ 다음 괄호 안의 단어들을 우리말에 맞도록 바르게 배열하시오.

**1** ▶ (Trip / A / Mongolia / to)
➡ _____

**2** ▶ (year, / this / had / I / a / summer / special / because / visited / I / for / Mongolia / the / for / first)
➡ _____
_____

**3** ▶ (friend / my / is / Altan / Mongolia. / from)
➡ _____

**4** ▶ (grandmother / his / me / invited / Ulaanbaatar, / to / capital / the / Mongolia. / of)
➡ _____

**5** ▶ (a / after / flight / four-hour / Seoul, / from / I / and / Altan / at / arrived / Khann / Chinggis / Airport / International / Ulaanbaatar. / in)
➡ _____
_____

**6** ▶ (took / it / minutes / thirty / taxi / by / the / from / airport / to / Altan's / house. / grandmother's)
➡ _____
_____

**7** ▶ (house / her / a / is / *ger*, / traditional / a / house. / Mongolian)
➡ _____

**8** ▶ (is / it / a / tent, / big / it / but / cozy / is / inside.)
➡ _____

**9** ▶ (we / when / entered, / smelled / something / wonderful.)
➡ _____

**10** ▶ (was / it / the / from / that / *khorkhog* / she / cookinig / was / us. / for)
➡ _____

**11** ▶ (is / *khorkhog* / a / barbecue. / Mongolian)
➡ _____

**12** ▶ (is / it / of / made / lamb / and / with / cooked / stones. / hot)
➡ _____

**13** ▶ (was / I / when / moved / said / Altan / serve / Mongolians / to / *khorkhog* / guests. / special)
➡ _____
_____

**1** 몽골 여행

**2** 나는 올해 몽골을 처음으로 방문해서 특별한 여름을 보냈다.

**3** 내 친구 알탄은 몽골 출신이다.

**4** 그의 할머니께서는 몽골의 수도인 울란바토르에 나를 초대하셨다.

**5** 서울에서 네 시간 비행 후 알탄과 나는 울란바토르의 칭기즈칸 국제공항에 도착했다.

**6** 공항에서 알탄의 할머니 댁까지 택시로 30분이 걸렸다.

**7** 할머니의 집은 몽골 전통 가옥인 게르이다.

**8** 큰 텐트이지만 내부는 아늑하다.

**9** 우리가 들어갔을 때, 뭔가 좋은 냄새가 났다.

**10** 그녀가 우리를 위해 요리하고 있던 호르호그에서 나는 냄새였다.

**11** 호르호그는 몽골식 바비큐이다.

**12** 그것은 양고기로 만들어졌으며 뜨거운 돌로 요리되었다.

**13** 나는 알탄이 몽골인들은 특별한 손님에게 호르호그를 대접한다고 말했을 때 감동을 받았다.

**14** (was / it / delicious / so / I / that / for / asked / more.)

➡ _____

**15** (dinner, / after / I / and / Altan / outside / went / see / to / night / the / sky.)

➡ _____

**16** (sky / the / full / was / of / stars. / bright)

➡ _____

**17** (felt / I / like / was / I / a / in / place. / magical)

➡ _____

**18** (the / during / three / next / days, / showed / Altan / around / me / and / me / helped / Mongolian / experience / culture.)

➡ _____

**19** (moment / every / fun / was / and / exciting, / I / but / the / had / most / fun / I / when / rode / camel / a / the / in / Desert. / Gobi)

➡ _____

**20** (first, / at / was / I / because / scared / camel / the / taller / was / I / than / expected.)

➡ _____

**21** (once / but / sat / I / its / on / back, / soon / I / used / got / its / to / movement.)

➡ _____

**22** (the / from / back, / camel's / view / the / of / desert / the / truly / was / amazing.)

➡ _____

**23** (visit / my / Mongolia / to / a / special / was / experience / many / in / ways.)

➡ _____

**24** (gave / it / me / great / a / to / chance / get / know / to / friend's / my / and / culture. / country)

➡ _____

**25** (want / I / visit / to / again / Mongolia / someday!)

➡ _____

**14** 그것은 너무 맛있어서 나는 더 달라고 했다.

**15** 저녁 식사 후, 알탕과 나는 밤하늘을 보기 위해 밖으로 나갔다.

**16** 하늘은 밝은 별들로 가득했다.

**17** 나는 신비한 장소에 있는 것처럼 느꼈다.

**18** 그 후 3일 동안, 알탕은 나를 구경시켜 주었고 몽골 문화를 경험할 수 있게 도와주었다.

**19** 매 순간이 재미있고 흥미진진했지만, 고비 사막에서 낙타를 탈 때가 가장 재미있었다.

**20** 처음에는 내가 예상했던 것보다 낙타의 키가 커서 무서웠다.

**21** 그러나 낙타 등에 앉자 곧 움직임에 익숙해졌다.

**22** 낙타의 등에서 보는 사막의 경치는 정말로 놀라웠다.

**23** 내가 몽골을 방문한 것은 여러 면에서 특별한 경험이었다.

**24** 내 친구의 나라와 문화를 알 수 있는 좋은 기회가 되었다.

**25** 나는 언젠가 몽골을 다시 방문하고 싶다!

※ 다음 우리말을 영어로 쓰시오.

**1** 몽골 여행

➡ _____

**2** 나는 올해 몽골을 처음으로 방문해서 특별한 여름을 보냈다.

➡ _____

**3** 내 친구 알탕은 몽골 출신이다.

➡ _____

**4** 그의 할머니께서는 몽골의 수도인 울란바토르에 나를 초대하셨다.

➡ _____

**5** 서울에서 네 시간 비행 후 알탕과 나는 울란바토르의 칭기즈 칸 국제공항에 도착했다.

➡ _____

**6** 공항에서 알탕의 할머니 댁까지 택시로 30분이 걸렸다.

➡ _____

**7** 할머니의 집은 몽골 전통 가옥인 게르이다.

➡ _____

**8** 큰 텐트이지만 내부는 아늑하다.

➡ _____

**9** 우리가 들어갔을 때, 뭔가 좋은 냄새가 났다.

➡ _____

**10** 그녀가 우리를 위해 요리하고 있던 호르호그에서 나는 냄새였다.

➡ _____

**11** 호르호그는 몽골식 바비큐이다.

➡ _____

**12** 그것은 양고기로 만들어졌으며 뜨거운 돌로 요리되었다.

➡ _____

**13** 나는 알탕이 몽골인들은 특별한 손님에게 호르호그를 대접한다고 말했을 때 감동을 받았다.

➡ _____

**14** 그것은 너무 맛있어서 나는 더 달라고 했다.

➡ _____

**15** 저녁 식사 후, 알탕과 나는 밤하늘을 보기 위해 밖으로 나갔다.

➡ _____

**16** 하늘은 밝은 별들로 가득했다.

➡ _____

**17** 나는 신비한 장소에 있는 것처럼 느꼈다.

➡ _____

**18** 그 후 3일 동안, 알탕은 나를 구경시켜 주었고 몽골 문화를 경험할 수 있게 도와주었다.

➡ _____

**19** 매 순간이 재미있고 흥미진진했지만, 고비 사막에서 낙타를 탈 때가 가장 재미있었다.

➡ _____

**20** 처음에는 내가 예상했던 것보다 낙타의 키가 커서 무서웠다.

➡ _____

**21** 그러나 낙타 등에 앉자 곧 움직임에 익숙해졌다.

➡ _____

**22** 낙타의 등에서 보는 사막의 경치는 정말로 놀라웠다.

➡ _____

**23** 내가 몽골을 방문한 것은 여러 면에서 특별한 경험이었다.

➡ _____

**24** 내 친구의 나라와 문화를 알 수 있는 좋은 기회가 되었다.

➡ _____

**25** 나는 언젠가 몽골을 다시 방문하고 싶다!

➡ _____

※ 다음 우리말과 일치하도록 빈칸에 알맞은 말을 쓰시오.

### Writing Workshop - Step 2

1. A _____ _____ Suncheon

2. My family _____ _____ _____ to Suncheon _____ _____.

3. We _____ the National Garden.

4. It was _____ large _____ _____ _____ _____ _____
   the whole garden.

5. _____ _____ _____ _____ _____, we were really hungry.

6. _____ _____, we had Gukbap _____ _____ _____
   _____.

7. Suncheon _____ _____ _____ Gukbap and we enjoyed it.

8. This trip was _____ good _____ I _____ _____ _____
   it for a long time.

1. 순천으로의 여행
2. 나의 가족은 작년 여름에 순천으로 여행을 갔다.
3. 우리는 순천 국가 정원을 방문했다.
4. 그곳은 너무 넓어서 우리는 정원 전체를 다 볼 수 없었다.
5. 세 시간 동안 걸은 후, 우리는 정말 배가 고팠다.
6. 저녁 식사로 우리는 부모님들이 좋아하시는 국밥을 먹었다.
7. 순천은 국밥으로 유명하고, 우리는 그것을 즐겼다.
8. 이번 여행은 너무 좋아서 나는 오랫동안 그것을 결코 잊지 않을 것이다.

### Wrap Up 1-2

1. G: _____ _____ your _____, Tony?

2. B: It was great. I _____ _____ the International Food Festival
   _____ _____ _____.

3. G: _____ _____ did you _____?

4. B: I had a _____ _____ _____, *tangyuan*.

5. G: _____ _____ you like it?

6. B: I enjoyed it. It's _____ _____ sweet rice balls. Chinese
   people _____ _____ it to guests _____ _____ _____.

1. G: 토니야, 주말 잘 보냈니?
2. B: 좋았어. 부모님과 함께 국제 음식 축제에 다녀왔어.
3. G: 무슨 음식 먹어 봤니?
4. B: 중국 전통 후식인 탕위안을 먹었어.
5. G: 어땠어?
6. B: 맛있었어. 그건 달콤하고 동그란 떡으로 만들었어. 중국 사람들은 보통 결혼식에서 손님들에게 이것을 대접해.

### Wrap Up 7

1. _____ _____ the restaurant _____ just opened _____
   _____ _____?

2. The restaurant was _____ _____ _____ I had to _____
   _____ an hour _____ _____ _____.

3. The cheese cake _____ _____ _____ _____
   _____ all of it.

4. The restaurant was _____ _____ _____ _____
   talk with my friends.

1. 모퉁이에 막 오픈한 그 식당은 어땠나요?
2. 그 식당은 매우 붐벼서 나는 안에 들어가기 위해 한 시간 동안 기다려야 했어요.
3. 그 치즈 케이크는 매우 맛있어서 나는 전부 먹어 치웠어요.
4. 그 식당은 매우 시끄러워서 나는 친구와 이야기할 수 없었어요.

# 구석구석 지문 Test

※ 다음 우리말을 영어로 쓰시오.

## Writing Workshop - Step 2

1. 순천으로의 여행
➡ _____

2. 나의 가족은 작년 여름에 순천으로 여행을 갔다.
➡ _____

3. 우리는 순천 국가 정원을 방문했다.
➡ _____

4. 그곳은 너무 넓어서 우리는 정원 전체를 다 볼 수 없었다.
➡ _____

5. 세 시간 동안 걸은 후, 우리는 정말 배가 고팠다.
➡ _____

6. 저녁 식사로 우리는 부모님들이 좋아하시는 국밥을 먹었다.
➡ _____

7. 순천은 국밥으로 유명하고, 우리는 그것을 즐겼다.
➡ _____

8. 이번 여행은 너무 좋아서 나는 오랫동안 그것을 결코 잊지 않을 것이다.
➡ _____

## Wrap Up 1-2

1. G: 토니야, 주말 잘 보냈니?
➡ _____

2. B: 좋았어. 부모님과 함께 국제 음식 축제에 다녀왔어.
➡ _____

3. G: 무슨 음식 먹어 봤니?
➡ _____

4. B: 중국 전통 후식인 탕위안을 먹었어.
➡ _____

5. G: 어땠어?
➡ _____

6. B: 맛있었어. 그건 달콤하고 동그란 떡으로 만들었어. 중국 사람들은 보통 결혼식에서 손님들에게 이것을 대접해.
➡ _____

## Wrap Up 7

1. 모퉁이에 막 오픈한 그 식당은 어땠나요?
➡ _____

2. 그 식당은 매우 붐벼서 나는 안에 들어가기 위해 한 시간 동안 기다려야 했어요.
➡ _____

3. 그 치즈 케이크는 매우 맛있어서 나는 전부 먹어 치웠어요.
➡ _____

4. 그 식당은 매우 시끄러워서 나는 친구와 이야기할 수 없었어요.
➡ _____

※ 다음 영어를 우리말로 쓰시오.

| | | |
|---|---|---|
| 01 | select | |
| 02 | intelligent | |
| 03 | teleport | |
| 04 | burn | |
| 05 | translate | |
| 06 | animated | |
| 07 | easily | |
| 08 | sense | |
| 09 | freeze | |
| 10 | impossible | |
| 11 | amusement | |
| 12 | predict | |
| 13 | without | |
| 14 | machine | |
| 15 | possible | |
| 16 | cross | |
| 17 | danger | |
| 18 | mean | |
| 19 | off | |
| 20 | perfect | |
| 21 | through | |

| | | |
|---|---|---|
| 22 | strange | |
| 23 | replace | |
| 24 | beat | |
| 25 | check | |
| 26 | situation | |
| 27 | closet | |
| 28 | space | |
| 29 | chance | |
| 30 | dictionary | |
| 31 | translator | |
| 32 | unbelievable | |
| 33 | lucky | |
| 34 | cloudy | |
| 35 | not just | |
| 36 | don't have to | |
| 37 | in danger | |
| 38 | no longer | |
| 39 | based on | |
| 40 | free from | |
| 41 | by the way | |
| 42 | be able to 동사원형 | |
| 43 | slow down | |

※ 다음 우리말을 영어로 쓰시오.

01 동영상의, 생기 있는 _____

02 기회 _____

03 구름의, 흐린 _____

04 가능한 _____

05 행운의 _____

06 번역가 _____

07 기계 _____

08 건너다 _____

09 위험 _____

10 즐거움, 오락 _____

11 쉽게 _____

12 선택하다 _____

13 (휴대 전화로) 문자를 보내다 _____

14 감지하다 _____

15 의미하다 _____

16 얼리다 _____

17 ~ 없이 _____

18 예측하다 _____

19 불가능한 _____

20 순간 이동하다 _____

21 불타다 _____

22 번역하다 _____

23 사전 _____

24 할인되어 _____

25 옷장 _____

26 완벽한 _____

27 대체하다 _____

28 똑똑한 _____

29 ~을 통해, ~ 사이로 _____

30 상황 _____

31 이상한 _____

32 믿기 어려운, 놀랄만한 _____

33 확인하다, 점검하다 _____

34 공간 _____

35 그런데, 그건 그렇고 _____

36 위험에 처한, 위험에 빠진 _____

37 더 이상 ~하지 않다 _____

38 ~할 수 있다 _____

39 ~에 근거하여 _____

40 속도를 늦추다 _____

41 조심하다 _____

42 ~의 염려가 없는 _____

43 (사전 · 참고 자료 · 컴퓨터 등에서 정보를) 찾아보다 _____

※ 다음 영영풀이에 알맞은 단어를 <보기>에서 골라 쓴 후, 우리말 뜻을 쓰시오.

1 _____ : to take the place of: _____

2 _____ : to defeat someone in a game: _____

3 _____ : the best possible: _____

4 _____ : to be destroyed by fire: _____

5 _____ : able to happen or be done: _____

6 _____ : to perceive or realize something: _____

7 _____ : to change words in another language: _____

8 _____ : to go from one side to the other side of an area: _____

9 _____ : having desirable things unexpectedly happen to you: _____

10 _____ : to say that an event will happen in the future: _____

11 _____ : to choose something from a number of things: _____

12 _____ : a large piece of furniture with a door used for storing clothes:
_____

13 _____ : when the sky is covered with a lot of clouds: _____

14 _____ : the enjoyment that you get from being entertained: _____

15 _____ : to create the sounds of powerful rhythm with the voice and the hands:
_____

16 _____ : a book that contains a list of words and phrases alphabetically with their
meanings or their translations in another language: _____

| 보기 | | | |
|---|---|---|---|
| dictionary | select | amusement | closet |
| perfect | beatbox | lucky | translate |
| beat | replace | sense | burn |
| cloudy | cross | predict | possible |

※ 다음 우리말과 일치하도록 빈칸에 알맞은 말을 쓰시오.

### Listen & Speak 1 A

**B:** _____ _____ _____ _____ a new VR game?

**G:** That _____ interesting.

**B:** 우리 새로운 VR 게임을 해 보는 게 어때?
**G:** 그거 재미있겠다.

### Listen & Speak 1 B

1. **B:** Do you _____ _____ ideas _____ our group _____?

   **G:** No. _____ _____ you?

   **B:** I'm _____ we should _____ _____ _____ jobs. _____ do you _____?

   **G:** That _____ _____ for our project. _____ _____ _____ some information _____ _____ _____.

2. **G:** The Robot Expo _____ next week. _____ _____ you go _____ me?

   **B:** Yes, I'd love _____. That _____ _____.

   **G:** We'll have a _____ _____ _____ _____ engineers.

   **B:** That'll be _____.

1. **B:** 우리 조별 프로젝트에 대한 좋은 생각이 있니?
   **G:** 아니. 너는 어때?
   **B:** 나는 미래 직업에 대해 이야기하면 좋겠다고 생각하고 있어. 너는 어떻게 생각해?
   **G:** 우리 프로젝트에 완벽한 것 같아. 인터넷에서 정보를 찾아보자.

2. **G:** 로봇 박람회가 다음 주에 시작돼. 나와 함께 가는 게 어때?
   **B:** 응, 가고 싶어. 그거 재미있겠는데.
   **G:** 우리는 로봇 공학자를 만날 기회가 있을 거야.
   **B:** 그거 아주 좋겠다.

### Listen & Speak 1 C

1. **A:** I'm _____ _____ _____ a _____.

   **B:** That sounds _____ _____.

2. **A:** I'm _____ to _____ a model car.

   **B:** That _____ _____ _____.

1. **A:** 난 드론을 날릴 거야.
   **B:** 그거 재미있겠다.

2. **A:** 난 모형 자동차를 조립할 거야.
   **B:** 그거 재미있겠다.

### Listen & Speak 2 A

**G:** Is _____ _____ for you _____ _____ _____ your smartphone?

**B:** No, it's _____ _____.

**G:** 네가 스마트폰 없이 사는 것이 가능할까?
**B:** 아니, 그건 불가능해.

### Listen & Speak 2 B

1. **G:** This computer _____ nice. _____ _____ is _____?

   **M:** It's 500 dollars. It's _____ _____ one.

   **G:** _____ _____ _____ _____ _____ _____ this coupon?

   **M:** _____ me _____. Yes, you can. So, you'll _____ 30 dollars _____.

   **G:** _____. I'll _____ it.

2. **B:** We _____ lots of _____ _____ our trip.

   **G:** We sure _____. We have _____ _____ 500 pictures.

   **B:** Is _____ _____ _____ _____ an _____ photo album _____ _____ them?

   **G:** Yes, it's _____. I _____ _____ _____ for that.

### Listen & Speak 2 C

1. **A:** _____ _____ _____ for you _____ _____ _____ your eyes _____?

   **B:** _____. I _____ _____ that.

2. **A:** Is it _____ _____ to _____ _____ Gangwondo _____ bicycle?

   **B:** _____. I _____ _____ _____ _____.

### Real-Life Zone A

**G:** _____ _____ those words on the board.

**B:** _____ d o _____ _____ _____? _____ _____ _____ _____ in the _____.

**G:** What _____ _____ the AI _____?

**B:** _____ do I _____ it?

**G:** You _____ your smartphone camera at the words and _____ AI _____ _____. You will _____ _____ _____.

**B:** Is it _____ _____ _____ _____ _____ _____ those words?

**Speaker:** Sure. I can _____ any language and _____ it.

**B:** Wow, that _____ _____. So, AI, _____ do those words _____?

**Speaker:** They _____ "Dreams _____ _____!"

**B:** That's _____.

1. G: 이 컴퓨터가 좋아 보이네요. 얼마예요?
   M: 500달러예요. 가장 최신 컴퓨터예요.
   G: 이 쿠폰을 사용하는 것이 가능한가요?
   M: 확인해 볼게요. 네, 사용할 수 있어요. 그러면, 30달러 할인돼요.
   G: 좋아요. 이걸로 살게요.

2. B: 우리는 여행 동안 사진을 많이 찍었어.
   G: 진짜 그랬어. 500장 넘게 있어.
   B: 그 사진들로 동영상 앨범을 만드는 것이 가능하니?
   G: 응, 가능해. 나는 그것을 위한 앱이 있어.

1. A: 눈 감고 문자 메시지 보내는 것이 가능하니?
   B: 물론이지. 할 수 있어.

2. A: 자전거로 강원도를 여행하는 것이 가능하니?
   B: 물론이지. 할 수 있어.

G: 저기 칠판에 있는 글자 좀 봐.
B: 무슨 뜻이지? 사전에서 찾아보자.
G: AI 번역기를 사용하는 게 어때?
B: 어떻게 사용하는 거니?
G: 스마트폰 카메라를 글자 위에 댄 후에 AI에게 번역해 달라고 해 봐. 아마 답을 해 줄 거야.
B: AI가 저런 글자를 읽는 것이 가능해?
Speaker: 물론이에요. 저는 어떤 언어도 읽을 수 있고 번역할 수 있어요.
B: 오, 정말 놀라워. 그럼 AI, 이 글자는 뜻이 뭐니?
Speaker: "꿈은 이루어진다."라는 뜻이에요.
B: 정말 대단하구나.

## 대화문 Test

※ 다음 우리말에 맞도록 대화를 영어로 쓰시오.

해석

### Listen & Speak 1 A

B: ______________________________

G: ______________________________

B: 우리 새로운 VR 게임을 해 보는 게 어때?
G: 그거 재미있겠다.

### Listen & Speak 1 B

1. B: ______________________________
   G: ______________________________
   B: ______________________________
   G: ______________________________
   ______________________________
2. G: ______________________________
   B: ______________________________
   G: ______________________________
   B: ______________________________

1. B: 우리 조별 프로젝트에 대한 좋은 생각이 있니?
   G: 아니. 너는 어때?
   B: 나는 미래 직업에 대해 이야기하면 좋겠다고 생각하고 있어. 너는 어떻게 생각해?
   G: 우리 프로젝트에 완벽한 것 같아. 인터넷에서 정보를 찾아보자.

2. G: 로봇 박람회가 다음 주에 시작돼. 나와 함께 가는 게 어때?
   B: 응, 가고 싶어. 그거 재미있겠는데.
   G: 우리는 로봇 공학자를 만날 기회가 있을 거야.
   B: 그거 아주 좋겠다.

### Listen & Speak 1 C

1. A: ______________________________
   B: ______________________________
2. A: ______________________________
   B: ______________________________

1. A: 난 드론을 날릴 거야.
   B: 그거 재미있겠다.

2. A: 난 모형 자동차를 조립할 거야.
   B: 그거 재미있겠다.

### Listen & Speak 2 A

G: ______________________________

B: ______________________________

G: 네가 스마트폰 없이 사는 것이 가능할까?
B: 아니, 그건 불가능해.

## Listen & Speak 2 B

1. **G:** _____

   **M:** _____

   **G:** _____

   **M:** _____

   **G:** _____

2. **B:** _____

   **G:** _____

   **B:** _____

   **G:** _____

1. **G:** 이 컴퓨터가 좋아 보이네요. 얼마예요?
   **M:** 500달러예요. 가장 최신 컴퓨터예요.
   **G:** 이 쿠폰을 사용하는 것이 가능한가요?
   **M:** 확인해 볼게요. 네, 사용할 수 있어요. 그러면, 30달러 할인돼요.
   **G:** 좋아요. 이걸로 살게요.

2. **B:** 우리는 여행 동안 사진을 많이 찍었어.
   **G:** 진짜 그랬어. 500장 넘게 있어.
   **B:** 그 사진들로 동영상 앨범을 만드는 것이 가능하니?
   **G:** 응, 가능해. 나는 그것을 위한 앱이 있어.

## Listen & Speak 2 C

1. **A:** _____

   **B:** _____

2. **A:** _____

   **B:** _____

1. **A:** 눈 감고 문자 메시지 보내는 것이 가능하니?
   **B:** 물론이지. 할 수 있어.

2. **A:** 자전거로 강원도를 여행하는 것이 가능하니?
   **B:** 물론이지. 할 수 있어.

## Real-Life Zone A

**G:** _____

**B:** _____

**G:** _____

**B:** _____

**G:** _____

**B:** _____

**Speaker:** _____

**B:** _____

**Speaker:** _____

**B:** _____

**G:** 저기 칠판에 있는 글자 좀 봐.
**B:** 무슨 뜻이지? 사전에서 찾아보자.
**G:** AI 번역기를 사용하는 게 어때?
**B:** 어떻게 사용하는 거니?
**G:** 스마트폰 카메라를 글자 위에 댄 후에 AI에게 번역해 달라고 해 봐. 아마 답을 해 줄 거야.
**B:** AI가 저런 글자를 읽는 것이 가능해?
**Speaker:** 물론이에요. 저는 어떤 언어도 읽을 수 있고 번역할 수 있어요.
**B:** 오, 정말 놀라워. 그럼 AI, 이 글자는 뜻이 뭐니?
**Speaker:** "꿈은 이루어진다."라는 뜻이에요.
**B:** 정말 대단하구나.

※ 다음 우리말과 일치하도록 빈칸에 알맞은 것을 골라 쓰시오.

**1** A _____ _____ the _____ Expo
A. AI        B. at        C. Day

**2** Jina and Suhan are _____ the _____ AI _____.
A. World     B. Expo      C. at

**3** They are _____ the _____ _____.
A. home      B. entering  C. AI

**4** Suhan: _____ _____ this! It's a house of the _____.
A. at        B. future    C. look

**5** Jina: Let's _____ _____ the bedroom first. Look, _____ a smart _____.
A. into      B. there's   C. go        D. closet

**6** Suhan: I'm standing in _____ of this screen on the _____ door and my clothes _____ _____.
A. keep      B. front     C. changing  D. closet

**7** Jina: The screen _____ clothes that _____ the _____.
A. suit      B. suggests  C. weather

**8** Suhan: That's amazing! We _____ _____ have to _____ about _____ for the weather.
A. longer    B. dressing  C. no        D. worry

**9** Jina: Right. Let's _____ _____ _____ the living room.
A. on        B. move      C. to

**10** Suhan: Oh, I like _____ _____ _____.
A. speaker   B. music     C. this

**11** AI Speaker: I'm _____ _____ a music _____.
A. just      B. speaker   C. not

**12** I can do _____ _____ you can _____.
A. than      B. imagine   C. more

**13** Jina: It's _____ to _____ that you can _____ us. What can you do?
A. believe   B. hard      C. understand

**14** AI Speaker: _____ _____ _____ a movie?
A. watching  B. how       C. about

**15** I'll _____ _____ for you.
A. one       B. play

**16** Suhan: Look, those _____ windows are _____ _____.
A. getting   B. smart     C. darker

**17** I _____ _____ I'm in a movie _____.
A. like      B. theater   C. feel

1 인공 지능 박람회에서의 하루

2 진아와 수한이가 세계 인공 지능 박람회에 있다.

3 그들은 인공 지능 집으로 들어가고 있다.

4 수한: 이것 봐! 미래의 집이야.

5 진아: 침실 먼저 들어가 보자. 이거 봐, 스마트 옷장이 있어.

6 수한: 옷장 문에 있는 스크린 앞에 서 있으니까 내 옷이 계속해서 바뀌어.

7 진아: 스크린이 날씨에 적합한 옷을 제안하는 거야.

8 수한: 놀라워! 우린 더 이상 날씨 때문에 무슨 옷을 입을지 걱정할 필요가 없겠다.

9 진아: 맞아. 이제 거실로 가 보자.

10 수한: 오, 이 음악 스피커 마음에 들어.

11 인공 지능 스피커: 저는 그냥 음악 스피커가 아니에요.

12 저는 당신이 상상하는 것 이상의 것을 할 수 있어요.

13 진아: 네가 우리를 이해한다니 믿기 어려운 걸! 넌 뭘 할 수 있어?

14 인공 지능 스피커: 영화 보는 건 어때요?

15 하나 틀어 줄게요.

16 수한: 이것 봐, 스마트 창문이 점점 어두워지고 있어.

17 마치 내가 영화관 안에 있는 것 같아.

**18** Jina: _____ _____ can you _____?
A. do    B. else    C. what

**19** AI Speaker: I can _____, _____. _____ _____, "cats and boots and cats and boots."
A. too    B. comes    C. beatbox    D. here

**20** Suhan: You're _____. _____!
A. job    B. good    C. funny

**21** Jina: _____! _____ a smart car station _____!
A. outside    B. hurry    C. there's

**22** _____ go and _____ _____ that red car.
A. ride    B. let's    C. in

**23** Suhan: This car is _____ _____. Let's _____ _____.
A. cool    B. in    C. so    D. get

**24** AI Car: Welcome. Are you _____ _____ _____?
A. to    B. ready    C. go

**25** Jina: Yes, _____ _____ we _____ now?
A. should    B. what    C. do

**26** It's my first _____ to _____ _____ a smart car.
A. ride    B. time    C. in

**27** AI Car: You don't _____ _____ do _____.
A. need    B. anything    C. to

**28** I will _____ and _____ you _____ the next station.
A. take    B. drive    C. to

**29** Suhan: Watch _____! I _____ a cat _____ the street.
A. out    B. crossing    C. see

**30** AI Car: Don't _____. I _____ just _____ it.
A. sensed    B. have    C. worry

**31** When I _____ _____ situations, I _____ _____ or stop.
A. down    B. dangerous    C. sense    D. slow

**32** Jina: _____ _____ you do _____?
A. that    B. how    C. can

**33** AI Car: I'm a very _____ _____ car.
A. robotic    B. intelligent

**34** I know _____ _____ _____.
A. about    B. all    C. driving

**35** I can _____ danger _____ _____ knowledge and _____.
A. on    B. predict    C. experience    D. based

**36** Suhan: _____ smart! You think and _____ _____ a person.
A. like    B. how    C. act

**37** You _____ really _____ a _____.
A. like    B. human    C. are

진아: 또 뭘 할 수 있어?

인공 지능 스피커: 비트박스도 할 수 있어요. "북치기 박치기 북치기 박치기."

수한: 넌 정말 재미있구나. 잘했어!

진아: 서둘러! 밖에 스마트 자동차 정류장이 있어.

가서 저 빨간 차를 타 보자.

수한: 이 차 정말 멋지다. 차에 타자.

인공 지능 자동차: 어서 오세요. 갈 준비 됐나요?

진아: 응, 우린 이제 뭘 해야 하지?

스마트 자동차에 타는 건 처음이야.

인공 지능 자동차: 아무 것도 하지 않아도 돼요.

제가 운전해서 다음 정류장까지 데려다줄 거니까요.

수한: 조심해! 고양이가 길을 건너고 있는 게 보여.

인공 지능 자동차: 걱정 말아요. 이미 감지했어요.

저는 어떤 위험 상황을 감지하면 속도를 늦추거나 멈춰요.

진아: 어떻게 그렇게 할 수 있어?

인공 지능 자동차: 전 아주 지능적인 로봇 차예요.

저는 운전에 대한 모든 걸 알고 있어요.

저는 제 지식과 경험을 바탕으로 위험을 예측할 수 있어요.

수한: 정말 똑똑하구나! 사람처럼 생각하고 행동하는구나.

정말 인간 같아.

※ 다음 우리말과 일치하도록 빈칸에 알맞은 말을 쓰시오.

**1** A Day _____ the _____ _____

**2** Jina and Suhan are _____ _____ _____ _____ _____.

**3** They _____ _____ the _____ _____.

**4** Suhan: Look at this! It's a house _____ _____ _____.

**5** Jina: Let's _____ _____ the bedroom first. Look, there's a _____ _____.

**6** Suhan: I'm standing in _____ of this screen _____ _____ _____ _____ and my clothes _____ _____.

**7** Jina: The screen _____ clothes _____ _____ _____.

**8** Suhan: That's amazing! We _____ _____ have to worry about _____ _____ _____ _____.

**9** Jina: Right. _____ _____ _____ _____ the living room.

**10** Suhan: Oh, I like _____ _____ _____.

**11** AI Speaker: _____ _____ _____ a music speaker.

**12** I can do _____ _____ you _____ _____.

**13** Jina: _____ _____ _____ _____ that you _____ _____ us. What can you do?

**14** AI Speaker: _____ _____ _____ a movie?

**15** I'll _____ _____ _____ you.

**16** Suhan: Look, those smart windows are _____ _____.

**17** I _____ _____ I'm in a _____ _____.

**1** 인공 지능 박람회에서의 하루

**2** 진아와 수한이가 세계 인공 지능 박람회에 있다.

**3** 그들은 인공 지능 집으로 들어가고 있다.

**4** 수한: 이것 봐! 미래의 집이야.

**5** 진아: 침실 먼저 들어가 보자. 이거 봐, 스마트 옷장이 있어.

**6** 수한: 옷장 문에 있는 스크린 앞에 서 있으니까 내 옷이 계속해서 바뀌어.

**7** 진아: 스크린이 날씨에 적합한 옷을 제안하는 거야.

**8** 수한: 놀라워! 우린 더 이상 날씨 때문에 무슨 옷을 입을지 걱정할 필요가 없겠다.

**9** 진아: 맞아. 이제 거실로 가 보자.

**10** 수한: 오, 이 음악 스피커 마음에 들어.

**11** 인공 지능 스피커: 저는 그냥 음악 스피커가 아니에요.

**12** 저는 당신이 상상하는 것 이상의 것을 할 수 있어요.

**13** 진아: 네가 우리를 이해한다니 믿기 어려운 걸! 넌 뭘 할 수 있어?

**14** 인공 지능 스피커: 영화 보는 건 어때요?

**15** 하나 틀어 줄게요.

**16** 수한: 이것 봐, 스마트 창문이 점점 어두워지고 있어.

**17** 마치 내가 영화관 안에 있는 것 같아.

**18** Jina: _____ _____ can you do?

**19** AI Speaker: I _____ beatbox, _____. _____ _____, "cats and boots and cats and boots."

**20** Suhan: You're _____. _____ _____!

**21** Jina: _____! _____ a smart car station _____!

**22** _____ _____ and _____ _____ that red car.

**23** Suhan: This car is _____ _____. Let's _____ _____.

**24** AI Car: Welcome. _____ you _____ _____ _____?

**25** Jina: Yes, _____ _____ we _____ now?

**26** It's _____ _____ _____ _____ in a smart car.

**27** AI Car: You _____ _____ _____ do anything.

**28** I will drive and _____ _____ _____ the next station.

**29** Suhan: _____ _____! I see a cat _____ the street.

**30** AI Car: _____ worry. I _____ _____ _____ it.

**31** When I _____ _____ _____, I slow _____ or stop.

**32** Jina: _____ _____ you _____ that?

**33** AI Car: I'm a very _____ _____ car.

**34** I know _____ _____ _____.

**35** I can predict danger _____ _____ knowledge and experience.

**36** Suhan: _____ smart! You think and act _____ a person.

**37** You are really _____ a _____.

18 진아: 또 뭘 할 수 있어?
19 인공 지능 스피커: 비트박스도 할 수 있어요. "북치기 박치기 북치기 박치기."
20 수한: 넌 정말 재미있구나. 잘했어!
21 진아: 서둘러! 밖에 스마트 자동차 정류장이 있어.
22 가서 저 빨간 차를 타 보자.
23 수한: 이 차 정말 멋지다. 차에 타자.
24 인공 지능 자동차: 어서 오세요. 갈 준비 됐나요?
25 진아: 응. 우린 이제 뭘 해야 하지?
26 스마트 자동차에 타는 건 처음이야.
27 인공 지능 자동차: 아무 것도 하지 않아도 돼요.
28 제가 운전해서 다음 정류장까지 데려다줄 거니까요.
29 수한: 조심해! 고양이가 길을 건너고 있는 게 보여.
30 인공 지능 자동차: 걱정 말아요. 이미 감지했어요.
31 저는 어떤 위험 상황을 감지하면 속도를 늦추거나 멈춰요.
32 진아: 어떻게 그렇게 할 수 있어?
33 인공 지능 자동차: 전 아주 지능적인 로봇 차예요.
34 저는 운전에 대한 모든 걸 알고 있어요.
35 저는 제 지식과 경험을 바탕으로 위험을 예측할 수 있어요.
36 수한: 정말 똑똑하구나! 사람처럼 생각하고 행동하는구나.
37 정말 인간 같아.

※ 다음 문장을 우리말로 쓰시오.

**1** A Day at the AI Expo

➡ _____

**2** Jina and Suhan are at the World AI Expo.

➡ _____

**3** They are entering the AI home.

➡ _____

**4** Suhan: Look at this! It's a house of the future.

➡ _____

**5** Jina: Let's go into the bedroom first. Look, there's a smart closet.

➡ _____

**6** Suhan: I'm standing in front of this screen on the closet door and my clothes keep changing.

➡ _____

**7** Jina: The screen suggests clothes that suit the weather.

➡ _____

**8** Suhan: That's amazing! We no longer have to worry about dressing for the weather.

➡ _____

**9** Jina: Right. Let's move on to the living room.

➡ _____

**10** Suhan: Oh, I like this music speaker.

➡ _____

**11** AI Speaker: I'm not just a music speaker.

➡ _____

**12** I can do more than you can imagine.

➡ _____

**13** Jina: It's hard to believe that you can understand us. What can you do?

➡ _____

**14** AI Speaker: How about watching a movie?

➡ _____

**15** I'll play one for you.

➡ _____

**16** Suhan: Look, those smart windows are getting darker.

➡ _____

**17** I feel like I'm in a movie theater.

➡ _____

**18** Jina: What else can you do?

➡ _____

**19** AI Speaker: I can beatbox, too. Here comes, "cats and boots and cats and boots."

➡ _____

**20** Suhan: You're funny. Good job!

➡ _____

**21** Jina: Hurry! There's a smart car station outside!

➡ _____

**22** Let's go and ride in that red car.

➡ _____

**23** Suhan: This car is so cool. Let's get in.

➡ _____

**24** AI Car: Welcome. Are you ready to go?

➡ _____

**25** Jina: Yes, what should we do now?

➡ _____

**26** It's my first time to ride in a smart car.

➡ _____

**27** AI Car: You don't need to do anything.

➡ _____

**28** I will drive and take you to the next station.

➡ _____

**29** Suhan: Watch out! I see a cat crossing the street.

➡ _____

**30** AI Car: Don't worry. I have just sensed it.

➡ _____

**31** When I sense dangerous situations, I slow down or stop.

➡ _____

**32** Jina: How can you do that?

➡ _____

**33** AI Car: I'm a very intelligent robotic car.

➡ _____

**34** I know all about driving.

➡ _____

**35** I can predict danger based on knowledge and experience.

➡ _____

**36** Suhan: How smart! You think and act like a person.

➡ _____

**37** You are really like a human.

➡ _____

※ 다음 괄호 안의 단어들을 우리말에 맞도록 바르게 배열하시오.

**1** (Day / at / A / AI / the / Expo)
➡ _____

**2** (Suhan / and / Jina / at / are / World / the / Expo. / AI)
➡ _____

**3** (they / entering / are / AI / the / home.)
➡ _____

**4** (Suhan: / at / look / this! // a / it's / of / house / future. / the)
➡ _____

**5** (Jina: / go / let's / the / into / first. / bedroom // look, / a / there's / closet. / smart)
➡ _____

**6** (Suhan: / standing / I'm / front / in / this / of / screen / the / on / door / closet / and / clothes / my / changing. / keep)
➡ _____

**7** (Jina: / screen / the / clothes / suggests / that / the / suit / weather.)
➡ _____

**8** (Suhan: / amazing! / that's // we / longer / no / to / have / about / worry / for / dressing / weather. / the)
➡ _____

**9** (Jina: / right. // move / let's / to / on / the / room. / living)
➡ _____

**10** (Suhan: / oh, / like / I / music / this / speaker.)
➡ _____

**11** (AI / Speaker: / not / I'm / a / just / speaker. / music)
➡ _____

**12** (I / do / can / than / more / imagine. / can / you)
➡ _____

**13** (Jina: / hard / it's / believe / to / you / that / understand / can / us. // what / you / can / do?)
➡ _____

**14** (Speaker: / AI / about / how / a / watching / movie?)
➡ _____

**15** (play / I'll / for / you. / one)
➡ _____

**16** (Suhan: / look, / smart / those / are / windows / darker. / getting)
➡ _____

**17** (feel / I / like / in / I'm / movie / theater. / a)
➡ _____

**1** 인공 지능 박람회에서의 하루

**2** 진아와 수한이가 세계 인공 지능 박람회에 있다.

**3** 그들은 인공 지능 집으로 들어가고 있다.

**4** 수한: 이것 봐! 미래의 집이야.

**5** 진아: 침실 먼저 들어가 보자. 이거 봐, 스마트 옷장이 있어.

**6** 수한: 옷장 문에 있는 스크린 앞에 서 있으니까 내 옷이 계속해서 바뀌어.

**7** 진아: 스크린이 날씨에 적합한 옷을 제안하는 거야.

**8** 수한: 놀라워! 우린 더 이상 날씨 때문에 무슨 옷을 입을지 걱정할 필요가 없겠다.

**9** 진아: 맞아. 이제 거실로 가 보자.

**10** 수한: 오, 이 음악 스피커 마음에 들어.

**11** 인공 지능 스피커: 저는 그냥 음악 스피커가 아니에요.

**12** 저는 당신이 상상하는 것 이상의 것을 할 수 있어요.

**13** 진아: 네가 우리를 이해한다니 믿기 어려운 걸! 넌 뭘 할 수 있어?

**14** 인공 지능 스피커: 영화 보는 건 어때요?

**15** 하나 틀어 줄게요.

**16** 수한: 이것 봐, 스마트 창문이 점점 어두워지고 있어.

**17** 마치 내가 영화관 안에 있는 것 같아.

**18** (Jina: / else / what / do? / you / can)
➡ _____

**19** (AI / Speaker: / can / I / too. / beatbox // comes, / here / and / "cats / boots / and / boots." / and / cats)
➡ _____

**20** (Suhan: / funny. / you're // job! / good)
➡ _____

**21** (Jina: / hurry! / a / there's / car / smart / outside! / station)
➡ _____

**22** (go / let's / ride / and / that / in / car. / red)
➡ _____

**23** (Suhan: / car / this / cool. / is / so // get / in. / let's)
➡ _____

**24** (AI / Car: / welcome. // you / are / to / ready / go?)
➡ _____

**25** (Jina: / yes, / should / what / do / we / now?)
➡ _____

**26** (my / it's / time / first / ride / to / in / a / car. / smart)
➡ _____

**27** (AI / Car: / don't / you / need / do / to / anything.)
➡ _____

**28** (will / I / drive / and / you / take / the / to / station. / next)
➡ _____

**29** (Suhan: / out! / watch // see / I / cat / a / the / crossing / street.)
➡ _____

**30** (Car: / AI / worry. / don't // have / I / sensed / it. / just)
➡ _____

**31** (I / when / sense / situations, / dangerous / slow / I / down / stop. / or)
➡ _____

**32** (Jina: / can / how / do / that? / you)
➡ _____

**33** (Car: / AI / a / I'm / intelligent / very / car. / robotic)
➡ _____

**34** (know / I / about / all / driving.)
➡ _____

**35** (can / I / danger / predict / on / based / experience. / and / knowledge)
➡ _____

**36** (Suhan: / smart! / how // think / you / and / like / act / a / person.)
➡ _____

**37** (are / you / like / really / human. / a)
➡ _____

**18** 진아: 또 뭘 할 수 있어?

**19** 인공 지능 스피커: 비트박스도 할 수 있어요. "북치기 박치기 북치기 박치기."

**20** 수한: 넌 정말 재미있구나. 잘했어!

**21** 진아: 서둘러! 밖에 스마트 자동차 정류장이 있어.

**22** 가서 저 빨간 차를 타 보자.

**23** 수한: 이 차 정말 멋지다. 차에 타자.

**24** 인공 지능 자동차: 어서 오세요. 갈 준비 됐나요?

**25** 진아: 응, 우린 이제 뭘 해야 하지?

**26** 스마트 자동차에 타는 건 처음이야.

**27** 인공 지능 자동차: 아무 것도 하지 않아도 돼요.

**28** 제가 운전해서 다음 정류장까지 데려다줄 거니까요.

**29** 수한: 조심해! 고양이가 길을 건너고 있는 게 보여.

**30** 인공 지능 자동차: 걱정 말아요. 이미 감지했어요.

**31** 저는 어떤 위험 상황을 감지하면 속도를 늦추거나 멈춰요.

**32** 진아: 어떻게 그렇게 할 수 있어?

**33** 인공 지능 자동차: 전 아주 지능적인 로봇 차예요.

**34** 저는 운전에 대한 모든 걸 알고 있어요.

**35** 저는 제 지식과 경험을 바탕으로 위험을 예측할 수 있어요.

**36** 수한: 정말 똑똑하구나! 사람처럼 생각하고 행동하는구나.

**37** 정말 인간 같아.

※ 다음 우리말을 영어로 쓰시오.

**1** 인공 지능 박람회에서의 하루

➡ _____

**2** 진아와 수한이가 세계 인공 지능 박람회에 있다.

➡ _____

**3** 그들은 인공 지능 집으로 들어가고 있다.

➡ _____

**4** 수한: 이것 봐! 미래의 집이야.

➡ _____

**5** 진아: 침실 먼저 들어가 보자. 이거 봐, 스마트 옷장이 있어.

➡ _____

**6** 수한: 옷장 문에 있는 스크린 앞에 서 있으니까 내 옷이 계속해서 바뀌어.

➡ _____

**7** 진아: 스크린이 날씨에 적합한 옷을 제안하는 거야.

➡ _____

**8** 수한: 놀라워! 우린 더 이상 날씨 때문에 무슨 옷을 입을지 걱정할 필요가 없겠다.

➡ _____

**9** 진아: 맞아. 이제 거실로 가 보자.

➡ _____

**10** 수한: 오, 이 음악 스피커 마음에 들어.

➡ _____

**11** 인공 지능 스피커: 저는 그냥 음악 스피커가 아니에요.

➡ _____

**12** 저는 당신이 상상하는 것 이상의 것을 할 수 있어요.

➡ _____

**13** 진아: 네가 우리를 이해한다니 믿기 어려운 걸! 넌 뭘 할 수 있어?

➡ _____

**14** 인공 지능 스피커: 영화 보는 건 어때요?

➡ _____

**15** 하나 틀어 줄게요.

➡ _____

**16** 수한: 이것 봐, 스마트 창문이 점점 어두워지고 있어.

➡ _____

**17** 마치 내가 영화관 안에 있는 것 같아.

➡ _____

**18** 진아: 또 뭘 할 수 있어?
➡ _____

**19** 인공 지능 스피커: 비트박스도 할 수 있어요. "북치기 박치기 북치기 박치기."
➡ _____

**20** 수한: 넌 정말 재미있구나. 잘했어!
➡ _____

**21** 진아: 서둘러! 밖에 스마트 자동차 정류장이 있어.
➡ _____

**22** 가서 저 빨간 차를 타 보자.
➡ _____

**23** 수한: 이 차 정말 멋지다. 차에 타자.
➡ _____

**24** 인공 지능 자동차: 어서 오세요. 갈 준비 됐나요?
➡ _____

**25** 진아: 응, 우린 이제 뭘 해야 하지?
➡ _____

**26** 스마트 자동차에 타는 건 처음이야.
➡ _____

**27** 인공 지능 자동차: 아무 것도 하지 않아도 돼요.
➡ _____

**28** 제가 운전해서 다음 정류장까지 데려다줄 거니까요.
➡ _____

**29** 수한: 조심해! 고양이가 길을 건너고 있는 게 보여.
➡ _____

**30** 인공 지능 자동차: 걱정 말아요. 이미 감지했어요.
➡ _____

**31** 저는 어떤 위험 상황을 감지하면 속도를 늦추거나 멈춰요.
➡ _____

**32** 진아: 어떻게 그렇게 할 수 있어?
➡ _____

**33** 인공 지능 자동차: 전 아주 지능적인 로봇 차예요.
➡ _____

**34** 저는 운전에 대한 모든 걸 알고 있어요.
➡ _____

**35** 저는 제 지식과 경험을 바탕으로 위험을 예측할 수 있어요.
➡ _____

**36** 수한: 정말 똑똑하구나! 사람처럼 생각하고 행동하는구나.
➡ _____

**37** 정말 인간 같아.
➡ _____

※ 다음 우리말과 일치하도록 빈칸에 알맞은 말을 쓰시오.

## Before You Read

1. _____ _____
2. AI _____ Human!
3. An AI program _____ _____ a human _____ a *baduk* _____.
4. The AI _____ _____ _____ _____ Lee Sedol, who is _____ _____ _____ _____ *baduk* _____.
5. *Baduk* is a board game, and the rules are _____ _____.
6. Many people _____ it would be impossible _____ _____ _____ _____ a human player.
7. However, the AI _____ _____ _____ _____ Lee's play, and it _____ _____ the game.
8. People _____ _____ that an AI can _____ _____ _____ _____ a human.

1. 데일리 뉴스
2. AI가 인간을 이기다!
3. 바둑 대국에서 AI 프로그램이 인간을 이겼다.
4. AI가 이세돌과 대국을 벌였는데, 그는 가장 위대한 바둑기사들 중의 한 명이다.
5. 바둑은 보드 게임이고, 그 규칙은 이해하기 어렵다.
6. 많은 사람들은 AI가 인간 기사를 이기는 것은 불가능할 것이라고 믿었다.
7. 그러나, AI는 이세돌의 경기를 예측할 수 있었고, 그리고 마침내 경기에서 이겼다.
8. 사람들은 AI가 인간보다 더 똑똑할 수 있다는 것에 충격을 받았다.

## Focus on Expressions

1. In 2099, people _____ _____ a flying car _____ _____ _____ the moon.
2. Kids _____ _____ _____ to the moon _____ the _____ _____ is there.
3. _____ _____, horse-riding is _____ _____ _____.
4. They _____ _____ to _____ _____ the horses.

1. 2099년에 사람들은 달에 가기 위해 날아다니는 차를 탑니다.
2. 아이들은 가장 멋진 놀이공원이 그곳에 있기 때문에 달에 가는 것을 좋아합니다.
3. 다른 무엇보다도, 말타기는 그들이 가장 좋아하는 활동입니다.
4. 그들은 말에서 내리기를 원하지 않습니다.

## Wrap Up 1-2

1. G: Minseok, there is a _____ _____ machine _____ _____. _____ _____ we _____ it?
2. B: That _____ interesting. We'll _____ _____ easily and fast _____ _____ it.
3. G: I hope so. _____ _____ _____, do you think maybe _____ will be possible _____ _____ _____ _____ humans someday?
4. B: I'm not sure. But we _____ _____ _____ _____ _____ danger _____ _____ robots.
5. G: _____ do you _____?
6. B: Robots can help people _____ _____. Robots can do the dangerous work _____ humans _____ _____ _____.
7. G: You're _____. We should _____ _____ _____ _____ _____ the bright side.

1. G: 민석아, 저쪽에 스마트 음식 주문 자판기가 있어. 가서 해 보지 않을래?
2. B: 재미있겠다. 저걸 사용하면 우린 쉽고 빠르게 주문할 수 있을 거야.
3. G: 그러길 바라. 그건 그렇고, 너는 로봇이 언젠가 인간을 대체할 수 있을 거라고 생각하니?
4. B: 잘 모르겠어. 하지만 우리는 로봇 덕분에 위험이 없어질 거야.
5. G: 무슨 뜻이야?
6. B: 로봇은 위험에 처한 사람들을 도울 수 있어. 로봇이 위험한 일을 할 수 있어서 사람들이 그 일을 하지 않아도 되지.
7. G: 네 말이 맞아. 우리는 항상 좋은 면을 보도록 해야 해.

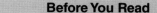

※ 다음 우리말을 영어로 쓰시오.

**Before You Read**

1. 데일리 뉴스
   ➡ _____

2. AI가 인간을 이기다!
   ➡ _____

3. 바둑 대국에서 AI 프로그램이 인간을 이겼다.
   ➡ _____

4. AI가 이세돌과 대국을 벌였는데, 그는 가장 위대한 바둑기사들 중의 한 명이다.
   ➡ _____

5. 바둑은 보드 게임이고, 그 규칙은 이해하기 어렵다.
   ➡ _____

6. 많은 사람들은 AI가 인간 기사를 이기는 것은 불가능할 것이라고 믿었다.
   ➡ _____

7. 그러나, AI는 이세돌의 경기를 예측할 수 있었고, 그리고 마침내 경기에서 이겼다.
   ➡ _____

8. 사람들은 AI가 인간보다 더 똑똑할 수 있다는 것에 충격을 받았다.
   ➡ _____

**Focus on Expressions**

1. 2099년에 사람들은 달에 가기 위해 날아다니는 차를 탑니다.
   ➡ _____

2. 아이들은 가장 멋진 놀이공원이 그곳에 있기 때문에 달에 가는 것을 좋아합니다.
   ➡ _____

3. 다른 무엇보다도, 말타기는 그들이 가장 좋아하는 활동입니다.
   ➡ _____

4. 그들은 말에서 내리기를 원하지 않습니다.
   ➡ _____

**Wrap Up 1-2**

1. G: 민석아, 저쪽에 스마트 음식 주문 자판기가 있어. 가서 해 보지 않을래?
   ➡ _____

2. B: 재미있겠다. 저걸 사용하면 우린 쉽고 빠르게 주문할 수 있을 거야.
   ➡ _____

3. G: 그러길 바라. 그건 그렇고, 너는 로봇이 언젠가 인간을 대체할 수 있을 거라고 생각하니?
   ➡ _____

4. B: 잘 모르겠어. 하지만 우리는 로봇 덕분에 위험이 없어질 거야.
   ➡ _____

5. G: 무슨 뜻이야?
   ➡ _____

6. B: 로봇은 위험에 처한 사람들을 도울 수 있어. 로봇이 위험한 일을 할 수 있어서 사람들이 그 일을 하지 않아도 되지.
   ➡ _____

7. G: 네 말이 맞아. 우리는 항상 좋은 면을 보도록 해야 해.
   ➡ _____

※ 다음 영어를 우리말로 쓰시오.

01 collect _____

02 affair _____

03 official _____

04 businessman _____

05 suffer _____

06 rule _____

07 dynasty _____

08 explain _____

09 unknown _____

10 fit _____

11 press _____

12 through _____

13 tourist _____

14 independence _____

15 community _____

16 store _____

17 modern _____

18 alive _____

19 another _____

20 movement _____

21 village _____

22 poem _____

23 waste _____

24 property _____

25 royal _____

26 society _____

27 found _____

28 pottery _____

29 support _____

30 meaning _____

31 taste _____

32 interest _____

33 architecture _____

34 Spanish _____

35 in danger _____

36 set foot _____

37 be known as _____

38 care for _____

39 fall off _____

40 thanks to _____

41 be famous for _____

42 in need _____

43 be in harmony with _____

※ 다음 우리말을 영어로 쓰시오.

| | |
|---|---|
| 01 전통 | |
| 02 현대의 | |
| 03 사회, 단체 | |
| 04 건축 | |
| 05 사업가 | |
| 06 저장하다, 보관하다 | |
| 07 왕조, 시대 | |
| 08 설명하다 | |
| 09 의미 | |
| 10 도자기 | |
| 11 알려지지 않은 | |
| 12 시 | |
| 13 공무원, 당국 | |
| 14 모으다, 수집하다 | |
| 15 설립하다 | |
| 16 독립 | |
| 17 사건, 일 | |
| 18 재산 | |
| 19 살아 있는 | |
| 20 관심, 흥미 | |
| 21 지원하다 | |

| | |
|---|---|
| 22 통치하다; 규칙, 원칙 | |
| 23 고통 받다, 시달리다 | |
| 24 여행객 | |
| 25 운동 | |
| 26 ~을 통하여 | |
| 27 적합하다 | |
| 28 왕의, 왕실의 | |
| 29 또 다른, 다른 하나의 | |
| 30 압박하다 | |
| 31 마을 | |
| 32 지역사회, 주민 | |
| 33 낭비하다 | |
| 34 자연 | |
| 35 (사업, 세력 등이) 쇠퇴하다 | |
| 36 ~으로 가득하다 | |
| 37 ~을 돌보다 | |
| 38 ~ 덕분에 | |
| 39 수백의, 수많은 | |
| 40 어려움에 처한 | |
| 41 ~으로 유명하다 | |
| 42 ~으로 알려지다 | |
| 43 ~와 조화를 이루다 | |

※ 다음 영영풀이에 알맞은 단어를 <보기>에서 골라 쓴 후, 우리말 뜻을 쓰시오.

1 _____ : not dead: _____

2 _____ : a man who works in business: _____

3 _____ : a family of rulers who rule over a country for a long period of time: _____

4 _____ : a long written story about imaginary people and events: _____

5 _____ : the art of planning, designing and constructing buildings: _____

6 _____ : connected with or belonging to the king or queen of a country: _____

7 _____ : to have the official power to control a country and the people who live there: _____

8 _____ : to give details about something or describe it so that it can be understood: _____

9 _____ : all the things that belong to someone or something that belongs to them: _____

10 _____ : a hard solid substance found in the ground and often used for building houses: _____

11 _____ : the place where someone lives or the town that they come from: _____

12 _____ : to get an institution, company, or organization started, often by providing the necessary money: _____

13 _____ : to bring things or people together from several places or from several people: _____

14 _____ : to put things in a container or other places and leave them there until they are needed: _____

15 _____ : an area of ground, especially one that is used for a particular purpose such as farming or building: _____

16 _____ : all the animals, plants, and other things in the world that are not made by people, and all the events and processes that are not caused by people: _____

| 보기 | | | |
|---|---|---|---|
| land | store | found | hometown |
| businessman | architecture | stone | rule |
| alive | collect | property | nature |
| royal | novel | explain | dynasty |

Step1

※ 다음 우리말과 일치하도록 빈칸에 알맞은 말을 쓰시오.

**Listen & Speak 1 B-2**

G: _____ you know _____ _____ Changdeokgung?

B: Yes, a _____. It's _____ _____ its beautiful garden.

G: I'm _____ _____ go there _____ my Chinese friend.

B: I _____ you'll _____ it.

G: 너는 창덕궁에 대해 아는 것이 있니?
B: 응, 조금. 그것은 아름다운 정원으로 유명해.
G: 난 내 중국인 친구와 함께 그곳에 갈 거야.
B: 그곳이 마음에 들 거야.

**Listen & Speak 2 A**

B: _____ you _____ this _____?

W: Sure. It's the *Two Sisters* _____ Renoir. He _____ it _____ 1881.

B: 이 그림에 대해 설명을 해 주시겠습니까?
W: 물론이죠. 이 그림은 르누아르의 "두 자매"예요. 그는 1881년에 이 그림을 그렸어요.

**Listen & Speak 2 B-1**

1. G: Can you _____ _____ _____?

   B: Sure. It _____ _____ _____ Yun Dongju.

   G: What's it _____?

   B: It's _____ him _____ his hometown.

2. B: Could you _____ _____ Helping Hands _____?

   G: It's a _____ _____ in our _____.

   B: Could you _____ me _____ _____ it?

   G: Well, they _____ _____ _____ children in need.

1. G: 이 시를 설명해 줄 수 있니?
   B: 그럼. 그것은 윤동주에 의해 씌어졌어.
   G: 그것은 무엇에 관한 거니?
   B: 그것은 고향을 그리워하는 작가에 관한 거야.
2. B: '도움의 손길'이 무엇인지 설명해 줄 수 있니?
   G: 그것은 우리 지역 사회에 있는 자원봉사 단체예.
   B: 그것에 관해 더 말해 줄 수 있니?
   G: 음, 그들은 어려움에 처한 어린이들을 돌봐.

**Listen & Speak 2 C**

A: _____ you _____ your plan _____ _____ money?

B: I _____ _____ my money _____ snacks.

A: 돈을 절약할 너의 계획에 대해 설명해 줄 수 있니?
B: 간식에 돈을 낭비하지 않을 거야.

**Real-Life Zone A**

G: _____ are *hanoks*? Do you know _____ _____ them?

M: *Hanoks* are traditional _____ _____. They _____ to be _____ _____ nature.

G: Could you _____ _____ _____ more about them?

M: *Hanoks* are _____ in the summer and _____ in the winter.

G: 한옥은 무엇이에요? 한옥에 대해 아는 것이 있으세요?
M: 한옥은 전통적인 한국 가옥이에요. 그것들은 자연과 조화를 이루도록 설계되었어요.
G: 그것들에 대해 좀 더 설명하실 수 있어요?
M: 한옥은 여름에는 시원하고 겨울에는 따뜻해요.

W: That _____ interesting. _____ can I _____ these _____ _____?

M: There's a *hanok* village _____ _____.

G: How _____ _____ there and _____ the *hanoks*?

W: Good _____! _____ can we _____ there?

M: You can _____ Bus Number 5 _____ _____ at the bus stop.

W: 그거 재미있네요. 이 전통 가옥을 어디에서 볼 수 있어요?

M: 이 근처에 한옥 마을이 있어요.

G: 거기 가서 한옥들을 보는 게 어때요?

W: 좋은 생각이구나! 그곳에 어떻게 갈 수 있죠?

M: 저기 버스 정류장에서 5번 버스를 타시면 돼요.

## Real-Life Zone B

1. A: Do you _____ _____ about the Great Wall of China?

   B: Yes. It is _____ _____ the _____ _____ in the world.

   A: Can you _____ _____ it is _____?

   B: It's _____ it is the _____ _____ in the world.

2. A: Do you know _____ _____ the _____ *The Old Man and the Sea*?

   B: Yes. It is a _____ _____ _____ _____ Ernest Hemingway.

   A: Can you _____ _____ it is famous?

   B: It's _____ Hemingway _____ the Pulitzer Prize in 1953 _____ this novel.

1. A: 중국의 만리장성에 대해 아는 것이 있나요?
   B: 네. 그것은 세계에서 멋진 광경들 중의 하나예요.
   A: 그것이 왜 유명한지 설명해 줄 수 있나요?
   B: 세계에서 가장 긴 성벽이기 때문이죠.

2. A: '노인과 바다'라는 소설에 대해 아는 것이 있나요?
   B: 네. 그것은 어니스트 헤밍웨이가 쓴 소설이에요.
   A: 그것이 왜 유명한지 설명해 줄 수 있나요?
   B: 헤밍웨이가 이 책으로 1953년 풀리쳐상을 받았기 때문이죠.

## Real-Life Zone B e.g.

A: Do you _____ _____ _____ the Eiffel Tower?

B: Yes. It _____ _____ _____ 1889 _____ Gustave Eiffel.

A: Can you _____ _____ it is _____?

B: _____ _____ it was the _____ _____ in the world _____ _____ _____.

A: 너는 에펠탑에 대해 아는 것이 있니?
B: 응. 그것은 1889년에 Gustave Eiffel에 의해 세워졌어.
A: 그것이 왜 유명한지 설명할 수 있니?
B: 그것은 그 당시 그 탑이 세계에서 가장 높은 탑이었기 때문이야.

## Wrap Up

B: Do you _____ _____ about a *dol* party?

G: Yes. It's the _____ party for a one-year-old _____.

B: Could you _____ me _____ about it?

G: Well, the family members _____ _____ for the party, and the birthday baby _____ a *hanbok*.

B: That _____ _____.

G: The family members _____ _____ and _____ _____ a _____ _____ for the baby. It's a _____ _____.

B: 넌 돌잔치에 대해 아는 것이 있니?
G: 응. 그건 한 살 먹은 아기를 위한 생일잔치야.
B: 그것에 대해 더 말해 줄 수 있니?
G: 음, 그 잔치를 위해 가족들이 함께 모이고 생일을 맞은 아기는 한복을 입어.
B: 그거 재미있구나.
G: 가족들은 음식을 함께 나누어 먹고 아기가 오래 살기를 바라. 그건 한국의 전통이야.

※ 다음 우리말에 맞도록 대화를 영어로 쓰시오.

해석

### Listen & Speak 1 B-2

G: _____

B: _____

G: _____

B: _____

G: 너는 창덕궁에 대해 아는 것이 있니?
B: 응, 조금. 그것은 아름다운 정원으로 유명해.
G: 난 내 중국인 친구와 함께 그곳에 갈 거야.
B: 그곳이 마음에 들 거야.

### Listen & Speak 2 A

B: _____

W: _____

B: 이 그림에 대해 설명을 해 주시겠습니까?
W: 물론이죠. 이 그림은 르누아르의 "두 자매"예요. 그는 1881년에 이 그림을 그렸어요.

### Listen & Speak 2 B-1

1. G: _____

   B: _____

   G: _____

   B: _____

2. B: _____

   G: _____

   B: _____

   G: _____

1. G: 이 시를 설명해 줄 수 있니?
   B: 그럼. 그것은 윤동주에 의해 씌어졌어.
   G: 그것은 무엇에 관한 거니?
   B: 그것은 고향을 그리워하는 작가에 관한 거야.
2. B: '도움의 손길'이 무엇인지 설명해 줄 수 있니?
   G: 그것은 우리 지역 사회에 있는 자원봉사 단체야.
   B: 그것에 관해 더 말해 줄 수 있니?
   G: 음, 그들은 어려움에 처한 어린이들을 돌봐.

### Listen & Speak 2 C

A: _____

B: _____

A: 돈을 절약할 너의 계획에 대해 설명해 줄 수 있니?
B: 간식에 돈을 낭비하지 않을 거야.

### Real-Life Zone A

G: _____

M: _____

G: _____

M: _____

G: 한옥은 무엇이에요? 한옥에 대해 아는 것이 있으세요?
M: 한옥은 전통적인 한국 가옥이에요. 그것들은 자연과 조화를 이루도록 설계되었어요.
G: 그것들에 대해 좀 더 설명하실 수 있어요?
M: 한옥은 여름에는 시원하고 겨울에는 따뜻해요.

W: _____

M: _____

G: _____

W: _____

M: _____

W: 그거 재미있네요. 이 전통 가옥을 어디에서 볼 수 있어요?

M: 이 근처에 한옥 마을이 있어요.

G: 거기 가서 한옥들을 보는 게 어때요?

W: 좋은 생각이구나! 그곳에 어떻게 갈 수 있죠?

M: 저기 버스 정류장에서 5번 버스를 타시면 돼요.

### Real-Life Zone B

1. A: _____

   B: _____

   A: _____

   B: _____

2. A: _____

   B: _____

   A: _____

   B: _____

1. A: 중국의 만리장성에 대해 아는 것이 있나요?

   B: 네. 그것은 세계에서 멋진 광경들 중의 하나예요.

   A: 그것이 왜 유명한지 설명해 줄 수 있나요?

   B: 세계에서 가장 긴 성벽이기 때문이죠.

2. A: '노인과 바다'라는 소설에 대해 아는 것이 있나요?

   B: 네. 그것은 어니스트 헤밍웨이가 쓴 소설이에요.

   A: 그것이 왜 유명한지 설명해 줄 수 있나요?

   B: 헤밍웨이가 이 책으로 1953년 퓰리쳐상을 받았기 때문이죠.

### Real-Life Zone B e.g.

A: _____

B: _____

A: _____

B: _____

A: 너는 에펠탑에 대해 아는 것이 있니?

B: 응. 그것은 1889년에 Gustave Eiffel에 의해 세워졌어.

A: 그것이 왜 유명한지 설명할 수 있니?

B: 그것은 그 당시 그 탑이 세계에서 가장 높은 탑이었기 때문이야.

### Wrap Up

B: _____

G: _____

B: _____

G: _____

B: _____

G: _____

B: 넌 돌잔치에 대해 아는 것이 있니?

G: 응. 그건 한 살 먹은 아기를 위한 생일잔치야.

B: 그것에 대해 더 말해 줄 수 있니?

G: 음, 그 잔치를 위해 가족들이 함께 모이고 생일을 맞은 아기는 한복을 입어.

B: 그거 재미있구나.

G: 가족들은 음식을 함께 나누어 먹고 아기가 오래 살기를 바라. 그건 한국의 전통이야.

Step1

※ 다음 우리말과 일치하도록 빈칸에 알맞은 것을 골라 쓰시오.

**1** The _____ of _____ in _____
    A. Architecture    B. King    C. Gyeongseong

**2** _____ you _____ _____ Bukchon?
    A. to    B. been    C. have

**3** _____ is a _____ *hanok* _____ in Bukchon.
    A. village    B. beautiful    C. there

**4** It is _____ with tourists _____ want to see Korea's _____ .
    A. who    B. popular    C. past

**5** However, not many people _____ that Bukchon was _____ _____ one man's _____ .
    A. created    B. efforts    C. through    D. know

**6** That man was Jeong Segwon, _____ _____ the King of Architecture _____ Gyeongseong.
    A. known    B. in    C. as

**7** Jeong Segwon was a _____ _____ _____ Geonyangsa in 1920.
    A. founded    B. who    C. businessman

**8** At the _____ , Korea was _____ by Japan, and the Japanese were changing Gyeongseong to _____ their _____ .
    A. ruled    B. fit    C. taste    D. time

**9** Many Japanese _____ _____ Gyeongseong were _____ Japanese or _____ houses.
    A. into    B. Western    C. building    D. moving

**10** Jeong Segwon _____ to _____ the *hanok* and help the _____ people.
    A. protect    B. suffering    C. wanted

**11** He said, "People are _____ . We Joseon people should _____ Jongno and not _____ the Japanese _____ foot here."
    A. keep    B. set    C. let    D. power

**12** He _____ the land _____ Gyeongbokgung _____ Changdeokgung.
    A. between    B. bought    C. and

**13** There he _____ small, _____ *hanoks* for the _____ .
    A. people    B. built    C. modern

**14** _____ his _____ , we now have Bukchon _____ _____ its beautiful *hanoks*.
    A. filled    B. through    C. with    D. efforts

**1** 경성의 건축왕

**2** 당신은 북촌에 다녀온 적이 있는가?

**3** 북촌에는 아름다운 한옥 마을이 있다.

**4** 그곳은 한국의 과거를 보고 싶어 하는 관광객들에게 인기가 있다.

**5** 그러나 북촌이 한 사람의 노력으로 만들어졌다는 것을 아는 사람은 많지 않다.

**6** 그 사람은 경성의 건축왕으로 알려진 정세권이었다.

**7** 정세권은 1920년에 건양사를 설립한 사업가였다.

**8** 그 당시 한국은 일본의 지배를 받았고, 일본인들은 경성을 그들의 취향에 맞게 바꾸고 있었다.

**9** 경성으로 이주하는 많은 일본인들은 일본식이나 서양식 집들을 짓고 있었다.

**10** 정세권은 한옥을 지키고 고통받는 사람들을 돕기를 원했다.

**11** 그는 말했다. "사람이 힘이다. 우리 조선 사람들은 종로를 지켜야 하며, 일본인들이 이곳에 발을 붙이지 못하게 해야 한다."

**12** 그는 경복궁과 창덕궁 사이의 땅을 샀다.

**13** 거기에 그는 사람들을 위해 작은 현대식 한옥들을 지었다.

**14** 그의 노력으로 북촌은 현재 아름다운 한옥으로 가득 차 있다.

**15** Jeong Segwon helped the _____ _____ in many
_____.

    A. movement       B. ways       C. independence

    15 정세권은 여러 방법으로 독립운동을 도왔다.

**16** For _____, he built the office building for the Joseon Language
Society and _____ its efforts to _____ the Joseon language
_____.

    A. keep       B. example       C. alive       D. supported

    16 예를 들면, 그는 조선어 학회를 위한 회관을 지었고 조선어를 지키려는 그들의 노력을 지원했다.

**17** When the Joseon Language Affair _____, he was _____ by
the police and _____ a lot.

    A. caught       B. happened       C. suffered

    17 조선어 학회 사건이 발생했을 때 그는 경찰에 잡혀 많은 고통을 겪었다.

**18** Japanese _____ _____ him to _____ Japanese houses.

    A. pressed       B. officials       C. build

    18 일본인 관리들은 그에게 일본식 가옥을 지으라고 압박했다.

**19** He said, "I don't know _____ _____ _____ Japanese
houses."

    A. how       B. build       C. to

    19 그는 말했다. "나는 일본식 가옥을 지울 줄 모르오."

**20** An _____ said, "You _____ how to build *hanoks*, _____
you can _____ Japanese houses, too."

    A. so       B. know       C. official       D. build

    20 한 관리가 말했다. "당신은 한옥을 지을 줄 아오. 그러니 일본식 가옥도 지을 수 있소."

**21** But he did not do _____ the Japanese _____ him to _____.

    A. what       B. do       C. told

    21 그러나 그는 그 일본인이 그에게 요구한 것을 하지 않았다.

**22** The _____ was _____.

    A. high       B. cost

    22 그 대가는 컸다.

**23** His business _____ _____, and he lost his _____.

    A. property       B. off       C. fell

    23 그의 사업은 쇠퇴했고, 그는 재산을 잃었다.

**24** However, in _____, thanks _____ Jeong Segwon, the
_____ of Korea _____ live with us today.

    A. still       B. part       C. traditions       D. to

    24 그러나 부분적으로나마, 정세권 덕분에 한국의 전통이 오늘날 여전히 우리와 함께 살아 있다.

※ 다음 우리말과 일치하도록 빈칸에 알맞은 말을 쓰시오.

1  _____ _____ of _____ _____ Gyeongseong

2  _____ you _____ _____ Bukchon?

3  _____ _____ a beautiful *hanok* _____ in Bukchon.

4  It is _____ with tourists _____ want to see Korea's _____.

5  _____, not many people _____ that Bukchon _____ _____ one man's _____.

6  That man was Jeong Segwon, _____ _____ the King of _____ in Gyeongseong.

7  Jeong Segwon was a businessman _____ _____ Geonyangsa in 1920.

8  _____ _____ _____, Korea _____ _____ _____ Japan, and the Japanese _____ _____ Gyeongseong to _____ their _____.

9  Many Japanese _____ _____ Gyeongseong _____ _____ _____ or _____ houses.

10  Jeong Segwon _____ _____ _____ the *hanok* and help the _____ people.

11  He said, "People are _____. We Joseon people _____ _____ Jongno and not _____ the Japanese _____ _____ here."

12  He _____ the land _____ Gyeongbokgung _____ Changdeokgung.

13  There he _____ small, _____ *hanoks* for the _____.

14  _____ his _____, we now have Bukchon _____ _____ its beautiful *hanoks*.

1  경성의 건축왕

2  당신은 북촌에 다녀온 적이 있는가?

3  북촌에는 아름다운 한옥 마을이 있다.

4  그곳은 한국의 과거를 보고 싶어 하는 관광객들에게 인기가 있다.

5  그러나 북촌이 한 사람의 노력으로 만들어졌다는 것을 아는 사람은 많지 않다.

6  그 사람은 경성의 건축왕으로 알려진 정세권이었다.

7  정세권은 1920년에 건양사를 설립한 사업가였다.

8  그 당시 한국은 일본의 지배를 받았고, 일본인들은 경성을 그들의 취향에 맞게 바꾸고 있었다.

9  경성으로 이주하는 많은 일본인들은 일본식이나 서양식 집들을 짓고 있었다.

10  정세권은 한옥을 지키고 고통받는 사람들을 돕기를 원했다.

11  그는 말했다. "사람이 힘이다. 우리 조선 사람들은 종로를 지켜야 하며, 일본인들이 이곳에 발을 붙이지 못하게 해야 한다."

12  그는 경복궁과 창덕궁 사이의 땅을 샀다.

13  거기에 그는 사람들을 위해 작은 현대식 한옥들을 지었다.

14  그의 노력으로 북촌은 현재 아름다운 한옥으로 가득 차 있다.

**15** Jeong Segwon helped the _____ _____ _____ _____ _____.

**16** _____ _____, he built the office building for the Joseon Language Society and _____ _____ _____ to _____ the Joseon language _____.

**17** When the Joseon Language Affair _____, he _____ _____ _____ the police and _____ _____ _____.

**18** Japanese officials _____ him _____ _____ Japanese houses.

**19** He said, "I don't know _____ _____ _____ Japanese houses."

**20** An _____ said, "You _____ _____ _____ build *hanoks*, _____ you can _____ Japanese houses, _____."

**21** But he did not do _____ the Japanese _____ him _____ _____.

**22** The _____ was _____.

**23** His business _____ _____, and he _____ his _____.

**24** However, in _____, _____ _____ Jeong Segwon, the _____ of Korea _____ _____ _____ us today.

---

**15** 정세권은 여러 방법으로 독립운동을 도왔다.

**16** 예를 들면, 그는 조선어 학회를 위한 회관을 지었고 조선어를 지키려는 그들의 노력을 지원했다.

**17** 조선어 학회 사건이 발생했을 때 그는 경찰에 잡혀 많은 고통을 겪었다.

**18** 일본인 관리들은 그에게 일본식 가옥을 지으라고 압박했다.

**19** 그는 말했다. "나는 일본식 가옥을 지을 줄 모르오."

**20** 한 관리가 말했다. "당신은 한옥을 지을 줄 아오. 그러니 일본식 가옥도 지을 수 있소."

**21** 그러나 그는 그 일본인이 그에게 요구한 것을 하지 않았다.

**22** 그 대가는 컸다.

**23** 그의 사업은 쇠퇴했고, 그는 재산을 잃었다.

**24** 그러나 부분적으로나마, 정세권 덕분에 한국의 전통이 오늘날 여전히 우리와 함께 살아 있다.

※ 다음 문장을 우리말로 쓰시오.

**1** The King of Architecture in Gyeongseong

➡ _____

**2** Have you been to Bukchon?

➡ _____

**3** There is a beautiful *hanok* village in Bukchon.

➡ _____

**4** It is popular with tourists who want to see Korea's past.

➡ _____

**5** However, not many people know that Bukchon was created through one man's efforts.

➡ _____

**6** That man was Jeong Segwon, known as the King of Architecture in Gyeongseong.

➡ _____

**7** Jeong Segwon was a businessman who founded Geonyangsa in 1920.

➡ _____

**8** At the time, Korea was ruled by Japan, and the Japanese were changing Gyeongseong to fit their taste.

➡ _____

**9** Many Japanese moving into Gyeongseong were building Japanese or Western houses.

➡ _____

**10** Jeong Segwon wanted to protect the *hanok* and help the suffering people.

➡ _____

**11** He said, "People are power. We Joseon people should keep Jongno and not let the Japanese set foot here."

➡ _____

**12** He bought the land between Gyeongbokgung and Changdeokgung.

➡ _____

**13** There he built small, modern *hanoks* for the people.

➡ _____

**14** Through his efforts, we now have Bukchon filled with its beautiful *hanoks*.

➡ _____

**15** Jeong Segwon helped the independence movement in many ways.

➡ _____

**16** For example, he built the office building for the Joseon Language Society and supported its efforts to keep the Joseon language alive.

➡ _____

**17** When the Joseon Language Affair happened, he was caught by the police and suffered a lot.

➡ _____

**18** Japanese officials pressed him to build Japanese houses.

➡ _____

**19** He said, "I don't know how to build Japanese houses."

➡ _____

**20** An official said, "You know how to build *hanoks*, so you can build Japanese houses, too."

➡ _____

**21** But he did not do what the Japanese told him to do.

➡ _____

**22** The cost was high.

➡ _____

**23** His business fell off, and he lost his property.

➡ _____

**24** However, in part, thanks to Jeong Segwon, the traditions of Korea still live with us today.

➡ _____

※ 다음 괄호 안의 단어들을 우리말에 맞도록 바르게 배열하시오.

**1** (King / The / Architecture / of / Gyeongseong / in)
➡ _____

**2** (you / have / to / been / Bukchon?)
➡ _____

**3** (is / there / a / *honok* / beautiful / Bukchon. / in / village)
➡ _____

**4** (is / it / with / popular / who / tourists / to / want / see / past. / Korea's)
➡ _____

**5** (not / however, / people / many / know / Bukchon / that / created / was / one / through / efforts. / man's)
➡ _____

**6** (man / that / Jeong / was / Segwon, / as / known / King / the / Architecture / of / Gyeongnseong. / in)
➡ _____

**7** (Segwon / Jeong / was / businessman / a / who / Geonyangsa / founded / 1920. / in)
➡ _____

**8** (the / at / time, / was / Korea / by / ruled / Japan, / and / Japanese / the / changing / were / to / Gyeongseong / fit / taste. / their)
➡ _____

**9** (Japanese / many / into / moving / Gyeongseong / were / Japanese / building / or / houses. / Western)
➡ _____

**10** (Segwon / Jeong / to / wanted / protect / *hanok* / the / help / and / suffering / the / people.)
➡ _____

**11** (said, / he / "people / power. / are // Joseon / we / people / keep / should / Jongno / not / and / the / let / Japanese / foot / here." / set)
➡ _____

**12** (bought / he / land / the / between / Changdeokgung. / and / Gyoengbokgung)
➡ _____

**13** (he / there / small, / built / *honoks* / modern / the / for / people.)
➡ _____

**14** (his / through / efforts, / now / we / have / filled / Bukchon / with / beautiful / its / *hanoks*.)
➡ _____

---

1 경성의 건축왕

2 당신은 북촌에 다녀온 적이 있는가?

3 북촌에는 아름다운 한옥 마을이 있다.

4 그곳은 한국의 과거를 보고 싶어 하는 관광객들에게 인기가 있다.

5 그러나 북촌이 한 사람의 노력으로 만들어졌다는 것을 아는 사람은 많지 않다.

6 그 사람은 경성의 건축왕으로 알려진 정세권이었다.

7 정세권은 1920년에 건양사를 설립한 사업가였다.

8 그 당시 한국은 일본의 지배를 받았고, 일본인들은 경성을 그들의 취향에 맞게 바꾸고 있었다.

9 경성으로 이주하는 많은 일본인들은 일본식이나 서양식 집들을 짓고 있었다.

10 정세권은 한옥을 지키고 고통받는 사람들을 돕기를 원했다.

11 그는 말했다. "사람이 힘이다. 우리 조선 사람들은 종로를 지켜야 하며, 일본인들이 이곳에 발을 붙이지 못하게 해야 한다."

12 그는 경복궁과 창덕궁 사이의 땅을 샀다.

13 거기에 그는 사람들을 위해 작은 현대식 한옥들을 지었다.

14 그의 노력으로 북촌은 현재 아름다운 한옥으로 가득 차 있다.

**15** (Segwon / Jeong / the / helped / movement / independence / in / ways. / many)

➡ _____

**16** (example, / for / built / he / office / the / for / building / the / Language / Joseon / Society / and / its / supported / to / efforts / keep / the / language / Joseon / alive.)

➡ _____

➡ _____

**17** (the / when / Joseon / Affair / Language / happened, / was / he / by / caught / the / police / suffered / and / lot. / a)

➡ _____

➡ _____

**18** (officials / Japanese / him / pressed / build / to / houses. / Japanese)

➡ _____

**19** (said, / he / "I / know / don't / to / how / Japanese / build / houses.")

➡ _____

**20** (official / an / said, / "you / how / know / to / build / *hanoks*, / you / so / build / can / houses, / Japanese / too.")

➡ _____

➡ _____

**21** (he / but / did / do / not / what / Japanese / the / him / told / do. / to)

➡ _____

**22** (cost / the / high. / was)

➡ _____

**23** (business / his / off, / fell / and / lost / he / property. / his)

➡ _____

**24** (however, / part, / in / to / thanks / Segwon, / Jeong / traditions / the / Korea / of / live / still / with / us / today. / us)

➡ _____

➡ _____

**15** 정세권은 여러 방법으로 독립운동을 도왔다.

**16** 예를 들면, 그는 조선어 학회를 위한 회관을 지었고 조선어를 지키려는 그들의 노력을 지원했다.

**17** 조선어 학회 사건이 발생했을 때 그는 경찰에 잡혀 많은 고통을 겪었다.

**18** 일본인 관리들은 그에게 일본식 가옥을 지으라고 압박했다.

**19** 그는 말했다. "나는 일본식 가옥을 지울 줄 모르오."

**20** 한 관리가 말했다. "당신은 한옥을 지을 줄 아오. 그러니 일본식 가옥도 지을 수 있소."

**21** 그러나 그는 그 일본인이 그에게 요구한 것을 하지 않았다.

**22** 그 대가는 컸다.

**23** 그의 사업은 쇠퇴했고, 그는 재산을 잃었다.

**24** 그러나 부분적으로나마, 정세권 덕분에 한국의 전통이 오늘날 여전히 우리와 함께 살아 있다.

※ 다음 우리말을 영어로 쓰시오.

**1** 경성의 건축왕

➡ _____

**2** 당신은 북촌에 다녀온 적이 있는가?

➡ _____

**3** 북촌에는 아름다운 한옥 마을이 있다.

➡ _____

**4** 그곳은 한국의 과거를 보고 싶어 하는 관광객들에게 인기가 있다.

➡ _____

**5** 그러나 북촌이 한 사람의 노력으로 만들어졌다는 것을 아는 사람은 많지 않다.

➡ _____

**6** 그 사람은 경성의 건축왕으로 알려진 정세권이었다.

➡ _____

**7** 정세권은 1920년에 건양사를 설립한 사업가였다.

➡ _____

**8** 그 당시 한국은 일본의 지배를 받았고, 일본인들은 경성을 그들의 취향에 맞게 바꾸고 있었다.

➡ _____

**9** 경성으로 이주하는 많은 일본인들은 일본식이나 서양식 집들을 짓고 있었다.

➡ _____

**10** 정세권은 한옥을 지키고 고통받는 사람들을 돕기를 원했다.

➡ _____

**11** 그는 말했다. "사람이 힘이다. 우리 조선 사람들은 종로를 지켜야 하며, 일본인들이 이곳에 발을 붙이지 못하게 해야 한다."

➡ _____

_____

**12** 그는 경복궁과 창덕궁 사이의 땅을 샀다.

➡ _____

**13** 거기에 그는 사람들을 위해 작은 현대식 한옥들을 지었다.

➡ _____

**14** 그의 노력으로 북촌은 현재 아름다운 한옥으로 가득 차 있다.

➡ _____

**15** 정세권은 여러 방법으로 독립운동을 도왔다.

➡ _____

**16** 예를 들면, 그는 조선어 학회를 위한 회관을 지었고 조선어를 지키려는 그들의 노력을 지원했다.

➡ _____
_____

**17** 조선어 학회 사건이 발생했을 때 그는 경찰에 잡혀 많은 고통을 겪었다.

➡ _____

**18** 일본인 관리들은 그에게 일본식 가옥을 지으라고 압박했다.

➡ _____

**19** 그는 말했다. "나는 일본식 가옥을 지울 줄 모르오."

➡ _____

**20** 한 관리가 말했다. "당신은 한옥을 지을 줄 아오. 그러니 일본식 가옥도 지을 수 있소."

➡ _____

**21** 그러나 그는 그 일본인이 그에게 요구한 것을 하지 않았다.

➡ _____

**22** 그 대가는 컸다.

➡ _____

**23** 그의 사업은 쇠퇴했고, 그는 재산을 잃었다.

➡ _____

**24** 그러나 부분적으로나마, 정세권 덕분에 한국의 전통이 오늘날 여전히 우리와 함께 살아 있다.

➡ _____

※ 다음 우리말과 일치하도록 빈칸에 알맞은 말을 쓰시오.

## Before You Read

1. _____ _____ _____ the Joseon people _____ _____ the Japanese language.
2. The Joseon people _____ _____ _____ the Joseon language _____.
3. The Joseon people _____ _____ _____ the country.
4. Soon, the _____ _____ _____ _____.

1. 일본 관리들은 조선 사람들에게 일본 어를 쓰도록 압박했다.
2. 조선 사람들은 조선어를 살아 있게 지 키려고 노력했다.
3. 조선 사람들은 나라를 지키기를 원했다.
4. 이윽고, 독립운동이 일어났다.

## Language in Use

1. A woman _____ _____ the building _____ _____ _____ _____.
2. She _____ _____ a new store.
3. Many people _____ _____ _____ to the woman's new store _____ _____ Joe's store.
4. _____ people _____ _____ _____ Joe's store.
5. His food business _____ _____.

1. 한 여인이 Joe의 가게 옆에 있는 건물 로 이사 왔다.
2. 그녀는 새로운 가게를 열었다.
3. 많은 사람들이 Joe의 가게 대신에 그 여인의 새 가게로 가기 시작했다.
4. Joe의 가게에 들어오는 사람들은 거의 없었다.
5. 그의 음식 장사는 쇠퇴했다.

## Writing Workshop

1. _____ is _____ Yongbok?
2. He lived _____ the _____ _____, and his job _____ _____ fish.
3. _____ he _____ _____, he _____ the Japanese people _____ _____ Ulleungdo.
4. He _____ Japan _____ and said that Ulleungdo and Dokdo _____ _____ _____ Korea.
5. In 1696, the _____ _____ _____ told the Japanese people _____ _____ _____ Ulleugdo and Dokdo.
6. He _____ _____ _____ _____ _____ Ulleungdo and Dokdo.

1. 안용복은 누구인가?
2. 그는 조선왕조 시대에 살았으며, 그의 직업은 물고기를 잡는 것이었다.
3. 그가 물고기를 잡고 있었을 때 그는 일본 사람들이 울릉도 근처에서 물고 기를 잡는 것을 보았다.
4. 그는 일본을 두 번 방문해서 울릉도와 독도는 한국에 속해 있다고 말했다.
5. 1696년에 일본인 통치자는 일본인들 에게 울릉도와 독도 근처에서 물고기 를 잡지 말라고 공식적으로 말했다.
6. 그는 울릉도와 독도를 지키기 위해 최 선을 다했다.

## 구석구석 지문 Test

※ 다음 우리말을 영어로 쓰시오.

### Before You Read

1. 일본 관리들은 조선 사람들에게 일본어를 쓰도록 압박했다.

   ➡ _____

2. 조선 사람들은 조선어를 살아 있게 지키려고 노력했다.

   ➡ _____

3. 조선 사람들은 나라를 지키기를 원했다.

   ➡ _____

4. 이윽고, 독립운동이 일어났다.

   ➡ _____

### Language in Use

1. 한 여인이 Joe의 가게 옆에 있는 건물로 이사 왔다.

   ➡ _____

2. 그녀는 새로운 가게를 열었다.

   ➡ _____

3. 많은 사람들이 Joe의 가게 대신에 그 여인의 새 가게로 가기 시작했다.

   ➡ _____

4. Joe의 가게에 들어오는 사람들은 거의 없었다.

   ➡ _____

5. 그의 음식 장사는 쇠퇴했다.

   ➡ _____

### Writing Workshop

1. 안용복은 누구인가?

   ➡ _____

2. 그는 조선왕조 시대에 살았으며, 그의 직업은 물고기를 잡는 것이었다.

   ➡ _____

3. 그가 물고기를 잡고 있었을 때 그는 일본 사람들이 울릉도 근처에서 물고기를 잡는 것을 보았다.

   ➡ _____

4. 그는 일본을 두 번 방문해서 울릉도와 독도는 한국에 속해 있다고 말했다.

   ➡ _____

5. 1696년에 일본인 통치자는 일본인들에게 울릉도와 독도 근처에서 물고기를 잡지 말라고 공식적으로 말했다.

   ➡ _____

6. 그는 울릉도와 독도를 지키기 위해 최선을 다했다.

   ➡ _____

※ 다음 영어를 우리말로 쓰시오.

| | | |
|---|---|---|
| 01 | blame | |
| 02 | century | |
| 03 | performance | |
| 04 | classical | |
| 05 | actually | |
| 06 | freely | |
| 07 | enjoyable | |
| 08 | healthy | |
| 09 | audience | |
| 10 | disturb | |
| 11 | secret | |
| 12 | appear | |
| 13 | work | |
| 14 | clap | |
| 15 | serious | |
| 16 | between | |
| 17 | imagine | |
| 18 | manners | |
| 19 | book fair | |
| 20 | memorable | |
| 21 | familiar | |

| | | |
|---|---|---|
| 22 | surprisingly | |
| 23 | dependent | |
| 24 | concerto | |
| 25 | trash can | |
| 26 | scene | |
| 27 | increased | |
| 28 | mostly | |
| 29 | nobleman | |
| 30 | noise | |
| 31 | orchestra | |
| 32 | correct | |
| 33 | movement | |
| 34 | result | |
| 35 | after some time | |
| 36 | as a result | |
| 37 | dependent on | |
| 38 | blame A for B | |
| 39 | for now | |
| 40 | go back in time | |
| 41 | at any time | |
| 42 | take care of | |
| 43 | with time | |

※ 다음 우리말을 영어로 쓰시오.

01 비난하다

02 박수치다

03 정지, 멈춤

04 올바른, 정확한

05 비밀

06 심각한, 진지한

07 방해하다

08 즐거운, 즐길 수 있는

09 나타나다

10 사회적인, 사교적인

11 놀랍게도

12 협주곡

13 관객

14 익숙한

15 움직임,
   (큰 교향곡 따위의) 악장(부분)

16 사실은

17 도서 박람회

18 결과

19 증가된

20 밝은

21 자유롭게

22 건강한

23 의존적인, 의존하는

24 예절

25 세기

26 고전의, 클래식 음악의

27 기억에 남을, 기억할 만한

28 공연

29 주로

30 상상하다

31 귀족

32 소음, 잡음

33 돌려주다, 반납하다

34 장면

35 그건 그렇고

36 ～을 살펴 보다

37 그 결과

38 우선은, 지금은

39 아무 때나

40 B 때문에 A를 비난하다

41 ～에 의존하는

42 얼마 후

43 더 이상 ～하지 않는

※ 다음 영영풀이에 알맞은 단어를 <보기>에서 골라 쓴 후, 우리말 뜻을 쓰시오.

1 _____ : full of light; shining strongly: _____

2 _____ : to start to be seen: _____

3 _____ : to hit your open hands together: _____

4 _____ : a loud or unpleasant sound: _____

5 _____ : to interrupt someone when they are trying to work, sleep, etc.:

_____

6 _____ : to make a high sound by blowing air through your lips or teeth:

_____

7 _____ : to stop talking or doing something for a short time before continuing:

_____

8 _____ : a fact or piece of information that is kept hidden from other people:

_____

9 _____ : a man from a family of high social rank; a female member of the

nobility: _____

10 _____ : the act of performing a play, concert, or some other form of

entertainment: _____

11 _____ : something that is caused by something else that happened or was done

before: _____

12 _____ : to think or say that someone or something is responsible for something

bad: _____

13 _____ : a piece of music for one or more solo instruments playing with an

orchestra: _____

14 _____ : something such as a book, song, or painting that is produced by a writer,

musician, artist, etc: _____

15 _____ : a group of musicians who play usually classical music together and who

are led by a conductor: _____

16 _____ : to bring something to the place that it came from or the place where it

should go: _____

| 보기 | | | |
|---|---|---|---|
| secret | performance | whistle | clap |
| noise | disturb | orchestra | concerto |
| result | work | return | nobleman |
| blame | pause | appear | bright |

※ 다음 우리말과 일치하도록 빈칸에 알맞은 말을 쓰시오.

**Listen & Speak 1 B**

1. **B:** Are you _____ _____ _____ to an opera? I have two _____.

   **G:** Yes, I love opera. _____ is it?

   **B:** It's _____ Saturday _____ 5:00. Can you _____ _____?

   **G:** Yes, _____ so much _____ _____ me.

2. **B:** _____ _____ we go to the new shoe shop _____ _____?

   **G:** Okay. _____ _____ at 2:00 _____ Saturday?

   **B:** Can you _____ _____ at 1:00? I _____ _____ _____ _____ _____ my sister at 3:00.

   **G:** Sure. _____ you _____.

해석

1. **B:** 너 오페라에 가는 것에 관심이 있니? 내게 표가 두 장 있어.
   **G:** 응, 나 오페라 아주 좋아해. 언제야?
   **B:** 이번 주 토요일 5시야. 갈 수 있니?
   **G:** 응. 나한테 물어봐 줘서 정말 고마워.

2. **B:** 우리 이번 주말에 새로 생긴 신발 가게에 가는 거 어때?
   **G:** 좋아. 토요일 2시 어때?
   **B:** 1시에 가능하니? 난 3시에 여동생을 돌봐야 해.
   **G:** 당연하지. 그때 보자.

**Listen & Speak 2 B**

1. **B:** We're _____ _____ Hangang this weekend. Do you _____?

   **G:** Of _____. _____ _____ to bring your camera.

   **B:** Okay. I _____. I'll _____ some snacks, _____.

   **G:** _____ great.

2. **G:** You _____ _____. What's your _____?

   **B:** Thanks. Well, I _____ _____ _____ _____. You should go with me _____.

   **G:** That _____ _____ fun. _____ things I _____ _____?

   **B:** _____ _____ _____ eat _____ _____ of fruits and vegetables, _____.

1. **B:** 우리 이번 주말에 한강 가잖아. 기억하니?
   **G:** 물론이지. 카메라 가져 오는 것 잊지 마.
   **B:** 알았어. 잊지 않을게. 나는 약간의 간식도 가져올게.
   **G:** 아주 좋아.

2. **G:** 너 건강해 보여. 비결이 뭐니?
   **B:** 고마워. 음, 나는 매일 수영하러 가. 너도 언젠가 나와 함께 가는 게 좋겠어.
   **G:** 재밌을 것 같은데. 내가 또 해야 하는 다른 것들이 있니?
   **B:** 다양한 종류의 과일과 채소를 먹는 것도 잊지 마.

### Real-Life Zone A

G: What are you _____ _____?

B: Classical music. I'm _____ _____ a concert tomorrow and I'd _____ _____ know about the music _____ I go.

G: I _____ it's _____ enjoyable _____ you know the music.

B: _____, I don't want to _____ at the _____ time.

G: _____ you just _____ _____ the music _____?

B: No. In classical music, one piece of music _____ have several _____. You should _____ and clap at the _____ _____.

G: I _____. _____ you _____ _____ _____ clap at the _____ _____. By the _____, can you _____ _____ to our soccer _____ tomorrow at 4:00?

B: Sure. I'll come to the _____ _____ the concert _____.

G: Okay. _____ you _____.

G: 무엇을 듣고 있니?

B: 클래식 음악. 나 내일 콘서트에 가는데 가기 전에 음악에 대해 알고 싶어.

G: 음악을 알면 더 즐길 수 있겠지.

B: 사실 박수를 잘못된 때에 치고 싶지 않아.

G: 그냥 음악이 멈추었을 때 박수를 치지 않니?

B: 아니야. 클래식 음악에선 음악 한 곡에 여러 번 멈춤이 있을 수가 있어. 기다렸다가 맨 마지막에 박수를 쳐야 해.

G: 그렇구나. 진짜 마지막에 박수를 치는 것을 잊지 마. 그건 그렇고, 내일 4시 축구 연습에 올 수 있니?

B: 물론이지. 콘서트가 끝난 후 연습에 갈게.

G: 좋아. 그때 보자.

### Real-Life Zone B

A: _____ _____ we go to the library on Monday _____ _____? Can you _____ it?

B: Sorry, but I _____. How _____ _____ Tuesday?

A: Okay. _____ _____ _____ _____ your library card.

B: All _____. I _____.

A: 월요일 방과 후에 도서관에 가는 게 어때? 갈 수 있니?

B: 미안하지만, 못 가. 화요일은 어때?

A: 좋아. 도서관 카드 가져오는 걸 잊지 마.

B: 알았어. 잊지 않을게.

### Wrap Up

G: Yunho! _____ you _____ about the Christmas concert at the city hall?

B: Yes. I _____ _____ a _____ opera singer _____ _____ on the stage.

G: Oh, then _____ _____ we go _____ Christmas Day? Can you _____ _____?

B: Sure. Do you know _____ _____ the concert starts?

G: It starts _____ 5:30. _____ _____ at the bus stop at 4:00.

B: Good. Don't _____ _____ dress _____.

G: Okay. I _____.

G: 윤호야! 너 시청에서 하는 크리스마스 콘서트에 대해 들어 봤어?

B: 응. 유명한 오페라 가수가 무대에 오를 것이라고 들었어.

G: 오, 그러면 크리스마스 날에 가는 게 어때? 갈 수 있니?

B: 물론이지. 너는 콘서트가 언제 시작하는지 아니?

G: 5시 30분에 시작해. 버스 정류장에서 4시에 만나자.

B: 좋아. 옷을 차려입는 것 잊지 마.

G: 알았어. 잊지 않을게.

※ 다음 우리말에 맞도록 대화를 영어로 쓰시오.

### Listen & Speak 1 B

1. B: _____
   G: _____
   B: _____
   G: _____

2. B: _____
   G: _____
   B: _____
   G: _____

1. B: 너 오페라에 가는 것에 관심이 있
      니? 내게 표가 두 장 있어.
   G: 응, 나 오페라 아주 좋아해. 언제야?
   B: 이번 주 토요일 5시야. 갈 수 있니?
   G: 응. 나한테 물어봐 줘서 정말 고마워.

2. B: 우리 이번 주말에 새로 생긴 신발
      가게에 가는 거 어때?
   G: 좋아. 토요일 2시 어때?
   B: 1시에 가능하니? 난 3시에 여동생
      을 돌봐야 해.
   G: 당연하지. 그때 보자.

### Listen & Speak 2 B

1. B: _____
   G: _____
   B: _____
   G: _____

2. G: _____
   B: _____
   G: _____
   B: _____

1. B: 우리 이번 주말에 한강 가잖아. 기
      억하니?
   G: 물론이지. 카메라 가져 오는 것 잊
      지 마.
   B: 알았어. 잊지 않을게. 나는 약간의
      간식도 가져올게.
   G: 아주 좋아.

2. G: 너 건강해 보여. 비결이 뭐니?
   B: 고마워. 음, 나는 매일 수영하러
      가. 너도 언젠가 나와 함께 가는
      게 좋겠어.
   G: 재밌을 것 같은데. 내가 또 해야
      하는 다른 것들이 있니?
   B: 다양한 종류의 과일과 채소를 먹는
      것도 잊지 마.

## Real-Life Zone A

G: _____

B: _____

_____

G: _____

B: _____

G: _____

B: _____

G: _____

_____

B: _____

G: _____

G: 무엇을 듣고 있니?

B: 클래식 음악. 나 내일 콘서트에 가는데 가기 전에 음악에 대해 알고 싶어.

G: 음악을 알면 더 즐길 수 있겠지.

B: 사실 박수를 잘못된 때에 치고 싶지 않아.

G: 그냥 음악이 멈추었을 때 박수를 치지 않니?

B: 아니야. 클래식 음악에선 음악 한 곡에 여러 번 멈춤이 있을 수가 있어. 기다렸다가 맨 마지막에 박수를 쳐야 해.

G: 그렇구나. 진짜 마지막에 박수를 치는 것을 잊지 마. 그건 그렇고, 내일 4시 축구 연습에 올 수 있니?

B: 물론이지. 콘서트가 끝난 후 연습에 갈게.

G: 좋아. 그때 보자.

## Real-Life Zone B

A: _____

B: _____

A: _____

B: _____

A: 월요일 방과 후에 도서관에 가는 게 어때? 갈 수 있니?

B: 미안하지만, 못 가. 화요일은 어때?

A: 좋아. 도서관 카드 가져오는 걸 잊지 마.

B: 알았어. 잊지 않을게.

## Wrap Up

G: _____

B: _____

G: _____

B: _____

G: _____

B: _____

G: _____

G: 윤호야! 너 시청에서 하는 크리스마스 콘서트에 대해 들어 봤어?

B: 응. 유명한 오페라 가수가 무대에 오를 것이라고 들었어.

G: 오, 그러면 크리스마스 날에 가는 게 어때? 갈 수 있니?

B: 물론이지. 너는 콘서트가 언제 시작하는지 아니?

G: 5시 30분에 시작해. 버스 정류장에서 4시에 만나자.

B: 좋아. 옷을 차려입는 것 잊지 마.

G: 알았어. 잊지 않을게.

※ 다음 우리말과 일치하도록 빈칸에 알맞은 것을 골라 쓰시오.

**1** The _____ of _____ Concert _____
A. Classical      B. History      C. Manners

**2** _____ _____ at a _____ music concert.
A. yourself      B. classical      C. imagine

**3** The _____ starts to _____ _____ of Mozart's piano _____.
A. one      B. orchestra      C. concertos      D. play

**4** The concert _____ is _____ and _____.
A. dark      B. hall      C. silent

**5** _____ makes a _____.
A. sound      B. nobody

**6** _____ looks _____.
A. serious      B. everybody

**7** The _____ only _____ after the concerto _____.
A. clap      B. audiences      C. finishes

**8** This is a _____ _____ _____ concerts today.
A. scene      B. at      C. familiar

**9** Let's go _____ in time and _____ a _____ at one of Mozart's concerts in the 18th _____.
A. take      B. century      C. back      D. look

**10** You are in a _____ hall _____ a _____ house.
A. nobleman's      B. bright      C. inside

**11** Mozart is _____ the _____.
A. playing      B. piano

**12** _____, however, the _____ are eating, drinking, and _____ _____.
A. audiences      B. freely      C. surprisingly      D. talking

**13** They _____ and _____ at any _____.
A. clap      B. time      C. whistle

**14** You are _____ by their _____ manners, but Mozart _____ would be _____ by today's quiet audiences.
A. himself      B. shocked      C. bad      D. surprised

**15** Concerts in Mozart's _____ were _____ _____ _____.
A. mostly      B. time      C. events      D. social

**16** They were _____ _____ _____ _____ people.
A. places      B. meet      C. good      D. to

**17** _____ was _____ _____ of the _____.
A. part      B. concert      C. noise      D. just

---

1 클래식 콘서트 관람 예절의 역사

2 당신이 클래식 공연장에 있다고 상상해 보아라.

3 오케스트라가 모차르트의 피아노 협주곡들 중 한 곡을 연주하기 시작한다.

4 콘서트장은 어둡고 조용하다.

5 아무도 소리를 내지 않는다.

6 모두가 진지하게 보인다.

7 청중은 오직 협주곡이 끝난 후에만 손뼉을 친다.

8 이것이 오늘날 콘서트에서 익숙한 장면이다.

9 과거로 거슬러 올라가서 18세기 모차르트의 콘서트들 중 하나를 살펴보자.

10 당신은 한 귀족의 집안 밝은 홀에 있다.

11 모차르트는 피아노를 치고 있다.

12 하지만 놀랍게도, 청중들은 먹고 마시며 자유롭게 대화하고 있다.

13 그들은 아무 때나 휘파람을 불고 박수를 친다.

14 당신은 그들의 나쁜 매너에 충격을 받지만, 모차르트 자신은 오늘날의 조용한 청중에게 놀랄지도 모른다.

15 모차르트 시대의 콘서트는 주로 사교적인 행사였다.

16 콘서트는 사람을 만나기에 좋은 장소였다.

17 소음은 그저 콘서트의 일부였다.

**18** Today's _____ concerts began in the 19th _____ _____ many big concert halls were _____.

    A. century        B. built        C. quiet        D. when

**19** _____ people, _____ _____ _____, went to concerts.

    A. noblemen        B. more        C. just        D. not

**20** Artists were _____ _____ _____ _____ noblemen for money.

    A. on        B. longer        C. dependent        D. no

**21** The artists had _____ power over their _____ and started to _____ their _____ power.

    A. increased        B. works        C. more        D. use

**22** _____ _____, Wagner _____ the audience for making _____.

    A. blamed        B. for        C. noise        D. example

**23** _____ some _____, a no-clapping-between-movements _____ _____.

    A. time        B. appeared        C. after        D. rule

**24** _____ a _____, here we are today, very _____ and _____.

    A. serious        B. result        C. quiet        D. as

**25** We do not know _____ concerts will look _____ in the future _____ manners _____ with time.

    A. because        B. like        C. what        D. change

**26** For now, _____, if you want to _____ _____ music concerts, just _____ this:

    A. classical        B. however        C. remember        D. enjoy

**27** _____ the music, but do not _____ those _____ you.

    A. disturb        B. enjoy        C. around

---

**18** 오늘날의 조용한 콘서트는 많은 대형 공연장이 생긴 19세기에 시작됐다.

**19** 귀족뿐만 아니라 더 많은 사람들이 콘서트에 갔다.

**20** 예술가들은 더 이상 돈을 벌기 위해 귀족들에게 의존하지 않았다.

**21** 예술가들은 자신의 작품에 더 많은 권한이 생겼고 그 힘을 사용하기 시작했다.

**22** 예를 들어, 바그너는 소음을 낸다는 것 때문에 관객들을 비난했다.

**23** 얼마 후에 '악장 사이 박수 금지 규칙'이 생겼다.

**24** 그 결과, 오늘날 우리는, 매우 조용하고 진지하다.

**25** 예절은 시대에 따라 변하기 때문에 우리는 콘서트가 미래에는 어떤 모습일지 모른다.

**26** 하지만 지금은 당신이 클래식 음악 공연을 즐기고 싶다면 이것만은 기억해라:

**27** 음악은 즐기되 당신 주변의 다른 사람들을 방해하지 마라.

※ 다음 우리말과 일치하도록 빈칸에 알맞은 말을 쓰시오.

1  The _____ of _____ Concert _____

2  _____ _____ at a _____ music concert.

3  The _____ starts to _____ _____ _____ Mozart's _____ concertos.

4  The concert _____ is _____ and _____.

5  _____ makes a _____.

6  _____ looks _____.

7  The _____ only _____ after the _____ _____.

8  This is a _____ _____ _____ concerts today.

9  _____ _____ _____ in _____ and _____ a _____ at _____ _____ Mozart's concerts in the 18th century.

10  You are in a _____ hall _____ a _____ house.

11  Mozart is _____ the _____.

12  _____, however, the _____ are eating, drinking, and _____ _____.

13  They _____ and _____ _____ _____ _____.

14  You are _____ _____ their _____ _____, but Mozart _____ would be _____ _____ today's _____ audiences.

15  Concerts in Mozart's time _____ _____ _____ events.

16  They were _____ _____ _____ _____ people.

17  _____ was _____ _____ _____ the concert.

1  클래식 콘서트 관람 예절의 역사

2  당신이 클래식 공연장에 있다고 상상해 보아라.

3  오케스트라가 모차르트의 피아노 협주곡들 중 한 곡을 연주하기 시작한다.

4  콘서트장은 어둡고 조용하다.

5  아무도 소리를 내지 않는다.

6  모두가 진지하게 보인다.

7  청중은 오직 협주곡이 끝난 후에만 손뼉을 친다.

8  이것이 오늘날 콘서트에서 익숙한 장면이다.

9  과거로 거슬러 올라가서 18세기 모차르트의 콘서트들 중 하나를 살펴보자.

10  당신은 한 귀족의 집안 밝은 홀에 있다.

11  모차르트는 피아노를 치고 있다.

12  하지만 놀랍게도, 청중들은 먹고 마시며 자유롭게 대화하고 있다.

13  그들은 아무 때나 휘파람을 불고 박수를 친다.

14  당신은 그들의 나쁜 매너에 충격을 받지만, 모차르트 자신은 오늘날의 조용한 청중에게 놀랄지도 모른다.

15  모차르트 시대의 콘서트는 주로 사교적인 행사였다.

16  콘서트는 사람을 만나기에 좋은 장소였다.

17  소음은 그저 콘서트의 일부였다.

**18** Today's _____ concerts began in the 19th _____ _____ many big concert halls _____ _____.

**19** More people, _____ _____ _____, went to concerts.

**20** Artists were _____ _____ _____ on noblemen _____ _____.

**21** The artists had _____ _____ over their _____ and started to _____ their _____ _____.

**22** _____ _____, Wagner _____ the audience _____ _____ _____.

**23** _____ _____ _____, a no-clapping-between-movements _____ _____.

**24** _____ _____ _____, here we are today, very _____ and _____.

**25** We do not know _____ _____ will _____ _____ in the future _____ manners _____ _____ _____.

**26** _____ _____, _____, if you want to _____ _____ music concerts, _____ _____ this:

**27** _____ the music, but _____ _____ _____ _____ _____ you.

**18** 오늘날의 조용한 콘서트는 많은 대형 공연장이 생긴 19세기에 시작됐다.

**19** 귀족뿐만 아니라 더 많은 사람들이 콘서트에 갔다.

**20** 예술가들은 더 이상 돈을 벌기 위해 귀족들에게 의존하지 않았다.

**21** 예술가들은 자신의 작품에 더 많은 권한이 생겼고 그 힘을 사용하기 시작했다.

**22** 예를 들어, 바그너는 소음을 낸다는 것 때문에 관객들을 비난했다.

**23** 얼마 후에 '악장 사이 박수 금지 규칙'이 생겼다.

**24** 그 결과, 오늘날 우리는, 매우 조용하고 진지하다.

**25** 예절은 시대에 따라 변하기 때문에 우리는 콘서트가 미래에는 어떤 모습일지 모른다.

**26** 하지만 지금은 당신이 클래식 음악 공연을 즐기고 싶다면 이것만은 기억해라:

**27** 음악은 즐기되 당신 주변의 다른 사람들을 방해하지 마라.

※ 다음 문장을 우리말로 쓰시오.

**1** The History of Classical Concert Manners

➡ _____

**2** Imagine yourself at a classical music concert.

➡ _____

**3** The orchestra starts to play one of Mozart's piano concertos.

➡ _____

**4** The concert hall is dark and silent.

➡ _____

**5** Nobody makes a sound.

➡ _____

**6** Everybody looks serious.

➡ _____

**7** The audiences only clap after the concerto finishes.

➡ _____

**8** This is a familiar scene at concerts today.

➡ _____

**9** Let's go back in time and take a look at one of Mozart's concerts in the 18th century.

➡ _____

**10** You are in a bright hall inside a nobleman's house.

➡ _____

**11** Mozart is playing the piano.

➡ _____

**12** Surprisingly, however, the audiences are eating, drinking, and talking freely.

➡ _____

**13** They whistle and clap at any time.

➡ _____

**14**  You are shocked by their bad manners, but Mozart himself would be surprised by today's quiet audiences.

➡ _____

**15**  Concerts in Mozart's time were mostly social events.

➡ _____

**16**  They were good places to meet people.

➡ _____

**17**  Noise was just part of the concert.

➡ _____

**18**  Today's quiet concerts began in the 19th century when many big concert halls were built.

➡ _____

**19**  More people, not just noblemen, went to concerts.

➡ _____

**20**  Artists were no longer dependent on noblemen for money.

➡ _____

**21**  The artists had more power over their works and started to use their increased power.

➡ _____

**22**  For example, Wagner blamed the audience for making noise.

➡ _____

**23**  After some time, a no-clapping-between-movements rule appeared.

➡ _____

**24**  As a result, here we are today, very quiet and serious.

➡ _____

**25**  We do not know what concerts will look like in the future because manners change with time.

➡ _____

**26**  For now, however, if you want to enjoy classical music concerts, just remember this:

➡ _____

**27**  Enjoy the music, but do not disturb those around you.

➡ _____

※ 다음 괄호 안의 단어들을 우리말에 맞도록 바르게 배열하시오.

**1** (History / The / Classical / of / Manners / Concert)
➡ _____

**2** (yourself / imagine / a / at / music / classical / concert.)
➡ _____

**3** (orchestra / the / to / starts / one / play / of / piano / Mozart's / concertos.)
➡ _____

**4** (concert / the / is / hall / silent. / and / dark)
➡ _____

**5** (makes / nobody / sound. / a)
➡ _____

**6** (looks / everybody / serious.)
➡ _____

**7** (audiences / the / clap / only / the / after / finishes. / concerto)
➡ _____

**8** (is / this / a / familiar / at / scene / today. / concerts)
➡ _____

**9** (go / let's / back / time / in / and / a / take / look / one / at / Mozart's / of / in / concerts / 18th / the / century.)
➡ _____
_____

**10** (are / you / a / in / bright / inside / hall / nobleman's / a / house.)
➡ _____

**11** (is / Mozart / the / piano. / playing)
➡ _____

**12** (however, / surprisingly, / audiences / the / eating, / are / drinking, / talking / and / freely.)
➡ _____
_____

**13** (whistle / they / clap / and / any / at / time.)
➡ _____

**14** (are / you / by / shocked / bad / their / manners, / Mozart / but / would / himself / surprised / be / today's / by / audiences. / quiet)
➡ _____
_____

**15** (in / concerts / time / Mozart's / mostly / were / events. / social)
➡ _____

**16** (were / they / places / good / meet / to / people.)
➡ _____

**17** (was / noise / part / just / concert. / the / of)
➡ _____

**1** 클래식 콘서트 관람 예절의 역사

**2** 당신이 클래식 공연장에 있다고 상상해 보아라.

**3** 오케스트라가 모차르트의 피아노 협주곡들 중 한 곡을 연주하기 시작한다.

**4** 콘서트장은 어둡고 조용하다.

**5** 아무도 소리를 내지 않는다.

**6** 모두가 진지하게 보인다.

**7** 청중은 오직 협주곡이 끝난 후에만 손뼉을 친다.

**8** 이것이 오늘날 콘서트에서 익숙한 장면이다.

**9** 과거로 거슬러 올라가서 18세기 모차르트의 콘서트들 중 하나를 살펴보자.

**10** 당신은 한 귀족의 집안 밝은 홀에 있다.

**11** 모차르트는 피아노를 치고 있다.

**12** 하지만 놀랍게도, 청중들은 먹고 마시며 자유롭게 대화하고 있다.

**13** 그들은 아무 때나 휘파람을 불고 박수를 친다.

**14** 당신은 그들의 나쁜 매너에 충격을 받지만, 모차르트 자신은 오늘날의 조용한 청중에게 놀랄지도 모른다.

**15** 모차르트 시대의 콘서트는 주로 사교적인 행사였다.

**16** 콘서트는 사람을 만나기에 좋은 장소였다.

**17** 소음은 그저 콘서트의 일부였다.

**18** (quiet / today's / began / concerts / in / 19th / the / when / century / big / many / halls / concert / built. / were)

➡ _____

_____

**19** (people, / more / just / not / noblemen, / to / went / concerts.)

➡ _____

**20** (were / artists / longer / no / dependent / noblemen / on / money. / for)

➡ _____

**21** (artists / the / more / had / over / power / their / works / and / to / started / use / increased / their / power.)

➡ _____

_____

**22** (example, / for / blamed / Wagner / audience / the / making / noise. / for)

➡ _____

_____

**23** (some / after / time, / no-clapping-between-movements / a / appeared. / rule)

➡ _____

**24** (a / as / result, / we / here / today, / are / quiet / very / serious. / and)

➡ _____

**25** (do / we / know / not / concerts / what / will / like / look / the / in / future / manners / because / with / change / time.)

➡ _____

**26** (now, / for / however, / you / if / to / want / classical / enjoy / concerts, / music / remember / just / this:)

➡ _____

_____

**27** (the / enjoy / music, / do / but / disturb / not / around / you. / those)

➡ _____

**18** 오늘날의 조용한 콘서트는 많은 대형 공연장이 생긴 19세기에 시작됐다.

**19** 귀족뿐만 아니라 더 많은 사람들이 콘서트에 갔다.

**20** 예술가들은 더 이상 돈을 벌기 위해 귀족들에게 의존하지 않았다.

**21** 예술가들은 자신의 작품에 더 많은 권한이 생겼고 그 힘을 사용하기 시작했다.

**22** 예를 들어, 바그너는 소음을 낸다는 것 때문에 관객들을 비난했다.

**23** 얼마 후에 '악장 사이 박수 금지 규칙'이 생겼다.

**24** 그 결과, 오늘날 우리는, 매우 조용하고 진지하다.

**25** 예절은 시대에 따라 변하기 때문에 우리는 콘서트가 미래에는 어떤 모습일지 모른다.

**26** 하지만 지금은 당신이 클래식 음악 공연을 즐기고 싶다면 이것만은 기억해라:

**27** 음악은 즐기되 당신 주변의 다른 사람들을 방해하지 마라.

※ 다음 우리말을 영어로 쓰시오.

**1** 클래식 콘서트 관람 예절의 역사
➡ _____

**2** 당신이 클래식 공연장에 있다고 상상해 보아라.
➡ _____

**3** 오케스트라가 모차르트의 피아노 협주곡들 중 한 곡을 연주하기 시작한다.
➡ _____

**4** 콘서트장은 어둡고 조용하다.
➡ _____

**5** 아무도 소리를 내지 않는다.
➡ _____

**6** 모두가 진지하게 보인다.
➡ _____

**7** 청중은 오직 협주곡이 끝난 후에만 손뼉을 친다.
➡ _____

**8** 이것이 오늘날 콘서트에서 익숙한 장면이다.
➡ _____

**9** 과거로 거슬러 올라가서 18세기 모차르트의 콘서트들 중 하나를 살펴보자.
➡ _____

**10** 당신은 한 귀족의 집안 밝은 홀에 있다.
➡ _____

**11** 모차르트는 피아노를 치고 있다.
➡ _____

**12** 하지만 놀랍게도, 청중들은 먹고 마시며 자유롭게 대화하고 있다.
➡ _____

**13** 그들은 아무 때나 휘파람을 불고 박수를 친다.
➡ _____

**14** 당신은 그들의 나쁜 매너에 충격을 받지만, 모차르트 자신은 오늘날의 조용한 청중에게 놀랄지도 모른다.
➡ _____

**15** 모차르트 시대의 콘서트는 주로 사교적인 행사였다.
➡ _____

**16** 콘서트는 사람을 만나기에 좋은 장소였다.
➡ _____

**17** 소음은 그저 콘서트의 일부였다.
➡ _____

**18** 오늘날의 조용한 콘서트는 많은 대형 공연장이 생긴 19세기에 시작됐다.

➡ _____

**19** 귀족뿐만 아니라 더 많은 사람들이 콘서트에 갔다.

➡ _____

**20** 예술가들은 더 이상 돈을 벌기 위해 귀족들에게 의존하지 않았다.

➡ _____

**21** 예술가들은 자신의 작품에 더 많은 권한이 생겼고 그 힘을 사용하기 시작했다.

➡ _____

**22** 예를 들어, 바그너는 소음을 낸다는 것 때문에 관객들을 비난했다.

➡ _____

**23** 얼마 후에 '악장 사이 박수 금지 규칙'이 생겼다.

➡ _____

**24** 그 결과, 오늘날 우리는, 매우 조용하고 진지하다.

➡ _____

**25** 예절은 시대에 따라 변하기 때문에 우리는 콘서트가 미래에는 어떤 모습일지 모른다.

➡ _____

**26** 하지만 지금은 당신이 클래식 음악 공연을 즐기고 싶다면 이것만은 기억해라.

➡ _____

**27** 음악은 즐기되 당신 주변의 다른 사람들을 방해하지 마라.

➡ _____

※ 다음 우리말과 일치하도록 빈칸에 알맞은 말을 쓰시오.

## Before You Read B

1. A _____ to Good _____ _____

2. _____ a classical music concert can be a _____ _____ if you _____ these tips _____ _____.

3. _____ You _____ In:

4. _____ _____ _____ 20-30 minutes before _____ _____.

5. _____ _____ what music _____ _____ _____ _____.

6. _____ Music _____ _____:

7. _____ _____ your cellphone!

8. _____ quiet. _____ talking, _____, singing _____ _____ the music.

9. _____ _____ until the whole _____ _____ _____.

10. _____ is safe _____ _____ when the audience starts _____.

1. 콘서트 예절에 대한 안내
2. 당신이 이와 같은 조언들을 명심한다면 클래식 콘서트를 보는 것은 기억에 남는 경험이 될 것이다.
3. 들어가기 전:
4. 콘서트 시간 20–30분 전에 도착하길 계획하라.
5. 어떤 음악이 연주될지 알아보아라.
6. 음악이 연주될 때:
7. 휴대 전화를 꺼라.
8. 조용히 머물러라. 말하거나 휘파람을 불거나 음악에 따라 노래하지 말아라.
9. 전체의 곡이 끝날 때까지 박수치지 말아라.
10. 관객들이 박수 치기 시작할 때 박수를 치는 것이 안전하다.

## Writing Workshop

1. Music Concert _____

2. _____ February 2, I went _____ _____ _____ _____ at the Seoul Arts Center _____ Jo Seongu's piano concert _____ _____.

3. It was a great _____ _____ _____ _____ _____ him _____ _____.

4. He _____ Chopin's _____ _____ No. 1.

5. I did not know _____ _____ _____ _____ _____ _____.

6. I liked his _____ _____.

7. I _____ _____ _____ this experience.

1. 음악 콘서트 리뷰
2. 2월 2일에 나는 조성우의 피아노 콘서트가 열린 서울아트 센터의 콘서트홀에 갔다.
3. 그가 라이브로 연주하는 것을 듣는 것은 훌륭한 기회였다.
4. 그는 쇼팽의 피아노 협주곡 1번을 연주했다.
5. 나는 클래식 공연이 얼마나 아름다운지 몰랐다.
6. 나는 그의 라이브 공연이 아주 마음에 들었다.
7. 나는 이 경험을 잊지 않을 것이다.

## Wrap Up 7

1. Reporter: _____ is your new album _____ _____?

2. Justin Otter: It's _____ _____ next month.

3. Reporter: What are _____ _____ _____ _____ the new album?

4. Justin Otter: I'm _____ _____ _____ a concert at the Super Stadium.

5. My hero Michael Johnson _____ _____ _____ his concerts _____ _____ _____ _____ at the place.

1. 기자: 당신의 새 앨범은 언제 나오나요?
2. 저스틴 오터: 다음 달에 나옵니다.
3. 기자: 새 앨범에 대한 계획은 무엇인가요?
4. 저스틴 오터: 저는 수퍼 스타디움에서 콘서트를 가질 계획입니다.
5. 저의 영웅인 마이클 존슨이 세계 공연 동안 콘서트들 중 하나를 그 장소에서 열었거든요.

Step2

※ 다음 우리말을 영어로 쓰시오.

### Before You Read B

1. 콘서트 예절에 대한 안내
➡ _____

2. 당신이 이와 같은 조언들을 명심한다면 클래식 콘서트를 보는 것은 기억에 남는 경험이 될 것이다.
➡ _____

3. 들어가기 전:
➡ _____

4. 콘서트 시간 20-30분 전에 도착하길 계획하라.
➡ _____

5. 어떤 음악이 연주될지 알아보아라.
➡ _____

6. 음악이 연주될 때:
➡ _____

7. 휴대 전화를 꺼라.
➡ _____

8. 조용히 머물러라. 말하거나 휘파람을 불거나 음악에 따라 노래하지 말아라.
➡ _____

9. 전체의 곡이 끝날 때까지 박수치지 말아라.
➡ _____

10. 관객들이 박수 치기 시작할 때 박수를 치는 것이 안전하다.
➡ _____

### Writing Workshop

1. 음악 콘서트 리뷰
➡ _____

2. 2월 2일에 나는 조성우의 피아노 콘서트가 열린 서울아트 센터의 콘서트홀에 갔다.
➡ _____

3. 그가 라이브로 연주하는 것을 듣는 것은 훌륭한 기회였다.
➡ _____

4. 그는 쇼팽의 피아노 협주곡 1번을 연주했다.
➡ _____

5. 나는 클래식 공연이 얼마나 아름다운지 몰랐다.
➡ _____

6. 나는 그의 라이브 공연이 아주 마음에 들었다.
➡ _____

7. 나는 이 경험을 잊지 않을 것이다.
➡ _____

### Wrap Up 7

1. 기자: 당신의 새 앨범은 언제 나오나요?
➡ _____

2. 저스틴 오터: 다음 달에 나옵니다.
➡ _____

3. 기자: 새 앨범에 대한 계획은 무엇인가요?
➡ _____

4. 저스틴 오터: 저는 수퍼 스타디움에서 콘서트를 가질 계획입니다.
➡ _____

5. 저의 영웅인 마이클 존슨이 세계 공연 동안 콘서트들 중 하나를 그 장소에서 열었거든요.
➡ _____

※ 다음 영어를 우리말로 쓰시오.

01 pig

02 dump

03 barn

04 enter

05 fair

06 above

07 ad

08 feed

09 die

10 spider

11 as

12 crowd

13 nobody

14 attention

15 human

16 without

17 last

18 dead

19 miracle

20 must

21 save

22 farm

23 sheep

24 narrator

25 excitement

26 shining

27 pen

28 rat

29 weave

30 web

31 terrific

32 out of

33 fatten up

34 look+형용사

35 care for

36 right away

37 get[win] a prize

38 share A with B

39 run out of

40 Why don't you ~?

41 between A and B

42 too 형용사 to 동사원형

※ 다음 우리말을 영어로 쓰시오.

| | | |
|---|---|---|
| 01 | 쥐 | |
| 02 | 거미줄 | |
| 03 | 거미 | |
| 04 | 군중, 무리 | |
| 05 | 죽다 | |
| 06 | 아무도 ~ 않다 | |
| 07 | ~하다시피 | |
| 08 | (가축의) 우리 | |
| 09 | 헛간 | |
| 10 | 흥분, 신남 | |
| 11 | 박람회 | |
| 12 | 양 | |
| 13 | 농장 | |
| 14 | ~보다 위에 | |
| 15 | 광고 | |
| 16 | 먹이를 주다 | |
| 17 | 구하다 | |
| 18 | 서술자, 내레이터 | |
| 19 | 죽은 | |
| 20 | 인간의 | |
| 21 | 관심 | |

| | | |
|---|---|---|
| 22 | 지속되다 | |
| 23 | ~해야 하다 | |
| 24 | 반짝이는, 빛나는 | |
| 25 | ~ 없이, ~하지 않고 | |
| 26 | 쓰레기 폐기장 | |
| 27 | 돼지 | |
| 28 | (~을) 출전시키다 | |
| 29 | 훌륭한 | |
| 30 | (실을) 엮다 | |
| 31 | 기적 | |
| 32 | 즉시, 곧바로 | |
| 33 | (재료) ~으로 | |
| 34 | ~을 돌보다 | |
| 35 | 살찌우다 | |
| 36 | A와 B 사이에 | |
| 37 | ~하게 보이다 | |
| 38 | 너무 ~해서 …할 수 없다 | |
| 39 | ~하는 게 어때? | |
| 40 | ~이 다 떨어지다 | |
| 41 | 상을 받다 | |
| 42 | A를 B와 나누다 | |

※ 다음 영영풀이에 알맞은 단어를 <보기>에서 골라 쓴 후, 우리말 뜻을 쓰시오.

1 _____ : relating to people: _____

2 _____ : higher than something else: _____

3 _____ : a place for depositing rubbish: _____

4 _____ : a feeling of enthusiasm and interest: _____

5 _____ : an animal that has a long tail and looks like a large mouse: _____

6 _____ : a thin net made by a spider to catch insects: _____

7 _____ : making or reflecting bright light: _____

8 _____ : to continue to exist or happen for a specified period of time: _____

9 _____ : a good event that is very surprising or difficult to believe: _____

10 _____ : a small area with a fence round it where farm animals are kept:

_____

11 _____ : a farm animal whose skin is covered with thick curly hair called wool:

_____

12 _____ : a creature with eight legs that catches insects for food: _____

13 _____ : to officially state that someone will participate in a competition, race, or

examination: _____

14 _____ : a large group of people who have gathered together in one place in a

disorganized way: _____

15 _____ : to form cloth by crossing threads over and under each other by hand or

by using a machine: _____

16 _____ : a person who tells a story in a book, movie, or play or gives an account

of something: _____

| 보기 | | | |
|---|---|---|---|
| weave | last | sheep | dump |
| above | enter | human | crowd |
| web | rat | miracle | pen |
| shining | narrator | spider | excitement |

※ 다음 우리말과 일치하도록 빈칸에 알맞은 것을 골라 쓰시오.

**1**  _____ _____
A. Web        B. Charlotte's

**2**  _____: The _____ of Wilbur the pig on Mr. and Mrs. Allen's _____
A. pen        B. setting        C. farm

**3**  _____: Narrator 1, 2, 3, Wilbur: A pig, Charlotte: A _____, Mr. and Mrs. Allen: Farm _____, Old Sheep, Duck, Rat
A. owners        B. spider        C. roles

**Scene 1**

**4**  Narrator 1: *Charlotte's Web* is a story of _____ _____ Wilbur the pig _____ Charlotte the spider.
A. and        B. between        C. friendship

**5**  Narrator 2: They _____ _____ Mr. and Mrs. Allen's _____ Old Sheep, Duck, and Rat.
A. on        B. with        C. lived        D. farm

**6**  Narrator 3: _____ day, Mr. and Mrs. Allen were talking _____ the _____.
A. outside        B. one        C. barn

**7**  Mrs. Allen: Wilbur _____ very _____.
A. good        B. looks

**8**  Mr. Allen: He'll _____ _____ _____ for Christmas.
A. bacon        B. make        C. good

**9**  Old Sheep: They _____ _____ Wilbur _____ for Christmas!
A. up        B. fattening        C. are

**10**  Duck: _____ _____!
A. bacon        B. for

**11**  Wilbur: No! I'm _____ young _____ _____!
A. to        B. too        C. die

**12**  Charlotte: You _____, Wilbur. I'll _____ you.
A. save        B. won't

**13**  _____: _____?
A. how        B. Wilbur

**14**  Charlotte: I don't _____ _____, but _____?
A. yet        B. remember        C. know

**15**  You _____ me when Mr. Allen tried to _____ my web _____!
A. clean        B. saved        C. off

**16**  Now it's my _____ _____ _____ you.
A. to        B. save        C. turn

1  샬럿의 거미줄

2  배경: 앨런 부부 농장의 돼지 윌버의 우리

3  배역: 서술자 1, 2, 3, 돼지 윌버, 거미 샬럿, 농장 주인 앨런 부부, 늙은 양, 오리, 쥐

**장면 1**

4  서술자 1: "샬럿의 거미줄"은 돼지 윌버와 거미 샬럿 사이의 우정 이야기다.

5  서술자 2: 그들은 늙은 양, 오리, 쥐와 함께 앨런 부부의 농장에서 살았다.

6  서술자 3: 어느 날, 앨런 부부는 헛간 밖에서 이야기하고 있었다.

7  앨런 부인: 윌버가 아주 좋아 보여요.

8  앨런 씨: 그는 크리스마스에 좋은 베이컨이 될 거예요.

9  늙은 양: 그들은 크리스마스를 위해 윌버를 살찌우고 있어.

10  오리: 베이컨을 위해!

11  윌버: 안 돼! 나는 죽기에 너무 어려.

12  샬럿: 죽지 않을 거야, 윌버. 내가 널 구할게.

13  윌버: 어떻게?

14  샬럿: 아직 잘 모르겠어. 그런데 기억나?

15  앨런 씨가 거미줄을 없애려고 했을 때 네가 나를 구했잖아.

16  이제 내가 너를 구할 차례야.

**Scene 2**

**17** Charlotte: _____ _____ I _____ Wilbur?

    A. can         B. save         C. how

**18** Hmm.... Oh, I _____ an _____!

    A. idea         B. have

**19** Narrator 1: That night, Charlotte started _____ _____ something _____ Wilbur's pen.

    A. weave         B. above         C. to

**20** She worked _____ all night _____ _____.

    A. without         B. hard         C. sleeping

**21** Narrator 2: The _____ morning, Mr. and Mrs. Allen came _____ _____ Wilbur.

    A. to         B. next         C. feed

**22** Mrs. Allen: Look! _____ are _____ in the _____. "Some Pig"!

    A. words         B. there         C. web

**23** Mr. Allen: _____ _____!

    A. miracle         B. a

**24** Narrator 3: Soon, a _____ _____ came to _____ Wilbur.

    A. crowd         B. large         C. see

**Scene 3**

**25** Narrator 1: _____ time _____, only a _____ people came.

    A. passed         B. few         C. as

**26** Charlotte _____ _____ _____.

    A. meeting         B. called         C. a

**27** Charlotte: _____ we saw, human _____ does not _____ long.

    A. attention         B. as         C. last

**28** If nobody _____ _____ Wilbur, he will _____ _____ before Christmas.

    A. for         B. dead         C. cares         D. be

**29** We _____ write _____ _____ soon.

    A. word         B. must         C. another

**30** Duck: I have an _____! _____ _____ "Terrific"?

    A. about         B. how         C. idea

**31** Old Sheep: I _____ _____!

    A. it         B. like

---

**장면 2**

**17** 샬럿: 내가 어떻게 윌버를 구할 수 있을까?

**18** 음… 오, 좋은 생각이 났어!

**19** 서술자 1: 그날 밤, 샬럿은 윌버의 우리 위에 무언가를 짜기 시작했다.

**20** 그녀는 밤새도록 자지 않고 열심히 일했다.

**21** 서술자 2: 다음 날 아침, 앨런 부부는 윌버에게 먹이를 주러 왔다.

**22** 앨런 부인: 보세요! 거미줄에 단어들이 있어요. '대단한 돼지'!

**23** 앨런 씨: 기적이야!

**24** 서술자 3: 곧 많은 군중들이 윌버를 보러 왔다.

**장면 3**

**25** 서술자 1: 시간이 지날수록 극소수의 사람들만이 왔다.

**26** 샬럿은 회의를 소집했다.

**27** 샬럿: 보았다시피 인간의 관심은 오래 지속되지 않아.

**28** 아무도 윌버를 돌보지 않는다면, 그는 크리스마스 전에 죽을 거야.

**29** 우리는 곧 다른 단어를 써야 해.

**30** 오리: 내게 생각이 있어. '훌륭한'은 어때?

**31** 늙은 양: 좋아!

**Scene 4**

**32** Narrator 2: Again, Charlotte _____ hard _____ _____ _____ .

    A. night          B. worked         C. all

**33** Two days _____ , a _____ _____ came.

    A. later            B. crowd          C. bigger

**34** Charlotte: This also _____ _____ _____ soon.

    A. be              B. will             C. forgotten

**35** We _____ _____ prepare the next word _____ .

    A. to              B. away          C. have          D. right

**36** Duck: Uh, oh. I have _____ _____ _____ ideas.

    A. out            B. run            C. of

**37** Rat: What's _____ _____ _____ ?

    A. the            B. all            C. excitement

**38** Old Sheep: _____ _____ _____ help us?

    A. don't          B. why           C. you

**39** Will you _____ some ads _____ the _____ ?

    A. from          B. bring          C. dump

**40** Duck: We're _____ _____ _____ new words.

    A. to              B. trying          C. find

**41** Charlotte: We're trying _____ _____ Wilbur's _____ .

    A. life            B. save           C. to

**42** Rat: Okay, _____ Wilbur _____ his meal _____ me.

    A. with          B. if            C. shares

**Scene 5**

**43** Narrator 3: _____ Rat's _____ , they _____ chose "Shining."

    A. help          B. with           C. finally

**44** The _____ _____ _____ came.

    A. ever          B. biggest         C. crowd

**45** Mr. Allen: You know _____ ? I won't _____ bacon _____ _____ Wilbur.

    A. make         B. what         C. of         D. out

**46** I'll _____ _____ in the _____ !

    A. him          B. enter         C. fair

**47** Mrs. Allen: Great idea! Our _____ Wilbur will _____ a _____ !

    A. prize         B. famous        C. get

**48** Wilbur: Did you _____ that? I'm _____ to the _____ !

    A. hear          B. fair         C. going

**49** Thank you, Charlotte! You _____ me. Thank you _____ !

    A. all          B. saved

---

**장면 4**

**32** 서술자 2: 다시 샬럿은 밤새도록 열심히 일했다.

**33** 이틀 후, 더 많은 군중이 왔다.

**34** 샬럿: 이것 또한 곧 잊힐 거야.

**35** 우리는 곧바로 다음 단어를 준비해야 해.

**36** 오리: 오. 나는 아이디어가 바닥이 나 버렸어.

**37** 쥐: 모두들 뭐가 그렇게 신나니?

**38** 늙은 양: 우릴 도와주는 게 어때?

**39** 쓰레기 더미에서 광고 몇 개를 가져다줄래?

**40** 오리: 우리는 새로운 단어를 찾으려고 노력하고 있어.

**41** 샬럿: 우리는 윌버의 생명을 구하려고 노력하고 있어.

**42** 쥐: 알았어. 윌버가 음식을 나와 나눈다면.

**장면 5**

**43** 서술자 3: 쥐의 도움으로, 그들은 마침내 '빛나는'을 선택했다.

**44** 이제껏 가장 많은 군중이 왔다.

**45** 앨런 씨: 그거 알아요? 나는 윌버로 베이컨을 만들지 않을 거예요.

**46** 나는 그를 박람회에 출전시킬 거예요.

**47** 앨런 부인: 좋은 생각이에요! 우리 유명한 윌버가 상을 받을 거예요!

**48** 윌버: 들었어? 내가 박람회에 나갈 거야!

**49** 고마워, 샬럿! 네가 나를 구했어. 모두들 고마워!

※ 다음 우리말과 일치하도록 빈칸에 알맞은 말을 쓰시오.

**1** Charlotte's _____

**2** _____: The _____ of Wilbur the _____ on Mr. and Mrs. Allen's _____

**3** _____: Narrator 1, 2, 3, Wilbur: A _____, Charlotte: A _____, Mr. and Mrs. Allen: Farm _____, Old Sheep, Duck, Rat

**Scene 1**

**4** Narrator 1: *Charlotte's Web* is a story of _____ _____ Wilbur the pig _____ Charlotte the _____.

**5** Narrator 2: They _____ _____ Mr. and Mrs. Allen's farm _____ Old Sheep, Duck, and Rat.

**6** Narrator 3: _____ _____, Mr. and Mrs. Allen _____ _____ _____ _____ _____.

**7** Mrs. Allen: Wilbur _____ very _____.

**8** Mr. Allen: He'll _____ _____ _____ for Christmas.

**9** Old Sheep: They _____ _____ Wilbur _____ for Christmas!

**10** Duck: _____ bacon!

**11** Wilbur: No! I'm _____ _____ _____ _____!

**12** Charlotte: You _____, Wilbur. I'll _____ you.

**13** Wilbur: _____?

**14** Charlotte: I don't know _____, but _____?

**15** You _____ me when Mr. Allen _____ _____ _____ my web _____!

**16** Now it's _____ _____ _____ _____ you.

**1** 샬럿의 거미줄

**2** 배경: 앨런 부부 농장의 돼지 윌버의 우리

**3** 배역: 서술자 1, 2, 3, 돼지 윌버, 거미 샬럿, 농장 주인 앨런 부부, 늙은 양, 오리, 쥐

**장면** 1

**4** 서술자 1: "샬럿의 거미줄"은 돼지 윌버와 거미 샬럿 사이의 우정 이야기다.

**5** 서술자 2: 그들은 늙은 양, 오리, 쥐와 함께 앨런 부부의 농장에서 살았다.

**6** 서술자 3: 어느 날, 앨런 부부는 헛간 밖에서 이야기하고 있었다.

**7** 앨런 부인: 윌버가 아주 좋아 보여요.

**8** 앨런 씨: 그는 크리스마스에 좋은 베이컨이 될 거예요.

**9** 늙은 양: 그들은 크리스마스를 위해 윌버를 살찌우고 있어.

**10** 오리: 베이컨을 위해!

**11** 윌버: 안 돼! 나는 죽기에 너무 어려.

**12** 샬럿: 죽지 않을 거야, 윌버. 내가 널 구할게.

**13** 윌버: 어떻게?

**14** 샬럿: 아직 잘 모르겠어. 그런데 기억나?

**15** 앨런 씨가 거미줄을 없애려고 했을 때 네가 나를 구했잖아.

**16** 이제 내가 너를 구할 차례야.

**Scene 2**

**17** Charlotte: _____ can I _____ Wilbur?

**18** Hmm.... Oh, I _____ _____ _____!

**19** Narrator 1: That night, Charlotte started _____ _____ something _____ Wilbur's pen.

**20** She _____ _____ all night _____ _____.

**21** Narrator 2: The next morning, Mr. and Mrs. Allen came _____ _____ Wilbur.

**22** Mrs. Allen: Look! _____ are _____ in the web. "_____ _____"!

**23** Mr. Allen: A _____!

**24** Narrator 3: Soon, a _____ _____ came _____ _____ Wilbur.

**Scene 3**

**25** Narrator 1: _____ time _____, _____ _____ _____ _____ people came.

**26** Charlotte _____ _____ _____.

**27** Charlotte: _____ we _____, _____ _____ does not _____ _____.

**28** If nobody _____ _____ Wilbur, he _____ _____ _____ _____ Christmas.

**29** We _____ _____ _____ _____ _____ soon.

**30** Duck: I have an idea! _____ _____ "Terrific"?

**31** Old Sheep: I like _____!

장면 2

**17** 샬럿: 내가 어떻게 윌버를 구할 수 있을까?

**18** 음… 오, 좋은 생각이 났어!

**19** 서술자 1: 그날 밤, 샬럿은 윌버의 우리 위에 무언가를 짜기 시작했다.

**20** 그녀는 밤새도록 자지 않고 열심히 일했다.

**21** 서술자 2: 다음 날 아침, 앨런 부부는 윌버에게 먹이를 주러 왔다.

**22** 앨런 부인: 보세요! 거미줄에 단어들이 있어요. '대단한 돼지'!

**23** 앨런 씨: 기적이야!

**24** 서술자 3: 곧 많은 군중들이 윌버를 보러 왔다.

장면 3

**25** 서술자 1: 시간이 지날수록 극소수의 사람들만이 왔다.

**26** 샬럿은 회의를 소집했다.

**27** 샬럿: 보았다시피 인간의 관심은 오래 지속되지 않아.

**28** 아무도 윌버를 돌보지 않는다면, 그는 크리스마스 전에 죽을 거야.

**29** 우리는 곧 다른 단어를 써야 해.

**30** 오리: 내게 생각이 있어. '훌륭한'은 어때?

**31** 늙은 양: 좋아!

**Scene 4**

**32** Narrator 2: Again, Charlotte _____ _____ _____ _____.

**33** Two days _____, a _____ _____ came.

**34** Charlotte: This also _____ _____ _____ soon.

**35** We _____ _____ the next word _____ _____.

**36** Duck: Uh, oh. I have _____ _____ _____ ideas.

**37** Rat: What's all the _____?

**38** Old Sheep: _____ _____ _____ help us?

**39** Will you _____ some ads _____ the _____?

**40** Duck: We're _____ _____ _____ new words.

**41** Charlotte: We're _____ _____ _____ Wilbur's life.

**42** Rat: Okay, if Wilbur _____ his meal _____ me.

**Scene 5**

**43** Narrator 3: _____ Rat's help, they _____ _____ "Shining."

**44** The _____ _____ crowd came.

**45** Mr. Allen: You know _____? I won't _____ bacon _____ _____ Wilbur.

**46** I'll _____ _____ in the _____!

**47** Mrs. Allen: Great idea! Our _____ Wilbur will _____ _____ _____!

**48** Wilbur: Did you hear that? I'm _____ _____ _____!

**49** Thank you, Charlotte! You _____ me. Thank you _____!

장면 4

**32** 서술자 2: 다시 샬럿은 밤새도록 열심히 일했다.

**33** 이틀 후, 더 많은 군중이 왔다.

**34** 샬럿: 이것 또한 곧 잊힐 거야.

**35** 우리는 곧바로 다음 단어를 준비해야 해.

**36** 오리: 오. 나는 아이디어가 바닥이 나 버렸어.

**37** 쥐: 모두들 뭐가 그렇게 신나니?

**38** 늙은 양: 우릴 도와주는 게 어때?

**39** 쓰레기 더미에서 광고 몇 개를 가져다줄래?

**40** 오리: 우리는 새로운 단어를 찾으려고 노력하고 있어.

**41** 샬럿: 우리는 윌버의 생명을 구하려고 노력하고 있어.

**42** 쥐: 알았어, 윌버가 음식을 나와 나눈다면.

장면 5

**43** 서술자 3: 쥐의 도움으로, 그들은 마침내 '빛나는'을 선택했다.

**44** 이제껏 가장 많은 군중이 왔다.

**45** 앨런 씨: 그거 알아요? 나는 윌버로 베이컨을 만들지 않을 거예요.

**46** 나는 그를 박람회에 출전시킬 거예요.

**47** 앨런 부인: 좋은 생각이에요! 우리 유명한 윌버가 상을 받을 거예요!

**48** 윌버: 들었어? 내가 박람회에 나갈 거야!

**49** 고마워, 샬럿! 네가 나를 구했어. 모두들 고마워!

※ 다음 문장을 우리말로 쓰시오.

**1** Charlotte's Web
➡ _____

**2** Setting: The pen of Wilbur the pig on Mr. and Mrs. Allen's farm
➡ _____

**3** Roles: Narrator 1, 2, 3, Wilbur: A pig, Charlotte: A spider, Mr. and Mrs. Allen: Farm owners, Old Sheep, Duck, Rat
➡ _____

**Scene 1**

**4** Narrator 1: Charlotte's Web is a story of friendship between Wilbur the pig and Charlotte the spider.
➡ _____

**5** Narrator 2: They lived on Mr. and Mrs. Allen's farm with Old Sheep, Duck, and Rat.
➡ _____

**6** Narrator 3: One day, Mr. and Mrs. Allen were talking outside the barn.
➡ _____

**7** Mrs. Allen: Wilbur looks very good.
➡ _____

**8** Mr. Allen: He'll make good bacon for Christmas.
➡ _____

**9** Old Sheep: They are fattening Wilbur up for Christmas!
➡ _____

**10** Duck: For bacon!
➡ _____

**11** Wilbur: No! I'm too young to die!
➡ _____

**12** Charlotte: You won't, Wilbur. I'll save you.
➡ _____

**13** Wilbur: How?
➡ _____

**14** Charlotte: I don't know yet, but remember?
➡ _____

**15** You saved me when Mr. Allen tried to clean my web off.
➡ _____

**16** Now it's my turn to save you.
➡ _____

**Scene 2**

**17** Charlotte: How can I save Wilbur?
➡ _____

**18** Hmm.... Oh, I have an idea!
➡ _____

**19** Narrator 1: That night, Charlotte started to weave something above Wilbur's pen.
➡ _____

**20** She worked hard all night without sleeping.
➡ _____

**21** Narrator 2: The next morning, Mr. and Mrs. Allen came to feed Wilbur.
➡ _____

**22** Mrs. Allen: Look! There are words in the web. "Some Pig"!
➡ _____

**23** Mr. Allen: A miracle!
➡ _____

**24** Narrator 3: Soon, a large crowd came to see Wilbur.
➡ _____

### Scene 3

**25** ▸ Narrator 1: As time passed, only a few people came.
➡ _____

**26** ▸ Charlotte called a meeting.
➡ _____

**27** ▸ Charlotte: As we saw, human attention does not last long.
➡ _____

**28** ▸ If nobody cares for Wilbur, he will be dead before Christmas.
➡ _____

**29** ▸ We must write another word soon.
➡ _____

**30** ▸ Duck: I have an idea! How about "Terrific"?
➡ _____

**31** ▸ Old Sheep: I like it!
➡ _____

### Scene 4

**32** ▸ Narrator 2: Again, Charlotte worked hard all night.
➡ _____

**33** ▸ Two days later, a bigger crowd came.
➡ _____

**34** ▸ Charlotte: This also will be forgotten soon.
➡ _____

**35** ▸ We have to prepare the next word right away.
➡ _____

**36** ▸ Duck: Uh, oh. I have run out of ideas.
➡ _____

**37** ▸ Rat: What's all the excitement?
➡ _____

**38** ▸ Old Sheep: Why don't you help us?
➡ _____

**39** ▸ Will you bring some ads from the dump?
➡ _____

**40** ▸ Duck: We're trying to find new words.
➡ _____

**41** ▸ Charlotte: We're trying to save Wilbur's life.
➡ _____

**42** ▸ Rat: Okay, if Wilbur shares his meal with me.
➡ _____

### Scene 5

**43** ▸ Narrator 3: With Rat's help, they finally chose "Shining."
➡ _____

**44** ▸ The biggest ever crowd came.
➡ _____

**45** ▸ Mr. Allen: You know what? I won't make bacon out of Wilbur.
➡ _____

**46** ▸ I'll enter him in the fair!
➡ _____

**47** ▸ Mrs. Allen: Great idea! Our famous Wilbur will get a prize!
➡ _____

**48** ▸ Wilbur: Did you hear that? I'm going to the fair!
➡ _____

**49** ▸ Thank you, Charlotte! You saved me. Thank you all!
➡ _____

※ 다음 괄호 안의 단어들을 우리말에 맞도록 바르게 배열하시오.

**1** (Web / Charlotte's)
➡ _____

**2** (Setting: / pen / the / Wilbur / of / pig / the / Mr. / on / and / Allen's / Mrs. / farm)
➡ _____

**3** (Roles: / 1, / narrator / 3, / 2, / Wilbur: / pig, / a / Charlotte: / spider, / a // Mr. and Mrs. Allen: / owners, / farm / Sheep, / Old / Rat / Duck,)
➡ _____

**Scene 1**

**4** (Narrator 1: / Web / Charlotte's / a / is / of / story / between / friendship / Wilbur / pig / the / and / the / Charlotte / spider.)
➡ _____

**5** (Narrator 2: / lived / they / on / Mrs. / and / Mr. / farm / Allen's / with / Sheep, / Old / and / Duck, / Rat.)
➡ _____

**6** (Narrator 3: / day, / one / Mr. / and / Allen / Mrs. / talking / were / the / outside / barn.)
➡ _____

**7** (Mrs. Allen: / looks / Wilbur / good. / very)
➡ _____

**8** (Mr. Allen: / make / he'll / bacon / good / Christmas. / for)
➡ _____

**9** (Old Sheep: / are / they / Wilbur / fattening / for / up / Christmas!)
➡ _____

**10** (Duck: / bacon! / for)
➡ _____

**11** (Wilbur: / no! // too / I'm / to / young / die!)
➡ _____

**12** (Charlotte: / won't, / you / Wilbur. // you. / save / I'll)
➡ _____

**13** (how? / Wilbur)
➡ _____

**14** (Charlotte: / don't / I / yet, / know / remember? / but)
➡ _____

**15** (saved / you / when / me / Allen / Mr. / to / tried / clean / to / web / off. / my)
➡ _____

**16** (it's / now / turn / my / save / to / you.)
➡ _____

1 샬럿의 거미줄

2 배경: 앨런 부부 농장의 돼지 월버의 우리

3 배역: 서술자 1, 2, 3, 돼지 월버, 거미 샬럿, 농장 주인 앨런 부부, 늙은 양, 오리, 쥐

**장면 1**

4 서술자 1: "샬럿의 거미줄"은 돼지 월버와 거미 샬럿 사이의 우정 이야기다.

5 서술자 2: 그들은 늙은 양, 오리, 쥐와 함께 앨런 부부의 농장에서 살았다.

6 서술자 3: 어느 날, 앨런 부부는 헛간 밖에서 이야기하고 있었다.

7 앨런 부인: 월버가 아주 좋아 보여요.

8 앨런 씨: 그는 크리스마스에 좋은 베이컨이 될 거예요.

9 늙은 양: 그들은 크리스마스를 위해 월버를 살찌우고 있어.

10 오리: 베이컨을 위해!

11 월버: 안 돼! 나는 죽기에 너무 어려.

12 샬럿: 죽지 않을 거야, 월버. 내가 널 구할게.

13 월버: 어떻게?

14 샬럿: 아직 잘 모르겠어. 그런데 기억나?

15 앨런 씨가 거미줄을 없애려고 했을 때 네가 나를 구했잖아.

16 이제 내가 너를 구할 차례야.

## Scene 2

**17** (Charlotte: / can / how / save / I / Wilbur?)

➡ _____

**18** (hmm.... // I / oh, / an / have / idea!)

➡ _____

**19** (Narrator 1: / night, / that / started / Charlotte / to / something / weave / above / pen. / Wilbur's)

➡ _____

**20** (worked / she / all / hard / sleeping. / night / without)

➡ _____

**21** (Narrator 2: / next / the / morning, / Mr. / and / Allen / Mrs. / to / came / Wilbur. / feed)

➡ _____

**22** (Mrs. Allen: / look! / are / there / in / words / the / web. // Pig"! / "Some)

➡ _____

**23** (Mr. Allen: / miracle! / a)

➡ _____

**24** (Narrator 3: / a / soon, / crowd / large / to / came / Wilbur. / see)

➡ _____

## Scene 3

**25** (Narrator 1: / time / as / passed, / a / only / few / came. / people)

➡ _____

**26** (called / Charlotte / meeting. / a)

➡ _____

**27** (Charlotte: / we / as / saw, / attention / human / not / does / long. / last)

➡ _____

**28** (nobody / if / for / cares / Wilbur, / will / he / dead / be / Christmas. / before)

➡ _____

**29** (must / we / another / write / soon. / word)

➡ _____

**30** (Duck: / have / I / idea! / an // about / how / "Terrific"?)

➡ _____

**31** (Old Sheep: / like / it! / I)

➡ _____

**장면 2**

**17** 샬럿: 내가 어떻게 월버를 구할 수 있을까?

**18** 음… 오, 좋은 생각이 났어!

**19** 서술자 1: 그날 밤, 샬럿은 월버의 우리 위에 무언가를 짜기 시작했다.

**20** 그녀는 밤새도록 자지 않고 열심히 일했다.

**21** 서술자 2: 다음 날 아침, 앨런 부부는 월버에게 먹이를 주러 왔다.

**22** 앨런 부인: 보세요! 거미줄에 단어들이 있어요. '대단한 돼지'!

**23** 앨런 씨: 기적이야!

**24** 서술자 3: 곧 많은 군중들이 월버를 보러 왔다.

**장면 3**

**25** 서술자 1: 시간이 지날수록 극소수의 사람들만이 왔다.

**26** 샬럿은 회의를 소집했다.

**27** 샬럿: 보았다시피 인간의 관심은 오래 지속되지 않아.

**28** 아무도 월버를 돌보지 않는다면, 그는 크리스마스 전에 죽을 거야.

**29** 우리는 곧 다른 단어를 써야 해.

**30** 오리: 내게 생각이 있어. '훌륭한'은 어때?

**31** 늙은 양: 좋아!

**Scene 4**

**32** (Narrator 2: / again, / worked / Charlotte / hard / night. / all)

➡ _____

**33** (days / two / later, / bigger / a / came. / crowd)

➡ _____

**34** (Charlotte: / also / this / be / will / soon. / forgotten)

➡ _____

**35** (have / we / prepare / to / next / the / right / word / away.)

➡ _____

**36** (Duck: / oh. / uh, // have / I / out / run / ideas. / of)

➡ _____

**37** (Rat: / all / what's / excitement? / the)

➡ _____

**38** (Old Sheep: / don't / why / help / you / us?)

➡ _____

**39** (you / will / bring / ads / some / the / from / dump?)

➡ _____

**40** (Duck: / trying / we're / find / to / words. / new)

➡ _____

**41** (Charlotte: / trying / we're / save / to / life. / Wilbur's)

➡ _____

**42** (Rat: / okay, / Wilbur / if / his / shares / with / meal / me.)

➡ _____

**Scene 5**

**43** (Narrator 3: / Rat's / with / help, / finally / they / "Shining." / chose)

➡ _____

**44** (biggest / the / crowd / ever / came.)

➡ _____

**45** (Allen: / Mr. / know / you / what? / won't / I / bacon / make / of / out / Wilbur.)

➡ _____

**46** (enter / I'll / in / him / fair! / the)

➡ _____

**47** (Mrs. Allen: / idea! / great // famous / our / will / Wilbur / a / get / prize!)

➡ _____

**48** (Wilbur: / you / did / hear / that? // going / I'm / the / to / fair!)

➡ _____

**49** (you, / thank / Charlotte! // saved / you / me. // you / thank / all!)

➡ _____

**장면 4**

**32** 서술자 2: 다시 샬럿은 밤새도록 열심히 일했다.

**33** 이틀 후, 더 많은 군중이 왔다.

**34** 샬럿: 이것 또한 곧 잊힐 거야.

**35** 우리는 곧바로 다음 단어를 준비해야 해.

**36** 오리: 오. 나는 아이디어가 바닥이 나 버렸어.

**37** 쥐: 모두들 뭐가 그렇게 신나니?

**38** 늙은 양: 우릴 도와주는 게 어때?

**39** 쓰레기 더미에서 광고 몇 개를 가져다줄래?

**40** 오리: 우리는 새로운 단어를 찾으려고 노력하고 있어.

**41** 샬럿: 우리는 윌버의 생명을 구하려고 노력하고 있어.

**42** 쥐: 알았어. 윌버가 음식을 나와 나눈다면.

**장면 5**

**43** 서술자 3: 쥐의 도움으로, 그들은 마침내 '빛나는'을 선택했다.

**44** 이제껏 가장 많은 군중이 왔다.

**45** 앨런 씨: 그거 알아요? 나는 윌버로 베이컨을 만들지 않을 거예요.

**46** 나는 그를 박람회에 출전시킬 거예요.

**47** 앨런 부인: 좋은 생각이에요! 우리 유명한 윌버가 상을 받을 거예요!

**48** 윌버: 들었어? 내가 박람회에 나갈 거야!

**49** 고마워, 샬럿! 네가 나를 구했어. 모두들 고마워!

※ 다음 우리말을 영어로 쓰시오.

**1** 샬럿의 거미줄
➡ _____

**2** 배경: 앨런 부부 농장의 돼지 윌버의 우리
➡ _____

**3** 배역: 서술자 1, 2, 3, 돼지 윌버, 거미 샬럿, 농장 주인 앨런 부부, 늙은 양, 오리, 쥐
➡ _____

**Scene 1**

**4** 서술자 1: "샬럿의 거미줄"은 돼지 윌버와 거미 샬럿 사이의 우정 이야기다.
➡ _____

**5** 서술자 2: 그들은 늙은 양, 오리, 쥐와 함께 앨런 부부의 농장에서 살았다.
➡ _____

**6** 서술자 3: 어느 날, 앨런 부부는 헛간 밖에서 이야기하고 있었다.
➡ _____

**7** 앨런 부인: 윌버가 아주 좋아 보여요.
➡ _____

**8** 앨런 씨: 그는 크리스마스에 좋은 베이컨이 될 거예요.
➡ _____

**9** 늙은 양: 그들은 크리스마스를 위해 윌버를 살찌우고 있어.
➡ _____

**10** 오리: 베이컨을 위해!
➡ _____

**11** 윌버: 안 돼! 나는 죽기에 너무 어려.
➡ _____

**12** 샬럿: 죽지 않을 거야, 윌버. 내가 널 구할게.
➡ _____

**13** 윌버: 어떻게?
➡ _____

**14** 샬럿: 아직 잘 모르겠어. 그런데 기억나?
➡ _____

**15** 앨런 씨가 거미줄을 없애려고 했을 때 네가 나를 구했잖아.
➡ _____

**16** 이제 내가 너를 구할 차례야.
➡ _____

**Scene 2**

**17** 샬럿: 내가 어떻게 윌버를 구할 수 있을까?
➡ _____

**18** 음… 오, 좋은 생각이 났어!
➡ _____

**19** 서술자 1: 그날 밤, 샬럿은 윌버의 우리 위에 무언가를 짜기 시작했다.
➡ _____

**20** 그녀는 밤새도록 자지 않고 열심히 일했다.
➡ _____

**21** 서술자 2: 다음 날 아침, 앨런 부부는 윌버에게 먹이를 주러 왔다.
➡ _____

**22** 앨런 부인: 보세요! 거미줄에 단어들이 있어요. '대단한 돼지'!
➡ _____

**23** 앨런 씨: 기적이야!
➡ _____

**24** 서술자 3: 곧 많은 군중들이 윌버를 보러 왔다.
➡ _____

### Scene 3

**25** 서술자 1: 시간이 지날수록 극소수의 사람들만이 왔다.
➡ _____

**26** 샬럿은 회의를 소집했다.
➡ _____

**27** 샬럿: 보았다시피 인간의 관심은 오래 지속되지 않아.
➡ _____

**28** 아무도 윌버를 돌보지 않는다면, 그는 크리스마스 전에 죽을 거야.
➡ _____

**29** 우리는 곧 다른 단어를 써야 해.
➡ _____

**30** 오리: 내게 생각이 있어. '훌륭한'은 어때?
➡ _____

**31** 늙은 양: 좋아!
➡ _____

### Scene 4

**32** 서술자 2: 다시 샬럿은 밤새도록 열심히 일했다.
➡ _____

**33** 이틀 후, 더 많은 군중이 왔다.
➡ _____

**34** 샬럿: 이것 또한 곧 잊힐 거야.
➡ _____

**35** 우리는 곧바로 다음 단어를 준비해야 해.
➡ _____

**36** 오리: 오. 나는 아이디어가 바닥이 나 버렸어.
➡ _____

**37** 쥐: 모두들 뭐가 그렇게 신나니?
➡ _____

**38** 늙은 양: 우릴 도와주는 게 어때?
➡ _____

**39** 쓰레기 더미에서 광고 몇 개를 가져다줄래?
➡ _____

**40** 오리: 우리는 새로운 단어를 찾으려고 노력하고 있어.
➡ _____

**41** 샬럿: 우리는 윌버의 생명을 구하려고 노력하고 있어.
➡ _____

**42** 쥐: 알았어, 윌버가 음식을 나와 나눈다면.
➡ _____

### Scene 5

**43** 서술자 3: 쥐의 도움으로, 그들은 마침내 '빛나는'을 선택했다.
➡ _____

**44** 이제껏 가장 많은 군중이 왔다.
➡ _____

**45** 앨런 씨: 그거 알아요? 나는 윌버로 베이컨을 만들지 않을 거예요.
➡ _____

**46** 나는 그를 박람회에 출전시킬 거예요.
➡ _____

**47** 앨런 부인: 좋은 생각이에요! 우리 유명한 윌버가 상을 받을 거예요!
➡ _____

**48** 윌버: 들었어? 내가 박람회에 나갈 거야!
➡ _____

**49** 고마워, 샬럿! 네가 나를 구했어. 모두들 고마워!
➡ _____

# MEMO

MEMO

적중100 plus

2학기 전과정

영어 기출 문제집

영어 기출 문제집

적중'100 plus
2학기 전과정

영어 기출 문제집

적중100

2학기

# 정답 및 해설

시사 | 송미정

중 2

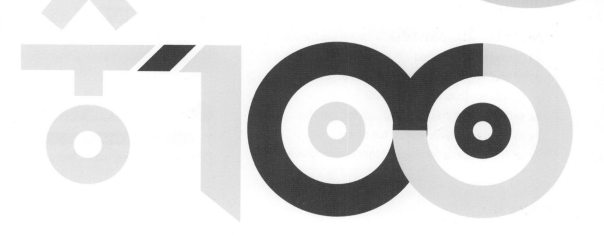

Lesson **6**

# New Places, New Experiences

**시험대비 실력평가**  p.08

01 (1) exciting  (2) disappointed    02 ②
03 ③        04 ①        05 ③
06 (1) (g)et used to  (2) show, around

01 감정을 나타내는 동사에 '-ing'를 붙이면 '~한 감정을 일으키는'의 의미가 되고, '-ed'를 붙이면 '~한 감정을 느끼는'의 의미가 된다. (1) excited: 신이 난 exciting: 신나게 하는 / 어젯밤의 축구 경기는 정말 신났다. (2) disappointing: 실망시키는 disappointed: 실망한 / 그는 시험 결과에 실망했다.

02 ②에는 'interested(흥미를 느끼는)'가 어울리며, 나머지 보기들은 'interesting(흥미로운)'이 적절하다. ① 수학은 내게 가장 흥미로운 과목이다. ② 내가 관심 있는 과목은 컴퓨터공학이다. ③ 이 부분이 이 영화에서 가장 재미있는 부분이다. ④ 신문에 무슨 재미있는 기사라도 있나요? ⑤ 나는 지난 주말에 아주 재미있는 쇼를 봤다.

03 as soon as: ~하자마자 Once: ~하자마자 / 그는 자리에 들자마자 잠들었다.

04 expect: 기대하다, 예상하다 / 나는 그를 거기서 볼 거라고 예상하지 못했기 때문에 놀랐다.

05 ① 감독은 전체 팀원들을 불러 모았다. ② 그럼 내가 충분히 연습을 하지 않는다는 의미인가요? ③ moved: 가슴 뭉클한 / 많은 사람들이 그의 노래와 아름다운 목소리에 감동 받았다. ④ 이 같은 순간을 오랫동안 기다려 왔어. ⑤ 자동차는 우리의 현대 생활 양식에 중요한 부분이 되어 왔다.

06 (1) get used to: ~에 익숙해지다 (2) show A around B: A에게 B를 여기저기 안내하다

**서술형 시험대비**  p.09

01 (1) boring  (2) amazed    02 are used to
03 (1) shooting star  (2) so (s)cared that
    (3) asleep, (b)oring  (4) capital
04 with      05 (1) up  (2) At  (3) for  (4) like
06 (1) I hope this year will be full of joy.
    (2) This place is so magical that I want to live here.

01 (1) bore: 지루하게 만들다 boring: 재미없는, 지루하게 하는 / 그 영화는 너무 지루해서 보는 도중에 잠들었다. (2) amaze: 놀라게 하다 amazed: 놀란 / 우리 모두는 그가 일하는 속도에 놀랐다.

02 be used to: ~에 익숙하다(= be familiar to) / 나는 이제 네가 나의 억양에 익숙하다고 생각한다.

03 (1) shooting star: 유성 (2) so 형용사/부사 that 주어+동사: 매우 ~해서 …하다 scared: 겁먹은, 무서워하는 (3) asleep: 잠이 든 boring: 재미없는, 지루하게 하는 (4) capital: 수도

04 be made with: ~로 만들어지다 / 여러분은 팥, 우유 그리고 얼음으로 만든 음식이 무엇인지 알고 있나요? be cooked with: ~으로 요리되다 / 보통, 스파게티는 토마토소스로 요리된다.

05 (1) wake up: 잠에서 깨다 / 그녀는 시계를 맞추어 놓았지만 일어나지 못하였다. (2) at first: 처음에는 / 처음에 나는 네가 말하는 것을 이해했다고 생각했다. (3) can't wait for: 빨리 ~하면 좋겠다 / 그는 그 파티를 기대하고 있다. (4) feel like+주어+동사: ~인 것처럼 느끼다 / 내가 키가 큰 것처럼 느껴진다.

06 (1) be full of: ~로 가득하다 (2) magical: 아주 멋진, 마법의 so 형용사/부사 that 주어+동사: 매우 …해서 ~하다

**교과서**

## Conversation

**핵심 Check**  p.10~11

1 (1) Have you ever run
  (2) I have never met any famous actor before
2 (C) → (B) → (A)
3 (1) How do you like this book
  (2) How did you like the movie?
4 What → How

### 교과서 대화문 익히기

**Check(√) True or False**  p.12

1 F  2 T  3 T  4 T

### 교과서 확인학습  p.14~15

**Listen & Speak 1 A**
Have you ever / have, tasty

**Listen & Speak 1 B**

(1) look / going, with, Have, been / coastline / can't, for

(2) Have, ever, rise / watched, on / tried, wake, early

**Listen & Speak 1 C**

(1) Have you ever / experience

(2) you ever ridden / experience

**Listen & Speak 2 A**

How do you / bigger

**Listen & Speak 2 B**

(1) How, vacation / went / How did / amazing

(2) Have you been to / had / How did you / won't

**Listen & Speak 2 C**

(1) How / colorful

(2) do you like / sweet

**Real-Life Zone A**

Have you ever traveled abroad / went / How / enjoyed / interesting, had / let, fried / How, like them / so, scared at first / imagine

**Communication Task**

Have you ever eaten / tasty, haven't, try

---

**시험대비 기본평가**     p.16

| 01 ④ | 02 ② | 03 (C) → (B) → (A) → (D) |
|---|---|---|
| 04 ② | | |

01 Have you ever+과거분사 ~?: 너는 ~해 본 적 있니? tasty: 맛있는

02 노래에 대한 만족 여부를 묻고 답하고 있다. How do you like ~?: ~는 어떠니? cheerful: 쾌활한, 유쾌한

03 (C) 인호가 신나 보여 무슨 일인지 이유를 묻는다. (B) 이유를 말하면서, 제주도에 가본 경험이 있는지 질문한다. (A) 여러 번 제주도를 가 봤다고 대답하며, 해안선을 좋아한다고 말한다. (D) 이번이 첫 제주도 여행이라며 주말이 빨리 왔으면 좋겠다고 얘기하면서 기대감을 표현한다.

04 'How do you like ~?'는 어떤 것에 대한 만족이나 불만족에 대해 물을 때 사용하며 '~는 어떠니?'라는 의미이다. 유사한 표현으로 'What do you think of[about] ~?'가 있다.

---

**시험대비 실력평가**     p.17~18

| 01 ② | 02 ④ | 03 ③ | 04 ⑤ |
|---|---|---|---|
| 05 ⑤ | 06 ① | 07 ④ | 08 ② |
| 09 ④ | | | |

01 Have you ever+과거분사 ~?: 너는 ~해 본 적 있니? sunrise(= sunrise): 일출, 해돋이. 남자아이가 강릉에서 새해 첫날에 해돋이를 본 경험이 있다고 말하고 있으므로, 해돋이를 본 경험이 있는지 질문하는 것이 적절하다.

02 ① 여자아이는 일출을 본 적이 있는가? ② 남자아이는 일출을 본 적이 있는가? ③ 언제 남자아이는 일출을 봤는가? ④ 남자아이는 일출을 몇 번 본 경험이 있는가? ⑤ 어디서 남자아이는 일출을 보았는가?

03 피자를 만들어 본 경험이 있는지 물어보는 질문에 있다고 대답했는데 곧바로 피자를 오직 여러 번 먹어보기만 했다는 것은 어색하다.

04 'How did you like ~?( ~는 어땠어?)'는 상대방의 만족여부에 대해 물어보는 표현이다. (C) 방학이 어땠는지 묻는 질문에. (D) 좋았다고 대답하면서, 가족과 독도를 다녀왔다고 얘기한다. (B) 독도가 어땠는지 묻는 질문에, (A) 굉장했다고 하며, 다시 한 번 가보고 싶다고 말한다.

05 Have you ever+과거분사 ~?: 너는 ~ 해 본 적 있니? 어떤 장소에 다녀온 적이 있는지 경험을 말할 때는 'have been to 장소'라는 표현을 사용함에 유의한다.

06 How did you like ~?: ~은 어땠어?

07 해외여행을 가 본 경험을 물어보니, (C) 지난여름에 캄보디아에 다녀왔다고 대답한다. (B) 여행이 어땠는지 물어보자, (D) 날씨는 더웠지만 여행은 즐거웠다고 대답한다. (E) 여행하면서 재미있었던 경험을 얘기해 달라는 말에, (A) 거미튀김을 먹었다고 대답한다.

08 (A) How was ~?: ~는 어땠어?(만족이나 불만족에 대해 묻기) (B) What ~: 어떤 ~ (C) How did you like ~?: ~는 어땠어?(만족이나 불만족에 대해 묻기)

09 친구가 아닌 부모님과 함께 다녀왔다.

---

**서술형 시험대비**     p.19

| 01 excited | 02 Have you ever been there? |
|---|---|
| 03 for | 04 How do you like your new house? |
| 05 ridden | 06 How did you like it? |
| 07 Have you ever traveled abroad | |
| 08 ⓐ I have been to Cambodia → I went to Cambodia | |

01 감정을 나타내는 동사에 '-ing'를 붙이면 '~한 감정을 일으키는' 의미가 되고, '-ed'를 붙이면 '~한 감정을 느끼는' 의미가 된다. excited: 신난

02 Have you (ever) been (to) ~?: ~에 가 본 적 있니?

03 can't wait for: 빨리 ~하면 좋겠다

04 How do you like ~?: ~는 어떠니?

05 현재완료(have/has+p.p)가 경험의 의미로 사용되면 '~한 적이

3

있다'라고 해석한다. ride-rode-ridden: 타다

06 How did you like ~?: ~는 어땠어?

07 Have you ever+과거분사 ~?: 너는 ~해 본 적 있니? travel: 여행하다 abroad: 해외에

08 'last summer(지난여름)'는 과거의 특정 시점을 나타내는 부사구이므로, 현재완료와 어울리지 않는다. 그러므로 과거 시제를 사용한다.

## Grammar
교과서

### 핵심 Check
p.20~21

1 (1) so  (2) that

2 (1) who[whom/that]  (2) which[that]

### 시험대비 기본평가
p.22

01 ②, ⑤   02 (1) which → that  (2) very → so
   (3) who → which[that]
   (4) which I left it → which I left

03 (1) He spoke so fast that I could not understand him.
   (2) The bike which[that] Eric wants to buy is very expensive.

04 ③

01 선행사가 the author로 사람이며 'I want to meet' 다음에 이어질 목적어 역할을 할 수 있는 목적격 관계대명사 who나 whom 그리고 that이 적절하다.

02 (1), (2) 'so+형용사+that+주어+동사'의 형태로 원인과 결과를 나타내야 한다. (3) 선행사 The mirror가 사물이므로 관계대명사는 which 또는 that으로 쓰는 것이 적절하다. (4) 목적격 관계대명사가 left의 목적어이므로 목적어 it을 또 쓰지 않는다.

03 (1) so를 추가하여 'so+부사+that+주어+동사'의 형태로 원인과 결과를 나타낸다. (2) 목적격 관계대명사 which나 that을 추가한다.

04 목적격 관계대명사 which 또는 that, 'so+형용사+that+주어+동사'이므로 공통으로 들어갈 단어는 that이다.

### 시험대비 실력평가
p.23~25

01 ⑤   02 ⑤   03 ⑤   04 ①

05 The chair was so comfortable that she fell asleep.

06 (1) which  (2) which  (3) that  (4) are
   (5) clearly  (6) so

07 (1) that  (2) who is   08 ③   09 ④

10 (1) O  (2) O  (3) X  (4) O  (5) X   11 ②

12 She is wearing the wedding dress which her mother left her.

13 He got up so early that he was sleepy all morning.

14 bags were, that, couldn't, them

15 (1) we can't, them  (2) too slow to win
   (3) cute enough, to

16 ④   17 ⑤   18 ③

19 (1) The boy band is BTS. + I like it most.
   (2) This is the picture. + I took it three days ago.
   (3) I know some people. + They work for Google.

01 모두 주격이나 목적격으로 사용된 관계대명사 that이 들어갈 수 있지만 ⑤번은 소유격 관계대명사 whose가 들어가야 한다.

02 주절이 과거이므로 that절의 동사도 과거로 쓴다. can't를 couldn't로 바꾸어야 한다.

03 ⑤번은 주격 관계대명사이고 나머지는 목적격 관계대명사이다.

04 ①번은 접속사이지만 나머지는 모두 관계대명사이다.

05 'so+형용사+that+주어+동사'로 '매우 …해서 ~하다'라는 의미를 나타낸다. fall asleep: 잠이 들다

06 (1), (2) 선행사가 사물이므로 which, (3) 선행사가 '사람+동물'이므로 that (4) 목적격 관계대명사가 꾸미고 있는 주어는 The boxes이므로 동사는 are를 쓴다. (5) 주절의 동사가 spoke이므로 so 다음에 부사를 쓴다. (6) 'so+형용사+that+주어+동사'로 '매우 …해서 ~하다'라는 의미를 나타낸다.

07 목적격 관계대명사와 '주격 관계대명사+be동사'는 생략할 수 있다.

08 enough는 부사일 때 형용사를 뒤에서 꾸며준다. 그러므로 easy enough로 쓰는 것이 적절하다.

09 ④는 'so+형용사+that+주어+동사'의 형태가 올바르고 주절의 주어가 that절의 목적어로 올바르게 쓰였다. ① Is he strong enough to lift it? ② The dinner yesterday was too awful to eat. ③ This watch is so expensive that I can't buy it. ⑤ I got up so late that I couldn't have breakfast this morning.

10 (1), (4)는 목적격 관계대명사로 생략할 수 있다. (2)는 주격 관계대명사이나 be동사와 함께 생략할 수 있다, (3)은 목적격 관계대명사이나 관계대명사가 그 앞에 전치사와 함께 있으므로 생략할 수 없다. (5)는 주격 관계대명사로 생략할 수 없다.

11 선행사가 사람이므로 who나 that을 이용하고 선행사 the woman이 두 번째 문장의 목적어이므로 목적격 관계대명사를 쓰고 목적어였던 her는 쓰지 말아야 한다.

12 목적격 관계대명사가 나올 자리이므로 '선행사+관계대명사+주어+동사'의 어순으로 쓴다.

13 'so+형용사+that+주어+동사'로 '매우 …해서 ~하다'라는 의미를 나타낸다.

14 남자가 가방을 두 개 들고 있으므로 주어는 the bags이고 'so … that ~' 구문을 이용하여 문장을 완성한다. 이때 주절의 주어가 that절의 목적어이므로 주절의 주어 the bags를 that절의 목적어 자리에 them으로 적절하게 써야 한다.

15 (1), (2) 'too+형용사/부사+to부정사'는 '원인과 결과'를 나타내는 'so+형용사/부사+that+주어+can't+동사원형'과 바꾸어 쓸 수 있다. (3) '형용사/부사+enough+to부정사'는 '원인과 결과'를 나타내는 'so+형용사/부사+that+주어+can+동사원형'과 바꾸어 쓸 수 있다.

16 주어진 문장과 ④에 쓰인 that은 선행사를 꾸며 주는 목적격 관계대명사이다. ① 지시대명사 ② 지시형용사 ③, ⑤ 접속사

17 주어진 문장과 ⑤의 that은 목적격 관계대명사로 쓰임이 같다. ①은 주격 관계대명사 ② 지시대명사 ③, ④ 접속사

18 첫 번째 문장에서는 to부정사가 있으므로 too와 enough 중에서 선택하는데, small 앞에 위치하므로 enough를 쓸 수 없다. 두 번째 문장에서는 접속사 that이 있으므로 so와 함께 쓰는 것이 적절하다.

19 (1), (2)는 모두 목적격 관계대명사가 있는 문장이므로 관계대명사 대신 선행사를 목적어로 해서 두 문장으로 쓴다. (3)은 주격 관계대명사가 있는 문장이므로 관계대명사 대신 선행사를 주어로 해서 두 문장으로 쓴다.

## 서술형 시험대비
p.26~27

01 (1) The story which she told me was surprising.
   (2) This is the money which I really need.
   (3) I have a friend who lives in Canada.
   (4) This is the movie which has a sad ending.
   (5) I met a person whose hobby is mountain climbing.

02 (1) This is the apartment which[that] she lives in.
   (2) I like the jacket which[that] my wife bought for me.
   (3) Aladdin is the movie which[that] I like best.
   (4) Look at the cloud which[that] is floating in the sky.

03 (1) so, that, I can't   (2) which

04 (1) The boy has no toys which[that] he can play with. 또는 The boy has no toys with which he can play.
   (2) He is the mechanic who[whom/that] I want to introduce to you.

   (3) The girls who I took care of were my nieces.
   (4) The pen that I'm writing with is Mike's.
   (5) Everything (that) I told you was true.

05 (1) cooks so well that   (2) runs so fast that
   (3) so smart that he, gets

06 (1) that you drink   (2) something that you listen to

07 (1) I was so tired that I could not work any more.
   (2) The cat moved so quietly that no one noticed it.
   (3) The stairs were so high and steep that I felt dizzy.

08 (1) This game console is so small that you can take it anywhere.
   (2) The bags are too heavy for you to carry to the airport.

01 (1), (2), (4) 선행사가 사물이므로 관계대명사 which를 써야 한다. (3) 선행사가 사람이므로 관계대명사 who를 써야 한다. (5) 접속사와 소유격으로 연결해야 하므로 소유격 관계대명사 whose를 써야 한다.

02 목적격 관계대명사의 선행사가 사물이나 동물이면 관계대명사를 which 또는 that으로 쓰고 생략할 수 있다. 주격관계대명사는 be동사와 함께 생략할 수 있다.

03 (1) 'too+형용사/부사+to부정사'는 '원인과 결과'를 나타내는 'so+형용사/부사+that+주어+can't+동사원형'과 바꾸어 쓸 수 있다. (2) 관계대명사 that은 사물인 경우 which로 바꾸어 쓸 수 있다.

04 (1) 관계대명사 앞에 전치사가 함께 쓰인 경우 that을 사용하지 않는다. 사람은 whom, 사물은 which를 쓴다. (2) 선행사가 사람이므로 관계대명사 who[whom]나 that을 써야 한다. mechanic 정비사 (3) 선행사인 주어가 복수이므로 동사를 was가 아닌 were로 쓴다. (4) 관계대명사가 전치사의 목적인 경우 그 전치사를 빠뜨리면 안 된다. (5) what은 선행사를 포함한 관계대명사가 필요할 때 쓴다. that으로 고치거나 생략하는 것이 적절하다.

06 목적격 관계대명사에서 선행사가 something이면 주로 that을 쓰고 그 다음에 주어 동사가 나온다.

07 (1), (3) 'so+형용사+that+주어+동사'로 '매우 …해서 ~하다'라는 의미를 나타낸다. 주절이 과거이므로 that절의 시제도 과거로 쓴다. (2) that절의 주어와 주절의 주어가 다르기 때문에 noticed 다음에 목적어 it(=the cat)을 써야 한다.

08 (1) 'so … that ~' 구문은 두 개의 절로 되어 있으므로 주절의 주어가 that절의 목적어인 경우 생략하지 않고 반드시 쓴다. (2) 'too … to ~' 구문은 하나의 절로 구성된 문장이므로 주어 the bags(=them)를 carry의 목적어로 다시 쓰지 않는다.

5

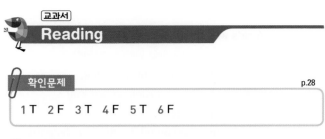

## Reading

### 확인문제      p.28

1 T   2 F   3 T   4 F   5 T   6 F

### 확인문제      p.29

1 T   2 F   3 T   4 F   5 T   6 F

### 교과서 확인학습 A      p.30~31

01 Trip
02 for the first time
03 is from
04 invited, to
05 a four-hour flight, arrived at
06 It took, by taxi
07 traditional
08 cozy inside
09 smelled wonderful
10 from, cooking for
11 Mongolian barbecue
12 is made of, with
13 was moved, serve, to
14 so, that
15 went outside
16 was full of
17 felt like
18 During, showed me around
19 had the most fun
20 At first, taller than
21 once, got used to
22 the view of the desert
23 in many ways
24 to get to know
25 again someday

### 교과서 확인학습 B      p.32~33

1 A Trip to Mongolia
2 This year, I had a special summer because I visited Mongolia for the first time.
3 My friend Altan is from Mongolia.
4 His grandmother invited me to Ulaanbaatar, the capital of Mongolia.
5 After a four-hour flight from Seoul, Altan and I arrived at Chinggis Khaan International Airport in Ulaanbaatar.
6 It took thirty minutes by taxi from the airport to Altan's grandmother's house.
7 Her house is a *ger*, a traditional Mongolian house.
8 It is a big tent, but it is cozy inside.
9 When we entered, something smelled wonderful.
10 It was from the *khorkhog* that she was cooking for us.
11 *Khorkhog* is a Mongolian barbecue.
12 It is made of lamb and cooked with hot stones.

13 I was moved when Altan said Mongolians serve *khorkhog* to special guests.
14 It was so delicious that I asked for more.
15 After dinner, Altan and I went outside to see the night sky.
16 The sky was full of bright stars.
17 I felt like I was in a magical place.
18 During the next three days, Altan showed me around and helped me experience Mongolian culture.
19 Every moment was fun and exciting, but I had the most fun when I rode a camel in the Gobi Desert.
20 At first, I was scared because the camel was taller than I expected.
21 But once I sat on its back, I soon got used to its movement.
22 From the camel's back, the view of the desert was truly amazing.
23 My visit to Mongolia was a special experience in many ways.
24 It gave me a great chance to get to know my friend's country and culture.
25 I want to visit Mongolia again someday!

### 시험대비 실력평가      p.34~37

01 ④
02 After a four-hour flight from Seoul
03 by a taxi → by taxi     04 ②
05 ⓐ a *ger*   ⓒ *khorkhog*
06 It was from the *khorkhog* that she was cooking for us.
07 filled with      08 ①, ④      09 ③
10 ⑤      11 ②      12 ③      13 flight
14 ②      15 ②      16 ⓐ so   ⓑ that
17 ②, ③, ⑤      18 ④      19 ①      20 taller
21 couldn't get → soon got      22 ③
23 ①, ④      24 forget → forget it      25 ①, ⑤
26 four thirty

01 ⓐ from: (출처·기원) … 출신의[에서 나온], ⓑ invited A to B: A를 B에 초대하다
02 '숫자+단위 명사'가 하나의 낱말로 형용사처럼 쓰일 경우에 하이픈으로 연결하고 four-hour처럼 단수로 쓰는 것이 적절하다.
03 교통이나 통신 수단을 나타낼 때: by+무관사 명사

04 ② Altan's 'grandmother' invited the writer to Ulaanbaatar.

05 ⓐ '게르', ⓒ '호르호그'를 가리킨다.

06 'from'을 보충하면 된다.

07 be full of = be filled with: ~로 가득 차 있다

08 get[come/learn] to 동사원형: ~하게 되다

09 ⓐ와 ③번: 한 번[일단] …하면, ~하자마자(접속사), ①, ④: 한 번(부사), ②, ⑤: (과거) 언젠가[한때]

10 이 글은 '몽골을 방문해서 겪은 특별한 경험'에 관한 글이다.

11 ⓐ와 ③, ⑤번: 관계대명사, ①, ②, ④번: 접속사

12 순천 국가 정원은 너무 넓어서 글쓴이의 가족은 정원 전체를 다 볼 수 없었다.

13 fly의 명사 flight를 쓰는 것이 적절하다.

14 ②번 다음 문장의 His에 주목한다. 주어진 문장의 My friend Altan을 받고 있으므로 ②번이 적절하다.

15 이 글은 글쓴이가 올해 몽골을 처음으로 방문해서 특별한 여름을 보냈다는 내용의 글이므로, 제목으로는 '내가 몽골에서 보낸 특별한 여름'이 적절하다.

16 so+형용사/부사+that: 매우 ~해서 …하다

17 ⓒ와 ②, ③, ⑤: 부사적 용법, ① 형용사적 용법, ④ 명사적 용법

18 호르호그가 뜨거운 돌로 요리되는 이유는 대답할 수 없다. ① It's a traditional Mongolian house. ② Altan's grandmother. ③ It is made of lamb. ⑤ They serve it to special guests.

19 ⓐ visit(명사)+to 장소, ⓑ 방법 앞에는 전치사 in을 쓰는 것이 적절하다.

20 처음에는 글쓴이가 예상했던 것보다 낙타의 '키가 커서' 무서웠다.

21 글쓴이는 낙타 등에 앉자 곧 움직임에 '익숙해졌다.'

22 ③ 만족한, ① 지루한, ② 실망한, ④ 자신감 있는, ⑤ 속상한

23 목적격 관계대명사 which나 that을 쓰는 것이 적절하다.

24 forget 다음에 목적어 it(=this trip)이 필요하다.

25 ⓐ와 ①, ⑤번: 완료 용법, ②, ③번: 경험 용법, ④ 계속 용법

26 half past/after four, thirty (minutes) past/after four도 가능하다.

서술형 시험대비          p.38~39

01 (A) special   (B) invited   (C) four-hour

02 It took four hours.

03 (A) Mongolia   (B) grandmother's          04 cozy

05 게르에 들어갔을 때 나던 좋은 냄새

06 (A) *khorkhog*   (B) night sky

07 to experience

08 I was scared because the camel was taller than I expected.

09 My visit to Mongolia      10 was moved

11 we could[might] / so that

12 (A) traditional Mongolian   (B) cozy

01 (A) '특별한' 여름을 보냈다고 해야 하므로 special이 적절하다. (B) 나를 '초대하셨다'고 해야 하므로 invited가 적절하다. visit: 방문하다, (C) '숫자+단위 명사'가 하나의 낱말로 형용사처럼 쓰일 경우에 하이픈으로 연결하고 단수로 써야 하므로 four-hour가 적절하다.

02 서울에서 울란바토르의 칭기즈 칸 국제공항까지 비행기로 '네 시간' 걸렸다.

03 올해 여름, 글쓴이는 '몽골'을 처음으로 방문했다. 알탕과 글쓴이는 알탕의 '할머니' 댁에 갔다.

04 cozy: 아늑한, 편리한

05 알탕과 글쓴이가 '게르에 들어갔을 때 나던 좋은 냄새'를 가리킨다.

06 알탕의 할머니는 알탕과 글쓴이를 위해 맛있는 '호르호그'를 요리해 주셨다. 그것을 먹은 후에, 알탕과 글쓴이는 밝은 별들로 가득한 '밤하늘'을 보기 위해 밖으로 나갔다.

07 help+목적어+to부정사 또는 원형부정사

08 'than'을 보충하면 된다.

09 '내가 몽골을 방문한 것'을 가리킨다.

10 감동을 받은 것이므로 수동태로 쓰는 것이 적절하다.

11 부사적 용법의 목적을 나타내는 to부정사는 'in order that 주어 can[may]' 또는 'so that 주어 can[may]'으로 바꿔 쓸 수 있다.

12 게르는 '몽골 전통' 가옥이다. 그것은 큰 텐트이지만 내부는 '아늑하다.'

영역별 핵심문제          p.41~45

01 ③

02 (1) is made   (2) show, around   (3) modern

03 ①          04 ①          05 ⑤          06 ⑤

07 guest      08 ⓑ, ⓒ, ⓓ, ⓔ          09 ②

10 ③          11 How did you like them?

12 ⑤          13 (1) warm enough   (2) so   (3) for

14 ①          15 ④

16 (1) The girls who[whom/that] I invited did not come to my birthday party.

  (2) There was a TV program which[that] I wanted to watch.

  (3) There are some cookies which[that] you can eat.

  (4) The bag is so strong that I can carry a lot of books in it.

(5) I was so busy that I couldn't go shopping. 또는
I was too busy to go shopping.

(6) It is so easy that anyone can do it.

**17** which

**18** (1) I bought the radio. + It isn't working.

(2) That's the coach. + I saw him at the soccer match.

**19** ⑤  **20** comes

**21** It took thirty minutes by taxi from the airport to Altan's grandmother's.

**22** ③

**23** so it isn't cozy inside → but it is cozy inside

**24** It was so delicious that I asked for more.

**25** It gave me a great chance to get to know my friend's country and culture.

**26** ①  **27** ④

**28** (A) This is  (B) had  (C) to see  **29** ⑤

**30** Welcome to Mongolia, a country full of the beauty of nature and culture.

---

**01** satisfying 만족감을 주는 be satisfied with: ~에 만족하다. boring 재미없는, 지루하게 하는

**02** (1) be made of: ~로 만들어지다 (2) show A around B: …에게 ~을 둘러보도록 안내하다 (3) modern: 현대의

**03** from A to B: A에서 B로 / 이 그림을 오른쪽에서 왼쪽으로 살펴보아라.

**04** chance: 기회 / 어떤 것을 할 기회

**05** Have you ever+과거분사 ~?(너는 ~해 본 적이 있니?)는 상대방에게 경험을 묻는 표현으로 ever 다음에는 동사의 과거분사형을 써야 한다.

**06** be made with: ~로 만들어지다

**07** guest: 손님 / 당신을 방문하도록 초대된 사람

**08** ⓐ 여자아이가 탕위안을 먹어 본 경험이 있는가? 토니가 국제음식 축제에 가서 먹었다는 내용은 나오지만 여자아이가 탕위안을 먹었는지 안 먹었는지에 대한 언급은 없다. ⓑ 토니는 누구와 함께 국제 음식 축제에 갔는가? 토니는 부모님과 같이 국제 음식 축제로 갔다. ⓒ 탕위안은 무엇인가? 중국의 전통 후식이다. ⓓ 토니는 주말에 어디를 갔는가? 토니는 국제 음식 축제에 갔다. ⓔ 토니는 국제 음식 축제에서 무엇을 먹었는가? 토니는 국제 음식 축제에서 탕위안을 먹었다.

**09** ⓑ No. → Yes. 새로 생긴 중국 음식점에 가 봤는지 질문하자 지난주 토요일에 거기서 저녁을 먹었다는 것으로 보아 간 경험이 있다고 대답해야 한다.

**10** 남자아이가 수진에게 여행하면서 재미있었던 경험을 이야기해 달라는 말에 생각해 본다고 대답하고 거미 튀김을 먹었다고 말해야 거미 튀김이 어땠는지 남자아이가 질문을 할 수 있으므로 ③이 적절하다.

**11** How did you like ~?: ~는 어땠어?

**12** 수진이는 거미 튀김이 너무 커서 처음에 무서웠지만 맛은 괜찮았다고 했다.

**13** (1) enough는 형용사/부사를 뒤에서 꾸며준다. (2) 'so … that ~' 구문으로 쓴다. (3) 'too … to ~'에서 의미상 주어가 필요할 때에는 'for+목적격'으로 쓴다.

**14** ①번은 목적을 나타내는 'so that ~' 구문의 that이고, 주어진 문장과 나머지 ②~⑤는 모두 원인과 결과를 나타내는 'so … that ~'이다.

**15** 목적격 관계대명사가 전치사의 목적어인 경우 그 전치사를 반드시 써야 한다. 그러므로 'The road which he was driving on was not safe.' 또는 'The road on which he was driving was not safe.'로 쓰는 것이 올바르다.

**16** (1), (2), (3) 관계대명사의 선행사가 '사람'이면 who나 that을 쓰고, 선행사가 '사물이나 동물'이면 which나 that을 쓴다. (4), (5), (6) 'so+형용사/부사+that+주어+동사'로 '매우 …해서 ~하다'라는 의미를 나타낸다. 주절과 that절의 시제를 일치하도록 쓴다.

**17** 첫 번째 문장의 빈칸에는 선행사 the skirt를 꾸며줄 목적격 관계대명사 which 또는 that이 필요하다. 두 번째 문장에서는 선택을 위해 사용되는 의문사 which가 나와야 한다. 그러므로 공통으로 들어갈 단어는 which가 적절하다.

**18** 관계대명사의 선행사가 '사람'이면 who나 that을 쓰고, 선행사가 '사물이나 동물'이면 which나 that을 쓴다.

**19** ⑤ I got up too late to catch the bus. 또는 I got up so late that I missed the bus.로 쓰는 것이 적절하다.

**20** be from = come from: ~ 출신이다

**21** 명사의 소유격 다음에 나오는 house는 생략할 수도 있다(소유격 다음의 명사가 무엇을 가리키는지 분명할 때).

**22** 주어진 문장의 It에 주목한다. ③번 앞 문장에서 말한 '좋은 냄새'를 받고 있으므로 ③번이 적절하다.

**23** 게르는 큰 텐트이지만 '내부는 아늑하다.'

**24** so+형용사/부사+that: 매우 …해서 ~하다

**25** gave 다음에 4형식 순서(간접목적어+직접목적어)로 쓰는 것이 적절하다.

**26** 이 글은 '글쓴이가 몽골을 방문한 것이 여러 면에서 특별한 경험이었다.'는 내용의 글이므로, 제목으로는 '특별한 경험, 몽골을 방문하기'가 적절하다.

**27** 글쓴이가 고비 사막에서 얼마나 오래 낙타를 탔는지는 대답할수 없다. ① For three days. ② The writer experienced Mongolian culture with Altan. ③ It was when the writer rode a camel in the Gobi Desert. ⑤ The writer's visit to Mongolia.

**28** (A) 기장이 방송으로 자신을 소개할 때는 This is가 적절하다. (B) 착륙할 때의 안내방송이므로 had가 적절하다. (C) hope는 to부정사를 목적어로 취하므로 to see가 적절하다.

29 위 글은 '기내 안내방송'이다. ① 생[실황] 방송, ② 탑승 안내 방송, ③ 기행문, ④ 교통 방송 안내[교통 정보]

30 Mongolia와 a country full of the beauty of nature and culture를 동격으로 처리하여 그 사이에 콤마(,)를 넣어야 한다. Welcome to ~.: ~에 오신 것을 환영합니다.

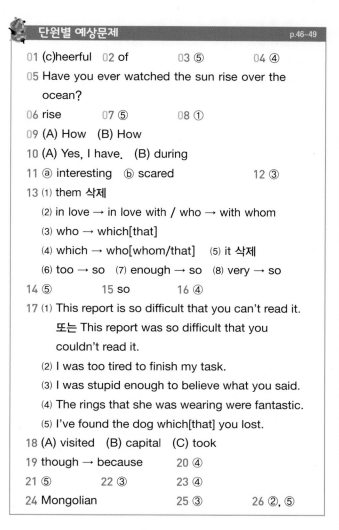

01 (c)heerful  02 of  03 ⑤  04 ④
05 Have you ever watched the sun rise over the ocean?
06 rise  07 ⑤  08 ①
09 (A) How  (B) How
10 (A) Yes, I have.  (B) during
11 ⓐ interesting  ⓑ scared  12 ③
13 (1) them 삭제
    (2) in love → in love with / who → with whom
    (3) who → which[that]
    (4) which → who[whom/that]  (5) it 삭제
    (6) too → so  (7) enough → so  (8) very → so
14 ⑤  15 so  16 ④
17 (1) This report is so difficult that you can't read it.
    또는 This report was so difficult that you couldn't read it.
    (2) I was too tired to finish my task.
    (3) I was stupid enough to believe what you said.
    (4) The rings that she was wearing were fantastic.
    (5) I've found the dog which[that] you lost.
18 (A) visited  (B) capital  (C) took
19 though → because  20 ④
21 ⑤  22 ③  23 ④
24 Mongolian  25 ③  26 ②, ⑤

01 cheerful: 쾌활한, 유쾌한 / 현저히 행복한

02 be full of: ~로 가득하다 / 그곳은 새로운 주인을 기다리는 동물들로 가득 차 있었다. be made of: ~로 만들어지다 / 이 핑크 드레스는 비단으로 만들어졌다.

03 ① bright: 밝은 / 어젯밤 달이 매우 밝았다. ② whole: 전체의, 모든 / 너는 완전한 그림을 보기 위해서 수많은 점들을 봐야만 한다. ③ modern: 현대의 / 고대의 건물부터 현대의 예술 작품에 이르기까지 당신은 그것들을 발견할 수 있다. ④ abroad: 해외에 / 나는 해외로 여행할 계획이다. ⑤ asleep: 잠이 든 / 그는 바쁜 하루를 끝내고, 잠이 든다.

04 expect: 기대하다, 예상하다 / 어떤 것이 발생할 것이라고 믿거나 생각하다

05 Have you ever+과거분사 ~?: 너는 ~해 본 적이 있니? rise: (해가) 뜨다

06 rise: (해가) 뜨다 / 지평선 위로 하늘에 나타나다

07 so → but

08 'Have you ever+과거분사 ~?'는 '너는 ~해 본 적이 있니?'의 뜻으로, 상대방에게 경험을 묻는 표현이다. 해 본 적이 있으면 'Yes, I have.'로, 해 본 적이 없으면 'No, I haven't.'로 답한다. 빈칸 뒤에 'It was a wonderful experience.(그것은 멋진 경험이었어.)'로 설명하고 있으므로, 긍정의 대답이 어울린다.

09 (A) How was ~?: ~는 어땠어? (B) How did you like ~?: ~는 어땠어?

10 (A) 해외여행을 한 경험을 묻는 질문에 지난여름에 캄보디아를 다녀왔다고 말하는 것으로 보아 긍정의 대답이 들어가야 한다. (B) during은 '특정 기간'이 이어지고, for는 보통 '숫자로 된 기간'이 이어진다.

11 감정을 나타내는 동사에 '-ing'를 붙이면 '~한 감정을 일으키는'의 의미가 되고, '-ed'를 붙이면 '~한 감정을 느끼는'의 의미가 된다. interesting: 흥미로운 scared: 겁먹은, 무서워하는

12 거미 튀김이 커서 처음에 조금 무서웠다. 하지만 맛은 괜찮았다는 내용이 어울리므로 But이 적절하다.

13 (1) 목적격 관계대명사는 접속사와 목적어의 결합이다. 그러므로 목적어 them은 삭제한다. (2) 목적격 관계대명사가 전치사의 목적어인 경우 그 전치사가 문장에 반드시 있어야 한다. 그러므로 전치사 with를 추가한다. be in love with: ~와 사랑에 빠지다 (3) 선행사가 사물이므로 관계대명사 which나 that을 써야 한다. (4) 선행사가 사람이므로 관계대명사 who나 whom, that을 써야 한다. (5) 목적격 관계대명사는 접속사와 목적어의 결합이다. 그러므로 목적어 it은 삭제한다. (6), (7), (8) 'so+형용사/부사+that+주어+동사'로 '매우 …해서 ~하다'라는 의미를 나타낸다.

14 ⑤의 관계대명사는 주격이므로 whom은 쓸 수 없다. who 또는 that으로 쓰는 것이 적절하다.

15 첫 번째 문장은 두 절을 원인과 결과의 관계로 연결해 줄 등위접속사 'so'가 필요하고, 두 번째 문장은 'so ... that ~'의 형태로 원인과 결과를 나타내는 문장이므로 'so'가 빈칸에 공통으로 들어간다.

16 ④는 목적격 관계대명사를 생략해서 쓴 올바른 문장이다. ① This is the video camera which he lent me. ② I'm listening to the music which you recommended. ③ I know a boy who speaks English very well. ⑤ I don't like people who tell a lie.

17 (1) 주절과 that절의 시제를 일치시켜야 한다. (2) too+형용사/부사+to부정사: 너무 …해서 ~할 수 없다 (3) 형용사/부사+enough+to부정사: 너무 …해서 ~할 수 있다 (4) 주어가 The rings이므로 were가 적절하다. (5) 선행사가 the dog으로 동물이므로 관계대명사 which나 that이 적절하다.

18 (A) 몽골을 처음으로 '방문했다'고 해야 하므로 visited가 적절하다. invite: 초대[초청]하다, (B) 몽골의 '수도'라고 해야 하므로 capital이 적절하다. capital: 수도, capitol: (미국) 주 의회

9

의사당, the Capitol: 미국 국회 의사당, (C) 30분이 '걸렸다'고 해야 하므로 took이 적절하다. It takes 시간: (얼마의 시간이) 걸리다, 행위자+spend+시간 ~ing/on 명사: ~하는 데 (시간을) 보내다[들이다]

19 몽골을 처음으로 '방문해서' 특별한 여름을 보냈다고 하는 것이 적절하다.

20 글쓴이가 울란바토르에 초대된 이유는 대답할 수 없다. ① This summer. ② No. ③ Altan's grandmother. ⑤ Thirty minutes.

21 'of'를 'for'로 고치는 것이 적절하다. ask for: 요청하다

22 이 글은 글쓴이가 경험한 몽골 전통 가옥인 게르와 몽골식 바비큐인 호르호그에 대한 내용의 글이므로, 제목으로는 '나는 게르와 호르호그를 즐겼다'가 적절하다.

23 몽골인들은 특별한 손님에게 호르호그를 대접한다.

24 'Mongolia'의 형용사형을 쓰는 것이 적절하다. Mongolian: 몽골의(형용사); 몽골 사람(명사)

25 주어진 문장의 But에 주목한다. ③번 앞 문장에 나오는 내용과 상반되는 내용이 뒤에 이어지므로 ③번이 적절하다.

26 ⓑ와 ①, ③, ④: 형용사적 용법, ②: 명사적 용법, ⑤: 부사적 용법

---

### 🦊 서술형 실전문제     p.50~51

01 The service was good. → The service was bad.

02 I have been to Jejudo many times. / I have been there many times.

03 (1) What do you think of[about] your ice cream?
  (2) What's your opinion of[about/on] your ice cream?

04 (1) Jack was so sleepy that he couldn't work any more.
  (2) Mason is so short that he can't ride a roller coaster.
  (3) The man is so busy that he can't play with his daughter.
  (4) It was so hot that children couldn't play outside.

05 (1) I want a robot which[that] I can control.
  (2) Look at the picture which[that] my classmate drew.
  (3) Daniel is the boy who[whom/that] I met at the concert.
  (4) The cathedral which[that] we visited last year was beautiful.

06 (1) He is so honest that he can't tell a lie.
  (2) He is so old that he can enter a university.

07 like     08 (A) wonderful (B) cooked (C) so

---

09 (A) Mongolian barbecue (B) special guests

10 got used to

11 It gave a great chance to get to know my friend's country and culture to me.

12 (A) Mongolian culture (B) special experience

---

01 새로 생긴 중국 음식점의 서비스가 좋다고 말하면서 그곳에 다시 가지 않을 거라고 하는 것은 어색하다.

02 have been to 장소/장소 부사: ~에 가 본 적이 있다

03 'How do you like ~?'는 어떤 것에 대한 만족이나 불만족에 대해 물을 때 사용하며 '~는 어떠니?'라는 의미이다. 유사한 표현으로 'What do you think of[about] ~?', 'What is your opinion of[on] ~?' 등의 표현을 사용한다.

04 'so+형용사/부사+that+주어+동사'로 '매우 …해서 ~하다'라는 의미를 나타낸다. that절의 주어와 주절의 주어가 같으면 that절의 주어는 대명사로 쓰는 것이 두 문장을 연결했을 때 자연스럽다.

05 관계대명사의 선행사가 '사람'이면 who나 that을 쓰고, 선행사가 '사물이나 동물'이면 which나 that을 쓴다.

07 feel+like+주어+동사: ~처럼 느끼다

08 (A) 감각동사 smell의 보어로 형용사를 써야 하므로 wonderful이 적절하다. (B) 수동태 it is cooked에서 it is를 생략한 것이므로 cooked가 적절하다. (C) 뒤에 형용사가 나오므로 so가 적절하다. so+형용사/부사+that: 매우 …해서 ~하다

09 호르호그는 양고기로 만들어졌고 뜨거운 돌로 요리되는 '몽골식 바비큐'이다. 몽골인들은 '특별한 손님'에게 호르호그를 대접한다.

10 get used to: ~에 익숙해지다

11 give는 'to'를 사용하여 3형식으로 고친다.

12 알탕은 글쓴이가 '몽골 문화'를 경험할 수 있게 도와주었고, 몽골을 방문한 것은 여러 면에서 '특별한 경험'이었다.

---

### 🐰 창의사고력 서술형문제     p.52

|모범답안|

01 A: Have you broken your arm?
  B: Yes, I have. / No, I haven't.

02 (1) was so small that, ride a roller coaster
  (2) was so shy that, say anything in public
  (3) was so young that, watch a movie for free
  (4) was so brave that, travel by myself

03 (A) Last summer (B) Ulleungdo (C) walked
  (D) the island

---

01 break one's arm: 팔이 부러지다

01 (1) of   (2) At, to   (3) of
02 (1) My friend is studying abroad now.
   (2) We expected to see each other again.
03 during     04 ⑤       05 ⑤
06 (1) How was your vacation?
   (2) How did like your vacation?
07 amazing       08 ③       09 ②
10 Have you been to the new Chinese restaurant?
11 ②     12 ③     13 ③     14 ③
15 (1) There is a shop which[that] sells good coffee in
    front of my office.
   (2) I like the game which[that] the boys are
    downloading now.
16 ①
17 (1) Tell me about the man whom you admire most.
   (2) She is the woman who lives next door.
   (3) Mandy swam so fast that she won the gold
    medal.
18 It's Ulaanbaatar.
19 It took thirty minutes by taxi from the airport to
Altan's grandmother's house. 또는 It took thirty
minutes from the airport to Altan's grandmother's
house by taxi.
20 ②, ⑤     21 touched       22 ③
23 (A) experience   (B) scared   (C) amazing
24 ③       25 ④

01 (1) be full of: ~로 가득하다 / 방이 연기로 가득차서 창문을 열었다. (2) at first: 처음에는, get used to: ~에 익숙해지다 / 처음에는 그의 억양이 이해하기 어려웠다. 하지만 곧, 우리는 그것에 익숙해졌다. (3) be made of: ~로 만들어지다 / Feijoada는 브라질의 국민요리이다. 그것은 검정 콩과 고기로 만들어진다.

02 (1) abroad: 해외에 (2) expect: 기대하다, 예상하다

03 during: ~동안(내내) 쉬는 시간 동안 스노보딩에 대해서 더 이야기해 봅시다. 나는 겨울 방학 동안 여행을 했다.

04 ① get used to: ~에 익숙해지다 / 어떤 사람이나 사물과 친숙해지다 ② kid: 농담하다 / 농담을 하다 ③ station: 역, 정거장 / 사람들이 타거나 내릴 수 있도록 지하철이나 버스가 멈추는 장소 ④ part: 부분, 일부/ 어떤 것의 전체를 만드는 조각, 부분품 또는 요소들 중의 하나 ⑤ modern: 현대의. designed and made using the latest ides or methods / 가장 최신의 생각이나 방법을 사용하여 디자인되고 만들어진

05 late → early 해가 뜨는 것을 보려고 했는데 늦게 일어나지 못했다는 것은 내용상 어색하다.

06 'How did you like ~?'는 과거의 어떤 것에 대한 만족이나 불만족에 대해 물을 때 사용하며 '~는 어땠니?'라는 의미이다. 같은

의미로 'How was ~?'가 있다.

07 amaze: 놀라게 하다 amazing: 놀라운

08 토니에게 주말을 잘 보냈는지 물어보니 (C) 부모님과 함께 국제 음식 축제에 다녀왔다고 대답한다. (A) 무슨 음식을 먹어 봤는지 물어보니, (B) 중국 전통 후식인 탕위안을 먹었다고 대답한다. (D) 이어, 탕위안이 어땠는지 물어보니, 맛있었다고 대답하며 탕위안에 대해 설명해 준다.

09 How did you like ~?: ~는 어땠어?

10 Have you been to ~?: ~에 가본 적 있니? Chinese: 중국의

11 주어진 문장에서 it은 Cambodia를 의미한다. 캄보디아에 대한 상대방을 의견을 묻고, 날씨가 더웠지만 여행은 즐거웠다는 말이 나와야 한다.

12 누구와 캄보디아를 갔는지는 언급되지 않았다. ① 수진이가 캄보디아를 갔을 때 날씨는 어땠는가? ② 수진이는 지난여름에 어디로 여행을 갔는가? ③ 수진이는 누구와 캄보디아로 여행을 갔는가? ④ 수진이는 해외로 여행한 적이 있는가? ⑤ 수진이는 캄보디아에서 무엇을 먹었는가?

13 목적격 관계대명사와 '주격관계대명사+be동사'는 생략이 가능하다. 그러므로 ③은 The boy who is playing the violin is my son. 또는 The boy playing the violin is my son.으로 쓰는 것이 적절하다.

14 첫 번째 문장은 선행사가 사물이므로 목적격 관계대명사 which 혹은 that이 필요하다. 두 번째 문장은 선행사가 '사람+사물'이므로 주격 관계대명사 that이 필요하다. 그러므로 공통으로 들어갈 단어는 that이다.

15 선행사가 사물이나 동물이면 which나 that을 쓴다.

16 주어 The man을 'I sat next to'가 꾸며주는 형태이므로 ①이 목적격 관계대명사 who(m) 또는 that이 생략된 곳이다.

17 (1) 목적격 관계대명사 whom을 사용하여 선행사 the man을 뒤에서 수식한다. (2) 주격 관계대명사 who를 사용하여 선행사 the woman을 뒤에서 수식한다. (3) 'so+형용사/부사+that+주어+동사'의 어순으로 '매우 …해서 ~하다'라는 의미를 나타낸다.

18 몽골의 수도는 '울란바토르'이다.

19 'by'를 보충하면 된다. by taxi: 택시로

20 목적격 관계대명사 that이나 which가 적절하다.

21 be moved = be touched: 감동받다

22 이 글은 글쓴이가 경험한 몽골 전통 가옥인 게르와 몽골식 바비큐인 호르호그에 대한 내용의 글이다.

23 (A) 'help+목적어+to부정사/원형부정사'이므로 experience가 적절하다. (B) 감정을 나타내는 동사는 수식받는 명사가 감정을 느끼게 되는 경우에 과거분사를 써야 하므로 scared가 적절하다. scared: 무서워하는, 겁먹은, scary: 무서운, 겁나는, (C) 경치가 정말로 '놀라웠던' 것이므로 amazing이 적절하다. (감정을 나타내는 동사는 감정을 유발할 때 현재분사를 쓰는 것이 적절하다.)

24 ⓐ, ①, ④, ⑤: 명사적 용법, ②: 형용사적 용법, ③: 부사적 용법

25 낙타의 등에서 보는 사막의 경치는 정말로 '놀라웠다.'

Lesson 7

# Living in the AI World

다. 너는 우산을 가져와야 할 것이다. (4) luck: 행운 lucky: 운이 좋은 / 나는 우연히 내가 좋아하는 영화 배우를 만났다. 운이 좋은 날이다! by chance: 우연히

## 시험대비 실력평가    p.60

| | | | |
|---|---|---|---|
| 01 ③ | 02 funny | 03 ① | 04 ③ |
| 05 ③ | 06 ② | 07 (1) no longer[more] | |

(2) don't (h)ave

01 ① 동물 중에는 지진을 예측하는 능력을 가진 것이 있다. ② 집의 수도관이 얼지 않기를 희망한다. ③ teleport: 순간 이동하다, 나는 시간과 공간을 통과해 순간 이동할 수 있습니다. ④ 암호를 확인한 다음 다시 시도해 보십시오. ⑤ 나는 아이를 위해 장난감을 골랐다.

02 fun: 재미 funny: 재미있는 / 너의 이야기가 너무 웃겨서 나는 웃음을 멈출 수가 없다.

03 translate: 번역하다 / 불어를 영어로 번역할 수 있는 사람을 아니?

04 beat: 이기다 / 그리스와의 첫 경기에서, 우리나라 팀은 그리스 팀을 이겼다.

05 ③의 like는 '좋아하다'의 의미로 사용하였고, 나머지는 '~와 같이, ~처럼'의 의미로 사용하였다. ① 숲속에서 배우는 것은 재미있을 것 같지 않나요? ② 그 옷을 입으니 완전히 다른 사람처럼 보여요. ③ 왜 그렇게 좋아하시죠? ④ 그것은 약간 체스 게임 같이 보이지 않는가? ⑤ 그들은 사람들처럼 오랫동안 슬퍼한다.

06 strange: 이상한 unusual: 특이한, 이상한 / 실험 후에 사람들에게 어떤 이상한 것을 보았는지 물어봤다.

07 (1) no longe[more]: 더 이상 ~하지 않다 (2) don't have to 동사원형: ~할 필요가 없다(= don't need to, need not)

## 서술형 시험대비    p.61

01 (1) greedy (2) funny (3) sunny, cloudy (4) lucky
02 (r)eplace
03 By, by
04 (1) translate (2) (p)ossible, finish
   (3) (e)lse (4) (h)ave, perfect
05 (1) in (2) to (3) off
06 (1) I saw him crossing the street.
   (2) He predicted that the GDP would go up.

01 (1) greed: 욕심 greedy: 욕심 많은 / Scrooge는 욕심 많은 노인이었다. (2) fun: 재미 funny: 재미있는 / 이야기가 재미있기 때문에 난 이 책을 좋아한다. (3) sun: 태양 sunny: 맑은 cloud: 구름 cloudy: 흐린 / 오늘은 날씨가 맑았지만 내일은 흐릴 것이

02 replace: 대체하다(= take the place of) / 새로운 세포들이 오래된 세포들을 대신한다.

03 by the way: 그런데, 그건 그렇고 / 그건 그렇고, 아직도 공립 도서관에서 일하시나요? by 동사ing: ~함으로써 / 그것을 함으로써 시간 관리 기술을 배울 수 있습니다.

04 (1) translate: 번역하다 (2) possible: 가능한 Is it possible (for 목적격) to 동사원형 ~?: (…가) ~하는 것이 가능할까? (3) else: 그 밖의 (4) don't have to 동사원형: ~할 필요가 없다(= need not) perfect: 완벽한

05 (1) get in: ~에 타다 / 차에 당장 타라, 안 그러면 늦을 거야. (2) get to: ~에 도착하다 / 내가 산 정상에 도착했을 때, 아주 어두워졌다. (3) get off: ~에서 내리다, ~에서 떨어지다 / 우리는 그를 곧 보게 될 것이다. 승객들이 지금 비행기에서 내리고 있는 중이다.

06 (1) cross: 건너다 (2) predict: 예측하다

## 교과서 Conversation

### 핵심 Check    p.62~63

1 Sounds
2 That sounds good / I think it's exciting
3 Is it possible that
4 Is it possible for him to finish this marathon?
  Can he finish this marathon?
5 Is it possible for you to make a cake?

## 교과서 대화문 익히기

### Check(√) True or False    p.64

1 F   2 T   3 F   4 T

## 교과서 확인학습    p.66~67

### Listen & Speak 1 A

don't / sounds

1 have any, for, project / What about / talk about future, What, think / sounds perfect, look for
2 begins, Why, with / to, sounds / chance to meet robotics / great

1 going, drone / like fun
2 going, build / like fun

possible, to live without / possible

1 looks, How much / newest / Is it possible to use / check, off / Perfect
2 took, picture during / did, than, it possible to make, out of / have

1 Is it possible, to text with, closed
2 possible for you / by

at / What, they mean, look them up, dictionary / about using / How / point, translate, get / possible for AI to read / read, translate / unvelievable, mean / amazing

## 시험대비 기본평가     p.68

| 01 ③ | 02 ① | 03 ② |

01 가능 여부를 나타내는 표현들로는 'Is it possible that 주어 동사 ~?', 'Is it possible for 목적격 to 동사원형 ~?', 'Can 주어 동사원형 ~?' 등이 있다.

02 여자아이는 남자아이의 의견을 좋아하면서, 인터넷에서 정보를 찾아보자고 제안하고 있다. sound 형용사: ~하게 들리다

03 로봇 박람회를 같이 가자고 제안하는 말에, (B) 제안을 수락하면서 박람회가 재미있겠다고 자신의 생각을 표현한다. (A) 로봇 공학자를 만날 기회가 있을 거라고 하자 (C) 그러면 좋겠다고 말한다. Why don't you ~?: ~하는 게 어때? exciting: 흥미진진한, 신나는 sound 형용사: ~하게 들리다 chance: 기회 look for: 찾다

## 시험대비 실력평가     p.69~70

| 01 ② | 02 ④ | 03 ⑤ | 04 ④ |
| 05 ④ | 06 ⑤ | 07 ② | 08 ③ |
| 09 ④ | | | |

01 sound 형용사: ~하게 들리다 exciting: 흥미진진한, 신나는

02 ① 남자아이는 로봇 박람회를 어떻게 생각하는가? 재미있을 것 같다고 생각한다. ② 그들은 로봇 박람회에서 누구를 만날 수 있을까? 로봇 공학자. ③ 여자아이는 남자아이와 어디를 같이 가기를 원하는가? 로봇 박람회. ④ 로봇 박람회를 가기 위해서 그들은 어디서 만날 것인가? 대화의 내용에 나와 있지 않으므로 대답할 수 없음. ⑤ 언제 로봇 박람회가 시작되는가? 다음 주에.

03 주어진 문장은 글자의 뜻을 물어보고 있는 질문이므로 글자의 뜻을 이야기해 주고 있는 'They mean "Dreams come true!"("꿈은 이루어진다!"라는 뜻이에요.)'라는 대답 앞에 오는 것이 적절하다.

04 사전을 찾지 않고 곧바로 AI 번역기를 사용하였다.

05 주어진 문장은 로봇이 위험에 처한 사람들을 도울 수 있다는 내용으로 ④번 다음 문장인 'Robots can do the dangerous work so humans don't have to.(로봇이 그 위험한 일을 할 수 있어서 사람들이 그 일을 하지 않아도 되지.)'가 주어진 문장을 좀 더 설명한 것으로 볼 수 있다.

06 스마트 음식 주문 자판기를 사용해 보자는 제안에, 쉽고 빠르게 주문을 할 수 있다고 말하고 있으므로, 제안에 대해 긍정하는 내용이 빈칸에 들어가는 것이 적절하다. sound 형용사: ~하게 들리다 interesting: 재미있는, 흥미로운

07 여자아이가 로봇이 인간을 대체할 수 있을 거라고 생각하는지 민석이에게 묻는 질문에 잘 모르겠다고 대답했다.

08 ③ Yes, I can. → Yes, you can. 또는 Is it possible that I keep a pet? → Is it possible that you keep a pet?

09 ④ 영화를 보자는 제안에 반대하는 말을 하고 재미있을 것 같다고 말하는 것은 앞뒤가 맞지 않는다.

## 서술형 시험대비     p.71

01 Can you
02 Is it possible to use this coupon?
03 She will pay 470 dollars.
04 (A) up (B) about
05 unbelievable
06 Is it possible for you to travel around Gangwondo by bicycle?

01 가능 여부를 나타내는 표현들로는 'Is it possible for 목적격 to 동사원형 ~?', 'Can 주어 동사원형 ~?' 등이 있다.

02 Is it possible (for 목적격) to 동사원형 ~?: (…가) ~하는 것이 가능할까?

03 컴퓨터 가격이 500 달러였는데 30달러 할인되는 쿠폰을 사용하였으므로 470달러를 낼 것이다.

04 (A) look ~ up: (사전·참고 자료·컴퓨터 등에서 정보를) 찾아 보다 (B) What about ~?: ~하는 게 어때?

05 unbelievable: 믿기 어려운, 놀랄만한

06 Is it possible (for 목적격) to 동사원형 ~?: (…가) ~하는 것이 가능할까? by bicycle: 자전거로

## 교과서 Grammar

### 핵심 Check                                        p.72~73

1 (1) doing  (2) sing  (3) washed
2 (1) to play  (2) to solve  (3) It

### 시험대비 기본평가                                   p.74

01 (1) sang → sing(또는 singing)
   (2) to fly → fly(또는 flying)
   (3) choose → to choose
   (4) That → It
02 (1) cry[또는 crying] (2) cleaned
   (3) play(또는 playing) (4) flow(또는 flowing)
03 ④
04 It is necessary for you to take a rest.

01 (1), (2) 지각동사의 목적어가 목적격보어의 행위의 주체가 될 때 목적격보어로 원형부정사나 현재분사를 쓰는 것이 적절하다. (3) 진주어로 to부정사가 적절하다. (4) 가주어로는 that이 아니라 it 을 쓴다.

02 (1) 지각동사의 목적격보어는 목적어와의 관계가 능동일 경우 원형부정사나 현재분사가 쓰인다. (2) 지각동사의 목적격보어는 목적어와의 관계가 수동일 경우 과거분사가 쓰인다. (3) 그들이 경기 하는 것이므로 play 또는 playing이 적절하다. (4) 물이 흐르는 것이므로 능동의 의미를 나타내 는 flow 또는 flowing이 적절하다.

03 가주어로는 that이 아니라 it을 쓰며 진주어로 to부정사를 이용한다.

04 가주어 it과 진주어 to부정사를 이용하여 문장을 쓴다. 또한 의미상의 주어로 'for+목적격'을 써야 하므로 for를 추가한다.

### 시험대비 실력평가                                   p.75~77

01 ⑤       02 ③       03 ①       04 It is
good to ride bicycles for fun on weekends.  05 ④
06 (1) waiting (2) playing (3) played (4) listen (5) It (6) to
swim (7) of    07 ④       08 This → It  09 ③, ④
10 ④       11 him turn[turning] off the stove

---

12 ①, ⑤       13 ③       14 ②       15 ③
16 (1) It is not easy to make her laugh.
   (2) It is my plan to read 10 books during winter
       vacation.
17 (1) to paint → paint[painting]
   (2) wears → to wear
   (3) of → for
18 (1) Minsu hears a dog bark[barking] whenever he
       passes by the house.
   (2) I saw a bird fly[flying] high in the sky.
   (3) It is exciting for me to watch baseball games
       with my friends.
   (4) It is dangerous to put paper near the fire.

01 목적어와의 관계가 능동이므로 지각동사의 목적격보어로 원형 부정사 혹은 현재분사가 적절하다. / It을 가주어로 하고 to부정사를 진주어로 쓰는 것이 적절하다.

02 feel은 지각동사이므로 목적격보어로 원형부정사 혹은 현재분사, 과거분사를 취한다. the dog이 his clothes를 끌고 가는 주체가 되므로 pull 또는 pulling이 적절하다.

03 가주어로는 that이 아니라 it을 쓰며 진주어로 to부정사가 적절하다.

04 가주어 it과 진주어로 to부정사를 이용하여 문장을 쓴다.

05 지각동사 feel의 목적격보어로 원형부정사 혹은 현재분사가 적절하다. At times, Nora felt him stare[staring] at her.

06 (1) 지각동사 see의 목적격보어로 원형부정사가 적절하다. (2) 지각동사 hear의 목적격보어로 현재분사가 적절하다. (3) the game이 play되는 것이므로 목적격보어로 수동의 의미를 갖는 과거분사가 적절하다 (4) make는 사역동사이므로 목적격보어로 원형부정사가 적절하다. (5) 가주어로는 that이 아니라 it을 쓴다. (6) 진주어로 to부정사를 쓰는 것이 적절하다. (7) to부정사의 의미상 주어를 나타낼 때 문장에 쓰인 형용사가 사람의 성질을 나타내는 말일 때는 'of+목적격'을 쓴다.

07 지각동사 watch의 목적격보어로 bake나 baking을 쓰는 것이 적절하다.

08 주어로 쓰인 'that'절의 경우에도 보통 가주어 'it'을 쓰고 'that' 절을 문장 뒤로 보낸다.

09 목적어와의 관계가 능동이므로 지각동사의 목적격보어로 원형 부정사 혹은 현재분사가 적절하다.

10 it을 가주어로 하고 to부정사를 진주어로 쓰는 것이 적절하다.

11 Bill이 난로를 끄는 것을 보았다는 의미이다. 목적어와 목적격보어의 관계가 능동이므로 원형부정사 또는 현재분사로 써야 한다.

12 ② I saw a boy solve[solving] math problems. ③ By the way, do you think it will be possible for robots to replace humans someday? ④ Is it possible to fly through a rainbow?

13 (A) 지각동사의 목적어와 목적격보어의 관계가 능동이므로 현재분사가 적절하다. (B) 지각동사의 목적어와 목적격보어의 관계가 능동이므로 원형부정사가 적절하다. (C) 지각동사의 목적어와 목적격보어의 관계가 수동 (이름이 불리는 것)이므로 과거분사가 적절하다.

14 ②번은 인칭대명사이지만 나머지는 모두 가주어 It이다. 가주어는 해석하지 않지만 인칭대명사는 '그것'이라고 해석한다.

15 주어진 문장과 ③번은 목적격보어로 쓰인 현재분사이다. ① 분사구문 ② 진행형을 만드는 현재분사 ④, ⑤ 동명사

16 it을 가주어로 하고 to부정사를 진주어로 하여 쓰는 것이 적절하다.

17 (1) 지각동사의 목적격보어로 원형부정사나 현재분사가 적절하다. (2) it을 가주어로 하고 to부정사를 진주어로 쓰는 것이 적절하다. (3) to부정사의 의미상 주어로 사람의 성질을 나타내는 형용사가 쓰인 것이 아니므로 'for+목적격'이 적절하다.

18 (1)~(3) 지각동사의 목적격보어로 원형부정사나 현재분사를 이용한다. (4), (5) it을 가주어로 하고 to부정사를 진주어로 하여 'It ~ to부정사' 구문으로 쓰는 것이 적절하다. to부정사의 의미상 주어로 사람의 성질을 나타내는 형용사가 쓰인 것이 아니므로 'for+목적격'이 적절하다.

## 🦉 서술형 시험대비                                        p.78~79

01 (1) I saw them play[playing] soccer in the playground.
   (2) Barbara felt her heart beat[beating] faster.
   (3) Aaron looked at Sylvia come[coming] with Alex hand in hand.
   (4) A farmer bought 43 sheep at the market and saw them stolen 24 hours later.
   (5) It is hard to take care of a baby.
   (6) It is a lot of fun to go on a picnic.
   (7) It is difficult for me to learn a new language.

02 I heard Sam baking some cookies.

03 (1) It was very difficult to answer the math questions.
   (2) It was a great experience to swim in the blue sea.
   (3) It is good for your health to exercise regularly.
   (4) It is not easy for me to learn English.
   (5) It is true that a friend in need is a friend indeed.

04 (1) to stay (2) pulled (3) sing[singing] (4) take

05 to read 50 novels

06 (1) for me to pass the driver's test
   (2) to watch the view as we went higher and higher
   (3) of you to help that old woman
   (4) that Annabelle didn't tell him a lie

07 make[또는 making]

08 (1) He heard them playing te drums.

   (2) Suhan looked at AI Speaker playing a movie.

09 (1) It is very smart of her to solve that problem.
   (2) It is not safe to swim in this river as it is very deep.

01 (1)~(3) 지각동사의 목적어와 목적격보어의 관계가 능동이므로 목적격보어로 원형부정사 혹은 현재분사가 적절하다 (4) 지각동사의 목적어와 목적격보어의 관계가 수동이므로 과거 분사가 적절하다 (5) It ~ to부정사' 구문으로 쓰는 것이 적절하다. (6) 가주어로는 that이 아니라 it을 쓴다. (7) to부정사의 의미상 주어로 사람의 성질을 나타내는 형용사가 쓰인 것이 아니므로 'for+목적격'이 적절하다.

02 진행형의 문장이므로 목적격보어로 현재분사가 적절하다.

03 (1)~(4) 문장의 주어로 쓰인 to부정사를 뒤로 보내고 대신 주어 자리에 가주어 it을 쓴다. (5) 주어로 쓰인 that절의 경우에도 긴 that절을 뒤로 보내고 주어 자리에 가주어 it을 쓴다.

04 (1) ask는 to부정사를 목적격보어로 받는다. (2) 지각동사의 목적어와 목적격보어의 관계가 수동일 때 목적격보어로 과거분사가 적절하다. (3) 목적어와 목적격보어의 관계가 능동일 때 목적격보어로 원형부정사나 현재분사가 적절하다. (4) 사역동사 make는 원형부정사를 목적격보어로 받는다.

05 가주어로 it이 나와 있으므로 진주어로 to부정사를 쓰는것이 적절하다.

06 (1) '하는데 어려움이 있다'는 것을 '~하기 어렵다'는 문장으로, (2) Watching을 to watch로 바꾸어서, '가주어(it) ~ 진주어(to부정사) …' 구문을 이용하여 쓴다. (4) In fact는 '사실은'이라는 뜻이므로 It is true 다음에 that절을 진주어로 쓴다.

07 지각동사 see의 목적어와 목적격보어의 관계가 능동이므로 목적격보어로 원형부정사나 현재분사가 적절하다.

08 지각동사의 목적어와 목적격보어의 관계가 능동이며, 진행형으로 쓰이고 있으므로 현재분사를 이용한다.

09 (1) to solve의 주어가 she이므로 of her로 의미상의 주어를 나타내야 한다. (2) 전치사 in의 목적어로 this river를 쓴다.

## 🐦 교과서 Reading

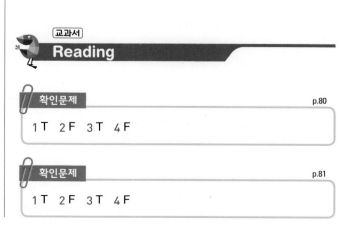

| 📎 확인문제 |       | p.80 |
| 1 T | 2 F | 3 T | 4 F |

| 📎 확인문제 |       | p.81 |
| 1 T | 2 F | 3 T | 4 F |

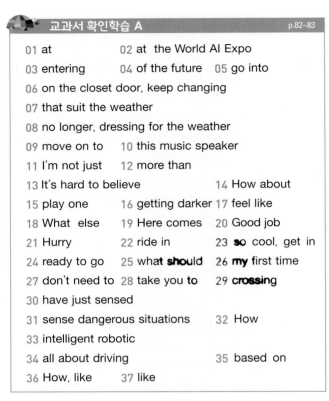
01 at    02 at the World AI Expo

03 entering    04 of the future    05 go into

06 on the closet door, keep changing

07 that suit the weather

08 no longer, dressing for the weather

09 move on to    10 this music speaker

11 I'm not just    12 more than

13 It's hard to believe    14 How about

15 play one    16 getting darker    17 feel like

18 What else    19 Here comes    20 Good job

21 Hurry    22 ride in    23 **so** cool, get in

24 ready to go    25 wha**t should**    26 **my** first time

27 don't need to    28 take you **to**    29 **crossing**

30 have just sensed

31 sense dangerous situations    32 How

33 intelligent robotic

34 all about driving    35 based on

36 How, like    37 like

**교과서 확인학습 B**    p.84~85

1 A Day **at** the AI Expo

2 Jina **and** Suhan are at the World AI Expo.

3 They **are** entering the AI home.

4 Suhan: Look at this! It's a house of the future.

5 Jina: Let's go into the bedroom first. Look, there's a smart closet.

6 Suhan: I'm standing in front of this screen on the closet door and my clothes keep changing.

7 Jina: The screen suggests clothes that suit the weather.

8 Suhan: That's amazing! We no longer have to worry about dressing for the weather.

9 Jina: Right. Let's move on to the living room.

10 Suhan: Oh, I like this music speaker.

11 AI Speaker: I'm not just a music speaker.

12 I can do more than you can imagine.

13 Jina: It's hard to believe that you can understand us. What can you do?

14 AI Speaker: How about watching a movie?

15 I'll play one for you.

16 Suhan: Look, those smart windows are getting darker.

17 I feel like I'm in a movie theater.

18 Jina: What else can you do?

19 AI Speaker: I can beatbox, too. Here comes, "cats

and boots and cats and boots."

20 Suhan: You're funny. Good job!

21 Jina: Hurry! There's a smart car station outside!

22 Let's go and ride in that red car.

23 Suhan: This car is so cool. Let's get in.

24 AI Car: Welcome. Are you ready to go?

25 Jina: Yes, what should we do now?

26 It's my first time to ride in a smart car.

27 AI Car: You don't need to do anything.

28 I will drive and take you to the next station.

29 Suhan: Watch out! I see a cat crossing the street.

30 AI Car: Don't worry. I have just sensed it.

31 When I sense dangerous situations, I slow down or stop.

32 Jina: How can you do that?

33 AI Car: I'm a very intelligent robotic car.

34 I know all about driving.

35 I can predict danger based on knowledge and experience.

36 Suhan: How smart! You think and act like a person.

37 You are really like a human.

**시험대비 실력평가**    p.86~89

01 Jina and Suhan    02 ②, ④, ⑤    03 ②

04 ⑤    05 (A) one (B) What else (C) comes

06 I feel like I'm in a movie theater.    07 ①, ④

08 ②, ⑤    09 ③    10 changing    11 ②, ⑤

12 ④    13 ③    14 ①, ④    15 ⑤

16 (A) music speaker (B) beatbox    17 ①

18 ④    19 ①, ④    20 beaten[beat]

21 it    22 who is one of the greatest baduk players    23 ④

01 '진아'와 '수한'을 가리킨다.

02 ⓑ와 ②, ④, ⑤번: 현재분사, ①, ③: 동명사

03 '진아'가 침실에 먼저 들어가 보자고 말한다.

04 주어진 문장의 you에 주목한다. ⑤번 앞 문장의 내용을 말한 AI Speaker를 가리키므로 ⑤번이 적절하다.

05 (A) 'a movie'를 지칭하므로 one이 적절하다. 'a+명사'는 one 으로, 'the+명사'는 it으로 받는다. (B) '또 뭘 할 수 있어?'라 고 해야 하므로 What else가 적절하다. (C) "cats and boots and cats and boots."는 비트박스를 하는 한 예에 해당하는 말 이므로 comes 가 적절하다. 비트박스: 사람의 입으로 디제잉 (DJing)의 소리를 흉내 내는 일종의 모사이다.

06 feel like: …한 느낌이 있다

07 '고양이가 길을 건너고 있는게 보인다'고 해야 하므로, 지각동사 see의 목적격보어 자리에 동사원형이나 현재분사가 오는 것이 적절하다.

08 ⓐ와 ②, ⑤번: 멋진, 끝내 주는, ①, ④: (날씨·공기 따위가) 서늘한, 시원한, ③ 차분한, 침착한

09 이 글은 '인공 지능 자동차는 지능적인 로봇 차이기 때문에 운전에 대한 모든 걸 알고 있고 위험을 예측하며 운전할 수 있다'는 내용의 글이므로, 제목으로는 '걱정 말아요! 저는 운전에 대한 모든 걸 알고 있어요.'가 적절하다.

10 keep ~ing: 계속 ~하다

11 worry about = be concerned[worried, anxious] about: ~에 대해 걱정하다, ② be anxious for: 갈망하다, ⑤ be concerned with: …에 관계가 있다, …에 관심이 있다

12 수한이의 옷이 어떻게 계속해서 바뀌는지는 대답할 수 없다. ① They are entering the AI home at the World AI Expo. ② They enter the bedroom first. ③ He is standing in front of the screen on the closet door. ⑤ It suggests clothes that suit the weather.

13 ③은 진아(와 수한)를 가리키고, 나머지는 다 'AI Speaker'를 가리킨다.

14 ⓐ와 ①, ④번: ~처럼(접속사), ② 좋아하다(동사), ③ ~처럼(전치사), ⑤ 비슷한(형용사)

15 이 글은 AI Speaker가 그냥 음악 스피커가 아니라 사람들이 상상하는 것 이상의 것을 할 수 있다는 내용의 글이므로, 주제로는 '그것의 원래 역할을 하는 외에 AI Speaker가 할 수 있는 것'이 적절하다.

16 AI Speaker는 '음악 스피커'일 뿐만 아니라 영화를 틀어 주고 '비트박스'도 할 수 있다.

17 (A) take+사람+to+장소: ~를 …에 데리고 가다, (C) based on: ~에 근거하여

18 지식과 경험을 바탕으로 '위험을 예측할 수 있다'고 하는 것이 적절하다. ① safety: 안전(함), ⑤ generate: 발생시키다

19 ⓐ와 ②, ③, ⑤: 부사적 용법, ① 형용사적 용법, ④ 명사적 용법

20 'beat'의 과거분사형 beaten과 beat이다.

21 가주어 'it'이 적절하다.

22 one+of+the+복수명사: ~ 중의 하나

23 AI는 이세돌의 경기를 예측할 수 있었고, 그리고 마침내 경기에서 이겼다.

## 서술형 시험대비 p.90~91

01 entering into → entering

02 We no longer have to worry about dressing for the weather.

03 (a) closet door (b) the weather

04 than

05 What about / Why don't you

06 becoming 또는 growing

07 (1) 영화를 틀어 줄 수 있다.
   (2) 비트박스도 할 수 있다.

08 Intelligence

09 (1) don't have to
   (2) need not

10 AI Car가 이미 고양이가 길을 건너고 있는 것을 감지했고, AI Car는 어떤 위험한 상황을 감지하면 속도를 늦추거나 멈추기 때문이다.

11 a cat crossing the street

12 (A) Suhan (B) his clothes

13 amazed → amazing

14 suggests clothes

01 enter: ~에 들어가다, enter into: (논의·처리 등을) 시작하다

02 no longer: 더 이상 …아닌

03 그것은 스마트 '옷장 문'에 있는 스크린이고 그 앞에 서 있는 사람에게 '날씨'에 적합한 옷을 제안한다.

04 비교급 뒤에 'than'이 적절하다.

05 How about ~ing? = What about ~ing? = Why don't you+동사원형?: ~하는 게 어때?

06 get[become/grow]+형용사의 비교급: 점점 ~해지다

07 인공 지능 스피커는 그냥 음악 스피커가 아니라 당신이 상상하는 것 이상의 것을 할 수 있다고 하면서, 두 가지 예를 설명하고 있다.

08 intelligent의 명사형인 intelligence를 쓰는 것이 적절하다. artificial intelligence = AI: (컴퓨터) 인공 지능

09 don't need to = don't have to = need not: ~할 필요가 없다

10 바로 뒤의 내용을 쓰는 것이 적절하다.

11 '길을 건너고 있는 고양이'를 가리킨다.

12 '수한'이가 실제로 그의 옷을 계속 바꿔 입는 것이 아니다. 그는 단지 옷장 문에 있는 스크린 앞에서 있으면 '그의 옷'이 계속해서 바뀐다.

13 감정을 나타내는 동사는 감정을 유발할 때 현재분사를 쓰는 것이 적절하다.

14 옷장 문에 있는 스크린이 날씨에 적합한 '옷을 제안해주기' 때문이다.

## 영역별 핵심문제 p.93~97

01 look
02 ①
03 (1) on (2) just (3) longer (4) if
04 (1) (b)eat (2) (i)ntelligent (3) (r)eplace
05 ④
06 ③
07 ⑤
08 ③
09 for
10 ③
11 ①
12 (A) for (B) Sure (C) do
13 ⑤
14 ⑤
15 (1) play(또는 playing)

17

     (2) swim(또는 swimming)

     (3) ride(또는 riding)

**16** ②     **17** ④

**18** (1) I saw him riding[ride] a bike in the park.

     (2) I smelled something burning in the kitchen.

     (3) It is not possible to talk on the moon.

     (4) It is exciting to play basketball with friends.

**19** (1) danced → dance[dancing]

     (2) burns → burning

     (3) tearing → torn

     (4) of → for

     (5) beating → to beat

     (6) make → to make

**20** ①, ⑤     **21** ④     **22** closet     **23** I can do more than you can imagine.     **24** ②

**25** Look out! 또는 Be careful!     **26** ④

**27** slow down or stop when you sense dangerous situations     **28** called     **29** ⑤

---

**01** look ~ up: (사전·참고 자료·컴퓨터 등에서 정보를) 찾아보다 / 그는 네가 그것들을 인터넷에서 찾을 충분한 시간을 줄 것이다. look for: 찾다 / 이 고래들은 무리지어 먹이를 찾는다.

**02** free from: ~이 없는 / 그녀에게는 걱정거리가 끊이지 않는다.

**03** (1) based on: ~에 근거하여 / 그 영화는 유명한 소설에 기반을 두고 있다. (2) not just: 단지 ~뿐이 아니다 / 그것은 단순히 돈의 문제만은 아니다. (3) no longer: 더 이상 ~하지 않는 / 그녀는 더 이상 아이가 아니다. (4) see if 주어 동사: ~인지 아닌지 확인하다 / 문이 잠겨 있는지 가서 확인해 보세요.

**04** (1) beat: 이기다 (2) intelligent: 똑똑한 (3) replace: 대체하다

**05** (A) '우리는 정말 그랬어.'란 의미로, did는 'took lots of pictures during our trip.'을 의미한다. (B) Is it possible (for 목적격) to 동사원형 ~?: (…가) ~하는 것이 가능할까?

**06** 사진으로 동영상 앨범을 만드는 것이 가능한지 물어보고 있으므로 가능한지 불가능한지 대답을 해야 한다. 또한 빈칸 뒤에 'I have an app for that.(나는 그것을 위한 앱이 있어.)'라고 말했으므로 가능하다고 대답하는 것이 적절하다.

**07** (A) Why don't we ~?: ~하는 게 어때?(제안, 권유) (B) sound 형용사: ~하게 들리다

**08** 주어진 문장은 상대방의 생각을 물어보는 'What do you think?(너는 어떻게 생각해?)'이다. 그러므로 자신의 생각을 표현한 'That sounds perfect for our project.(우리 프로젝트에 완벽한 것 같아.)' 앞의 질문으로 어울린다.

**09** (A) perfect for: ~에 완벽한, ~에 안성맞춤인 (B) look for: 찾다

**10** 여자아이는 남자아이의 의견이 프로젝트에 완벽하다고 생각한다. disagree: 동의하지 않다

**11** 로봇 박람회에 같이 가자고 제안하는 말에, 'That sounds exciting.(그거 재미있겠는데.)'이라고 했으므로 빈칸에는 제안에 긍정하는 말이 어울린다.

**12** (A) to부정사의 행위에 대하여 행위를 하는 주체가 있을 때 to부정사 앞에 의미상 주어를 넣는다. 의미상의 주어는 일반적으로 'for+목적격'을 사용하며 주절에 사람의 '성질이나 성격 등'을 나타내는 형용사가 쓰였을 경우 'of+목적격'을 사용한다. Is it possible (for 목적격) to 동사원형 ~?: (…가) ~하는 것이 가능할까? (B) 'I can do that.(할 수 있어.)'으로 대답하고 있으므로, 가능하다고 말하는 것이 어울린다. (C) read를 의미하므로 do가 적절하다.

**13** 첫 문장에는 smell이 나왔으므로 목적격보어로 현재분사가 나와야 한다. 두 번째 문장에서는 지각동사이므로 목적격보어로 동사원형이나 현재분사가 나와야 한다.(사람들이 수영하는 것이므로 능동)

**14** 가주어로 it이 나와야 하며 진주어로 to부정사가 적절하다.

**15** (1)~(3) 지각동사의 목적어가 목적격보어의 행위의 주체가 될 경우 목적격보어로 원형부정사나 현재분사를 쓴다.

**16** that이 나오려면 뒤에 주어와 동사가 있는 절이 이어져야 한다. It was interesting to compare their situation and ours.

**17** see가 지각동사이므로 목적격보어로 serve나 serving이 적절하다.

**18** (1) 지각동사의 목적어와 목적격보어의 관계가 능동일 경우 목적격보어로 원형부정사와 현재분사를 모두 사용할 수 있으나 의미상 그 동작이 진행 중인 것을 나타낼 때에는 주로 현재분사를 사용한다. (2) smell은 목적격보어로 현재분사를 사용한다. (3)~(4) it이 나와 있으므로 '가주어(it) ~ 진주어(to 부정사)' 구문을 이용하여 쓴다.

**19** (1), (3) 지각동사의 목적어와 목적격보어가 능동의 관계에 있을 경우 목적격보어로 원형부정사나 현재분사를 쓰고, 수동일 경우 과거분사를 쓴다. (2) smell은 목적격보어로 현재분사를 쓴다. (4) to부정사의 의미상 주어로 사람의 성질을 나타내는 형용사가 쓰인 것이 아니므로 'for+목적격'이 적절하다. (5) for an AI가 의미상의 주어로 나와 있으므로 to beat을 써야 한다. (6) it을 가주어로 하고 to부정사를 진주어로 쓰는 것이 적절하다.

**20** 주격 관계대명사 'that'이나 'which'가 적절하다.

**21** 이 글은 인공 지능 집에서 옷장 문에 있는 스크린이 날씨에 적합한 옷을 제안하는 내용의 글이므로, 제목으로는 '옷을 제안하는 스크린'이 적절하다. ⑤ suitable for: …에 알맞은[어울리는]

**22** closet: 벽장; 보관 장소로 사용되는 작은 방이나 캐비닛

**23** more than you can imagine: 당신이 상상하는 것 이상의 것

**24** (A)와 ②번: 가주어, ①, ④: 비인칭 주어 <시간·날짜·거리·날씨 등에 대해 말할 때 동사의 주어 자리에 씀> ③ 가목적어 ⑤ 그것(앞에 이미 언급 되었거나 현재 이야기되고 있는 사물·동물을 가리킴)

25 watch out = look out = be careful: (특히 위험이 있을 때 경고하는 말로) 조심하다

26 ⓑ와 ①번: 완료 용법, ② 경험 용법, ③, ⑤: 계속 용법, ④ 결과 용법

27 앞 문장 '저는 어떤 위험 상황을 감지하면 속도를 늦추거나 멈춰요.'를 가리킨다.

28 "Alpha-Foot"이라고 '불리는' 축구 로봇이라고 해야 하므로, 과거분사로 쓰는 것이 적절하다.

29 ⑤ 위 글은 '학교 신문 기사'이다. ① (책, 연극, 영화 등에 대한) 논평[비평], 감상문, ② 독후감, ③ 수필

### 단원별 예상문제  p.98~101

01 (b)urn / burn  02 cloudy  03 ②
04 (1) in danger (2) based on  05 (t)ranslator  06 ⑤
07 Is it possible for AI to read those words?
08 dictionary  09 (C) – (D) – (B) – (A)
10 (D) – (A) – (C) – (B)  11 if  12 Is it possible to freeze fire?  13 ②  14 ②
15 ①, ③  16 ②, ⑤  17 ②  18 suits → suit  19 ⑤  20 ④  21 ②
22 ③  23 ②  24 ④
25 (A) robotic car (B) do anything

01 burn: 불타다 / 불에 의해서 파괴되다 / 불을 낮춰, 그렇지 않으면 그게 탈 거야.

02 cloud: 구름 cloudy: 구름이 낀, 흐린

03 ① freeze, freeze: 얼리다 / 얼음 한 판 얼리는 데 하루 종일 걸린다. ② slow, slow down: 속도를 늦추다 / 이것은 노화를 늦추는 데 널리 사용되고 있습니다. ③ texting, text: (휴대전화로) 문자를 보내다 / 친구들과 문자를 주고 받거나 온라인에서 말하는 것을 좋아하나요? ④ point, point (at/toward): 돌리다, 향하게 하다 / 공공장소에서 낯선 사람들을 손가락으로 가리키는 것은 예의 없는 행동이다. ⑤ take, take: 선택하다, 사다 / 어른 표 두 장을 사겠습니다.

04 (1) in danger: 위험에 처한, 위험에 빠진 (2) based on: ~에 근거하여

05 translate: 번역하다 translator: 번역가

06 AI 번역기를 사용하는 방법에 대해 묻고 대답하고 있다.

07 Is it possible (for 목적격) to 동사원형 ~?: (…가) ~하는 것이 가능할까? AI: 인공지능(artificial intelligence)

08 dictionary: 사전 / 알파벳순으로 그것의 의미 또는 다른 언어로의 번역이 있는 일련의 단어와 구를 포함하는 책

11 see if 주어 동사: ~인지 아닌지 확인하다

12 Is it possible (for 목적격) to 동사원형 ~?: (~가) ~하는 것이 가능할까? freeze: 얼리다

13 가주어로는 it을 쓰며 진주어로 to부정사를 이용한다. 또한 의미

상의 주어로 문장에 쓰인 형용사가 사람의 성질을 나타내는 말이 아니므로 'for+목적격'을 쓴다.

14 첫 번째 문장에서는 지각동사의 목적격보어로 원형부정사나 현재분사가 적절하다. 두 번째 문장에서는 it을 가주어로 하고 to부정사를 진주어로 하여 'It ~ to부정사' 구문으로 쓰는 것이 적절하다.

15 ② I heard my name called repeatedly. ④ Mick watched them fight[fighting] each other. ⑤ He was looking at the dog eat[eating] the bones.

16 ① It is necessary to come early in the morning. ③ It is helpful to read many kinds of books. ④ It was really boring for me to memorize English words.

17 (A) worry about: ~에 대해 걱정하다, (B) dress for: … 에 적합한 옷을 입다

18 주격 관계대명사 that의 선행사가 clothes이므로 'suit'로 고치는 것이 적절하다.

19 ⓑ와 ①, ③, ④번: 동명사(목적이나 용도), ②, ⑤번: 현재분사(동작이나 상태, 진행)

20 ⓐ: Suhan(과 Jina), ⓑ, ⓓ, ⓔ: AI Speaker, ⓒ: Suhan과 Jina를 가리킨다.

21 ⓑ와 ②, ④, ⑤번: 명사적 용법, ① 형용사적 용법, ③ 부사적 용법

22 스마트 창문이 점점 어두워지고 있다.

23 ②번 다음 문장의 do that에 주목한다. 주어진 문장의 내용을 받고 있으므로 ②번이 적절하다.

24 이 글은 '인공 지능 자동차는 운전에 대한 모든 걸 알고 운전한다.'는 내용의 글이다.

25 그것은 운전에 대한 모든 걸 알고 있는 아주 지능적인 '로봇차'이다. 사람들은 스마트 자동차에 타고 있는 동안 '아무것도 하지' 않아도 된다.

### 서술형 실전문제  p.102~103

01 Is that possible → Is it possible
02 I think that is perfect for our project.
03 Is it possible for you to text with your eyes closed?
04 (1) To save energy in our daily lives is important.
   (2) It is important to save energy in our daily lives.
   (1) To feel tired after work is natural.
   (2) It is natural to feel tired after work.
05 riding a horse
06 enter
07 The screen suggests clothes that[which] suit the weather.
08 any longer

09 (A) what (B) How (C) based

10 speed up → slow down

11 What a smart car (you are)!

01 가주어 it은 to부정사를 받고 있는 것이므로 that을 가주어 it 대신에 쓸 수 없다.

02 자신의 의견을 표현하는 말에는 'That sounds ~.', 'I think (that) ~.' 등이 있다.

03 Is it possible (for 목적격) to 동사원형 ~?: (…가) ~하는 것이 가능할까? text: (휴대전화로) 문자를 보내다 with+명사+p.p: ~가 ~된 채로

04 to부정사가 문장의 주어로 쓰일 때 주어 자리에 가주어 it을 두고 to부정사 부분(진주어)을 문장 뒤로 보낸다. 또한 to부정사가 문장의 주어일 때는 단수로 받는다.

05 지각동사의 목적어가 목적격보어의 행위의 주체가 될 때 목적격 보어로 원형부정사나 현재분사를 쓴다. 목적격보어 자리에 원형 부정사와 현재분사를 모두 사용할 수 있으나 의미상 그 동작이 진행 중인 것을 나타낼 때에는 주로 현재분사를 사용한다.

06 go into = enter: ~에 들어가다

07 주격 관계대명사 that[which]을 사용하는 것이 적절하다.

08 no longer = not ~ any longer: 더 이상 … 아닌

09 (A) 'do'의 목적어가 와야 하므로 what이 적절하다. (B) '어떻게' 그렇게 할 수 있냐고 해야 하므로 How가 적절하다. (C) 지식과 경험을 '바탕으로'라고 해야 하므로 based가 적절하다. based on: ~에 근거하여

10 어떤 위험 상황을 감지하면 '속도를 늦추거나' 멈춘다고 해야 하므로 'slow down'으로 고쳐야 한다. speed up: 속도를 높이다

11 How+형용사[부사]+(주어+동사)! = What+a/an+형용사 +명사+(주어+동사)!

창의사고력 서술형 문제 p.104

|모범답안|

01 A: Is it possible to fry an egg on the street[road]?
   B: Yes, I think it's possible. / No, I don't think it's possible.

02 (1) singing   (2) a girl eating   (3) a boy looking at

03 (A) AI Cook
   (B) vegetables and meat
   (C) a delicious meal
   (D) vegetables and meat

01 Is it possible (for 목적격) to 동사원형 ~?: (…가) ~하는 것이 가능할까? fry an egg: 계란을 부치다

단원별 모의고사 p.105~108

01 getting   02 (1) to  (2) on  (3) of   03 ③

04 Is it possible for you to live without your smartphone?

05 impossible 06 ④   07 ①   08 ②

09 (A) interesting   (B) to replace

10 (C) from   (D) of   11 ⑤   12 possible

13 (1) It is good for your health to eat a lot of vegetables.
   (2) It is possible that people may not want to talk to each other anymore.

14 ④   15 ⑤

16 (1) Mina smelled onions frying.
   (2) We heard them whispering[whisper] to each other.
   (3) It is interesting to find and create new things.
   (4) It is easy for you to send e-mails.

17 ③   18 ③   19 The screen suggests clothes that suit the weather.   20 ④

21 like   22 that → those   23 ②, ③

24 I can predict danger based on knowledge and experience.   25 ⑤

01 get 비교급: 점점 더 ~해지다 / 이야기는 점점 더 재미있게 된다 get in: ~에 타다 / 그는 택시 앞좌석에 타고 있다.

02 (1) face to face: (~와) 서로 얼굴을 맞대고 / 그들은 마주보고 앉아 서로를 바라보고 있다. (2) move on: ~로 이동하다 / 자, 이제 다음 이야기입니다 (3) out of: (원천·출처) ~에서, ~으로부터 / 그들은 옥수수와 콩 같은 식물 재료를 사용하여 플라스틱 제품을 만든다.

03 off: 할인되어 / 개장일에 가구를 구입하시면 25퍼센트 할인해 드립니다.

04 Is it possible (for 목적격) to 동사원형 ~?: (…가) ~하는 것이 가능할까? without: ~ 없이

05 impossible: 불가능한

06 ④는 가주어이며, 나머지는 this computer를 받는 대명사이다.

07 so: 그럼, 그러면

08 ② 현금으로 낼지 카드로 낼지에 대해서는 언급되지 않았다. ① 여자가 가진 쿠폰을 사용할 수 있는가? 사용할 수 있다. ③ 그들은 어디에 있는가? 컴퓨터 가게 ④ 그녀는 얼마나 할인을 받았는가? 30달러 ⑤ 여자는 무엇을 사기를 원하는가? 컴퓨터

09 (A) interesting: 재미있는, 흥미로운 (B) Is it possible for 목적격 to 동사원형 ~?: …가 ~하는 것이 가능할까? replace: 대체하다

10 (C) free from: ~이 없는 (D) because of 명사: ~ 때문에

11 ⓔ dark → bright 로봇이 위험한 일을 할 수 있어서 사람들이 위험이 없어진다는 내용은 좋은 면을 보고 있는 것이다.

12 possible: 가능한 / 일어나거나 발생할 수 있는

13 (1) 문장의 주어로 쓰인 to부정사를 뒤로 보내고 대신 주어 자

리에 가주어 it을 쓴다. (2) 주어로 쓰인 that절의 경우에도 긴 that절을 뒤로 보내고 주어 자리에 가주어 it을 쓴다.

**14** 지각동사의 목적어와 목적격보어가 능동의 관계에 있을 경우 목적격보어로 원형부정사나 현재분사를 쓴다.

**15** to부정사의 의미상 주어로 사람의 성질을 나타내는 형용사가 쓰였으므로 'of+목적격'이 적절하다. It is very kind of you to help us.

**16** (1) smell은 목적격보어로 현재분사를 쓴다. (2) 지각동사의 목적어와 목적격보어가 능동의 관계에 있을 경우 목적격보어로 원형부정사나 현재분사를 쓴다. 의미상 그 동작이 진행 중인 것을 나타낼 때에는 주로 현재분사를 사용한다. (3), (4) it을 가주어로 하고 to부정사를 진주어로 쓰는 것이 적절하다. to부정사의 의미상 주어로 사람의 성질을 나타내는 형용사가 쓰인 것이 아니므로 'for+목적격'이 적절하다.

**17** ⓑ We heard Yena play(playing) the violin. ⓓ Jeniffer felt him come(coming) closer. ⓖ Is it safe to swim in this river?

**18** ⓐ와 ②, ⑤번: 관계대명사, ①, ③, ④: 접속사

**19** 앞 문장의 내용을 가리킨다.

**20** (That's) right.: 그렇습니다, ④ 괜찮아요. ① You got it. 맞습니다. ② You can say that again. 정말 그렇다[(당신 말에) 전적으로 동의한다]. ③ I agree with you. 당신 의견에 동의해요. ⑤ You said it. 맞습니다.

**21** (A) like: 좋아하다(동사), (B) like ~처럼(접속사)

**22** 뒤에 복수명사(smart windows)가 나오기 때문에, 지시형용사도 복수형으로 고치는 것이 적절하다.

**23** ⓐ와 ②, ③: 형용사적 용법, ①, ④: 명사적 용법, ⑤ 부사적 용법

**24** 'on'을 보충하면 된다.

**25** 인공 지능 자동차는 '자신의' 지식과 경험을 바탕으로 위험을 예측할 수 있다.

# The Unknown Hero

### 시험대비 실력평가     p.112

01 (1) Chinese   (2) Spanish    02 ③      03 ①
04 ④      05 ②
06 (1) harmony   (2) Thanks

01 China: 중국 Chinese: 중국어; 중국의 Spain: 스페인 Spanish: 스페인의; 스페인어

02 ① 내 취미는 우표를 수집하는 것이다. ② 내가 충분히 연습을 하지 않았다는 의미인가요? ③ waste: 낭비하다 / 왜 필요하지도 않은 옷에 돈을 낭비하니? ④ 색깔과 스타일은 개인적인 취향의 문제이다. ⑤ 다른 사람들의 재산을 침해하지 않도록 조심하라.

03 be famous for: ~으로 유명하다 take care of: ~을 돌보다

04 store: 저장하다, 보관하다 / 우리는 창고에 상품을 보관한다.

05 ② loyal: 충실한, 충성스러운 royal: 왕의, 왕실의 ① 우리는 그가 살았는지 죽었는지 모른다. ② 배움에는 왕도가 없다. ③ 나는 또 다른 컴퓨터가 필요하다. ④ 그 도둑은 창문을 통해 들어갔다. ⑤ 그 회사는 유럽 내에 있는 고객들을 지원할 것이다.

06 (1) in harmony with: ~와 조화를 이루어 (2) thanks to: ~ 덕분에

### 서술형 시험대비     p.113

01 (1) interested   (2) amazed
02 care, take
03 (1) Hundreds   (2) set   (3) filled
04 found
05 (1) At   (2) in   (3) for   (4) as
06 (1) I hope this year will be full of joy.
    (2) I tried the dress on but it didn't fit.

01 (1) interest: 흥미, 관심 interested: 흥미가 있는 / Jackson은 미술에 아주 흥미가 있다. (2) amaze: 놀라게 하다 amazed: 놀란 / 우리 모두는 그 뉴스에 놀랐다.

02 care for: ~을 돌보다 take care of: ~을 돌보다 / 그녀는 연로한 부모님을 보살피기 위해 다시 집으로 이사를 했다.

03 (1) hundreds of: 수백의, 수많은 (2) set foot: 발을 들여놓다 (3) be filled with: ~으로 가득 차다

04 found: find(발견하다)의 과거형; 설립하다 / Smith씨는 내년

에 회사를 설립할 것이다. Mike는 방에서 무엇인가 먹을 것을 발견했다.

05 (1) at last: 마침내, 결국 / 결국 우리가 경기에 이겼다. (2) in danger: 위험에 처한 / 그 아이들이 지금 위험에 처해 있다. (3) can't wait for: ~을 몹시 기대하다 / 그는 그 파티를 몹시 기대하고 있다. (4) be known as: ~으로 알려지다 / Ann의 아버지는 위해한 과학자로 알려져 있다.

06 (1) be full of: ~로 가득하다 (2) fit: 맞다 tried the dress on: tried on the dress: 그 드레스를 입어 보았다.

### 교과서 Conversation

#### 핵심 Check     p.114~115

1 Do you know anything about / Do you know (that)
2 explain / Could, explain
3 Could you explain your plan to save money?

### 교과서 대화문 익히기

#### Check(√) True or False     p.116

1 F   2 T   3 T   4 F

### 교과서 확인학습     p.118~119

**Listen & Speak 1 B-2**
Do, anything / little, famous for / going to, with / think, like

**Listen & Speak 2 A**
explain, painting / painted

**Listen & Speak 2 B-1**
1. explain / was written / about / about, missing
2. explain / volunteer group / tell, more / take care

**Listen & Speak 2 C**
Could, explain / waste, on

**Real-Life Zone A**
What, anything about / Korean houses, are

designed, in harmony / a little / cool, warm / sounds, Where, see / near here / about going, seeing / idea, How, get / take, over there

**Real-Life Zone B**

1. know anything / greatest sights / why, famous / because, longest wall
2. about, novel / short novel / explain why / won, for

**Real-Life Zone B e.g.**

know anything / was built / explain why / It's because, tallest tower

**Wrap Up**

know anything / birthday / tell, more / get together, wears / interesting / share food, wish for / Korean tradition

## 시험대비 기본평가 p.120

01 ④　　02 (C) → (B) → (A) → (D)　　03 ②

01 Do you know anything about ~?은 어떤 것에 대해 알고 있는지 묻는 표현이다.

02 (C) 창덕궁에 대해 알고 있는 것이 있는지 묻는다. (B) 조금 안다고 말하면서, 그것은 아름다운 정원으로 유명하다고 대답한다. (A) 친구와 함께 그곳에 갈 예정이라고 말한다. (D) 그곳이 마음에 들 것이라고 대답한다.

03 'Could you explain ~?'은 어떤 것에 대한 설명을 요청할 때 사용하며 could 대신에 can을 쓸 수 있다.

## 시험대비 실력평가 p.121~122

01 ②　　02 was written　　03 ④
04 ④　　05 ⑤　　06 ①
07 돌잔치를 위해 가족이 함께 모이고 생일을 맞는 아기가 한복을 입는 것
08 share　　09 ④　　10 written　　11 ②
12 He won the Pulitzer Prize.

01 대화의 흐름으로 보아 이 시에 대한 설명을 요청하는 물음이 와야 한다.

02 시가 윤동주에 의해 쓰여진 것이므로 수동태가 되어야 한다.

03 ① 여자아이가 시를 좋아하는지는 알 수 없다. ② 이 시의 제목은 알 수 없다. ③ 남자아이가 윤동주를 좋아하는지는 알 수 없다. ④ 이 시는 고향을 그리워하는 작가에 관한 것이다. ⑤ 이 소녀가 이 시에 관심이 있는 이유는 알 수 없다.

04 세종대왕을 아느냐고 물어보는 질문에 모른다고 대답하고 곧바로 한글을 창제한 왕이라고 말하는 것은 어색하다.

05 (C) 에펠탑에 대해 아느냐고 묻는 질문에, (D) 1889년에 Gustave Eiffel에 의해 세워졌다고 대답한다. (B) 그것이 유명한 이유를 묻자, (A) 그 당시 세계에서 가장 높은 탑이었기 때문이라고 대답한다.

06 ① 그것에 대해 더 말해 주겠느냐는 표현이 알맞다.

07 That은 지시대명사로 앞 문장의 내용을 받는다.

08 어떤 것을 다른 사람과 함께 가지거나 사용하거나 점거하다: share: 공유하다, 나눠 갖다

09 ④ 남자아이가 돌잔치에 참석하기를 원하는지는 알 수 없다.

10 수동의 의미이므로 과거분사가 알맞다.

11 ② 유명한 이유를 설명해 달라는 표현이므로 explain이 알맞다.

## 서술형 시험대비 p.123

01 in　　02 cool　　03 interesting
04 Shall　　05 how to　　06 sight → sights
07 (B) why　(C) because

01 be in harmony with: ~와 조화를 이루다

02 여름에는 시원하고 겨울에는 따뜻하다는 말이 자연스럽다.

03 감정을 나타내는 동사에 '-ing'를 붙이면 '~한 감정을 일으키는'의 의미가 되고, '-ed'를 붙이면 '~한 감정을 느끼는'의 의미가 된다. interesting: 흥미 있는

04 How about ~ing?는 제안을 나타내는 말로 Shall we ~?로 바꿔 쓸 수 있다.

05 길을 묻는 표현이다.

06 'one of the 최상급+복수명사'의 구문이다.

07 (B) 이유를 묻는 의문부사 why가 알맞다. (C) It's because ~: ~이기 때문이다

교과서

# Grammar

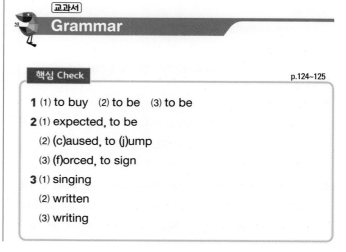

## 핵심 Check p.124~125

1 (1) to buy　(2) to be　(3) to be
2 (1) expected, to be
　(2) (c)aused, to (j)ump
　(3) (f)orced, to sign
3 (1) singing
　(2) written
　(3) writing

01 ⑤

02 (1) eating   (2) hidden   (3) talking   (4) invited

03 (1) I want you to clean the windows.

    (2) Timothy got an email sent by a stranger this morning.

    (3) Who are the boys playing soccer on the ground?

    (4) Tell her to buy a comfortable pair of shoes!

04 (1) Jack gave his wife a necklace made of pearls.

    (2) Who is the man cutting the beef sandwiches with a knife?

    (3) Mike advised her to go to bed early.

01 ask의 목적격보어는 to부정사이다.

02 (1) 진행의 의미이므로 현재분사 eating을 쓴다. (2) 수동의 의미이므로 과거분사 hidden을 쓴다. (3) 진행의 의미이므로 현재분사 talking을 쓴다. (4) 수동의 의미이므로 과거분사 invited를 쓴다.

03 (1), (4) want, tell은 to부정사를 목적격보어로 취하는 동사이다. (2) email이 보내지는 것이므로 과거분사가 적절하다. (3) 소년들이 축구를 하는 것이므로 현재분사가 적절하다.

01 ③     02 ③     03 ⑤     04 ②

05 ②     06 (1) carrying   (2) written   (3) sleeping cat     07 ①     08 ①

09 (1) to help   (2) to go   (3) to stay   (4) not to take

10 (1) kick → kicking

    (2) the playing badminton man → the man playing badminton

    (3) baby crying → crying baby

11 ②     12 ④     13 ③     14 ③

15 ⑤     16 writing, written     17 ①

18 ④

19 (1) My parents always tell me to do my best in school.

    (2) Good health enabled him to carry out the plan.

20 ③

01 have는 목적어와 목적격보어의 관계가 수동인 경우 목적격보어로 과거분사를 사용하는 동사이다. 신발에 광이 나게 한다는 의미이므로 과거분사를 쓰는 것이 적절하다.

02 ① Do you want me to clean your house for you? ② He told Perry to put on a yellow shirt. ④ The doctor advised Ted to stop smoking. ⑤ Ms. Green asked him to carry the boxes.

03 ⑤번은 동명사이고 나머지는 다 현재분사이다.

04 현재분사가 뒤에서 앞의 명사를 수식하도록 한다. / expect는 목적격보어로 to부정사를 취한다.

05 첫 번째 문장은 5형식이고 두 번째 문장은 3형식이다. 3형식과 5형식에 쓰이면서, to부정사를 목적격보어와 목적어로 받을 수 있는 동사는 want이다.

06 (1) 현재분사가 뒤에서 앞의 명사를 수식하도록 한다. (2) e-mail이 쓰여진 것이므로 과거분사가 적절하다. (3) 현재분사가 단독으로 쓰일 때는 명사 앞에 와서 명사를 수식한다.

07 warn과 ask는 목적격보어로 to부정사가 오며, to부정사의 부정형은 'not[never]+to 동사원형'이다

08 축구를 하고 있는 것이므로 '수동이나 완료'의 의미로 쓰이는 과거분사가 아니라 '진행'을 나타내는 현재분사를 쓰는 것이 적절하다.

09 (1), (2), (3), (4) ask, allow, order, warn의 목적격보어로 to부정사가 적절하다. to부정사의 부정형은 'not to 동사원형'으로 쓴다.

10 (1) 현재분사가 뒤에서 the boy를 수식하도록 하는 것이 적절하다. (2) 현재분사가 목적어나 부사구를 수반할 때에는 명사 뒤에 와서 앞의 명사를 수식한다. (3) 현재분사가 단독으로 쓰일 때는 명사 앞에 와서 명사를 수식한다.

11 ② make는 사역동사이므로 목적격보어로 동사원형이 와야 하며, 나머지는 모두 to부정사가 와야 한다.

12 ④ find는 목적격보어로 현재분사를 쓴다. 동사원형은 쓸 수 없다.

13 want는 목적격보어로 to부정사를 쓴다.

14 '전화를 받고 있는'의 의미이므로 현재분사를 쓴다. '저녁식사에 초대된'의 의미이므로 과거분사를 쓴다.

15 allow는 목적격보어로 to부정사를 취한다.

16 '~을 쓰고 있는 소년'이라는 의미이므로 현재분사로 the boy를 수식하고, '한국어로 쓰여진'이라는 의미이므로 과거분사로 the letter를 수식하는 것이 적절하다.

17 make는 목적격보어로 to부정사가 아니라 원형부정사를 쓴다.

18 '태권도를 배우고 있는 여자아이'이므로 현재분사를 이용하여 뒤에서 명사를 수식하도록 해야 한다.

19 (1), (2) tell과 enable은 목적격보어로 to부정사가 온다.

20 ③번은 동명사이고 나머지는 모두 현재분사이다.

01 (1) helping → to help   (2) go → to go

    (3) left → to leave   (4) excited → exciting

    (5) throws → throwing   (6) to repair → repair

02 (1) beginning   (2) dancing   (3) frightened

(4) taken

03 (1) to come (2) to do (3) expects (4) to go

04 (1) The teacher asked me to close the door.

(2) Mom told me to walk the dog.

(3) Kate climbed the mountain covered with snow.

(4) When are you going to fix the broken window?

(5) Mariko looked at her daughter playing[play] in the park.

05 (1) The business woman running a big company is Sophie.

(2) There is a bridge built long time ago.

06 (1) not to drive so fast

(2) to play the piano for us

07 (1) playing (2) exciting (3) repaired (4) amazing

(5) hit

08 (1) The woman asked the man to carry her bag.

(2) Emma advised me to wait till tomorrow.

(3) Peter told Sylvia to dance with him.

(4) They expected him to participate in the festival.

(5) Good health enabled him to finish the plan.

09 (1) cheering

(2) sliced

10 (1) 현재분사 → 이유: '~하는 중'이라고 해석된다.

(2) 동명사 → 이유: 현재분사로 해석하면 '방이 기다리고 있다는' 것이 되어 어색하며 room의 용도를 나타내어 '대기실'이라는 의미이다.

01 (1), (2), (3) ask, want, advise는 목적격보어로 to부정사를 취한다. (4) bowling game이 흥분을 유발하는 것이므로 exciting을 써야 한다. (5) 소년이 공을 던지는 주체이므로 현재분사로 수식하는 것이 적절하다. (6) have는 목적격보어로 원형부정사를 취한다.

02 (1), (2) 분사가 목적어나 부사구를 수반할 때에는 명사 뒤에 와서 앞의 명사를 수식한다. (3) 뉴스에 놀라는 것이므로 과거분사가 적절하다. (4) 사진이 찍히는 것이므로 과거분사가 적절하다.

03 (1), (2), (4) tell, want, allow는 목적격보어로 to부정사를 취한다. (3) hope는 5형식으로 쓰이지 않는다.

04 (1), (2) ask, tell은 목적격보어로 to부정사를 취한다. (3) 눈으로 덮인 것이므로 과거분사를 쓴다. (4) 창문이 깨진 것이므로 과거분사를 쓴다. (5) look at이 지각동사이므로 현재분사나 동사원형을 쓴다.

05 분사가 목적어나 부사구를 수반할 때에는 명사 뒤에 와서 앞의 명사를 수식한다. 이때 명사와 분사 사이에 '관계대명사+be동사'가 생략되어 있다고 볼 수 있다.

06 order와 ask는 목적격보어로 to부정사를 쓰고 부정사의 부정은 not[never]을 앞에 붙인다.

07 (1) 배드민턴을 치고 있는 그 소녀는 나의 여동생이다. (2) 나는 너에게 해 줄 흥미진진한 이야기가 있어. (3) 우리는 그 차가 Potter와 Parker에 의해 수리되게 하였다. (4) Jina는 놀라운 농구 선수이다. (5) 너는 그 건물이 덤프트럭에 의해 부딪친 것을 보았니?

08 ask, advise, tell, expect, enable 등은 모두 목적격보어로 to부정사가 와야 한다.

09 (1) 진행의 의미이므로 현재분사를 쓴다. (2) 수동의 의미이므로 과거분사를 쓴다.

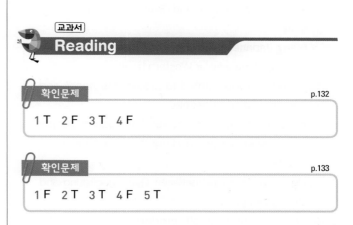

**Reading** 교과서

확인문제 　　　　　　　　　　p.132

1 T　2 F　3 T　4 F

확인문제 　　　　　　　　　　p.133

1 F　2 T　3 T　4 F　5 T

교과서 확인학습 A 　　　　　　p.134~135

01 Architecture 02 Have, been

03 There is 04 popular, who, past

05 know, was created, efforts

06 known as 07 who founded

08 time, was ruled, fit, taste

09 moving into, Japanese, Western

10 wanted, protect, suffering

11 power, keep, let, set foot

12 between, and

13 modern, people

14 efforts, filled with

15 independence movement, ways

16 example, supported, keep, alive

17 happened, caught, suffered

18 pressed, build

19 how to

20 official, know, so, build 21 what, told

22 cost, high

23 fell, property

24 part, to, traditions, still

1 The King of Architecture in Gyeongseong.

2 Have you been to Bukchon?

3 There is a beautiful *hanok* village in Bukchon.

4 It is popular with tourists who want to see Korea's past.

5 However, not many people know that Bukchon was created through one man's efforts.

6 That man was Jeong Segwon, known as the King of Architecture in Gyeongseong.

7 Jeong Segwon was a businessman who founded Geonyangsa in 1920.

8 At the time, Korea was ruled by Japan, and the Japanese were changing Gyeongseong to fit their taste.

9 Many Japanese moving into Gyeongseong were building Japanese or Western houses.

10 Jeong Segwon wanted to protect the *hanok* and help the suffering people.

11 He said, "People are power. We Joseon people should keep Jongno and not let the Japanese set foot here."

12 He bought the land between Gyeongbokgung and Changdeokgung.

13 There he built small, modern *hanoks* for the people.

14 Through his efforts, we now have Bukchon filled with its beautiful *hanoks*.

15 Jeong Segwon helped the independence movement in many ways.

16 For example, he built the office building for the Joseon Language Society and supported its efforts to keep the Joseon language alive.

17 When the Joseon Language Affair happened, he was caught by the police and suffered a lot.

18 Japanese officials pressed him to build Japanese houses.

19 He said, "I don't know how to build Japanese houses."

20 An official said, "You know how to build hanoks, so you can build Japanese houses, too."

21 But he did not do what the Japanese told him to do.

22 The cost was high.

23 His business fell off, and he lost his property.

24 However, in part, thanks to Jeong Segwon, the traditions of Korea still live with us today.

01 who[that]    02 moved → moving    03 ②

04 우리 조선 사람들은 조선을 지켜야 하며, 일본인들이 이곳에 발을 들여놓지 못하게 해야 한다.

05 ⑤      06 ④

07 It is popular with tourists who want to see Korea's past.

08 known    09 ①    10 ②    11 ③

12 ①    13 ③    14 ⑤    15 ④

16 ③    17 ⑤    18 ②

19 a beautiful hanok village      20 past

21 ②      22 Jeong Segwon was a businessman who founded Geonyangsa in 1920.    23 ⑤

24 ③      25 They were building Japanese or Western houses.

26 ①      27 alive

28 was happened → happened

01 선행사가 사람이고 주격이므로 관계대명사 who나 that을 쓴다.

02 '경성으로 이사 오는 많은 일본인들'의 뜻이 되어야 하므로 능동의 의미를 나타내는 현재분사가 알맞다.

03 문맥상 '한옥을 지키기를 원했다'가 자연스럽다.

04 set foot: 발을 들여놓다

05 정세권은 일본인들이 종로에 발을 들여놓지 않도록 해야 한다고 말했다.

06 ⓐ have been to: ~에 다녀온 적이 있다 ⓑ through: ~을 통하여

07 be popular with: ~에게 인기가 있다

08 수동의 의미이므로 과거분사가 알맞다.

09 in many ways: 여러 방법으로

10 ⓑ, ② 형용사적 용법 ①, ④ 명사적 용법 ③, ⑤ 부사적 용법

11 press는 목적격보어로 to부정사를 취한다.

12 ① 정세권이 왜 독립운동을 도왔는지는 위 글에서 언급되지 않았다.

13 ⓐ와 ②, ③, ④는 선행사를 포함하는 관계대명사이고, ①, ⑤는 의문대명사이다.

14 fall off: 쇠퇴하다 thanks to: ~ 덕분에

15 주어진 문장의 There는 경복궁과 창덕궁 사이의 땅을 가리킨다.

16 목적보어가 원형부사 set이므로 사역동사 make나 let이 와야 하는데, 문맥상 '일본인들이 발을 들여놓지 않도록 해야 한다'이므로 허용을 나타내는 let이 알맞다.

17 ⓑ, ⑤ ~에 의하여, ~ 때문에 ①, ② ~을 뚫고, ~을 관통하여 ③ ~의 처음부터 끝까지 ④ ~을 사이에 두고

18 filled with: ~으로 가득 찬

19 It은 인칭대명사로 앞에 나온 단수 명사를 받고 있다.

20 현재 이전의 시기와 일어난 일들: past(과거)

21 보기와 ②의 as는 전치사로 '~으로'의 뜻으로 쓰였다.

22 관계대명사 who 대신 that을 써도 좋다.

23 ⓑ, ⑤ 부사적 용법 ①, ③, ④ 명사적 용법 ② 형용사적 용법

24 ① 창의적인 ② 부정적인 ③ 애국적인 ④ 친절한 ⑤ 정렬적인

25 많은 일본인들은 일본식이나 서양식 집을 짓고 있었다.

26 for example: 예를 들면

27 '조선어를 살아 있게 지키다'의 뜻이 되어야 하므로 alive가 알맞다.

28 happen은 자동사이므로 수동태로 쓸 수 없다.

---

## 서술형 시험대비 p.142~143

01 He said (that) he didn't know how to build Japanese houses.

02 ⓑ so ⓑ what ⓒ to

03 (A) build   (B) property

04 They pressed him to build Japanese houses.

05 to set

06 land

07 (A) and   (B) Through   (C) with

08 independence

09 For

10 When the Joseon Language Affair happened, he was caught by the police and suffered a lot.

11 (A) to build   (B) how

12 It made an effort to keep the Joseon language alive.

13 (A) to   (B) with   (C) through

14 has

15 known

---

01 피전달문을 이끄는 접속사 that은 생략할 수 있다.

02 (A) so: 그래서 (B) 선행사를 포함하는 관계대명사 what이 알맞다. (C) thanks to: ~ 덕분에

03 한 일본인 관리의 압력에도 불구하고, 정세권은 일본식 집을 짓지 않았다. 그 결과 그는 그의 재산을 잃었다.

05 let은 목적격보어로 원형부정사를 취하고 allow는 to부정사를 취한다.

06 특히 농사나 건축과 같은 특수한 목적을 위해 사용되는 일정한 지역의 땅: land(땅, 토지)

07 (A) between A and B: A와 B 사이에 (B) through: ~을 통하여, ~으로 (C) filed with: ~으로 가득 찬

08 depend: 의존하다 independence: 독립

09 for example: 예를 들면

10 수동태이므로 'by'를 보충하면 된다.

---

11 (A) press는 to부정사를 목적격보어로 취한다. (B) build의 목적어인 Japanese가 있으므로 what은 올 수 없다.

13 (A) have been to: ~에 다녀오다 (B) be popular with: ~에게 인기가 있다 (C) through: ~으로, ~을 통해

14 There is ~ 구문은 have[has] 동사를 써서 바꿔 쓸 수 있다.

15 수동의 뜻을 나타내므로 과거분사로 고쳐야 한다.

---

## 영역별 핵심문제 p.145~149

01 (1) French   (2) architect

02 (1) interested   (2) part   (3) modern        03 ②

04 ①              05 ⑤              06 (D) → (A) → (C) → (B)

07 ④              08 ①

09 They are designed to be in harmony with nature.

10 ③              11 ④              12 ③

13 (1) give → to give

　　(2) to wait → wait

　　(3) to repair → repair

　　(4) played → play[playing]

　　(5) writing → written

14 ④              15 ④              16 ⑤

17 (1) Lucy's dad wants her to be a police officer.

　　(2) My mother asked me to buy some milk on my way home.

　　(3) The teacher told the students to bring some water.

　　(4) She got her two sons to divide a cake exactly in half.

18 (1) We like to walk[walking] on fallen leaves.

　　(2) He hit the flying ball.

19 (1) 해석: Jane은 얇게 썰어진 치즈를 좋아한다.

　　(2) 해석: Jane은 치즈를 얇게 써는 것을 좋아한다.

　　(3) 어법상 차이: sliced는 '썰어진 (치즈)'라는 의미의 과거분사로 cheese를 수식하고, slicing은 '(치즈를) 써는 것'이라는 의미로 동명사로 쓰였다.

20 ③              21 ②              22 ruler              23 ③

24 여러분은 이런 종류의 항아리를 본 적이 있나요?

25 painted

26 They used it for storing rice.

27 Why           28 national           29 ③, ⑤           30 body

31 Western       32 ②                33 ⑤

---

01 (1) 나라와 언어명의 관계이다. (2) 명사와 그 명사의 행위자의 관계이다.

02 (1) be interested in: ~에 관심이 있다 (2) part: 부분 (3) modern: 현대의

03 be famous for: ~으로 유명하다

**04** 상상의 사람들과 사건들에 관해 쓴 긴 이야기: novel(소설)

**05** 설명을 요청하는 문장이 되어야 한다.

**06** (D) 설명 요청→ (A) 설명 → (C) 더 자세한 설명 요청 → (B) 대답

**07** ⓓ You should. → You shouldn't. 뒤에 이어지는 문장이 책이 재미있지 않았다는 뜻이므로 책을 사지 말라는 대답이 자연스럽다.

**08** 한옥에 대해 알고 있는지 묻는 문장이므로 ①이 적절하다.

**09** They가 가리키는 것이 traditional Korean houses이므로 수동태의 문장이 되어야 한다.

**10** 어떤 장소에 가는 방법을 묻는 표현이므로 How가 알맞다.

**11** 남자는 전통 마을이 이곳에서 가깝다고 대답했다.

**12** 주어진 문장의 밑줄 친 부분은 동명사이다. 따라서 '~하는 중인'이라는 의미의 현재분사로 쓰인 ③번이 답이다.

**13** (1) ask의 목적격보어로 to부정사가 와야 한다. (2), (3) make, have는 사역동사이므로 목적격보어로 동사원형이 와야 한다. (4) 지각동사의 목적격보어이므로 동사원형이나 현재분사를 쓴다. (5) '쓰인'의 뜻으로 수동의 의미이므로 과거분사를 쓴다.

**14** ask의 목적격보어로 to부정사가 적절하다.

**15** ④ '웃고 있는'의 의미가 알맞으므로 현재분사 smiling을 쓴다.

**16** (A) '고장난 카메라'라는 의미이므로 과거분사를 쓰는 것이 적절하다. (B) 사물을 수식하는 것이므로 현재분사를 쓰는 것이 적절하다.(C) '잠긴 문'이라는 의미이므로 과거분사를 쓰는 것이 적절하다.

**17** (1) want, (2) ask, (3) tell, (4) get 등의 동사는 목적격보어로 to부정사가 와야 한다.

**18** (1) 낙엽은 떨어진 잎을 말하는 것이므로 'fallen leaves'라고 쓸 수 있다. (2) '날아오는 공'이므로 현재분사로 ball을 수식하도록 문장을 만든다.

**19** like는 동명사를 목적어로 취할 수 있는 동사이며, 위 문장에서 치즈는 slice의 주체가 될 수 없으므로 slicing이 현재분사라고 볼 수 없다.

**20** 글의 흐름상 그가 일본인들이 울릉도 근처에서 고기 잡는 것을 보았다는 문장 다음에 이어져야 하므로 ③번이 적절하다.

**21** ⓐ, ② 동명사 ①, ③, ④, ⑤ 현재분사

**22** 나라를 다스리는 사람: ruler(통치자)

**23** 안용복이 고기를 잘 잡았는지는 위 글의 내용에서 알 수 없다.

**24** pot: 항아리, 냄비

**25** 꽃들이 그려진 것이므로 수동의 뜻을 나타내는 과거분사가 적절하다.

**26** 쌀을 저장하기 위해 사용했다.

**27** How about ~ing?=Why don't you ~?: ~하는 게 어때?

**28** nation의 형용사형은 national이다.

**29** ⓒ, ③, ⑤ 관계대명사 ① 진주어 ② 동사의 목적어가 되는 명사

**30** 사람의 머리, 팔, 다리를 포함한 육체의 모든 부분: body(몸, 신체)

**31** West의 형용사형은 Western이다.

**32** set foot: 발을 들여놓다

**33** ⑤ 정세권이 어떻게 종로를 지켰는지는 대답할 수 없다.

### 단원별 예상문제　　　　　　　　p.150~153

| | | | |
|---|---|---|---|
| 01 ④ | 02 in | 03 ⑤ | 04 ③ |
| 05 돌잔치 | 06 ② | 07 tradition | 08 ④ |

09 on the land between Gyeongbokgung and Changdeokgung

| | | |
|---|---|---|
| 10 Gyeongseong | | 11 movement 12 ③ |
| 13 ③ | 14 (1) to help, comes | (2) to feed |
| 15 ② | 16 ② | 17 ⑤ |

18 (A) happened   (B) to build   (C) what　19 ③

| | |
|---|---|
| 20 ③ | 21 wearing |

22 (A) painted   (B) holding　23 ④　　24 has

| | |
|---|---|
| 25 ③ | 26 created → was created |
| 27 ⑤ | 28 ① |

**01** take care of=care for: ~을 돌보다

**02** in danger: 위험에 빠진 / 그는 생명의 위험을 느꼈다. be interested in: ~에 흥미가 있다 / Jake는 체스에 흥미가 있다.

**03** ① meaning: 의미 / 이 단어의 의미가 뭐죠? ② explain: 설명하다 / 먼저, 경기 규칙을 설명해 드리겠습니다. ③ waste: 낭비하다 / 왜 필요하지도 않은 옷에 돈을 낭비했니? ④ abroad: 해외에 / 나는 해외로 여행할 계획이다. ⑤ unknown: 알려지지 않은 / 그 소년은 무슨 알려지지 않은 이유 때문에 별들을 세느라 애를 쓰고 있었다.

**04** 신체 또는 마음의 고통을 느끼다: suffer(시달리다, 고통 받다)

**05** It은 인칭대명사로 앞에 나온 a dol party를 받는다.

**06** wish for: ~을 바라다

**07** 오랫동안 존재해 온 관습이나 믿음: tradition(전통)

**08** ④ 몇 명의 가족이 돌잔치를 위해 모이는지는 대답할 수 없다.

**09** there는 앞에 나온 장소의 부사구를 받는다.

**10** it은 인칭대명사로 앞에 나온 단수명사를 받는다.

**11** move의 명사형은 movement이다.

**12** ③ 경복궁과 창덕궁 사이에 많은 한옥이 있는지는 위 글에서 알 수 없다.

**13** '책을 읽는' 소녀이므로 현재분사로, '깨진 유리창'이므로 과거분사로 각각 수식하는 것이 적절하다.

**14** 때의 부사절에서는 현재시제를 사용하여 미래를 나타내며 ask와 tell은 목적격보어로 to부정사가 나온다.

**15** ② '~라고 이름 지어진'이라는 의미이므로 과거분사로 수식한다.

**16** ② ask의 목적격보어로 to부정사가 적절하다.

17 tell의 목적격보어로 to부정사가 적절하다.

18 (A) happen은 자동사이므로 수동태로 쓸 수 없다. (B) press는 목적격보어로 to부정사를 취한다. (C) 선행사를 포함하는 관계대명사가 알맞다.

19 '대가는 컸다'의 뜻으로 cost가 주어일 때는 형용사 high가 적절하다.

20 ③ 정세권은 일본식 집을 짓기를 원하지 않았다.

21 능동의 의미이므로 현재분사가 적절하다.

22 (A) 수동의 의미이므로 과거분사가 적절하다. (B) 능동의 의미이므로 현재분사가 적절하다.

23 위 글의 주제는 행복해 하는 Johnsy이므로 희망에 찬 분위기가 적절하다.

24 There is[are] ~ 구문은 have[has] 동사를 써서 바꿔 쓸 수 있다.

25 be popular with: ~에게 인기가 있다

26 문맥상 수동태가 적절하다.

27 주어진 문장은 음식 사업이 쇠퇴했다는 뜻이므로 사람들이 가게에 오지 않았다는 말 다음에 와야 한다.

28 문맥상 사람들이 가게에 거의 오지 않았다는 말이므로 Few가 적절하다.

서술형 실전문제  p.154~155

01 I don't know much about it and I'm interested in it. → I don't know much about it but I'm interested in it.

02 Yes, I know a little about Changdeokgung.

03 to Changdeokgung

04 explain

05 (1) to tell  (2) to study  (3) (to) push

06 (1) named  (2) talking

07 (1) not to be  (2) not to give

08 (1) This is the only book written by him.
   (2) The boy living in this house is Andy.
   (3) The teacher told us to gather at the gym.
   (4) Jiho asked Dohun to clean the window.

09 during

10 to not fish → not to fish

11 He was a fisherman.

12 storing

13 현대적인 옹기

01 나는 그것에 대해 많이 알지 못하며 그것에 흥미가 있다고 말하는 것은 어색하다.

02 a little: 조금

03 there는 앞에 나온 장소를 나타내는 부사구를 가리킨다.

04 Could you explain ~?은 설명을 요청하는 표현이다.

05 ask, encourage, help는 to부정사를 목적격보어로 취하는 동사이다. help는 동사원형을 쓸 수도 있다.

06 (1) '~라고 이름 지어진'이라는 의미이므로 과거분사로 수식한다. (2) 로봇이 말하는 주체가 되므로 현재분사로 수식한다.

07 ask와 encourage는 목적격보어로 to부정사를 쓰고 부사의 부정은 not을 to ~ 앞에 붙인다.

08 (1) 과거분사 written은 명사 book 뒤에서 수식한다. (2) 현재분사 living은 명사 boy 뒤에서 수식한다. (3) tell의 목적격보어로 to부정사가 나온다. (4) ask의 목적격보어로 to부정사가 나온다.

09 '~ 중에, ~ 동안에'의 뜻으로 특정한 기간을 나타내는 명사가 올 때는 during을 쓴다.

10 to부정사의 부정은 to부정사 앞에 not을 붙인다.

11 안용복의 직업은 물고기를 잡는 것이라고 했다.

12 전치사의 목적어이므로 동명사형이 되어야 한다.

13 it은 인칭대명사로 앞에 언급된 a modern onggi를 가리킨다.

창의사고력 서술형 문제  p.156

|모범답안|

01 (1) Dad wants me to come home early.
   (2) My classmates asked me to be quiet in class.
   (3) She told him to fix the computer.
   (4) She didn't allow us to play the piano.
   (5) I advised her to go home early after the concert.
   (6) The teacher forced the students to attend the classes.
   (7) We persuaded him to come to Ann's birthday party.

02 (A) between
   (B) building
   (C) moving
   (D) taste
   (E) protect
   (F) independence
   (G) example
   (H) building

단원별 모의고사  p.157~160

01 ②      02 ⑤      03 ④

04 한 살 먹은 아기를 위한 생일 잔치

05 wears      06 ④      07 ③      08 ④

09 경복궁과 창덕궁 사이에 있는 땅에

10 You are also helping the independence movement in many ways.

11 ③　　　12 ⑤　　　13 ④　　　14 ①

15 She bought a smartphone made in Korea.

16 shocked　17 ①　　　18 ②　　　19 ③

20 caught → was caught　21 ①　　　22 ②

23 job　　　24 officially　25 ④

01 hundreds of: 수백의, 수많은 / 허리케인 시즌만 되면 수백 명의 사람들이 목숨을 잃습니다. thanks to: ~ 덕분에 / 그녀의 발명 덕분에 많은 사람들이 좀 더 나은 생활을 하고 있다.

02 '살아 있는'의 뜻으로 living은 한정적 용법, alive는 서술적 용법으로 쓰인다. other는 뒤에 복수 명사가 오고, another는 단수 명사가 온다.

03 ④ stone: 돌

04 it은 앞 문장의 the birthday party for a one-year-old baby를 받는다.

05 옷, 신발, 장갑과 같은 것을 여러분의 신체 또는 신체의 부분에 걸치다: wear(입다, 신다, 쓰다)

06 ④ 돌잔치에 가족들이 어떤 음식을 먹는지는 알 수 없다.

07 (C) 만리장성에 대해 아는 것이 있느냐고 묻는다. (A) 그렇다고 대답한다. (B) 그것이 유명한 이유를 다시 묻는다. (D) 세계에서 가장 긴 벽이기 때문이라고 대답한다.

08 일본인들이 경성에 와서 그들의 취향에 맞게 경성을 바꾼다는 문장 다음에 와야 한다.

09 there는 on the land between Gyeongbokgung and Changdeokgung을 가리킨다.

10 also는 보통 be동사와 일반동사 사이에 위치한다. 여러 방법으로: in many ways

11 ③ Jeong이 일본식 집을 짓는 법을 모르는지는 위 대화의 내용으로 보아 알 수 없다.

12 make는 사역동사로 동사원형을 목적격보어로 취한다. 나머지는 모두 to부정사를 목적격보어로 취하는 동사들로 to do가 들어가야 한다.

13 모두 '~을 사용하는'이라는 의미의 현재분사가 쓰이지만 ④번에는 과거분사 used가 쓰여 '중고차'라는 의미를 만든다.

14 cause, expect, ask, want, tell 모두 목적격보어로 to부정사가 나와야 한다. ceremony: 식, 의식

15 분사가 명사 뒤에서 명사를 꾸며줄 때, 분사 앞에는 '주격 관계대명사+be동사'가 생략되었다고 볼 수 있다.

16 충격을 느끼는 것이므로 과거분사로 주어를 설명하는 것이 적절하다.

17 빈칸에는 to부정사를 목적격보어로 취할 수 있는 동사가 들어가야 한다.

18 ⓐ, ② 경험 ①, ④ 계속 ③ 완료 ⑤ 결과

19 보기와 ③ ~으로 ① ~할 때 ② ~하는 대로, ~처럼 ④ ~이기 때문에 ⑤ ~함에 따라, ~할수록

20 문맥상 수동태가 되어야 한다.

21 문맥상 결과를 나타내는 접속사 so가 적절하다.

22 앞 문장과 대조되는 내용이 나오므로 상반을 나타내는 접속부사 however가 알맞다.

23 어떤 사람이 돈을 벌기 위해 하는 일: job(직업)

24 동사를 수식하므로 official의 부사형이 와야 한다.

25 ④ 안용복은 일본을 두 번 방문했다.

# Manners Make the Man

## 시험대비 실력평가 p.164

01 tourist    02 ④    03 ④    04 ③
05 ⑤    06 ②
07 (1) bright    (2) freely    (3) concerto

01 도서관 : 사서 / 관광 : 관광객
02 increase: 증가하다
03 disturb: 방해하다(=interrupt)
04 누군가 또는 무언가가 어떤 나쁜 일에 책임이 있다고 생각하거나 말하다를 가리키는 단어는 'blame(비난하다)'이다.
05 <보기>와 ⑤는 '작품'이라는 의미로 쓰였고, 나머지는 '일, 직장'이라는 의미로 쓰였다.
06 be on time: 제시간에 오다 / take a look at: ~을 보다
07 (1) bright: 밝은 (2) freely: 자유롭게 (3) concerto: 협주곡

## 서술형 시험대비 p.165

01 (1) artist    (2) scientist    (3) novelist    (4) tourist
02 clap
03 (1) blame    (2) audience    (3) serious    (4) mostly
04 (C)onsequently
05 (1) no longer    (2) dependent on    (3) at any time
06 (1) I need a small trash can.
   (2) Noise was just part of the concert.
   (3) Concerts in Mozart's time were mostly social events.

01 (1) artist: 예술가 (2) scientist: 과학자 (3) novelist: 소설가 (4) tourist: 관광객
02 두 손뼉을 마주 치다: clap(박수치다)
03 (1) blame: 비난하다 (2) audience: 청중 (3) serious: 심각한 (4) mostly: 주로
04 as a result: 그 결과(=consequently)
05 (1) no longer: 더 이상 ~ 않다 (2) dependent on: ~에 의존하는 (3) at any time: 아무 때나
06 (1) trash can: 쓰레기통 (2) part of: ~의 일부 (3) mostly: 주로 / social: 사교적인

## 교과서 Conversation

### 핵심 Check p.166~167

1 (1) make it / fine    (2) about going / problem
2 (1) Don't forget to    (2) Remember to    (3) Make sure to    (4) won't

## 교과서 대화문 익히기

### Check(√) True or False p.168

1 F    2 T    3 T    4 F

## 교과서 확인학습 p.170~171

**Listen & Speak 1 B**
1. interested in, tickets / When / this, at, make it / thanks, asking
2. Why don't, this / What about / make it, have to / See

**Listen & Speak 2 B**
1. going to, remember / Don't forget / won't / Sounds
2. look, secret / go swimming, sometime / sounds like, Any other / forget to, many kinds

**Real-Life Zone A**
listening to / going to, like to, before / guess, more, if / clap, wrong / when, stops / may, pauses, wait, very end / see, Make sure, forget to, real ending, way, make it, practice, after, finishes, See

**Real-Life Zone B**
Why don't, after, make / can't, about / Don't forget / right, won't

**Wrap Up**
Have, heard, that, will be, why don't, make it / what time / at, Let's meet / forget to / won't

## 시험대비 기본평가 p.172

01 ④    02 (C) → (B) → (D) → (A)    03 ②

01 갈 수 있느냐고 묻는 표현이 와야 한다.

02 (C) 주말에 신발 가게에 가겠느냐고 묻는다. (B) 좋다고 말하면서, 토요일 2시에 가자고 제안한다. (D) 1시에 갈 수 있느냐고 묻는다. (A) 좋다고 대답한다.

03 'Don't forget to ~.'는 어떤 일을 잊지 말고 하라고 상기시키는 표현이다.

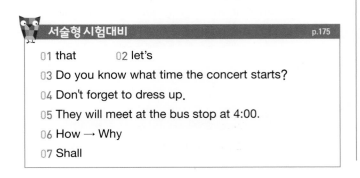
01 healthy
02 Are there any other things that[which] I should do?    03 ①     04 Remember 05 ⑤
06 ③, ④
07 ②     08 ①     09 ③     10 ④
11 I'll come to the practice after the concert finishes.
12 ②

01 health의 형용사형이 와야 한다. healthy: 건강한

02 앞에 Are there가 생략된 문장이다. things 다음에는 관계대명사 목적격 that이나 which가 생략되었다.

03 ① 소녀는 소년에게 건강해 보이는 비결을 묻고 있다.

04 Remember는 '기억하다'의 뜻이므로 Don't forget과 의미가 같다.

05 (C) 월요일에 도서관에 가자는 제안에, (D) 월요일 대신 화요일에 가자고 대답한다. (A) 좋다고 말하며 도서관 카드를 가져오라고 말하자, (B) 알겠다고 대답한다.

06 Can you make it at ~?은 약속 시간을 정할 때 쓰는 표현이다.

07 listen to: ~을 듣다

08 before: ~하기 전에 if: ~한다면

09 ⓑ와 ③의 may는 '~일지도 모르다'의 뜻으로 약한 추측을 나타낸다.

10 make it to: ~에 오다

11 때를 나타내는 부사절은 미래의 일을 나타낼 때 현재형을 쓴다.

12 ② 소년이 종종 잘못된 때에 박수를 치는지는 알 수 없다.

01 that     02 let's
03 Do you know what time the concert starts?
04 Don't forget to dress up.
05 They will meet at the bus stop at 4:00.
06 How → Why
07 Shall

---

01 heard의 목적어가 되는 명사절을 이끄는 접속사 that이 필요하다.

02 why don't we ~?는 제안을 나타내는 말로 let's ~로 바꾸어 쓸 수 있다.

03 간접의문문으로 바꾼다. 간접의문문은 '의문사+주어+동사'의 어순이 된다.

04 dress up: 옷을 차려 입다

06 Why don't we ~?: ~하는 게 어때?

07 How about ~?은 Shall we ~?나 Let's ~로 바꿔 쓸 수 있다.

핵심 Check      p.176~177

1 (1) when    (2) where    (3) why    (4) how / the way
2 (1) what you bought
   (2) if[whether] you like
   (3) Who do you think will

01 ②
02 (1) when    (2) where    (3) when    (4) why
03 ①
04 (1) where    (2) when    (3) why    (4) how

01 간접의문문은 '의문사+주어+동사'의 형태로 다른 문장 안에서 목적어 역할을 한다.

02 (1) 선행사 the month는 때를 나타내므로 관계부사 when을 쓴다. (2) 선행사 the restaurant는 장소를 나타내므로 관계부사 where를 쓴다. (3) 선행사 the day는 때를 나타내므로 관계부사 when을 쓴다. (4) 선행사 the reason은 이유를 나타내므로 관계부사 why를 쓴다.

03 간접의문문의 어순은 '의문사+주어+동사'이며 의문사가 없는 경우는 'if[whether]+주어+동사'로 쓴다.

04 (1) 선행사가 장소이므로 관계부사 where (2) 선행사가 때이므로 관계부사 when (3) 선행사가 이유이므로 관계부사 why (4) 방법을 나타내므로 관계부사 how

01 ⑤      02 ①      03 ⑤

04 (1) where   (2) the way   (3) for which

05 (1) Do you know who that tall guy over there is?

   (2) Tell me who made this chocolate cake.

   (3) I wonder if[whether] Marianne got married.

   (4) Where do you think Snow White is?

06 ②      07 ⑤      08 ①

09 (1) I know who won the race.

   (2) Do you know when the bus will come?

   (3) The man is asking her how long it takes to get to TIG Market.

   (4) Who do you think will win the game?

   (5) What do you guess she wants to buy?

10 ①

11 (1) when does the show start → when the show starts

   (2) that does the bag have → if[whether] the bag has

   (3) Do you think who → Who do you think

12 ②, ④      13 ⑤

14 (1) I know how she solved the problem.

   (2) I know (the reason) why Jerry was angry.

   (3) This is the library where I often stop by on my way home.

15 ④      16 ④      17 ③, ⑤

18 (1) How long does it take to reach the top?

   (2) Was the thief a man or a woman?

   (3) What is the secret of his success?

---

01 간접의문문은 '의문사+주어+동사'의 어순이다. It으로 받고 있으므로 단수가 적절하다.

02 선행사가 때(the day)를 나타내므로 때의 관계부사 when 또는 '전치사+관계대명사'인 on which가 와야 하는데, on이 빈칸 앞에 있으므로 which가 적절하다.

03 간접의문문의 어순은 '의문사+주어+동사'의 형태임에 유의한다.

04 (1) 선행사가 장소이므로 관계부사로 where를 써야 한다. which를 쓰려면 staying 다음에 전치사 in[at]이 있어야 한다. (2) the way와 관계부사 how는 함께 쓸 수 없다. (3) 관계부사 why 대신에 for which를 쓸 수 있다.

05 간접의문문의 어순은 '의문사+주어+동사'이며 의문사가 없는 경우는 'if[whether]+주어+동사'로 쓴다. 의문사가 주어인 경우에는 의문사가 주어 역할을 동시에 하므로 직접의문문처럼 '의문사+동사'의 어순임에 유의해야 한다. think 동사가 주절에 있을 경우 간접의문문의 의문사를 문장 맨 앞에 써야 함에도 유의한다.

06 나머지는 모두 '언제'를 뜻하는 의문부사인 반면 ②는 관계부사이다.

07 의문사가 없는 간접의문문의 어순은 'if[whether]+주어+동사'이지만, if를 쓸 경우 or not을 바로 붙여 쓰지 않는다.

08 (1) 선행사가 이유이므로 관계부사로 why를 써야 한다. (2) the way와 관계부사 how는 함께 쓸 수 없다. how 대신 the way를 써도 좋다.

09 간접의문문의 어순은 '의문사+주어+동사'이며 의문사가 없는 경우는 'if[whether]+주어+동사'로 쓴다. think나 guess 동사가 주절에 있을 경우 간접의문문의 의문사를 문장 맨 앞으로 배치한다.

10 ①은 때를 나타내는 선행사를 취하는 관계부사 when을 쓰고 나머지는 모두 where를 쓴다.

11 (1) 간접의문문의 어순은 '의문사+주어+동사'이다. (2) 의문사가 필요 없는 자리이므로 'if[whether]+주어+동사'로 써야 한다. (3) think 동사가 주절에 있을 경우 간접의문문의 의문사를 문장 맨 앞에 써야 한다.

12 관계부사 where 대신 to which를 써도 좋다.

13 간접의문문의 어순은 '의문사+주어+동사'이다.

14 (1) how 대신 the way를 써도 좋다. (2) 선행사가 이유이므로 관계부사 why가 적절하다. (3) 선행사가 장소이므로 관계부사 where가 적절하다.

15 주어진 문장과 ④에서 when은 관계부사로 쓰였고, 나머지는 모두 접속사로 쓰였다.

16 올바른 문장은 This is the house where I live with my parents.이다.

17 선행사가 계절이므로 관계부사 when 대신 in which를 써도 좋다.

18 간접의문문의 어순은 '의문사+주어+동사'이며 의문사가 없는 경우는 'if[whether]+주어+동사'로 쓴다. (3)에서 believe 동사가 주절에 있을 경우 간접의문문의 의문사를 문장 맨 앞으로 배치한다.

---

01 (1) Tell me what you want for Christmas.

   (2) She asks me how much sugar there is in the bottle.

   (3) Do you know where Greece is on the map?

   (4) I wonder if[whether] he is a singer.

   (5) I have no idea if[whether] he will join us soon.

   (6) Where do you think your soul goes after you die?

02 (1) This is the house where[in which] I was born.

(2) December 25th is the day when[on which] Christmas is celebrated.

(3) There is a small bed where[on which] I always sleep.

(4) This is the way[how] I solved the problem.

03 (1) I ate  (2) she left  (3) he is  (4) if

04 (1) why  (2) which[that]  (3) the way 또는 how  (4) when

05 (1) The doctor will ask you what you ate for breakfast.

(2) Please let us know if[whether] you are able to attend the meeting.

(3) What do you suppose they are thinking?

06 (1) where  (2) why  (3) when

07 (1) Daniel told us how he became a singer.

(2) It is doubtful whether he will come or not.

08 (1) Do you remember the day when you first saw your little sister?

(2) A park is a place where people take a walk.

(3) Mariel wants to know whether he is going to meet Asako.

09 (1) Nobody knows. Why did Lauren leave the office early?

(2) It is difficult to understand. What does the teacher say?

(3) Steve didn't tell me. When did the movie begin?

(4) Do you think? What is the most typical Korean dish?

(5) They wonder. Can they borrow some books today?

01 간접의문문의 어순은 '의문사+주어+동사'이며 의문사가 없는 경우는 'if[whether]+주어+동사'로 쓴다. think 동사가 주절에 있을 경우 간접의문문의 의문사를 문장 맨 앞으로 배치한다.

02 (1) the house를 수식하는 관계부사는 where를 쓴다. '전치사+관계대명사'로 바꿔 써도 좋다. (2) the day를 수식하는 관계부사는 when을 쓴다. (3) a small bed를 수식하는 관계부사는 where를 쓴다. (4) the way how는 쓸 수 없다. the way나 how를 별개로 써야 한다.

03 (1), (2), (3) 간접의문문의 어순은 '의문사+주어+동사'이다. (4) I konw 뒤에는 that절, know 뒤에는 if[whether]절이 온다.

04 (1) 선행사가 이유를 나타내는 말이므로 why를 써야 한다. (2) 관계사절에 전치사 in이 쓰였으므로 where를 which[that]로 써야 한다. (3) the way와 how를 같이 쓸 수 없으므로 the way 또는 how만을 써야 한다. (4) 선행사가 때를 나타내는 말

이므로 when을 써야 한다.

05 (1), (2), (3) 간접의문문의 어순은 '의문사+주어+동사'이며 의문사가 없는 경우는 'if[whether]+주어+동사'로 쓴다. suppose 동사가 주절에 있을 경우 간접의문문의 의문사를 문장 맨 앞으로 배치한다.

06 (1) 선행사가 장소이므로 where를 쓴다. (2) 선행사가 이유이므로 why를 쓴다. (3) 선행사가 때이므로 when을 쓴다.

08 (1) when은 선행사 the day 뒤에 쓰여 수식한다. (2) 관계부사 where는 장소를 나타내는 선행사 a place를 수식한다. (3) whether가 이끄는 명사절이 know의 목적어가 된다.

09 간접의문문의 어순은 '의문사+주어+동사'이며 의문사가 없는 경우는 'if[whether]+주어+동사'로 쓴다. think 동사가 주절에 있을 경우 간접의문문의 의문사를 문장 맨 앞으로 배치한다.

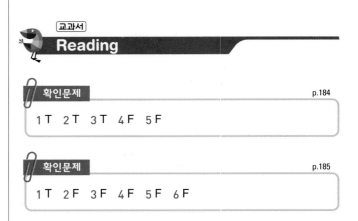

교과서
## Reading

확인문제                                    p.184

1 T  2 T  3 T  4 F  5 F

확인문제                                    p.185

1 T  2 F  3 F  4 F  5 F  6 F

교과서 확인학습 A                          p.186~187

01 Classical, Manners
02 Imagine yourself, classical
03 orchestra, play one, piano
04 hall, dark, silent
05 Nobody, sound
06 Everybody, serious
07 audiences, clap, finishes
08 familiar scene at
09 go back, time, take, look
10 bright, inside, nobleman's
11 playing, piano
12 Surprisingly, audiences, talking freely
13 whistle, clap
14 shocked, bad, himself, surprised, quiet
15 were mostly social
16 good places to meet

17 just part

18 quiet, century when, were built

19 not just noblemen

20 no longer dependent

21 more power, use, increased

22 For example, blamed, for

23 After, rule appeared

24 As a result, quiet

25 what concerts, look like, because, change

26 however, enjoy classical, just remember

27 Enjoy, disturb those

1 The History of Classical Concert Manners

2 Imagine yourself at a classical music concert.

3 The orchestra starts to play one of Mozart's piano concertos.

4 The concert hall is dark and silent.

5 Nobody makes a sound.

6 Everybody looks serious.

7 The audiences only clap after the concerto finishes.

8 This is a familiar scene at concerts today.

9 Let's go back in time and take a look at one of Mozart's concerts in the 18th century.

10 You are in a bright hall inside a nobleman's house.

11 Mozart is playing the piano.

12 Surprisingly, however, the audiences are eating, drinking, and talking freely.

13 They whistle and clap at any time.

14 You are shocked by their bad manners, but Mozart himself would be surprised by today's quiet audiences.

15 Concerts in Mozart's time were mostly social events.

16 They were good places to meet people.

17 Noise was just part of the concert.

18 Today's quiet concerts began in the 19th century when many big concert halls were built.

19 More people, not just noblemen, went to concerts.

20 Artists were no longer dependent on noblemen for money.

21 The artists had more power over their works and started to use their increased power.

22 For example, Wagner blamed the audience for making noise.

23 After some time, a no-clapping-between-movements rule appeared.

24 As a result, here we are today, very quiet and serious.

25 We do not know what concerts will look like in the future because manners change with time.

26 For now, however, if you want to enjoy classical music concerts, just remember this:

27 Enjoy the music, but do not disturb those around you.

01 ①, ④, ⑤

02 The concert hall is dark and silent. Nobody makes a sound. Everybody looks serious. The audiences only clap after the concerto finishes.

03 ①　　　　04 ③

05 today's quiet audiences　06 ②, ⑤

07 in which　　08 ②　　09 ①, ②, ④

10 (A) what　(B) manners　(C) those

11 ①　　　12 ②　　　13 ①, ②, ⑤

14 concerto → concertos　15 ⑤　　　16 ④

17 ①, ④　　18 ④　　　19 ④

20 built → were built　　21 ①

22 ④　　　23 ②

01 ⓐ와 ①, ④, ⑤번: 명사적 용법, ② 부사적 용법, ③번: 형용사적 용법

02 'This가 가리키는 것은 오늘날의 연주회 장면이다.

03 오늘날의 연주회장은 어둡고 조용하다.

04 ⓐ take a look at ~을 보다, ⓒ be surprised by[at] ~에 놀라다

05 모차르트는 오늘날의 조용한 관객에 의해서 놀라게 될 것이다.

06 ⓑ와 ①, ③, ④번: 진행 시제를 나타내는 현재분사, ②, ⑤: 동명사

07 관계부사 when = 전치사+which

08 이 글은 오늘날의 조용한 콘서트가 어떻게 시작되었는지 그 유래를 설명하고 있다.

09 ① 19세기에 큰 연주회장이 많이 지어졌다. ② 예술가들이 돈에 대하여 귀족에게서 독립했다. ④ 바그너는 소음을 내는 청중을 싫어했다. (③ 그들의 작품이 더 우수했는지는 알 수 없다.) ⑤ 악장사이 박수 안 치는 규칙을 누가 만들었는지는 알 수 없다.

10 (A) look like의 목적어가 되는 의문대명사 what이 적절하다.
(B) "예의범절"이라는 뜻은 manners이다. manner는 "방법"

35

이라는 뜻이다. (C) "~하는 사람들"이라는 뜻은 복수를 나타내어 those를 쓴다.

11 연주회장에서의 예의범절이 현재는 과거와 달라졌고 미래에는 어떻게 변할지 알 수 없지만, 그것과 상관없이 현재의 바람직한 관람 태도를 나타내는 대조의 표현이 적절하다.

12 연주회장에서 지켜야 하는 것은 주변 사람들에게 피해를 주지 않는 것이기 때문에 "주변의"를 가리키는 around가 적절하다.

13 ⓐ와 ③, ④: 재귀 용법, ①, ②, ⑤번: 강조 용법

14 "~ 중에서 하나"라는 뜻일 때는 "one of the/소유격+복수명사"의 형태를 가지기 때문에 concerto를 concertos로 바꾸어야 한다.

15 ⑤ 왜 오케스트라가 모차르트의 피아노 콘체르토를 연주했는지는 이 글에서 소개되지 않았다.

16 ④ 이 글은 오늘날과 다르게 Mozart 시대의 콘서트가 어떠했는지를 보여준다. 따라서 글의 주제는 "Mozart 시대의 콘서트는 어떠했는가?"이다.

17 ⓐ와 ②, ③, ⑤번: 형용사적 용법, ① 명사적 용법, ④ 부사적 용법

18 ④ 그 당시의 연주회에서는 관객이 아무 때나 박수치고, 휘파람을 불었다.

19 ④: "A를 ~ 때문에 비난하다"는 의미일 때는 "blame A for ~"라고 한다.

20 부사절의 주어 many big concert halls는 짓는 입장이 아니라 지어지는 위치에 있기 때문에 수동태가 되어서 "were builit"가 되어야 한다.

21 오늘날의 조용한 콘서트는 19세기에 시작되었다.

22 "~처럼 보이다"는 "look like"이다. look after 돌보다, look into 조사하다, look at 보다, look out 밖을 내다보다

23 (A) 오늘날의 연주회는 조용하므로 quiet (B) 문장을 연결할 때는 접속사가 있어야 한다. because of는 뒤에 명사(구)가 온다. (C) 연주회에서는 남에게 방해가 되지 않아야 하므로 disturb

## 🦉 서술형 시험대비     p.194~195

01 번호: ⑤ 틀린 것: look 올바른 형태: looks

02 audience

03 콘서트장은 어둡고 조용하다. 아무도 소리를 내지 않는다. 모두가 진지해 보인다. 청중은 오직 협주곡이 끝난 후에만 손뼉을 친다.

04 take

05 nobleman

06 freely

07 noise

08 weren't

09 (A) be built   (B) power

10 what

11 ⓐ because   ⓑ those

12 음악은 즐기되 주변의 다른 사람들을 방해하지 마라.

13 Nobody

14 Everybody[Everyone] looks serious.

15 (A) dark   (B) silent   (C) clap

01 ⑤ 주어 Everybody는 단수 취급하기 때문에 단수 동사 looks가 되어야 한다.

02 "공공장소에서 하는 연설이나 공연을 보고, 듣는 사람의 무리"는 "관객, 청중"을 나타낸다.

03 This는 보통 앞 문장을 가리키지만 여기서는 앞에 주어진 콘서트 장소에 대한 설명 전체를 가리킨다.

04 접속사 and로 연결되는 병렬 구조에서 동사원형 go와 같은 형태인 take가 되어야 한다.

05 "사회적으로 높은 계층에 있으며 공작 등과 같은 호칭을 가지는 사람"은 "귀족"이다.

06 동사 eat, drink, talk를 수식하는 단어는 부사가 되어야 한다.

07 바그너는 소음을 내는 것 때문에 관객을 비난했다.

08 "더 이상 ~하지 않는"에 해당하는 의미의 "no longer"는 "not ~ any longer"로 바꾸어 쓸 수 있다.

09 19세기에는 많은 대규모 공연장이 건설되고, 예술가들은 자신의 작품에 대해 더 많은 권력을 가지게 되었다.

10 전치사 like의 목적어 역할을 하는 의문대명사 what이 적절하다.

11 ⓐ 절과 절을 연결하는 접속사 because가 적절하다. ⓑ "~하는 사람들"이라는 의미로 지시대명사 those가 적절하다.

12 주어진 문장에서 this가 가리키는 것은 뒤에 이어지는 문장을 가리킨다.

13 콘서트장은 조용하기 때문에 "누구도 소음을 내지 않는다."고 해야 한다.

14 "~해 보이다"에 해당하는 동사는 look이다.

15 오늘날의 연주회장은 어둡고 조용하며, 관객은 협주곡이 끝난 후에만 박수를 친다.

## 🐞 영역별 핵심문제     p.197~201

01 unfamiliar   02 ⑤     03 ④

04 (1) at any time   (2) for now   (3) As a result

05 ⑤     06 (D) → (A) → (C) → (B)     07 ②

08 ①     09 Actually   10 remember   11 ⑤

12 ③

13 (1) why   (2) which   (3) where   (4) which   (5) how

14 ④       15 I know the reason why Jane is

crying.　16 ③

17 This is the house where Shakespeare was born. / This is the house in which Shakespeare was born.

18 (1) what it is　(2) where it is

19 (1) 해석: 이곳은 내가 어렸을 때 방문하고 했던 공원이다.
　(2) 해석: 이곳은 내가 어렸을 때 가곤 했던 공원이다.
　(3) 어법상 차이: (1) which는 관계대명사이다. (2) where는 관계부사이다.

20 (A) yourself　(B) concertos　(C) finishes

21 ④　22 ③　23 ④　24 ②, ⑤

25 ③　26 ②　27 ④　28 ③

29 (A) what　(B) because　(C) remember

01 주어진 단어의 관계는 반의어 관계이다. appear (나타나다) : disappear (사라지다) = familiar (친숙한) : unfamiliar (친숙하지 않은)

02 어떤 것을 원래 있던 곳이나 가야 할 곳으로 가져가다를 나타내는 말은 return(돌려주다, 반납하다)이다.

03 dependent: 의존적인

04 (1) at any time: 아무 때나 (2) for now: 지금은 (3) as a result: 그 결과

05 How about ~ing?: ~하는 것은 어때?

06 (D) 오페라에 관심 있느냐고 질문 → (A) 그렇다고 대답하며 오페라가 언제 있느냐고 질문 → (C) 토요일이라고 대답하며 갈 수 있느냐고 질문 → (B) 갈 수 있다고 대답

07 ⓑ bringing → to bring (미래의 일은 'forget+to부정사'의 형을 쓴다.

08 글의 흐름상 조건을 나타내는 접속사 if가 알맞다.

09 actual의 부사형이 와야 한다.

10 not forget은 remember와 같은 뜻이다.

11 ⑤ 소년은 콘서트가 끝난 후에 연습하러 갈 것이라고 말했다.

12 간접의문문의 어순은 '의문사+주어+동사'의 형태임에 유의한다.

13 (1) 선행사가 이유이므로 why를 쓴다. (2) 선행사가 the date(날짜)이므로 관계부사 when이나 '전치사+관계대명사'인 on which가 와야 한다. 전치사 on이 있기 때문에 which를 써야 한다. (3) 선행사가 장소이므로 where를 쓴다. (4) 선행사 the day가 spent의 목적어이므로 관계대명사 which를 쓴다. (5) the way나 how를 써야 한다.

14 의문사가 없는 간접의문문의 어순은 'if[whether]+주어+동사'이며 if는 or not과 붙여 쓰지 않는다.

15 이유를 나타내는 관계부사와 선행사의 위치에 주의한다.

16 ⓐ why he came here ⓒ 의문사가 없으므로 if he will

come ⓔ 주절의 동사가 think이므로 Where do you think Ann spent her spring vacation?

17 the house를 수식하는 관계부사 where나 '전치사+대명사'인 in which를 쓴다.

18 간접의문문의 어순은 '의문사+주어+동사'이며 (1)에는 무엇인지를 묻는 표현이, (2)에는 장소를 묻는 표현이 들어가는 것이 적절하다.

19 (1)은 선행사 the park이 visit의 목적어이므로 관계대명사 which가 와야 한다. (2)는 go to the park의 관계이므로 관계부사 where가 와야 한다.

20 (A) 명령문은 주어 You가 생략된 것이기 때문에 목적어는 재귀대명사 yourself가 되어야 한다. (B) "one of the 복수명사"가 되어야 하기 때문에 concertos가 되어야 한다. (C) 시간의 부사절에서는 미래 대신 현재를 쓴다.

21 ⓐ와 ④번: 부정사의 명사적 용법 ①, ②, ③, ⑤ 부정사의 부사적 용법

22 본문에는 관객이 박수를 치는 이유에 대하여서는 언급이 없다.

23 (A) "시간상으로, 시간에서"의 의미로 "in time", (B) "~에 의해서"의 의미로 행위자를 나타낼 때는 by

24 ⓐ와 ②, ⑤: 현재분사, ①, ③, ④: 동명사

25 모차르트 시대에는 연주회장에서 아무 때나 박수를 치고 휘파람을 불었다.

26 관계부사는 "전치사+which"로 바꾸어 쓸 수 있다. the 19th century를 선행사로 하는 관계부사 when은 in which로 바꾸어 쓸 수 있다.

27 이 글은 19세기에 예술가들에 대한 권한이 증가하면서 조용한 연주회가 시작된 과정을 소개하고 있다.

28 예절이 변하기 때문에 미래의 연주회가 어떠할 지는 알 수 없다.

29 (A) look like의 목적어가 될 수 있는 의문대명사 what이 적절하다. (B) 내용상 이유를 나타내는 접속사 because가 적절하다. (C) 음악을 즐기기 위해서 지켜야 할 예의범절은 "기억하라"고 해야 한다.

### 단원별 예상문제　　p.202~205

01 ②　02 ④　03 concerto　04 ③
05 ②　06 on　07 ④
08 about meeting　09 ③　10 ⑤
11 ③　12 ⑤　13 ③　14 ④
15 ③　16 ③　17 ②
18 shocked　19 social
20 (A) bright　(B) whistled　(C) clapped
21 (A) quiet　(B) just　(C) increased
22 ④　23 ③
24 We do not know what concerts will look like in

the future because manners change with time

25 however    26 to enjoy

27 음악을 즐겨라, 그러나 여러분 주위에 있는 사람들을 방해하지 는 마라.

01 blame: 비난하다

02 take a look at: ~을 보다

03 오케스트라와 연주하는 하나 이상의 독주 악기를 위한 음악: concerto(협주곡)

04 with time: 시간이 지남에 따라 / by the way: 그건 그렇고

05 ① century: 세기 / 우리는 21세기에 살고 있다. ② movement: 움직임 / 그는 움직임이 느리다. ③ classical: 클래식의 / 그녀는 클래식 공연에 갔다. ④ volunteer: 자원봉사하다 / 그들은 어린이 센터에서 자원봉사를 한다. ⑤ social: 사교적인 / 새로운 친구를 사귀기 위해 사교 모임에 가입하라.

06 be on the stage: 무대에 서다

07 크리스마스에 갈 수 있느냐고 묻고 있으므로 make it이 알맞다.

08 Let's ~는 How about ~ing?로 바꿔 쓸 수 있다.

09 ③ 소녀는 소년에게 콘서트에 가자고 제안했다.

10 기다렸다가 맨 마지막에 박수를 쳐야 한다는 뜻이므로 클래식 음악에서는 한 곡에 여러 반 멈춤이 있다는 말 다음에 와야 한다.

11 글의 흐름상 콘서트에 가기 전에 클래식 음악에 대해 알고 싶다는 말이 알맞다.

12 '그런데'의 뜻으로 화제를 바꿀 때 쓰는 by the way가 알맞다.

13 ③ 소년이 종종 콘서트에 가는지는 알 수 없다.

14 의문사가 없는 간접의문문은 'if[whether]+주어+동사'로 쓴다.

15 선행사 the town 뒤에 관계부사 where를 쓴다.

16 I wonder 다음에는 if나 whether로 시작하는 간접의문문이 온다.

17 ②번은 조건절에 쓰인 if이지만 나머지는 모두 간접의문문을 이끌고 있다.

18 shock은 "충격을 주다"의 의미로 그 당시의 방식에 주어가 놀라게 되는 수동의 입장이기 때문에 과거분사가 되어야 한다.

19 이어지는 문장에서 사람들을 만나기에 좋은 장소라고 하는 것으로 보아 "사교적인"에 해당하는 social이 적절하다.

20 Mozart 시대의 연주회장은 밝고, 소음이 많았으며 아무 때나 휘파람을 불고 박수를 쳤다.

21 (A) 오늘날의 공연장의 분위기를 나타내는 것은 quiet이다. (B) "~뿐만 아니라"의 뜻으로는 "not just"가 적절하다. (C) "증가된"의 의미로 수동의 의미를 포함하는 것은 과거분사 increased이다.

22 ⓐ와 ④번: 관계부사 ①, ②: 접속사, ③, ⑤: 의문부사(간접의문)

23 ③ 얼마나 많은 예술가들이 귀족에게 의존했는지에 대한 언급은 없다.

24 what으로 시작하는 부분은 간접의문으로 간접의문은 "의문사+주어+동사"의 어순이다.

25 앞뒤의 내용이 대조적이기 때문에 however가 적절하다.

26 동사 want의 목적어는 to부정사이다.

27 those around you= people who are around you

서술형 실전문제     p.206~207

01 Sure, I can. → Sorry, but I can't.

02 swimming

03 Any other things I should do?

04 to eat

05 (1) I'll tell you where he has been since last Monday.
　(2) I'd like to know if[whether] you met her.
　(3) Where do you think I can find some fruit?

06 when

07 Could you tell me when the next train comes?

08 where

09 (1) Do you know if[whether] Anna loves me?
　(2) I don't know why Kate was so surprised.
　(3) Cathy will tell me who broke the window yesterday.
　(4) Which book can you imagine Jennifer bought?

10 yourself

11 ⑤ The audiences only clap after the concerto will finish. → The audiences only clap after the concerto finishes.

12 clap

13 to

14 bad

15 Concerts in Mozart's time were good places to meet people.

01 월요일에 도서관에 가자는 제안에 화요일이 어떠냐고 묻고 있으므로 Sure, I can.은 어색하다.

02 go swimming: 수영하러 가다

03 문장 앞에 Are there와 관계대명사 목적격 that이나 which가 생략되었다.

04 문맥상 미래의 일을 나타내는 to부정사가 와야 한다.

05 간접의문문의 어순은 '의문사+주어+동사'이며 의문사가 없는 경우는 'if[whether]+주어+동사'로 쓴다. think 동사가 주절에 있을 경우 간접의문문의 의문사를 문장 맨 앞으로 배치한다.

06 선행사가 때를 나타내므로 관계부사 when을 쓴다.

07 간접의문문의 어순은 '의문사+주어+동사'이다.

08 선행사가 장소를 나타내므로 장소의 관계부사 where를 써야 한다.

09 간접의문문의 어순은 '의문사+주어+동사'이며 의문사가 없는 경우는 'if[whether]+주어+동사'로 쓴다. 의문사가 주어인 경우에는 직접의문문처럼 '의문사+동사'의 어순임에 유의해야 하며 imagine 동사가 주절에 있을 경우 간접의문문의 의문사를 문장 맨 앞에 써야 함에도 유의한다.

10 "자신이 ~한 상황에 있다는 것을 상상해 보라"는 의미로 목적어는 자신을 가리키는 재귀 대명사가 적절하다.

11 시간이나 조건의 부사절에서는 미래의 의미에 해당하는 경우에도 현재시제를 사용한다.

12 클래식 연주회에서 협주곡이 끝나면 위 글에 따르면 청중이 하는 일은 박수를 치는 것이다.

13 and 이하를 목적을 나타내는 to부정사의 부사적 용법으로 바꾸어 쓸 수 있다.

14 Mozart 시대의 콘서트를 감상하는 방식은 오늘날의 관점에서 보았을 때는 "나쁜 예의 범절"에 해당할 수 있다.

15 모차르트 시대의 연주회 = concerts in Mozart's time, 사람들을 만나기 좋은 장소 = good places to meet people

### 창의사고력 서술형 문제 p.208

|모범답안|

01 (1) Tell me whom you will vote for?

(2) Did you ask Ann why she was absent?

(3) Do you know who fixed the computer?

(4) I wonder if Max can play the piano.

(5) I don't know when he went to the concert.

(6) Can you tell me which flower he likes better?

(7) Which do you think she chose?

02 (A) if[whether]

(B) that

(C) going

(D) meet

(E) not

(F) to

### 단원별 모의고사 p.209~212

01 independent          02 ③          03 ⑤

04 (1) By the way   (2) a look at   (3) dependent on

05 ③          06 ②          07 ①          08 ①

09 ①          10 That sounds like fun.

11 ④          12 ④          13 ②

14 (1) The girl is asking where the nearest bus stop is.

(2) Do you know if[whether] the leaves will turn yellow in autumn?

(3) Will you tell me when you met her?

15 ③

16 (1) I remember where the girl lived.

(2) Anna asked me if[whether] I loved Angelina.

17 in which     18 (A) independent   (B) appeared

19 were built, went

20 번호: ①   틀린 것: which   올바른 형태: when

21 ④          22 ④          23 ②, ⑤

24 (A) Surprisingly   (B) himself   (C) mostly

25 ④          26 ③

01 두 단어는 반의어 관계이다. dark (어두운) : bright (밝은) / dependent (의존적인) : independent (독립적인)

02 work: 직장, 작품

03 일을 하거나 잠을 자려고 할 때 누군가를 방해하다: interrupt (방해하다)

04 (1) by the way: 그건 그렇고 (2) take a look at: ~을 보다 (3) dependent on: ~에 의존하는

05 갈 수 있냐고 묻는 말이므로 크리스마스에 가자고 제안하는 말 다음에 와야 한다.

06 Why don't we ~?: ~하는 게 어때?

07 dress up: 옷을 차려 입다

08 ① 그 소녀가 언제 콘서트에 대해 들었는지는 알 수 없다.

09 문맥상 소년이 건강해 보이는 비결을 묻는 말이므로 You look healthy. 다음에 와야 한다.

10 fun은 명사이므로 like와 함께 쓰여야 한다.

11 forget+동명사: ~한 것을 잊다 / forget+to부정사: ~할 것을 잊다

12 B가 동의하고 5시에 만나자고 말했으므로 약속 시간을 정하는 표현인 ④가 알맞다.

13 선행사가 장소인 관계부사는 where, 때인 관계부사는 when이다.

14 (1), (2), (3) 간접의문문의 어순은 '의문사+주어+동사'이며, 의문사가 없는 경우는 'if[whether]+주어+동사'로 쓴다.

15 ③은 '~할 때'를 뜻하는 접속사인 반면에 나머지는 모두 관계부사이다

16 (1), (2) 간접의문문의 어순은 '의문사+주어+동사'이며 의문사가 없는 경우는 'if[whether]+주어+동사'로 쓴다.

17 the way how는 쓸 수 없지만, how를 in which로 바꿔 쓸 수 있다.

18 19세기에 많은 사람들이 공연장을 찾게 되면서 예술가들이 귀족으로부터 독립적이 되고 작품 중간에 박수를 치지 않는 규칙이 생겨났다.

19 19세기에 큰 연주회장이 지어지고, 많은 사람들이 연주회장에 가게 되면서 예술가들이 귀족에게 의존하지 않을 수 있게 되었다.

20 ① the 19th century를 선행사로 하는 관계부사 when이 들어가야 한다.

21 ⓐ와 ④번: 간접의문문, ①, ②: 관계대명사절 ③: 관계부사절, ⑤ 접속사절

22 (A) 시간이 흐름에 따라 = with time, (B) 너의 주변에 = around you

23 ⓑ와 ②, ⑤: 부사절을 유도하는 접속사 if, ①, ③, ④: 간접의문문을 유도하는 접속사 if

24 (A) 문장 전체를 수식하는 부사 Surprisingly가 적절하다. (B) 강조 용법의 재귀대명사를 쓸 수 있는 위치이다. (C) "주로"의 의미로 부사 mostly가 적절하다.

25 (D)와 ④번: 부정사의 형용사적 용법, ①, ⑤번: 부정사의 명사적 용법, ②, ③: 부정사의 부사적 용법

26 위 글에서 18세기 연주회는 오늘날과 달랐다는 것을 알 수 있지만, 얼마나 많은 연주회장을 지었는지는 알 수 없다.

## Lesson S

# Charlotte's Web

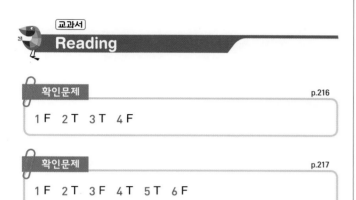

교과서
**Reading**

---

**확인문제**　　　　　　　　　　p.216

1 F　2 T　3 T　4 F

---

**확인문제**　　　　　　　　　　p.217

1 F　2 T　3 F　4 T　5 T　6 F

---

### 교과서 확인학습 A　　　　　　p.218~219

| | |
|---|---|
| 01 Web | 02 Setting, pen |
| 03 Roles | 04 friendship between, and |
| 05 lived on | 06 outside the barn |
| 07 looks, good | 08 make good bacon |
| 09 are fattening, up | 10 For　　11 too, to |
| 12 won't, save | 13 How　　14 yet |
| 15 clean, off | 16 my turn　17 How |
| 18 have | 19 to weave, above |
| 20 hard, without sleeping | 21 to feed |
| 22 words, Some Pig | 23 miracle |
| 24 large crowd | 25 As, only a few |
| 26 called a meeting | 27 As, human attention, last |
| 28 cares, will be dead | 29 another word |
| 30 How about | 31 it　　32 all night |
| 33 later | 34 will be forgotten |
| 35 right away | 36 run out of 37 excitement |
| 38 Why don't you | 39 bring, from |
| 40 trying to | 41 to save　42 shares, with |
| 43 With, finally | 44 biggest ever |
| 45 what, make, out of | 46 enter him |
| 47 get a prize | 48 the fair　49 saved |

---

### 교과서 확인학습 B　　　　　　p.220~221

1 Charlotte's Web

2 Setting: The pen of Wilbur the pig on Mr. and Mrs. Allen's farm

---

3 Roles: Narrator 1, 2, 3, Wilbur: A pig, Charlotte: A spider, Mr. and Mrs. Allen: Farm owners, Old Sheep, Duck, Rat

4 Narrator 1: *Charlotte's Web* is a story of friendship between Wilbur the pig and Charlotte the spider.

5 Narrator 2: They lived on Mr. and Mrs. Allen's farm with Old Sheep, Duck, and Rat.

6 Narrator 3: One day, Mr. and Mrs. Allen were talking outside the barn.

7 Mrs. Allen: Wilbur looks very good.

8 Mr. Allen: He'll make good bacon for Christmas.

9 Old Sheep: They are fattening Wilbur up for Christmas!

10 Duck: For bacon!

11 Wilbur: No! I'm too young to die!

12 Charlotte: You won't, Wilbur. I'll save you.

13 Wilbur: How?

14 Charlotte: I don't know yet, but remember?

15 You saved me when Mr. Allen tried to clean my web off.

16 Now it's my turn to save you.

17 Charlotte: How can I save Wilbur?

18 Hmm…. Oh, I have an idea!

19 Narrator 1: That night, Charlotte started to weave something above Wilbur's pen.

20 She worked hard all night without sleeping.

21 Narrator 2: The next morning, Mr. and Mrs. Allen came to feed Wilbur.

22 Mrs. Allen: Look! There are words in the web. "Some Pig"!

23 Mr. Allen: A miracle!

24 Narrator 3: Soon, a large crowd came to see Wilbur.

25 Narrator 1: As time passed, only a few people came.

26 Charlotte called a meeting.

27 Charlotte: As we saw, human attention does not last long.

28 If nobody cares for Wilbur, he will be dead before Christmas.

29 We must write another word soon.

30 Duck: I have an idea! How about "Terrific"?

31 Old Sheep: I like it!

32 Narrator 2: Again, Charlotte worked hard all night.

33 Two days later, a bigger crowd came.

34 Charlotte: This also will be forgotten soon.

35 We have to prepare the next word right away.

36 Duck: Uh, oh. I have run out of ideas.

37 Rat: What's all the excitement?

38 Old Sheep: Why don't you help us?

39 Will you bring some ads from the dump?

40 Duck: We're trying to find new words.

41 Charlotte: We're trying to save Wilbur's life.

42 Rat: Okay, if Wilbur shares his meal with me.

43 Narrator 3: With Rat's help, they finally chose "Shining."

44 The biggest ever crowd came.

45 Mr. Allen: You know what? I won't make bacon out of Wilbur.

46 I'll enter him in the fair!

47 Mrs. Allen: Great idea! Our famous Wilbur will get a prize!

48 Wilbur: Did you hear that? I'm going to the fair!

49 Thank you, Charlotte! You saved me. Thank you all!

---

## 서술형 실전문제　　　　　　　p.222~223

01 (1) As　(2) as　(3) as

02 excitement

03 (l)asted

04 (1) of　(2) with　(3) for　(4) of

05 (1) (e)nter　(2) (m)ust　(3) pen　(4) fattening up
　　(5) (t)errific

06 (1) weave　(2) enter　(3) dump　(4) narrator

07 (1) I have run out of ideas.
　　(2) Bring some ads from the dump, will you?
　　(3) If Wilbur shares his meal with me, I'll bring some ads from the dump.
　　(4) A prize will be got[gotten] by our famous Wilbur. 또는 Our famous Wilbur will get a prize.
　　(5) John needed someone to talk with about his troubles.
　　(6) As we saw, human attention does not last long.

08 (1) As　(2) If　(3) when

09 (A) Scene　(B) How　(C) yet

10 ⓐ Wilbur the pig and Charlotte the spider
　　ⓑ Mr. and Mrs. Allen

11 I'm so young that I can't die!

01 (1) ~하다시피, ~이듯이 (2) ~이기 때문에 (3) ~하면서 (1) 보시다시피 나는 아직도 갈 길이 멀어요. (2) 그들이 나에게 상당한 양의 돈을 제안하기 때문에 거절하기가 힘들다. (3) 그들은 서로 작별인사를 하면서 울었습니다.

02 excitement: 흥분, 신남

03 last: 지속되다 / 우리의 작업은 끝없이 지속될 것처럼 보인다.

04 (1) run out of: ~이 다 떨어지다 (2) share A with B: A를 B와 나누다 (3) care for: ~를 돌보다 (4) out of: (재료) ~으로

05 (1) enter: (~를) 출전시키다 (2) must: ~해야 하다 (3) pen: 우리 (4) fatten up: 살찌우다 (5) terrific: 훌륭한

06 (1) weave: (실을) 엮다 / 손이나 기계를 이용해 위아래로 서로 실을 교차함으로써 천을 만들다 (2) enter: (~를) 출전시키다 / 어떤 사람이 대회, 경주, 또는 시험에 참여할 것이라고 공식적으로 언급하다 (3) dump: 쓰레기 폐기장 / 쓰레기를 두는 장소 (4) narrator: 서술자, 내레이터 / 책, 영화, 또는 연극에서 이야기를 말해 주거나 어떤 것을 설명해 주는 사람

07 (1) 현재완료는 'have+pp'의 형태이다. (2) 명령문의 부가의문문으로 'will you'가 적절하다. (3) 조건의 부사절에서는 현재시제로 미래를 나타낸다. (4) A prize를 주어로 하는 수동태가 되거나 Wilbur를 주어로 하는 능동태가 되어야 한다. (5) to부정사가 someone을 수식하는 형용사적 용법으로 쓰는 것이 자연스러우며 이때 someone을 말하는 것이 아니므로 전치사 with를 넣어 '함께' 말하는 것이 되어야 한다. (6) 서로 대조되는 내용이 나오는 것이 아니므로 '양보'를 나타내는 though가 아니라 '…하는 것과 같이, …하는 대로, (…와) 마찬가지로(양태)'를 뜻하는 as로 고치는 것이 적절하다.

08 (1) '…함에 따라(추이)'를 뜻하는 As가 적절하다. (2) 앞 절은 현재시제이고 이어지는 절은 미래시제이므로 조건의 접속사 if가 적절하다. (3) 때를 나타내는 when이 적절하다.

09 (A) '장면 1'이라고 해야 하므로 Scene이 적절하다. scenery: 경치, (B) '어떻게'라고 해야 하므로 How가 적절하다. (C) 부정문이므로 yet이 적절하다. already는 주로 긍정문에서 '이미'의 뜻으로 사용한다.

10 ⓐ는 '돼지 윌버와 거미 샬럿'을, ⓑ는 '앨런 부부'를 가리킨다.

11 too ~ to = so ~ that ... can't

---

## 단원별 예상문제　　　　　　　p.224~228

01 ②　　　02 ②, ④　　03 ④　　　04 ④

05 (1) crowd　(2) dead　(3) dump　(4) excitement

06 (1) The sun is above the clouds.
　　(2) Her parents tried to fatten her up.
　　(3) I ran out of money.
　　(4) I have to go right away.
　　(5) She moved back home to care for her parents.

07 ⑤　　　　08 ②

09 I'm so sleepy that I can't drive.

10 (1) Ruth was given a nice present by Eddie. A nice present was given to Ruth by Eddie.
　　(2) A pretty dress was bought for Stephanie by Alex.

(3) An interesting question was asked of Charlotte by Wilbur.

| 11 ⑤ | 12 ② | 13 ② | 14 ④ |
| 15 ⑤ | 16 ③ | 17 weave | |
| 18 ②, ③, ⑤ | 19 (A) wove  (B) pen | | |
| 20 (A) a few  (B) called  (C) Terrific | | | |
| 21 will care → cares | 22 ⑤ | 23 ② | |
| 24 ③ | 25 ⑤ | 26 ③, ⑤ | |
| 27 The biggest ever crowd came. | | 28 Wilbur | |

01 nobody: 아무도 ~않다 / Ella는 그녀 자신에게만 관심을 가진다. 아무도 그녀의 친구가 되기를 원하지 않는다.

02 get/win a prize: 상을 받다

03 ④ save: 구하다 / 그는 너를 구할 수 있는 사람이다.

04 right away: 즉시, 곧바로, too 형용사 to 동사원형: 너무 …해서 ~할 수 없다

05 (1) crowd: 군중, 무리 (2) dead: 죽은 (3) dump: 쓰레기 폐기장 (4) excitement: 흥분, 신남

06 (1) above: ~보다 위에 (2) fatten up: 살찌우다 (3) run out of: ~이 다 떨어지다 (4) right away: 즉시, 곧바로 (5) care for: ~를 보살피다[돌보다]

07 주어진 문장의 make는 become의 뜻을 가지며 '주어+동사+보어'의 2형식 문장이다. ① 4형식 ② 5형식 ③ 3형식 ④ 5형식 ⑤ 2형식

08 주어진 문장의 to save는 to부정사의 형용사적 용법이다. ①, ③ 명사적 용법 ② 형용사적 용법 ④, ⑤ 부사적 용법

09 too ~ to … = so ~ that 주어 can't ... 너무 ~해서 …할 수 없다

10 직접목적어를 주어로 한 수동태에서 간접목적어 앞에 (1) give는 전치사 to를, (2) buy는 for를, (3) ask는 of를 쓴다. 또한 buy는 간접목적어(사람)를 주어로 수동태를 만들지 않는다.

11 조동사가 있는 문장의 수동태는 '조동사+be+p.p.' 형식을 갖는다.

12 ① I need someone very honest to depend upon. ③ Dan looks very honest. ④ "Shining" was finally chosen by them. ⑤ If nobody cares for Wilbur, he will be dead before Christmas.

13 위 글은 '연극 대본'이다. ① (책, 연극, 영화 등에 대한) 논평 [비평], 감상문, ③ 독후감, ④ 수필, ⑤ (신문, 잡지의) 글, 기사

14 ④ me는 'Charlotte'을 가리키고, 나머지는 다 'Wilbur'를 가리킨다.

15 ⓐ와 ⑤번: 구하다, ① (돈을) 모으다, 저축하다, ② (나중에 쓰거나 먹으려고) 남겨 두다, ③ 절약하다, ④ 저장하다

16 '앨런 부인'이 아니라 '앨런 씨'가 말한다.

17 weave: 짜다[엮다], 짜서[엮어서] 만들다, 틀이나 기계를 사용하여 각각의 실을 위 아래로 교차시켜 천이나 카펫을 만들다

18 ⓑ와 ①, ④: 부사적 용법, ② 형용사적 용법, ③, ⑤: 명사적 용법

19 샬럿은 윌버의 '우리' 위의 거미줄에 '대단한 돼지'라는 단어를 '짰다'.

20 (A) 복수 명사 people이 뒤에 나오므로 a few가 적절하다. a little+단수 명사, (B) 샬럿은 회의를 '소집했다'고 해야 하므로 called가 적절하다. cancel: 취소하다, (C) '훌륭한'이라고 해야 하므로 Terrific이 적절하다. terrible: 끔찍한

21 조건 부사절에서는 현재시제가 미래를 대신한다.

22 샬럿이 거미줄에 처음 짠 단어가 무엇이었는지는 대답할 수 없다. ① No. ② Charlotte. hold a meeting: 회의를 개최하다, 회의를 열다, ③ No. ④ Because Wilbur will be dead before Christmas if nobody cares for him.

23 일손이 많으면 일이 가벼워진다.(백짓장도 맞들면 낫다), ① 남에게 받고 싶은 대로 남에게 해 주어라. ③ 제때의 바늘 한 뜸이 아홉 번의 수고를 던다. (때를 놓치지 않고 신속하게 행동해야 생길 수 있는 문제를 예방할 수 있다.) ④ 사공이 많으면 배가 산으로 올라간다. (요리사가 너무 많으면 국을 망친다.) ⑤ 콩 심은데 콩 나고 팥 심은데 팥 난다. (뿌린 대로 거둘 것이다.)

24 '늙은 양'이 아니라 '오리'의 아이디어가 바닥이 나버렸다.

25 ⑤ 이 글은 모두의 도움으로 윌버가 베이컨이 되는 대신에 박람회에 출전하게 되었다는 내용의 글이므로, 제목으로는 '모두들 고마워! 나는 박람회에 나갈 거야!'가 적절하다.

26 ③ 완전히, ⑤ 즉시, ⓐ와 나머지는 모두 '마침내'

27 'The'를 보충하면 된다. ever는 [비교급·최상급 뒤에서 그 말을 강조하여] 이제까지, 지금까지

28 '윌버'를 가리킨다.

43

# 교과서 파헤치기

9 guest, 손님   10 modern, 현대의
11 Mongolian, 몽골의   12 expect, 기대하다, 예상하다
13 view, 경관, 전망   14 airport, 공항   15 part, 부분, 일부
16 station, 역, 정거장

Lesson
**6**

## 단어 TEST Step 1 · p.02

| | | |
|---|---|---|
| 01 해외에 | 02 낙타 | 03 쾌활한, 유쾌한 |
| 04 시작, 처음 | 05 화려한, (색이) 다채로운 | |
| 06 밝은 | 07 달콤한, 단 | 08 ~할 만큼 (충분히) |
| 09 경관, 전망 | 10 비행 | 11 수도 |
| 12 손님 | 13 현대의 | 14 양고기 |
| 15 해안선 | 16 겁먹은, 무서워하는 | |
| 17 언어 | 18 아주 멋진, 마법의, 마술의 | |
| 19 잠이 든 | 20 기대하다, 예상하다 | |
| 21 전체, 모든 | 22 순간 | 23 굉장한, 놀라운 |
| 24 문화 | 25 가슴 뭉클한 | 26 맛있는 |
| 27 ~하자마자 | 28 결혼(식) | |
| 29 (해가) 뜨다, 일어나다 | | 30 아늑한 |
| 31 제공하다 | 32 상상하다 | 33 기회 |
| 34 전통적인 | 35 ~로 가득하다 | 36 ~에 익숙해지다 |
| 37 ~로 만들어지다 | 38 …에게 ~을 둘러보도록 안내하다 | |
| 39 ~으로 요리되다 | 40 ~에 가 본 적 있니? | |
| 41 빨리 ~하면 좋겠다 | | 42 ~인 것처럼 느끼다 |
| 43 잠에서 깨다 | | |

## 단어 TEST Step 2 · p.03

| | | |
|---|---|---|
| 01 chance | 02 colorful | 03 moment |
| 04 cozy | 05 asleep | 06 enough |
| 07 camel | 08 flight | 09 guest |
| 10 imagine | 11 beginning | 12 serve |
| 13 kid | 14 abroad | 15 view |
| 16 lamb | 17 tasty | 18 bright |
| 19 magical | 20 cheerful | 21 wedding |
| 22 modern | 23 amazing | 24 capital |
| 25 once | 26 culture | 27 part |
| 28 coastline | 29 rise | 30 scared |
| 31 moved | 32 traditional | 33 expect |
| 34 whole | 35 wake up | 36 from A to B |
| 37 feel like+주어+동사 | | 38 get used to |
| 39 can't wait to | 40 at first | 41 be full of |
| 42 be made of | 43 Have you been (to) ~? | |

## 단어 TEST Step 3 · p.04

1 bright, 밝은   2 asleep, 잠이 든   3 kid, 농담하다
4 cheerful, 쾌활한, 유쾌한   5 rise, (해가) 뜨다
6 chance, 기회   7 abroad, 해외에   8 magical, 마법의

## 대화문 TEST Step 1 · p.05~06

**Listen & Speak 1 A**
Have you ever tried / have, tasty

**Listen & Speak 1 B**
1 look excited, up / going to, with, Have, ever been / coastline, How about / can't wait for
2 Have, ever, rise over / How about / watched, rise, on / tried several times, wake up early

**Listen & Speak 1 C**
1 Have you ever, another country / have, experience
2 Have you ever ridden / wonderful experience

**Listen & Speak 2 A**
How do you like / bigger room

**Listen & Speak 2 B**
1 How, vacation / went to, with / How did, like / amazing, to visit
2 Have you been to / had dinner / How did you like / won't go back

**Listen & Speak 2 C**
1 How, like / colorful
2 How do you like / sweet

**Real-Life Zone A**
Have you ever traveled abroad / went, last summer / How did, like / hot, enjoyed / interesting experiences, had during / let, think, fried / How, like them / so, scared at first / imagine eating spiders

**Communication Task**
Have you ever eaten / tasty, haven't, try someday

## 대화문 TEST Step 2 · p.07~08

**Listen & Speak 1 A**
B: Have you ever tried Spanish food?
G: Yes, I have. It's really tasty.

**Listen & Speak 1 B**
1 G: You look excited, Inho. What's up?
 B: I'm going to Jejudo with my family this weekend. Have you ever been there?
 G: Yes, many times. I love the coastline. How about you?
 B: It'll be my first visit to Jejudo. I can't wait for this weekend!

2 B: Have you ever watched the sun rise over the ocean?

G: No. How about you?

B: I watched the sun rise in Gangneung on New Year's Day. It was great.

G: I tried several times, but I just couldn't wake up early enough.

### Listen & Speak 1 C

1 A: Have you ever traveled to another country?

B: Yes, I have. It was a wonderful experience.

2 A: Have you ever ridden a horse?

B: Yes, I have. It was a wonderful experience.

### Listen & Speak 2 A

G: How do you like your new house?

B: It's great. I have a bigger room now.

### Listen & Speak 2 B

1 G: How was your vacation?

B: Great. I went to Dokdo with my family.

G: How did you like it?

B: It was amazing. I want to visit there again.

2 B: Have you been to the new Chinese restaurant?

G: Yes. I had dinner there last Saturday.

B: How did you like it?

G: The service was bad. I won't go back there again.

### Listen & Speak 2 C

1 A: How do you like this shirt?

B: It's colorful. I like it.

2 A: How do you like your ice cream?

B: It's sweet. I like it.

### Real-Life Zone A

B: Have you ever traveled abroad, Sujin?

G: Yes, I went to Cambodia last summer.

B: Wow. How did you like it?

G: It was really hot, but I enjoyed the trip.

B: Tell me some interesting experiences you had during the trip.

G: Hmm... let me think. I ate fried spiders!

B: What? You're kidding. How did you like them?

G: They were really big, so I was a little scared at first. But the taste was okay.

B: Really? I cannot imagine eating spiders.

### Communication Task

A: Have you ever eaten tacos?

B: Yes, I have. They were tasty. / No, I haven't. I want to try some someday.

01 Trip, Mongolia

02 special, because, for, time

03 My, is from     04 invited, to, capital

05 After, flight, arrived at     06 took, by, from, to

07 Her, traditional Mongolian

08 tent, cozy inside

09 entered, smelled wonderful

10 from, that, cooking for     11 Mongolian barbecue

12 made of, cooked with

13 moved, serve, to, guests

14 so, that, for     15 After, went outside

16 was full of     17 felt like, magical

18 During, showed, around, experience

19 moment, exciting, most, rode

20 At, scared, than, expected

21 once, back, used to

22 From, back, view, amazing

23 visit, special, in, ways

24 gave, chance, get, culture

25 visit, again someday

01 Trip to Mongolia

02 This year, special summer, for the first time

03 is from Mongolia     04 invited, to, the capital

05 After a four-hour flight, arrived at

06 It took, by taxi from, to

07 traditional Mongolian house

08 big tent, cozy inside

09 When, entered, smelled wonderful

10 from, cooking for     11 Mongolian barbecue

12 is made of, cooked with

13 was moved, serve, to special guests

14 so, that, asked for     15 went outside to see

16 was full of bright

17 felt like, magical place

18 During, showed me around, helped me experience

19 Every moment, had the most fun, rode

20 At first, scared, taller than, expected

21 once, sat on, got used to

22 the view of the desert, truly amazing

23 in many ways

24 to get to know, country, culture

25 visit, again someday

45

1 몽골 여행

2 나는 올해 몽골을 처음으로 방문해서 특별한 여름을 보냈다.

3 내 친구 알탕은 몽골 출신이다.

4 그의 할머니께서는 몽골의 수도인 울란바토르에 나를 초대하셨다.

5 서울에서 네 시간 비행 후 알탕과 나는 울란바토르의 칭기즈 칸 국제공항에 도착했다.

6 공항에서 알탕의 할머니 댁까지 택시로 30분이 걸렸다.

7 할머니의 집은 몽골 전통 가옥인 게르이다.

8 큰 텐트이지만 내부는 아늑하다.

9 우리가 들어갔을 때, 뭔가 좋은 냄새가 났다.

10 그녀가 우리를 위해 요리하고 있던 호르호그에서 나는 냄새였다.

11 호르호그는 몽골식 바비큐이다.

12 그것은 양고기로 만들어졌으며 뜨거운 돌로 요리되었다.

13 나는 알탕이 몽골인들은 특별한 손님에게 호르호그를 대접한다고 말했을 때 감동을 받았다.

14 그것은 너무 맛있어서 나는 더 달라고 했다.

15 저녁 식사 후, 알탕과 나는 밤하늘을 보기 위해 밖으로 나갔다.

16 하늘은 밝은 별들로 가득했다.

17 나는 신비한 장소에 있는 것처럼 느꼈다.

18 그 후 3일 동안, 알탕은 나를 구경시켜 주었고 몽골 문화를 경험할 수 있게 도와주었다.

19 매 순간이 재미있고 흥미진진했지만, 고비 사막에서 낙타를 탈 때가 가장 재미있었다.

20 처음에는 내가 예상했던 것보다 낙타의 키가 커서 무서웠다.

21 그러나 낙타 등에 앉자 곧 움직임에 익숙해졌다.

22 낙타의 등에서 보는 사막의 경치는 정말로 놀라웠다.

23 내가 몽골을 방문한 것은 여러 면에서 특별한 경험이었다.

24 내 친구의 나라와 문화를 알 수 있는 좋은 기회가 되었다.

25 나는 언젠가 몽골을 다시 방문하고 싶다!

1 A Trip to Mongolia

2 This year, I had a special summer because I visited Mongolia for the first time.

3 My friend Altan is from Mongolia.

4 His grandmother invited me to Ulaanbaatar, the capital of Mongolia.

5 After a four-hour flight from Seoul, Altan and I arrived at Chinggis Khaan International Airport in Ulaanbaatar.

6 It took thirty minutes by taxi from the airport to Altan's grandmother's house.

7 Her house is a *ger*, a traditional Mongolian house.

8 It is a big tent, but it is cozy inside.

9 When we entered, something smelled wonderful.

10 It was from the *khorkhog* that she was cooking for us.

11 *Khorkhog* is a Mongolian barbecue.

12 It is made of lamb and cooked with hot stones.

13 I was moved when Altan said Mongolians serve *khorkhog* to special guests.

14 It was so delicious that I asked for more.

15 After dinner, Altan and I went outside to see the night sky.

16 The sky was full of bright stars.

17 I felt like I was in a magical place.

18 During the next three days, Altan showed me around and helped me experience Mongolian culture.

19 Every moment was fun and exciting, but I had the most fun when I rode a camel in the Gobi Desert.

20 At first, I was scared because the camel was taller than I expected.

21 But once I sat on its back, I soon got used to its movement.

22 From the camel's back, the view of the desert was truly amazing.

23 My visit to Mongolia was a special experience in many ways.

24 It gave me a great chance to get to know my friend's country and culture.

25 I want to visit Mongolia again someday!

**Writing Workshop - Step 2**

1. Trip to

2. took a trip, last summer

3. visited

4. so, that we could not see

5. After three hours' walking

6. For dinner, that my parents like

7. is famous for

8. so, that, would never forget

**Wrap Up 1-2**

1. How was, weekend

2. went to, with my parents

3. What food, try

4. traditional Chinese dessert

5. How did

6. made with, usually serve, at a wedding

**Wrap Up 7**

1. How was, that, around the corner

2. so crowded that, wait for, to get in

3. tasted so good that I ate

4. so noisy that I couldn't

---

**구석구석지문 TEST** Step 2                    p.20

**Writing Workshop - Step 2**

1. A Trip to Suncheon

2. My family took a trip to Suncheon last summer.

3. We visited the National Garden.

4. It was so large that we could not see the whole garden.

5. After three hours' walking, we were really hungry.

6. For dinner, we had Gukbap that my parents like.

7. Suncheon is famous for Gukbap and we enjoyed it.

8. This trip was so good that I would never forget it for a long time.

**Wrap Up 1-2**

1. G: How was your weekend, Tony?

2. B: It was great. I went to the International Food Festival with my parents.

3. G: What food did you try?

4. B: I had a traditional Chinese dessert, *tangyuan*.

5. G: How did you like it?

6. B: I enjoyed it. It's made with sweet rice balls. Chinese people usually serve it to guests at a wedding.

**Wrap Up 7**

1. How was the restaurant that just opened around the corner?

2. The restaurant was so crowded that I had to wait for an hour to get in.

3. The cheese cake tasted so good that I ate all of it.

4. The restaurant was so noisy that I couldn't talk with my friends.

---

Lesson **7**

**단어 TEST** Step 1                    p.21

| | | |
|---|---|---|
| 01 선택하다 | 02 똑똑한 | 03 순간 이동하다 |
| 04 불타다 | 05 번역하다 | 06 동영상의, 생기 있는 |
| 07 쉽게 | 08 감지하다 | 09 얼리다 |
| 10 불가능한 | 11 즐거움, 오락 | 12 예측하다 |
| 13 ~ 없이 | 14 기계 | 15 가능한 |
| 16 건너다 | 17 위험 | 18 의미하다 |
| 19 할인되어 | 20 완벽한 | 21 ~을 통해, ~ 사이로 |
| 22 이상한 | 23 대체하다 | 24 이기다 |
| 25 확인하다, 점검하다 | | 26 상황 |
| 27 옷장 | 28 공간 | 29 기회 |
| 30 사전 | 31 번역가 | 32 믿기어려운,놀랄만한 |
| 33 행운의 | 34 구름의, 흐린 | 35 단지 ~뿐이 아니다 |
| 36 ~할 필요가 없다 | 37 위험에 처한, 위험에 빠진 | |
| 38 더 이상 ~하지 않다 | 39 ~에 근거하여 | 40 ~의 염려가 없는 |
| 41 그런데, 그건 그렇고 | 42 ~할 수 있다 | 43 속도를 늦추다 |

**단어 TEST** Step 2                    p.22

| | | |
|---|---|---|
| 01 animated | 02 chance | 03 cloudy |
| 04 possible | 05 lucky | 06 translator |
| 07 machine | 08 cross | 09 danger |
| 10 amusement | 11 easily | 12 select |
| 13 text | 14 sense | 15 mean |
| 16 freeze | 17 without | 18 predict |
| 19 impossible | 20 teleport | 21 burn |
| 22 translate | 23 dictionary | 24 off |
| 25 closet | 26 perfect | 27 replace |
| 28 intelligent | 29 through | 30 situation |
| 31 strange | 32 unbelievable | 33 check |
| 34 space | 35 by the way | 36 in danger |
| 37 no longer | 38 be able to 동사원형 | |
| 39 based on | 40 slow down | 41 watch out |
| 42 free from | 43 look ~ up | |

**단어 TEST** Step 3                    p.23

1 replace, 대체하다    2 beat, 이기다

3 perfect, 완벽한    4 burn, 불타다    5 possible, 가능한

6 sense, 감지하다    7 translate, 번역하다

8 cross, 건너다    9 lucky, 행운의    10 predict, 예측하다

11 select, 선택하다    12 closet, 옷장

13 cloudy, 구름의, 흐린　14 amusement, 즐거움, 오락
15 beatbox, 비트박스를 하다　16 dictionary, 사전

**Listen & Speak 1 A**

Why don't we try, prefer

**Listen & Speak 1 B**

1 have any, for, project / What about / thinking, talk about future, What, think / sounds perfect, Let's look for, on the Internet

2 begins, Why don't, with / to, sounds exciting / chance to meet robotics / great

**Listen & Speak 1 C**

1 going to fly, drone / like fun

2 going, build / sounds like fun

**Listen & Speak 2 A**

it possible, to live without / not possible

**Listen & Speak 2 B**

1 looks, How much, it / the newest / Is it possible to use / Let, check, get, off / Perfect, take

2 took, pictures during / did, more than / it possible to make, animated, out of / possible, have an app

**Listen & Speak 2 C**

1 Is it possible, to text with, closed / Sure, can do

2 possible for you, travel around, by / Sure, can do that

**Real-Life Zone A**

Look at / What, they mean, Let's look them up, dictionary / about using, translator / How, use / point, ask, to translate, get an answer / possible for AI to read / read, translate / sounds unvelievable, what, mean / mean, come true / amazing

**Listen & Speak 1 A**

B: Why don't we try a new VR game?

G: That sounds interesting.

**Listen & Speak 1 B**

1 B: Do you have any ideas for our group project?

G: No. What about you?

B: I'm thinking we should talk about future jobs. What do you think?

G: That sounds perfect for our project. Let's look for some information on the Internet.

2 G: The Robot Expo begins next week. Why don't you go with me?

B: Yes, I'd love to. That sounds exciting.

G: We'll have a chance to meet robotics engineers.

B: That'll be great.

**Listen & Speak 1 C**

1 A: I'm going to fly a drone.

B: That sounds like fun.

2 A: I'm going to build a model car.

B: That sounds like fun.

**Listen & Speak 2 A**

G: Is it possible for you to live without your smartphone?

B: No, it's not possible.

**Listen & Speak 2 B**

1 G: This computer looks nice. How much is it?

M: It's 500 dollars. It's the newest one.

G: Is it possible to use this coupon?

M: Let me check. Yes, you can. So, you'll get 30 dollars off.

G: Perfect. I'll take it.

2 B: We took lots of pictures during our trip.

G: We sure did. We have more than 500 pictures.

B: Is it possible to make an animated photo album out of them?

G: Yes, it's possible. I have an app for that.

**Listen & Speak 2 C**

1 A: Is it possible for you to text with your eyes closed?

B: Sure. I can do that.

2 A: Is it possible for you to travel around Gangwondo by bicycle?

B: Sure. I can do that.

**Real-Life Zone A**

G: Look at those words on the board.

B: What do they mean? Let's look them up in the dictionary.

G: What about using the AI translator?

B: How do I use it?

G: You point your smartphone camera at the words and ask AI to translate. You will get an answer.

B: Is it possible for AI to read those words?

Speaker: Sure. I can read any language and translate it.

B: Wow, that sounds unbelievable. So, AI, what do those words mean?

Speaker: They mean "Dreams come true!"

B: That's amazing.

01 Day at, AI    02 at, World, Expo
03 entering, AI home    04 Look at, future
05 go into, there's, closet
06 front, closet, keep changing
07 suggests, suit, weather
08 no longer, worry, dressing
09 move on to    10 this music speaker
11 not just, speaker
12 more than, imagine
13 hard, believe, understand
14 How about watching    15 play one
16 smart, getting darker
17 feel like, theater    18 What else, do
19 beatbox, too, Here comes
20 funny, Good job
21 Hurry, There's, outside    22 Let's, ride in
23 so cool, get in    24 ready to go
25 what should, do    26 time, ride in
27 need to, anything    28 drive, take, to
29 out, see, crossing
30 worry, have, sensed
31 sense dangerous, slow down    32 How can, that
33 intelligent robotic
34 all about driving
35 predict, based on, experience    36 How, act like
37 are, like, human

01 at, AI Expo    02 at the World AI Expo
03 are entering, AI home    04 on the future
05 go into, smart closet
06 front, on the closet door, keep changing
07 suggests, that suit the weather
08 no longer, dressing for the weather
09 Let's move on to
10 this music speaker
11 I'm not just
12 more than, can imagine
13 It's hard to believe, can understand
14 How about watching    15 play one for
16 getting darker
17 feel like, movie theater    18 What else
19 can, too, Here comes
20 funny, Good job
21 Hurry, There's, outside

22 Let's go, ride in    23 so cool, get in
24 Are, ready to go    25 what should, do
26 my first time to ride    27 don't need to
28 take you to    29 Watch out, crossing
30 Don't, have just sensed
31 sense dangerous situations, down
32 How can, do    33 intelligent robotic
34 all about driving    35 based on
36 How, like    37 like, human

1 인공 지능 박람회에서의 하루
2 진아와 수한이가 세계 인공 지능 박람회에 있다.
3 그들은 인공 지능 집으로 들어가고 있다.
4 수한: 이것 봐! 미래의 집이야.
5 진아: 침실 먼저 들어가 보자. 이거 봐, 스마트 옷장이 있어.
6 수한: 옷장 문에 있는 스크린 앞에 서 있으니까 내 옷이 계속해서 바뀌어.
7 진아: 스크린이 날씨에 적합한 옷을 제안하는 거야.
8 수한: 놀라워! 우린 더 이상 날씨 때문에 무슨 옷을 입을지 걱정할 필요가 없겠다.
9 진아: 맞아. 이제 거실로 가 보자.
10 수한: 오, 이 음악 스피커 마음에 들어.
11 인공 지능 스피커: 저는 그냥 음악 스피커가 아니에요.
12 저는 당신이 상상하는 것 이상의 것을 할 수 있어요.
13 진아: 네가 우리를 이해한다니 믿기 어려운 걸! 넌 뭘 할 수 있어?
14 인공 지능 스피커: 영화 보는 건 어때요?
15 하나 틀어 줄게요.
16 수한: 이것 봐, 스마트 창문이 점점 어두워지고 있어.
17 마치 내가 영화관 안에 있는 것 같아.
18 진아: 또 뭘 할 수 있어?
19 인공 지능 스피커: 비트박스도 할 수 있어요. "북치기 박치기 북치기 박치기."
20 수한: 넌 정말 재미있구나. 잘했어!
21 진아: 서둘러! 밖에 스마트 자동차 정류장이 있어.
22 가서 저 빨간 차를 타 보자.
23 수한: 이 차 정말 멋지다. 차에 타자.
24 인공 지능 자동차: 어서 오세요. 갈 준비 됐나요?
25 진아: 응, 우린 이제 뭘 해야 하지?
26 스마트 자동차에 타는 건 처음이야.
27 인공 지능 자동차: 아무 것도 하지 않아도 돼요.
28 제가 운전해서 다음 정류장까지 데려다줄 거니까요.
29 수한: 조심해! 고양이가 길을 건너고 있는 게 보여.
30 인공 지능 자동차: 걱정 말아요. 이미 감지했어요.
31 저는 어떤 위험 상황을 감지하면 속도를 늦추거나 멈춰요.

32 진아: 어떻게 그렇게 할 수 있어?

33 인공 지능 자동차: 전 아주 지능적인 로봇 차예요.

34 저는 운전에 대한 모든 걸 알고 있어요.

35 저는 제 지식과 경험을 바탕으로 위험을 예측할 수 있어요

36 수한: 정말 똑똑하구나! 사람처럼 생각하고 행동하는구나.

37 정말 인간 같아.

32 Jina: How can you do that?

33 AI Car: I'm a very intelligent robotic car.

34 I know all about driving.

35 I can predict danger based on knowledge and experience.

36 Suhan: How smart! You think and act like a person.

37 You are really like a human.

1 A Day at the AI Expo

2 Jina and Suhan are at the World AI Expo.

3 They are entering the AI home.

4 Suhan: Look at this! It's a house of the future.

5 Jina: Let's go into the bedroom first. Look, there's a smart closet.

6 Suhan: I'm standing in front of this screen on the closet door and my clothes keep changing.

7 Jina: The screen suggests clothes that suit the weather.

8 Suhan: That's amazing! We no longer have to worry about dressing for the weather.

9 Jina: Right. Let's move on to the living room.

10 Suhan: Oh, I like this music speaker.

11 AI Speaker: I'm not just a music speaker.

12 I can do more than you can imagine.

13 Jina: It's hard to believe that you can understand us. What can you do?

14 AI Speaker: How about watching a movie?

15 I'll play one for you.

16 Suhan: Look, those smart windows are getting darker.

17 I feel like I'm in a movie theater.

18 Jina: What else can you do?

19 AI Speaker: I can beatbox, too. Here comes, "cats and boots and cats and boots."

20 Suhan: You're funny. Good job!

21 Jina: Hurry! There's a smart car station outside!

22 Let's go and ride in that red car.

23 Suhan: This car is so cool. Let's get in.

24 AI Car: Welcome. Are you ready to go?

25 Jina: Yes, what should we do now?

26 It's my first time to ride in a smart car.

27 AI Car: You don't need to do anything.

28 I will drive and take you to the next station.

29 Suhan: Watch out! I see a cat crossing the street.

30 AI Car: Don't worry. I have just sensed it.

31 When I sense dangerous situations, I slow down or stop.

**Before You Read**

1. DAILY NEWS

2. Beats

3. has beaten, in, match

4. had a match with, one of the greatest, players

5. difficult to understand

6. believed, for an AI to beat

7. was able to predict, finally won

8. are shocked, be more intelligent than

**Focus on Expressions**

1. get in, to get to

2. love to go, because, greatest amusement park

3. Above all, their favorite activity

4. don't want, get off

**Wrap Up 1-2**

1. smart food-ordering, over there, Why don't, try

2. sounds, be able to order, by using

3. By the way, for robots to replace

4. will be free from, because of

5. What, mean

6. in danger, so, don't have to

7. right, always try to look on

**Before You Read**

1. DAILY NEWS

2. AI Beats Human!

3. An AI program has beaten a human in a *baduk* match.

4. The AI had a match with Lee Sedol, who is one of the greatest *baduk* players.

5. *Baduk* is a board game, and the rules are difficult to understand.

6. Many people believed it would be impossible for an AI to beat a human player.

7. However, the AI was able to predict Lee's play, and it finally won the game.

8. People are shocked that an AI can be more intelligent than a human.

### Focus on Expressions

1. In 2099, people get in a flying car to get to the moon.

2. Kids love to go to the moon because the greatest amusement park is there.

3. Above all, horse-riding is their favorite activity.

4. They don't want to get off the horses.

### Wrap Up 1-2

1. G: Minseok, there is a smart food-ordering machine over there. Why don't we try it?

2. B: That sounds interesting. We'll be able to order easily and fast by using it.

3. G: I hope so. By the way, do you think maybe it will be possible for robots to replace humans someday?

4. B: I'm not sure. But we will be free from danger because of robots.

5. G: What do you mean?

6. B: Robots can help people in danger. Robots can do the dangerous work so humans don't have to.

7. G: You're right. We should always try to look on the bright side.

10 stone, 돌, 석조    11 hometown, 고향
12 found, 설립하다    13 collect, 모으다, 수집하다
14 store, 저장하다    15 land, 토지, 땅    16 nature, 자연

## 단어 TEST Step 1                                   p.40

01 모으다, 수집하다  02 사건, 일      03 공무원, 당국
04 사업가        05 고통 받다, 시달리다
06 통치하다; 규칙, 원칙           07 왕조, 시대
08 설명하다      09 알려지지 않은
10 적합하다      11 압박하다      12 ~을 통하여
13 여행객        14 독립          15 지역사회, 주민
16 저장하다, 보관하다             17 현대의
18 살아 있는     19 또 다른, 다른 하나의
20 운동          21 마을          22 시
23 낭비하다      24 재산          25 왕의, 왕실의
26 사회, 단체     27 설립하다      28 도자기
29 지원하다      30 의미          31 맛, 취향
32 관심, 흥미     33 건축          34 스페인의
35 위험에 빠진    36 발을 들여놓다  37 ~으로 알려지다
38 ~을 돌보다    39 (사업, 세력 등이) 쇠퇴하다
40 ~ 덕분에      41 ~으로 유명하다  42 어려움에 처한
43 ~와 조화를 이루다

## 단어 TEST Step 2                                   p.41

01 tradition     02 modern       03 society
04 architecture  05 businessman  06 store
07 dynasty       08 explain      09 meaning
10 pottery       11 unknown      12 poem
13 official      14 collect      15 found
16 independence  17 affair       18 property
19 alive         20 interest     21 support
22 rule          23 suffer       24 tourist
25 movement      26 through      27 fit
28 royal         29 another      30 press
31 village       32 community    33 waste
34 nature        35 fall off     36 be filled with
37 care for      38 thanks to    39 hundreds of
40 in need       41 be famous for 42 be known as
43 be in harmony with

## 단어 TEST Step 3                                   p.42

1 alive, 살아 있는   2 businessman, 사업가, 실업가
3 dynasty, 왕조    4 novel, 소설
5 architecture, 건축, 건축학   6 royal, 왕의, 왕실의
7 rule, 통치하다   8 explain, 설명하다   9 property, 재산

## 대화문 TEST Step 1                                 p.43~44

**Listen & Speak 1 B-2**

Do, anything about / little, famous for / going to, with
/ think, like

**Listen & Speak 2 A**

Could, explain, painting / by, painted, in

**Listen & Speak 2 B-1**

1 explain this poem / was written by / about / about,
  missing
2 explain what, is / volunteer group, community / tell,
  more about / take care of

**Listen & Speak 2 C**

Could, explain, to save / won't waste, on

**Real-Life Zone A**

What, anything about / Korean houses, are designed,
in harmony with / explain a little / cool, warm /
sounds, Where, see, traditional houses / near here /
about going, seeing / idea, How, get / take, over there

**Real-Life Zone B**

1 know anything / one of, greatest sights / explain
  why, famous / because, longest wall
2 anything about, novel / short novel written by /
  explain why / because, won, for

**Real-Life Zone B e.g.**

know anything about / was built in, by / explain why,
famous / It's because, tallest tower, at that time

**Wrap Up**

know anything / birthday, baby / tell, more / get together,
wears / sounds interesting / share food, wish for, long life
/ Korean tradition

## 대화문 TEST Step 2                                 p.45~46

**Listen & Speak 1 B-2**

G: Do you know anything about Changdeokgung?
B: Yes, a little. It's famous for its beautiful garden.
G: I'm going to go there with my Chinese friend.
B: I think you'll like it.

**Listen & Speak 2 A**

B: Could you explain this painting?
W: Sure. It's the *Two Sisters* by Renoir. He painted it
   in 1881.

1 G: Can you explain this poem?

B: Sure. It was written by Yun Dongju.

G: What's it about?

B: It's about him missing his hometown.

2 B: Could you explain what Helping Hands is?

G: It's a volunteer group in our community.

B: Could you tell me more about it?

G: Well, they take care of children in need.

A: Could you explain your plan to save money?

B: I won't waste my money on snacks.

G: What are *hanoks*? Do you know anything about them?

M: *Hanoks* are traditional Korean houses. They are designed to be in harmony with nature.

G: Could you explain a little more about them?

M: *Hanoks* are cool in the summer and warm in the winter.

W: That sounds interesting. Where can I see these traditional houses?

M: There's a *hanok* village near here.

G: How about going there and seeing the *hanoks*?

W: Good idea! How can we get there?

M: You can take Bus Number 5 over there at the bus stop.

1 A: Do you know anything about the Great Wall of China?

B: Yes. It is one of the greatest sights in the world.

A: Can you explain why it is famous?

B: It's because it is the longest wall in the world.

2 A: Do you know anything about the novel *The Old Man and the Sea*?

B: Yes. It is a short novel written by Ernest Hemingway.

A: Can you explain why it is famous?

B: It's because Hemingway won the Pulitzer Prize in 1953 for this novel.

A: Do you know anything about the Eiffel Tower?

B: Yes. It was built in 1889 by Gustave Eiffel.

A: Can you explain why it is famous?

B: It's because it was the tallest tower in the world at that time.

B: Do you know anything about a *dol* party?

G: Yes. It's the birthday party for a one-year-old baby.

B: Could you tell me more about it?

G: Well, the family members get together for the party, and the birthday baby wears a *hanok*.

B: That sounds interesting.

G: The family members share food and wish for a long life for the baby. It's a Korean tradition.

## 본문 TEST Step 1 p.47~48

01 King, Architecture, Gyeongseong

02 Have, been to

03 There, beautiful, village

04 popular, who, past

05 know, created through, efforts

06 known as, in

07 businessman who founded

08 time, ruled, fit, taste

09 moving into, building, Western

10 wanted, protect, suffering

11 power, keep, let, set

12 bought, between, and

13 built, modern, people

14 Through, efforts, filled with

15 independence movement, ways

16 example, supported, keep, alive

17 happened, caught, suffered

18 officials pressed, build

19 how to build

20 official, know, so, build

21 what, told, do                22 cost, high

23 fell off, property

24 part, to, traditions, still

## 본문 TEST Step 2 p.49~50

01 The King, Architecture in        02 Have, been to

03 There is, village

04 popular, who, past

05 However, know, was created through, efforts

06 known as, Architecture        07 who founded

08 At the time, was ruled by, were changing, fit, taste

09 moving into, were building Japanese, Western

10 wanted to protect, suffering

11 power, should keep, let, set, foot

12 bought, between, and

13 built, modern, people

14 Through, efforts, filled with

15 independence movement in many ways

16 For example, supported its efforts, keep, alive

17 happened, was caught by, suffered a lot

18 pressed, to build          19 how to build

20 official, know how to, so, build, too

21 what, told, to do          22 cost, high

23 fell off, lost, property

24 part, thanks to, traditions, still live with

1 경성의 건축왕

2 당신은 북촌에 다녀온 적이 있는가?

3 북촌에는 아름다운 한옥 마을이 있다.

4 그곳은 한국의 과거를 보고 싶어 하는 관광객들에게 인기가 있다.

5 그러나 북촌이 한 사람의 노력으로 만들어졌다는 것을 아는 사람은 많지 않다.

6 그 사람은 경성의 건축왕으로 알려진 정세권이었다.

7 정세권은 1920년에 건양사를 설립한 사업가였다.

8 그 당시 한국은 일본의 지배를 받았고, 일본인들은 경성을 그들의 취향에 맞게 바꾸고 있었다.

9 경성으로 이주하는 많은 일본인들은 일본식이나 서양식 집들을 짓고 있었다.

10 정세권은 한옥을 지키고 고통받는 사람들을 돕기를 원했다.

11 그는 말했다. "사람이 힘이다. 우리 조선 사람들은 종로를 지켜야 하며, 일본인들이 이곳에 발을 붙이지 못하게 해야 한다."

12 그는 경복궁과 창덕궁 사이의 땅을 샀다.

13 거기에 그는 사람들을 위해 작은 현대식 한옥들을 지었다.

14 그의 노력으로 북촌은 현재 아름다운 한옥으로 가득 차 있다.

15 정세권은 여러 방법으로 독립운동을 도왔다.

16 예를 들면, 그는 조선어 학회를 위한 회관을 지었고 조선어를 지키려는 그들의 노력을 지원했다.

17 조선어 학회 사건이 발생했을 때 그는 경찰에 잡혀 많은 고통을 겪었다.

18 일본인 관리들은 그에게 일본식 가옥을 지으라고 압박했다.

19 그는 말했다. "나는 일본식 가옥을 지을 줄 모르오."

20 한 관리가 말했다. "당신은 한옥을 지을 줄 아오, 그러니 일본식 가옥도 지을 수 있소."

21 그러나 그는 그 일본인이 그에게 요구한 것을 하지 않았다.

22 그 대가는 컸다.

23 그의 사업은 쇠퇴했고, 그는 재산을 잃었다.

24 그러나 부분적으로나마, 정세권 덕분에 한국의 전통이 오늘날 여전히 우리와 함께 살아 있다.

1 The King of Architecture in Gyeongseong.

2 Have you been to Bukchon?

3 There is a beautiful *hanok* village in Bukchon.

4 It is popular with tourists who want to see Korea's past.

5 However, not many people know that Bukchon was created through one man's efforts.

6 That man was Jeong Segwon, known as the King of Architecture in Gyeongseong.

7 Jeong Segwon was a businessman who founded Geonyangsa in 1920.

8 At the time, Korea was ruled by Japan, and the Japanese were changing Gyeongseong to fit their taste.

9 Many Japanese moving into Gyeongseong were building Japanese or Western houses.

10 Jeong Segwon wanted to protect the *hanok* and help the suffering people.

11 He said, "People are power. We Joseon people should keep Jongno and not let the Japanese set foot here."

12 He bought the land between Gyeongbokgung and Changdeokgung.

13 There he built small, modern *hanoks* for the people.

14 Through his efforts, we now have Bukchon filled with its beautiful *hanoks*.

15 Jeong Segwon helped the independence movement in many ways.

16 For example, he built the office building for the Joseon Language Society and supported its efforts to keep the Joseon language alive.

17 When the Joseon Language Affair happened, he was caught by the police and suffered a lot.

18 Japanese officials pressed him to build Japanese houses.

19 He said, "I don't know how to build Japanese houses."

20 An official said, "You know how to build *hanoks*, so you can build Japanese houses, too."

21 But he did not do what the Japanese told him to do.

22 The cost was high.

23 His business fell off, and he lost his property.

24 However, in part, thanks to Jeong Segwon, the traditions of Korea still live with us today.

**Before You Read**

1. Japanese officials pressed, to use
2. tried to keep, alive
3. wanted to protect
4. independence movement rose up

**Language in Use**

1. moved into, next to Joe's store
2. opened up
3. started to go, instead of
4. Few, set foot in
5. fell off

**Writing Workshop**

1. Who, An
2. during, Joseon Dynasty, was catching
3. When, was fishing, saw, fishing near
4. visited, twice, were part of
5. Japanese ruler officially, not to fish near
6. did his best to protect

Dokdo.
6. He did his best to protect Ulleungdo and Dokdo.

**Before You Read**

1. Japanese officials pressed the Joseon people to use the Japanese language.
2. The Joseon people tried to keep the Joseon language alive.
3. The Joseon people wanted to protect the country.
4. Soon, the independence movement rose up.

**Language in Use**

1. A woman moved into the building next to Joe's store.
2. She opened up a new store.
3. Many people started to go to the woman's new store instead of Joe's store.
4. Few people set foot in Joe's store.
5. His food business fell off.

**Writing Workshop**

1. Who is An Yongbok?
2. He lived during the Joseon Dynasty, and his job was catching fish.
3. When he was fishing, he saw the Japanese people fishing near Ulleungdo.
4. He visited Japan twice and said that Ulleungdo and Dokdo were part of Korea.
5. In 1696, the Japanese ruler officially told the Japanese people not to fish near Ulleugdo and

## 단어 TEST Step 1 p.59

01 비난하다 02 세기, 100년 03 공연
04 고전의, 클래식 음악의 05 사실은
06 자유롭게 07 즐거운, 즐길 수 있는
08 건강한 09 관객 10 방해하다
11 비밀 12 나타나다 13 작품
14 박수치다 15 심각한, 진지한
16 (위치가) ~ 사이에[중간]에 17 상상하다
18 예절 19 도서 박람회
20 기억에 남을, 기억할 만한 21 익숙한
22 놀랍게도 23 의존적인, 의존하는
24 협주곡 25 쓰레기통 26 장면
27 증가된 28 주로 29 귀족
30 소음, 잡음 31 오케스트라 32 올바른, 정확한
33 움직임, (큰 교향곡 따위의) 악장(부분) 34 결과
35 얼마 후 36 그 결과 37 ~에 의존하다
38 B 때문에 A를 비난하다
39 우선은, 현재로는, 지금은
40 과거로 거슬러 올라가다 41 아무 때나
42 ~을 돌보다 43 시간이 지남에 따라

## 단어 TEST Step 2 p.60

01 blame 02 clap 03 pause
04 correct 05 secret 06 serious
07 disturb 08 enjoyable 09 appear
10 social 11 surprisingly 12 concerto
13 audience 14 familiar 15 movement
16 actually 17 book fair 18 result
19 increased 20 bright 21 freely
22 healthy 23 dependent 24 manners
25 century 26 classical 27 memorable
28 performance 29 mostly 30 imagine
31 nobleman 32 noise 33 return
34 scene 35 by the way 36 take a look at
37 as a result 38 for now 39 at any time
40 blame A for B 41 dependent on 42 after some time
43 no longer

## 단어 TEST Step 3 p.61

1 bright, 밝은 2 appear, 나타나다 3 clap, 박수치다
4 noise, 소음, 잡음 5 disturb, 방해하다

6 whistle, 휘파람을 불다 7 pause, 정지하다, 멈추다
8 secret, 비밀 9 nobleman, 귀족
10 performance, 공연 11 result, 결과
12 blame, 비난하다 13 concerto, 협주곡
14 work, 작품 15 orchestra, 오케스트라
16 return, 돌려주다, 반납하다

## 대화문 TEST Step 1 p.62~63

**Listen & Speak 1 B**

1 interested in going, tickets / When / this, at, make it / thanks, for asking
2 Why don't, this weekend / What about, on / make it, have to take care of / See, then

**Listen & Speak 2 B**

1 going to, remember / course, Don't forget / won't, bring, too / Sounds
2 look healthy, secret / go swimming every day, sometime / sounds like, Any other, should do / Don't forget to, many kinds, too

**Real-Life Zone A**

listening to / going to, like to, before / guess, more, if / Actually, clap, wrong / Don't, clap when, stops / may, pauses, wait, very end / see, Make sure, don't forget to, real ending, way, make it, practice / practice after, finishes / See, then

**Real-Life Zone B**

Why don't, after school, make / can't, about on / Don't forget to bring / right, won't

**Wrap Up**

Have, heard / heard that, famous, will be / why don't, on, make it / what time / at, Let's meet / forget to, up / won't

## 대화문 TEST Step 2 p.64~65

**Listen & Speak 1 B**

1 B: Are you interested in going to an opera? I have two tickets.
 G: Yes, I love opera. When is it?
 B: It's this Saturday at 5:00. Can you make it?
 G: Yes, thanks so much for asking me.
2 B: Why don't we go to the new shoe shop this weekend?
 G: Okay. What about at 2:00 on Saturday?
 B: Can you make it at 1:00? I have to take care of my sister at 3:00.

G: Sure. See you then.

1 B: We're going to Hangang this weekend. Do you remember?

G: Of course. Don't forget to bring your camera.

B: Okay. I won't. I'll bring some snacks, too.

G: Sounds great.

2 G: You look healthy. What's your secret?

B: Thanks. Well, I go swimming every day. You should go with me sometime.

G: That sounds like fun. Any other things I should do?

B: Don't forget to eat many kinds of fruits and vegetables, too.

**Real-Life Zone A**

G: What are you listening to?

B: Classical music. I'm going to a concert tomorrow and I'd like to know about the music before I go.

G: I guess it's more enjoyable if you know the music.

B: Actually, I don't want to clap at the wrong time.

G: Don't you just clap when the music stops?

B: No. In classical music, one piece of music may have several pauses. You should wait and clap at the very end.

G: I see. Make sure you don't forget to clap at the real ending. By the way, can you make it to our soccer practice tomorrow at 4:00?

B: Sure. I'll come to the practice after the concert finishes.

G: Okay. See you then.

**Real-Life Zone B**

A: Why don't we go to the library on Monday after school? Can you make it?

B: Sorry, but I can't. How about on Tuesday?

A: Okay. Don't forget to bring your library card.

B: All right. I won't.

**Wrap Up**

G: Yunho! Have you heard about the Christmas concert at the city hall?

B: Yes. I heard that a famous opera singer will be on the stage.

G: Oh, then why don't we go on Christmas Day? Can you make it?

B: Sure. Do you know what time the concert starts?

G: It starts at 5:30. Let's meet at the bus stop at 4:00.

B: Good. Don't forget to dress up.

G: Okay. I won't.

01 History, Classical, Manners

02 Imagine yourself, classical

03 orchestra, play one, concertos

04 hall, dark, silent

05 Nobody, sound

06 Everybody, serious

07 audiences, clap, finishes

08 familiar scene at

09 back, take, look, century

10 bright, inside, nobleman's

11 playing, piano

12 Surprisingly, audiences, talking freely

13 whistle, clap, time

14 shocked, bad, himself, surprised

15 time, mostly social events

16 good places to meet

17 Noise, just part, concert

18 quiet, century when, built

19 More, not just noblemen

20 no longer dependent on

21 more, works, use, increased

22 For example, blamed, noise

23 After, time, rule appeared

24 As, result, quiet, serious

25 what, like, because, change

26 however, enjoy classical, remember

27 Enjoy, disturb, around

01 History, Classical, Manners

02 Imagine yourself, classical

03 orchestra, play one of, piano

04 hall, dark, silent

05 Nobody, sound

06 Everybody, serious

07 audiences, clap, concerto finishes

08 familiar scene at

09 Let's go back, time, take, look, one of

10 bright, inside, nobleman's

11 playing, piano

12 Surprisingly, audiences, talking freely

13 whistle, clap at any time

14 shocked by, bad manners, himself, surprised by, quiet

15 were mostly social

57

16 good places to meet
17 Noise, just part of
18 quiet, century when, were built
19 not just noblemen
20 no longer dependent, for money
21 more power, works, use, increased power
22 For example, blamed, for making noise
23 After some time, rule appeared
24 As a result, quiet, serious
25 what concerts, look like, because, change with time
26 For now, however, enjoy classical, just remember
27 Enjoy, do not disturb those around

24 그 결과, 오늘날 우리는, 매우 조용하고 진지하다.
25 예절은 시대에 따라 변하기 때문에 우리는 콘서트가 미래에는 어떤 모습일지 모른다.
26 하지만 지금은 당신이 래식 음악 공연을 즐기고 싶다면 이것만은 기억해라.
27 음악은 즐기되 당신 주변의 다른 사람들을 방해하지 마라.

1 클래식 콘서트 관람 예절의 역사
2 당신이 클래식 공연장에 있다고 상상해 보아라.
3 오케스트라가 모차르트의 피아노 협주곡들 중 한 곡을 연주하기 시작한다.
4 콘서트장은 어둡고 조용하다.
5 아무도 소리를 내지 않는다.
6 모두가 진지하게 보인다.
7 청중은 오직 협주곡이 끝난 후에만 손뼉을 친다.
8 이것이 오늘날 콘서트에서 익숙한 장면이다.
9 과거로 거슬러 올라가서 18세기 모차르트의 콘서트들 중 하나를 살펴보자.
10 당신은 한 귀족의 집안 밝은 홀에 있다.
11 모차르트는 피아노를 치고 있다.
12 하지만 놀랍게도, 청중들은 먹고 마시며 자유롭게 대화하고 있다.
13 그들은 아무 때나 휘파람을 불고 박수를 친다.
14 당신은 그들의 나쁜 매너에 충격을 받지만, 모차르트 자신은 오늘날의 조용한 청중에게 놀랄지도 모른다.
15 모차르트 시대의 콘서트는 주로 사교적인 행사였다.
16 콘서트는 사람을 만나기에 좋은 장소였다.
17 소음은 그저 콘서트의 일부였다.
18 오늘날의 조용한 콘서트는 많은 대형 공연장이 생긴 19세기에 시작됐다.
19 귀족뿐만 아니라 더 많은 사람들이 콘서트에 갔다.
20 예술가들은 더 이상 돈을 벌기 위해 귀족들에게 의존하지 않았다.
21 예술가들은 자신의 작품에 더 많은 권한이 생겼고 그 힘을 사용하기 시작했다.
22 예를 들어, 바그너는 소음을 낸다는 것 때문에 관객들을 비난했다.
23 얼마 후에 '악장 사이 박수 금지 규칙'이 생겼다.

1 The History of Classical Concert Manners
2 Imagine yourself at a classical music concert.
3 The orchestra starts to play one of Mozart's piano concertos.
4 The concert hall is dark and silent.
5 Nobody makes a sound.
6 Everybody looks serious.
7 The audiences only clap after the concerto finishes.
8 This is a familiar scene at concerts today.
9 Let's go back in time and take a look at one of Mozart's concerts in the 18th century.
10 You are in a bright hall inside a nobleman's house.
11 Mozart is playing the piano.
12 Surprisingly, however, the audiences are eating, drinking, and talking freely.
13 They whistle and clap at any time.
14 You are shocked by their bad manners, but Mozart himself would be surprised by today's quiet audiences.
15 Concerts in Mozart's time were mostly social events.
16 They were good places to meet people.
17 Noise was just part of the concert.
18 Today's quiet concerts began in the 19th century when many big concert halls were built.
19 More people, not just noblemen, went to concerts.
20 Artists were no longer dependent on noblemen for money.
21 The artists had more power over their works and started to use their increased power.
22 For example, Wagner blamed the audience for making noise.
23 After some time, a no-clapping-between-movements rule appeared.
24 As a result, here we are today, very quiet and serious.
25 We do not know what concerts will look like in the

future because manners change with time.

26 For now, however, if you want to enjoy classical music concerts, just remember this:

27 Enjoy the music, but do not disturb those around you.

---

## 구석구석지문 TEST Step 1 p.76

### Before I Read B

1. Guide, Concert Manners
2. Watching, memorable experience, keep, in mind
3. Before, Go
4. Plan to arrive, concert time
5. Find out, will be played
6. When, Is Playing
7. Turn off
8. Stay, No, whistling, along to
9. Don't clap, piece is over
10. It, to clap, clapping

### Writing Workshop

1. Review
2. On, to a concert hall, where, was held
3. opportunity to listen to, play live
4. played, Piano Concerto
5. how beautiful the classical music was
6. live performance
7. will not forget

### Wrap Up 7

1. When, coming out
2. coming out
3. your plans for
4. planning to have
5. held one of, during his world tour

---

8. Stay quiet. No talking, whistling, singing along to the music.
9. Don't clap until the whole piece is over.
10. It is safe to clap when the audience starts clapping.

### Writing Workshop

1. Music Concert Review
2. On February 2, I went to a concert hall at the Seoul Arts Center where Jo Seongu's piano concert was held.
3. It was a great opportunity to listen to him play live .
4. He played Chopin's Piano Concerto No. 1.
5. I did not know how beautiful the classical music was .
6. I liked his live performance.
7. I will not forget this experience.

### Wrap Up 7

1. Reporter: When is your new album coming out?
2. Justin Otter: It's coming out next month.
3. Reporter: What are your plans for the new album?
4. Justin Otter: I'm planning to have a concert at the Super Stadium.
5. My hero Michael Johnson held one of his concerts during his world tour at the place.

---

## 구석구석지문 TEST Step 2 p.77

### Before I Read B

1. A Guide to Good Concert Manners
2. Watching a classical music concert can be a memorable experience if you keep these tips in mind.
3. Before You Go In:
4. Plan to arrive 20-30 minutes before concert time.
5. Find out what music will be played.
6. When Music Is Playing :
7. Turn off your cellphone!

13 enter, (~을) 출전시키다　14 crowd, 군중, 무리

15 weave, (실을) 엮다　16 narrator, 서술자, 내레이터

## 단어 TEST Step 1　p.78

01 돼지　02 쓰레기 폐기장　03 헛간

04 (~을) 출전시키다　05 박람회　06 ~보다 위에

07 광고　08 먹이를 주다　09 죽다

10 거미　11 ~하다시피　12 군중, 무리

13 아무도 ~ 않다　14 관심　15 인간의

16 ~ 없이, ~하지 않고　17 지속되다

18 죽은　19 기적　20 ~해야 하다

21 구하다　22 농장　23 양

24 서술자, 내레이터　25 흥분, 신남　26 반짝이는, 빛나는

27 (가축의) 우리　28 쥐　29 (실을) 엮다

30 거미줄　31 훌륭한　32 (재료) ~으로

33 살찌우다　34 ~하게 보이다　35 ~을 돌보다

36 즉시, 곧바로　37 상을 받다　38 A를 B와 나누다

39 ~이 다 떨어지다　40 ~하는 게 어때?　41 A와 B 사이에

42 너무 ~해서 …할 수 없다

## 단어 TEST Step 2　p.79

01 rat　02 web　03 spider

04 crowd　05 die　06 nobody

07 as　08 pen　09 barn

10 excitement　11 fair　12 sheep

13 farm　14 above　15 ad

16 feed　17 save　18 narrator

19 dead　20 human　21 attention

22 last　23 must　24 shining

25 without　26 dump　27 pig

28 enter　29 terrific　30 weave

31 miracle　32 right away　33 out of

34 care for　35 fatten up

36 between A and B　37 look+형용사

38 too 형용사 to 동사원형　39 Why don't you ~?

40 run out of　41 get[win] a prize

42 share A with B

## 단어 TEST Step 3　p.80

1 human, 인간의　2 above, ~보다 위에

3 dump, 쓰레기 폐기장　4 excitement, 흥분, 신남

5 rat, 쥐　6 web, 거미줄　7 shining, 반짝이는, 빛나는

8 last, 지속되다　9 miracle, 기적　10 pen, (가축의) 우리

11 sheep, 양　12 spider, 거미

## 본문 TEST Step 1　p.81~83

01 Charlotte's Web　02 Setting, pen, farm

03 Roles, spider, owners

04 friendship between, and

05 lived on, farm with

06 one, outside, barn　07 looks, good

08 make good bacon

09 are fattening, up　10 For bacon

11 too, to die　12 won't, save

13 Wilbur, How　14 know yet, remember

15 saved, clean, off　16 turn to save

17 How can, save　18 have, idea

19 to weave, above　20 hard, without sleeping

21 next, to feed　22 There, words, web

23 A miracle　24 large crowd, see

25 As, passed, few　26 called a meeting

27 As, attention, last 28 cares for, be dead

29 must, another word

30 idea, How about　31 like it

32 worked, all night　33 later, bigger crowd

34 will be forgotten　35 have to, right away

36 run out of　37 all the excitement

38 Why don't you　39 bring, from, dump

40 trying to find　41 to save, life

42 if, shares, with　43 With, help, finally

44 biggest ever crowd

45 what, make, out of　46 enter him, fair

47 famous, get, prize　48 hear, going, fair

49 saved, all

## 본문 TEST Step 2　p.84~86

01 Web　02 Setting, pen, pig, farm

03 Roles, pig, spider, owners

04 friendship between, and, spider

05 lived on, with

06 One day, were talking outside the barn

07 looks, good　08 make good bacon

09 are fattening, up　10 For

11 too young to die　12 won't, save

13 How　14 yet, remember

15 saved, tried to clean, off

16 my turn to save 17 How, save

18 have an idea 19 to weave, above

20 worked hard, without sleeping

21 to feed 22 There, words, Some Pig

23 miracle 24 large crowd, to see

25 As, passed, only a few

26 called a meeting

27 As, saw, human attention, last long

28 cares for, will be dead before

29 must write another word

30 How about 31 it

32 worked hard all night

33 later, bigger crowd

34 will be forgotten 35 have to prepare, right away

36 run out of 37 excitement

38 Why don't you 39 bring, from, dump

40 trying to find 41 trying to save

42 shares, with 43 With, finally chose

44 biggest ever 45 what, make, out of

46 enter him, fair 47 famous, get a prize

48 going to the fair 49 saved, all

## 본문 TEST Step 3  p.87~88

1 샬럿의 거미줄

2 배경: 앨런 부부 농장의 돼지 월버의 우리

3 배역: 서술자 1, 2, 3, 돼지 월버, 거미 샬럿, 농장 주인 앨런 부부, 늙은 양, 오리, 쥐

4 서술자 1: "샬럿의 거미줄"은 돼지 월버와 거미 샬럿 사이의 우정 이야기다.

5 서술자 2: 그들은 늙은 양, 오리, 쥐와 함께 앨런 부부의 농장에서 살았다.

6 서술자 3: 어느 날, 앨런 부부는 헛간 밖에서 이야기하고 있었다.

7 앨런 부인: 월버가 아주 좋아 보여요.

8 앨런 씨: 그는 크리스마스에 좋은 베이컨이 될 거예요.

9 늙은 양: 그들은 크리스마스를 위해 월버를 살찌우고 있어.

10 오리: 베이컨을 위해!

11 월버: 안 돼! 나는 죽기에 너무 어려.

12 샬럿: 죽지 않을 거야, 월버. 내가 널 구할게.

13 월버: 어떻게?

14 샬럿: 아직 잘 모르겠어. 그런데 기억나?

15 앨런 씨가 거미줄을 없애려고 했을 때 네가 나를 구했잖아.

16 이제 내가 너를 구할 차례야.

17 샬럿: 내가 어떻게 월버를 구할 수 있을까?

18 음… 오, 좋은 생각이 났어!

19 서술자 1: 그날 밤, 샬럿은 월버의 우리 위에 무언가를 짜기 시작했다.

20 그녀는 밤새도록 자지 않고 열심히 일했다.

21 서술자 2: 다음 날 아침, 앨런 부부는 월버에게 먹이를 주러 왔다.

22 앨런 부인: 보세요! 거미줄에 단어들이 있어요. '대단한 돼지'!

23 앨런 씨: 기적이야!

24 서술자 3: 곧 많은 군중들이 월버를 보러 왔다.

25 서술자 1: 시간이 지날수록 극소수의 사람들만이 왔다.

26 샬럿은 회의를 소집했다.

27 샬럿: 보았다시피 인간의 관심은 오래 지속되지 않아.

28 아무도 월버를 돌보지 않는다면, 그는 크리스마스 전에 죽을 거야.

29 우리는 곧 다른 단어를 써야 해.

30 오리: 내게 생각이 있어. '훌륭한'은 어때?

31 늙은 양: 좋아!

32 서술자 2: 다시 샬럿은 밤새도록 열심히 일했다.

33 이틀 후, 더 많은 군중이 왔다.

34 샬럿: 이것 또한 곧 잊힐 거야.

35 우리는 곧바로 다음 단어를 준비해야 해.

36 오리: 오, 나는 아이디어가 바닥이 나 버렸어.

37 쥐: 모두들 뭐가 그렇게 신나니?

38 늙은 양: 우릴 도와주는 게 어때?

39 쓰레기 더미에서 광고 몇 개를 가져다줄래?

40 오리: 우리는 새로운 단어를 찾으려고 노력하고 있어.

41 샬럿: 우리는 월버의 생명을 구하려고 노력하고 있어.

42 쥐: 알았어, 월버가 음식을 나와 나눈다면.

43 서술자 3: 쥐의 도움으로, 그들은 마침내 '빛나는'을 선택했다.

44 이제껏 가장 많은 군중이 왔다.

45 앨런 씨: 그거 알아요? 나는 월버로 베이컨을 만들지 않을 거예요.

46 나는 그를 박람회에 출전시킬 거예요.

47 앨런 부인: 좋은 생각이에요! 우리 유명한 월버가 상을 받을 거예요!

48 월버: 들었어? 내가 박람회에 나갈 거야!

49 고마워, 샬럿! 네가 나를 구했어. 모두들 고마워!

## 본문 TEST Step 4-Step 5  p.89~93

1 Charlotte's Web

2 Setting: The pen of Wilbur the pig on Mr. and Mrs. Allen's farm

3 Roles: Narrator 1, 2, 3, Wilbur: A pig, Charlotte: A spider, Mr. and Mrs. Allen: Farm owners, Old Sheep, Duck, Rat

4 Narrator 1: *Charlotte's Web* is a story of friendship between Wilbur the pig and Charlotte the spider.

5 Narrator 2: They lived on Mr. and Mrs. Allen's farm with Old Sheep, Duck, and Rat.

6 Narrator 3: One day, Mr. and Mrs. Allen were talking outside the barn.

7 Mrs. Allen: Wilbur looks very good.

8 Mr. Allen: He'll make good bacon for Christmas.

9 Old Sheep: They are fattening Wilbur up for Christmas!

10 Duck: For bacon!

11 Wilbur: No! I'm too young to die!

12 Charlotte: You won't, Wilbur. I'll save you.

13 Wilbur: How?

14 Charlotte: I don't know yet, but remember?

15 You saved me when Mr. Allen tried to clean my web off.

16 Now it's my turn to save you.

17 Charlotte: How can I save Wilbur?

18 Hmm.... Oh, I have an idea!

19 Narrator 1: That night, Charlotte started to weave something above Wilbur's pen.

20 She worked hard all night without sleeping.

21 Narrator 2: The next morning, Mr. and Mrs. Allen came to feed Wilbur.

22 Mrs. Allen: Look! There are words in the web. "Some Pig"!

23 Mr. Allen: A miracle!

24 Narrator 3: Soon, a large crowd came to see Wilbur.

25 Narrator 1: As time passed, only a few people came.

26 Charlotte called a meeting.

27 Charlotte: As we saw, human attention does not last long.

28 If nobody cares for Wilbur, he will be dead before Christmas.

29 We must write another word soon.

30 Duck: I have an idea! How about "Terrific"?

31 Old Sheep: I like it!

32 Narrator 2: Again, Charlotte worked hard all night.

33 Two days later, a bigger crowd came.

34 Charlotte: This also will be forgotten soon.

35 We have to prepare the next word right away.

36 Duck: Uh, oh. I have run out of ideas.

37 Rat: What's all the excitement?

38 Old Sheep: Why don't you help us?

39 Will you bring some ads from the dump?

40 Duck: We're trying to find new words.

41 Charlotte: We're trying to save Wilbur's life.

42 Rat: Okay, if Wilbur shares his meal with me.

43 Narrator 3: With Rat's help, they finally chose "Shining."

44 The biggest ever crowd came.

45 Mr. Allen: You know what? I won't make bacon out of Wilbur.

46 I'll enter him in the fair!

47 Mrs. Allen: Great idea! Our famous Wilbur will get a prize!

48 Wilbur: Did you hear that? I'm going to the fair!

49 Thank you, Charlotte! You saved me. Thank you all!

# MEMO

# 적중 100 + 특별부록

# Plan B

# 우리학교 최신기출

시사·송미정 교과서를 배우는

학교 시험문제 분석·모음·해설집

전국단위 학교 시험문제 수집 및 분석
출제 빈도가 높은 문제 위주로 선별
문제 풀이에 필요한 상세한 해설

### 중2-2 영어

## 시사·송미정

◎ 선택형 문항의 답안은 컴퓨터용 수정 싸인펜을 사용하여 OMR 답안지에 바르게 표기하시오.
◎ 서술형 문제는 답을 답안지에 반드시 검정 볼펜으로 쓰시오.
◎ 총 29문항 100점 만점입니다. 문항별 배점은 각 문항에 표시되어 있습니다.

[충남 ○○중]

**01** 다음 주어진 단어의 영영 풀이로 적절하지 <u>않은</u> 것은? (3점)

① hurry: to move or act quickly
② ticket: a piece of paper that lets you go inside
③ stadium: a very large building that is used for sports
④ surfing: the activity of riding ocean waves on a board
⑤ suggest: to say that something is not good to be chosen

[서울 양천구 ○○중]

**02** 다음 중 밑줄 친 부분의 해석이 <u>어색한</u> 것은? (3점)

① You look <u>terrific</u> in those pants. (멋진)
② It was sad to see the animals in the <u>pen</u>. (우리)
③ I tried to <u>weave</u> her a scarf for Christmas. (짜다, 엮다)
④ The flowers are beautiful, but they won't <u>last</u> long. (끝나다)
⑤ The <u>crowd</u> gathered around to watch the show. (군중)

[전북 ○○중]

**03** 다음 밑줄 친 부분 중 어법상 <u>틀린</u> 것은? (3점)

ⓐThe vase ⓑis made ⓒby ⓓme ⓔlast year.

① ⓐ
② ⓑ
③ ⓒ
④ ⓓ
⑤ ⓔ

[충남 ○○중]

**04** 다음 짝지어진 동사의 시제 변화 중 형태가 바르지 <u>않은</u> 것은? (3점)

① lose - lost - lost
② mean - meant - meant
③ begin - began - begun
④ draw - drew - drawn
⑤ wear - wore - wore

[충남 ○○중]

**05** 다음 중 부가의문문의 쓰임이 적절한 문장은? (3점)

① He is tall, is he?
② The rumor is not true, is it?
③ He will read it, will he?
④ She likes tigers, don't she?
⑤ You can speak English, don't you?

**06** 다음 그림을 설명하는 문장을 주어진 〈조건〉에 맞추어 영작하시오. (4점)

<조건>
• 과거시제를 사용한다.
• be동사+과거분사의 수동태를 사용한다.
• <보기>의 단어를 적절한 형태로 변형한다.

<보기>
throw / the man

→ The stick _____.

**08** 다음 보기의 빈칸과 똑같은 부가의문문이 필요한 문장은? (3점)

<보기>
You forgot to bring your umbrella, _____?

① Mr. Park goes shopping every Sunday, _____?
② You will travel to Europe, _____?
③ Jenny wasn't at the party last night, _____?
④ You had a pen, _____?
⑤ Emily is tired, _____?

**07** 다음 중 어법상 올바른 문장은? (3점)

① The house cleaned by Tim every Sunday.
② My uncle's house destroyed by the flood.
③ Where did your dog found yesterday?
④ Was the letter delivered by David?
⑤ These cookies made by my mom.

**09** 다음 대화의 빈칸 (A), (B)에 들어갈 단어가 바르게 짝지어진 것은? (4점)

A: Which sport do you like (A)_____, surfing or swimming?
B: I like to (B)_____ surfing.

|  | (A) | (B) |
|---|---|---|
| ① | better | go |
| ② | well | play |
| ③ | well | do |
| ④ | better | be |
| ⑤ | best | go |

[10~13] 다음 대화를 읽고 물음에 답하시오.

Jiyeon: Oh, I can't believe it's still Wednesday.
Yeongji: I know, I know. There isn't any holiday this week.
Jiyeon: You know what? I have a new bike. This gives me some energy.
Yeongji: Wow. When did you get it?
Jiyeon: Yesterday my father bought it for me. Do you want to see my new mountain bike?
Yeongji: Sure.
Jiyeon: Can you come to my house this afternoon?
Yeongji: Of course. Plus, don't forget that we're going rock climbing this weekend!
Jiyeon: Don't worry. I won't forget.
Yeongji: Anyway, did you hear about Solmi?
Jiyeon: What about her? (A)She lives in Canada, _____.
Yeongji: No, she came back to Korea last month. She wants to see you.
Jiyeon: Oh, I can't wait (B)_____ (C)see her.

**10** 위 대화의 내용과 일치하는 것은? [전북 ○○중] (4점)

① 오늘은 금요일이다.
② 이번 주에는 쉬는 날이 많다.
③ 솔미는 지금 캐나다에 있다.
④ 솔미는 지난달에 한국에 돌아왔다.
⑤ 지연이는 지난주에 새 자전거를 샀다.

**11** 위 대화의 밑줄 친 (A)의 주어와 동사에 주의하여 부가의문문을 만들어 쓰시오. [전북 ○○중] (4점)

→ _____ _____

**12** 위 대화의 밑줄 친 (C)에 주의하여 빈칸 (B)에 들어갈 말로 가장 적절한 것은? [전북 ○○중] (3점)

① to
② on
③ in
④ for
⑤ from

**13** 위 대화의 영지가 지연의 집으로 오기로 한 시간을 주어진 일정표에서 고르면? [전북 ○○중] (4점)

|  | Wed | Thurs | Fri | Sat | Sun |
|---|---|---|---|---|---|
| morning | ⓐ |  |  | ⓑ |  |
| after-noon | ⓒ |  |  | ⓓ |  |
| evening |  |  |  | ⓔ |  |

① ⓐ     ② ⓑ     ③ ⓒ

④ ⓓ     ⑤ ⓔ

G: I'm thinking about (A)＿＿＿＿＿ a pet. Do you have a pet?

B: Yes, I do. I have a dog and a cat.

G: What do you think? Which pet is better for me? A cat or a dog?

B: Why don't you come to my house someday and play with my pets? Then you can decide.

G: Okay! I will.

*G: Girl, B: Boy

**14** 위 대화의 흐름상 빈칸 (A)에 들어갈 단어로 가장 적절한 것은? (3점)

① giving

② getting

③ feeding

④ touching

⑤ teaching

**15** 위 대화의 내용으로 적절하지 않은 것은? (3점)

① The boy has two kinds of animals.

② The girl can't decide the pet to keep.

③ The girl is asking for the boy's opinion.

④ The boy will take an animal to the girl.

⑤ The girl will go to the boy's house someday.

**16** 다음 중 대화의 내용이 어색한 것은? (3점)

① A: What are you doing?

B: I'm looking at a world map.

② A: Which storybook do you like better, Peter Pan or Snow White?

B: I like Peter Pan better.

③ A: Did you get the tickets?

B: Yes! I don't have to watch the game.

④ A: Don't forget to close the door!

B: Don't worry. I won't forget.

⑤ A: Do you want to see my new bike?

B: Sure. When did you get it?

**17** 다음 대화를 읽고 대답할 수 없는 것은? (4점)

Mingyu: Jiheon, which sport do you like? Soccer or table tennis?

Jiheon: I love table tennis. How about you, Mingyu?

Mingyu: I like soccer. I'm a big fan of James Hood. He's a great soccer player.

Jiheon: Oh, really? There's a soccer match this weekend between Korea and Turkey. Have you heard about it?

Mingyu: Of course. I already have a ticket. I'm going to see the game on Saturday. I can't wait.

Jiheon: That's fantastic.

① Which sport does Jiheon like?

② Which sport does Mungyu like?

③ What will Jiheon do this weekend?

④ What will Mungyu do this weekend?

⑤ Who is Mungyu's favorite soccer player?

### A Trip to Suncheon

My family took a trip to Suncheon last summer. We visited the National Garden. It was so large (A)_____ we could not see the whole garden. After three hours' walking, we were really hungry. For dinner, we had Gukbap that my parents like. Suncheon is famous for Gukbap and we enjoyed it. This trip was very good. So I would never forget it for a long time.

[충남 ○○중]

**18** 위 글의 흐름상 빈칸 (A)에 알맞은 것은? (3점)

① when

② before

③ which

④ that

⑤ because

[충남 ○○중]

**19** 위 글을 읽고 답할 수 없는 질문은? (4점)

① When did the writer go to Suncheon?

② Who did the writer go to Suncheon with?

③ Why didn't the writer see the whole garden?

④ How long did the writer visit Suncheon?

⑤ How did the writer feel about the trip to Suncheon?

A: Jiho, why are you in such a hurry?

J: Hi, Alex! I have to be home before 6:00. The game between the Thunders and the Cobras starts at 6:00 today.

A: Oh, are you a baseball fan? ⓐ너는 어느 팀을 응원하니? The Cobras or the Thunders?

J: The Cobras.

A: Me, too! I don't want to miss the game either.

J: Hurry up! We only have thirty minutes left.

A: Okay. Maybe we can watch a game together sometime.

J: That's a great idea! How about going to the next Cobras home game together?

A: Okay. They have a game next Saturday. We can eat fried chicken while watching the game!

J: That sounds great. ⓑ너무 기대된다.

*A: Alex, J: Jiho

[충남 ○○중]

**20** 위 대화의 밑줄 친 ⓐ의 영작으로 적절한 것은? (4점)

① Who is your team player?

② Which team do you want?

③ Which team do you support?

④ What is the name of your team?

⑤ What is the symbol of your team?

**21** 위 대화의 밑줄 친 ⓑ의 영작으로 적절한 것은? (3점)

① I love it!

② Let's do it!

③ I can't wait!

④ It's really nice!

⑤ I shouldn't wait!

[23~25] 다음 글을 읽고 물음에 답하시오.

The players are warming up.

Jian: Who's your favorite player?

Jihun: Number 77.

Jian: What does the number mean?

Jihun: Hmm... Players choose a number they like.

Dad: You know what? In the past, the numbers (A)결정되었다 by the players' batting order.

Jihun: That means there were no players with number 77!

Now, Jihun's favorite player is (B)_____ bat. Jihun looks anxious.

Jian: Your favorite player is at bat.

Jihun: Yes. He has hit 21 home runs already this year. If he hits one more today, he will be the home run leader this season.

The batter misses several balls. Now he has a full count. He is waiting for the next pitch.

Jihun: HOME RUN! HOME RUN!

Crack! The ball flies fast. It is going, going, going, gone!

**22** 위 대화의 내용으로 적절하지 않은 것은? (4점)

① Alex와 Jiho는 야구 팬이다.

② 오늘 6시에 야구 경기가 시작한다.

③ Alex와 Jiho는 같은 팀을 응원한다.

④ 오늘의 경기가 시작하기까지 30분 남았다.

⑤ Cobras 팀의 홈 경기가 다음 주 일요일에 있다.

**23** 위 글의 밑줄 친 (A)에 들어갈 적절한 형태의 단어를 고르면? (4점)

① determined

② were determined

③ was determined

④ has determined

⑤ determine

**24** 위 글의 흐름상 빈칸 (B)에 가장 적절한 것은? (3점)

① to
② on
③ with
④ for
⑤ at

**25** 위 글의 내용과 일치하는 것은? (4점)

① Jihun's favorite player never missed any balls.
② The players can't choose a number they like.
③ Jihun's favorite player has hit 25 home runs this year.
④ Jihun's favorite player hit a home run in this game.
⑤ Jihun looks relaxed when his favorite player is about to bat.

**[26~29] 다음 글을 읽고 물음에 답하시오.**

Today the Thunders and the Cobras have a game. Jihun's family is at the baseball stadium.

Jihun: Jian, this is your first time to come to the baseball stadium, (가)_____?

Jian: Yes, I'm so excited. I can't wait for the game to start.

Dad: Look, the players are coming out now!

Jian: Which team is the Thunders?

Jihun: Over there, behind third base. They are ⓐ<u>wear</u> dark gray uniforms because they are the visiting team.

Jian: Does the visiting team always ⓑ<u>wear</u> a dark color?

Jihun: Yes, that's (나)<u>the rule</u>. Home teams have bright uniforms and visiting teams have dark uniforms.

Jian: Why is that?

Mom: There is an interesting story about that. In the past, visiting teams could not wash their uniforms after every game. So they started ⓒ<u>wear</u> dark colors to hide the dirt.

Jian: Hahaha! That was a good idea!

**26** 위 글의 빈칸 (가)에 들어갈 말로 가장 적절한 것은? (3점)

① is it
② isn't it
③ is this
④ isn't this
⑤ aren't it

**28** 위 글의 밑줄 친 (나)가 뜻하는 것으로 가장 적절한 것은? (3점)

① 홈팀은 3루로 나와야 한다.
② 홈팀은 어두운 색 유니폼을 입는다.
③ 원정팀은 밝은 색 유니폼을 입는다.
④ 원정팀은 어두운 색 유니폼을 입는다.
⑤ 원정팀은 모든 경기 후에 유니폼을 세탁해야 한다.

**27** 위 글의 밑줄 친 ⓐ, ⓑ, ⓒ에 wear의 형태를 바르게 짝지은 것은? (4점)

| | ⓐ | ⓑ | ⓒ |
|---|---|---|---|
| ① | wear | wearing | wear |
| ② | wear | wearing | wearing |
| ③ | wearing | wear | wearing |
| ④ | wearing | wear | wear |
| ⑤ | to wear | wear | to wear |

**29** 위 글의 내용과 일치하는 것은? (4점)

① In the past, visiting teams could wash their uniforms after every game.
② This is Jihun's first time to come to the baseball stadium.
③ The Thunders are wearing bright uniforms.
④ Home teams wear bright uniforms.
⑤ Jian is very nervous now.

# 2학년 영어 2학기 중간고사(6과) 1회

문항수 : 선택형(27문항) 서술형(3문항)

20 . . .

반 이름

점수

◎ 선택형 문항의 답안은 컴퓨터용 수정 싸인펜을 사용하여 OMR 답안지에 바르게 표기하시오.
◎ 서술형 문제는 답을 답안지에 반드시 검정 볼펜으로 쓰시오.
◎ 총 30문항 100점 만점입니다. 문항별 배점은 각 문항에 표시되어 있습니다.

[서울 동작구 ○○중]

## 01 Which one fits the blank (A), (B) and (C)? (4점)

| (A)_____ | : think that something will happen |
| (B)_____ | : everything that can be seen from a particular place |
| (C)_____ | : a particular time |

| | (A) | (B) | (C) |
|---|---|---|---|
| ① | except | moment | flight |
| ② | view | flight | magical |
| ③ | expect | view | moment |
| ④ | relate | magic | move |
| ⑤ | appreciate | moment | special |

[서울 양천구 ○○중]

## 02 다음 빈칸에 들어가기에 <u>어색한</u> 단어는? (3점)

He was _____ after having dinner.

① bored
② moved
③ fatten up
④ pleased
⑤ disappointed

[서울 양천구 ○○중]

## 03 다음 빈칸 (A)에 들어가기에 가장 알맞은 것은? (3점)

(A)_____ who I met in the park like cooking.

① A boy
② A story
③ A friend
④ People
⑤ The student

[충남 ○○중]

## 04 다음 두 문장의 의미가 같도록 알맞은 단어를 고르면? (3점)

He bought me the book.
= He bought the book _____ me.

① about
② for
③ of
④ at
⑤ to

[서울 동작구 ○○중]

## 05 다음 관계대명사의 문장을 두 문장으로 만드시오. (5점)

The cookies which Susan made for me were delicious.

(1)_____
(2)_____

**06** 다음 중 밑줄 친 It과 쓰임이 같은 것은? (3점)

> It is important to work out regularly.

① It is sunny today.

② Put this letter in it.

③ It is a famous meat dish.

④ It is dangerous to swim in the sea.

⑤ It is usually cool and dry in winter.

**07** 다음 두 문장을 한 문장으로 연결할 때 빈칸에 알맞은 단어를 두 개 고르면? (3점)

> • The boy is cute. My friend introduced the boy to me.
> → The boy _____ my friend introduced to me is cute.

① who

② which

③ whom

④ where

⑤ why

**08** 다음 우리말과 같도록 괄호 안의 어휘를 이용하여 시제에 맞게 관계대명사 which의 문장으로 쓰시오. (4점)

> 그들이 살고 있던 텐트는 컸다.
> = The tent _____.
>  (The tent 포함 총 8단어 / in)

→ _____

**09** 다음 그림을 올바르게 표현한 문장은? (3점)

① The bags were so heavy that he couldn't carry.

② The bags were too heavy that he can carry them.

③ The man was so heavy that he couldn't carry them.

④ The bags were so heavy that he couldn't carry them.

⑤ The man was too heavy that he couldn't carry them.

**10** 다음 중 어법상 올바른 문장은? (4점)

① After taking a shower, I felt relaxing.

② The boy is cute which my friend introduced to me.

③ Diana is wearing a dress which Mrs. Barry made it for her.

④ My sister was so exciting about her first win at the match.

⑤ The beginning of the movie was interesting, but at the last part, I was disappointed.

---

**[12~13] 다음 대화를 읽고 물음에 답하시오.**

Ben:   Have you ever traveled abroad, Sujin?
Sujin: Yes, I went to Cambodia last summer.
Ben:   Wow. (A)
Sujin: It was really hot, but I enjoyed the trip.
Ben:   Tell me some interesting experiences you had during the trip. (B)
Sujin: Hmm... let me think. I ate fried spiders!
Ben:   What? You're kidding. (C)
Sujin: They were really big, so I was a little scared at first. (D) But the taste was okay.
Ben:   Really? (E) I cannot imagine eating spiders.

---

**11** 다음 문장을 주어진 〈조건〉에 맞추어 완성하시오. (4점)

> 그가 너무 빠르게 말해서 나는 그를 이해할 수 없다.

**조건**
- 원인과 결과를 나타낼 수 있도록 so와 that을 적절한 위치에 사용한다.
- 〈보기〉의 단어를 뜻에 맞도록 적절히 활용하여 문장을 완성한다.
- 문장의 시제에 주의한다.

**보기**

speak / understand

→ He _____ that I _____.

---

**12** 위 대화의 (A)~(E) 중 다음 문장이 들어갈 곳으로 가장 적합한 곳은? (3점)

> How did you like it?

① (A)      ② (B)      ③ (C)
④ (D)      ⑤ (E)

**13** 위 대화의 내용과 일치하지 <u>않는</u> 것은? (3점)

① Sujin은 지난여름 Cambodia에 다녀왔다.

② Sujin이 먹은 거미튀김은 작지만 맛있었다.

③ Sujin은 거미튀김을 먹을 때 처음에는 무서워했다.

④ Ben과 Sujin은 여행 경험에 관해서 이야기하고 있다.

⑤ 더운 날씨를 제외하고 Sujin은 캄보디아 여행을 즐거워했다.

**15** 다음 대화가 자연스러운 대화가 되도록 올바른 순서대로 배열한 것은? (3점)

(A) The service was bad. I won't go there again.
(B) Have you been to the new Spanish restaurant?
(C) Yes, I had dinner there last Sunday.
(D) How did you like it?

① (A) - (B) - (C) - (D)
② (B) - (C) - (D) - (A)
③ (B) - (A) - (D) - (C)
④ (C) - (A) - (D) - (B)
⑤ (C) - (B) - (D) - (A)

**14** 다음 대화의 빈칸에 들어갈 단어가 바르게 짝지어진 것은? (3점)

G: You look excited, Inho. What's up?
B: I'm (A)_____ to Jejudo with my family this weekend. Have you ever been there?
G: Yes, (B)_____. I love the coastline. How about you?
B: It'll be my first visit to Jejudo. I (C)_____ wait for this weekend!

|   | (A) | (B) | (C) |
|---|-----|-----|-----|
| ① | go | sometimes | can |
| ② | gone | little times | won't |
| ③ | went | many times | can't |
| ④ | will go | sometimes | will |
| ⑤ | going | many times | can't |

**16** 다음 글의 흐름상 밑줄 친 ⓐ~ⓔ 중 <u>어색한</u> 것은? (3점)

I love ⓐ<u>reading</u>. In Grandfather's room, there are many shelves which are full of books. The shelves are ⓑ<u>made of</u> wood. When I first ⓒ<u>went out of</u> the room, I didn't like the smell of the old books, but I soon ⓓ<u>got used to</u> it. Grandfather's room became my ⓔ<u>favorite</u> place.

① ⓐ        ② ⓑ        ③ ⓒ
④ ⓓ        ⑤ ⓔ

**17** 다음 글의 내용과 일치하지 <u>않는</u> 것을 <u>두 개</u> 고르면? (3점)

> This is your captain speaking. We have just arrived at the airport. Welcome to Mongolia, a country full of the beauty of nature and culture. The time in Ulaanbaatar is now 4:30 p.m. and there is a chance of rain. We hope you had a nice flight. Thank you for flying with us. We hope to see you again.

① 비행기 기장의 안내 멘트이다.

② 비행기가 공항에서 막 이륙했다.

③ 울란바토르에 비가 내리고 있다.

④ 울란바토르의 지금 시간은 오후 4시 30분이다.

⑤ 몽골은 자연과 문화의 아름다움으로 가득 찬 나라이다.

[18~20] 다음 글을 읽고 물음에 답하시오.

**[A]**
Her house is a ger, a traditional Mongolian house. (A) It is a big tent, but it is cozy inside. (B) It was from the khorhog that she was cooking for us. (C) Khorkhog is a Mongolian barbecue. (D) It is made of lamb and cooked with hot stones. (E) I was moved when Atlan said Mongolians serve khorkhog to special guests. It was so delicious that I asked for more. After dinner, Altan and I went outside to see the night sky. The sky was full of bright stars. I felt like I was in a magical place.

**[B]**
Atlan's grandmother lives in the ⓐ<u>small tent</u>. It is a ⓑ<u>traditional</u> house in Mongolia. It is cozy inside. ⓒ<u>Altan</u> cooked a Mongolian barbecue for me. It is made of ⓓ<u>beef</u> and cooked with hot stones. I was moved when Altan sad Mongolians served Khorkhog to ⓔ<u>many</u> guests.

**18** 위 글의 [B]는 [A]의 내용을 요약한 글이다. [B]의 밑줄 친 ⓐ~ⓔ 중 [A]의 내용과 일치하는 것은? (4점)

① ⓐ      ② ⓑ      ③ ⓒ

④ ⓓ      ⑤ ⓔ

**19** Where is the best place for the sentence in the box among (A)~(E) in [A]? (4점)

> When we entered, something smelled wonderful.

① (A)    ② (B)    ③ (C)

④ (D)    ⑤ (E)

During the next three days, Altan showed me (A)_____ and helped me experience Mongolian culture. Every moment was fun and (가)_____, but I had the most fun when I rode a camel in the Gobi Desert. At first, I was scared because the camel was taller than I expected. But (a)_____ I sat (B)_____ its back, I soon got used to its movement. From the camel's back, the view of the (나)_____ was truly wonderful.

My visit to Mongolia was a special experience (C)_____ many ways. It gave me a great chance to get to know my friend's country and culture. I want to visit Mongolia again someday!

**21** 위 글의 흐름상 빈칸 (가), (나)에 알맞은 단어는? (4점)

|  | (가) | (나) |
|---|---|---|
| ① | exciting | desert |
| ② | exciting | mountains |
| ③ | excite | ocean |
| ④ | excited | mountains |
| ⑤ | excited | desert |

**20** 위 글 [A] 문단의 내용과 일치하지 않는 것은? (3점)

① ger는 몽골의 전통 가옥이다.

② ger는 텐트인데 안은 좁고 불편하다.

③ khorkhog는 특별한 손님에게 대접하는 음식이다.

④ 글쓴이와 Altan은 저녁을 먹은 후 밤하늘을 구경했다.

⑤ 글쓴이는 저녁으로 몽골의 전통 음식인 khorkhog를 먹었다.

**22** 위 글의 빈칸 (A)~(C)에 알맞은 단어로 연결한 것은? (3점)

|  | (A) | (B) | (C) |
|---|---|---|---|
| ① | about | for | at |
| ② | about | for | on |
| ③ | around | in | in |
| ④ | around | on | in |
| ⑤ | for | in | at |

**23** Which one is right for the blank (a)? (3점)

① once

② that

③ both

④ also

⑤ if

**24** 위 글의 camel riding에 대한 글쓴이의 심정 변화로 적절한 것은? (3점)

① scared → fun

② scared → tired

③ disappointed → fun

④ disappointed → tired

⑤ relaxed → scared

**25** Which statement is NOT mentioned according to the passage? (3점)

① The writer rode a camel in the Gobi Desert.

② The writer hopes to visit Mongolia again someday.

③ The writer got to know Altan's country and culture.

④ The writer felt scared at first when he met a camel.

⑤ The writer had the most fun when he looked at the view of the desert.

---

[26~30] 다음 글을 읽고 물음에 답하시오.

This year, I had a special summer because I visited Mongolia for the first time. My friend Altan is from Mongolia. (A) His grandmother invited me to Ulaanbaatar, the capital of Mongolia. (B)

After a four-hour flight from Seoul, Altan and I arrived at Chinggis Khaan International Airport in Ulaanbaatar. It took thirty minutes by taxi from the airport to Altan's grandmother's house.

Her house is a ger, a traditional Mongolian house. It is a big tent, but it is cozy inside. When we entered, something smelled wonderful. (가)그것은 그녀가 우리를 위해 요리하고 있던 홀호그로에서 나오는 것이다. Khorkhog is a Mongolian barbecue. (C) It is made of lamb and cooked with hot stones. (D) I was moved when Altan said Mongolians serve khorkhog to special guests. It was very delicious. So I asked for more. After dinner, Altan and I went outside to see the night sky. The sky was full of bright stars. (E)

**26** 위 글에서 아래 문장의 밑줄 친 someone에 해당하는 것은? (3점)

> Someone invited the writer to Ulaanbaatar.

① Altan's grandmother

② a taxi driver

③ a special guest

④ a Mongolian

⑤ a cook

**27** 위 글의 내용과 일치하는 것은? (3점)

① Many modern buildings are in Ulaanbaatar, the capital of Mongolia.

② It took four hours to go from Seoul to Chinggis Khaan International Airport.

③ Altan's grandmother lives in a ger which is a modern, big tent.

④ Altan and the writer took a taxi from the airport to Altan's house.

⑤ The writer thought the khorkhog Altan's grandmother made for him was not tasty.

**29** 위 글의 흐름으로 보아 (A)~(E) 중 주어진 문장이 들어가기에 가장 적절한 곳은? (3점)

| I felt like I was in a magical place. |
| --- |

① (A)  ② (B)  ③ (C)

④ (D)  ⑤ (E)

**28** Which question CANNOT be answered from the above? (4점)

① Where is Altan from?

② When did the writer visit Mongolia?

③ What's the capital of Mongolia?

④ Who invited the writer to Ulaanbaatar?

⑤ How did Altan and the writer get to know each other?

**30** 위 글의 밑줄 친 (가)를 바르게 영작한 것은? (3점)

① It was from the thing that she was cooking for us khorkhog.

② It was from the khorkhog she was cooking for us.

③ She was cooking the khorkhog that it was from.

④ The khorkhog was from something that was cooking for us.

⑤ She cooked the khorkhog that it was from the khorkhog.

반
이
름

점수

문항수 : 선택형(25문항) 서술형(5문항)

20 .   .   .

◎ 선택형 문항의 답안은 컴퓨터용 수정 싸인펜을 사용하여 OMR 답안지에 바르게 표기하시오.
◎ 서술형 문제는 답을 답안지에 반드시 검정 볼펜으로 쓰시오.
◎ 총 30문항 100점 만점입니다. 문항별 배점은 각 문항에 표시되어 있습니다.

[경기 ○○중]
[서울 동작구 ○○중]

**01** 다음 빈칸에 공통으로 들어갈 것은?               (3점)

- Tom, _____ in my car. I'll give you ride.
- He didn't _____ off at the right stop again.

① get                    ② take
③ do                     ④ have
⑤ make

[서울 양천구 ○○중]

**02** 다음 중 빈칸에 들어갈 단어로 알맞지 않은 것은?     (3점)

- This is a love story (A)_____ a girl and her horse.
- Let's go grocery shopping. We've run (B)_____ of milk.
- The sun rose (C)_____ the horizon.
- Son, you know your mom cares (D)_____ you a lot.
- What can we make out (E)_____ these ingredients?

*ingredient 재료

① between                ② out
③ over                   ④ about
⑤ of

[서울 동작구 ○○중]

**03** 다음 중 어법상 옳은 것은?                        (3점)

① Look at the boys who is playing soccer.
② I don't know the boy who Jane is talking.
③ The man bought the bike that he doesn't need it.
④ The singer is the man I met at the fashion show.
⑤ He came with a friend whom he comes from China.

[서울 동작구 ○○중]

**04** 다음 중 밑줄 친 어휘의 쓰임이 알맞은 것은?         (3점)

① The last part was <u>disappointed</u>.
② After taking a shower, I felt <u>relaxing</u>.
③ My sister was so <u>exciting</u> about the game.
④ The movie was so <u>bored</u> that I fell asleep.
⑤ We were all <u>amazed</u> at his speed of working.

**05** 다음 주어진 단어를 참고하여 빈칸에 들어갈 어휘를 어법에 맞게 쓰시오. (6점)

> • Mike heard his phone (A)_____.
> (ring)
> • I heard my name (B)_____ in the street. (call)
> • Alice saw Mike (C)_____ toward her. (run)

(A)_____

(B)_____

(C)_____

**06** 다음 문장에서 의미상 가장 잘 통하는 것끼리 연결한 것은? (3점)

> ⓐ The wind was so strong
> ⓑ that everybody likes her
> ⓒ The stairs were so high
> ⓓ that I couldn't open the window
> ⓔ He spoke so fast
> ⓕ that I could not understand him

① ⓐ, ⓑ

② ⓐ, ⓓ

③ ⓒ, ⓑ

④ ⓒ, ⓕ

⑤ ⓔ, ⓓ

**07** 다음 중 어법상 적절하지 않은 문장은? (3점)

① Tom opened the door.

② My bike was stolen last Friday.

③ The picture was drawn by her.

④ The cookies make by her today.

⑤ He was known as a marathon winner.

**08** 다음 중 밑줄 친 부분의 쓰임이 나머지와 다른 하나는? (3점)

① He said <u>that</u> he would invite Sam to dinner.

② My wallet <u>that</u> I lost yesterday is blue.

③ She likes the present <u>that</u> her boyfriend sent to her.

④ The plant <u>that</u> he watered needs a lot of light.

⑤ She is wearing the sunglasses <u>that</u> her mother bought for her.

**09** 다음 두 문장을 'so ~ that' 구문을 사용하여 한 문장으로 쓰시오. (5점)

> (A) The stairs were very high and steep. + I felt dizzy.
> → The stairs were _____.
>
> (B) I was very tired. + I could not work anymore.
> → _____.

(A)_____

(B)_____

**11** 다음 중 어법상 <u>어색한</u> 곳을 찾아 쓰고 바르게 고쳐 쓰시오. (6점)

> (A) Have you ever rode a water slide?
> (B) It would be impossible for she to beat you.
> (C) We are so luck to get seats in this restaurant.

|  | 어색한 것 | 바르게 고친 것 |
|---|---|---|
| (A) | _____ → | _____ |
| (B) | _____ → | _____ |
| (C) | _____ → | _____ |

**10** 다음 두 문장을 주어진 〈조건〉에 맞추어 한 문장으로 쓰시오. (4점)

> • I like the song.
> • My friend uploaded a song on Youtube last week.
>
> ┌─ 조건 ─
> • whom과 which 중 적절한 목적격 관계대명사를 사용한다.
> • 첫 번째 문장을 주절로 쓴다.

→ _____

**12** 다음 중 어법상 <u>잘못된</u> 문장은? (3점)

① She is the girl I told you about.
② The tent that they lived in was very big.
③ The mirror whom you broke is my sister's.
④ Did you see the book which I left on the desk?
⑤ The cookies which Susan made for me were delicious.

Eunseong: Have you ever traveled abroad, Seojin?

(A) Tell me some interesting experiences you had during the trip.
(B) Hmm... let me think. I ate fried spiders!
(C) It was really hot, but I enjoyed the trip.
(D) Yes, I went to Cambodia last summer.
(E) Wow. How did you like it?

Seojin:　　What? You're kidding. How did you like them?
Eunseong: They were really big, so I was a little scared at first. But the taste was okay.
Seojin:　　Really? I cannot imagine eating spiders.
Eunseong: How about you? Have you ever been to another country?
Seojin:　　My family had a plan, but as you know, we cannot go abroad now because of Covid-19.
Eunseong: That's so sad. I hope we can go abroad next year.

[전북 ○○중]

**14** 위 대화를 읽고 주어진 질문에 대한 답으로 가장 적절한 것은?
(3점)

| Why can't Seojin go abroad? |

① Because he is too young.
② Because Covid-19 broke out.
③ Because he hates the hot weather.
④ Because he cannot speak English.
⑤ Because he doesn't like fried spiders.

[충남 ○○중]

**13** 위의 주어진 문장에 자연스럽게 이어지는 대화가 되도록 (A)~(E)를 바르게 배열한 것은?
(3점)

① (A) - (B) - (C) - (D) - (E)
② (A) - (B) - (E) - (D) - (C)
③ (C) - (E) - (B) - (A) - (D)
④ (D) - (E) - (C) - (A) - (B)
⑤ (D) - (E) - (B) - (A) - (C)

[서울 양천구 ○○중]

**15** 위 대화의 내용과 일치하지 않는 것은?
(3점)

① 캄보디아는 매우 더웠다.
② Eunseong은 캄보디아 여행을 즐겼다.
③ Eunseong은 지난 여름에 캄보디아에 갔다.
④ Eunseong은 거미 튀김을 먹을 때 처음에는 겁이 났다.
⑤ Eunseong이 먹은 거미 튀김은 작지만 매우 맛이 있었다.

This is your captain speaking. We _____ just arrived at the _____. Welcome to Mongolia, a country _____ the beauty of nature and culture. The time in Ulaanbaatar is now 4:30 p.m. and there is a _____ of rain. We hope you had a nice _____. Thank you for flying with us. We hope to see you again.

[서울 동작구 ○○중]

**16** Which one is <u>NOT</u> appropriate for the blank?　　(3점)

① fly

② have

③ chance

④ airport

⑤ full of

[서울 양천구 ○○중]

**17** 위 글을 읽고 알 수 있는 사실이 <u>아닌</u> 것은?　　(3점)

① 비행 시간

② 현재의 위치

③ 현지 시각

④ 화자의 직업

⑤ 현지의 예상 날씨

[전북 ○○중]

**18** 다음 글을 읽고 주어진 표의 내용과 일치하는 것은?　　(3점)

A Trip to Mongolia

This year, I had a special summer because I visited Mongolia for the first time. My friend Altan is from Mongolia. His grandmother invited me to Ulaanbaatar, the capital of Mongolia.

After a four-hour flight from Seoul, Altan and I arrived at Chinggis Khaan International Airport in Ulaanbaatar. It took thirty minutes by taxi from the airport to Altan's grandmother's house.

| | ⓐ | ⓑ | ⓒ | ⓓ | ⓔ |
|---|---|---|---|---|---|
| Seoul →Ulaanbaatar (hours) | 2 | 2 | 2 | 4 | 4 |
| Chinggis Khaan airport →Altan's grandmother's house (minutes) | 30 | 10 | 30 | 10 | 30 |
| Transportation | bus | bus | taxi | taxi | taxi |

① ⓐ　　　　② ⓑ　　　　③ ⓒ

④ ⓓ　　　　⑤ ⓔ

[A]

This year, I had a special summer because I visited Mongolia for the first time. My friend Altan is from Mongolia. His grandmother invited me to Ulaanbaatar, the capital of Mongolia.

After a four-hour flight from Seoul, Altan and I arrived at Chinggis Khaan International Airport in Ulaanbaatar. (가)공항에서 Altan의 할머니 집까지는 택시로 30분이 걸렸다.

[B]

Her house is a ger, a traditional Mongolian house. It is a big tent, but it is cozy inside. When we entered, something smelled (A)_____. ㉠It was from the khorkhog that she was cooking for us. Khorkhog is a Mongolian barbecue. It is made (B)_____ lamb and cooked with hot stones. I was moved when Altan said Mongolians serve Khorkhog to special guests. It was so delicious (C)_____ I asked for more. After dinner, Altan and I went outside to see the night sky. The sky was full (D)_____ bright stars. I felt like I was in a magical place.

[C]

During the next three days, Man showed me around and helped me ⓐexperience Mongolian culture. Every moment was fun and ⓑexcited, but I had the most fun when I rode a camel in the Gobi Desert. ㉡_____, I was ⓒscared because the camel was taller than I expected. But once I sat on its back, I soon got used to its movement. From the camel's back, the view of the desert was truly ⓓamazing.

My visit to Mongolia was a special experience in many ways. (나)It gave me a great chance ⓔto get to know my friend's (다)_____ and (라)_____. I want to visit Mongolia again someday.

**19** 위 글 [A]〜[C] 전체의 주제로 가장 알맞은 것은? (3점)

① 몽골의 자연
② 몽골 여행 경험
③ 몽골인 친구 소개
④ 몽골의 가볼 만한 곳 소개
⑤ 몽골의 전통 가옥과 전통 음식

**20** 위 글에 드러난 글쓴이의 심정으로 가장 알맞은 것은? (3점)

① upset
② lonely
③ excited
④ nervous
⑤ depressed

**21** 위 글 [A]의 내용과 일치하지 <u>않는</u> 것은? (3점)

① 몽골의 수도는 울란바토르이다.

② 글쓴이는 Altan과 함께 몽골을 방문했다.

③ Altan의 할머니는 글쓴이를 몽골로 초대하셨다.

④ 글쓴이는 올해 처음으로 몽골을 방문했다.

⑤ 서울에서 Altan 할머니의 댁까지는 모두 네 시간이 걸렸다.

**23** 위 글 [B]의 밑줄 친 ㉠이 가리키는 바로 가장 적절한 것은? (3점)

① a big tent

② the smell

③ hot stones

④ a Mongolian barbecue

⑤ a traditional Mongolian house

**24** 위 글 [C]의 밑줄 친 ⓐ~ⓔ 중 어법상 <u>어색한</u> 것은? (3점)

① ⓐ      ② ⓑ      ③ ⓒ

④ ⓓ      ⑤ ⓔ

**22** 위 글의 빈칸 (A)~(D)에 알맞은 단어로 묶인 것은? (3점)

| | (A) | (B) | (C) | (D) |
|---|---|---|---|---|
| ① | wonderfully | from | which | with |
| ② | wonderfully | from | that | of |
| ③ | wonderfully | of | which | with |
| ④ | wonderful | of | that | of |
| ⑤ | wonderful | of | which | with |

**25** 위 글 [B]~[C]의 내용과 일치하는 것은? (3점)

① 몽골의 전통 가옥은 작지만 아늑했다.

② 글쓴이는 특별한 손님으로 대접받았다.

③ 낙타의 등에서 바라본 밤하늘에는 별이 가득했다.

④ Altan은 글쓴이를 위해 몽골식 바비큐를 요리해 주었다.

⑤ 글쓴이는 Altan의 할머니께 다시 방문하겠다고 약속했다.

**26** 위 글 [C]의 빈칸 ⓒ에 들어갈 표현으로 문맥상 가장 적합한 것은? (3점)

① So
② If
③ Finally
④ At first
⑤ The next morning

**29** 위 글 [C] 문단의 (나)It이 가리키는 것은? (3점)

① Riding a camel
② The Gobi Desert
③ Mongolian culture
④ Visiting Mongolia
⑤ The view of the desert

**27** 위 글의 내용상 글쓴이가 여행 중 가장 즐거웠던 경험은? (3점)

① riding a camel
② eating Khorkhog
③ watching stars
④ visiting a ger
⑤ riding an airplane

**28** 위 글의 밑줄 친 (가)의 우리말과 일치하도록 'take'를 이용하여 어법과 시제에 맞게 문장을 완성하시오. (4점)

(A)공항에서 Altan의 할머니 집까지 택시로 30분이 걸렸다.

→ _____ _____ _____ _____
_____ _____ from the airport to
Altan's grandmother's house.

**30** 위 글 [C] 문단의 빈칸 (다), (라)에 들어갈 가장 적절한 단어를 보기에서 <u>모두</u> 고르면? (3점)

보기
ⓐ animal      ⓑ clothes
ⓒ country     ⓓ culture
ⓔ weather

① ⓐ, ⓑ
② ⓑ, ⓒ
③ ⓒ, ⓓ
④ ⓓ, ⓔ
⑤ ⓐ, ⓔ

◎ 선택형 문항의 답안은 컴퓨터용 수정 싸인펜을 사용하여 OMR 답안지에 바르게 표기하시오.

◎ 서술형 문제는 답을 답안지에 반드시 검정 볼펜으로 쓰시오.

◎ 총 30문항 100점 만점입니다. 문항별 배점은 각 문항에 표시되어 있습니다.

[경기 ○○중]

**01** To which one canNOT the following rule be applied?
(3점)

> \<Rule>
> noun + -y → adjective

① luck

② snow

③ cloud

④ salt

⑤ friend

[서울 동작구 ○○중]

**02** 다음 (A)와 (B)에 해당하는 영영풀이가 있는 문장은? (정답 2개)
(4점)

> (A) to say that an event will happen in the future
> (B) a large piece of furniture with a door used for storing clothes

① Philip still acts like a child.

② My red dress is not in the closet.

③ We can predict danger based on experience.

④ Dave is not only handsome but also intelligent.

⑤ Above all, horse-riding is their favorite activity.

[경기 ○○중]

**03** 다음 빈칸에 알맞은 말을 순서대로 고른 것은?
(3점)

> In the future, you may get (A)_____ a flying car to get (B)_____ Mars. You will get (C)_____ to get (D)_____ of the car. On Mars, people will love to take the train to look around, and nobody wants to get (E)_____.

| | (A) | (B) | (C) | (D) | (E) |
|---|---|---|---|---|---|
| ① | off | up | in | to | out |
| ② | to | out | off | in | up |
| ③ | in | to | up | out | off |
| ④ | out | in | to | off | up |
| ⑤ | up | off | out | on | to |

[경기 ○○중]

**04** Which one is the best for the following blanks in common?
(3점)

> (A) Frank saw Mike _____ toward her.
> (B) I know that _____ every day is good for the health.

① run

② to run

③ ran

④ running

⑤ have run

[경기 ○○중]

**05** 다음 중 밑줄 친 It의 성격이 다른 하나는?
(3점)

① It is not possible to talk on the moon.

② It isn't true that I fell in love with her.

③ It is important to save energy in our lives.

④ It is sunny today, so we can go on a picnic.

⑤ It is dangerous to cross the street without looking around.

**06** 다음 주어진 우리말을 <조건>에 맞게 영작하시오. (5점)

> 여름에 선글라스를 쓰는 것은 도움이 된다.

> <조건>
> 1. helpful, in, to를 반드시 사용한다.
> 2. It 포함 총 9단어로 완성한다.
> 3. 시제와 어법에 맞게 문장을 완성한다.

→ It _____.

**07** 다음 괄호 (A), (B), (C) 안에 들어갈 올바른 형태의 단어들로만 연결된 것은? (4점)

> • Jack heard someone (A)[come / to come] up the stairs.
> • I saw the flowers (B)[picking / picked] at the garden.
> • I can smell the bread (C)[burning / to burn].

|  | (A) | (B) | (C) |
|---|---|---|---|
| ① | come | picking | burning |
| ② | come | picked | burning |
| ③ | come | picked | to burn |
| ④ | to come | picking | burning |
| ⑤ | to come | picked | to burn |

**08** 다음 대화의 빈칸에 들어갈 알맞은 것은? (3점)

> A: There is a smart food-ordering machine over there. _____?
> B: That sounds like fun. We'll be able to order easily and fast by using it.

① How were they?
② How can we use it?
③ What do you mean?
④ Why don't we try it?
⑤ Can you tell me what it is?

**09** 다음 짝지어진 대화 중 <u>어색한</u> 것은? (3점)

① A: Do you have any ideas for our group project?
　B: No, what about you?
② A: The Robot Expo begins next week. Why don't you go with me?
　B: Yes, I'd love to.
③ A: We took lots of pictures during our trip.
　B: We sure did. We took more than 500 pictures.
④ A: This computer looks nice. How much is it?
　B: I will buy it with a special coupon.
⑤ A: What food did you try at the festival?
　B: I had a traditional Chinese dessert, tangyuan.

**10** 다음 대화의 빈칸 (A)에 들어갈 말로 알맞은 것은? (3점)

> B: Why don't we try a new VR game?
> G: (A)_____

① Don't worry.
② What do you think?
③ It looks good on you.
④ That sounds interesting.
⑤ Why do you want to buy it?

## 11 다음 대화의 두 사람이 말하고 있는 프로젝트는 무엇에 관한 것인가? (3점)

B: Do you have any ideas for our group project?
G: No. What about you?
B: I'm thinking we should talk about future jobs. What do you think?
G: That sounds perfect for our project. Let's look for some information on the Internet.

① Future jobs
② Saving energy
③ Some information
④ The Robot Expo
⑤ The science museum

G: Look at those words on the board.
B: What do they mean? ⓐLet's look them up in the dictionary. (A)
G: ⓑWhat about using the AI translator?
B: How do I use it?
G: You point your smartphone camera at the words and ask AI to translate. (B)
B: ⓒCan AI read those words?
Speaker: Sure. I can read any language and translate it. (C)
B: Wow. ⓓThat sounds unbelievably. (D) So, AI, what do those words mean?
Speaker: They mean "Dreams come true!"
B: ⓔThat's fantastic. (E)

## 13 위 대화의 (A)~(E) 중 주어진 대화문이 들어가기에 가장 적절한 곳은? (3점)

And then, you will get an answer.

① (A)　　　② (B)　　　③ (C)
④ (D)　　　⑤ (E)

## 12 Which one is appropriate for the blank? (3점)

B: Have you been to the new Chinese restaurant?
G: Yes. I had dinner there last Saturday.
B: _____?
G: The service was bad. I won't go back there again.

① Was that right?
② You know what?
③ What's the reason?
④ How did you like it?
⑤ What did you mean?

## 14 위 대화의 밑줄 친 ⓐ~ⓔ 중 어법상 어색한 것은? (3점)

① ⓐ　　　② ⓑ　　　③ ⓒ
④ ⓓ　　　⑤ ⓔ

**15** What are they talking about? (3점)

① Their future dreams

② The advantage of AI programs

③ How to use an AI translator

④ The price of a smart phone with an AI translator

⑤ A game between a human and an AI program

[17~19] 다음 대화를 읽고 물음에 답하시오.

> G: Minseok, there is a smart food-ordering machine over there. Why don't we try it?
>
> B: That sounds interesting. We'll be able to order easily and fast by using it.
>
> G: I hope so. By the way, do you think maybe it will be possible (A)_____ robots to replace humans someday?
>
> B: I'm not sure. But we will be free from danger because of robots.
>
> G: What do you mean?
>
> B: Robots can help people in danger. Robots can do the dangerous work so humans don't have to.
>
> G: You're right. (B)_____

**16** 다음 그림의 상황을 가장 잘 나타내는 대화를 고르면? (3점)

① A: Is it possible for you to read 50 novels during summer vacation?

　B: Yes, I think it's possible.

② A: Is it possible for you to read a text with your eyes closed?

　B: No, I don't think it's possible.

③ A: Is it possible for you to travel around Gangwondo by bicycle?

　B: No, I don't think it's possible.

④ A: Is it possible for you to fly a drone?

　B: Yes, I think it's possible.

⑤ A: Is it possible for you to live without a car?

　B: No, I think it's possible.

**17** According to the conversation, where are the boy and the girl? (3점)

① in a restaurant

② in a science lab

③ at a robot expo

④ in a classroom

⑤ at home

**18** Which is the best for (A)? (3점)

① at

② in

③ for

④ of

⑤ with

**19** Which one is the best for (B)? (4점)

① We need to look before we leap.

② We should try to look on the bright side.

③ We should keep in mind that walls have ears.

④ Remember that time and tide wait for no man.

⑤ As you know, actions speak louder than words.

**21** 위 글의 마지막 Jina의 말 다음에 이어질 내용으로 알맞은 것은? (3점)

① 미래의 거실 모습

② 옷을 잘 입는 방법

③ 날씨와 옷의 연관성

④ 미래 영화관의 모습

⑤ 박람회에서 유행한 아이템 소개

**[20~21]** 다음 글을 읽고 물음에 답하시오.

Jina and Suhan are at the World AI Expo. They are entering the AI home.

Suhan: Look at this! It's a house of the future.

Jina: Let's go into the bedroom first. Look, there's a smart closet.

Suhan: I'm standing in front of this screen on the closet door and my clothes keep changing.

Jina: The screen suggests clothes that suit the weather.

Suhan: That's great! We no longer have to worry about dressing for the weather.

Jina: Right. Let's move on to the living room.

**22** 주어진 글 다음에 이어지는 문장의 순서로 가장 적절한 것은? (4점)

AI Beats Human!

An AI program has beaten a human in a baduk match. The AI had a match with Lee Sedol, who is one of the greatest baduk players.

(A) Many people believed it would be impossible for an AI to beat a human player.

(B) Baeduk is a board game, and the rules are difficult to understand.

(C) However, the AI was able to predict Lee's play, and it finally won the game.

(D) People are shocked that an AI can be more intelligent than a human.

① (B) - (A) - (C) - (D)

② (B) - (C) - (D) - (A)

③ (A) - (C) - (B) - (D)

④ (D) - (A) - (B) - (C)

⑤ (D) - (B) - (C) - (A)

**20** 위 글의 내용과 일치하는 것은? (4점)

① There is a smart desk in the AI home.

② Jina and Suhan will move to the kitchen.

③ Jina and Suhan are going to the bedroom first.

④ The screen on the closet door suggests clothes that suit the trend.

⑤ When Suhan stands next to the mirror on the closet door, his clothes keep changing.

| | |
|---|---|
| Suhan: | Oh, I like this music speaker. |
| AI speaker: | I'm not just a music speaker. ⓐI can do more than you can imagine. |
| Jina: | (A)네가 우리를 이해한다는 것을 믿기 어려워. What can you do? |
| AI speaker: | How about watching a movie? I'll play one for you. |
| Suhan: | Look, those smart windows are getting darker. ⓑI feel like I'm in a movie theater. |
| Jina: | What else can you do? |
| AI Speaker: | I can beatbox, too. Here comes, "cats and boots and cats and boots." |
| Suhan: | This car is cool. Let's get in. |
| AI Car: | Welcome. ⓒAre you ready to go? |
| Jina: | Yes, what should we do now? It's my first time to ride in a smart car. |
| AI Car: | You don't need to do anything. I will drive and take you to the next station. |
| Suhan: | Watch out! I see a cat crossing the street. |
| AI Car: | ⓓDon't worry. I have just sensed it. When I sense dangerous situations, I slow down or stop. |
| Jina: | How can you do that? |
| AI Car: | I'm a very intelligent robotic car. I know all about driving. ⓔI can predict danger based on knowledge and experience. |
| Suhan: | How smart! You think and act like a person. You are really like a human. |

**23** 위 글의 우리말 (A)를 영작한 것으로 가장 적절한 것은? (3점)

① It's hard to believe what you understand.

② That you can understand us is hard to me.

③ What you can understand is hard to believe.

④ It's not possible for you to believe his understanding.

⑤ It's hard to believe that you can understand us.

**24** 위 글의 내용과 흐름을 고려할 때, 밑줄 친 ⓐ~ⓔ를 우리말로 해석한 것으로 어색한 것은? (4점)

① ⓐ 나는 네가 상상하는 것 이상을 할 수 있어.

② ⓑ 나는 영화관에 있는 것 같아.

③ ⓒ 갈 준비가 되었니?

④ ⓓ 걱정하지 마.

⑤ ⓔ 나는 지식과 경험에 근거해 위험을 막을 수 있어.

**25** 위 글의 내용과 일치하지 않는 것은? (3점)

① Jina는 스마트 자동차를 처음 탄다.

② Suhan은 음악 스피커가 마음에 든다.

③ Suhan은 스마트 자동차에 감탄했다.

④ 인공지능 스피커는 비트박스를 할 수 없다.

⑤ Suhan은 고양이가 길을 건너는 것을 보았다.

Jina and Suhan are at the World AI Expo. They are entering the AI home.

Suhan: Look at this! It's a house of the future.

Jina: Let's go into the bedroom first. Look, there's a smart closet.

Suhan: I'm standing in front of this screen on the closet door and my clothes keep changing.

Jina: The screen suggests clothes that suit the weather.

Suhan: That's amazing! We no longer have to worry about dressing ⓐ_____ the weather.

Jina: Right. Let's move ⓑ_____ to the living room.

Suhan: Oh, I like this music speaker.

AI Speaker: I'm not just a music speaker. I can do more than you can imagine.

Jina: (A)It's hard to believe that you can understand us. What can you do?

AI Speaker: How about watching a movie? I'll play one for you.

Suhan: Look, those smart windows are getting darker. I feel ⓒ_____ I'm in a movie theater.

Jina: What else can you do?

AI Speaker: I can beatbox, too. Here comes, "cats and boots and cats and boots."

Suhan: You're funny. Good job!

Jina: (B)Hurry! There's a smart car station outside! Let's go and ride in that red car.

Suhan: This car is so cool. Let's get in.

AI Car: Welcome. Are you ready to go?

Jina: Yes, what should we do now? It's my first time to ride in a smart car.

AI Car: You don't need to do anything. I will drive and take you to the next station.

Suhan: Watch ⓓ_____! I see a cat crossing the street.

AI Car: Don't worry. I have just sensed it. When I sense dangerous situations, I slow down or stop.

Jina: How can you do that?

AI Car: I'm a very intelligent robotic car. I know all about driving. I can predict danger based ⓔ_____ knowledge and experience.

Suhan: How smart! You think and act like a person. You are really like a human.

[서울 양천구 ○○중]

**26** 위 글의 밑줄 친 (A)와 쓰임이 같은 것은? (3점)

① It is not what I ordered.

② It is really cold and windy.

③ It is really nice to meet you.

④ Can you make it to the finish line?

⑤ It takes ten minutes from my house to school.

**27** 위 글의 빈칸 ⓐ~ⓔ 중 들어갈 단어로 알맞지 <u>않은</u> 것은? (4점)

① ⓐ : for

② ⓑ : on

③ ⓒ : like

④ ⓓ : out

⑤ ⓔ : in

**29** 위 글에서 AI Speaker가 주어진 것 이상 더 할 수 있는 두 가지를 찾아 우리말로 쓰시오. (4점)

(1) 음악 재생

(2)_____

(3)_____

**30** 위 글의 내용으로 볼 때, 다음 글에 등장하는 수한이의 박람회 감상문 (가)~(마) 중 내용상 <u>잘못된</u> 것은? (3점)

I went to the World AI Expo with Jina.

(가) When I was standing in front of the screen on the smart closet door, my clothes kept changing.

(나) The AI speaker changed the room into a movie theater.

(다) At the car station, I saw a smart car and it took us home.

(라) The car slowed down as soon as it sensed a cat on the road.

(마) It thought and acted like a person. I thought that the AI program was so smart!

① (가)　　　② (나)　　　③ (다)

④ (라)　　　⑤ (마)

**28** 위 글의 흐름으로 보아, 밑줄 친 (B)에 드러난 Jina의 심정으로 알맞은 것은? (3점)

① angry

② scared

③ excited

④ nervous

⑤ disappointed

◎ 선택형 문항의 답안은 컴퓨터용 수정 싸인펜을 사용하여 OMR 답안지에 바르게 표기하시오.
◎ 서술형 문제는 답을 답안지에 반드시 검정 볼펜으로 쓰시오.
◎ 총 30문항 100점 만점입니다. 문항별 배점은 각 문항에 표시되어 있습니다.

[대구 ○○중]
[서울 동작구 ○○중]

**01** 다음 중 밑줄 친 어휘의 쓰임이 <u>어색한</u> 것은?　　(3점)

① Gimchi is a traditional <u>Korean</u> food.
② Pablo Picasso was a <u>Spanish</u> painter.
③ A book written by an <u>England</u> novelist became a best-seller.
④ People around the world enjoy <u>Japanese</u> food such as sushi.
⑤ Many <u>Chinese</u> people believe that the number 8 brings good luck.

[서울 동작구 ○○중]

**02** 다음 빈칸에 들어갈 어휘가 <u>아닌</u> 것은? (순서 상관 없음)　(3점)

- Katy is _____ as a pop singer.
- The students are leading a _____.
- I like the Renaissance style of _____.
- The hat will _____ you from the sun light.
- The _____ of the damage from the fire was great.

① movement
② architecture
③ cost
④ property
⑤ known

[서울 동작구 ○○중]

**03** 다음 중 밑줄 친 어휘의 쓰임이 알맞은 것은?　　(3점)

① She's <u>into</u> making pottery.
② The singer is famous <u>of</u> the song "Memory."
③ Feel free to ask me questions <u>in</u> any time.
④ Can you help me <u>to</u> my history homework?
⑤ I am new here, so I am not familiar <u>of</u> this place.

[서울 동작구 ○○중]

**04** 다음 밑줄 친 어휘를 어법에 맞게 고쳐 쓰시오.　　(6점)

The woman ⓐ<u>wear</u> a red dress opens the window. The sun is shining in the sky. John looks at a leaf ⓑ<u>paint</u> on the wall. John looks happy. The man ⓒ<u>hold</u> a brush sees her happy face.

ⓐ wear → _____
ⓑ paint → _____
ⓒ hold → _____

[서울 동작구 ○○중]

**05** 다음 주어진 단어를 우리말에 맞게 배열하시오.　　(4점)

길을 건너는 사람들은 바빠 보였다.
(필요시 형태를 바꿀 것)
→ _____.
(looked, cross, the, the, people, busy, street)

→ _____

**06** 다음 중 문법적으로 옳은 것을 〈보기〉에서 고른 것은? (3점)

> **보기**
> ⓐ I had my students to study.
> ⓑ She told her dog to wait outside.
> ⓒ Emily advised her friends to go to bed early.
> ⓓ They are expecting her to bringing good news.

① ⓐ, ⓑ
② ⓐ, ⓒ
③ ⓑ, ⓒ
④ ⓑ, ⓓ
⑤ ⓒ, ⓓ

**08** 다음 빈칸에 알맞은 동사의 형태를 바르게 짝지은 것은? (3점)

> • I like the girl (A)_____ to music on the bench.
> • Read the memo (B)_____ in English.
> • The man (C)_____ a brush sees her happy face.

|  | (A) | (B) | (C) |
|---|---|---|---|
| ① | listening | writing | holding |
| ② | listening | written | held |
| ③ | listening | written | holding |
| ④ | listened | writing | held |
| ⑤ | listened | written | holding |

**07** 다음 대화에 대한 상황을 나타내는 문장 중 어법상 옳지 않은 것은? (3점)

> Cinderella: When is the party?
> Drizella: This weekend.
> Cinderella: Take me to the party, please.
> Drizella: You have to clean the house first.

① Cinderella wants to go to the party.
② Cinderella must clean the house first.
③ Drizella doesn't let Cinderella go to the party.
④ Cinderella asks Drizella to take her to the party.
⑤ Drizella doesn't allow Cinderella go to the party.

**09** 다음 대화를 읽고 상황을 나타내는 문장을 완성하시오. (5점)

> A: Will you marry me?
> B: Yes, I will.
> A: Can you wait for me?
> B: Yes. Please come back soon.
> *A: Tom / B: Jane

> (A) Tom asked _____.
> Tom은 그녀에게 자기와 결혼해 줄 것을 부탁했다. (Tom asked 포함 총 6단어)

> (B) Tom _____.
> Tom은 그녀가 자기를 기다려 줄 것을 원했다. (Tom 포함 총 7단어)

(A)_____

(B)_____

**10** 다음 밑줄 친 단어 (A), (B), (C)의 형태가 바르게 짝지어진 것은? (3점)

> The woman (A)<u>wear</u> a pink dress opens the window. The sun is shining in the sky. Johnsy looks at a leaf (B)<u>paint</u> on the wall. Johnsy looks happy. The man (C)<u>hold</u> a brush sees her happy face.

|     | (A)      | (B)      | (C)     |
|-----|----------|----------|---------|
| ①   | wearing  | painted  | holding |
| ②   | wearing  | painting | held    |
| ③   | wore     | painted  | holding |
| ④   | wore     | painting | holding |
| ⑤   | wore     | painted  | held    |

**11** 다음 중 대화의 흐름이 <u>어색한</u> 것은? (3점)

① A: Do you know anything about Korean history?
　 B: I don't know much about it, but I'm interested in it.

② A: I'm going to go to Changdeokgung with my Chinese friend.
　 B: I won't waste my money on snacks.

③ A: Could you explain this painting?
　 B: Sure. It's *Two Sisters* by Renoir.

④ A: What is this poem about?
　 B: It's about a boy missing his hometown.

⑤ A: Can you help me with my history homework?
　 B: Sure. Why don't we go to the library?

[12~13] 다음 대화를 읽고 물음에 답하시오.

> B: Do you know anything about a dol party?
> G: Yes. It's the birthday party for a one-year-old baby.
> B: (A)_____?
> G: Well, the family members get together for the party, and the birthday baby wears a hanbok.
> B: That sounds interesting.
> G: The family members share food and wish for a long life for the baby. It's a Korean tradition.
> 　　　　　　　　　　　　　　　　　*B: Tom / G: Amy

**12** According to the dialog, which statement is true? (3점)

① The family members share their party food.
② The family members don't gather for the party.
③ The family members wish for a long life for the guests.
④ The family members have to wear a hanbok for the party.
⑤ The dol party is a birthday party for celebrating 100 days.

**13** 위 대화의 빈칸 (A)에 들어갈 말로 알맞은 것은? (3점)

① When did you know about it?
② Could you tell me more about it?
③ Have you had a dol party before?
④ When are they going to wear a hanbok?
⑤ How about having the birthday party?

**14** 다음 글의 밑줄 친 ⓐ~ⓔ 중 문맥상 낱말의 쓰임이 적절하지 않은 것은?　　　　(4점)

A woman moved into the building next to Joe's store. She opened up a new store. Many people started to go to the woman's new store instead of Joe's store. Only few people ⓐset foot in Joe's store. As the time went by, his food business ⓑfell off. Joe decided to prepare a surprising event which provided pizza 50% off. It seemed to be successful at the beginning, but the sale kept ⓒincreasing. People still ⓓpreferred the woman's burger, and her store became popular. After all, Joe couldn't stand anymore and decided to ⓔquit his business.

① ⓐ　　　　② ⓑ　　　　③ ⓒ

④ ⓓ　　　　⑤ ⓔ

**15** 위 대화의 (A)에 들어가기에 가장 알맞은 표현은?　　(3점)

① harmony

② harmony in

③ in harmony

④ to harmony in

⑤ in harmony with

**16** 위 대화의 밑줄 친 ⓐ~ⓔ 중, 어법상 어색한 것은?　　(3점)

① ⓐ　　　　② ⓑ　　　　③ ⓒ

④ ⓓ　　　　⑤ ⓔ

[15~16] 다음 대화를 읽고 물음에 답하시오.

A: What are hanoks?
B: Hanoks are traditional Korean houses. They are ⓐdesigned to be (A)~와 조화를 이루다 nature.
A: Could you explain ⓑa little more about them?
B: Hanoks are cool in the summer and warm in the winter.
C: That ⓒsound interesting. Where can I see these traditional houses?
B: There's a hanok village near here.
A: How about going there and seeing the hanoks?
C: Good idea! How can we ⓓget there?
B: You can ⓔtake Bus Number 5 over there at the bus stop.

**17** 다음 글의 빈칸에 들어갈 말로 가장 적절한 것은?　　(3점)

An Yongbok lived during the Joseon Dynasty, and his job was catching fish. When he was fishing, he saw the Japanese people fishing near Ulleungdo and Dokdo which were part of Korea. Finally, in 1696, the Japanese ruler officially told the Japanese people to _____.
He did his best to protect Ulleungdo and Dokdo, which led to a good result.

① prepare to attack Joseon

② take a break for a second

③ get permission to take a trip

④ keep fishing as long as they want

⑤ stay away from Ulleungdo and Dokdo

Jeong Segwon helped the independence movement in many ways. For example, he built the office building for the Joseon Language Society and (A)[encouraged / discouraged] its efforts to keep the Joseon language alive. When the Joseon Language Affair happened, he was caught by the police and suffered a lot. Japanese officials (B)[asked / forced] him to build Japanese houses. He said, "I don't know how to build Japanese houses." An official said, "You know how to build hanoks, so you can build Japanese houses, too." He knew a lot about architecture, but he didn't want to do what the Japanese told him to do. The cost was high. His business went bad, and he (C)[gained / lost] his property. Above all, in part, thanks to Jeong Segwon, _____.

**19** 위 글의 빈칸에 들어갈 말로 가장 적절한 것은? [대전 ○○중] (3점)

① the Joseon language became endangered

② we can hand down Korean traditions

③ the Japanese kept building Japanese houses

④ Korea becomes one of the advanced nations

⑤ various hanoks developed and spread worldwide

**18** 위 글의 (A), (B), (C)에서 문맥상 낱말의 쓰임이 적절한 것끼리 짝지은 것은? [대전 ○○중] (4점)

| | (A) | (B) | (C) |
|---|---|---|---|
| ① | encouraged | made | gained |
| ② | encouraged | forced | lost |
| ③ | discouraged | made | lost |
| ④ | discouraged | forced | lost |
| ⑤ | discouraged | forced | gained |

**20** 위 글의 내용을 간략히 요약했을 때, 빈칸 (A), (B)에 들어갈 말로 가장 적절한 것은? [대전 ○○중] (3점)

Jeong Segwon supported Joseon's independence and (A)_____ what the Japanese told him to do, which made his business (B)_____.

| | (A) | (B) |
|---|---|---|
| ① | refused | weaken |
| ② | refused | successful |
| ③ | accepted | successful |
| ④ | accepted | weaken |
| ⑤ | took | worse |

Jeong Segwon was a businessman who founded Geonyangsa in 1920 ⓐ<u>that</u> built houses. At the time, Korea was ruled by Japan, and the Japanese were changing Gyeongseong to fit their taste. Many Japanese moving into Gyeongseong were building Japanese or Western houses. They pressed Jeong Segwon ⓑ<u>to help</u> what they were doing. He wanted to protect the hanok and help people who ⓒ<u>were suffered</u> from this pressure.

He said, "People are power. We Joseon people should keep Jongno and not let the Japanese ⓓ<u>step</u> in here." He bought the land between Gyeongbokgung and Changdeokgung. There he built small, modern hanoks for the people. Through his efforts, we now see ⓔ<u>that</u> Bukchon is filled with its beautiful hanoks.

*Jeong Segwon = J.S

## 21 위 글의 밑줄 친 ⓐ~ⓔ에서 어법상 어색한 것은? (4점)

① ⓐ      ② ⓑ      ③ ⓒ

④ ⓓ      ⑤ ⓔ

## 22 위 글을 읽고 유추할 수 <u>없는</u> 것은? (3점)

① Geonyangsa was a company building houses.

② Many Japanese were pushed to move into Joseon to build Japanese houses.

③ J.S didn't give up protecting hanoks and did his best.

④ J.S thought Joseon people should kick out the Japanese from Jongno.

⑤ J.S built modern hanoks, which made it possible to see today's Bukchon.

## 23 다음 글의 밑줄 친 부분이 가리키는 대상이 <u>다른</u> 것은? (3점)

Have you been to Bukchon? You can see a beautiful hanok village ⓐ<u>there</u>. Now ⓑ<u>it</u> is popular with tourists who want to see Korea's past. Even many foreigners who visit Korea consider ⓒ<u>it</u> natural that they upload a picture of hanoks onto their SNS. Many people choose ⓓ<u>this place</u> as one of the best-known tourists attractions in Korea. However, not many people know that ⓔ<u>it</u> was created through one man's efforts. That man was Jeong Segwon, known as the King of Architecture in Gyeongseong

① ⓐ      ② ⓑ      ③ ⓒ

④ ⓓ      ⑤ ⓔ

Have you been to Bukchon? There is a beautiful hanok village in Bukchon. It is popular (가)_____ tourists who want to see Korea's past. (A)_____, not many people know that Bukchon was created through one man's efforts. That man was Jeong Segwon, known as the King of Architecture in Gyeongseong.

Jeong Segwon was a businessman who founded Geonyangsa in 1920. At the time, Korea was ruled by Japan, and the Japanese were changing Gyeongseong to fit their taste. Many Japanese ⓐ moving into Gyeongseong were building Japanese or Western houses. Jeong Segwon wanted to protect the hanok and ⓑhelp the suffering people. He said, "People are power. We Joseon people should keep Jongno and not let the Japanese ⓒset foot here." He bought the land between Gyeongbokgung and Changdeokgung. There he built small, modern hanoks for the people. Through his efforts, we now have Bukchon filled (나)_____ its beautiful hanoks.

Jeong Segwon helped the independence movement in many ways. For example, he built the office building for the Joseon Language Society and supported its efforts to keep the Joseon language alive. When the Joseon Language Affair happened, he ⓓcaught by the police and suffered a lot. Japanese officials pressed him to build Japanese houses. He said, "I don't know how to build Japanese houses." An official said, "You know how to build hanoks, so you can build Japanese houses, too." But he did not do what the Japanese told him ⓔto do. The cost was high. His business fell off, and he lost his property. However, in part, thanks to Jeong Segwon, the traditions of Korea still live with us today.

**24** Which one is the best for the blank (A)? (3점)

① For instance
② As a result
③ Therefore
④ On the other hand
⑤ Also

**25** 위 글의 빈칸 (가), (나)에 공통으로 들어갈 단어를 활용하여 문장을 만들 때 알맞지 않은 문장은? (4점)

① She can text _____ her eyes closed.
② This community helps people _____ danger.
③ Don't forget to take an umbrella _____ you.
④ Can you help me _____ my history homework?
⑤ Hanoks are designed to be in harmony _____ nature.

**26** 위 글의 밑줄 친 동사의 형태가 <u>어색한</u> 것은? (3점)

① ⓐ      ② ⓑ      ③ ⓒ

④ ⓓ      ⑤ ⓔ

**29** 위 글을 읽고 정세권이 한 일이 <u>아닌</u> 것을 고르면? (3점)

① to keep Jongno

② to protect hanoks

③ to help suffering people

④ to change Gyeongseong

⑤ to build modern hanoks

**27** 위 글을 읽고 정세권에 대한 설명 중 옳은 것은? (3점)

① He built many Western buildings.

② He believed that people are power.

③ He was not interested in Joseon Language Affair.

④ He couldn't create Bukchon by himself.

⑤ He did not want to help the independence movement.

**30** 다음은 위 글을 읽은 후 학생들의 반응이다. 다음 중 <u>잘못된</u> 것은? (3점)

① Hyojung: I feel sad to know that many people don't know Jeong Segwon today.

② Yooa: Jeong Segwon protected not only the hanbok but also Jongno.

③ Arin: Jeong Segwon also paid much money to protect his property.

④ Binnie: I'm upset to know that Jeong Segwon suffered from the Japanese officials.

⑤ Mimi: Through Jeong Segwon's effort, we can enjoy Bukchon and its beautiful hanoks

**28** Which is the best title of the passages above? (3점)

① The Korean Tradition at the Present Time

② The History of a Hanok Village in Bukchon

③ The Works of the Joseon Language Society

④ The Independence Movements Against Japan

⑤ Jeong Segwon's Effort as an independence Activist

# 2학년 영어 2학기 기말고사(9과) 1회

문항수 : 선택형(28문항)　서술형(2문항)　　20 ．　．　．

◎ 선택형 문항의 답안은 컴퓨터용 수정 싸인펜을 사용하여 OMR 답안지에 바르게 표기하시오.
◎ 서술형 문제는 답을 답안지에 반드시 검정 볼펜으로 쓰시오.
◎ 총 30문항 100점 만점입니다. 문항별 배점은 각 문항에 표시되어 있습니다.

[대구 ○○중]
[서울 양천구 ○○중]

**01** 다음 빈칸에 공통으로 들어갈 단어로 알맞은 것은?　　(3점)

- The women's _____ first started in New Zealand.
- There is a cello solo in the second _____.

① piece
② affair
③ harmony
④ movement
⑤ community

[서울 양천구 ○○중]

**02** 다음 각각의 빈칸에 들어갈 수 <u>없는</u> 단어는?　　(3점)

- There were crowds of people waiting to get ⓐ_____ the bus.
- What time do you get ⓑ_____ in the morning?
- How can I get ⓒ_____ the supermarket?
- The kids didn't want to get ⓓ_____ the horses.
- The family members get ⓔ_____ for a dol party.

① up　　　　② to
③ off　　　　④ with
⑤ together

[서울 동작구 ○○중]

**03** 다음 우리말에 맞게 문장을 완성하시오.　　(5점)

(A) _____ _____ your help, we were able to do the work.
(너의 도움 덕분에 우리는 그 일을 할 수 있었다.)

(B) Judy is _____ _____ a child. She is over 18 now.
(Judy는 더 이상 어린애가 아니다.)

(A)_____

(B)_____

[서울 동작구 ○○중]

**04** 다음 두 문장을 한 문장으로 만드시오.　　(5점)

I'm not sure. + What did the man steal from this store?
→ I'm not sure _____.

→ _____

[서울 동작구 ○○중]

**05** Which one is grammatically correct?　　(3점)

① This is the reason why he is late.
② I like Sundays where I can sleep till late.
③ Tell me the way how you solved the problem.
④ Can you see the table on that he put the apple?
⑤ Monday is the day which I wash clothes.

## 06 다음 중 어법상 <u>잘못된</u> 것은? (3점)

① Daniel asked me where my pen was.

② Do you know what time the movie starts?

③ I'm not sure who the girl standing over there is.

④ Please tell me where were you during the weekend.

⑤ I remember when I went to a concert for the first time.

## 07 다음 중 어법상 <u>어색한</u> 문장은? (3점)

① The sun is shining in the sky.

② He gave cookies to the crying baby.

③ Johnsy looked at the leaf painting on the wall.

④ The man holding a brush sees her happy face.

⑤ The woman wearing a pink dress opens the window.

## 08 다음 중 어법상 <u>어색한</u> 문장은? (3점)

① I don't know when Mom left home.

② Please tell me when the zoo closes.

③ Do you know how old Mr. Martin is?

④ Do you know what are the title of the book?

⑤ I want to know when the English lesson finishes.

## 09 다음 중 어법상 올바른 문장의 개수를 고른 것은? (4점)

ⓐ That house build on the hill is beautiful.

ⓑ We are expecting Tom bring the good news.

ⓒ John's parents did not let John going out at night.

ⓓ He was one of the most famous scientists in the world.

ⓔ I'm planning to have a concert at the Super Stadium.

ⓕ It is popular with the tourists who want to see Korea's past.

① 2개　　　② 3개　　　③ 4개

④ 5개　　　⑤ 없음

## 10 다음 중 어법상 올바른 문장의 개수는? (3점)

ⓐ Tom is the student which every teacher likes.

ⓑ We're expecting Tom bring the good news.

ⓒ My parents didn't let me going out at night.

ⓓ BTS is planning to have a concert in Seoul.

ⓔ I miss the day which we went on a picnic at the lake.

ⓕ Do you know who the girl singing over there is?

① 2개　　　② 3개　　　③ 4개

④ 5개　　　⑤ 없음

## 11 다음 중 어법상 <u>어색한</u> 문장은? (3점)

① I know the town when she grew up.

② This is the park where I walk my dog.

③ I didn't know the time when she arrived at the airport.

④ Bill knows a good restaurant where we can have lunch.

⑤ Sue can't forget the day when she first opened her store.

## 12 다음 중 대화의 흐름이 <u>어색한</u> 것은? (3점)

① A: How about going to the new shoe store this weekend? Can you make it?

B: Yes. That would be great.

② A: Let's go to a PC room after the final exam. Can you make it at 2 p.m.?

B: Yes. I plan to go out with my girlfriend in the afternoon.

③ A: We are going to go to Daejeoncheon to ride a bike.

B: Don't forget to wear sunscreen.

④ A: The news said that it's very cold today.

B: Don't forget to put on a coat and neck warmer.

⑤ A: A lot of people have gotten Covid-19 again these days.

B: Don't forget to wear a mask at school.

## [13~15] 다음 대화를 읽고 물음에 답하시오.

G: What are you listening to?

B: Classical music. I'm going to a concert tomorrow and I'd like to know about the music before I go. (A)

G: I guess it's more enjoyable if you know the music. (B)

B: Actually, I don't want to clap at the wrong time.

G: Don't you just clap when the music stops? (C)

B: No. In classical music, one piece of music may have several pauses. (D)

G: I see. Make sure you don't forget to clap at the real ending. By the way, (가)_____ our soccer practice tomorrow at 4:00? (E)

B: Sure. I'll come to the practice after the concert finishes.

G: Okay. See you then.

*G: 여자/ B: 남자

## 13 위 대화의 내용과 일치하지 <u>않는</u> 것은? (4점)

① 남자는 내일 콘서트에 갈 예정이다.

② 여자는 음악을 알고 가면 더 즐거울 것이라고 말한다.

③ 남자의 말에 따르면, 음악 작품마다 여러 멈추는 부분이 있다.

④ 여자는 남자에게 연주의 첫 부분에서 박수치는 걸 잊지 말라고 조언한다.

⑤ 남자와 여자는 모두 내일 4시에 밴드 연습에 참여할 예정이다.

**14** 위 대화의 (A)~(E) 중 주어진 말이 들어갈 위치로 알맞은 곳은? (3점)

> You should wait and clap at the very end.

① (A)　　　② (B)　　　③ (C)

④ (D)　　　⑤ (E)

**15** Which one is proper in the blank (가)? (3점)

① can you make to

② can you make it to

③ what do you like to

④ can you explain why

⑤ why do you come to

**16** 다음이 자연스러운 대화가 되도록 ⓐ~ⓓ를 바르게 배열한 것은? (3점)

> ⓐ How did you like it?
> ⓑ How was your vacation?
> ⓒ Great. I went to Dokdo with my family.
> ⓓ It was amazing. I want to visit there again.

① ⓐ-ⓒ-ⓑ-ⓓ

② ⓐ-ⓓ-ⓑ-ⓒ

③ ⓑ-ⓒ-ⓐ-ⓓ

④ ⓑ-ⓓ-ⓐ-ⓒ

⑤ ⓓ-ⓒ-ⓑ-ⓐ

[17~18] 다음 글을 읽고 물음에 답하시오.

Let's go back in time and take a look at one of Mozart's concerts in the 18th century. You are in a bright hall inside a nobleman's house. Mozart is playing the piano. Surprisingly, however, the audiences are eating, drinking, and talking freely. They whistle and clap anytime. You are shocked by their bad manners, but Mozart himself would be surprised by today's quiet audiences. Concerts in Mozart's time were mostly social events. They were good places to meet people. (A)＿＿＿＿＿＿＿＿ ＿＿＿＿＿＿＿＿＿＿＿＿＿＿＿.

**17** What's the fact that we can know in the above passage? (4점)

① Mozart blamed the audience for making noise.

② Concerts in Mozart's time were mostly social events.

③ The audiences in 18th century only clapped after the music finished.

④ Audiences in the 18th century did not eat or drink during the concert.

⑤ Scenes at concerts in the 18th century were not different from those of today.

**18** Which one is proper in the blank (A)? (3점)

① Nobody made a sound.

② Noise was just part of the concert.

③ Audience could break the magic of the moment.

④ Mozart supported the audience for making noise.

⑤ The orchestra started to play Mozart's piano concerto.

Today's quiet concerts began in the 19th century (A)_____ many big concert halls were built. More people, not just noblemen, went to concerts. Artists were no longer dependent on noblemen for money. The artists had more power over their works and started to use their increased power. For example, Wagner blamed the audience for making noise. After some time, a no-clapping-between-movements rule appeared.

As a result, here we are today, very quiet and serious. (가)We do not know. What will concerts look like in the future because manners change with time. For now, however, if you want to enjoy classical music concerts, just remember this: Enjoy the music, but do not disturb those around you.

[충남 ○○중]

**20** 위 글의 밑줄 친 두 문장 (가)를 한 문장으로 만들 때 옳은 것은? (3점)

① We do not know what concerts will look like in the future

② We do not know what concerts looked like in the future

③ We do not know that concerts look like in the future

④ What we don't know look like in the future

⑤ What will concerts look like in the future

[대전 ○○중]

**21** 위 글에서 필자가 주장하는 바로 가장 적절한 것은? (4점)

① It is necessary to study the history of classical concert manners.

② Artists should be respected for their great efforts in their works.

③ Everyone has a different point of view of what good manners are.

④ We need not to think how the future classical concert will look like.

⑤ The important rule in concerts is behaving appropriately, not making others annoyed.

[충남 ○○중]

**19** 위 글의 빈칸 (A)에 들어갈 단어는? (3점)

① where　　　② what

③ when　　　④ in which

⑤ why

[22~25] 다음 글을 읽고 물음에 답하시오.

> Watching a classical music concert can be a memorable experience if you _____ these tips in mind.
>
> Before You Go In:
> · Plan to _____ 20-30 minutes before concert time.
> · 무슨 음악이 연주될 것인지 알아보아라.
>
> When Music Is Playing:
> · Turn off your cellphone!
> · Stay quiet. No talking, whistling, singing _____ or humming.
> · Don't clap until the whole piece is _____. It is safe to clap when the _____ starts clapping.

**23** 위의 공연 관람 예절에 대한 안내문의 내용과 일치하는 것은? (3점)

① 안내문의 내용을 따르지 않으면 공연에서 퇴장당할 수 있다.
② 공연 시간에 꼭 맞추어 공연장에 도착해야 한다.
③ 휴대폰은 반드시 꺼야만 한다.
④ 공연 중에 노래를 따라 불러도 좋다.
⑤ 다른 관객들이 박수를 치기 전에는 박수를 쳐서는 안된다.

**24** 위 글의 제목으로 가장 적절한 것은? (4점)

① Things Not to Do at a Concert
② Tips for Good Concert Manners
③ A Guide to Get Concert Tickets
④ When to Clap in a Classical Concert
⑤ What You Should Do during a Concert

**22** Which one is NOT proper for the blanks? (순서 관계 없음) (3점)

① arrive
② audience
③ over
④ keep
⑤ to

**25** 위 글의 밑줄 친 우리말과 일치하도록 〈보기〉의 단어를 모두 활용하여 영작할 때 5번째에 오는 단어는? (4점)

> **보기**
> find / music / will / played / what / out / be

① be          ② out          ③ will
④ what          ⑤ music

(A) Imagine yourself at a classical music concert. The orchestra starts to play one of Mozart's piano concertos. The concert hall is dark and silent. Nobody makes a sound. (B) Everybody looks serious. The audiences only clap after the concerto finishes. This is a familiar scene at concerts today. (C)

Let's go back in time and take a look at one of Mozart's concerts in the 18th century. (D) You are in a bright hall inside a nobleman's house. Mozart is playing the piano. Surprisingly, however, the audiences are eating, drinking, and talking freely. They whistle and clap at any time. You are shocked by their bad manners, but Mozart himself would be surprised by today's quiet audiences. Concerts in Mozart's time were mostly social events. They were good places to meet people. (E)

[경기 ○○중]

**27** 위 글의 내용을 아래와 같이 요약하고자 한다. 빈칸 (A), (B)에 들어갈 말로 가장 적절한 것은? (3점)

In today's classical music concert, the concert hall is dark and silent, and the audiences are (A)_____. In Mozart's time, however, the concert hall was bright and (B)_____ since it was a place for social events.

|   | (A) | (B) |
|---|-----|-----|
| ① | delightful | beautiful |
| ② | speechless | cozy |
| ③ | confident | spectacular |
| ④ | moved | quiet |
| ⑤ | serious | noisy |

[충남 ○○중]

**26** 위 글의 흐름으로 볼 때 주어진 문장이 들어갈 위치로 가장 적절한 곳은? (3점)

Noise was just part of the concert.

① (A)  ② (B)  ③ (C)

④ (D)  ⑤ (E)

[충남 ○○중]

**28** 위 글의 내용과 일치하지 <u>않는</u> 것은? (3점)

|   | [현재 모습] | [과거 모습] |
|---|-----------|-----------|
| ① | dark hall | bright hall |
| ② | just clap | whistle at any time |
| ③ | for study | for social event |
| ④ | silent | noisy |
| ⑤ | concert hall | nobleman's house |

Classical Music Concert Etiquette

### 1. Mind your Time
Plan to arrive 20-30 minutes before concert time. Give yourself enough time to find your seat.

### 2. Stay Quiet
No talking, whispering, whistling, singing along or humming.

### 3. Hold your Applause
Don't clap until the whole piece is over. If you do not know the exact timing for clapping, it is safe to clap when the audience starts clapping.

### 4. _____
During the concert, there is a short break when you can leave your seat. If you need to, you can go to the restroom, call someone, or get a drink or a snack outside the concert hall.

### 5. Dress Appropriately.
It's best to wear something that's in between; not too casual and yet not too formal. For example, wear something that you would wear for a job interview or a business meeting.

[대전 ○○중]

**29** 위 글의 내용을 잘못 이해한 사람은? (3점)

① 나리: 콘서트가 시작하기 20~30분 전에 도착해야 해.

② 지혜: 옆 사람에게 속삭이거나 노래를 따라 불러서는 안 돼.

③ 규동: 박수는 다른 관객이 칠 때 치는 게 안전하겠구나.

④ 원석: 공연 중간 쉬는 시간에는 화장실만 다녀올 수 있네.

⑤ 민주: 너무 캐주얼한 옷보다는 면접이나 비즈니스 회의에 입는 옷을 입고 가면 돼.

[대전 ○○중]

**30** 위 글의 빈칸에 들어갈 내용으로 적절한 것은? (3점)

① Alarm off, Flash off

② Listen Attentively

③ Show Respect to Others

④ Take Advantage of Intermissions

⑤ Find out What Music Will Be Played

# 정답 및 해설

## Lesson 5 (중간)

| | | | | |
|---|---|---|---|---|
| 01 ⑤ | 02 ④ | 03 ② | 04 ⑤ | 05 ② |
| 06 was thrown by the man | | 07 ④ | 08 ④ | 09 ① | 10 ④ |
| 11 doesn't she? | | 12 ① | 13 ④ | 14 ② | 15 ④ | 16 ③ |
| 17 ③ | 18 ④ | 19 ④ | 20 ③ | 21 ③ | 22 ⑤ | 23 ② | 24 ⑤ |
| 25 ④ | 26 ② | 27 ③ | 28 ④ | 29 ④ |

**01** ⑤ suggest는 '제안하다'라는 뜻을 가진 동사이다.

**02** ④ last는 '지속하다'라는 뜻을 가진 동사이다.

**03** last year가 있으므로 is made를 was made로 고쳐야 한다.

**04** 동사 wear의 시제 변화형은 wear-wore-worn이다.

**05** ① is he → isn't he / ③ will he → won't he / ④ don't she → doesn't she / ⑤ don't you → can't you로 고쳐야 어법상 적절한 문장이 된다.

**06** 막대기가 남자에 의해 던져졌다는 의미의 문장이다. 막대기라는 대상이 주어 자리에 있으므로 동사는 과거시제의 수동태인 was thrown이 되는 것이 적절하다.

**07** ① cleaned → is cleaned / ② destroyed → was destroyed / ③ Where did your dog found → Where was your dog found / ⑤ made → were made로 고쳐야 어법상 적절한 문장이 된다.

**08** 부가의문문은 평서문 뒤에 쓰여 평서문의 내용을 다시 한번 확인하는 문장이다. 평서문이 긍정문일 때 부가의문문은 부정문으로, 평서문이 부정문일 때 부가의문문은 긍정문으로 쓴다. 따라서 <보기> 문장의 부가의문문으로는 'didn't you'가 들어가는 것이 적절하다.

**09** (A) A가 B에게 서핑과 수영 중에 어떤 스포츠를 더 좋아하냐고 묻고 있다. 따라서 better가 적절하다.
(B) B가 서핑가는 것을 좋아한다고 대답하고 있으므로 동사 go가 적절하다.

**10** 위 대화에 따르면, 영지는 지연이에게 솔미가 지난달에 한국으로 돌아왔다고("No, she came back to Korea last month.") 언급하고 있다.

**11** 부가의문문은 평서문 뒤에 쓰여 평서문의 내용을 다시 한번 확인하는 문장이다. 평서문이 긍정문일 때 부가의문문은 부정문으로, 평서문이 부정문일 때 부가의문문은 긍정문으로 쓴다.

**12** "I can't wait to ~"는 "빨리 ~하고 싶다"라는 뜻으로 어떤 일에 대한 기대감을 나타내는 표현이다. 따라서 빈칸 (B)에는 ① to가 적절하다.

**13** 위 대화에 따르면, 지연이는 영지에게 오늘(수요일) 오후에 집으로 놀러올 수 있냐고 물었고 영지는 승낙했다.

**14** 위 대화에 따르면, 여학생은 반려 동물을 들이는 것을 생각 중이라고 말하고 있다. 따라서 빈칸에는 ② getting이 적절하다.

**15** 위 대화에 따르면 남학생은 한 마리의 개와 고양이를 키우고 있다. ④ The boy will take an animal to the girl.(남학생은 여학생에게 어떤 동물을 가져갈 것이다.)는 언급된 바 없다.

**16** "표를 샀니?"라는 A의 질문에 대해 "응! 난 경기를 볼 필요가 없어."라는 B의 대답은 흐름상 자연스럽지 않다.

**17** 위 글에서는 ③ What will Jiheon do this weekend?(지현이는 이번 주말에 무엇을 할 예정인가?)에 대해서는 언급된 바 없다.

**18** '너무 ~해서 …하다'라는 의미의 표현으로 'so+형용사/부사+that+주어+동사'를 쓸 수 있다.

**19** 위 글에서는 ④ How long did the writer visit Suncheon?(글 쓴이는 얼마나 오래 순천을 방문했는가?)에 대해서는 언급된 바 없다.

**20** support는 '지원하다' 또는 '응원하다'라는 뜻을 가진 동사이다. 따라서 주어진 우리말을 영작하면, "③ Which team do you support?"라고 할 수 있다.

**21** "I can't wait."는 "기다릴 수가 없다."라는 뜻으로 어떤 일에 대한 기대감을 나타내는 표현이다.

**22** 위 대화에서 Alex에 따르면, Cobras 팀의 홈 경기가 다음 주 토요일에 있을 것이라고("Okay. They have a game next Saturday.") 언급되었다.

**23** 아버지는 과거에는 선수들의 등번호가 선수들이 타석에 서는 순서로 결정되었다고 말하고 있다. 따라서 과거 시제의 수동형 동사인 ② were determined가 적절하다.

**24** be at bat: 타석에 서다

**25** 위 글에 따르면, 지훈이가 제일 좋아하는 선수가 공을 쳤고 그것이 빠르게 날라 갔다고('Crack! The ball flies fast. It is going, going, going, gone!') 말하고 있다.

**26** 부가의문문은 평서문 뒤에 쓰여 평서문의 내용을 다시 한번 확인하는 문장이다. 평서문이 긍정문일 때 부가의문문은 부정문으로, 평서문이 부정문일 때 부가의문문은 긍정문으로 쓴다. 따라서 주어와 동사가 'this is ~'인 문장의 부가의문문으로는 ② isn't it이 어법상 적절하다.

**27** ⓐ be동사인 are가 쓰였으므로 현재분사인 wearing이 적절하다. / ⓑ Does로 시작하는 일반동사의 의문문이므로 동사원형인 wear가 적절하다. / ⓒ 동사 started가 쓰였으므로 to wear 또는 wearing이 들어가는 것이 적절하다.

**28** 위 글에 따르면, 지안이가 원정팀은 항상 어두운 색을 입는지 물어보았고, 지훈이는 그것이 규칙이라고 대답했다.

**29** 위 글에 따르면, 홈팀은 밝은 색의 유니폼을 입으며 원정팀은 항상

어두운 색의 유니폼을 입는다고('Home teams have bright uniforms and visiting teams have dark uniforms.') 언급되어 있다.

## Lesson 6 (중간)

1회

01 ③  02 ③  03 ④  04 ②
05 (1) The cookies were delicious.
   (2) Susan made the cookies for me.
06 ④  07 ①, ③
08 which they lived in was big 또는 in which they lived was big
09 ④  10 ⑤  11 speaks so fast, can't understand him 12 ①
13 ②  14 ⑤  15 ②  16 ③  17 ②, ③  18 ②  19 ②
20 ②  21 ①  22 ④  23 ①  24 ①  25 ⑤  26 ①  27 ②
28 ⑤  29 ⑤  30 ②

01 (A) expect: 예상하다 / (B) view: 풍경, 광경 / (C) moment: 순간

02 빈칸에는 문맥상 주어 He를 보충 설명하는 보어가 들어가는 것이 적절하다. ③ fatten은 동사 원형이므로 빈칸에 들어가기 위해서는 과거분사형인 fattened가 되는 것이 어법상 적절하다.

03 관계대명사로 선행사가 사람일 때 쓸 수 있는 who가 쓰였으며, 동사는 like로서 주어는 복수형이다. 따라서 빈칸에는 ④ People이 들어가는 것이 적절하다.

04 수여동사를 4형식 문장에서 쓸 때는, 「주어 + 수여동사 + 간접목적어 + 직접목적어」의 순으로, 3형식 문장에서 쓸 때는, 「주어 + 수여동사 + 직접목적어 + for/of/to+ 직접목적어」 순으로 쓴다. make, cook, buy와 같은 동사는 3형식 문장에서 직접 목적어 앞에 전치사로 for를 쓴다.

05 두 문장을 연결할 때 겹치는 부분을 선행사로 만들고 관계대명사를 이용해 연결할 수 있다. 반대로 관계대명사로 이어진 문장을 두 문장으로 나눌 때는, 공통되는 부분을 반복해서 쓴다.

06 보기의 It은 가주어 It이다. 이와 쓰임이 같은 것은 ④ It is dangerous to swim in the sea.(바다에서 수영하는 것이 위험하다.)이다. / ①, ⑤: 비인칭 주어 ②, ③: 인칭대명사

07 두 문장을 연결할 때 겹치는 부분을 선행사로 만들고 관계대명사를 이용해 연결할 수 있다. 이때 관계대명사가 이끄는 절에서 관계대명사 who, which 또는 that이 목적어 역할을 할 때 목적격 관계대명사라고 한다. 선행사가 사람일 때 who나 whom을 쓸 수 있다.

08 두 문장을 연결할 때 겹치는 부분을 선행사로 만들고 관계대명사를 이용해 연결할 수 있다. 이때 관계대명사가 이끄는 절에서 관계대

명사 who, which 또는 that이 목적어 역할을 할 때 목적격 관계대명사라고 한다. who(m)는 선행사가 사람일 때, which는 선행사가 사물일 때, that은 두 경우 모두 쓸 수 있다.

09 'so+형용사/부사+that+주어+동사' 구문은 '너무 ~해서 …하다'라는 의미로 인과 관계를 나타낸다.

10 ① relaxing → relaxed / ② The boy is cute which my friend introduced to me. → The boy who(m) my friend introduced to me is cute. / ③ which Mrs. Barry made it → which Mrs. Barry made / ④ exciting → excited로 고쳐야 어법상 적절한 문장이 된다.

11 'so+형용사/부사+that+주어+동사' 구문은 '너무 ~해서 …하다'라는 의미로 인과 관계를 나타낸다.

12 "그건 어땠니?"라는 문장이 들어가기에 가장 적절한 곳은 캄보디아 여행에 대해서 설명하는 곳 앞인 (A)이다.

13 위 대화에 따르면, 수진이가 캄보디아 여행에서 먹은 거미 튀김은 커서 처음에는 좀 무서웠다고("They were really big, so I was a little scared at first.") 언급되어 있다.

14 (A) 이번 주말에 가족과 제주도에 갈 예정이라는 내용이므로 현재진행형인 going이 적절하다. / (B) G가 제주도에 가봤다고 대답했으므로, many times가 적절하다. / (C) "I can't wait."는 "기다리기 힘들다."라는 뜻으로 어떤 일에 대한 기대감을 나타내는 표현이다.

15 A가 새로 생긴 스페인 식당에 가보았냐고 묻자(B), B는 지난주 일요일에 저녁을 그곳에서 먹었다고 대답한다(C). A가 그곳이 어땠냐고 묻자(D), B가 서비스가 별로여서 다시 가고 싶지 않다고(A) 말하는 순서로 이어지는 것이 흐름상 가장 자연스럽다.

16 ⓒ went out of → went into로 고쳐야 문맥상 적절한 문장이 된다.

17 위 글에 따르면, 울란바토르 공항에 막 도착했다고('We have just arrived at the airport.') 언급했다. 또한 비가 내릴 가능성이 있다고('there is a chance of rain.') 말하고 있다.

18 위 글에 따르면, ⓐ 몽골 전통 가옥인 ger는 큰 텐트이다. / ⓒ 요리를 한 것은 Atlan의 할머니였다. / ⓓ Atlan의 할머니가 요리한 음식은 양고기로 만든 것이다. / ⓔ Khorkhog는 특별한 손님에게 대접하는 것이라고 언급되어 있다.

19 '우리가 들어갔을 때, 무언가 좋은 냄새가 났다.'라는 문장이 들어가기에 가장 적절한 곳은 텐트에서 만들고 있는 요리는 khorhog라고 말하는 곳 앞인 (B)이다.

20 위 글에 따르면, ger는 큰 텐트로 안은 아늑했다고('It is a big tent, but it is cozy inside.) 언급되어 있다.

21 (가) 몽골에서의 모든 순간이 재밌고 흥미진진했다는 내용이므로 현재분사형 형용사 exciting이 적절하다. / (나) 낙타 등에 타고 고비 사막에 갔던 것이 가장 즐거웠다는 내용이므로 desert(사막)가

적절하다.

**22** (A) show around: ~을 여기저기 구경시켜 주다

(B) sit on: ~ 위에 앉다

(C) in many ways: 많은 면에서, 많은 방식으로

**23** 위 글에 따르면, 글쓴이는 처음에는 낙타가 자신의 키보다 커서 무서웠지만 일단 낙타의 등에 앉게 되자 움직임에 익숙해졌다고 말하고 있다. 따라서 빈칸 (a)에는 ① once(일단 ~하자)가 적절하다.

**24** 위 글에 따르면, 글쓴이는 처음에는 낙타가 자신의 키보다 커서 무서웠지만 곧 움직임에 익숙해졌고 그 위에서 보는 풍경이 멋졌다고 언급하고 있다.

**25** 위 글에 따르면, 글쓴이가 몽골 여행 중에 가장 즐거웠던 일은 고비 사막에서 낙타를 탄 것이라고('I had the most fun when I rode a camel in the Gobi Desert.') 언급되어 있다.

**26** 첫 문단에 따르면, 글쓴이의 몽골인 친구 Altan의 할머니가 그를 울란바토르로 초대했다고('His grandmother invited me to Ulaanbaatar, the capital of Mongolia.') 언급되어 있다.

**27** 위 글에 따르면, 서울에서 칭기즈칸 공항까지 4시간이 소요되었다고 언급되어 있다.

**28** 위 글에서는 ⑤ How did Altan and the writer get to know each other?(글쓴이와 Altan이 어떻게 서로를 알게 되었는가?)에 대해서는 언급된 바 없다.

**29** '나는 내가 마법의 장소에 있다는 느낌을 받았다.'라는 문장이 들어가기에 가장 적절한 곳은 밤하늘을 구경했고 그곳에 가득 찬 밝은 별들을 보았다는 곳인 (E)이다.

**30** '그것(그 냄새)은 그녀가 우리를 위해 요리하고 있던 홀호그에서 나오는 것이었다.'는 문장은 it을 주어로 써서 ② It was from the khorkhog she was cooking for us.라고 영작할 수 있다.

## Lesson 6 (중간)

**01** ①  **02** ③  **03** ④  **04** ⑤

**05** (A) ringing[ring]  (B) called  (C) running[run]

**06** ②  **07** ④  **08** ①

**09** (A) so high and steep that I felt dizzy

(B) I was so tired that I could not work anymore.

**10** I like the song which my friend uploaded on Youtube last week.

**11** (A) rode → ridden / (B) she → her / (C) luck → lucky

**12** ③  **13** ④  **14** ②  **15** ⑤  **16** ①  **17** ①  **18** ⑤  **19** ②

**20** ③  **21** ⑤  **22** ④  **23** ②  **24** ②  **25** ②  **26** ④  **27** ①

**28** It took thirty minutes by taxi from the airport to Altan's grandmother's house.

**29** ④  **30** ③

**01** get in a car: 자동차에 타다 / get off: ~에서 내리다

**02** 위에서부터 순서대로, between(~ 사이의), run out of(~가 떨어지다), above(~ 위에), care about(~에게 마음을 쓰다, 관심을 가지다), out of(~으로)가 들어가는 것이 문맥상 가장 자연스럽다.

**03** ① who is → who are / ② talking → talking to / ③ doesn't need it → didn't need / ⑤ whom he comes → who comes로 고쳐야 어법상 적절한 문장이 된다.

**04** ① disappointed → disappointing / ② relaxing → relaxed / ③ exciting → excited / ④ bored → boring으로 고쳐야 어법상 적절한 문장이 된다.

**05** 지각동사 see, look, hear, watch, listen to, feel 등은 5형식 문장에서 쓰일 경우 목적보어로 동사원형 또는 현재분사(~ing)를 취한다. 한편 목적어와 목적보어의 관계가 수동일 경우에는 과거분사(p.p.)를 쓴다.

**06** 'so+형용사/부사+that+주어+동사' 구문은 '너무 ~해서 …하다'라는 의미로 인과 관계를 나타낸다. 따라서 ⓐ-ⓓ, ⓔ-ⓕ가 인과 관계로 이어지는 문장들이다.

**07** ④ make → were made로 고쳐야 어법상 적절한 문장이 된다.

**08** ① that은 두 문장을 연결하는 접속사 that이다. 나머지는 모두 관계대명사 역할을 하는 that이다.

**09** 'so+형용사/부사+that+주어+동사' 구문은 '너무 ~해서 …하다'라는 의미로 인과 관계를 나타낸다.

**10** 두 문장을 연결할 때 겹치는 부분을 선행사로 만들고 관계대명사를 이용해 연결할 수 있다. 이때 관계대명사가 이끄는 절에서 관계대명사 who, which 또는 that이 목적어 역할을 할 때 목적격 관계대명사라고 한다. who(m)는 선행사가 사람일 때, which는 선행사가 사물일 때, that은 두 경우 모두 쓸 수 있다.

**11** (A) ride의 과거분사형은 ridden이다. / (B) 의미상 주어 for 뒤에는 주격인 she가 아니라 목적격인 her가 적절하다. / (C) 명사인 luck는 형용사형인 lucky로 고치는 것이 어법상 적절하다.

**12** ③ whom → which로 고쳐야 어법상 적절한 문장이 된다.

**13** 은성이가 해외 여행을 해 본적 있냐고 묻자, 수진이는 작년 여름에 캄보디아에 갔었다고 대답한다(D). 은성이는 여행이 어땠냐고 묻고(E), 수진이는 더웠지만 즐거웠다고 대답한다(C). 은성이가 여행 중에 한 재밌는 경험에 대해 말해달라고 요청하자(A), 수진이가 거미 튀김을 먹었다고(B) 말하는 순서로 이어지는 것이 흐름상 가장 자연스럽다.

**14** 위 글에 따르면, 서진이는 코로나 바이러스 때문에 여행 계획이 있었지만 가지 못한다고("My family had a plan, but as you know, we cannot go abroad now because of Covid-19.") 언급했다.

**15** 위 대화에 따르면, Eunseong이 먹은 거미 튀김은 컸지만 매우 맛

이 있었다고("They were really big, so I was a little scared at first. But the taste was okay.") 언급했다.

**16** 위에서부터 순서대로, have, airport, full of, chance, trip이 들어가는 것이 문맥상 가장 자연스럽다.

**17** 위 글에서는 ① '비행 시간'에 대해서는 언급되어 있지 않다.

**18** 위 글에 따르면, 서울에서 울란바토르 공항까지 4시간이 소요되었고, 공항에서 Altan의 할머니 집까지는 택시로 30분이 걸렸다고 한다.

**19** 위 글에서는 친구 가족의 초대로 몽골의 울란바토르에 가서 경험한 여행에 대해서 이야기하고 있다.

**20** 위 글에 따르면, 글쓴이에게 몽골 여행은 특별한 경험이었으며 친구의 나라와 문화를 알 수 있던 좋은 경험이었다고 말하고 있다. 또한 다시 한번 방문하고 싶다고 말하고 있으므로, 글쓴이의 심정으로 가장 적절한 것은 ③ excited(신이 난)이다.

**21** 위 글에서 서울에서 Altan 할머니의 댁까지는 비행기로 4시간, 공항에서 할머니 댁까지 택시로 30분 걸렸다고 언급되어 있다.

**22** (A) 지각동사 smell이 사용되었으므로 보어로는 형용사 wonderful이 적절하다.
(B) be made of: ~로 만들어지다
(C) 'so+형용사/부사+that+주어+동사' 구문은 '너무 ~해서 … 하다'라는 의미로 인과 관계를 나타낸다.
(D) full of: ~로 가득찬

**23** ㉠It은 앞서 언급된 텐트에 들어가서 맡은 좋은 냄새를 가리킨다.

**24** ⓑ excited → exciting으로 고쳐야 어법상 적절한 문장이 된다.

**25** 위 글에 따르면, 글쓴이에게 Altan의 할머니가 대접한 Khorkhog는 특별한 손님에게 대접하는 음식이라고 언급되어 있다.

**26** 위 글에 따르면, 글쓴이는 낙타가 자신의 키보다 커서 처음에는 무서웠지만 곧 낙타의 움직임에 익숙해졌다고 이야기하고 있다. 따라서 빈칸 ㉡에는 ④ At first(처음에는)가 적절하다.

**27** 위 글에 따르면, 글쓴이가 몽골 여행 중에 가장 즐거웠던 일은 고비 사막에서 낙타를 탄 것이라고('I had the most fun when I rode a camel in the Gobi Desert.') 언급되어 있다.

**28** It took ~: 시간이 ~ 걸렸다 / from A to B: A에서 B까지

**29** (나)It는 바로 앞 문장에서 언급된 'My visit to Mongolia'를 가리킨다.

**30** 위 글에 따르면, 글쓴이에게 몽골 여행은 특별한 경험이었으며 친구의 나라와 문화를 알 수 있던 좋은 경험이었다고 말하고 있다. 따라서 빈칸 (다), (라)에는 country(나라)와 culture(문화)가 적절하다.

# Lesson 7 (기말) ①회

| | | | | |
|---|---|---|---|---|
| **01** ⑤ | **02** ②, ③ | **03** ③ | **04** ④ | **05** ④ |
| **06** is helpful to wear sunglasses in the summer | | | | **07** ② |
| **08** ④ | **09** ④ | **10** ④ | **11** ① | **12** ④ | **13** ② | **14** ④ | **15** ③ |
| **16** ② | **17** ① | **18** ④ | **19** ② | **20** ④ | **21** ① | **22** ① | **23** ⑤ |
| **24** ⑤ | **25** ④ | **26** ③ | **27** ⑤ | **28** ③ | | | |
| **29** 비트박스 / 영화 재생 | | | **30** ③ | |

**01** <보기>에서는 명사에 y를 더하면 형용사가 된다는 규칙을 설명하고 있다. 명사 friend의 형용사형은 friendly(친절한)이다.

**02** (A) '미래에 일이 일어날 것이라고 말하다'라는 영영 풀이가 가리키는 것은 predict(예측하다)이다. / (B) '옷을 보관하는 데 사용하는 큰 가구'라는 영영 풀이가 가리키는 것은 closet(옷장)이다.

**03** (A) get in: ~에 타다 / (B) get to: ~에 가다[도착하다] / (C) get up: 기상하다/ (D) get out of: ~에서 나가다/ (E) get off: 내리다

**04** (A)에는 지각동사의 목적보어로 run 또는 running이 적절하다. (B) 매일 달리는 것은 건강에 좋다는 의미의 문장으로, 주어 자리에는 동명사형인 running이 적절하다.

**05** ④It은 날씨를 나타낼 때 쓰는 비인칭 주어이다. 나머지는 모두 문장의 주어로 쓰인 to부정사가 수식어로 인해 길어진 경우, 보통 to 부정사를 뒤로 보내고 대신 주어 자리에 쓰이는 가주어 It이다.

**06** 문장의 주어로 쓰인 to부정사가 수식어로 인해 길어진 경우, 보통 to부정사를 뒤로 보내고 대신 주어 자리에 가주어 it을 둔다. 이때 쓰인 it은 가주어이므로 구체적인 뜻이 없으며, '...하는 것은 ~하다'로 해석한다.

**07** 지각동사 see, look at, hear, watch, listen to, feel 등은 5형식 문장에서 쓰일 경우 목적보어로 동사원형 또는 현재분사(~ing)를 취한다. 목적어와 목적보어의 관계가 수동일 경우에는 과거분사(p.p)를 쓴다. 따라서 (A)에는 come, (B)에는 picked, (C)에는 burning이 들어가는 것이 적절하다.

**08** A의 말에 대한 B의 대답이 스마트 음식 주문 기계에 대해 "재밌게 들린다. 우리는 그걸 이용해서 빠르고 쉽게 주문할 수 있을 거야." 였다. 따라서 빈칸에 들어갈 A의 말로 가장 적절한 것은 ④ Why don't we try it?(우리 저걸 시도해 보는게 어때니?)이다.

**09** "이 컴퓨터 멋지게 보이네요. 가격이 얼마입니까?"라는 A의 질문에 대해 "저는 특별 쿠폰을 이용해 구매하겠습니다."라는 B의 대답은 흐름상 자연스럽지 않다.

**10** "Why don't we ~?"는 "~하는 게 어때니?"라는 뜻으로 상대방에게 제안을 하는 표현이다. 따라서 B가 VR게임을 하자고 제안했으므로 빈칸에 들어갈 말로 가장 적절한 것은 ④ That sounds interesting.(좋은 생각이야.)이다.

**11** 위 대화에 따르면, B가 미래의 직업에 대해서 발표해야 한다고 생

각한다고 말했고("I'm thinking we should talk about future jobs. What do you think?"), G가 동의하고 있다.

**12** A의 말에 대한 B의 대답이 지난번에 방문했던 중식당의 "서비스가 좋지 않았어. 다시는 안 가려고."였다. 따라서 빈칸에 들어갈 A의 말로 가장 적절한 것은 ④ How did you like it?(그곳은 어땠니?)이다.

**13** "그리고 나서, 넌 답을 얻게 될 거야."라는 문장이 들어가기에 가장 적절한 곳은 카메라를 단어에 갖다대고 AI에게 번역해 달라고 부탁하면 답을 얻게 된다고 말하고 있는 곳인 (B)이다.

**14** ⓓ That sounds unbelievably. → That sounds unbelievable.로 고쳐야 어법상 적절한 문장이 된다.

**15** 위 대화에서는 모르는 단어나 언어에 대해 번역을 해주는 AI 번역기와 그 사용법에 대해서 이야기하고 있다.

**16** 위 그림에서는 눈을 감고 글을 읽으려고 하고 있다. 따라서 "네가 눈을 감고 글을 읽는 것이 가능해?"라는 A의 물음에 대해 B가 "아니, 가능하다고 생각하지 않아."라는 대답이 가장 적절하다.

**17** 위 대화의 초반에 따르면, 여학생과 남학생은 스마트 음식 주문 기계를 사용하자고 제안하고 동의하고 있다.

**18** 가주어 It - 진주어 to부정사 구문의 의미상 주어로 'for, of+ 목적격'의 형태로 쓸 수 있는데, for는 일반적인 상황에서, of는 사람의 성격이나 태도를 나타낼 때 쓴다.

**19** 위 대화에 따르면, 여학생은 로봇이 인간을 대체할까봐 걱정하고 있지만 남학생은 로봇이 인간에게 위험한 일을 대신해줄 수 있다고 생각하고 있다. 따라서 이에 대한 여학생의 반응으로 적절한 것은 ② We should try to look on the bright side.(우리는 긍정적으로 보려고 노력해야겠구나.)이다.

**20** 위 글에 따르면, 지나와 수한이는 AI 엑스포에서 AI 집으로 들어갔고 침실을 먼저 둘러보자고 이야기하고 있다.

**21** 위 글의 후반부에 AI엑스포에서 AI 집을 둘러보고 있는 지나는 수한이에게 거실로 가자고 이야기하고 있다.

**22** AI 프로그램이 위대한 바둑 선수 중 한 명인 이세돌과 시합을 해서 이겼다고 한다. 바둑은 보드 게임의 일종으로 규칙을 이해하기 어렵다(B). 많은 사람들이 AI가 인간을 이기는 것이 어렵다고 생각했지만(A), 이세돌의 수를 예측했고 마침내 바둑 시합에서 이겼다(C). 사람들은 AI가 인간보다 지능이 높다는 것에 충격을 받았다고(D) 말하는 순서로 이어지는 것이 흐름상 가장 자연스럽다.

**23** 문장의 주어로 쓰인 to부정사가 수식어로 인해 길어진 경우, 보통 to부정사를 뒤로 보내고 대신 주어 자리에 가주어 it을 둔다. 이때 쓰인 it은 가주어이므로 구체적인 뜻이 없으며, '...하는 것은 ~하다'로 해석한다. 이때 의미상 주어는 일반적인 상황에서는 for를 쓸 수 있다.

**24** ⓔI can predict danger based on knowledge and experience.는 "나는 지식과 경험에 근거해 위험을 예측할 수 있

어."라는 의미의 문장이다.

**25** 인공지능 스피커는 비트박스를 할 수 있다고("I can beatbox, too.") 직접 말하고 있다.

**26** (A)It은 가주어 It이다. 이와 쓰임이 같은 것은 ③ It is really nice to meet you.(만나서 정말 반갑습니다.)이다.

**27** ⓔ에는 on이 들어가는 것이 적절하다. / based on: ~에 근거하여

**28** 위 글에 따르면, 지나는 신이 난 채로 야외에 있는 스마트 자동차 역에서 빨간 자동차를 타보자고("Hurry! There's a smart car station outside! Let's go and ride in that red car.") 말하고 있다.

**29** 위 글에 따르면, 인공지능 스피커는 자신이 단순한 음악 재생기가 아니라고 말하면서, 영화를 재생할 수 있고("How about watching a movie? I'll play one for you.") 비트박스("I can beatbox, too.")도 할 수 있다고 말하고 있다.

**30** 위 글에 따르면, 수한이는 스마트 자동차를 타고 집에 간 것이 아니라 다음 역으로 이동했다("You don't need to do anything. I will drive and take you to the next station.").

## Lesson 8 (기말) 1회

**01** ③ **02** ④ **03** ①
**04** ⓐ wear → wearing ⓑ paint → painted ⓒ hold → holding
**05** The people crossing the street looked busy.
**06** ③ **07** ⑤ **08** ③
**09** (A) her to marry him (B) wanted her to wait for him
**10** ① **11** ② **12** ① **13** ② **14** ③ **15** ⑤ **16** ③ **17** ④
**18** ② **19** ② **20** ① **21** ③ **22** ② **23** ③ **24** ④ **25** ②
**26** ④ **27** ② **28** ② **29** ④ **30** ③

**01** ③은 '영국인 소설가에 의해 쓰인 책은 베스트셀러가 되었다.'라는 의미의 문장이다. 따라서 밑줄 친 England는 형용사인 English(영국인의)로 바꾸는 것이 적절하다.

**02** 위에서부터 순서대로, known as(~로서 알려진), movement(운동; 움직임), architecture(건축), protect(보호하다), cost(비용)가 들어가는 것이 문맥상 가장 자연스럽다.

**03** ② of → for / ③ in → at / ④ to → with / ⑤ of → with로 고쳐야 어법상 적절한 문장이 된다.

**04** 현재분사는 '동사+ing'의 형태로 명사를 수식하는 형용사 역할을 한다. 동명사와 형태는 동일하지만, 동명사는 명사 취급, 현재분사는 형용사로 취급한다. 과거분사는 일반적으로 '동사+ed'의 형태로 명사를 수식하는 형용사 역할을 할 수 있다.

**05** 현재분사는 '동사+ing'의 형태로 명사를 수식하는 형용사 역할을 한다.

**06** ⓐ to study → study / ⓓ to bringing → to bring으로 고쳐야 어법상 적절한 문장이 된다.

**07** ⑤ go → to go

**08** 현재분사와 과거분사는 be동사와 함께 진행형이나 수동태를 만들거나 명사를 수식하는 형용사 역할을 한다. 따라서 (A) listening, (B) written, (C) holding이 들어가는 것이 적절하다.

**09** (A) ask A to B: A에게 B를 부탁하다
(B) want A to B: A가 B하는 것을 원하다

**10** 현재분사와 과거분사는 명사를 수식하는 형용사 역할을 할 수 있다. 따라서 (A) wearing, (B) painted, (C) holding이 들어가는 것이 적절하다.

**11** "난 중국인 친구와 창덕궁에 갈 거야."라는 A의 말에 대해 "난 간식에 돈을 낭비하지 않을 거야."라는 B의 대답은 흐름상 자연스럽지 않다.

**12** 위 대화에 따르면, 돌 잔치에 모인 가족들은 잔치 음식을 다 같이 나눠 먹는다고("The family members share food and wish for a long life for the baby") 언급되어 있다.

**13** B의 질문에 대한 대답으로 G가 돌잔치에 대해 더 자세히 설명하고 있다. 따라서 빈칸에 들어갈 B의 말로 가장 적절한 것은 ② Could you tell me more about it?(그것에 대해 더 자세히 설명해줄 수 있니?)이다.

**14** ⓒ increasing → decreasing으로 고쳐야 문맥상 적절한 문장이 된다.

**15** in harmony with: ~와 조화를 이루는

**16** ⓒ sound → sounds로 고쳐야 어법상 적절한 문장이 된다.

**17** 위 글에 따르면, 조선시대 사람인 안용복은 조선 영토인 울릉도와 독도에서 일본인들이 불법으로 어업을 하는 것을 보았다. 후에 일본의 통치자가 일본인들에게 원하는 만큼 어업을 해도 된다고 말하자, 안용복은 울릉도와 독도를 지키기 위해 노력했다고 언급되어 있다.

**18** 위 글에 따르면, 정세권은 조선말 학회를 만들어 조선말이 살아남을 수 있도록 장려했으며, 일제가 그에게 일본식 가옥을 지으라고 강요했지만, 그는 거절했기 때문에 그 댓가로 사업이 악화되어 재산을 잃었다고 언급되어 있다. 따라서 빈칸에는 각각 (A) encouraged, (B) forced, (C) lost가 들어가는 것이 적절하다.

**19** 위 글에 따르면, 조선말과 한국식 건축을 지키려 했던 정세권의 노력으로 한국의 전통이 사라지지 않고 현대까지 계승되었다고 이야기하고 있다. 따라서 빈칸에는 ② we can hand down Korean traditions(우리는 한국의 전통을 계승할 수 있다.)가 들어가는 것이 적절하다.

**20** 위 글에 따르면, 일제가 그에게 일본식 가옥을 지으라고 강요했지만, 정세권은 거절했기 때문에 그 댓가로 사업이 악화되어 재산을 잃었다고 언급되어 있다. 따라서 빈칸에는 각각 (A) refused, (B)

weaken이 적절하다.

**21** ⓒ were suffered → suffered로 고쳐야 어법상 적절한 문장이 된다.

**22** 위 글에서는 ② Many Japanese were pushed to move into Joseon to build Japanese houses.(많은 일본인들이 한국으로 이주해 일본식 가옥을 지으라고 강요당했다.)라는 내용은 언급되어 있지 않다.

**23** ⓒ it은 'that they upload a picture of hanoks onto their SNS'라는 명사절을 대신하는 가목적어이다. 나머지는 모두 북촌을 가리킨다.

**24** 첫 문단에 따르면, 북촌 한옥 마을은 한국의 과거를 보기 위해 방문하는 관광객들에게는 인기 있지만, 많은 사람들이 북촌이 어떤 한 사람의 노력으로 만들어졌다는 것은 모른다고 언급하고 있다. 따라서 빈칸에는 ④ On the other hand(반면에)가 적절하다.

**25** 빈칸 (가), (나)에 공통으로 들어갈 단어는 with이다. ②의 빈칸에는 in이 들어가는 것이 적절하다.

**26** ⓓ caught → was caught로 고쳐야 어법상 적절한 문장이 된다.

**27** 두 번째 문단에 따르면, 정세권은 사람이 힘이라고 생각했다고 ('Segwon wanted to protect the hanok and help the suffering people. He said, "People are power."') 언급되어 있다.

**28** 위 글에서는 정세권이라는 조선시대 인물이 어떻게 종로의 북촌 한옥 마을을 지키고 조성하려 했는지에 대해서 이야기하고 있다. 따라서 위 글의 제목으로 가장 적절한 것은 ② The History of a Hanok Village in Bukchon(북촌 한옥 마을의 역사)이다.

**29** 위 글에 따르면, 경성을 자신들의 입맛에 맞게 바꾸려고 한 것은 정세권이 아니라 한국을 지배했던 일제이다.

**30** 위 글에 따르면, 정세권이 자신의 재산을 지키기 위해서 많은 돈을 지불했다는 내용은 언급되어 있지 않다.

## Lesson 9 (기말)  1회

| | | |
|---|---|---|
| **01** ④ **02** ④ **03** (A) Thanks to / (B) no longer | | |
| **04** what the man stole from this store **05** ① **06** ④ **07** ③ | | |
| **08** ④ **09** ② **10** ① **11** ① **12** ② **13** ⑤ **14** ④ **15** ② | | |
| **16** ③ **17** ② **18** ② **19** ③ **20** ① **21** ⑤ **22** ⑤ **23** ③ | | |
| **24** ② **25** ③ **26** ⑤ **27** ⑤ **28** ③ **29** ④ **30** ④ | | |

**01** 빈칸에는 공통적으로 movement(운동; 음악의 한 부분)가 들어가는 것이 문맥상 가장 자연스럽다.

**02** ⓐ get on: ~를 타다
ⓑ get up: 기상하다
ⓒ get to: ~에 도달하다, 가다

ⓓ get off: 내리다

ⓔ get together: 모이다

**03** (A) thanks to: ~ 덕분에 (B) no longer: 더 이상 ~ 아닌

**04** 간접의문문은 의문문이 '의문사+주어+동사' 형태로 다른 문장 안에서 주어, 목적어, 보어 역할을 하는 것을 말한다.

**05** ② where → when / ③ the way how → the way 또는 how / ④ on that → on which 또는 where/ ⑤ which → on which 또는 when으로 고쳐야 어법상 적절한 문장이 된다.

**06** ④ where were you → where you were로 고쳐야 어법상 적절한 문장이 된다.

**07** ③ painting → painted로 고쳐야 어법상 적절한 문장이 된다.

**08** ④ what are the title of the book → what the title of the book is로 고쳐야 어법상 적절한 문장이 된다.

**09** ⓐ build → built / ⓑ bring → to bring / ⓒ going → go로 고쳐야 어법상 적절한 문장이 된다.

**10** ⓐ which → that 또는 who / ⓑ bring → to bring / ⓒ going → go / ⓔ the days which → the days when으로 고쳐야 어법상 적절한 문장이 된다.

**11** ① when → where로 고쳐야 어법상 적절한 문장이 된다.

**12** "기말 고사 끝나고 PC방에 가자. 오후 2시에 올 수 있니?"라는 A의 질문에 대해 "응. 나는 오후에 여자친구와 나가기로 했어."라는 B의 대답은 흐름상 자연스럽지 않다.

**13** 위 대화에 따르면, 남자와 여자는 모두 내일 4시에 축구 연습에 참여할 예정이다.

**14** "넌 마지막까지 기다렸다가 박수를 쳐야 한다."라는 문장이 들어가기에 가장 적절한 곳은 클래식 음악에는 중간에 멈추는 경우도 있다고 말하고 있는 곳인 (D)이다.

**15** "Can you make it to ~?"는 "~에 오는 것이 가능하니?"라는 의미로, 어떤 행사에 참여하는 것이 가능한지 묻는 문장이다.

**16** A가 휴가가 어땠냐고 묻자(ⓑ), B는 좋았다고 말하면서 가족들과 독도에 갔다고 대답한다(ⓒ). A가 어땠냐고 묻자(ⓐ), B가 놀라웠다고 말하면서 다시 방문하고 싶다고(ⓓ) 말하는 순서로 이어지는 것이 흐름상 가장 자연스럽다.

**17** 위 글에 따르면, 모차르트 시대의 콘서트는 주로 사교 행사였다고('Concerts in Mozart's time were mostly social events.) 언급되어 있다.

**18** 위 글에서 모차르트 시대의 콘서트는 주로 사교 행사였기 때문에 콘서트 중간에 먹거나 이야기하거나 박수치는 것이 당연한 일이었다고 설명하고 있다. 따라서 빈칸에는 ② Noise was just part of the concert.(소음은 그저 공연의 일부였다)라는 문장이 들어가는 것이 가장 자연스럽다.

**19** 선행사로 시간을 나타내는 the 19th century가 왔으므로 빈칸 (A)에는 관계부사 when이 들어가는 것이 적절하다.

**20** 직접의문문이 문장 내에서 목적어나 주어로 쓰일 때는 '의문사+주어+동사' 형식의 간접의문문으로 바꿔야 어법상 적절하다. 따라서 주어진 두 문장을 한 문장으로 만들면 ① We do not know what concerts will look like in the future가 가장 적절하다.

**21** 위 글에서 필자는 시대에 따라 공연 매너가 바뀐다고 말하면서 현재로서는 음악을 즐기되 주변에 있는 사람들을 방해하지 말아야 한다고 말하고 있다. 따라서 필자가 주장하는 바로 ⑤ The important rule in concerts is behaving appropriately, not making others annoyed.(공연에서 중요한 규칙은 적절하게 행동하고 다른 사람들을 짜증나게 하지 않는 것이다.)가 가장 적절하다.

**22** 위에서부터 순서대로, keep, arrive, along, over, audience가 들어가는 것이 문맥상 자연스럽다.

**23** 위 글에 따르면, 음악이 연주될 때에는 핸드폰을 꺼야 한다고('Turn off your cellphone!) 언급했다.

**24** 위 글에서는 공연장에서 지켜야 할 매너들에 대해서 설명하고 있다. 따라서 제목으로 가장 적절한 것은 ② Tips for Good Concert Manners(좋은 공연 매너를 위한 조언)이다.

**25** 직접의문문이 문장 내에서 목적어나 주어로 쓰일 때는 '의문사+주어+동사' 형식의 간접의문문으로 바꿔야 어법상 적절하다. 따라서 주어진 우리말을 영작하면, 'Find out what music will be played.'가 된다.

**26** '소음은 그저 공연의 일부였다.'라는 문장이 들어가기에 가장 적절한 곳은 모차르트 시대에는 콘서트가 주로 사교 행사였기 때문에 사람들을 만나는 좋은 장소였다고 말하고 있는 곳인 (E)이다.

**27** 위 글에 따르면, 과거 모차르트 시대의 공연은 사교 행사로서 소음이 공연의 일부였지만, 현대에서는 공연장은 어둡고 조용하며 관객들은 진지하게 감상하는 것이 매너라고 말하고 있다. 따라서 빈칸에는 (A) serious, (B) noisy가 들어가는 것이 적절하다.

**28** 위 글에 따르면, 현재 공연 관람의 목적이 연구나 공부를 위한 것이라는 내용은 언급되어 있지 않다.

**29** 위 글에 따르면, 공연장 관람 매너 중 하나로 공연 중간 쉬는 시간에는 화장실을 다녀오는 것 뿐만 아니라 필요하다면 공연장 밖에서 간식이나 음료를 먹을 수 있다고 언급하고 있다.

**30** 위 글에 따르면, 공연장 관람 매너 중 하나로 공연 중간 쉬는 시간에는 화장실을 다녀오는 것 뿐만 아니라 필요하다면 공연장 밖에서 간식이나 음료를 먹을 수 있다고 언급하고 있다. 따라서 빈칸에 들어갈 내용으로 가장 적절한 것은 ④ Take Advantage of Intermissions(공연 중간 쉬는 시간을 이용해라.)이다.